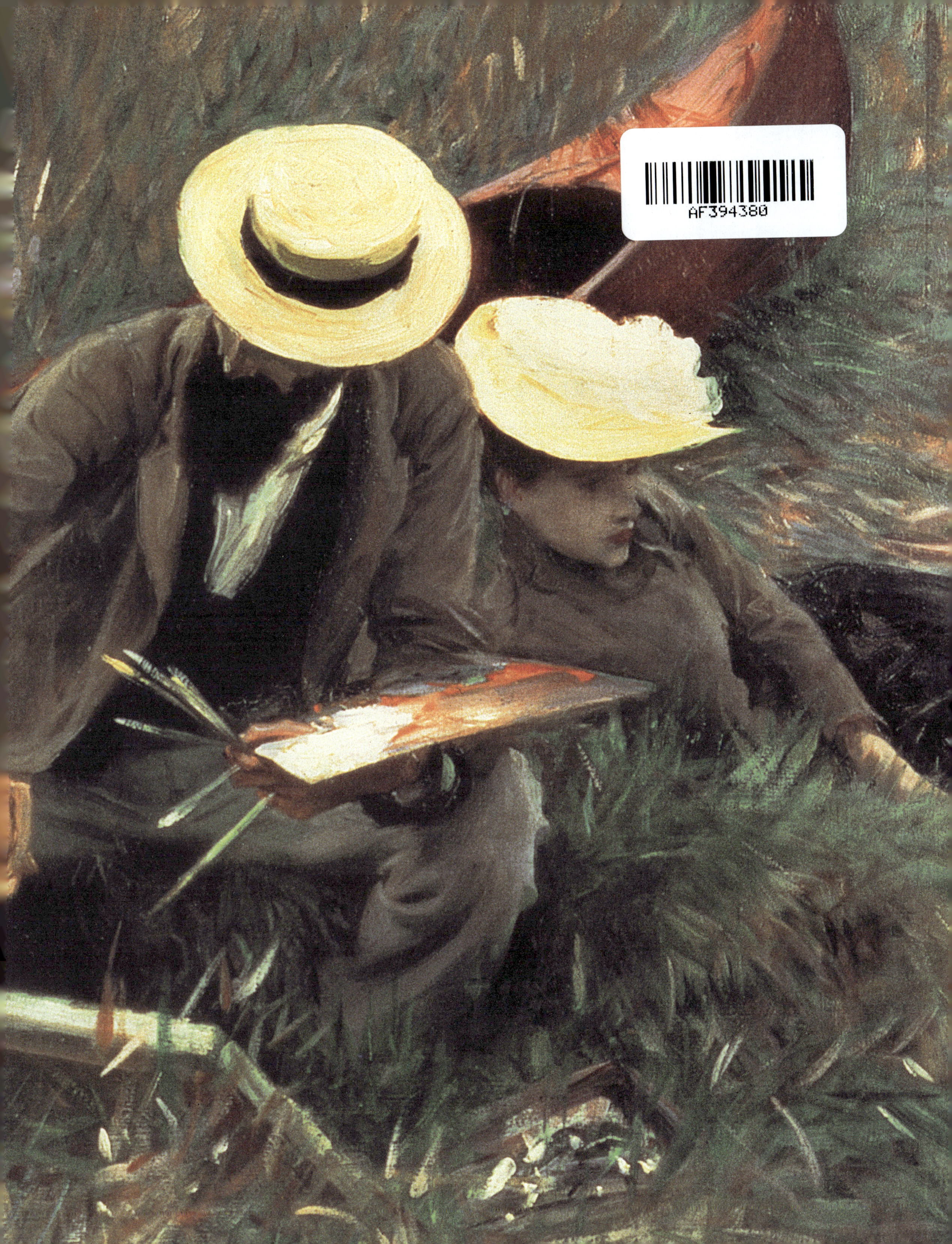
AF394380

JOHN SINGER SARGENT

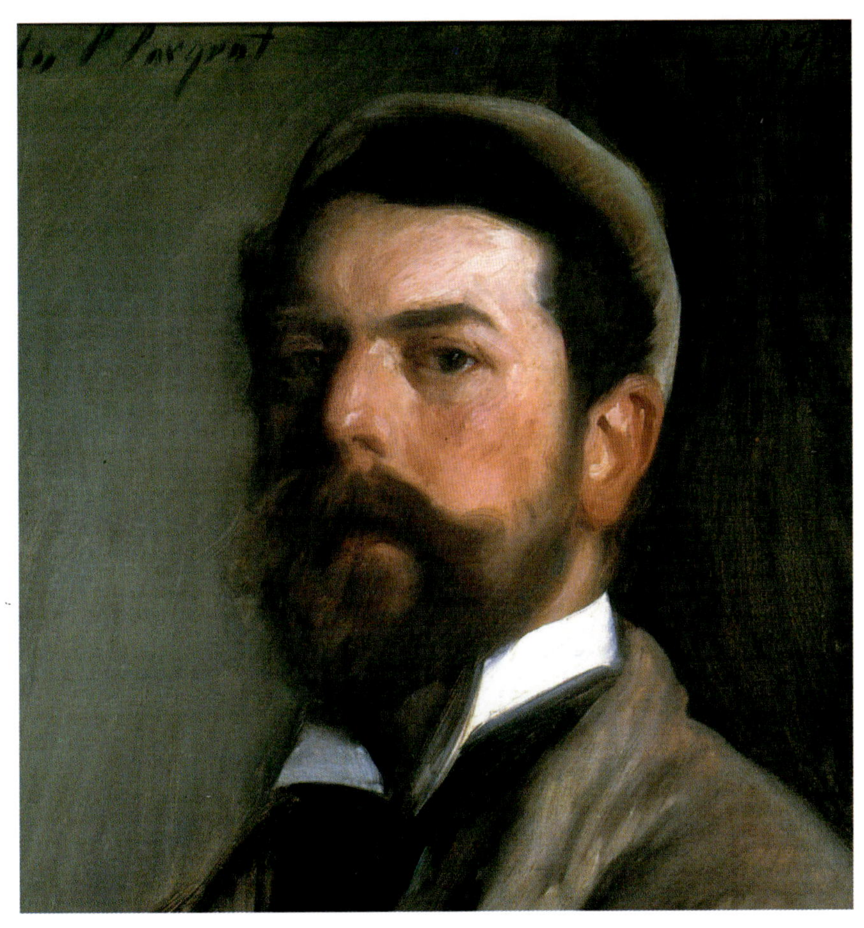

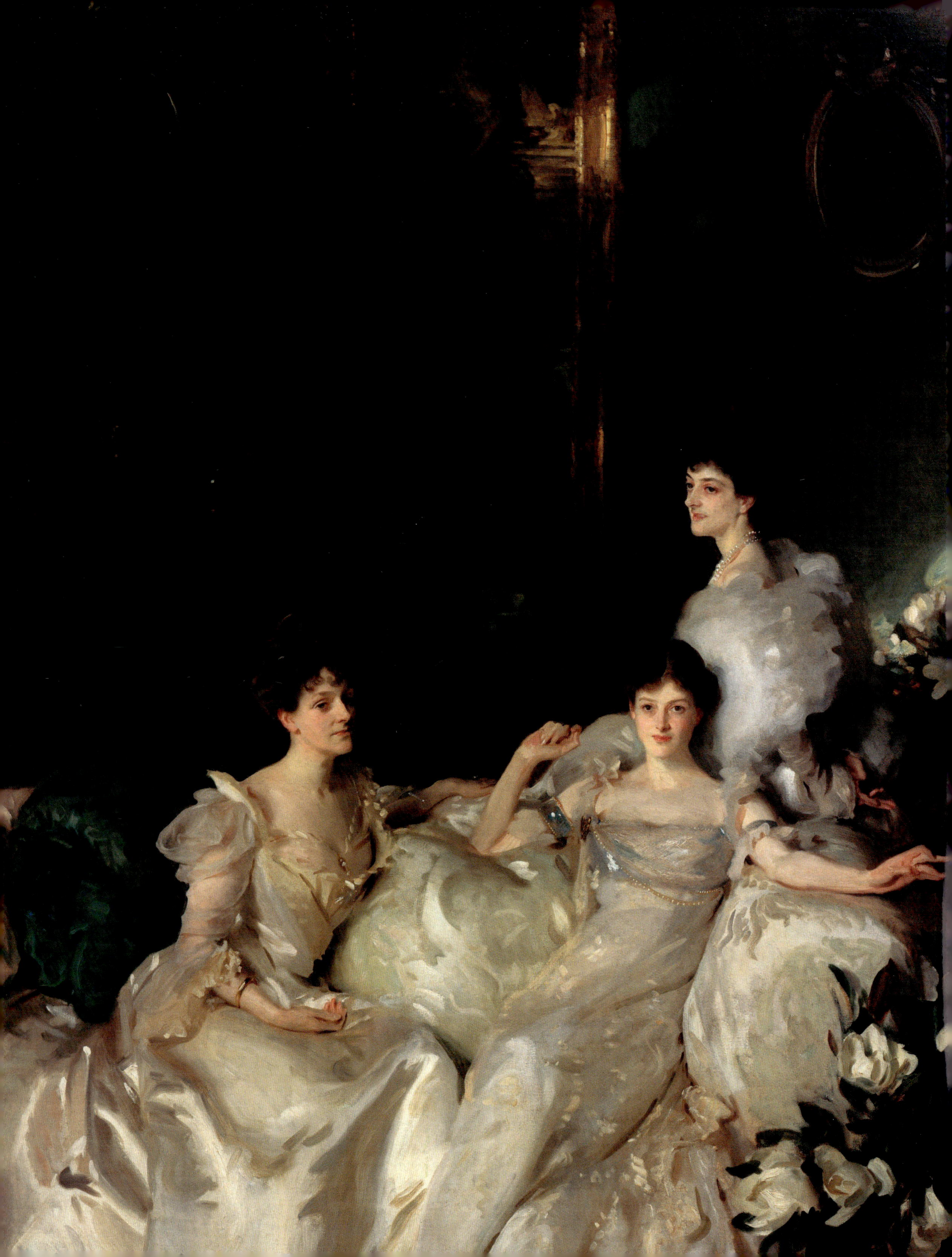

JOHN SINGER SARGENT

HIS LIFE AND WORK IN 500 IMAGES

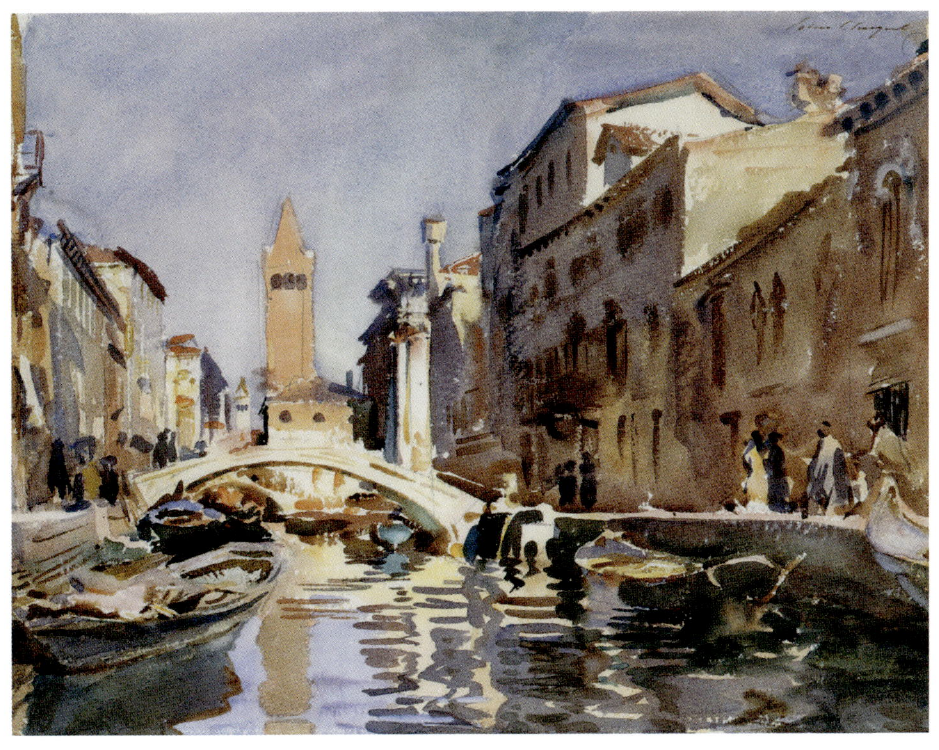

AN ILLUSTRATED EXPLORATION OF THE ARTIST, HIS LIFE AND
CONTEXT, WITH A GALLERY OF 300 PAINTINGS AND DRAWINGS

SUSIE HODGE

LORENZ BOOKS

This edition is published by Lorenz Books
an imprint of Anness Publishing Ltd
info@anness.com
www.lorenzbooks.com; www.annesspublishing.com

A CIP catalogue record for this book is available from the
British Library.

Publisher: Joanna Lorenz
Designer: Tina Vaughan
Editor: Tricia Wright
Assistant: Dylan Vaughan-Streater
Index: Marie Lorimer

Page 1: Self-portrait, 1892.
Page 2: The Wyndham Sisters, 1899.
Page 3: Venetian Canal, 1913.
Page 4: Schreckhorn, Eismeer, 1870 – painted in watercolour
by Sargent when he was just 14 years old.
Page 5: In a Medici Villa, 1906; Lady Agnew of Lochnaw,
c.1892–93; The Hotel Room, c.1908.

PICTURE CREDITS

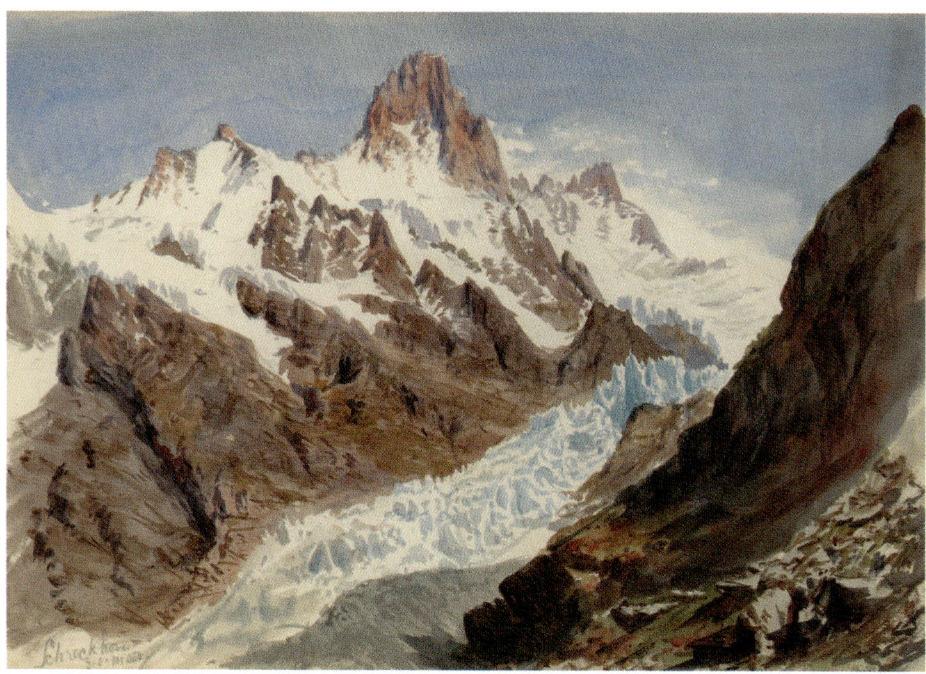

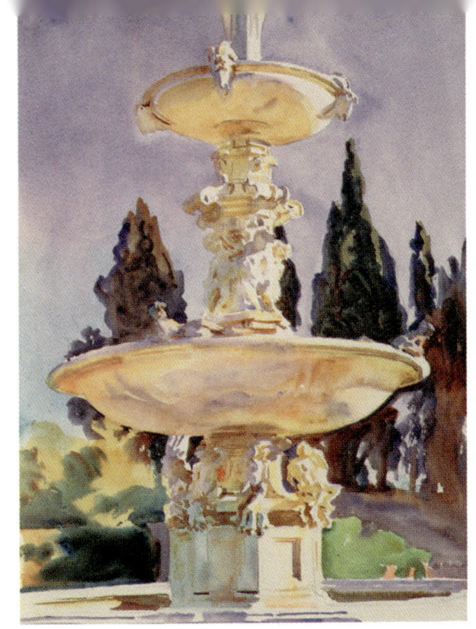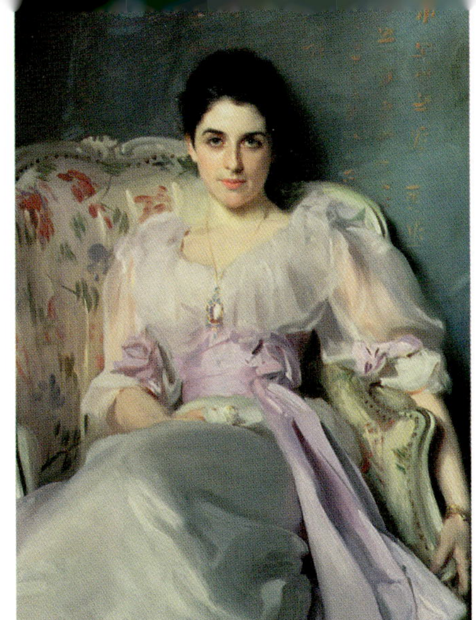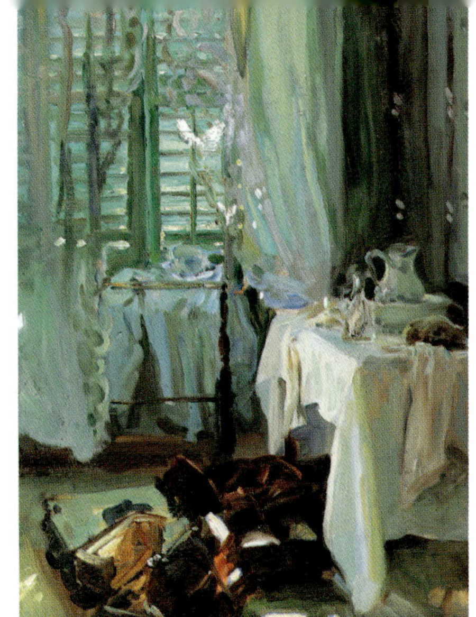

CONTENTS

INTRODUCTION

An American who spent most of his life in Europe, a portraitist who painted landscapes, a family man who never married, and an accomplished pianist who often entertained his sitters. John Singer Sargent (1856–1925) was one of the most influential portrait painters of his time, but he is also an enigma.

Over the course of his career, Sargent created roughly 900 oil paintings, more than 2,000 watercolours and a vast number of sketches and charcoal drawings, but despite his huge body of work, we know little about Sargent the man. Truly international, he was acclaimed on both sides of the Atlantic, and was close friends with many of the leading artists, writers, actors and musicians of his generation. He travelled extensively, to Venice, the Tyrol, Capri, Corfu, Spain, France, England, Holland, the Middle East, Canada and across America. Wherever he went, he captured the people and the surroundings. Using the fluid brushwork that had been introduced by his friends the Impressionists, his portraits are intimate and experimental, conveying both superficial appearances and psychological depths, and his landscapes are atmospheric and immediate. His style fuses the spectacular Impressionistic brushwork with techniques he learned from both Old and Modern masters, plus an acute interest in human psychology, all consolidated by his own adroit artistry.

DIVERSE AND PROLIFIC

Reflecting the decadence and elegance of the Edwardian era with a natural theatricality, Sargent became celebrated as the favourite portrait painter of the upper classes and a diverse, skilful and prolific artist of landscapes, figures and murals. In 1897, the Metropolitan Museum in New York called him: 'the Van Dyck of our times,' and in 1910, Walter Sickert (1860–1942) published an article questioning the overpowering enthusiasm for his work, calling it 'Sargentolatry'. Yet during his life, as well as attracting such acclamation from across Europe and America, he also provoked both scandal and condemnation, and after his death, he became judged adversely for not participating in the avant-garde movements of the period, such as Cubism and Fauvism, and so being inconsistent with the artistic sentiments of the time. He became rejected as nothing more than a relic of the Gilded Age, especially after the influential English art critic Roger Fry (1866–1934) dismissed his work as lacking aesthetic quality at the 1926 retrospective of his work in London. As with many artists however, the wheel of favour eventually turned and once again, in the early 21st century, Sargent's work began to be reassessed and revalued.

'HIS PRINCIPLES ARE EQUAL TO HIS TALENTS'

From early in his life, Sargent showed precocious artistic abilities and as a young man, his work was sought after by the rich and famous. Like other American artists such as James Abbott McNeill Whistler (1834–1903) and Mary Cassatt (1844–1926), Sargent was trained in Paris, and in 1874 a fellow art student wrote: "I met this last week a young Mr Sargent about 18 years old and one of the most talented fellows

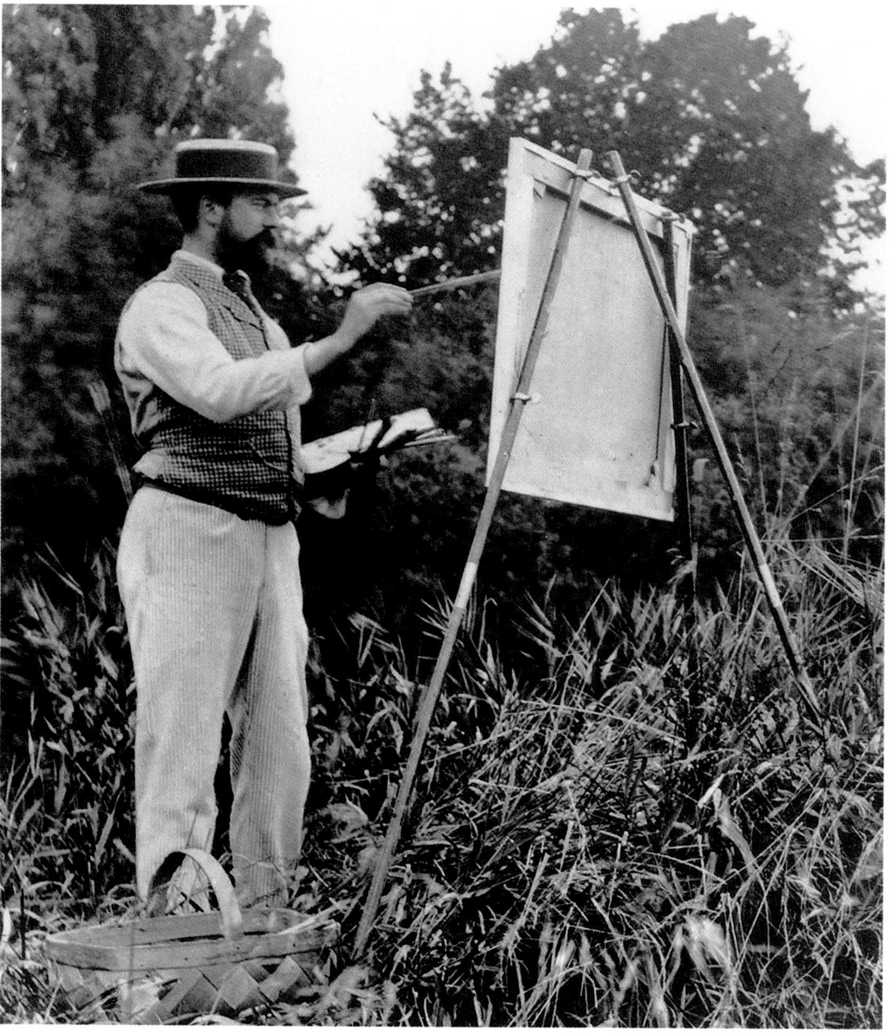

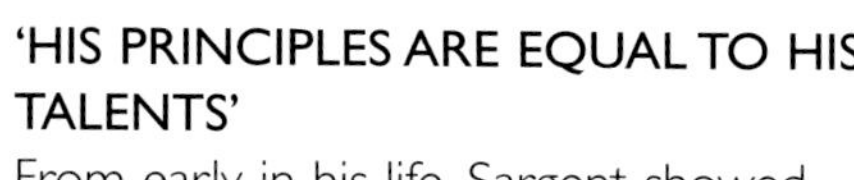

Left: John Singer Sargent painting in the countryside as a young man.

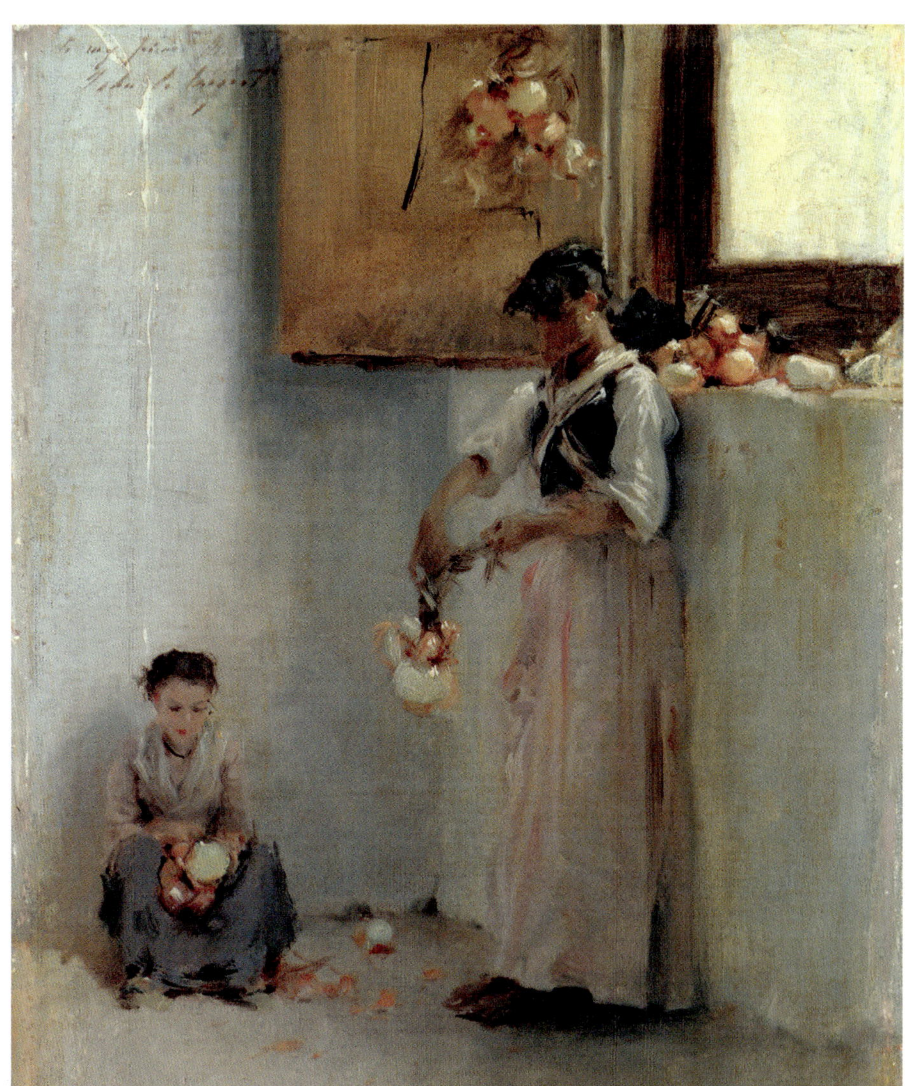

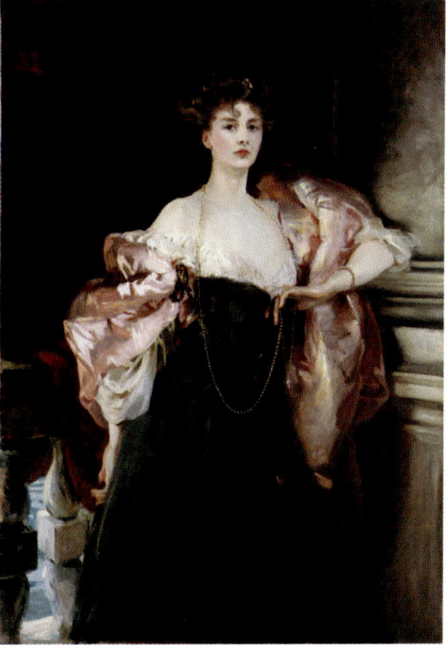

Left: Stringing Onions, *painted by Sargent in Capri during the summer of 1878.*

Above: Lady Helen Vincent, Viscountess D'Abernon — *one of the most celebrated hostesses of the time, Sargent painted her portrait in 1904 (see also page 185).*

Below: The Brook, *a vibrant watercolour painted by Sargent in 1907.*

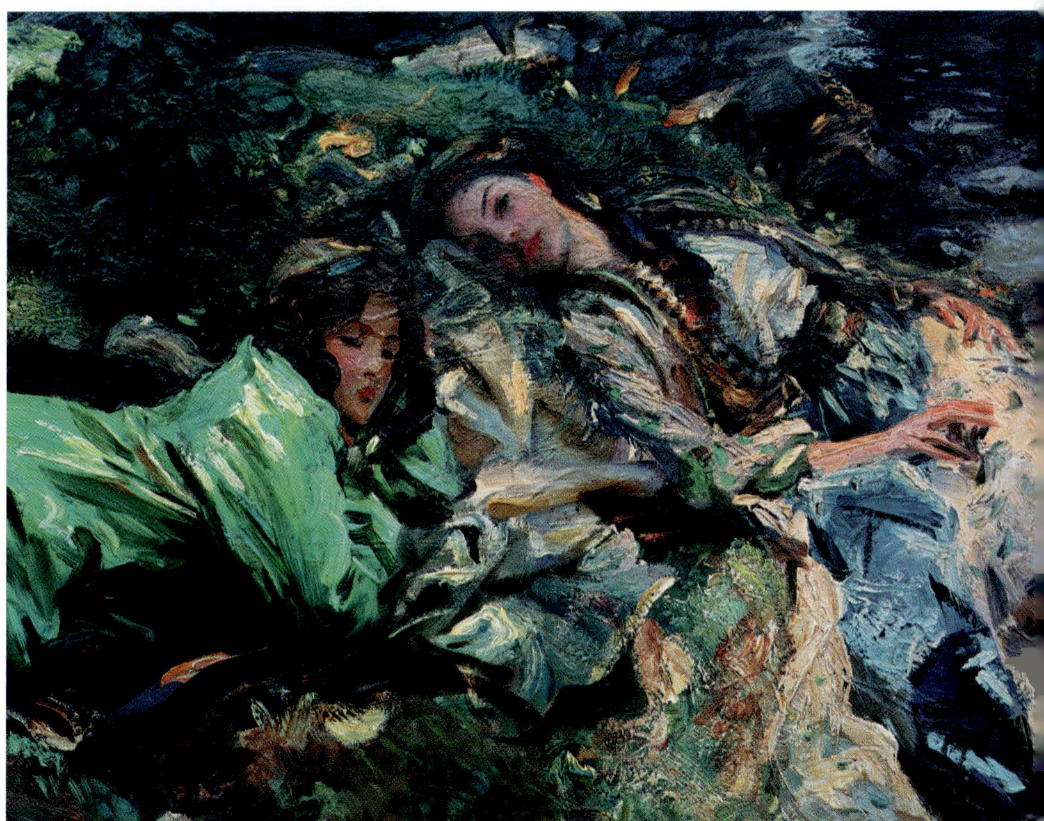

I have ever come across; his drawings are like Old Masters, and his colours are equally fine… Such men wake one up, and as his principles are equal to his talents, I hope to have his friendship."

CONTRASTING APPROACH

By the time he was 22, Sargent began to exhibit at the annual Salon in Paris, arguably the most prestigious exhibition in Europe at the time. He developed a way of making his subjects seem both close and distant, distinct and yet obscure, capturing a vivid sense of life along with an effect of detachment. He did not flatter his subjects, yet his portrayals made them seem alluring.

Sargent's use of costume and pose was dramatic, and his painting style demonstrates both a strong command of brushstrokes and tonal contrast, along with a loose, sketchy manner. These dichotomies gave his work particular appeal, and when he was only in his mid-20s, he was in great demand.

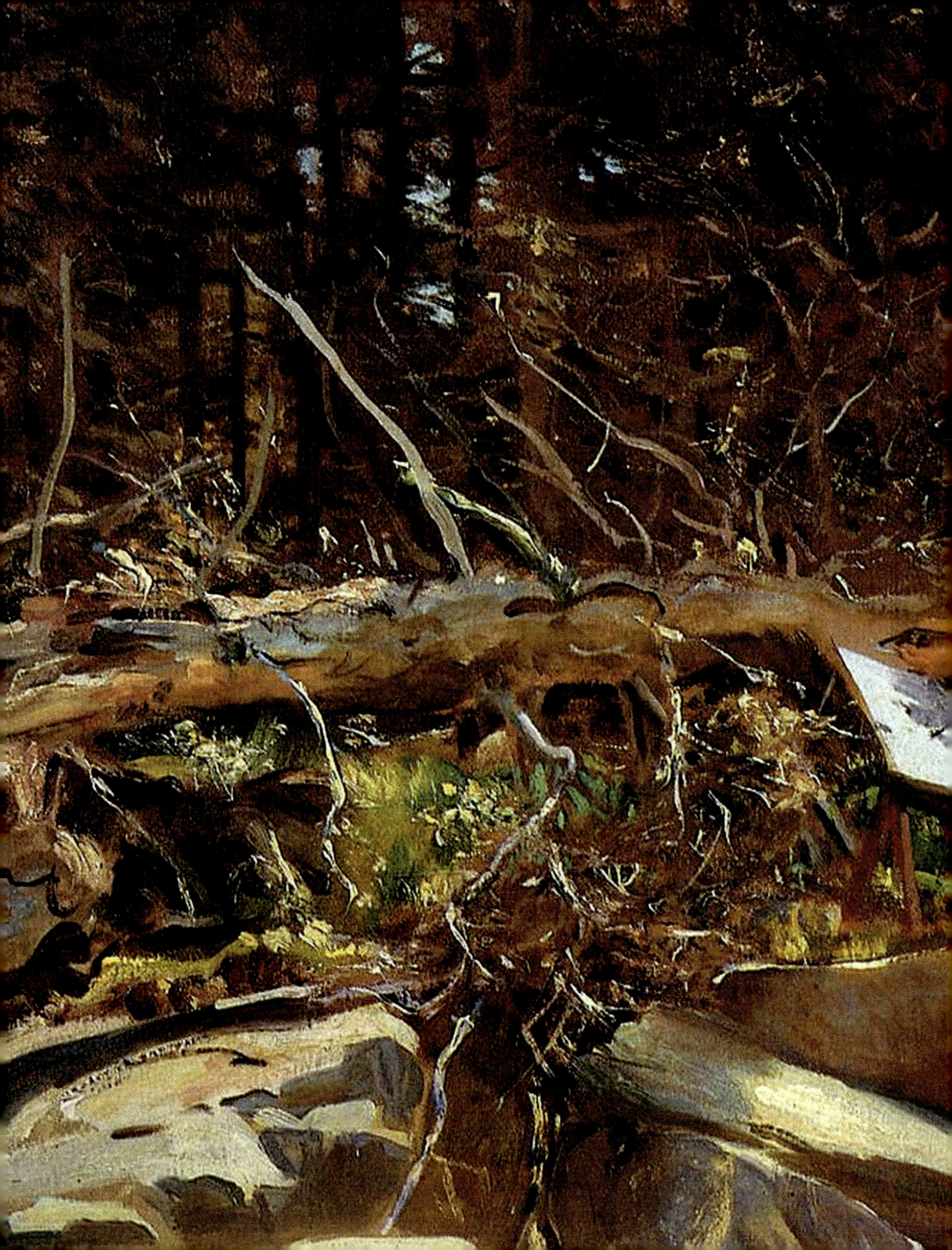

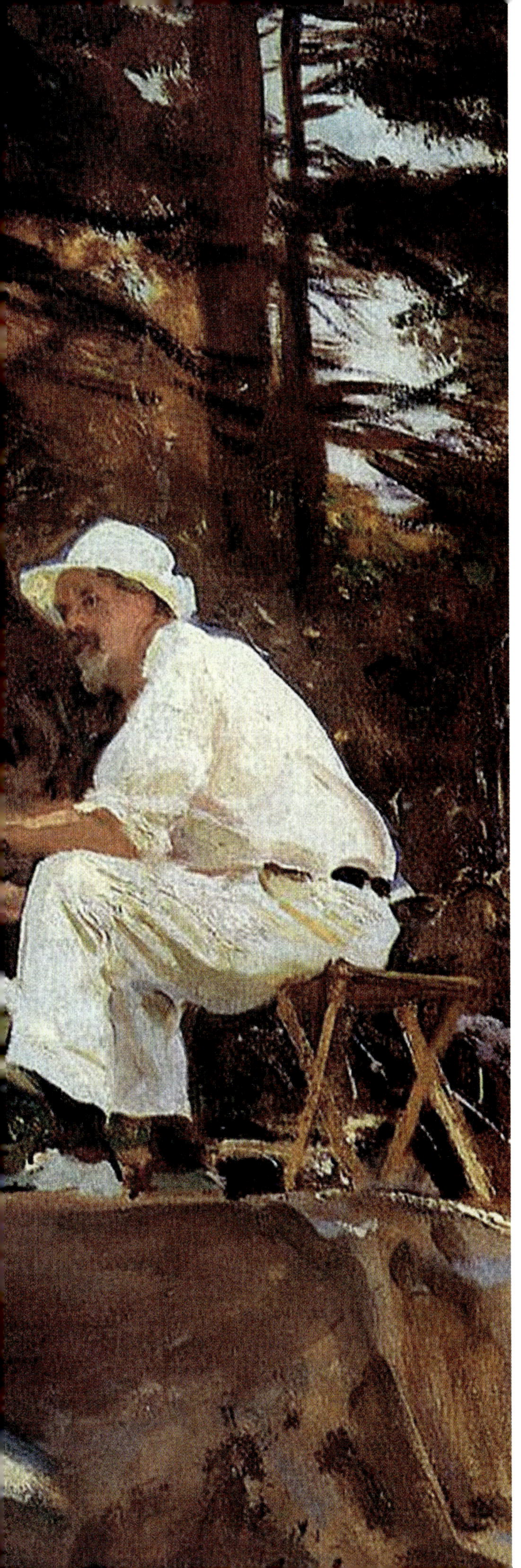

THE ENIGMA

Sargent was an accomplished pianist and dancer, fluent in French, Italian and German. Elegant and polite, he was also genial and well read. Throughout his career he was in demand for his portraits on both sides of the Atlantic, and during his lifetime he was perceived as a far more significant artist than contemporary avant-garde painters such as Paul Cézanne (1839–1906) and Paul Gauguin (1848–1903). But he had the opportunity and the ability to be as unconventional as any of the artists who later became linked to various modern art movements, and from the start, rather than choosing the more conventional studios that were taught by academic artists he allied himself with one of the most progressive, independent ateliers in Paris.

Left: An open-air sketch of one of Sargent's friends, Dwight Blaney, in 1922 on Ironbound Island in Maine, USA.

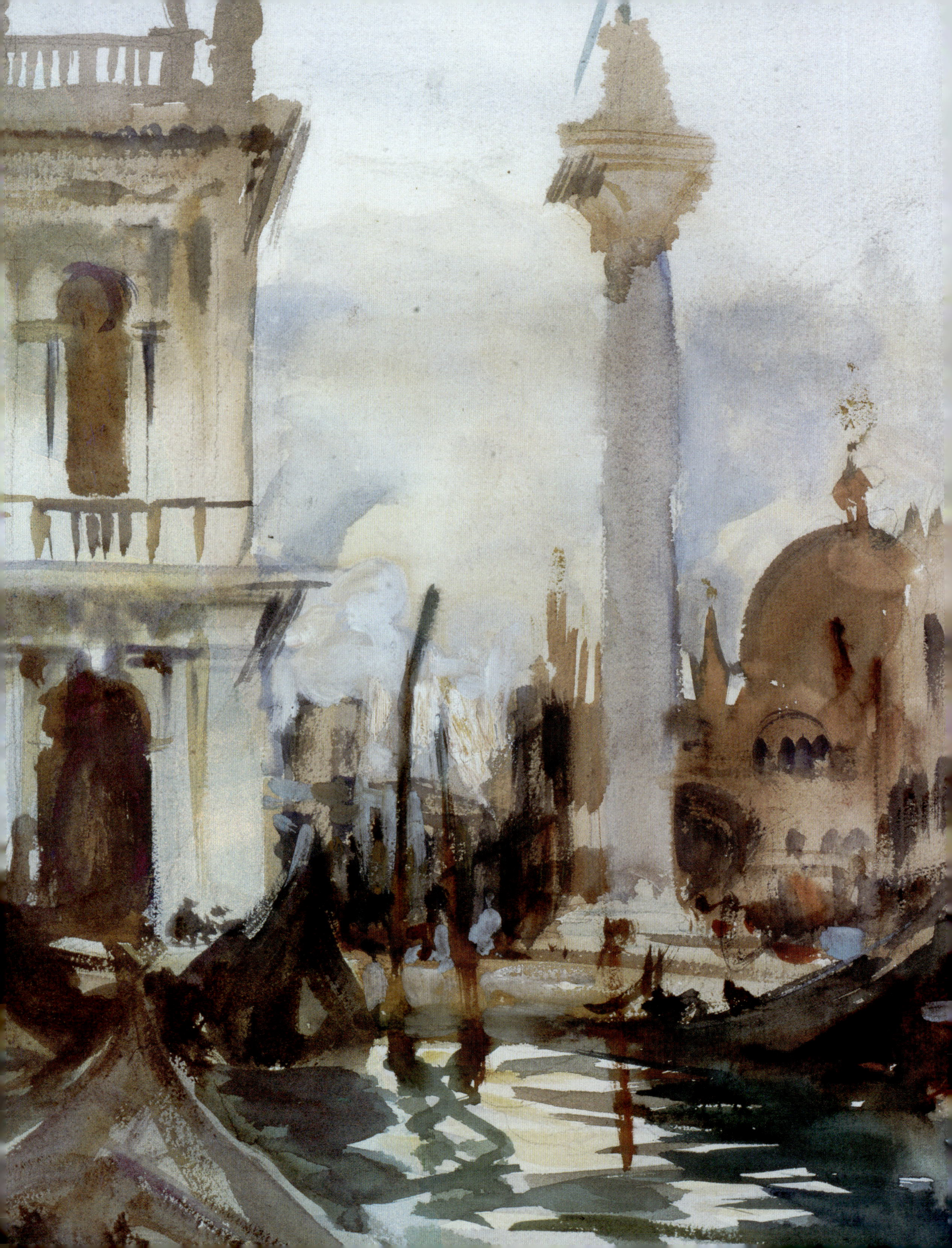

THE PRODIGY

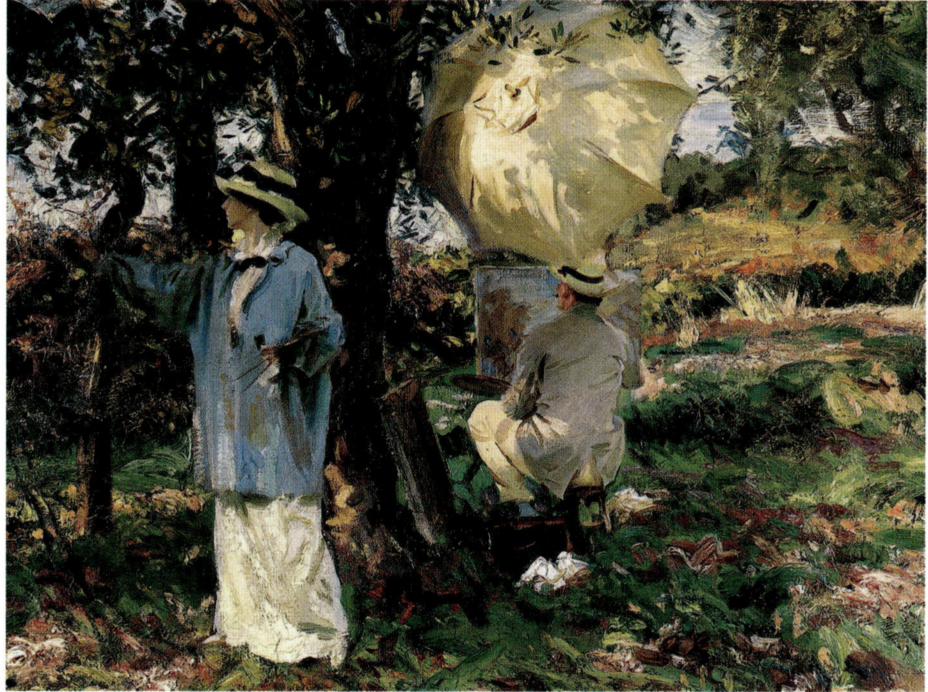

Although they were living in Europe, Sargent's father had hopes that when his only son grew up, he would join the American Navy. Mrs Sargent however, had other ideas. After seeing her young son's precocity with a pencil and paintbrush, she was sure that he would become an artist. From the first time his mother took him sketching in the Swiss Alps, he showed a remarkable talent, and his competence continued to improve and expand as he worked with pencil, charcoal, oils and watercolour, moving from portraits to landscapes and cityscapes, to murals and lively figure groups. At the time of Sargent's death in 1925, his close friend Violet Paget, the writer known as Vernon Lee (1856–1935), wrote: 'the summing up of a would-be biographer must, I think be: He painted.' This more or less encapsulates Sargent's life.

Above: The Sketchers, *1913, oil on canvas (see page 237).*

Left: Piazzetta di San Marco, *c.1904, watercolour.*

BIRTH AND EARLY LIFE

John Singer Sargent was born in Italy to American parents, surgeon Dr Fitzwilliam Sargent (1820–89) and Mary Newbold Singer (1826–1906), a wealthy merchant's daughter. The couple had moved to Florence in the autumn of 1854, following the death of their first child, in an attempt to restore Mrs Sargent's spirits.

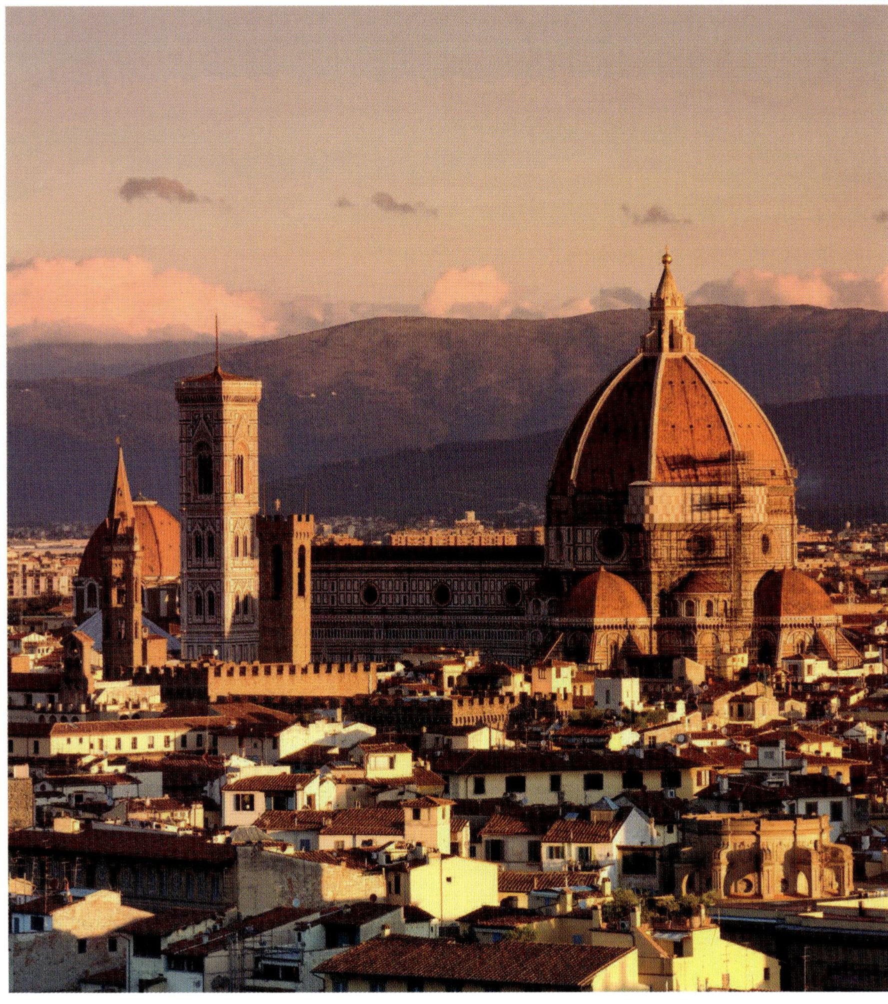

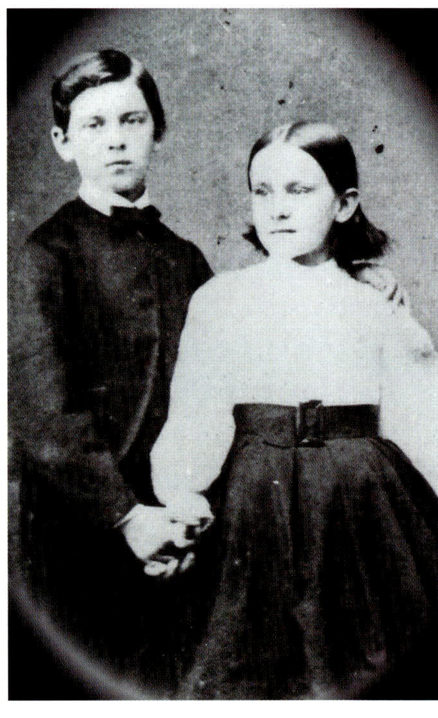

Left: Sargent was born on 12 January in Florence, three years after his elder sister's death.

Below: Because of their itinerant lifestyle, John and his younger sister Emily were together more than most siblings as they grew up, and remained close as adults.

Intending to return to the US after his wife's convalescence, Fitzwilliam Sargent had taken leave of absence from his prominent position as Attending Surgeon at Wills Hospital in Philadelphia. The couple spent most of their time in Paris, but when Mary became pregnant again they went to Florence in Tuscany, to avoid a cholera epidemic in France. On 12 January, 1856, their son John was born. They stayed in Florence until the summer and then went to Geneva and spent the winter in Rome, where their daughter Emily (1857–1936) was born. After Emily's birth, the family spent the spring and summer in Vienna, and at last,

Fitzwilliam reluctantly yielded to his wife's pleas to remain in Europe, and resigned his post in Philadelphia. For the rest of their lives they lived a quiet, nomadic existence, travelling constantly around Europe, never staying in one city for too long, surviving modestly on a small inheritance and savings, and generally avoiding society, except for mixing with a few expatriate friends.

A CLOSE FAMILY

Through an accident when she was four, Emily damaged her spine and from then on had to live a quiet life. Her elder brother became exceptionally protective and close to her, caring for her all his life and involving her in his activities. As adults, they were each other's closest companions, and neither married.

Sargent's mother was an avid amateur painter with a passion for culture and travel. She instigated the family's travels around Europe. In February 1861, while they were in Switzerland, she gave birth to another daughter, Mary Winthrop, nicknamed Minnie. By that time, the American Civil War had started, and Fitzwilliam followed events in the press avidly. The family spent that winter in Nice, living in the Maison Virello, rue Grimaldi. The continual change of local nannies as they settled in different cities and countries exposed John to various European languages, and subsequently, he picked them up without any foreign accent.

CONFLICTING SYMPATHIES

The family travelled to London to consult doctors about Emily's back, and in response to growing English sympathies for the South in the Civil War, Fitzwilliam published a pamphlet entitled *England, the United States, and the Southern Confederacy*, pleading for English reason and requesting that people did not simply consider short-term self-interest – that is in the supply of cotton to English mills – but that they considered the larger implications of the conflict. He was deeply saddened to discover that their fellow American expatriates were in the main similarly narrow-minded. In 1865, the Civil War came to an end. Sadly, four-year-old Minnie caught a bronchial infection, and despite medical attention, died.

Right: The Sargents spent the spring and summer of 1857 in Vienna. This is the interior of the Kunsthistorisches Museum, where the family were frequent visitors.

Below: Mary took her children to the Musée du Louvre in Paris, depicted here in Four O'Clock at the Salon *by François-Auguste Biard, 1847.*

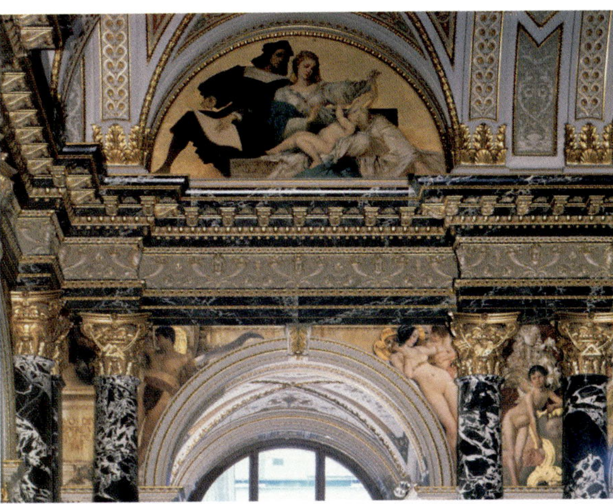

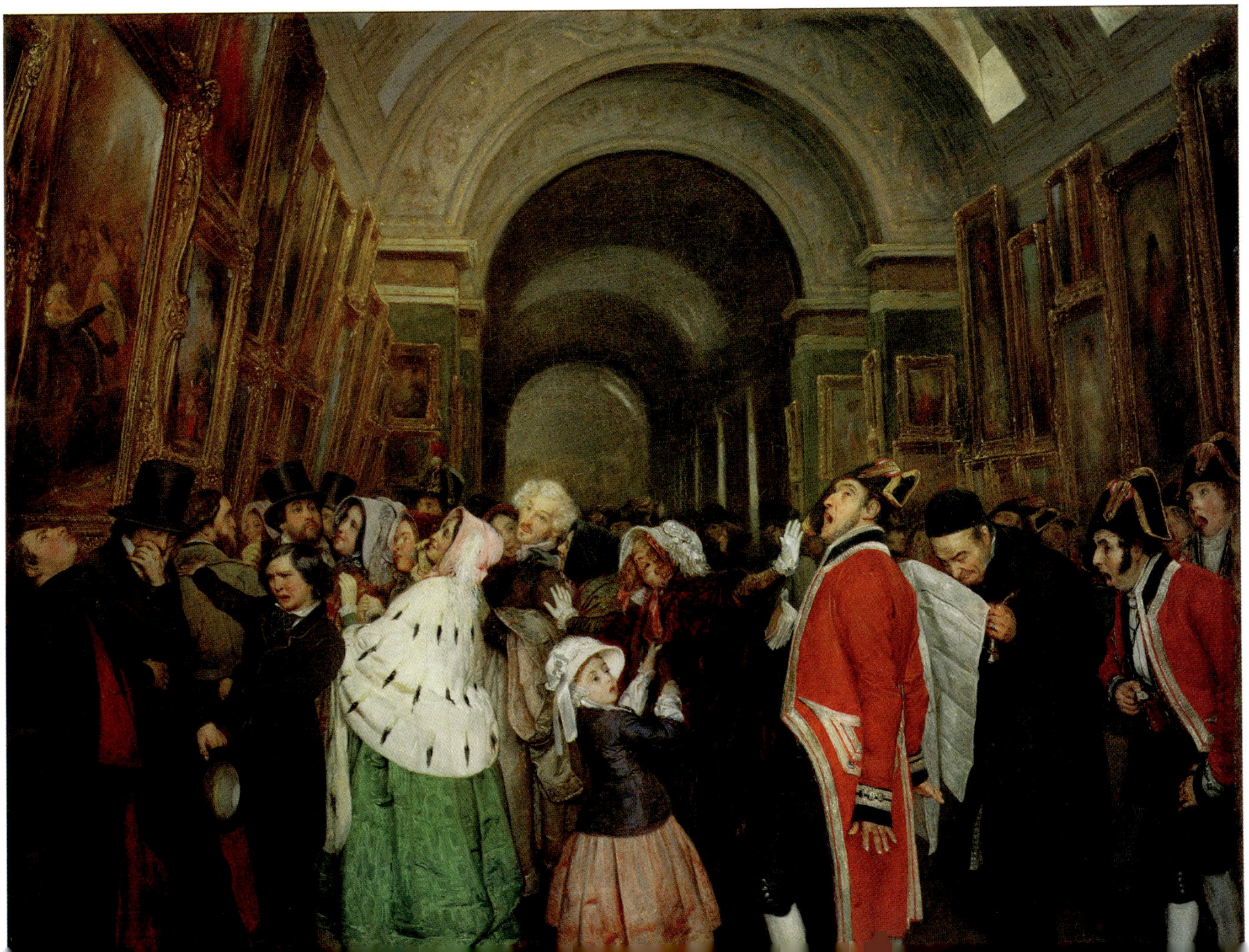

THE AMERICAN CIVIL WAR

From 1861 to 1865, fellow Americans fought each other to determine whether the Union would survive or whether the Confederacy would gain independence. Among the 34 states in January 1861, seven Southern States individually formed the Confederate States of America, which increased to 11. Those states that did not declare this secession were together known as the Union, or the North. The origins of the conflict arose over the slavery issue. In the 1860 presidential election, the Republicans, led by Abraham Lincoln (1809–65), backed the banning of slavery in all US territories, but those in the Southern States saw this as a violation of their constitutional rights. After four years of combat, with over 700,000 soldiers killed, the Confederacy collapsed and slavery was abolished. The ensuing Reconstruction of the nation took a further 12 years.

LEARNING HIS ART

By the age of 10, young John Sargent was fluent in French and Italian and could also speak German. He and Emily had piano teachers and were sent to dancing classes. They were both intelligent, well read, musical, and showed artistic talents. They made several close friends with children of other expatriates.

In the winter of 1866–67, John Sargent met Violet Paget, who lived next door to them in the garden of Maison Virello in Nice. He and Violet were 11, while Emily was nine. In later life, writing under her pseudonym Vernon Lee, Violet described the 'gruesome, historical charades' they played there. She was born in France to British expatriate parents, and like the Sargent children, grew up travelling around Europe. She too loved art, literature and music, and she played the harpsichord. As an adult writer, she was celebrated for her essays on travel in Italy, France, Germany and Switzerland. The Sargent children also became friends with Rafael Ben Nunez del Castillo. The same age as John and Violet, Ben also lived next door for a period of time, and he and John later corresponded with each other for many years.

PAINTING AFTERNOONS

After travelling to Paris, the Rhine, Munich, the Tyrol, Salzburg, Milan and Genoa, the Sargents and the Pagets were no longer neighbours, but whenever possible, Mary Sargent invited Violet to join her two children for afternoons spent painting, dancing or learning to play the piano. Mary also took her children to museums in whatever city they were living in at the time. Once a week, she held social receptions for their friends – expatriate Americans were numerous enough to have formed colonies in the major European cities.

All attempts to have John formally schooled failed however, mainly because of his itinerant life. Mary however, was convinced that travelling around Europe and visiting museums and churches would give him a satisfactory education. Early on, she had given John and Emily their own sketchbooks, and took them on drawing excursions, and she introduced them to art wherever they travelled in Europe.

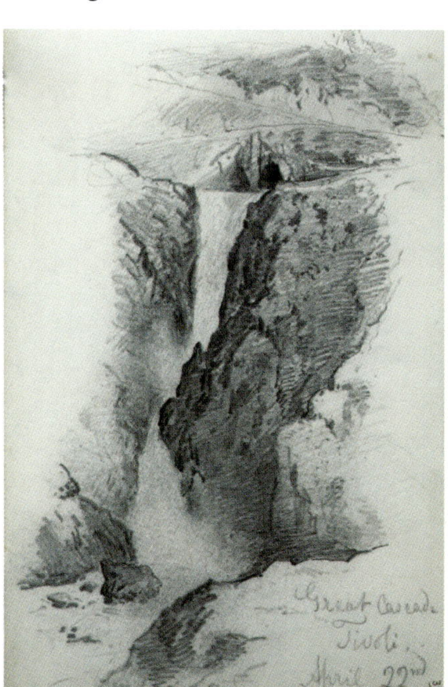

Above: The Great Cascade, *Tivoli, Italy, from Sargent's Alpine sketchbook of 1869.*

Above right: Showing Sargent's precocity, this is Templum Vestas *in Rome that he painted in a sketchbook in 1869, age 13.*

Right: Switzerland, 1869. One of a number of accomplished and mature watercolours from the sketchbook Sargent took to Switzerland when he was 13.

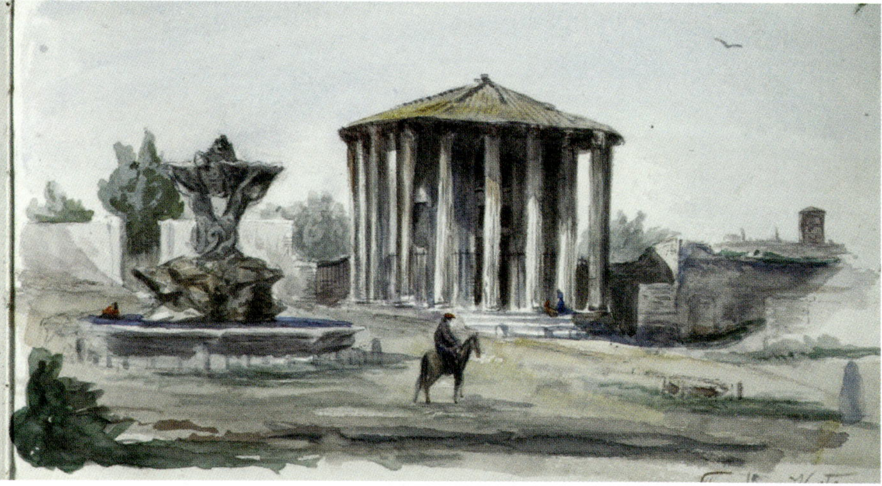

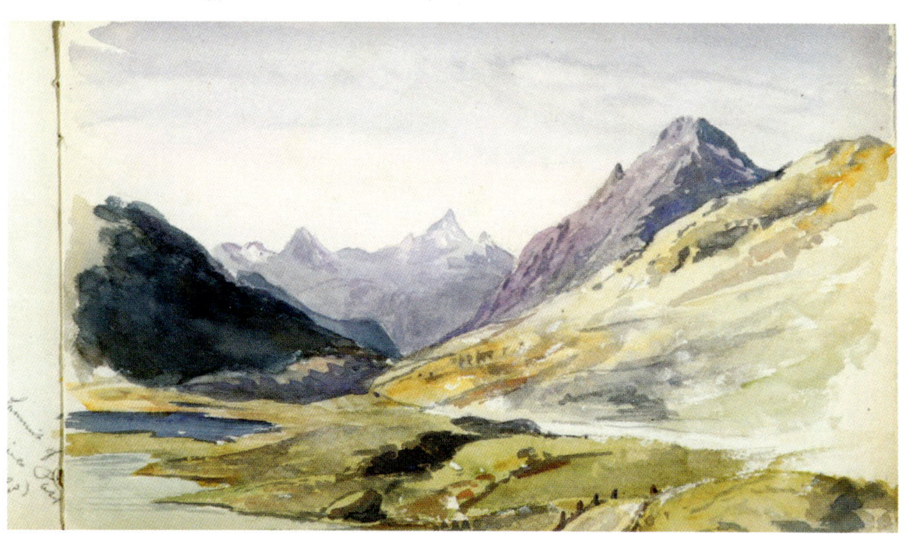

PRECOCIOUS TALENTS

By the time John was 13, Mary wrote that he: 'sketches quite nicely, and has a remarkably quick and correct eye. If we could afford to give him really good lessons, he would soon be quite a little artist.' During the winter of 1868–69, while the family was living above the Piazza di Spagna in Rome, he had some watercolour lessons from Carl Welsch (1828–1904), a German-American landscape painter. Sargent helped Welsch in his studio, and copied several of his watercolours. That year, the family travelled to Naples, Capri, Sorrento, Pompeii, Padua, Bolzano, St Moritz and Florence, where the young John was enrolled in the Accademia di Belle Arti.

While they were still in Florence, in February 1870, Violet Sargent was born (1870–1955), the youngest and last of the Sargent children. In Florence, John attended M. Joseph Domengés day school in the former Convent dei Servi di Maria in the Piazza della Santissima Annunziata and he took dancing lessons at 43 via Romana.

Next, the family travelled to Venice and Lake Maggiore, Switzerland and finally to Florence again. During the summer, John painted several Alpine watercolours that demonstrate his advanced abilities. However, in order have their son formally educated, the Sargents moved to Dresden, where John studied Latin, Greek, mathematics, geography, history and German, in preparation for the entrance exams for Das Gymnasium zum Heilige Kreuz (School of the Cross). While in Dresden, he also copied several paintings in the Albertina gallery.

RETURN TO ITALY

Unaccustomed to cold, damp winters, Emily became seriously ill and, terrified that they would lose another child, the Sargents abruptly ended John's education and travelled to Berlin, then to Leipzig, Munich and Venice, before returning to Florence. John and Emily also went on holiday for ten days in Bologna with Violet Paget and her family. Teenagers now, they spent their time discussing art and aesthetics.

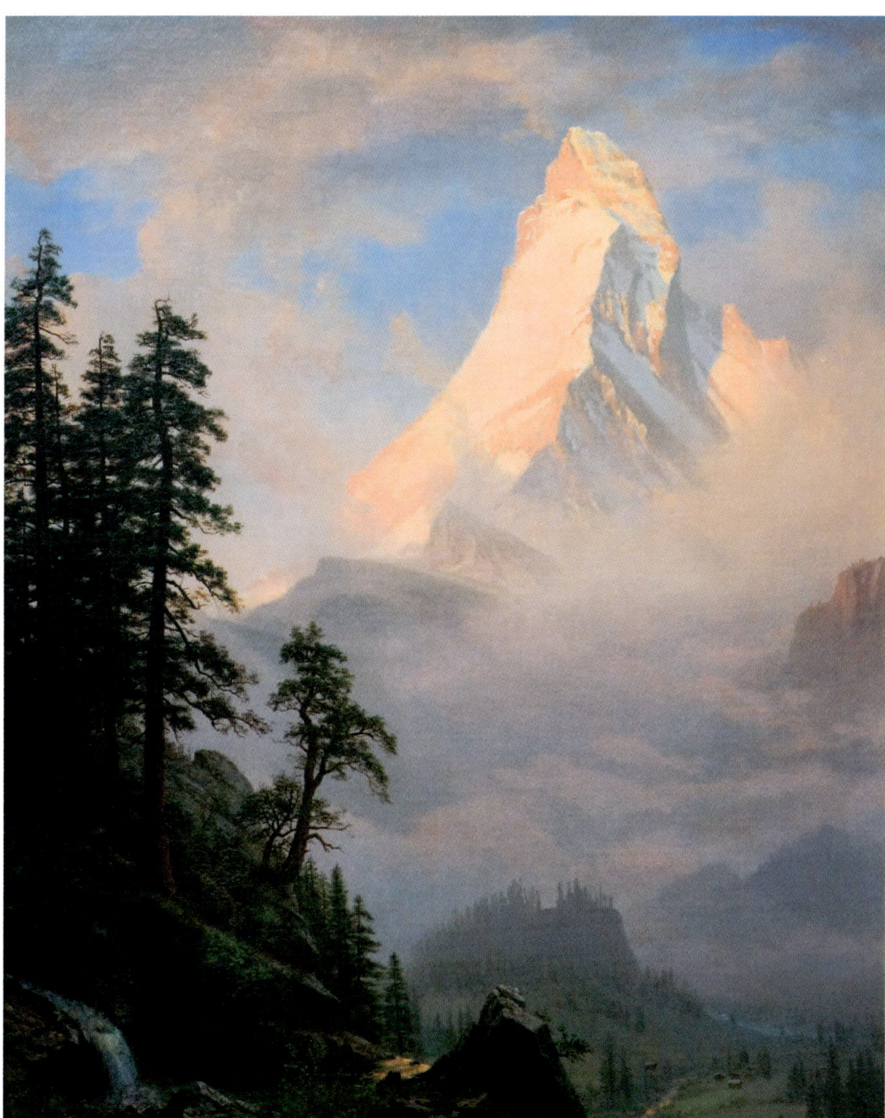

Above: Sunrise on the Matterhorn *by Albert Bierstadt (1830–1902), after 1875. Sargent travelled to numerous natural beauty spots.*

Below: In Florence, Sargent regularly visited the Galleria dell'Accademia, depicted by Odoardo Borrani, 1863.

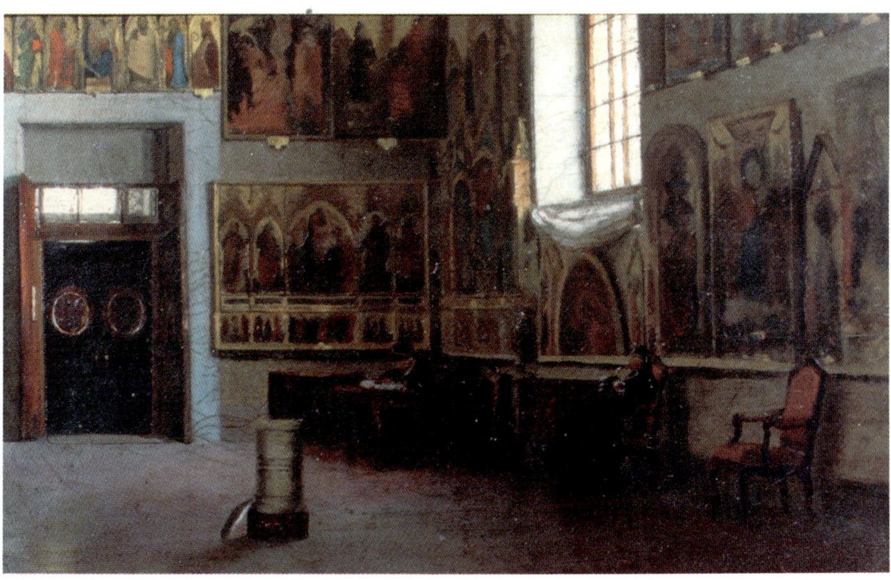

IN PARIS

In the summer of 1873, Mary Sargent and her children stayed in Venice while Fitzwilliam travelled to America. He met them in Switzerland in July, and that autumn, at the age of 17, Sargent enrolled at the Accademia di Belle Arti in Florence, where he studied art alongside British and American expatriate students.

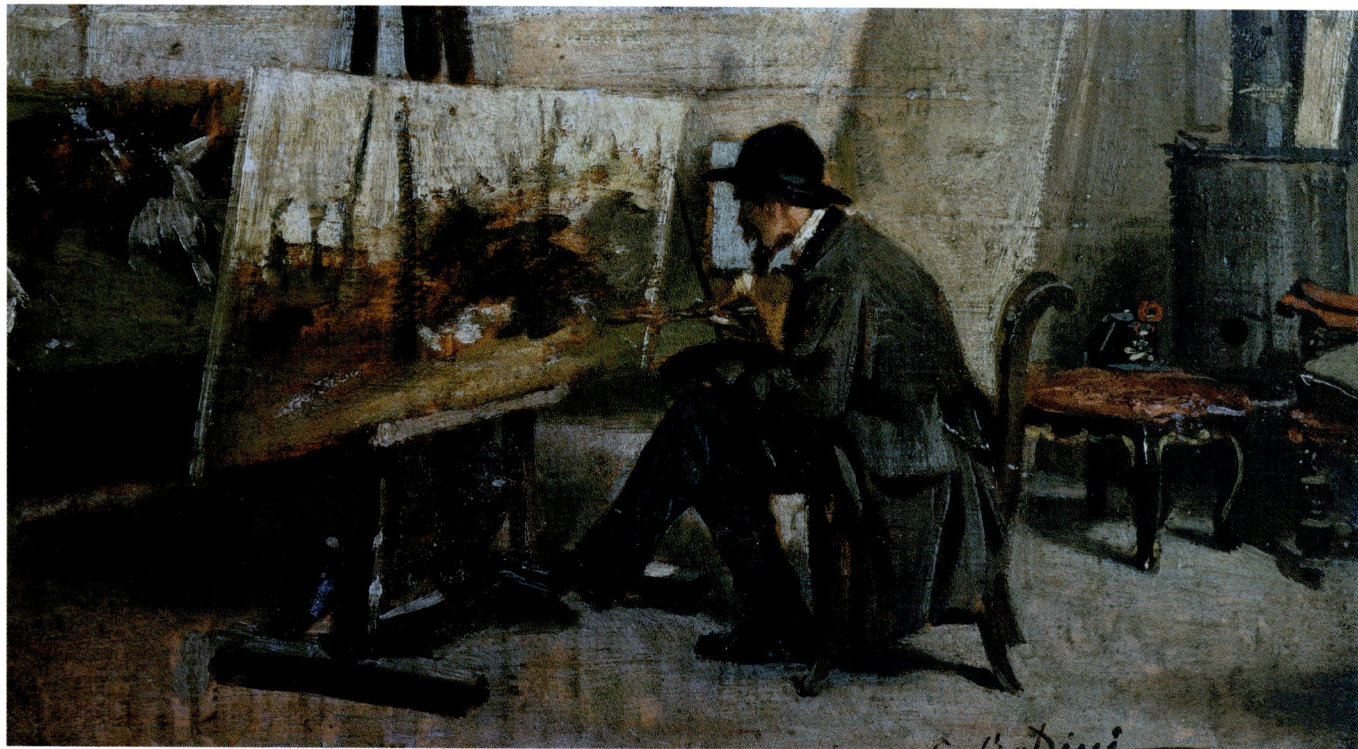

Above: A contemporary artist in a studio painted in 1866–67 by Sargent's friend Giovanni Boldini (1842–1931).

THE DAY AFTER

Sargent's fellow students at the Accademia di Belle Arti in Florence were Walter Launt Palmer (1854–1932), Edwin White (1817–77), Edward Clifford (1844–1907) and Heath Wilson (1849–1927). However, by December, the Accademia closed temporarily for lack of funds. It reopened the following March, but by then, Sargent was dissatisfied with the teaching. Determining to study in Paris as it was the art capital of the world, he spent weeks drawing and painting in efforts to convince his father to take his ambition of becoming an artist seriously. His diligence paid off, as in the spring of 1874, he and his father travelled to Paris. As they left Italy, in Paris, the artists who were soon be known as the Impressionists were holding their first independent exhibition. The exhibition ran from 15 April to 15 May 1874; Sargent and

Below: Impression, Sunrise, 1872; Claude Monet's paintings of the port of Le Havre earned the Impressionists their name.

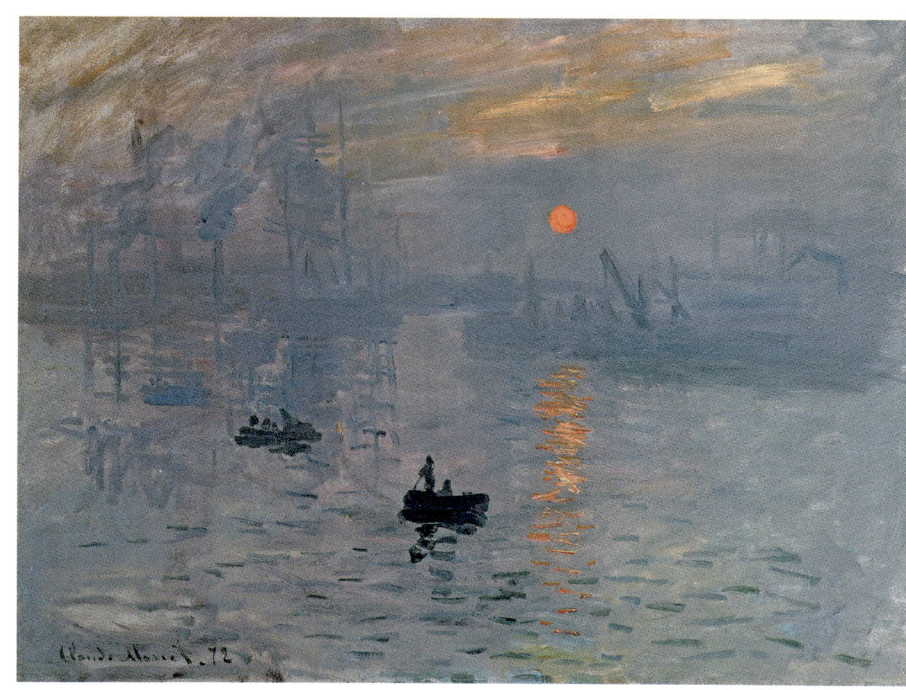

his father arrived in Paris on 16 May. However they did not know then that the exhibition would prove to be significant; the group of artists were unknown, and perceived by many as rather arrogant and lacking in talent.

GROWTH AS AN ARTIST

When Sargent and his father arrived in Paris they found that most of the main studios were full. Then, on 26 May, they visited the studio of Charles Auguste Émile Durand, known as Carolus-Duran (1837–1917), who was celebrated for his portraits of members of high society. An admirer of the Spanish master, Diego Velázquez (1599–1660), Carolus-Duran taught his students not to prepare a painting by making sketches or drawings, but instead insisted that: 'the main planes of the face must be laid directly on the unprepared canvas with a broad brush.' After studying Sargent's portfolio, Carolus-Duran accepted him as a student. Sargent also decided to sit

the rigorous exams to study drawing at the École des Beaux-Arts. His father left him in Paris, and for the first time John was on his own. He befriended fellow student, the American James Carroll Beckwith (1852–1917) and often worked in his studio. In July Sargent travelled to Caen to meet his family, and then they travelled on to Rouen together. By September they had all returned to Paris, moving into 52, rue Abbatrice. Sargent sat the Beaux-Arts exams in perspective and anatomy, ornament drawing and life drawing, coming 37th out of 162 entrants; the only one of Carolus-Duran's students to achieve success that year. After that, he became immensely industrious and remained so for the rest of his life. His routine then was a full day at Carolus-Duran's atelier, followed by two hours at the École des Beaux-Arts, at the coveted life classes of Adolphe Yvon (1817–93), then two more hours at the studio of artist Léon Bonnat (1833–1922).

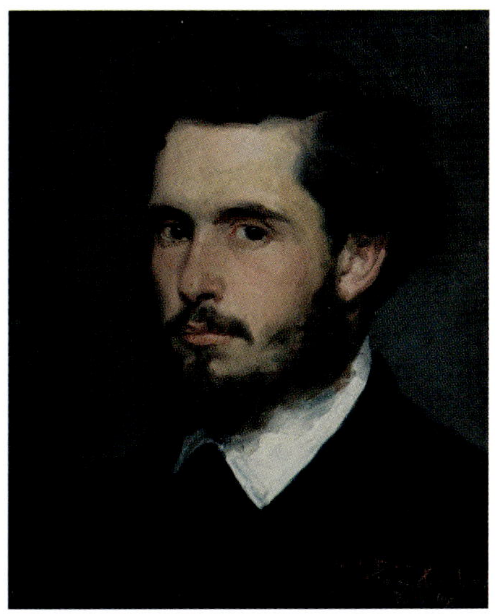

Above: The most highly regarded portraitist in Paris when Sargent arrived, Carolus-Duran painted this portrait of Monet in 1867.

Below: Sargent's painting, Two Wine Glasses, *c.1875, suggests familiarity with the early work of the Impressionists.*

THE IMPRESSIONISTS

The term 'Impressionist' was first used as an insult by a commentator in response to the 1874 exhibition in Paris. Put on by 30 unknown artists, including Claude Monet (1840–1926), Auguste Renoir (1841–1919), Camille Pissarro (1830–1903), Paul Cézanne (1839–1906), Alfred Sisley (1839–99), Frederic Bazille (1841–70) and Mary Cassatt (1844–1926), they had no one style, but called themselves the Société Anonyme Coopérative des Artistes, Peintres, Sculpteurs, Graveurs. All had been rejected by the art establishment for their radical approach to painting. Capturing transitory moments, often en plein air, they applied sketchy, rapid brushmarks, bright colours and few details. To contemporary viewers, their paintings looked unfinished. Critic Louis Leroy (1812–85), wrote of one of Monet's exhibited paintings *Impression, Sunrise*: 'Impression [...] Wallpaper in its embryonic state is more finished than that seascape.' The name Impressionism stuck.

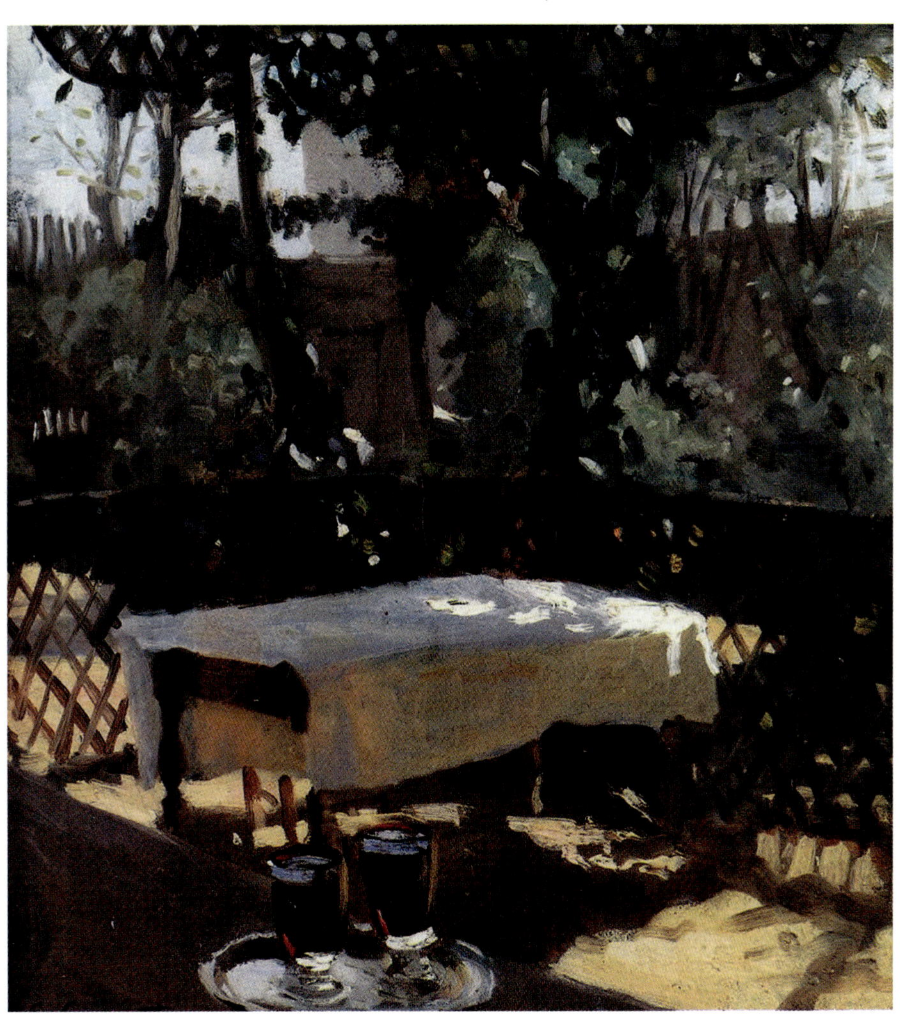

ACADEMIC V. AVANT-GARDE

From the 17th to the 19th centuries, the official art academies that had been established across Europe wielded great power in the art world, particularly the Académie des Beaux-Arts in Paris. To have any hope of success, artists followed the preferred academic art style of precision and refinement with a moralistic undercurrent.

As Sargent was growing up, academic art was the style most art students aspired to, with its careful drawing, imperceptible brushmarks and strict hierarchy of subjects. The style was directly influenced by the European art academies, and held to standards set by the French Académie des Beaux-Arts. It favoured a synthesis of Neoclassicism and Romanticism, and subjects that included history, religion, mythology and portraiture, reflecting the popular tastes of the upper middle classes. The academic style is exemplified in the paintings of William-Adolphe Bouguereau (1825–1905), Thomas Couture (1815–79), and Hans Makart (1840–84). The academies wielded great power, both over how art was made and over which artists became successful. They were in charge of art schools, they organized exhibitions and awarded prestigious art prizes. At the time, independent art exhibitions were rare,

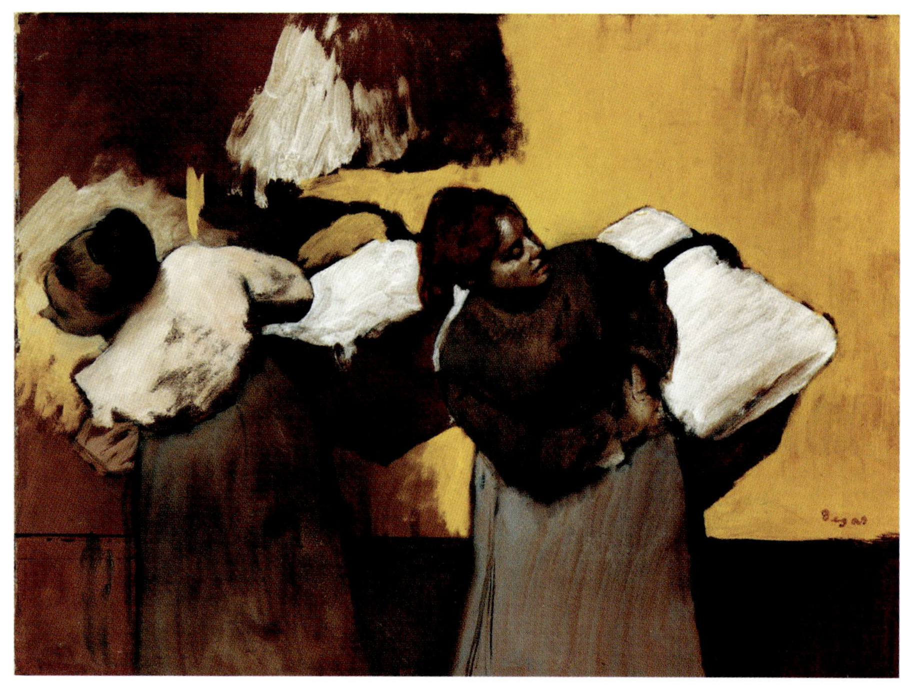

Below: Odalisque, *Thomas Couture, c.1870. Smooth, imperceptible brushmarks and a classical style were valued components of Academic art.*

Above: Laundresses, *c.1876. Flat brushstrokes, solid colour and unconventional compositions depicting modern life were some of Edgar Degas's avant-garde methods.*

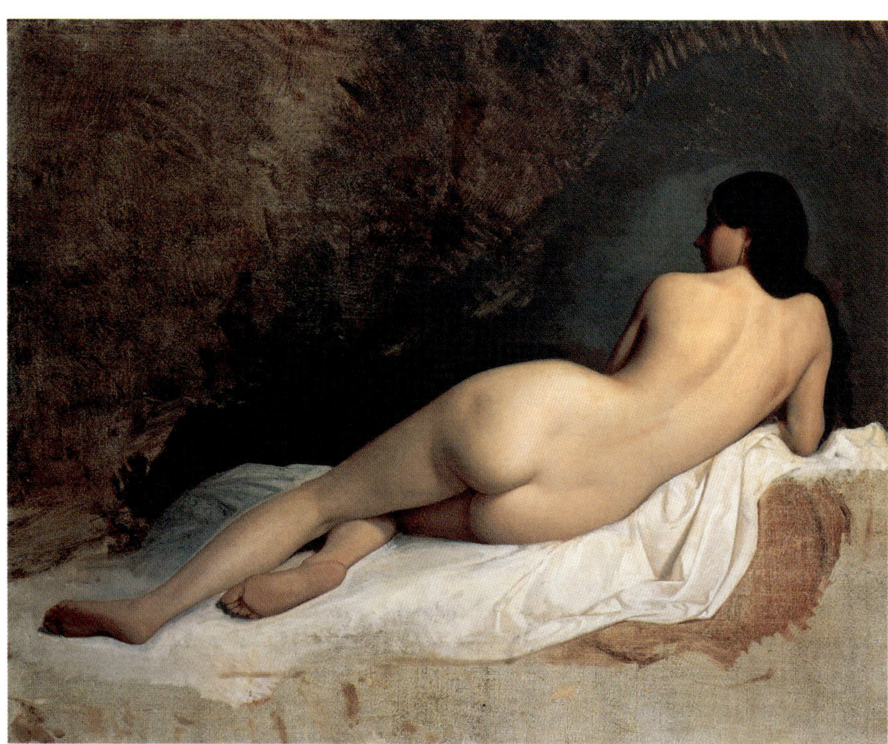

THE SALON

The Salon, the official art exhibition of the Parisian Académie des Beaux-Arts, began in 1667 and was held either annually or bi-annually for over 200 years. Between 1748 and 1890, it was the greatest art event in the Western world. Art was selected by a conservative jury, and as the only major art exhibition in France, it could hugely influence artists' career prospects. Artists who did not conform to academic conventions and expectations were rarely, if ever, approved by the jury, and so found it almost impossible to forge a successful career. Paintings were exhibited on every available wall space, from floor to ceiling, and artists aimed not only to be chosen, but also to be displayed where they could be seen.

most artists sought to be chosen for their national academy's official shows, where panels of experts selected the work and decided where on the walls it would be displayed – prominently or less obviously – depending on its perceived merits.

BREAKAWAY GROUPS

From the second half of the 19th century, especially in France and England, some artists, such as the Pre-Raphaelites and the Realists, began breaking away from the dominance of the Académie des Beaux-Arts and the Royal Academy. The French Revolution of 1848, in which both the working classes and middle classes were involved, prepared the way for Realism and artists who followed, such as Édouard Manet (1832–83) and Edgar Degas (1834–1917) chose to paint modern life rather than the preferred academic subjects. The Impressionists then began painting in a manner that went against long-held academic values and stylistic conventions. Their art captured fleeting moments, sensations of light, and aspects of modern life, all abhorred by the Salon jury. The Impressionists staged their own exhibitions and endured ridicule and contempt in efforts to produce an art they believed in. It was a struggle; the first Impressionist exhibition in 1874 attracted 3,500 visitors, while the Salon that opened two weeks later had 450,000 visitors. However, their art soon became accepted, and it led to more experimental art movements, such as Post-Impressionism, Expressionism and Fauvism.

AVANT-GARDE ART

The difference between what these modern artists produced and what the public expected resulted in hostility. Used to academic art, onlookers saw transgressions of traditions as insults rather than innovations, and accused the new artists of fraud, vulgarity and lunacy, while the press repudiated them. However, a few critics defended them. In 1863, the poet Charles Baudelaire (1821–67) used the term 'avant-garde,' from the French for 'vanguard,' meaning

ahead of the rest, to describe his ideal artist in an influential essay: *The Painter of Modern Life*. The term became used to describe any artist, group or style that explored new artistic methods or new techniques. From early in his career Sargent admired the modern approach of the Impressionists, and he joined with them in seeking new ways to record the world. He was perceived as an artistic innovator who challenged the conventional representations, but pleasingly so.

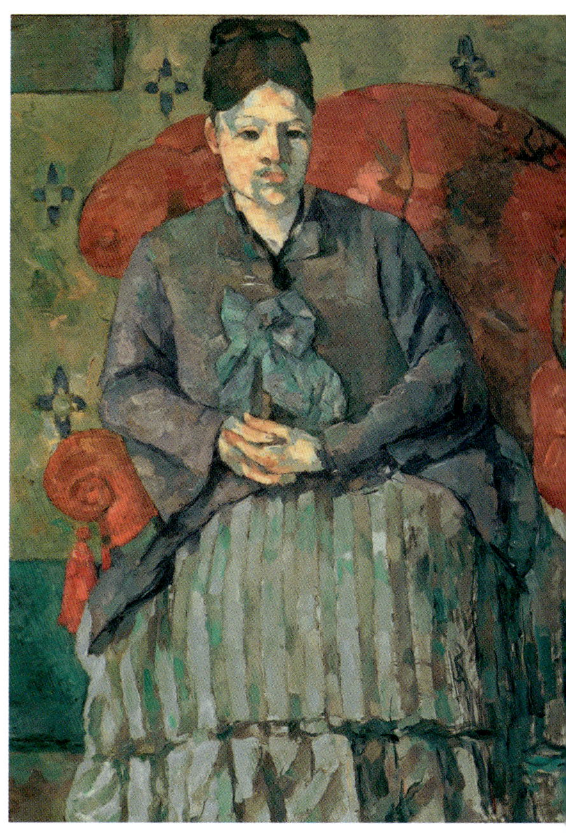

Right: Madame Cézanne in an Armchair, c.1877. *Paul Cézanne applied small patches of colour in subtle variations, and experimented with form in an attempt to create a completely new style.*

Below: Charity, William-Adolphe Bouguereau, 1878. *Beauty combined with morality epitomized the academic style depicted in this painting.*

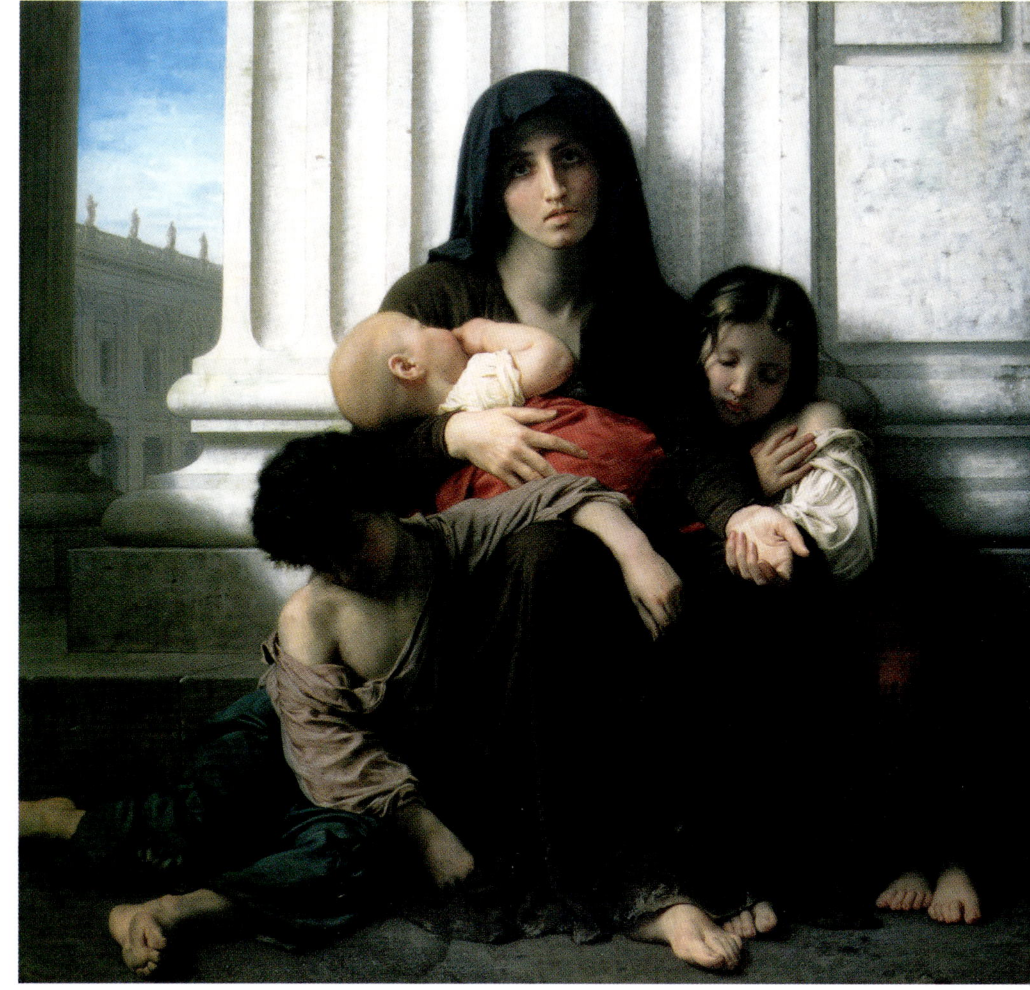

NEW WORLDS

Every January the students of Carolus-Duran held a banquet for him. In 1875 after this event, he took Sargent and two other students on a painting trip to Nice. The following May, Sargent sailed to America with his mother and sister Emily. At 20 years old, he was required to go there to retain US citizenship.

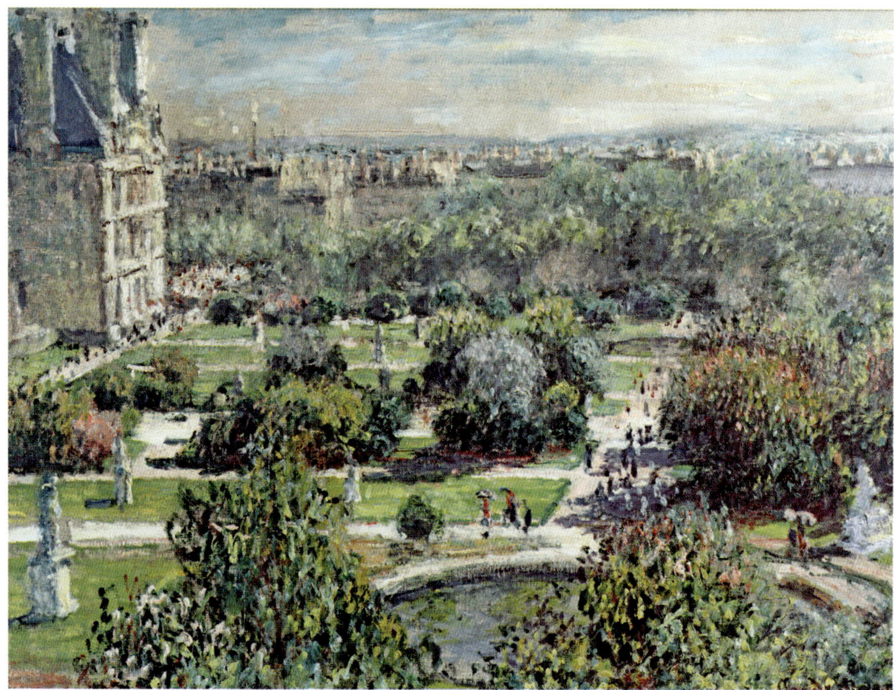

Above: Claude Monet's View of the Tuileries *of 1876 is an aerial view of Paris, painted at the time Sargent was studying there.*

A FAVOURITE STUDENT

Will H. Low (1853–1933), a fellow student at Carolus-Duran's studio, recalled Sargent's arrival there in 1874: 'He made his appearance... bringing a great roll of canvases and papers...an amazement to the class... Having a foundation in drawing which none among his new comrades could equal, this genius – surely the correct word – quickly acquired the methods then prevalent in the studio, and then proceeded to act as a stimulating force, which far exceeded the benefits of instruction given by Carolus himself.' Sargent soon became Carolus-Duran's favourite student. Although the other students nicknamed him 'teacher's pet,' it was in jest as they acknowledged his efforts and superior skills, and he was popular with them. His peripatetic childhood had prepared him for socializing with people of all ages and backgrounds.

In June 1875, the atelier closed for the summer and Sargent joined his family in Brittany. A couple of months later, he and Chicago-born Beckwith rented a studio together in Paris. That summer, Sargent stayed at Madame Darode's boarding house in the rue de l'Odéon, and at Christmas, Beckwith joined the Sargent family at Saint Malo.

THE SECOND IMPRESSIONIST EXHIBITION

On 1 April 1876, the second Impressionist exhibition opened in Paris at the gallery of the art dealer, Paul Durand-Ruel (1831–1922). Among the 252 works, Degas showed 24 paintings and Monet 18, although some exhibitors had no connection with the Impressionists. Despite the many negative reviews in newspapers and journals, Sargent visited the show and greatly admired the new painting ideas. It is probable that he met Claude Monet and Auguste Rodin (1840–1917) there. His mind was ignited by the exhibition and almost immediately, Sargent began incorporating looser, freer brushmarks and brighter colours into his own work.

SARGENT'S AMERICAN VISIT

The following month, on 13 May, while his father and younger sister Violet holidayed in Switzerland, Sargent sailed to America for the first time with his mother and Emily. During the voyage he made sketches of life on board ship. Once in America they visited the Centennial International Exhibition in Philadelphia; the first official World's Fair in the United States, held to celebrate 100 years of American cultural and industrial progress. Thirty-seven countries participated in the exposition, which attracted nearly 10 million visitors. Sargent was particularly fascinated by the marine paintings of American landscape artist Winslow Homer (1836–1910). Also while in America, he met his Newbold and Sargent cousins, and he and his mother and sister stayed on Rhode Island in New England as guests of his parents' friend, Augustus Ludlow Case (1812–93), a rear admiral in the US Navy who had served during the American Civil War. Sargent became good friends with Case's son-in-law, Charles Deering (1852–1927), who was an amateur artist, businessman, art collector and philanthropist. During the trip, Sargent also visited Chicago, Washington DC and Canada, where he visted Niagara Falls. At the beginning of October, the family set sail for England and by November, Sargent had returned to Paris where he took up his studies once more with Carolus-Duran and at the École des Beaux-Arts.

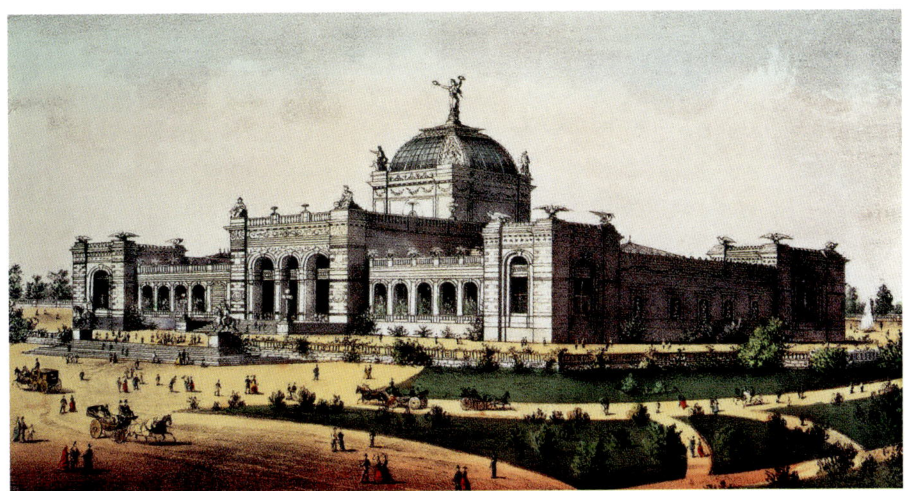

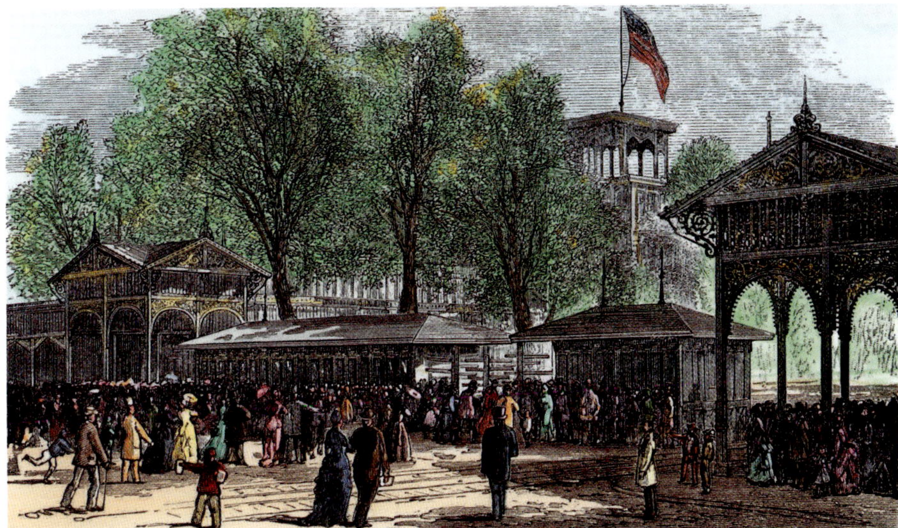

THE LUXEMBOURG MURAL

During the winter of 1875, Carolus-Duran received a public commission to paint a mural for the Luxembourg Palace in Paris, which had been used as a parliamentary building since the end of the 18th century. The immense canvas, which depicted *The Triumph of Marie de' Medici*, needed assistants and Carolus-Duran employed his best pupils: Singer Sargent, Beckwith and another American student Frank Fowler (1852–1910). They painted large sections of the work, and within it, Sargent and Beckwith added portraits of each other and of Carolus-Duran.

Above Left: The Art Gallery of the Centennial Exhibition in Philadelphia that Sargent visited, specifically studying paintings by Homer.

Left: Crowds at the main entrance to the Centennial Exhibition that fascinated Sargent during his first visit to the US.

Below: While in Canada, Sargent visited Niagara Falls, painted here by F. E. Church (1826–1900) in 1856.

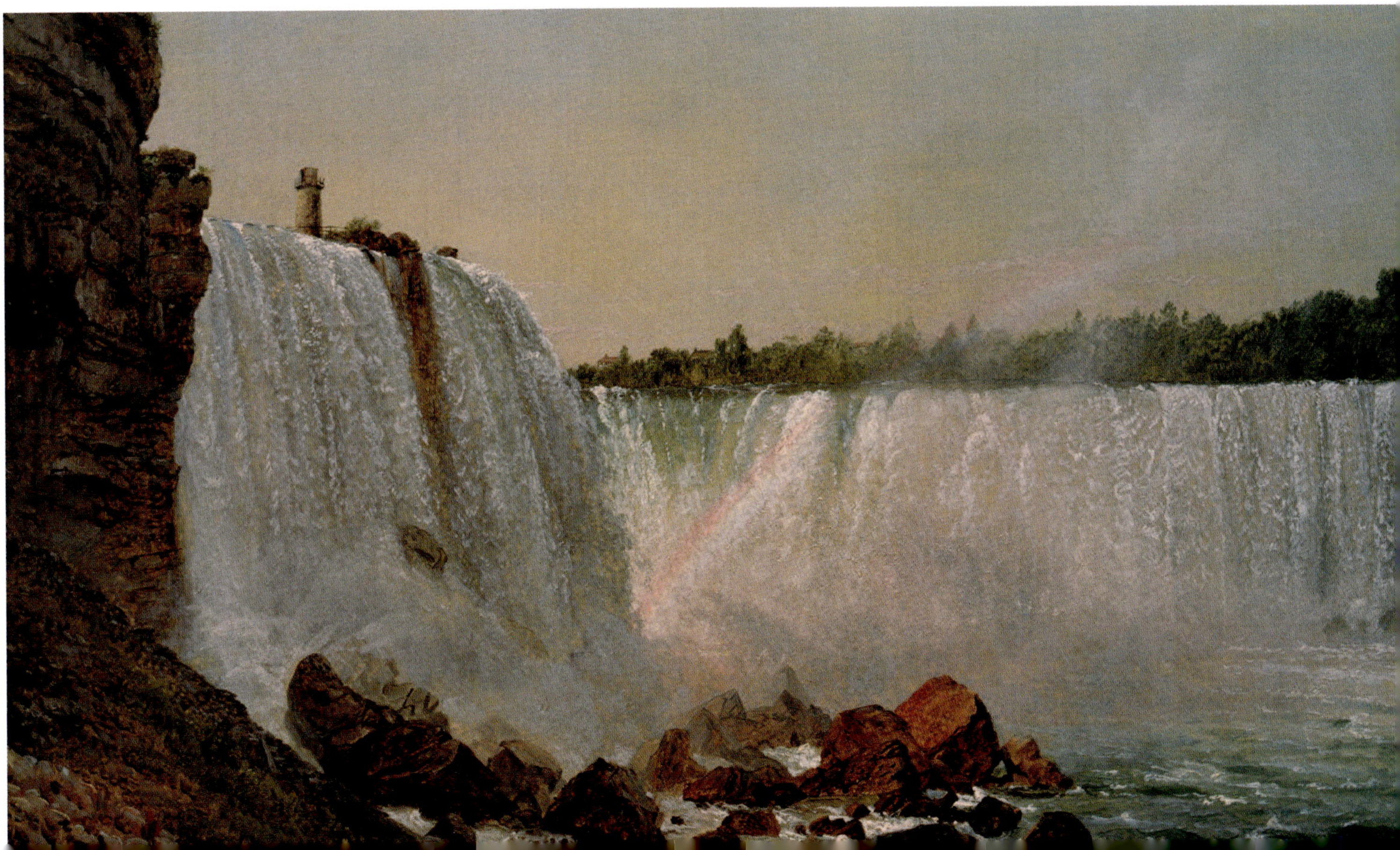

THE SALON AND BRITTANY

In 1877, at age 21, Sargent had his first Salon success. In the summer, he had taken a holiday with his family to Cancale on the Brittany coast where he made several sketches of locals fishing for oysters, which later became the subject of a colourful and expressive painting – and his second Salon success.

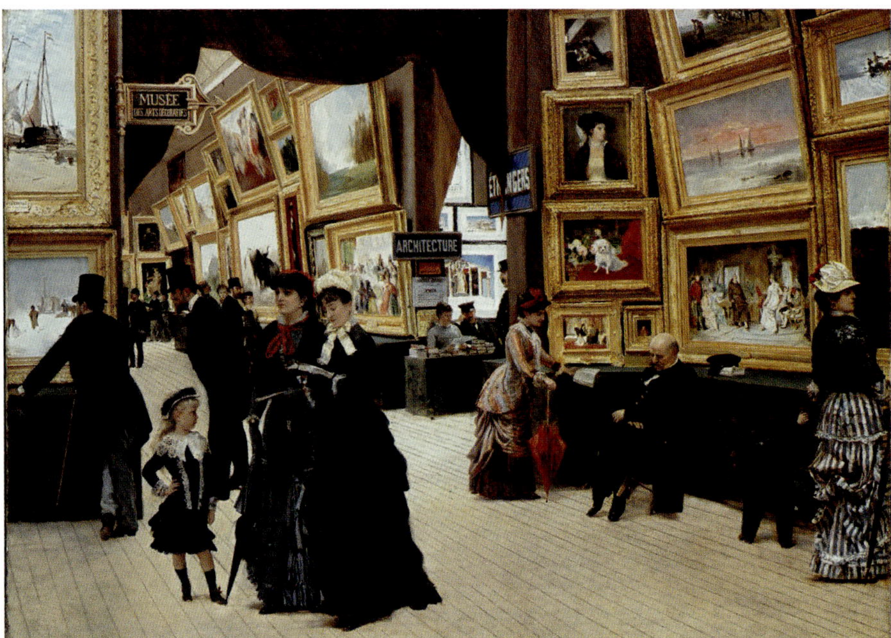

Above: The Salon, *c.1850. The Salon originally displayed the work of graduates of the École des Beaux-Arts, but it soon became open to any artist to enter.*

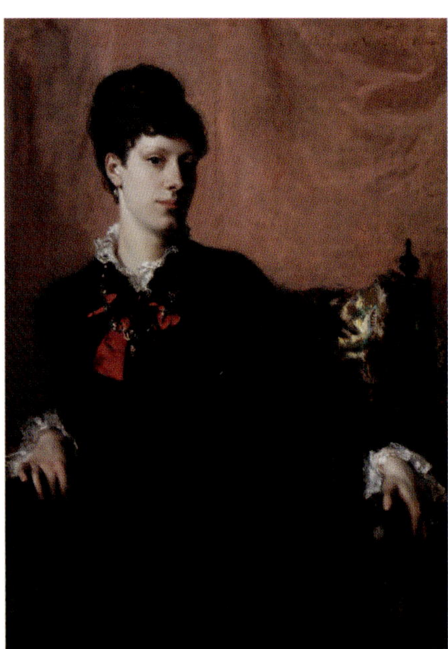

Above: Miss Fanny Watts, *1877. The early success of this portrait at the Salon heralded Sargent's rise to public acclaim in Paris.*

FIRST SUCCESSFUL PORTRAIT

Sargent had completed less than three years at the studio of Carolus-Duran when one of his portraits – of a family friend, Frances Sherborne Ridley Watts, known as Fanny (1858–1927) – was accepted by the Salon jury. Although his brushwork was a little freer than in most academic paintings, it was not as sketchy as the Impressionists' work, and a portrait of a friend was an acceptable subject for aspiring artists. Portraits displayed young artists' skills for those Salon visitors who might wish to make a commission. However, in contrast to traditional and upright compositions, Sargent presented his friend Fanny in an asymmetrical, leaning pose, resembling a portrait painted the previous year by Édouard Manet of the French poet and critic Stéphane Mallarmé (1842–98). Mallarmé's leaning position implies a sense of informality and familiarity, and the work was perceived as modern and daring. But although Sargent presented a similar pose as the Manet portrait, he did not adopt the same broken brushwork, so the painting was not perceived as too audacious; it was a blend of ideas Sargent had seen in the work of Manet, Monet, Degas, and especially in the portraits of Velázquez, who was Carolus-Duran's favourite artist.

Fanny was one of Sargent's friends from childhood, along with Violet Paget and Ben Castillo. Her parents were part of the group of expatriate Americans living in and travelling around Europe. When they found themselves in the same cities, they socialized and became rather like an extended family, writing to each other when apart. While Fanny was in Paris, it was perhaps only natural that Sargent would choose her as his sitter for his first Salon entry. He painted the portrait under Carolus-Duran's instruction, using warm tones to contrast with the black and white of her clothing. He captured her with apparent sensitivity and fondness: her slender, elegant fingers are relaxed on the arms of the chair; her sideways glance is calm. There is no tension in the image, and the splash of red against her black dress serves to enliven her face and highlight her lips. The handling of light is mature and closer to the tonal modelling of Velázquez. than to the bright, less modulated colour of the Impressionists that Sargent admired.

THE OYSTER GATHERERS

That summer in Brittany, Sargent spent time sketching the locals – mainly women and children – he watched each day walking across the beaches to fish, and back again in the evenings. Fascinated by the light, colour and movement, when he returned to his Paris studio, he created two large compositions of the subject. The first was *Oyster Gatherers of Cancale*. As with his portrait of Fanny Watts, it is not a simple blend of academic and avant-garde, but a personal expression and amalgamation of various artistic methods. The painting was selected by the jury for the Salon of 1878, where it also won an honourable mention. Carolus-Duran also entered his mural to that year's Salon, where it attracted positive reviews and additionally helped to promote Sargent's reputation. With such positive attention, Carolus-Duran subsequently agreed to sit for a portrait.

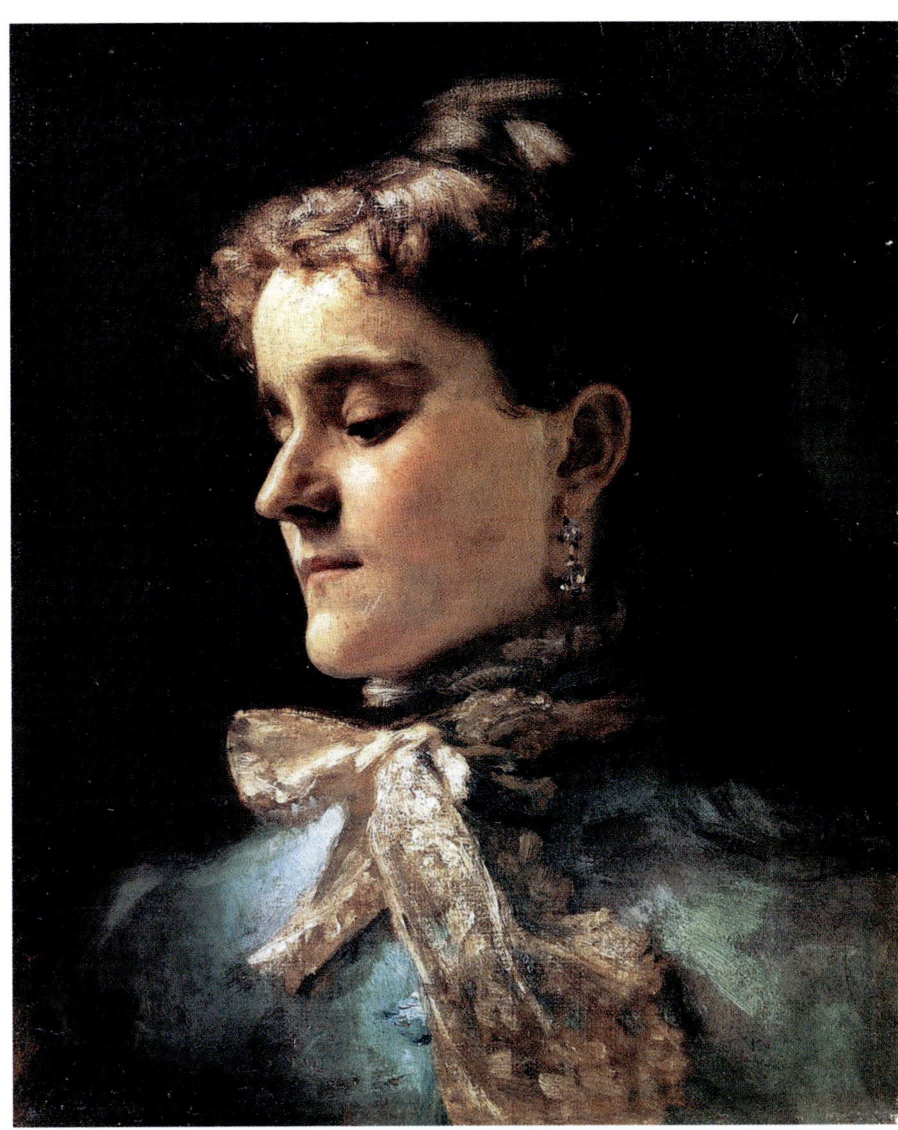

Right: Emily Sargent, 1877. *This is one of Sargent's earliest portraits of his beloved younger sister Emily.*

Below: Fishing for Oysters at Cancale. *In 1878, Sargent sent this sketch to the newly-formed Society of American Artists, New York, before submitting his finished painting of the subject to the Paris Salon (see page 105).*

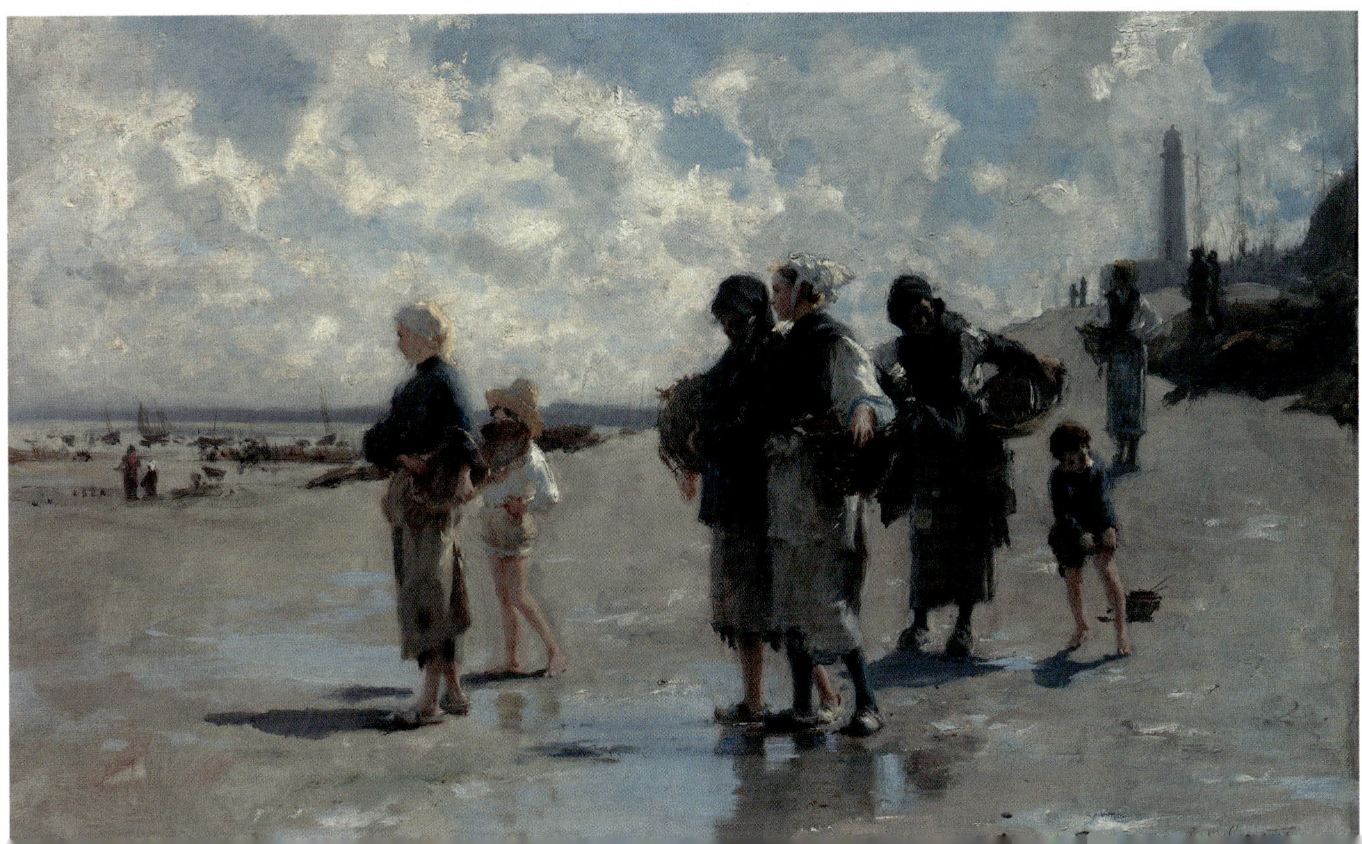

THE MEDITERRANEAN

In late July 1878, Sargent left Paris and his unfinished portrait of Carolus-Duran, and travelled to Naples. A week later he continued to the island of Capri, a favourite destination for artists because of its light, beauty and dramatic coastline. While there, he was befriended by an English painter, Frank Hyde (1849–1937).

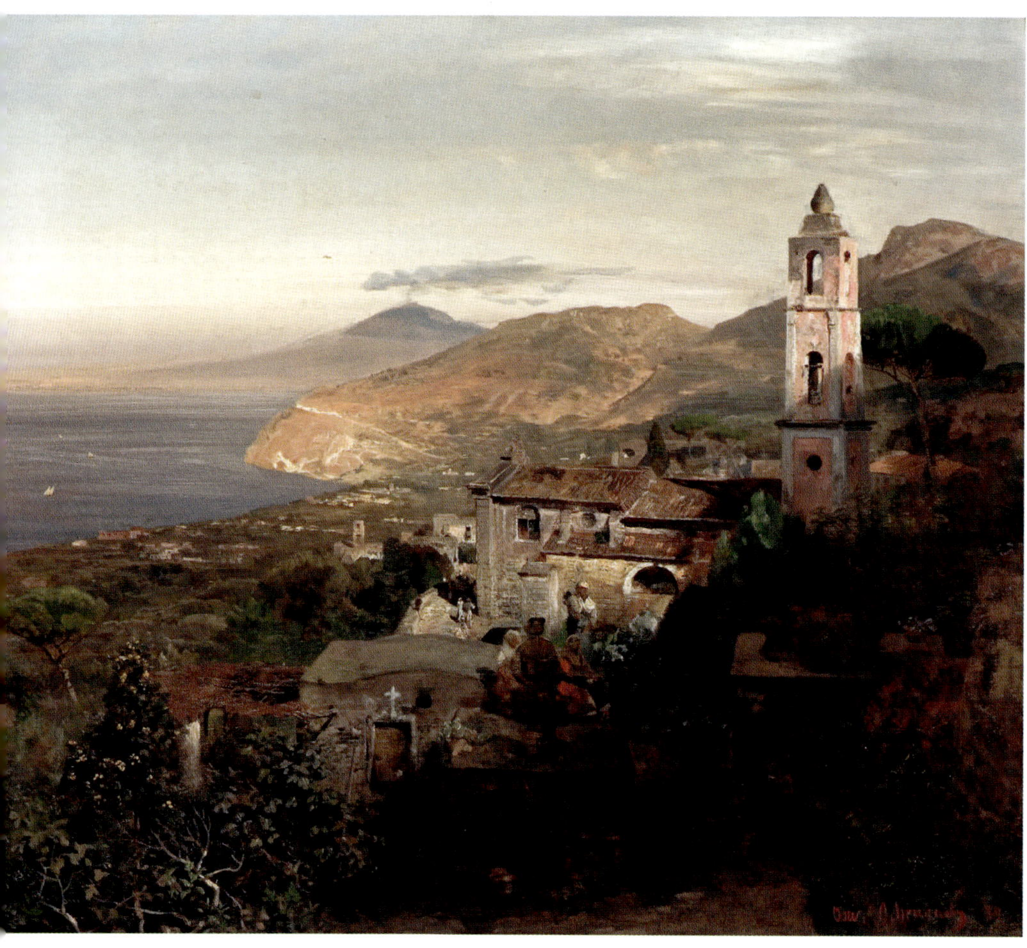

Above: Evening on Capri, *1860 by the German landscape painter Oswald Achenbach (1827–1905).*

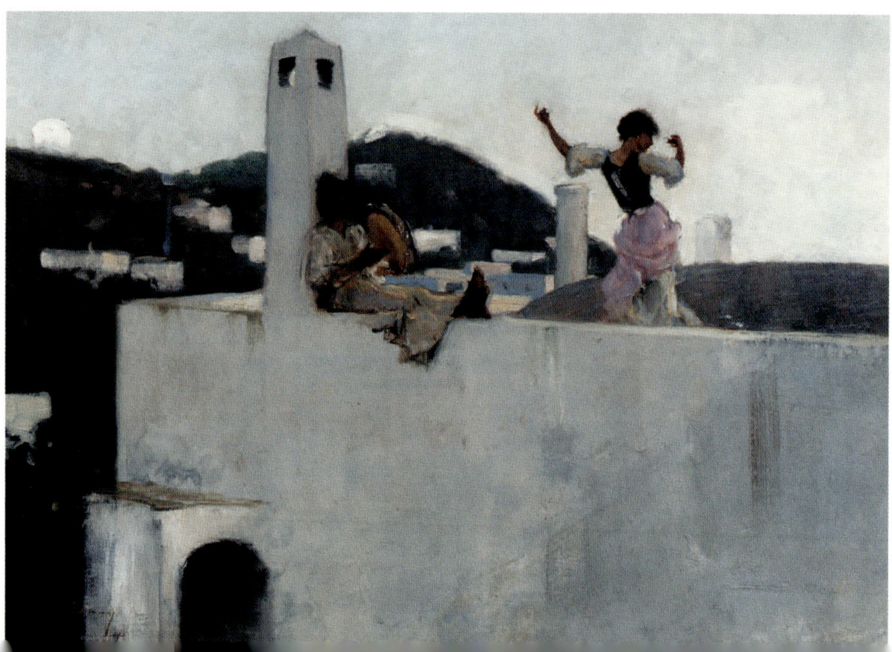

Below: Capri Girl on a Rooftop, *1878. One of Sargent's paintings of Rosina dancing the tarantella as dusk is falling.*

Sargent's summer travels in 1878 took him first to Aix-Les-Bains in south-eastern France, then to Naples to spend a week with his family. At the beginning of August, he left for Capri, which was said to be full of beautiful women, bright colours, distinctive scenery and interesting architecture. He managed to convince the captain of a small market boat laden with fruit and vegetables to take him to the island, but once there, he discovered that the oppressive heat had discouraged tourists and he booked into the deserted Marina Hotel. For the first few days, he sketched and painted, but felt somewhat lonely; it was the first time he had been anywhere without knowing anyone. He wrote to his friend Ben Castillo in Paris:

'Dear Ben... Naples is simply superb and I spent a delightful week there. Of course it was very hot, and one generally feels used up... I am painting away very hard and shall be here a long time. So if you write soon, as I should like, address Capri otherwise P.R. Naples... Your affect. old friend, John S. Sargent.'

ROSINA FERRARA

A few weeks later, Frank Hyde heard that a new artist was on the island and went to visit Sargent. He invited the young man to join him at the abandoned monastery of Santa Teresa which he was using as a studio. Sargent was delighted, and at Hyde's studio he met 16-year-old Rosina Ferrara (1862–1938) who often modelled for local artists. Rosina was from a small community of Anacapriote peasants, who were descended from the island's early Greek colonists, as Hyde wrote: 'The Anacapriotes were almost isolated from the rest of the island on account of the dangerous approach to their village, for a slip on the roughly hewn steps meant being hurled 1,000 feet to the rocks below. So small a colony were they that they were all related one to the other; you could see at a glance that they were a distinct type for the strain of the Arab was very marked in them.' Rosina was later described in a biography about Sargent by his friend, Sir Evan Charteris (1864–1940): 'An Ana-Capri girl, a magnificent type, about seventeen years of age, her complexion a rich nut-brown, with a mass of blue-black hair, very beautiful and of an Arab type.' In a magazine in 1882, the American artist Charles Sprague Pearce (1851–1914) described her as: 'the tawney-skinned [sic], panther-eyed, elf-like Rosina, wildest and lithest of all the creatures on the savage isle of Capri.'

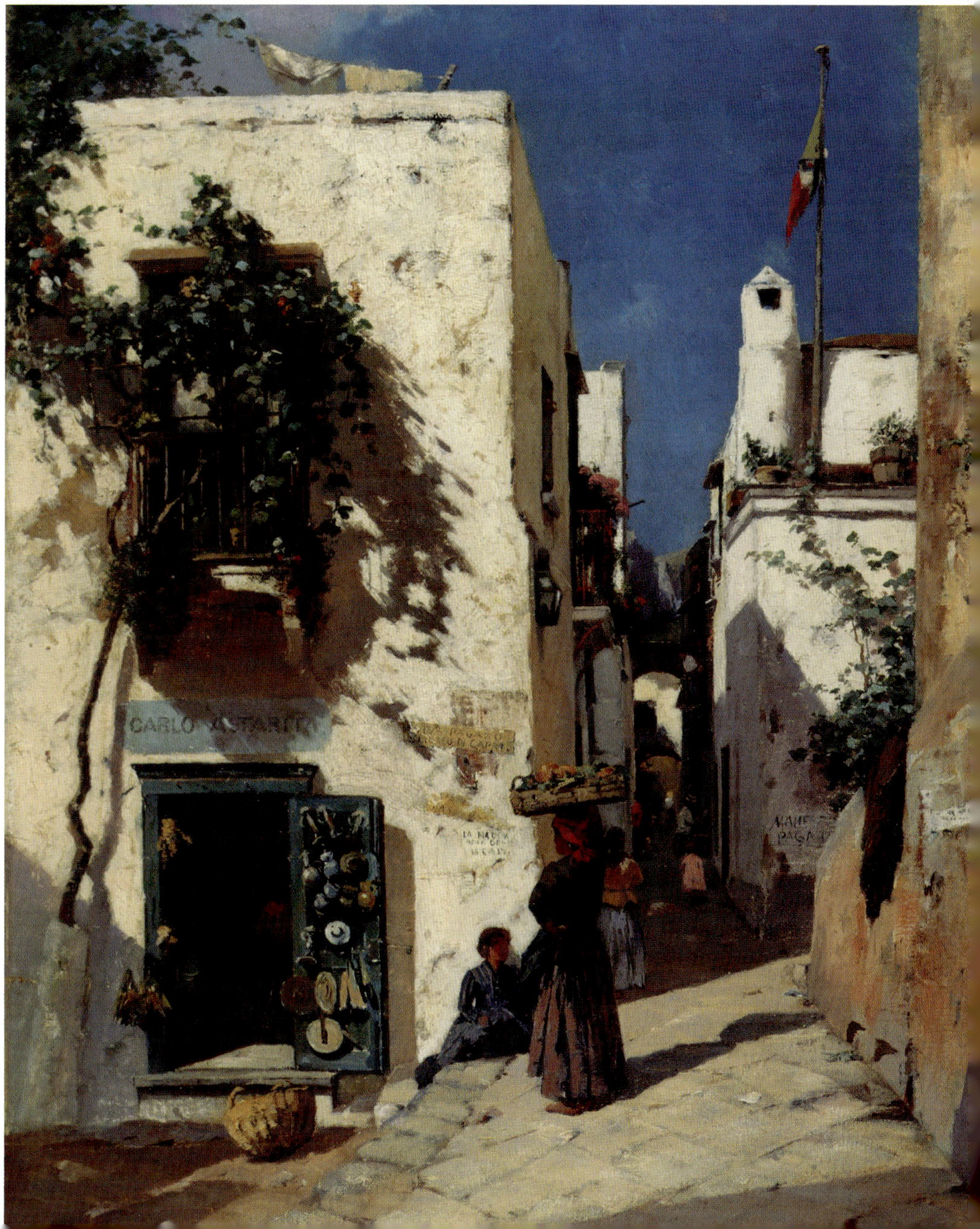

AN ARTISTS' COMMUNITY

Through Hyde, Sargent met other artists staying in Capri, and settled in, a part of the small community. The artists included Édouard Alexandre Sain (1830–1910), Henri-Lucien Doucet (1856–95), Charles-Edmond Daux (1855–1937), Hyde and a few others. Ever sociable, Sargent helped to make things particularly convivial. Because of the intense heat, he only painted in the evenings, and he also entertained the others. One evening he held a party on the rooftop with hired musicians playing tambourines and guitars. The view was spectacular, the evening air pleasant and the setting sun cast warm tints against the white stucco walls of the surrounding buildings. The festivities became lively, the 'tarantella was danced,' and that evening, he painted Rosina dancing on the rooftop against the darkening sky, in *Capri Girl on a Rooftop*.

Rosina's exotic appearance captivated Sargent, and he painted several works featuring her, including *A Beach at Capri* and *Head of a Capri Girl* (see page 106). Having learned how to capture skin tones convincingly in the atelier of Carolus-Duran, he created luminous, lyrical images of her. The skin tones may have derived from Carolus-Duran's instruction, but the palette and compositions were also akin to those of the French artist Jean-Baptiste-Camille Corot (1796–1875).

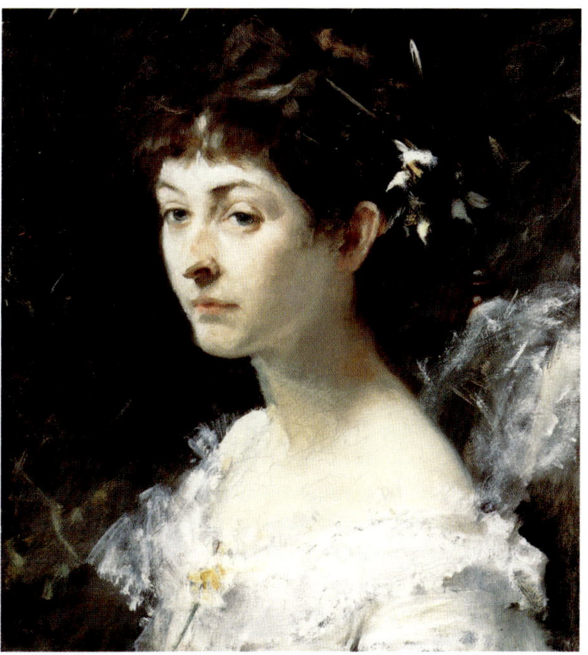

Left: Mary Turner Austin was one of Sargent's cousins, and like him, was an American expatriate in Europe. Sargent painted this portrait in c.1878.

Below: Alleys of Capri, 1894 by Adolf Gustav Thamm (1859–1925).

CAROLUS-DURAN

Charles Auguste Émile Durand, known as Carolus-Duran, was born in Lille, the son of a hotelier with distant Spanish ancestry. He began training as an artist from an early age at the Lille Academy, and from 1853 at the Académie Suisse in Paris. Six years later, his first painting was accepted for the Salon.

At Lille, Durand was taught drawing by the sculptor Jean-Baptiste Cadet de Beaupré (1758–1823), then he studied painting for two years with François Souchon (1787–1857). In Paris, he assumed his pseudonym Carolus-Duran, and in about 1855, he met Henri Fantin-Latour (1836–1904) as they both copied paintings at the Louvre. Fantin-Latour introduced Carolus-Duran to his avant-garde circle of friends, including Gustave Courbet (1819–77) who led the Realist movement, the sculptor, painter, poet and art critic Zacharie Astruc (1833–1907), Édouard Manet, Alphonse Legros (1837–1911) and Félix Henri Bracquemond (1833–1914). Sharing Courbet and Manet's interests in Realism, Carolus-Duran painted with striking tonal contrasts and bold brushwork. In 1862, he won a scholarship to Italy where he studied the work of the great Italian masters for four years. He then stayed in Spain until 1868. He became captivated by the work of Velázquez, and his own paintings began to show a

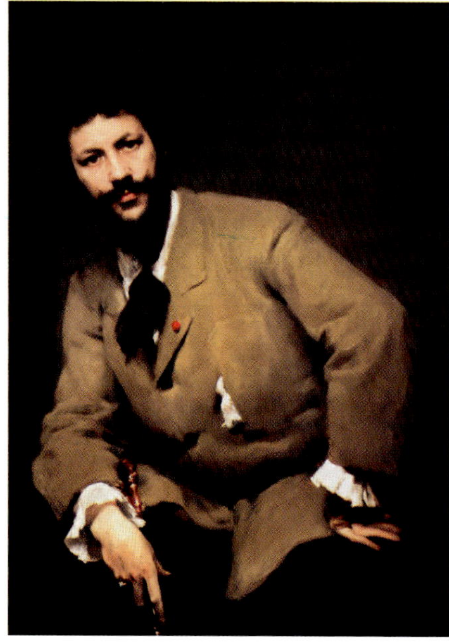

Above: Sargent painted this portrait of Carolus-Duran in 1879, just after his tutor was made Officer of the Legion of Honour.

Below: Courbet painted The Artist's Studio *in 1854, saying: 'It's the whole world coming to me to be painted.'*

THE PARIS COMMUNE

The Commune occurred in Paris after France's defeat in the Franco-Prussian war and the collapse of Emperor Napoleon III's Second Empire in 1870. The National Assembly, which was elected in February 1871, had a royalist majority, reflecting the conservative attitude of the provinces, and the republican Parisians feared that it would reinstate the monarchy. The next month, Parisians rose against the new government and proclaimed their city independent from the rest of France, forming the Commune government. However, when the National Assembly sent in troops, the Commune set up barricades in the streets and burned public buildings. Overall, about 20,000 Communards were killed and about 750 soldiers. The government arrested approximately 38,000 of the insurgents and deported more than 7,000 — Courbet was one of these.

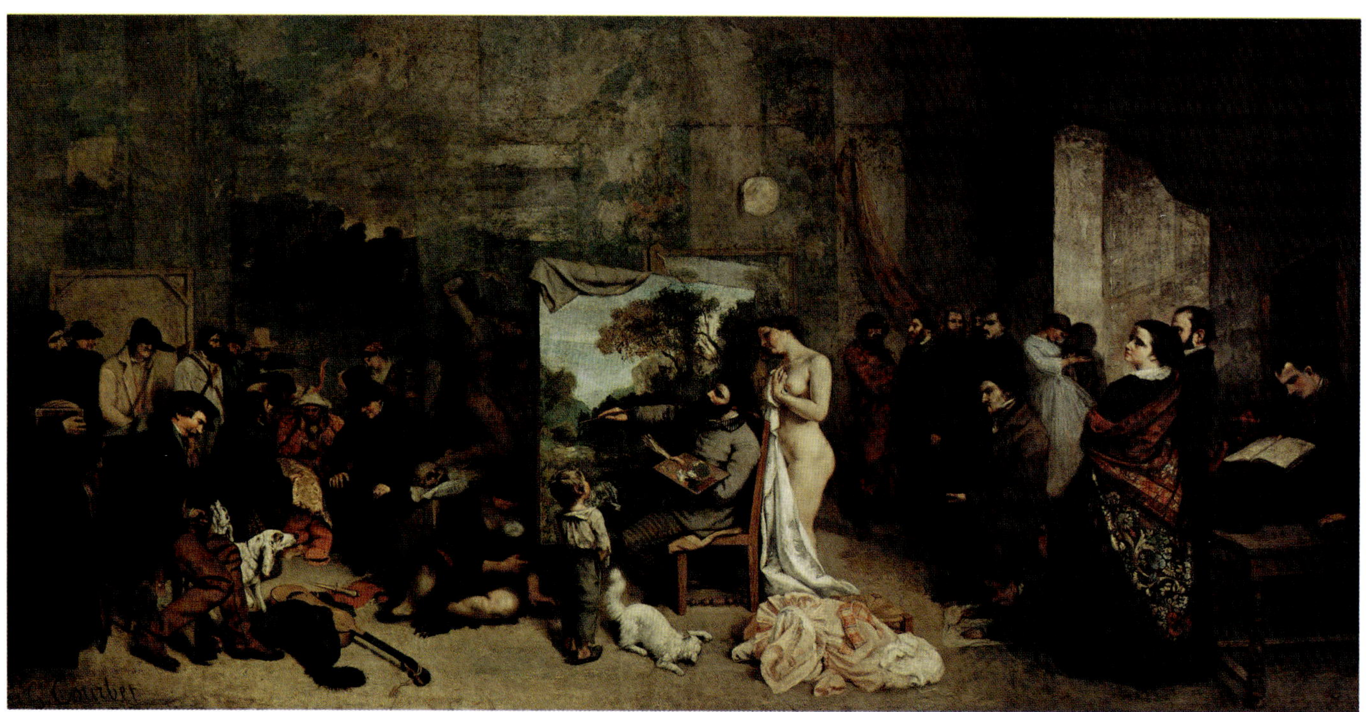

suited Sargent. Less rigid than the École des Beaux-Arts, the studio was also appealing because of Carolus-Duran's warmth and popularity. He repeatedly taught his students to: 'Express the maximum with the minimum of means.' Going against the basic teaching of the École des Beaux-Arts, that emphasized drawing, he said painting was the most important aspect of art and encouraged his students to draw and paint simultaneously using a loaded brush and without any preparatory drawing. Next, five or six main surfaces of the face were marked on without blending, and details built up from there using smaller amounts of paint. He stressed focusing attention on the effects of light. Sargent also learned to retain a certain informality in his portraits, to combine elegance and realism, to contrast the highlighted face and hands with thinly painted dark backgrounds, and to contrast detailed facial features with more loosely painted bodies. Overall, this created a balance of psychological depth and bravura, and was the approach Sargent consistently employed throughout his career.

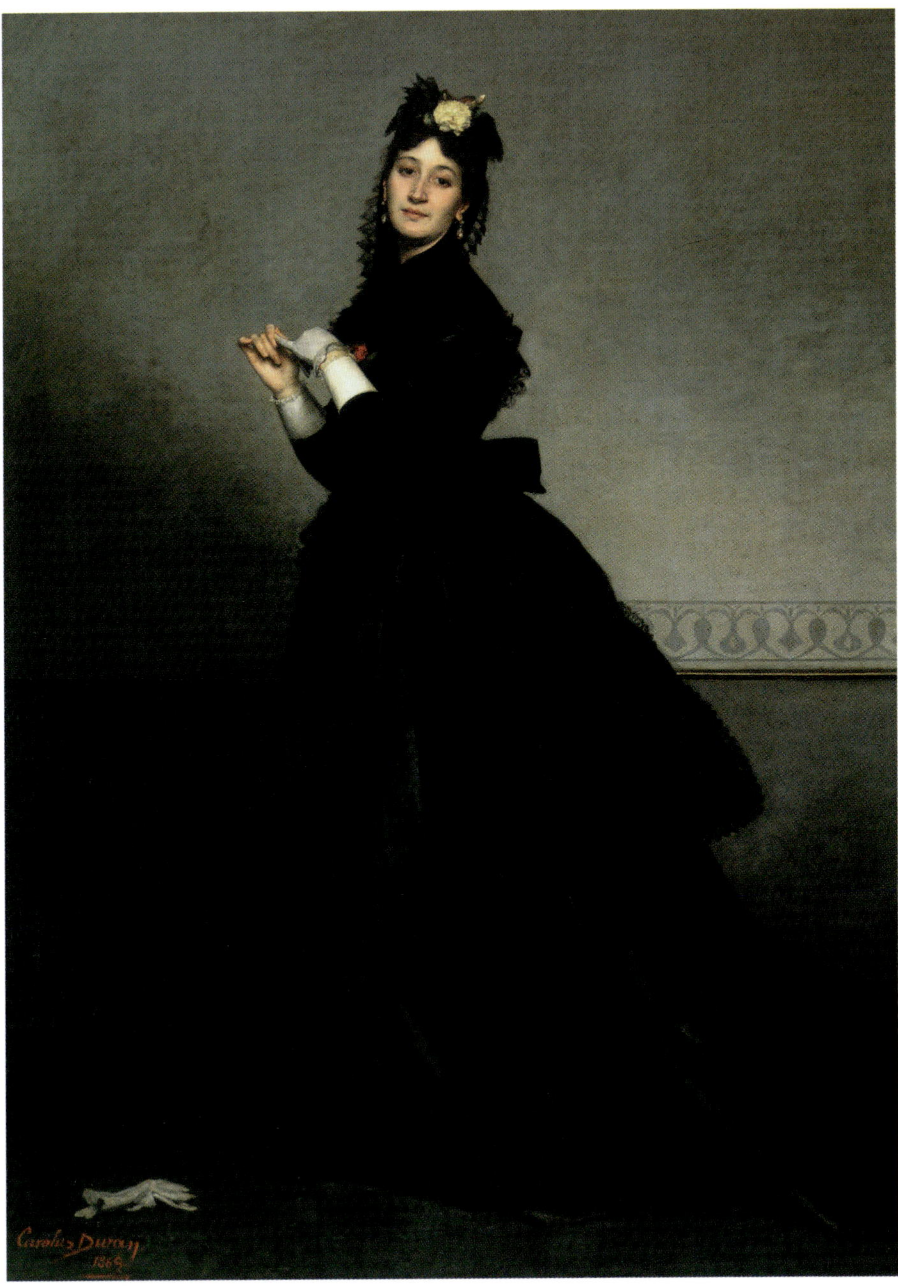

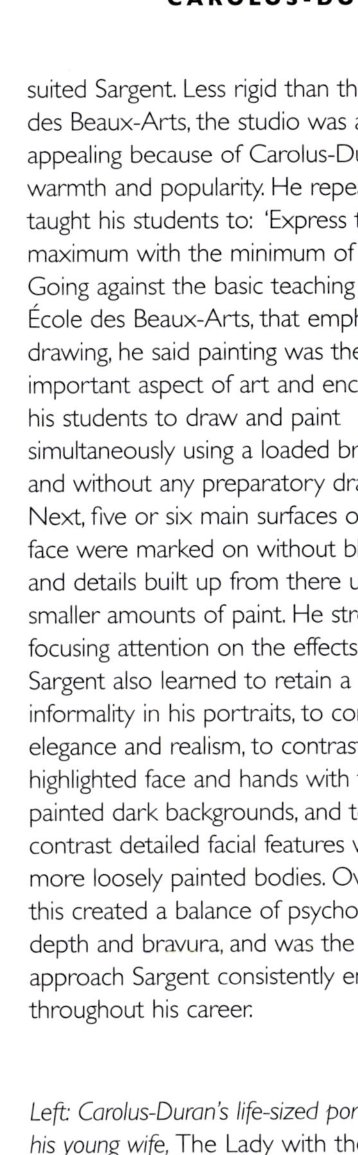

Left: Carolus-Duran's life-sized portrait of his young wife, The Lady with the Glove, *won a medal at the Salon of 1869.*

Below: Carolus-Duran's success was meteoric. Here, using the bold brushstrokes of the Realists, he painted his friend Manet, c.1880.

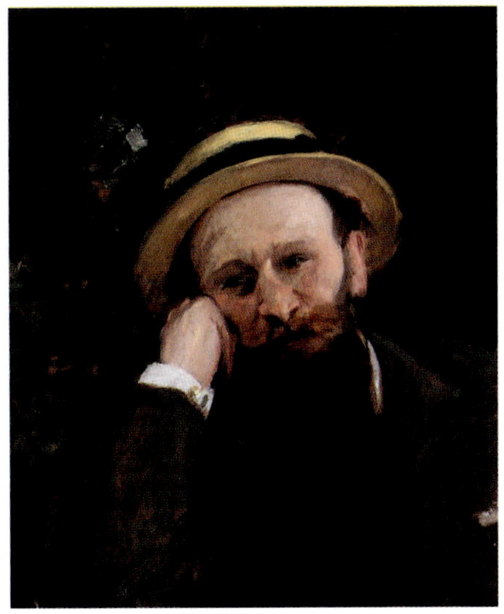

strong influence of the Spanish master. Returning from Brussels to Paris after the Commune, he became known as a fashionable society portraitist and opened a studio at 81, Boulevard du Montparnasse. Students paid for heating and models, but not their tuition.

HIGH PROFILE ARTIST

In 1872, Carolus-Duran was appointed a Knight of the Legion of Honour, promoted to Officer in 1878, Commander in 1889, and Grand Officer in 1900. In 1890, he helped to create the National Society of French Art (Société Nationale des Beaux Arts).

He became a member of the Académie des Beaux-Arts in 1904, and in 1905, Carolus-Duran was appointed director of the French Academy in Rome, a position he held until 1913.

CAROLUS-DURAN'S STUDIO

Sargent was attracted to Carolus-Duran's studio for its pleasant atmosphere, mix of foreign students, and its independence from the academic system – which he was additionally involved with at the École des Beaux-Arts. Among approximately 25 students, two-thirds were British and American, and one-third French; a lively mix that especially

ON HIS OWN

After his trip to Capri, Sargent had more or less finished studying and was working on his own as a professional artist. His painting *Among the Olive Trees, Capri* (1878) was accepted at the following year's Salon along with his finished portrait of Carolus-Duran.

PAUL HELLEU

In September 1878, back in Paris, Sargent intermittently attended Carolus-Duran's studio. He became friends with 18-year-old Paul-César Helleu (1859–1927), whom he had met at the second Impressionist exhibition in 1876, and whose father had recently died. Against his widowed mother's wishes, Helleu had become an art student, and as she had predicted, he was now poverty-stricken. According to Sargent's friend and biographer, Evan Charteris (1864-1940), on hearing of this, Sargent visited Helleu and praised one of his pastels. Flattered, Helleu offered the work to

Sargent. Sargent replied: "I shall gladly accept, Helleu, but not as a gift. I sell my own pictures, and I know what they cost me by the time they are out of my hand. I should never enjoy this pastel if I hadn't paid you a fair and honest price for it." He gave Helleu a thousand-franc note. Sargent also introduced him to his artist friends and the two became friends for life.

RISING REPUTATION

In October and November, Sargent travelled to Nice with his family, returning to Paris in December. The following year, he went to Spain and Morocco. After his paintings had been shown at the Salon, his reputation increased again. The magazine *L'Illustration* reproduced his portrait of Carolus-Duran on its cover as a tribute to the sitter, but it was also a huge success for Sargent. After seeing the painting at the Salon, his father Fitzwilliam Sargent wrote to their relatives that: 'there was always a little crowd around it, and one heard constantly remarks in favour of its excellence. But the proof of the pudding is in the eating, so the best or one of the best evidences of a portrait's success is in the receiving by the artist of commissions to execute others. And John received six such evidences from French people. He was very busy during the two months we were in Paris.'

Among Sargent's six commissions mentioned by Fitzwilliam, were portraits of Édouard Pailleron (1834–99), (see page 32) and of a little boy, Robert de Cevrieux (1872–unknown). Both show Carolus-Duran's influence, and particularly the approach of Velázquez and of Frans Hals (1580–1666). As Carolus-Duran had just been made an Officer of the Legion of Honour, Sargent capitalized on his tutor's celebrity and his own rising success by also exhibiting the portrait in New York and Boston in 1880, London in 1882 and Paris again in 1883.

INTRODUCTION TO SOCIETY

Édouard Pailleron was a lawyer, notary clerk, soldier and successful writer from a bourgeois Parisian family. After sitting for Sargent, the two men became friends, and Sargent went on to paint several portraits of Pailleron, his family and his larger circle, rapidly

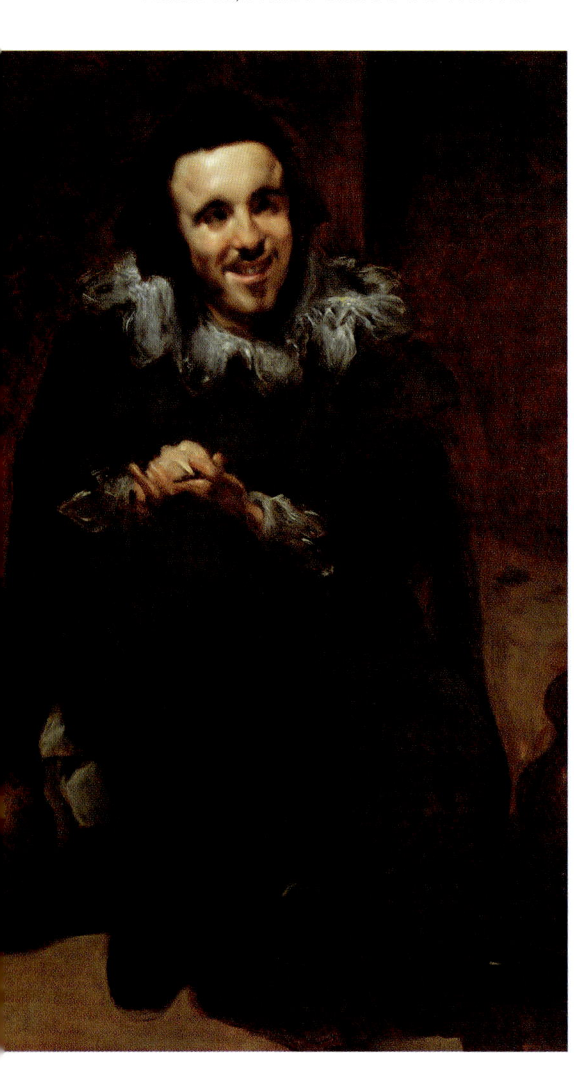

Left: In 1879, Sargent travelled to Spain and Morocco and copied works by Velázquez on display in the Prado. This painting is Don Juan de Calabazas, *after* The Jester Calabacillas, *1639.*

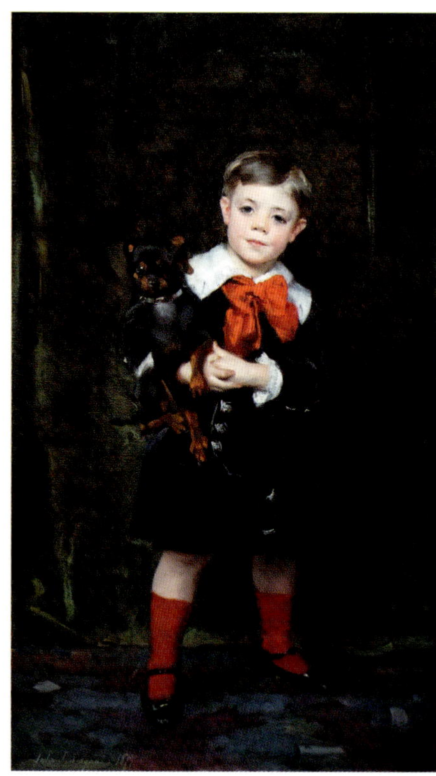

Right: Commissioned soon after Sargent's 1879 Salon success, this is his portrait of seven-year-old Robert de Cévrieux.

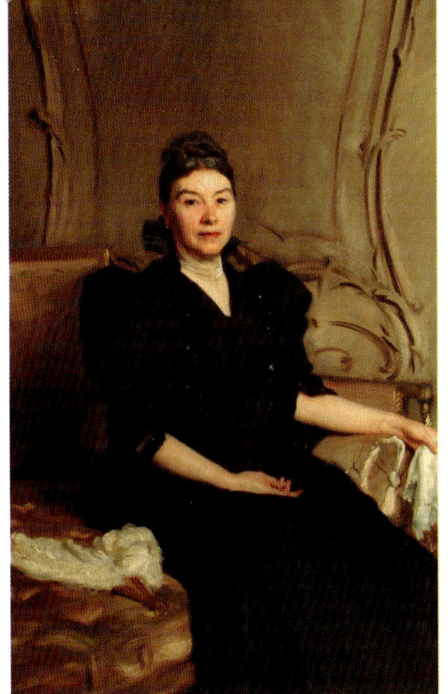

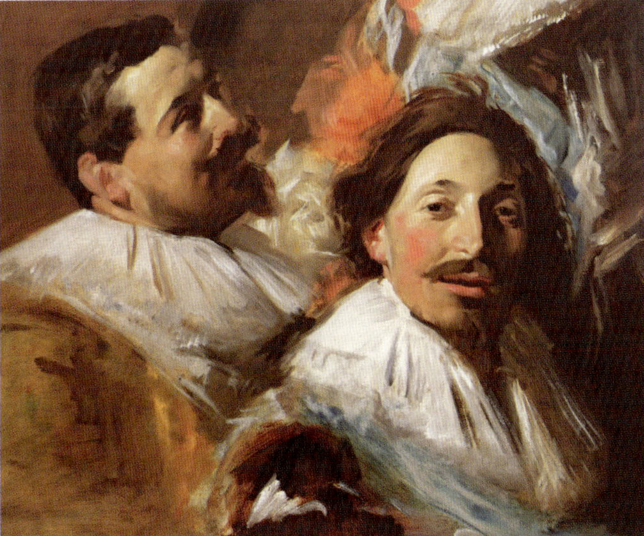

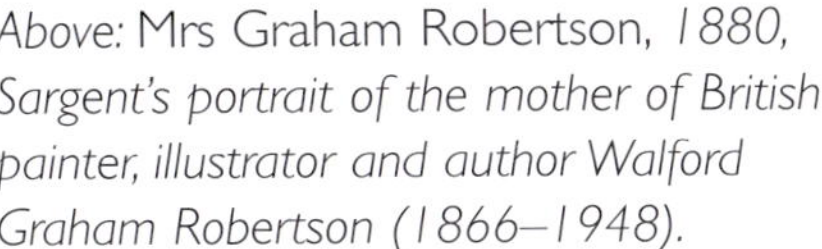

Above: Mrs Graham Robertson, 1880,
Sargent's portrait of the mother of British
painter, illustrator and author Walford
Graham Robertson (1866–1948).

becoming established as a society
portraitist. At the time, approximately
one-third of Sargent's commissions
were for portraits of children, which
had become increasingly fashionable.
His painting of seven-year-old Robert
de Cevrieux (left) was one of these.
Robert stands on an expensive
oriental carpet, fashionably dressed and
holding his pet dog. Designed to charm
viewers, the painting also reflects the
work of Carolus-Duran, who had
shown pictures of his own children
holding their pets at previous Salon
exhibitions.

DRAMATIC AND DYNAMIC

Sargent left Carolus-Duran's studio
in 1879, but the artistic influence
of his mentor continued. He also
began experimenting with elements
of the Impressionists' work, but did
not abandon traditional methods of
portraying tonal contrasts as they
had done. In Spain, Sargent became
captivated by the people, the culture
and the music and he produced several
dramatically lit, sketchy paintings of
Spanish scenes, often of dancers,
asymmetrically composed and full
of dynamism. His painting El Jaleo,
completed in 1882, was his greatest
success at the Salon.

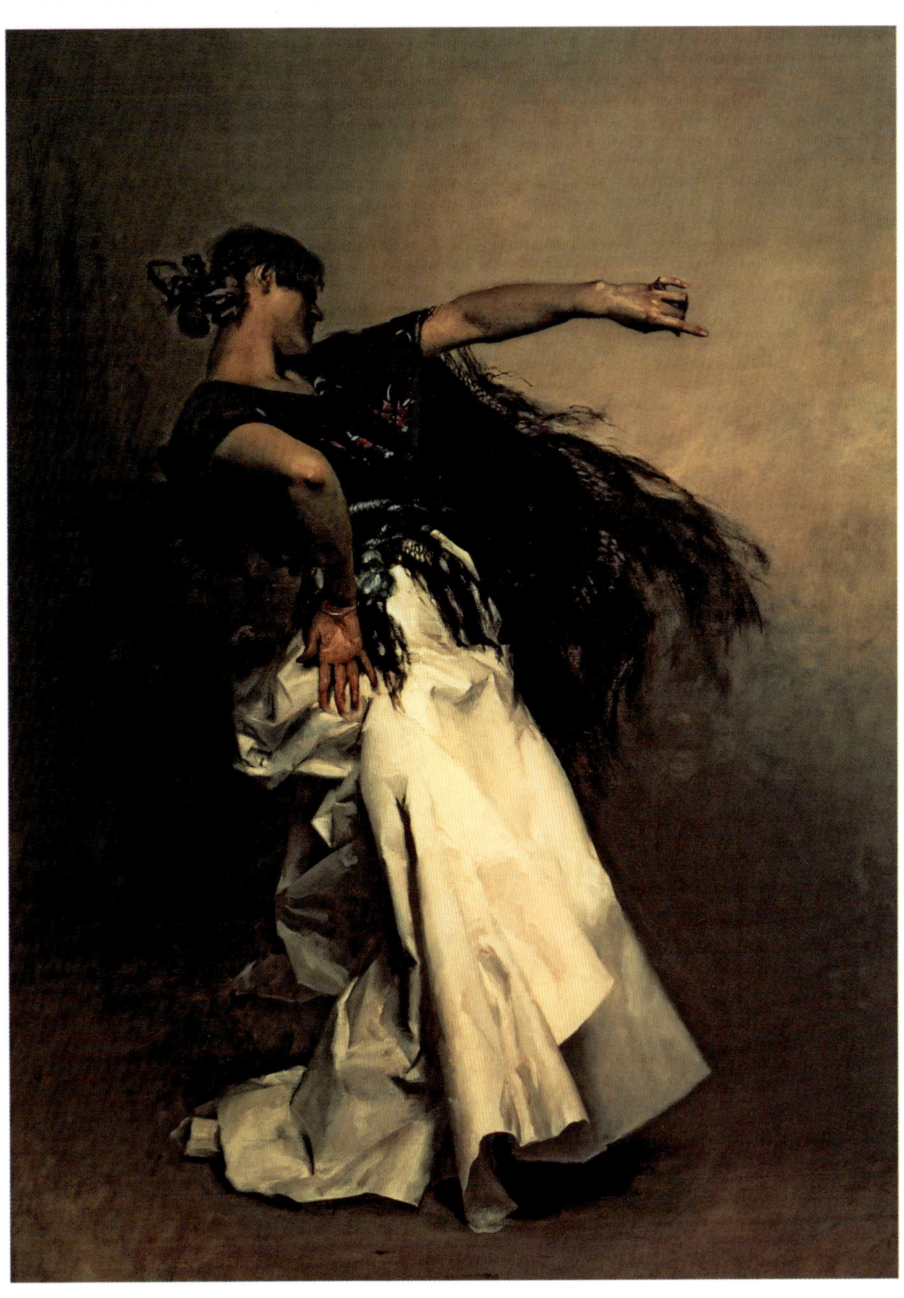

VISION AND ATMOSPHERE

As his career took off, Sargent became known as a portrait painter, although he tried to resist the label by creating and exhibiting works that showed his imaginative vision and ability to capture atmosphere. Additionally, to avoid being categorized, he imbued his portraits with a sense of freedom and character.

Since the 1850s, portraits had been created by photographers as much as by painters, and this new, uncharted competition posed a challenge for artists. A 'straight' likeness was no longer necessarily the goal, instead, many painters aspired to capture a sense of the spirit or character of their sitters. In 1867, the French art critic Charles Blanc (1813–82) published an influential book, *Grammaire des Arts du Dessin*. In it, he criticized photographic images: 'Who does not know how deceptive is the truth of the photographic image, which pretends to be infallible? The painter, endowed with a mind, can evoke the mind of his model, but how can a machine evoke a soul?' While portrait commissions were an excellent means

to earn a living and to become known, Sargent nonetheless adhered to Blanc's notion of making them expressive, often set within atmospheric scenes. Some of these, such as the paintings he produced of the Pailleron children (see pages 32–33), and scenes from Capri, Venice and Spain, were almost ambiguous – were they portraits or were they simply captured moments in time?

POWERFUL INFLUENCES

In January 1880, Sargent spent some weeks in Morocco capturing the brilliant colours and dramatic contrasts and shadows that the light created on the white stucco Moorish buildings. By the end of February, he returned to Paris and worked on a painting

inspired by his trip. *Fumée d'Ambre Gris* became another Salon success in May, along with his portrait of Marie Buloz Pailleron (1840–1913) the wife of his friend Édouard (see page 110). Almost simultaneously, his portrait of Carolus-Duran (see page 26) also made a strong impact at the Society of American Artists in New York. Travelling was second nature to Sargent and in August, he went to the Netherlands with friends, two American artists also living in Europe: Ralph Wormeley Curtis (1854–1922) and Francis Brooks

Below: A Street in Spain, 1880. Wherever he travelled, Sargent painted atmospheric, views of his surroundings (see page 114).

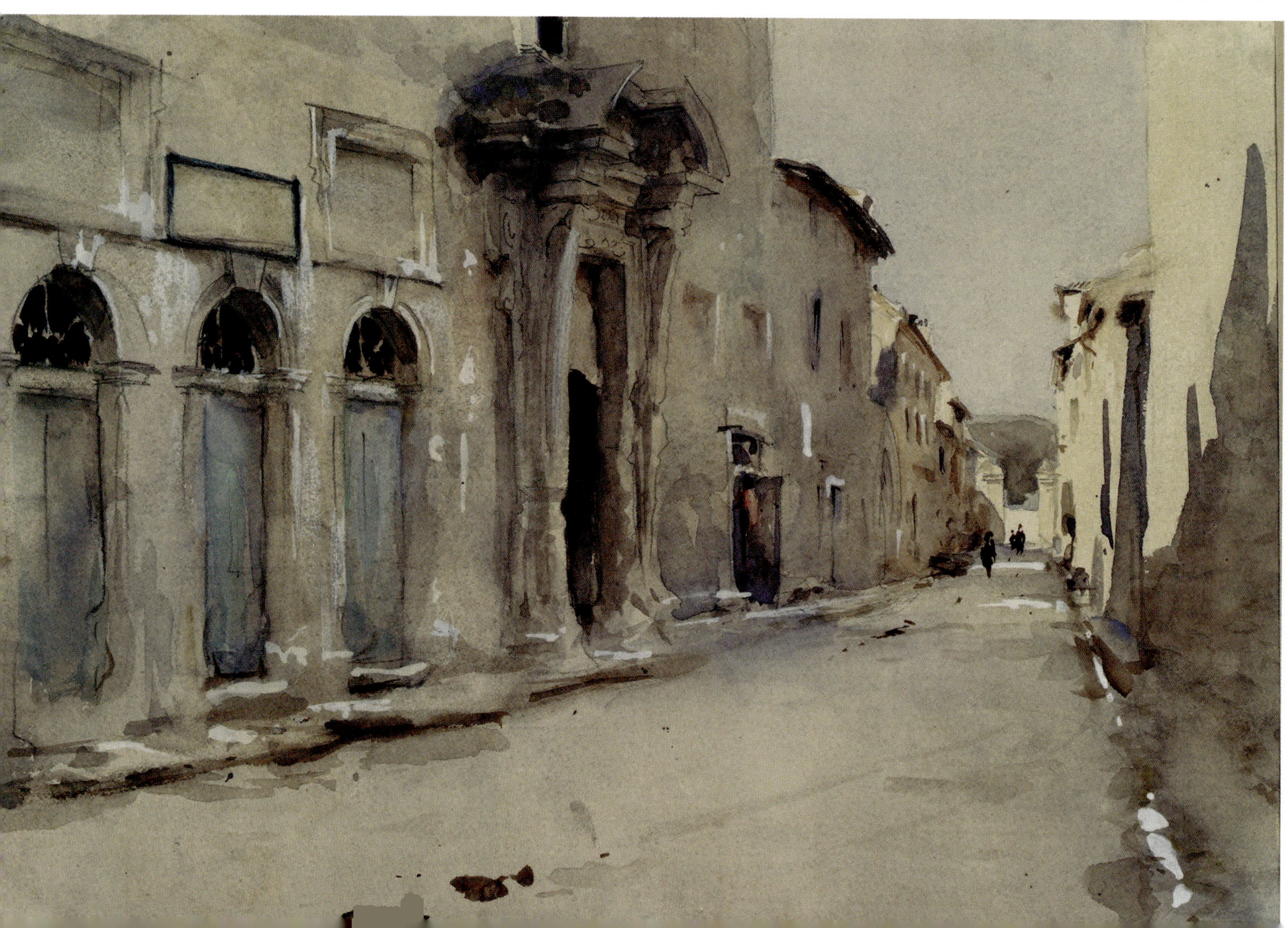

Chadwick (1850–1942). He painted portraits of both men in a loose, fresh style, capturing something of their characters. While in the Netherlands, he also copied work he saw there by Frans Hals (1580–1666), and later advised an art student: 'Begin with Frans Hals, copy and study Frans Hals, after that go to Madrid and copy Velázquez, but leave Velázquez till you have got all you can out of Frans Hals.'

By the middle of September, Sargent went to meet his family at Aix-Les-Bains, then travelled with them to Venice, where they stayed at the Hotel d'Italie. In Venice, he found studio space with other artists at the Palazzo Rezzonico, and after his family had left, he stayed on through the winter. While there, he met Boldini and possibly also Whistler. Sargent's Venetian studies are in marked contrast with the scenes usually chosen by artists. Dark, sultry and expressive, they portray back streets and squares, and deep, shadowy interiors often peopled with local figures seemingly unaware of him. Compositions are complex, atmospheric and show a marked influence of Hals and Velázquez.

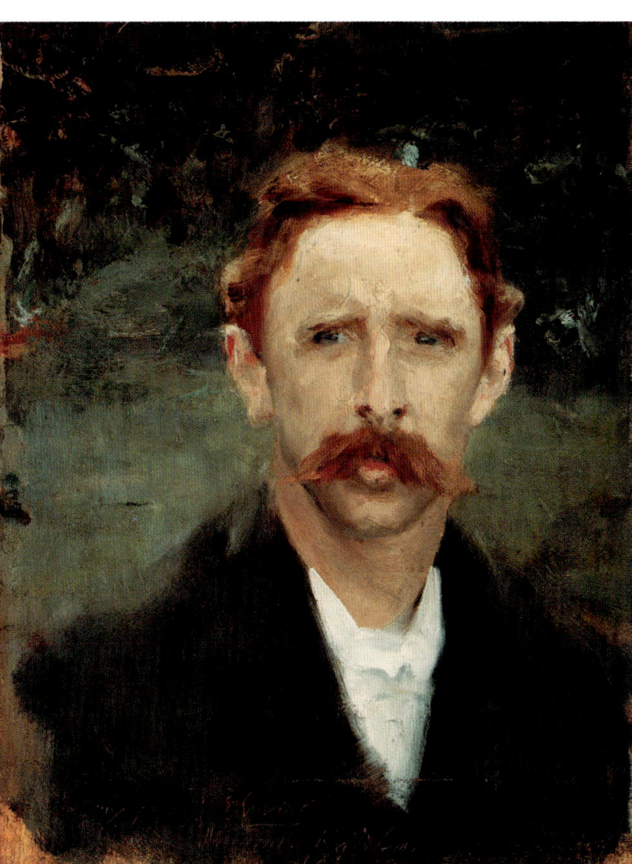

Left: My Friend Chadwick, *1880. Francis Chadwick was born in Boston, but he met Sargent while in Paris.*

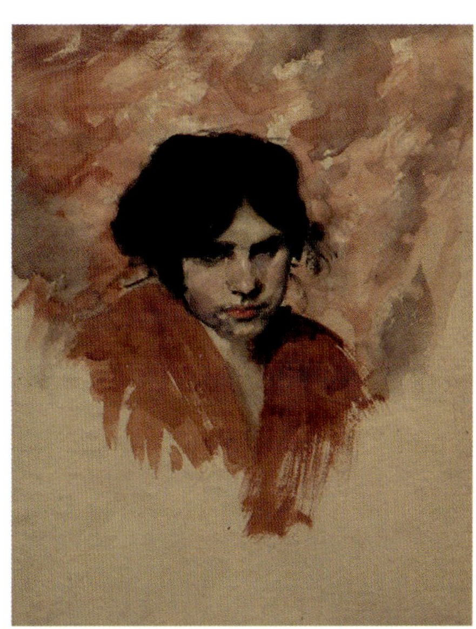

Right: Sargent painted Head of a Venetian Model *in watercolour while in Venice in 1880–81.*

Below: Street in Venice, *1882. Painted on Sargent's return to Venice in 1882, this illustrates his ability to capture atmosphere and evoke moods.*

SARGENT'S VENICE

Venice in the late 19th century was a city in decline, and had been since it fell to Napoleon Bonaparte (1769–1821) in 1797. The buildings were decaying, the people living in hardship. Much of the art had been looted by Napoleon's army. Yet Sargent saw beauty in the degeneration. He probably visited Venice for the first time in 1870. On his return in 1880, it inspired him perhaps more than any other place, and it continued to do so for the rest of his life. Sargent was attracted to aspects of the city that others had perhaps not depicted, but which allowed him to express his own personal vision.

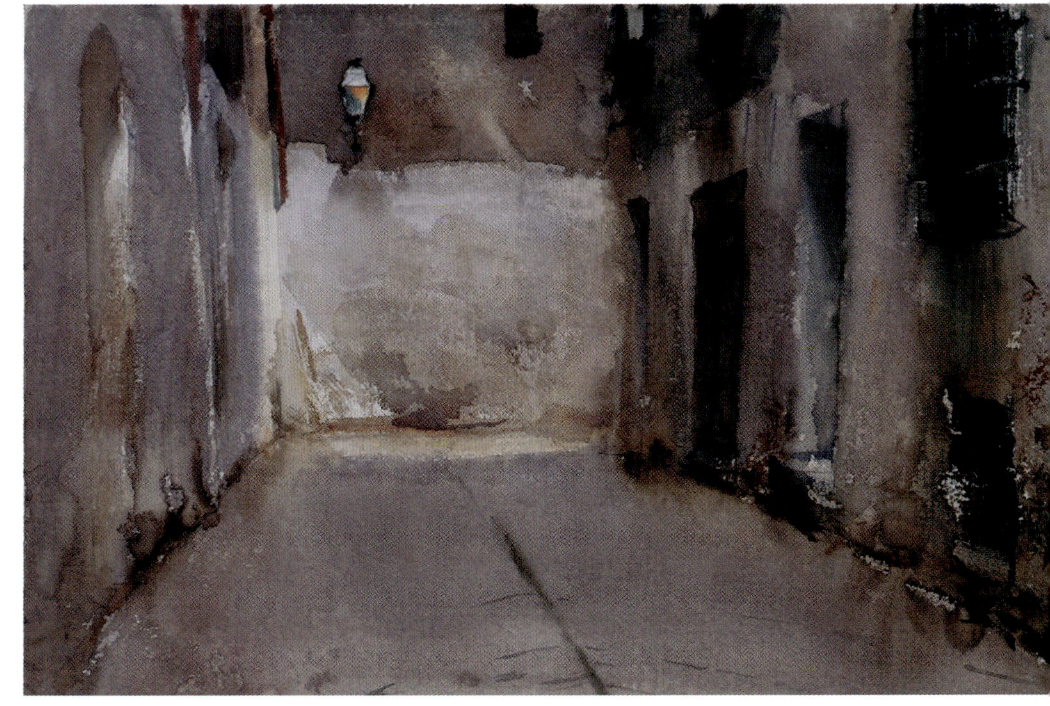

SOCIETY PORTRAITS

Between 1877–82, Sargent submitted many types of paintings to the Salon, although his portraits attracted the most positive attention. Returning from Venice to Paris in 1881, he began working immediately on numerous portraits, including one of the Pailleron children and one of Dr Samuel Jean Pozzi (1846–1918).

INTIMATE IMAGES

Édouard Pailleron had introduced Sargent to the Parisian upper-middle class circle. In May 1881, along with two Venetian watercolours, three of Sargent's society portraits were accepted by the Salon: the children of Édouard and Marie-Louise Pailleron, and the beautiful, 20-year-old Madame Ramón Subercaseaux (1860–1930), the newly married wife of the Chilean consul to Paris. Sargent's portrait shows her sitting at her piano, turning to look over her shoulder at viewers, and was awarded a second-class medal. Madame Subercaseaux wrote in her diary: 'It was in Paris during the Spring of 1880 that Sargent painted my portrait... the artist himself seemed a very attractive gentleman and therefore we treated him as a real friend. He was very young at the time, only 24 years of age, but he was a man of very pleasant manners. He came to our apartment... and was entirely free to arrange the composition of the portrait as he wished. It was not difficult to pose for him as his hours of work were neither long nor heavy. His way of painting was light, as his work showed afterwards.

He concentrated on each detail and took great care of the effect of each object and colour... He was very fond of music... He had been in Spain a short time and everything about that country left its impressions on him and from it he drew his inspirations. His teacher was Carolus-Duran, and from him he became a great admirer of the great Spaniard Velázquez.'

The painting of Édouard Pailleron's children was Sargent's first double portrait, featuring 11-year-old Marie-Louise and her 13-year-old brother, Édouard. It was created over several

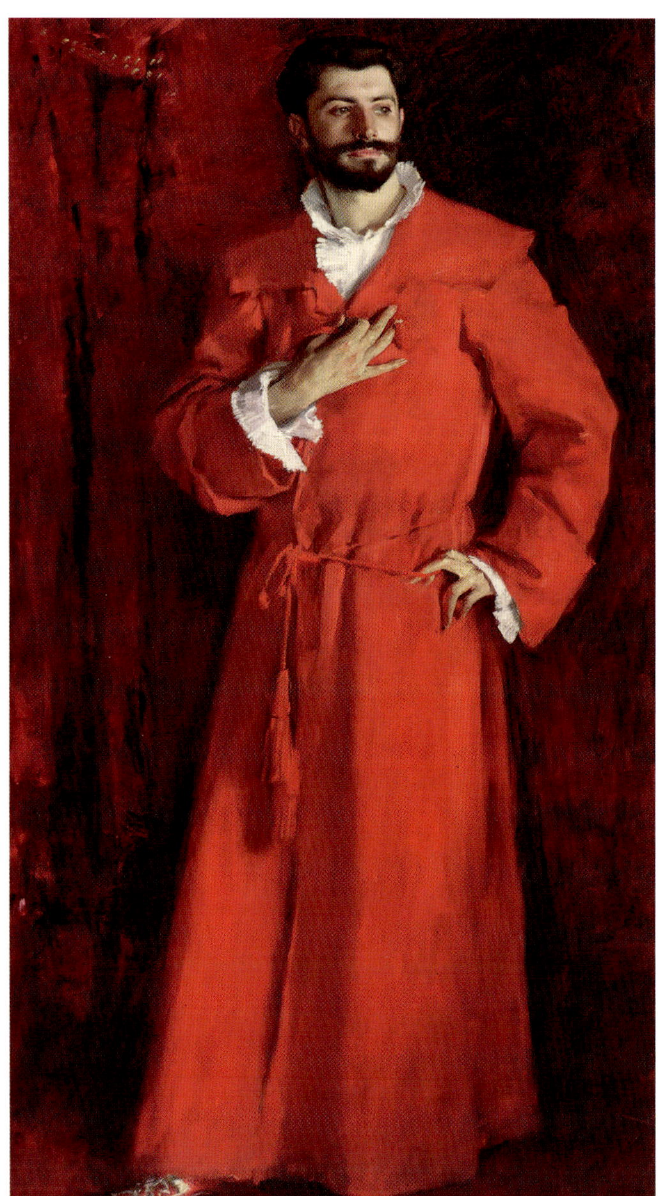

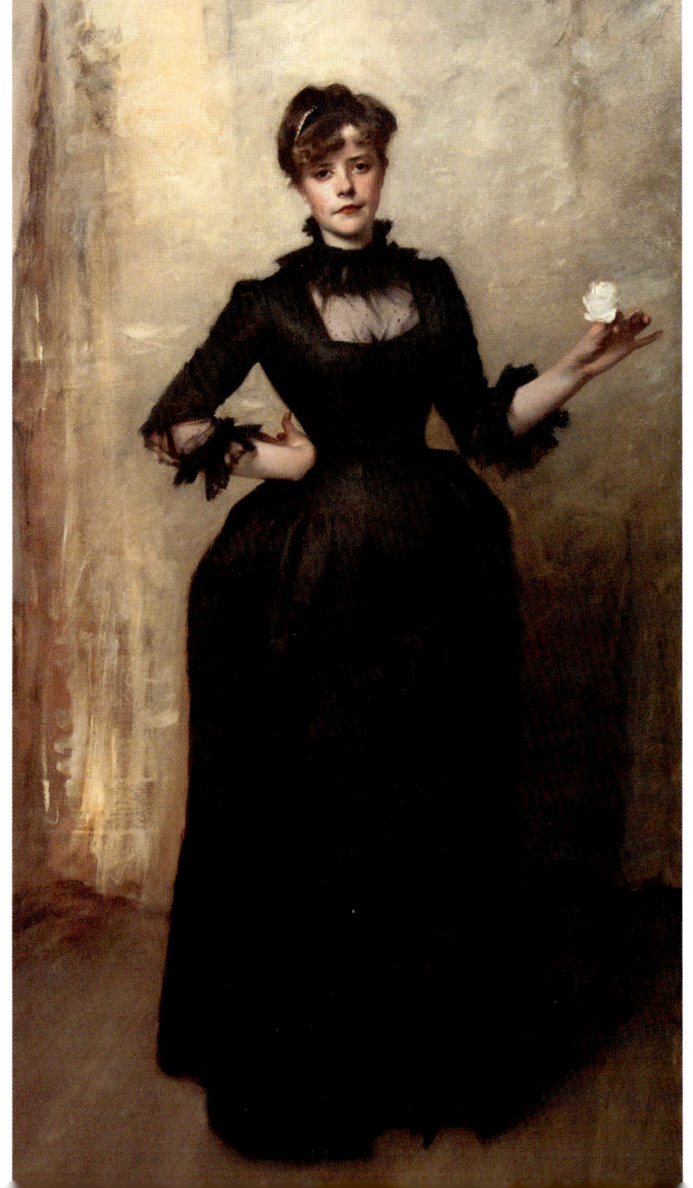

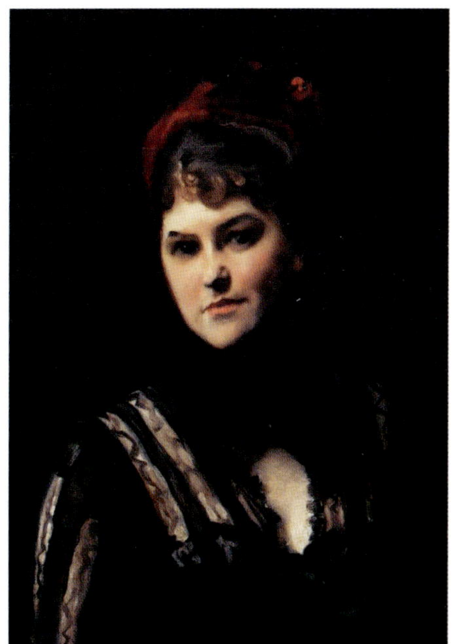

Above: Rich Pittsburg socialite, Mrs Kate Moore *(1846–1917). In Sargent's words: 'She is like a great frigate under full sail with homeward-bound steamers flying.'*

Far left: Sargent painted 35-year-old Dr Pozzi at Home *in 1881, showing a sensitive, dashing and relaxed individual.*

Left: Lady with the Rose, *or Charlotte Louise Burckhardt was a Salon success of 1882, along with Sargent's Spanish triumph,* El Jaleo *(see page 121).*

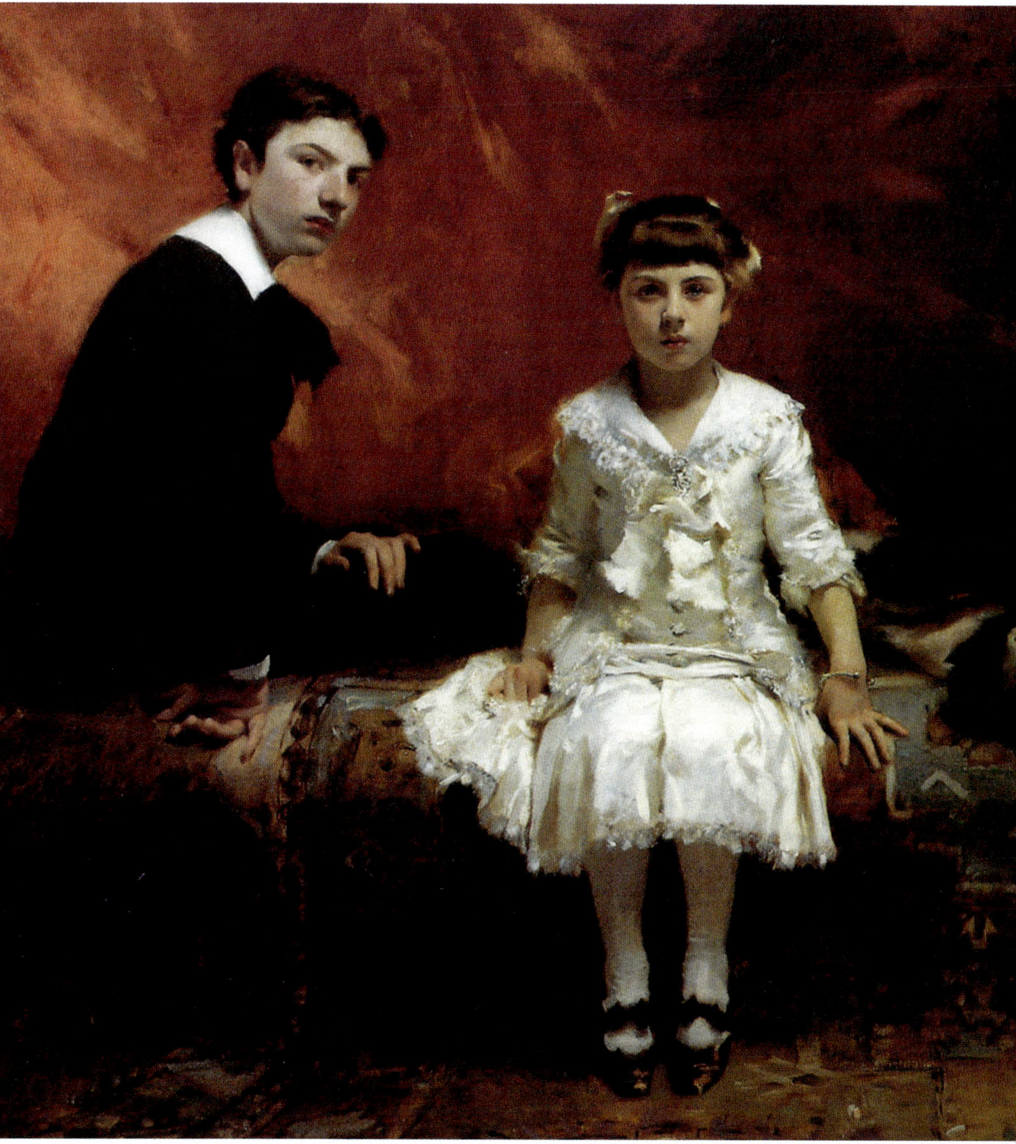

Above: Sargent's first double portrait, produced in 1881, of Édouard and Marie-Louise Pailleron.

months, and was not the easiest painting to execute; Marie-Louise later remembered 83 sittings in Sargent's studio at 73 rue Notre Dame des Champs. The children were also fairly difficult to work with. First of all, Marie-Louise argued with the 24-year-old artist about the length of the sittings, the arrangement of her hair and the soft cotton stockings she had to wear (she preferred shiny silk). Although the children's parents had portraits that can be seen to complement each other, Sargent did not attempt to make this part of a group of Pailleron portraits. While their playwright father posed in a contemporary interior and their mother was in a breezy garden, the children are set on a predominantly red Persian carpet draped over a backless divan with a heavy orange-red curtain behind. The impression created is of softness and warmth, perhaps reflecting Sargent's recent visits to Spain and Morocco. The portrait was shown at the 1881 Salon and it was enthusiastically received, although mostly for the charm of the children rather than the exotic setting.

THE LOVE DOCTOR

Samuel Jean Pozzi was a French surgeon and gynaecologist, nicknamed 'the love doctor' for his pioneering work to advance reproductive safety and the dignity of women. Handsome, charismatic and friends with famous Parisians, he also became something of a celebrity. He had a number of affairs including with the opera singer Georgette Leblanc (1869–1941), actresses Gabrielle Rejane (1856–1920) and Sarah Bernhardt (1844–1923), the Parisian socialite Virginie Gautreau (1859–1915), and the married daughter of an art dealer, Emma Sedelmeyer Fischof (1862–1927), who remained his mistress from 1890 for the rest of his life. He had three children with his wife, Therese Loth-Cazalis (1856–1932), but the marriage was unhappy. In 1918, he was shot by a former patient. Sargent has captured his handsome elegance; the scarlet dressing gown and frothy white lace evokes images of cardinals, or more specifically the *Portrait of Pope Innocent X* by Velázquez in c.1650.

MADAME X

In 1883, the year in which Sargent exhibited *The Daughters of Edward Darley Boit* at the Salon to great success, he began planning and painting a portrait of Virginie Amélie Avegno Gautreau – or Madame Pierre Gautreau, an American-born Parisian socialite, well known for her style and beauty.

The previous year, while Sargent was painting a portrait of Louise Burckhardt (see page 32), a rumour developed that they were having an affair. Whether the rumour was true or not was never established, and whether it enhanced his appeal, or the merits of the painting did that by itself is impossible to know. Further factors such as the originality of his bravura Spanish masterpiece *El Jaleo* (see page 121) probably made him more conspicuous, but from that time, Sargent became something of a celebrity artist. With rising confidence, he planned to paint a portrait for the Salon that was completely his choice and style.

A MAN OF PRODIGIOUS TALENT

Fashionable and notorious, Virginie Gautreau was born in New Orleans, but moved to France at the age of eight after her father's death in the American Civil War. She grew up to become an elegant member of French high society, known throughout Paris for her pale skin that she enhanced with lavender-coloured powder, dark henna-enhanced hair and shapely figure. Although she married a wealthy French banker and shipping magnate, she continued to have affairs, including with Dr Pozzi (see page 32–33). It was possibly through Pozzi that Sargent first met her in 1880. She was also a friend of the del Castillo family, and Sargent wrote to Ben: 'I have a great desire to paint her portrait and have reason to think she would allow it and is waiting for someone to propose this homage to her beauty. If you are 'bien avec elle' and will see her in Paris, you might tell her that I am a man of prodigious talent!'

Whether she needed persuading or not, Madame Gautreau agreed to sit for Sargent in the spring of 1883, but she was distracted and busy with social engagements, so only sat for

a few drawings. Sargent wrote to Vernon Lee: '...still in this country house struggling with the unpaintable beauty and hopeless laziness of Mme Gautreau.' After several trips abroad during the year, he resumed work on the portrait in the autumn, but he was not confident that it would stun Paris through its skill and bravado as he intended. He wrote to Ben del Castillo: 'The painting is much changed and far more advanced than when you last saw it. One day I was dissatisfied with it and dashed a tone of light rose over the former gloomy background. I turned the painting upside down, retired to the other end of the studio and looked at it under my arm... Carolus has been to see it and said: "Vous pouver l'envoyer au Salon avec confiance" ["*You can send it to the Salon with confidence*"]. Encouraging, but false. I have made up my mind to be refused.'

THE SCANDAL

In late autumn 1883, Sargent moved to a new studio in a more stylish

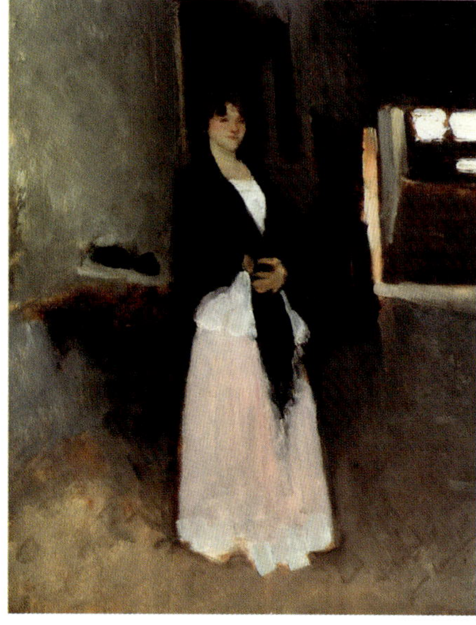

Above: Sargent painted numerous sultry women in Venice and Spain; A Venetian Woman is from 1881.

Below: Madame Gautreau Drinking a Toast, *1882–83, this small, intimate painting was a gift from Sargent to Madame Gautreau's mother.*

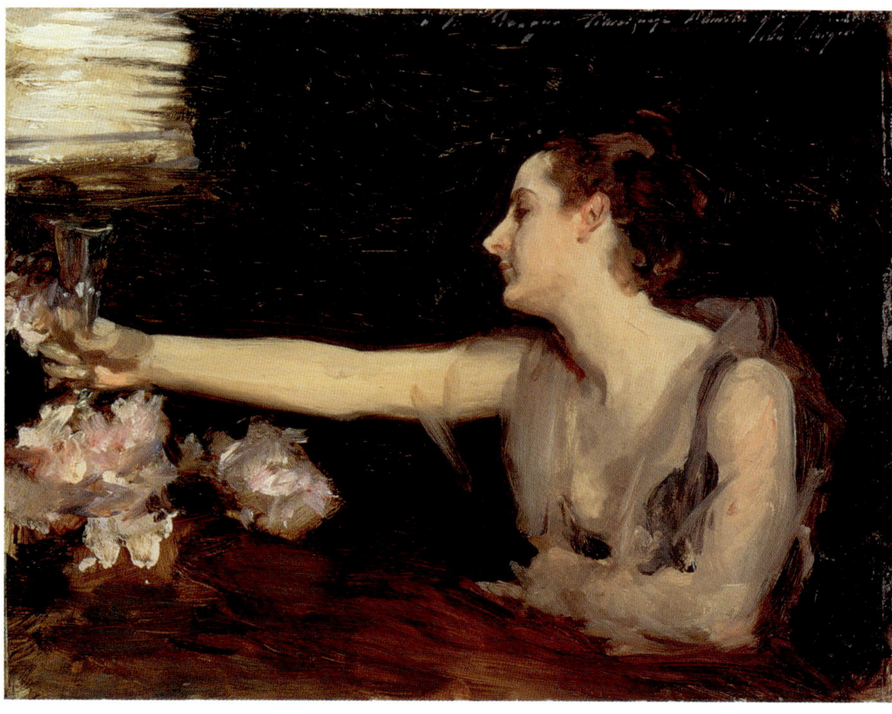

part of Paris. He continued painting commissioned portraits, but his portrait of Madame Gautreau preoccupied him. In 1884, it was, in fact, accepted for exhibition at the Salon. On the opening day, even though it was the seventh successive year that he had exhibited, Sargent was apprehensive. He was proved right. From the moment the Salon doors opened, the portrait (which he labelled *Madame XXX)* was lambasted, both by the public and by the critics. Everything about the painting offended visitors, from Madame Gautreau's provocative clothing (one of her flimsy, jewelled straps had fallen down), to her unnatural pallor and the expanse of flesh on show, to her distinctive profile, which was not found beautiful. Sargent's remarkable technical ability was disregarded as the public reacted to the painting with horror and moral indignation.

Below left: Madame X (Madame Pierre Gautreau). *A painting filled with contrasts, Sargent depicts a pale woman in a black dress that both reveals and hides at once.*

Below right: Sargent's unfinished copy of Madame X (Madame Pierre Gautreau), *(see both on page 125).*

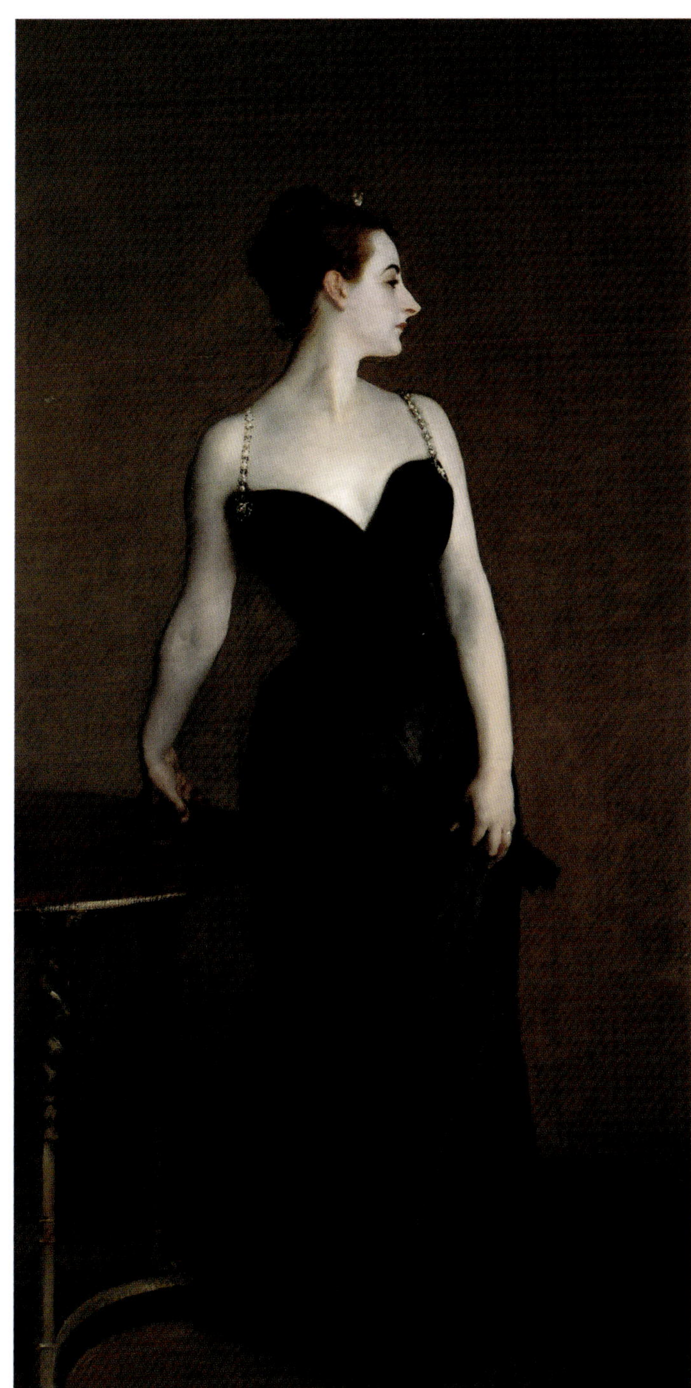

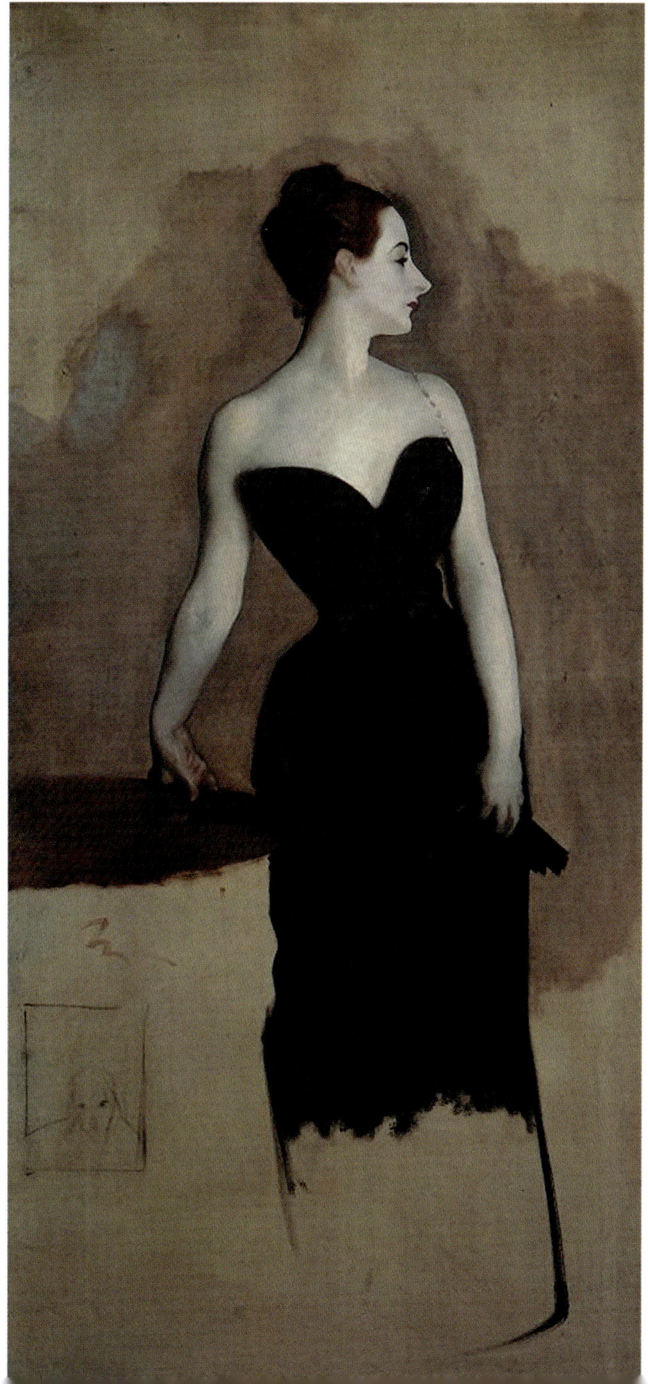

VISITING MONET

The scandal of Sargent's portrait of *Madame X* and the repercussions it caused destroyed Sargent's rising reputation in France. All his previous successes were immediately forgotten. Forced to rethink his career, he now turned to a man who had also been rejected before rising to fame: Claude Monet.

Madame X (see page 35) was considered shocking on several levels. One was that Sargent had painted the natural redness of her ear, which contrasted with the contrived whiteness of the rest of her skin, and highlighted the artifice of her powdering. At the time, her pose was considered sexually suggestive, not to mention her fallen shoulder strap. The painting also incorporates subtle classical references: sirens of Greek mythology adorn the table legs, while Madame Gautreau's tiara symbolizes the goddess Diana, the huntress. After the Salon closed, Sargent kept the painting with him until 1916, at which time he sold it to the Metropolitan Museum of Art in New York. In his letter to the director Sargent wrote: 'I suppose it is the best thing I have ever done.'

SIMILAR INTERESTS, DIFFERENT VISIONS

As a fashionably dressed 20-year-old art student in 1876, Sargent had met 36-year-old Monet who was still struggling to make a living. The two had dinner together at the Café du Helder where several of Monet's paintings were on display, and despite their differences in age and experience, it marked for them the beginning of a 50-year friendship.

Even though their painting styles and methods differed, they shared some common ground. Both artists painted landscapes and sought to portray transitory or fleeting moments, but Sargent had also been able to earn his living painting society portraits, regularly exhibiting his work at the Salon, and he was wealthy by the age of 30. Monet, who had shunned the Salon, did not paint commissioned portraits, and his work was not appreciated until he was 50 years old. Sargent greatly admired Monet's style and was also fascinated

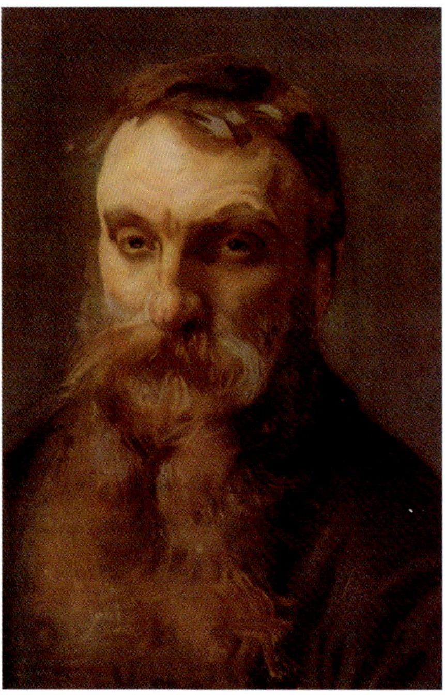

Above: Sargent painted this portrait of the sculptor Auguste Rodin in 1884; the year in which they both participated in Les XX.

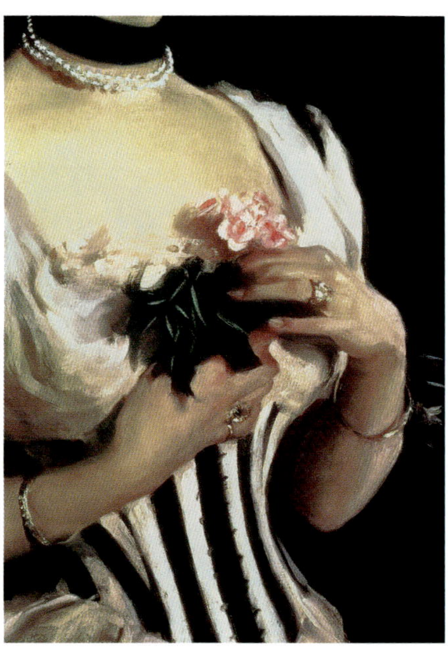

Above: Mrs Wilton Phipps, c.1884 (detail). Although Sargent's brushwork was often loosely Impressionistic, his society portraits were more carefully detailed.

by light, but his methods of depicting it were different. Unlike Monet who translated visual information into colour, Sargent focused on tonal contrasts. Years later, Sargent wrote that Monet's perception of light and its effects on objects: 'added a new perception to artists in the same way that man who invented perspective added a new perception to artists.' When Monet was asked to comment on Sargent's lavish praise, he said: 'I am very proud of his praise, but he has made me greater than I am. I only have the merit of painting directly in front of nature while searching to render my impressions of extremely transient effects.'

SUPPORTIVE RELATIONSHIP

Nine years after their first meeting, and the year after Sargent's humiliation at the Salon, he visited Monet at his country house in Giverny, a village 50 miles (80 km) from Paris. There, Sargent painted a richly-coloured scene of Monet at work painting in the open air, and over the next few years, Sargent purchased four of Monet's paintings. In his turn, Monet was also a supportive friend, always ready to offer advice. The two artists no doubt discussed how best Sargent should proceed after his career in Paris had faced such a setback.

Three years after he had stayed in Giverny, Sargent wrote to Monet: 'It is with great difficulty that I tear myself away from your delightful painting to tell you again how much I admire it. I sit in front of it for hours at a time in a state of enchantment. I am delighted to have in my home such a source of pleasure. I am sending to you what I should have sent to you a long time ago. If you have trouble getting money, the bankers at such-and-such a bank know my signature. Dear Monet, I thank you and I love you. As an artist, I worship you. John S. Sargent. PS I am not tipsy.'

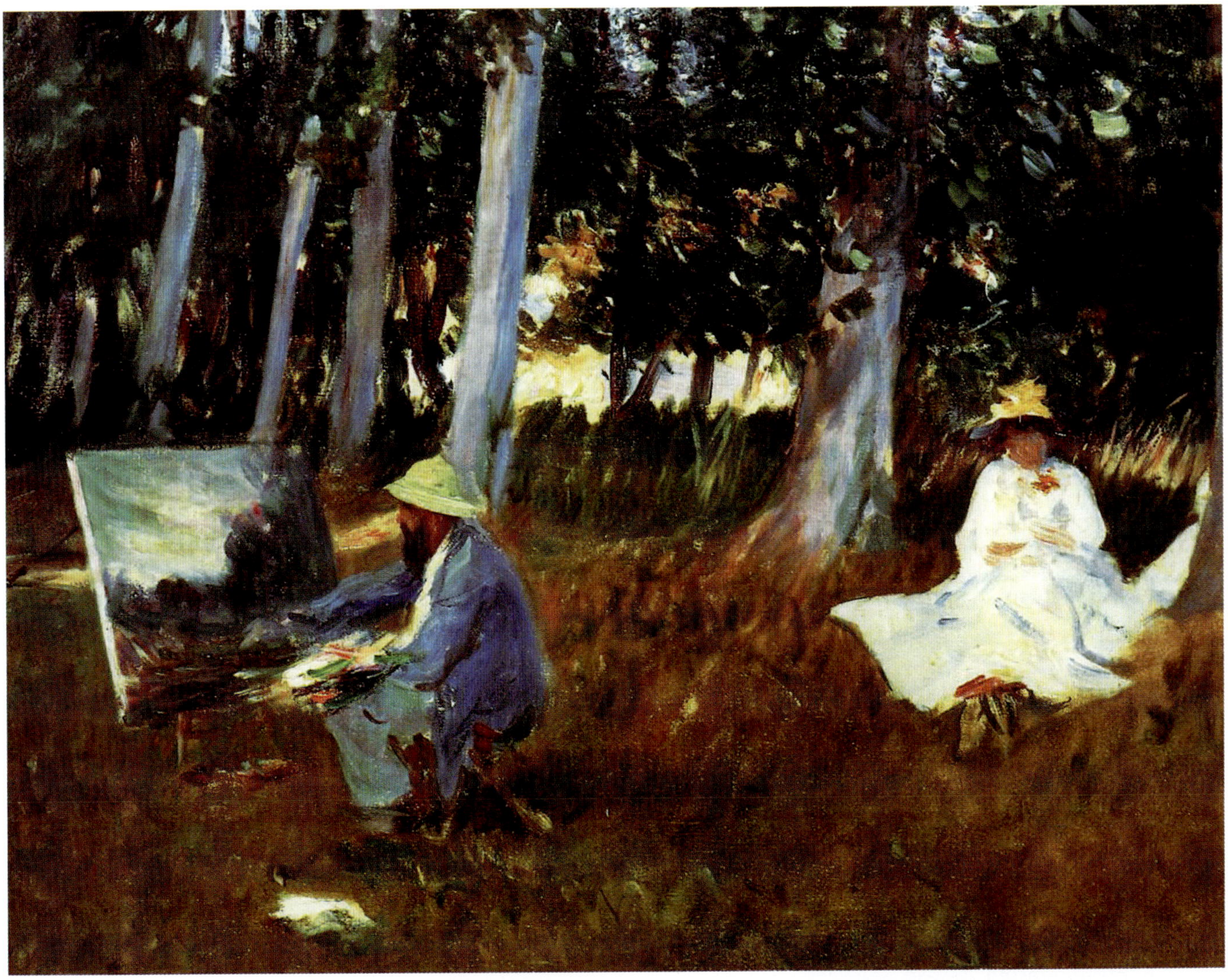

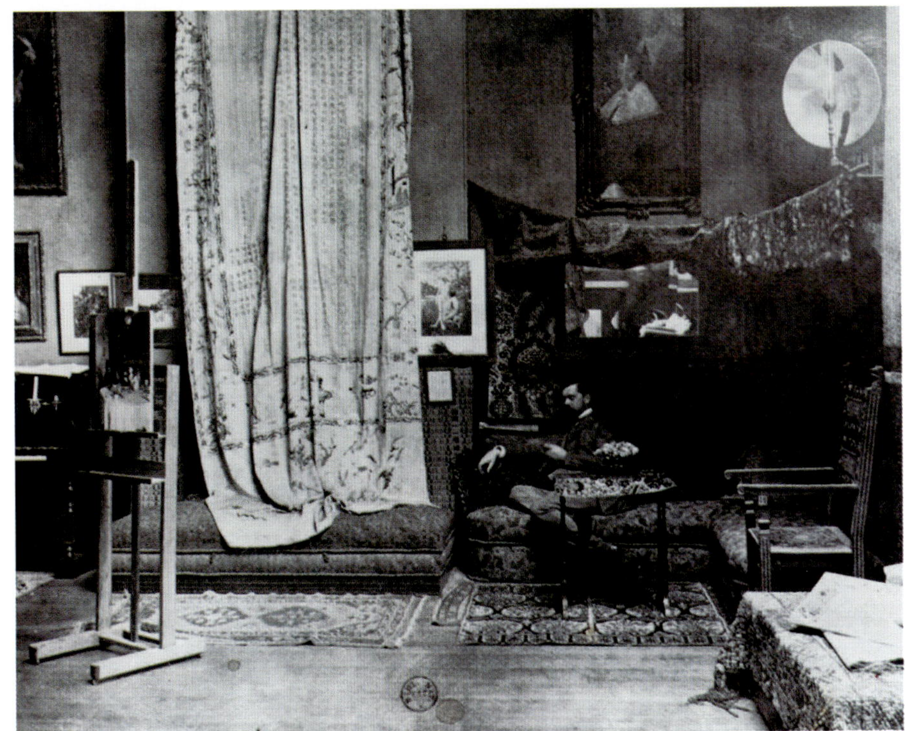

Above: Claude Monet Painting at the Edge of a Wood, *painted by Sargent during his stay with Monet in 1887.*

Right: Sargent in his studio, c.1885.

THE SOCIÉTÉ DES XX

The Société des XX, Les XX or Les Vingt, was a group of 20 Belgian painters, designers and sculptors, formed in 1883 by Brussels lawyer, publisher and entrepreneur Octave Maus (1856–1919). For a period of 10 years the member artists held an annual exhibition of their art, during which time they would also invite 20 international artists to participate. In 1884, Sargent and Rodin were among the foreign artists invited to exhibit with them.

MOVE TO LONDON

Even before the *Madame X* debacle, Sargent had been considering a move to England. In about 1882, he had met Henry James (1843–1916), an American novelist who lived in Britain, who tried to persuade Sargent to move there too. Initially hesitant, Sargent eventually began watching the British portrait market with interest.

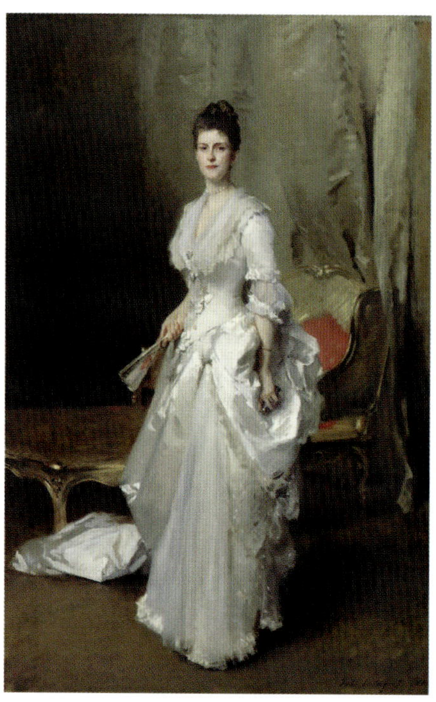

Left: Margaret Stuyvesant Rutherfurd White (Mrs Henry White), *1883.*

Below: Garden Study of the Vickers Children, *1884, an animated and Impressionistic scene of Albert and Edith's children in their garden.*

THE ROYAL ACADEMY

In 1882, Sargent had sent his flamboyant portrait of *Dr Pozzi at Home* (see page 32) to the Royal Academy in London. Even though the painting was a little too extravagant for most British tastes in portraiture, Sargent was encouraged by its acceptance at the Royal Academy – the British equivalent of the Salon and just as strict. Additionally, in the year before he had started painting *Madame X*, Sargent had been commissioned to paint the portrait of a fashionable American socialite, Margaret 'Daisy' Stuyvesant Rutherfurd White (1857–1916), the wife of the American diplomat Henry White (1850–1927) whom he knew in Paris. The couple were about to move to London, and Sargent realised the value of showing the portrait in both Paris and London. However, in late 1882, Daisy's ill-health prevented Sargent from completing the painting until the following year, when it was accepted by both the Salon and the Royal Academy. It was the year before the *Madame X* scandal, and the work's success helped to spread Sargent's good name to the portrait-buying public in England as well as France.

THE VICKERS FAMILY

In June 1884, Sargent travelled to England twice, and stayed each time at Lavington Rectory in Sussex, the home of his friends, Albert Vickers (1838–1919) and his wife Edith (1854–1909). While there, he painted a full-length portrait of Edith and several oil sketches, including one of Albert and Edith's children playing in their garden of lilies in the soft evening light. He also painted Albert and Edith in their cosy dining room. These informal, loosely painted works, similar in approach to several of his recent Venetian and Spanish paintings, suggest casual, passing moments. In July, he stayed with Albert's brother Thomas Vickers (1833–1915) and his wife Frances Mary (1841–1904) in Sheffield. They had commissioned him to paint a portrait of their three daughters, Florence Evelyn (1867–1947), Mabel Frances (1862–94) and Clara Mildred (1865–1952), whom he had met in Paris about a year before when the girls were studying art. He wrote to Vernon Lee about the commission: 'I am to paint portraits in the country and three ugly young women in Sheffield.' Whether

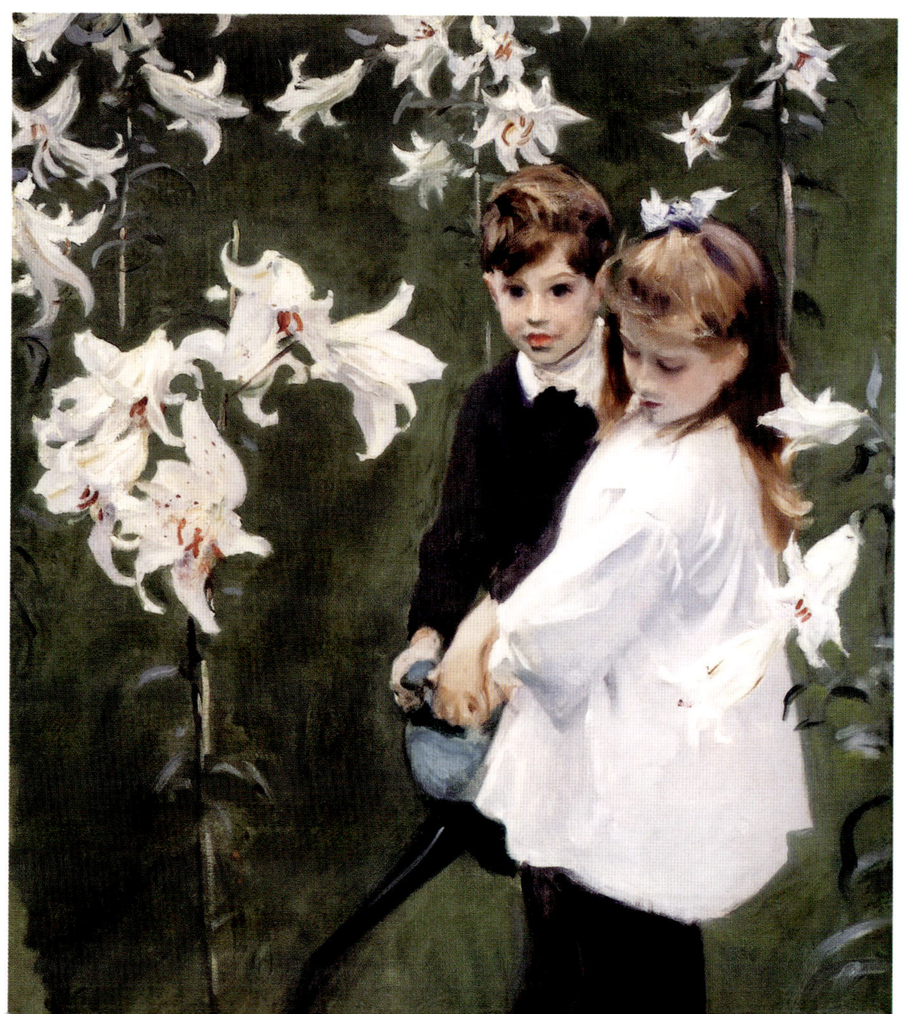

his skills overrode the young women's ugliness, or whether they were not ugly to begin with, his portrait of the three Misses Vickers (see page 124) with its complex composition and strong tonal contrasts, shows them to be rather attractive. However, when the portrait was shown at the Salon in May 1885, it was disdained by critics and dubbed 'pseudo-Velázquez.' The following year, he showed it at the Royal Academy, and it was voted the 'Worst Picture of the Year' by The Pall Mall Gazette visitors' poll. Critics found his use of perspective 'shallow and pretentious.'

THE GROSVENOR GALLERY

Henry James continued trying to convince Sargent to move to England. In the summer of 1884, he introduced Sargent to J. Comyns Carr (1849–1916), one of the directors of the Grosvenor Gallery that had displayed Sargent's portrait, *Mrs Wodehouse Legh* (1859–1931), earlier that year. Soon after, he returned briefly to Paris, but was back in London the following year, staying in Whistler's old studio at Tite Street in Chelsea. In September, while on a boat trip on the River Thames with a fellow student from Carolus-Duran's studio, Edwin Austin Abbey (1852–1911), he sustained a bad head wound and Abbey took him to recuperate in nearby Broadway, a village in the Cotswold hills that was the home of a small colony of mainly Anglo-American artists. Instantly Sargent felt at home there and forged some firm friendships. That October, he travelled to Bournemouth to paint the novelist and poet, Robert Louis Stevenson (1850–94) and his wife Fanny (1840–1914), (see pages 127 and 132).

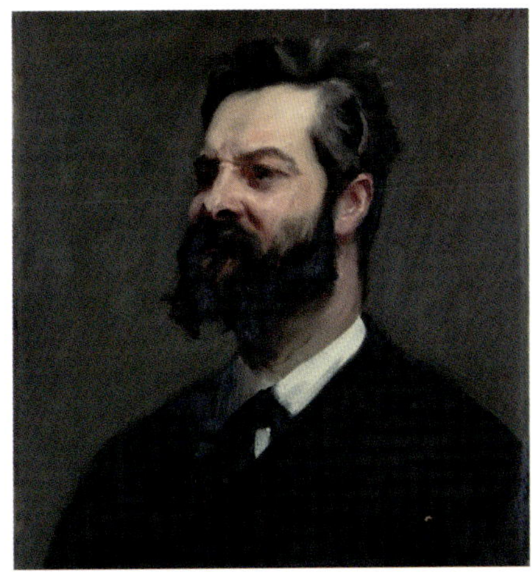

Above right: Art critic, writer and poet, Louis de Fourcaud was one of the prominent art critics in Paris when Sargent painted him in 1884, just before he moved to London.

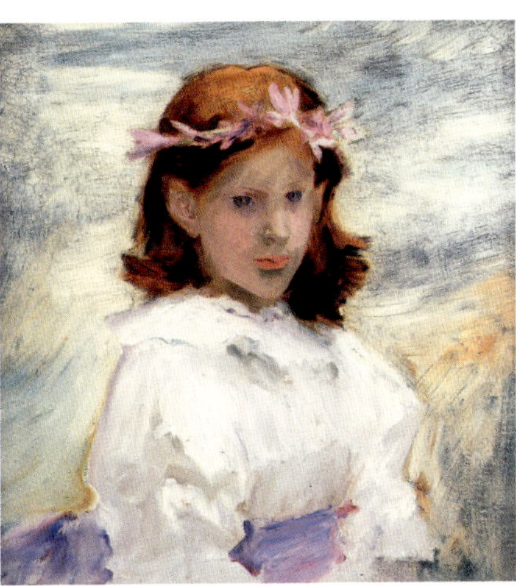

Right: Portrait of Teresa Gosse, 1885, daughter of Sir Edmund Gosse (1849–1928), an English poet, author and critic.

Below: An expressive work in watercolour and gouache. Sargent painted The Brook *as a quick plein air sketch.*

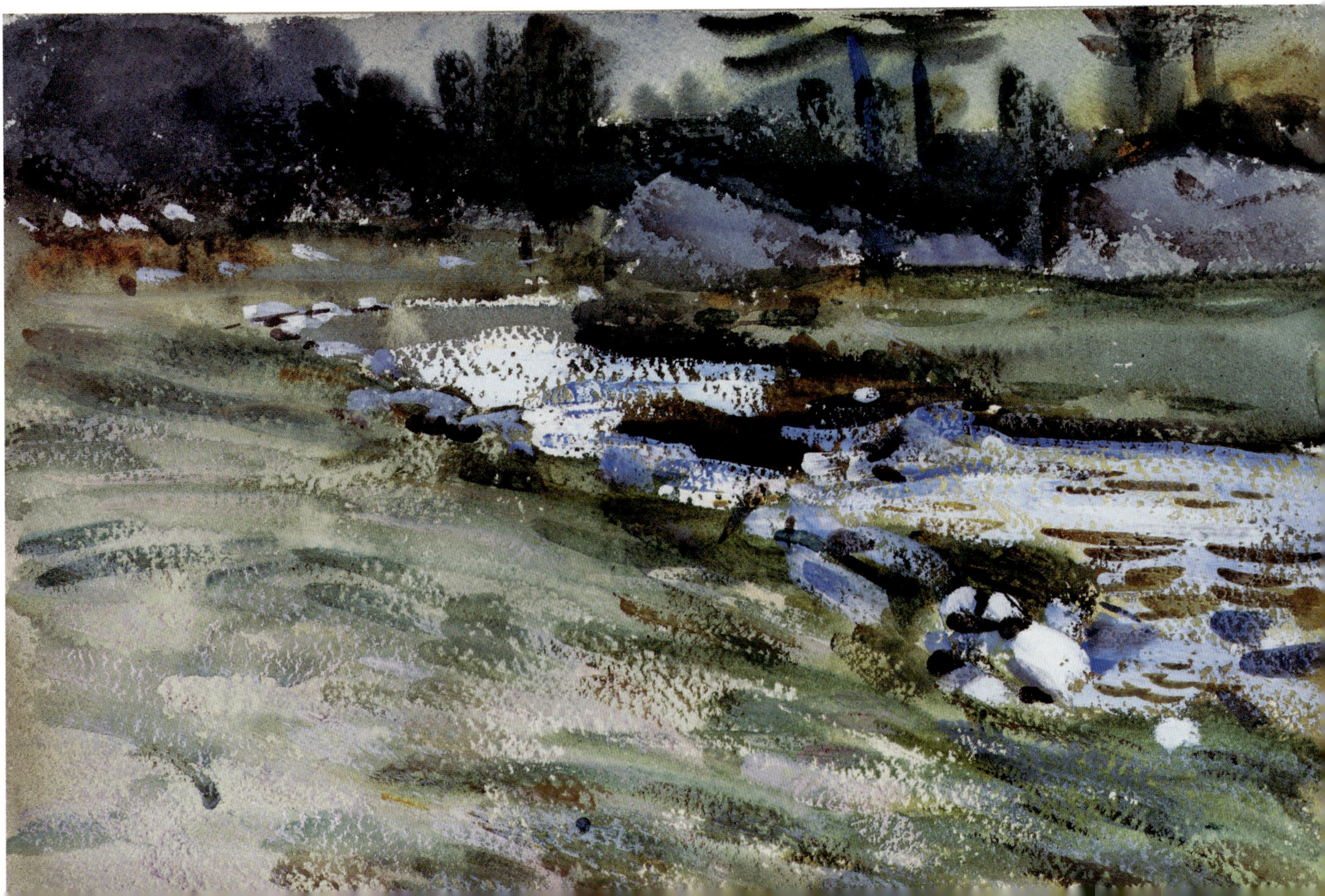

THE COTSWOLDS

After Sargent's boating accident, Abbey took him to stay with Frank (1848–1912) and Elizabeth Millet (1853–1932) in the Cotswolds. While there Sargent recalled a scene he had passed in Pangbourne while boating with Abbey one evening, of glowing Chinese lanterns hanging in a garden amid trees and lilies.

IMPRESSIONIST STYLE

It was September 1885, and Sargent was still inspired by Monet's intricately modulated, broken brushstrokes he had witnessed in Giverny. From that time, Monet's ideas affected Sargent's approach to painting, and are clearly evident in a work he painted while staying in the Cotswolds. As he recuperated, Sargent began planning a painting based on the Chinese lantern scene he had witnessed along the River Thames. He made several preliminary sketches and included elements from the previous year's *Garden Study of the Vickers Children* (see page 38).

CARNATION, LILY, LILY, ROSE

Sargent began painting his picture in Frank and Elizabeth's garden, and

continued working on it until early November, when he put it aside until the following summer. The entire work was painted en plein air, as Monet had worked, and progress was slow because Sargent needed the same light and weather conditions each time. It had to be late summer to autumn, not raining or windy and just after sunset when the sky was tinged with an orange-mauve light. Initially conceived as a painting of one little girl lighting a Chinese lantern, Sargent began using five-year-old Kate Millet (1880–unknown) as his model. As Kate had dark hair and Sargent wanted a blonde child, he put her in a wig, but

then he discovered that the daughters of the illustrator Fred Barnard (1846–96) and his wife Alice (1847–1924) who lived nearby were blonde, so he used them instead.

Each day when the required conditions were present, Sargent placed his easel and paints in the garden in readiness, and he asked his young models, Dorothy (Dolly) (1878–1949) and Marion Polly Barnard (1874–1946) to pose. As the sun set, he began to paint quickly, surrounded companionably by his new friends. He could only work for a few minutes before the light changed, and as winter neared and

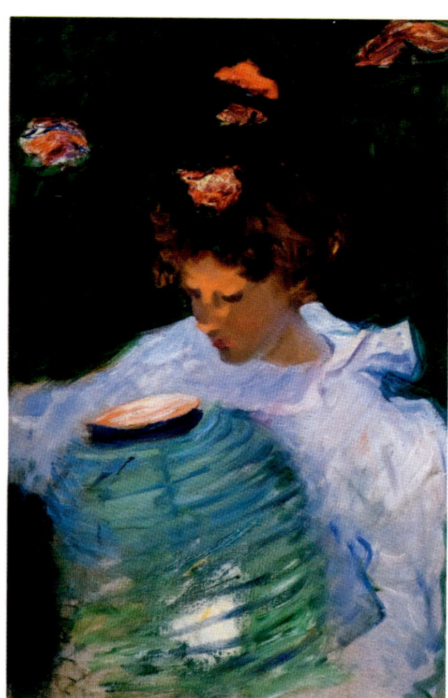

Above: One of several studies for Carnation, Lily, Lily, Rose.

Right: Carnation, Lily, Lily, Rose, *1885–86, a painting that helped to establish Sargent in Britain (see also page 129).*

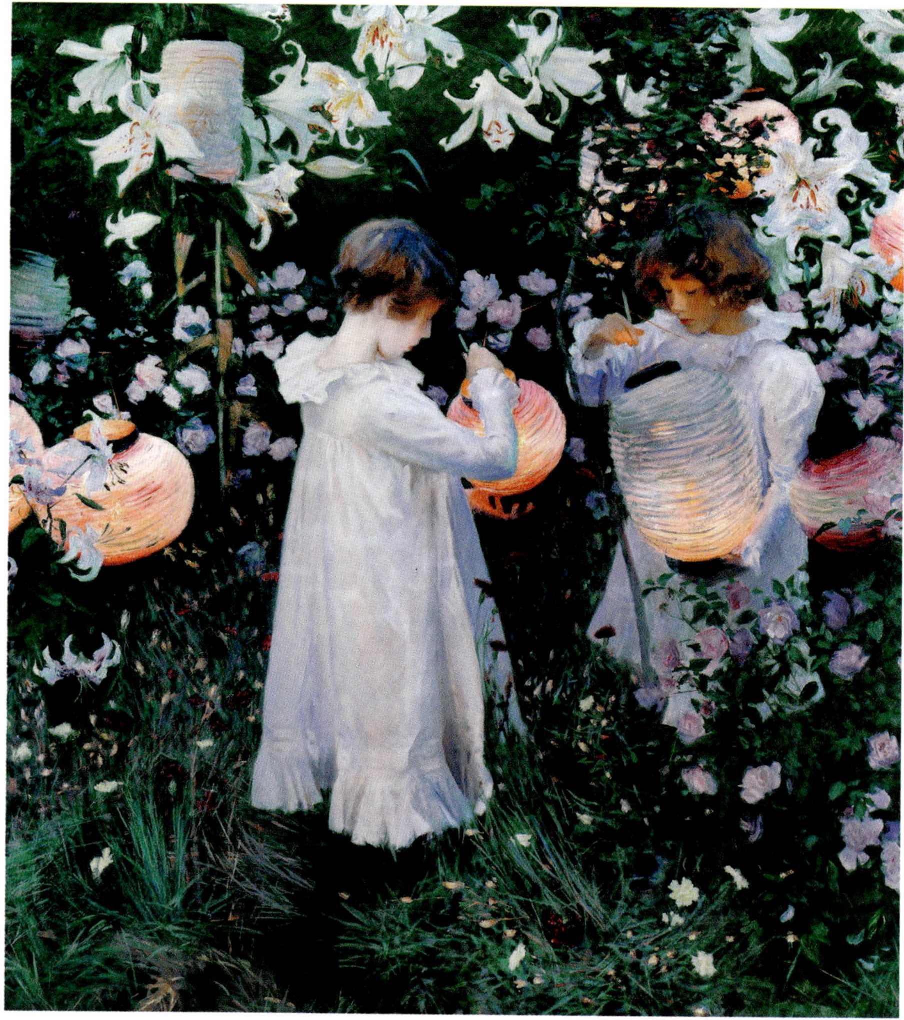

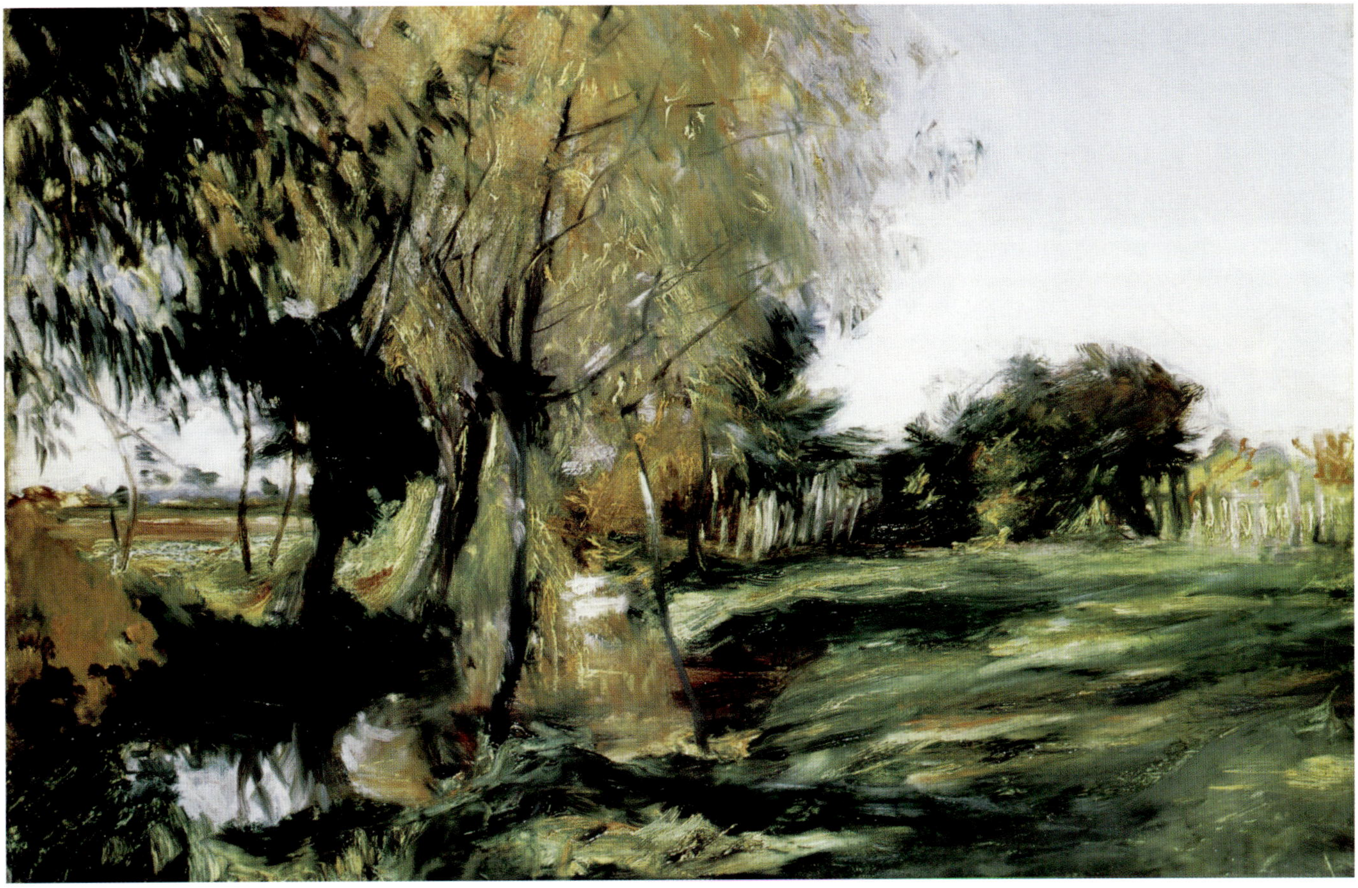

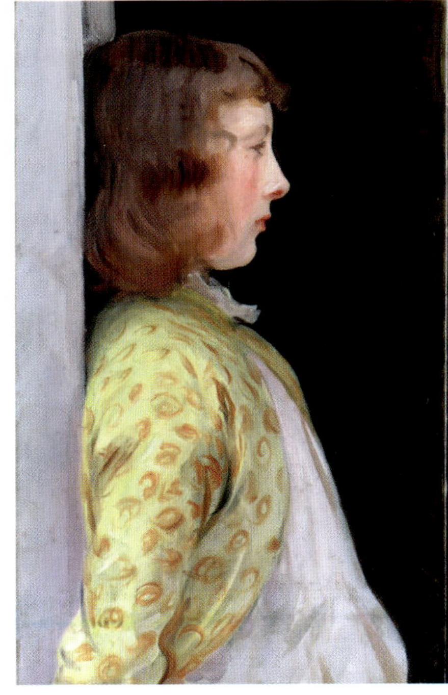

the flowers died, he replaced them with artificial flowers. The painting was one of the few figure compositions he made out of doors, and he completed it by the end of October 1886. He wrote to Emily about it: 'Fearful difficult subject. Impossible brilliant colours of flowers, and lamps and brightest green lawn background. Paints are not bright enough, and then the effect only lasts ten minutes.' While working, Sargent cut down the rectangular canvas, turning it into an approximately square shape. The completed painting *Carnation, Lily, Lily, Rose* was named after a popular song of the time, *The Wreath,* by Joseph Mazzinghi (that Sargent and his friends often sang around the piano in Broadway). It was ultimately a great success, despite some negative criticism at the Royal Academy exhibition in 1887 for his 'Frenchified' style. Yet it was also greatly acclaimed, and Sir Frederic Leighton (1830–96), President of the Royal Academy, encouraged the Tate Gallery to buy it. It subsequently became the first of Sargent's works to be acquired by a public museum.

THE BROADWAY SET

Many members of the small colony of artists who had settled in the village of Broadway were, like Sargent, expatriate Americans. Frank D. Millet had been the first to see the village as an artists' retreat and move there. It was a picturesque rural location in the Cotswolds overlooking the Vale of Evesham. The group included Millet, Edwin Abbey, the writer and landscapist George Boughton (1833–1905), the illustrator, landscape painter and garden designer Alfred Parsons (1847–1920), Edwin Blashfield (1848–1936), Fred Barnard, and the writers Henry James and Edmund Gosse. They were together an assorted, warm and high-spirited bunch, who became close through their intellectual and artistic interests, and were accepted by the locals. Although they all pursued their artistic careers, they also enjoyed themselves enormously, playing tennis, and sharing teas, musical evenings and dances together.

Above: At Broadway, *1885. Another radidly painted plein air work, painted while Sargent lived with the Millet family.*

Below: Portrait of Dorothy Barnard, *1889. Dolly was one of Sargent's models for* Carnation, Lily, Lily, Rose.

BRITAIN AND AMERICA

'I want him to come here to live and work,' wrote Henry James to a friend about Sargent. But Sargent remained tentative until *Carnation, Lily, Lily, Rose* was admired at the Royal Academy, inspiring several portrait commissions. Within a short time, he did as James wished and settled permanently in London.

In May 1887, Sargent signed a three-year lease on the studio in Tite Street, deciding that a studio in Chelsea was the best base from which to paint English society portraits. However, despite some early interest, such commissions were slow, as the scandal surrounding *Madame X* in Paris had made many women uneasy about how the artist might depict them. *Carnation,*

Lily, Lily, Rose was radical for both Britain and the period, but it caused Sargent's reputation to gradually increase. His method of paint application, of separate strokes of pure colour, made the work appear to flicker and glow, while the combination of natural twilight and the artificial candlelight of the lanterns reflected charmingly on the children's faces and lily petals.

ASSIMILATING IMPRESSIONISM

Sargent continued trying to absorb and assimilate the Impressionist techniques he had learned from Monet, while retaining the style of painting that had so far helped him achieve acclaim. Like Monet, he was particularly fascinated with light, and became highly skilled at portraying it, but in contrast with the Impressionists, he remained fairly literal in his interpretations, continuing to capture deep tonal qualities that did not dissolve into streaks of colour as Monet's paintings did. He had learned many other things from Monet as well, including using a boat as a floating studio for working en plein air, and he constructed his own bateau-atelier (studio boat), so he could capture reflections and the movement of light and colour on water. He began working from a small boat wherever he was near water, whether on the River Thames, or in a harbour in the

Above: Gathering Flowers at Twilight, *c.1883. After staying with Monet, Sargent spent more time painting en plein air.*

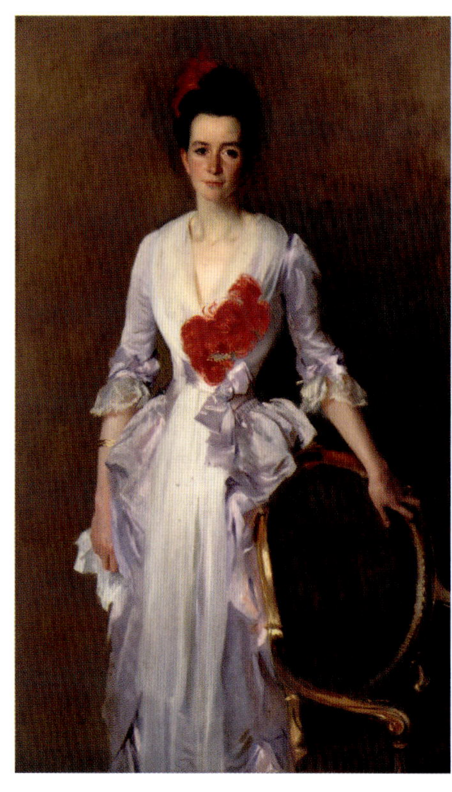

Right: Isabelle Parrott, or Mrs Archibald Douglas Dick, 1886, one of the wealthy Americans who commissioned Sargent.

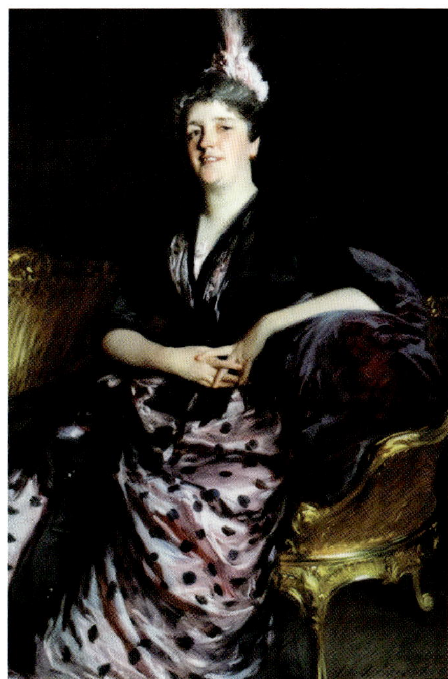

Above: Painted in 1887, Mary Louisa Cushing *was an heiress, married to Ned Darley Boit, Sargent's friend who trained as a lawyer but devoted himself to art.*

Mediterranean, Maine or Florida. In 1887, he acquired Monet's painting *Vagues à la Manneporte* of 1885, and the Frenchman's influence became even more apparent, but Sargent's work always defined form and space more precisely than Monet's, with thinner paint and fewer juxtapositions of colour. Many of his works of the time, such as *A Boating Party* (see page 141), *Paul Helleu Sketching with his Wife* (see page 53), *Gathering Flowers at Twilight* and *Two Girls with Parasols* are particularly Impressionistic, giving him the opportunity to express himself more personally and individually away from his commissioned portraits.

SUCCESS IN THE US

During that same year, Sargent travelled to the United States where many members of the American high society were eager for him to paint their portraits. Distanced from both the scandal of *Madame X* and the rigidity of academic expectations, they admired Sargent's method of capturing his sitters expressively and individually, often seemingly in the middle of a movement.

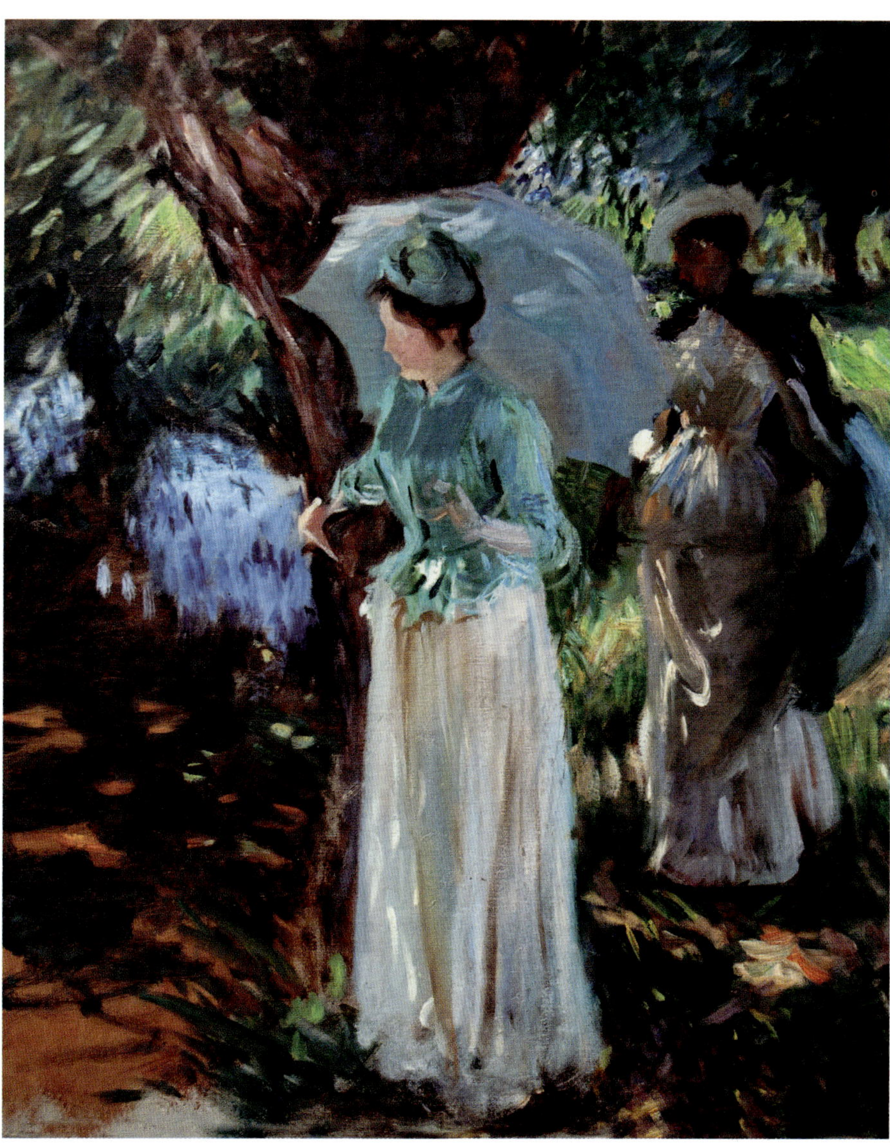

Above: Two Girls with Parasols, *1888. This is an unfinished, Impressionistic canvas of friends on a country walk.*

FIRST ONE-MAN SHOW

Sargent settled into life in Britain, and still travelled around Europe, occasionally also visiting the US. In September 1887, he stayed with some old family friends; Admiral and Mrs Goodrich in Newport, Rhode Island. The following year, he had his first solo exhibition in Boston. It was a great success.

While staying with the Goodrich family, Sargent painted the portrait of Elizabeth Allen Marquand (1862–1951), the wife of Henry Gurdon Marquand (1819–1902), an American financier, philanthropist and art collector. Although he thought the portrait: 'a dreary subject,' it was received with delight by Mr and Mrs Marquand. Next he went to New York to visit his old friend Beckwith, with whom he had shared a studio in Paris and who was working in New York as a portraitist, and after New York, he travelled to Boston, where he had been commissioned by General Lucius Fairchild (1831–96) and his wife Frances Bull Fairchild (1845–1924). While there, he also painted Isabella Stewart Gardner (1840–1924) and Mrs Edward Darley Boit – or Mary Louisa Cushing (known as Isa), (see page 43). Although in recent works he had used thicker, brighter and more opaque paints, for these portraits he returned to his previous method of using thin paint and translucent glazes to create luminous and dramatic tonal contrasts. Once again, his style owes much to the influences of Carolus-Duran, Manet, and especially Velázquez.

MRS JACK

Isabella Stewart Gardner (known as Mrs Jack) had been introduced to Sargent by Henry James in 1886. She loved his work and had been given his *El Jaleo* by her cousin Thomas Jefferson Coolidge (1831–1920). Married to John 'Jack' Lowell Gardner II (1837–98), a businessman, art collector and philanthropist, she perceived herself as wild, scandalous and alluring, having had several lovers. So she asked Sargent to paint her portrait to echo some of the risqué elements of *Madame X*. Beginning in December 1887, Isabella paid him $3000 for her portrait.

However, she was not easy to paint. She constantly fidgeted and turned to look out of the window. Ultimately, Sargent made eight renderings of her face before they were both satisfied with it.

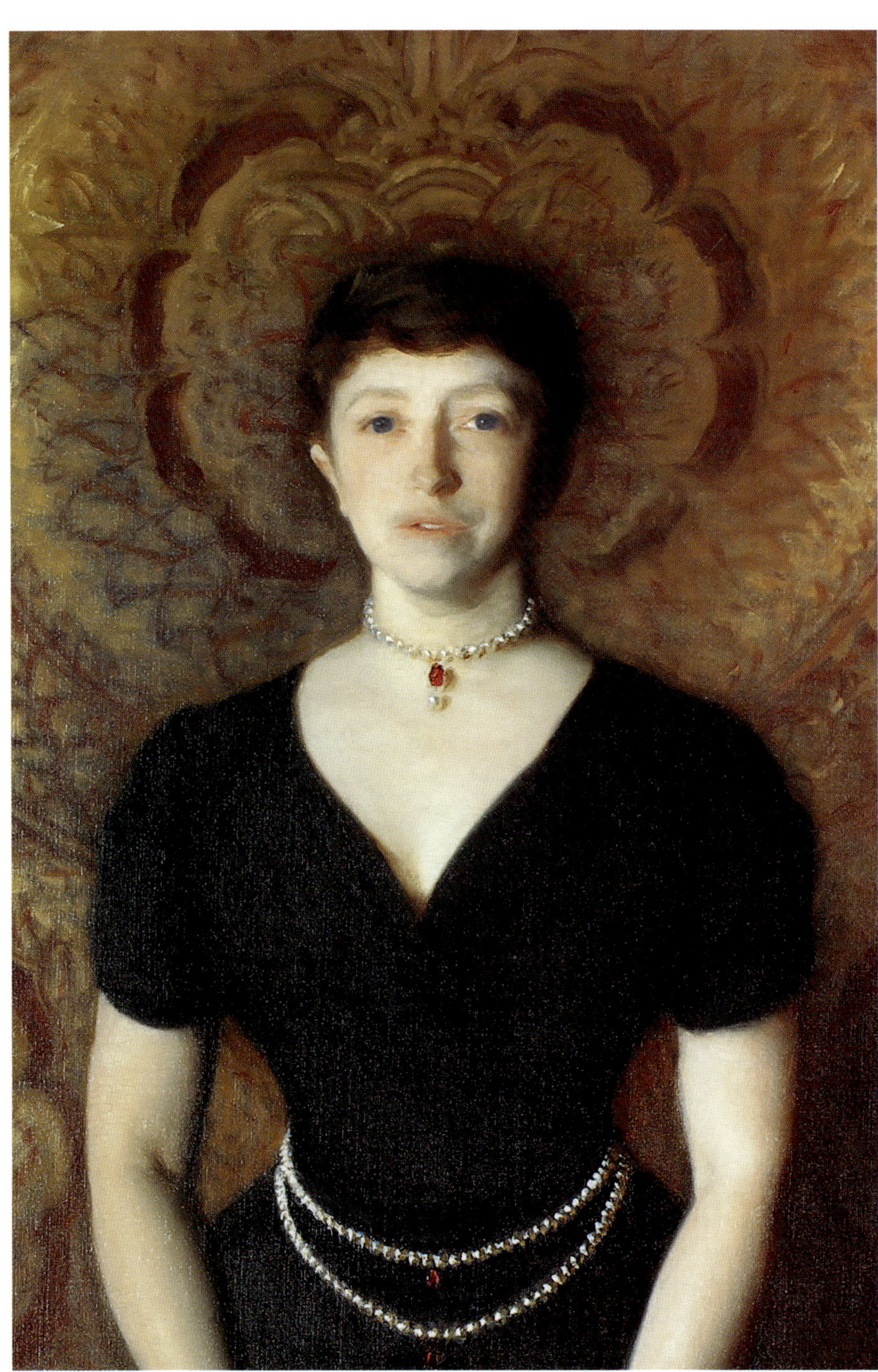

Above: Detail of Sargent's full-length portrait of Isabella Stewart Gardner (Mrs Jack), 1888 (see also page 135). Her sensuous form is emphasized by the double string of pearls at her waist.

The resulting image is rather strange. With a somewhat static pose and a tight black dress with pearls at the waist, it projects a sensuous display of flesh, while the 15th century velvet brocade background encircles her head like a heart-shaped halo. James described her as resembling a 'Byzantine Madonna.' Although she was 46 years old, she looks younger, and she loved it, declaring that it was the best portrait Sargent ever did. It was exhibited in 1888 in Sargent's solo show, but her husband asked her not to show it again publicly while he was alive. She duly respected his wishes and it remained in their home until after her death. Perhaps the greatest consequence of the portrait was that Sargent and Mrs Jack became close friends, and she subsequently encouraged many of her other wealthy friends to commission him too.

THE ST BOTOLPH'S EXHIBITION

The St Botolph Club was founded in Boston in 1880 as a private men's club. In December 1887, Sargent had shown his portrait of Robert Louis Stevenson in a group exhibition there, and from the end of January to mid-February 1888, the club hosted a solo exhibition of his work. It was Sargent's first one-man show, featuring 21 oil paintings and one watercolour. Among the works on display was *The Daughters of Edward Darley Boit* (see page 120), which Henry James believed was the best work Sargent had ever painted. Over 1300 visitors visited the exhibition, and James and other writers published comprehensive essays about Sargent in both American and British publications.

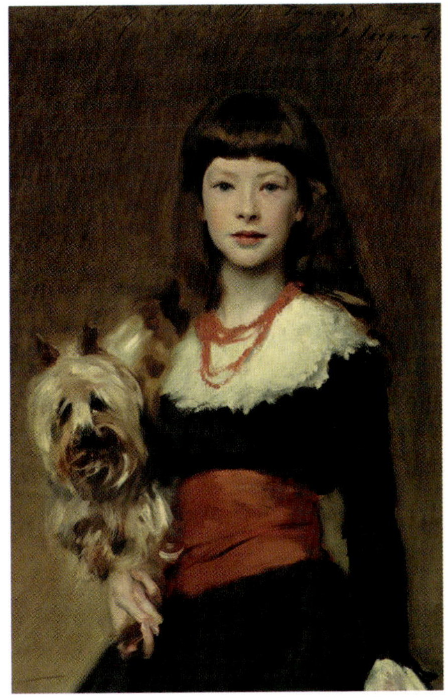

Above: In 1882, Sargent painted 12-year-old Eleanor Beatrice Townsend, daughter of a friend, capturing her lively personality as she clutches her terrier.

Above right: The huge success of Sargent's exhibition at the St Botolph Club resulted in many more portrait commissions for him. This is his Portrait of Leroy King as a Young Boy, *painted in 1888.*

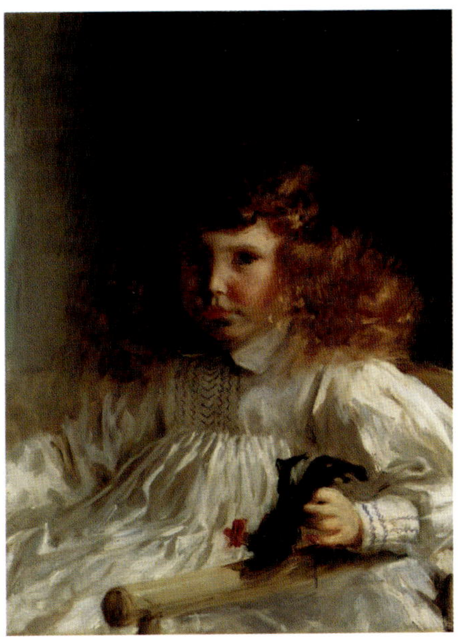

Sargent was often described as shy, retiring and socially awkward, but he was actually remarkably sociable in his own circle and a devoted and generous friend. He went out nearly every night, was a proficient pianist, and frequently entertained his friends and sitters by playing the piano for them. Many of his friendships inspired experiments in painting.

Right: J. Comyns Carr, director of the Grosvenor Gallery, spent the summers of 1885 and 1886 in Broadway. Comyns in a Punt, 1888, was painted from memory.

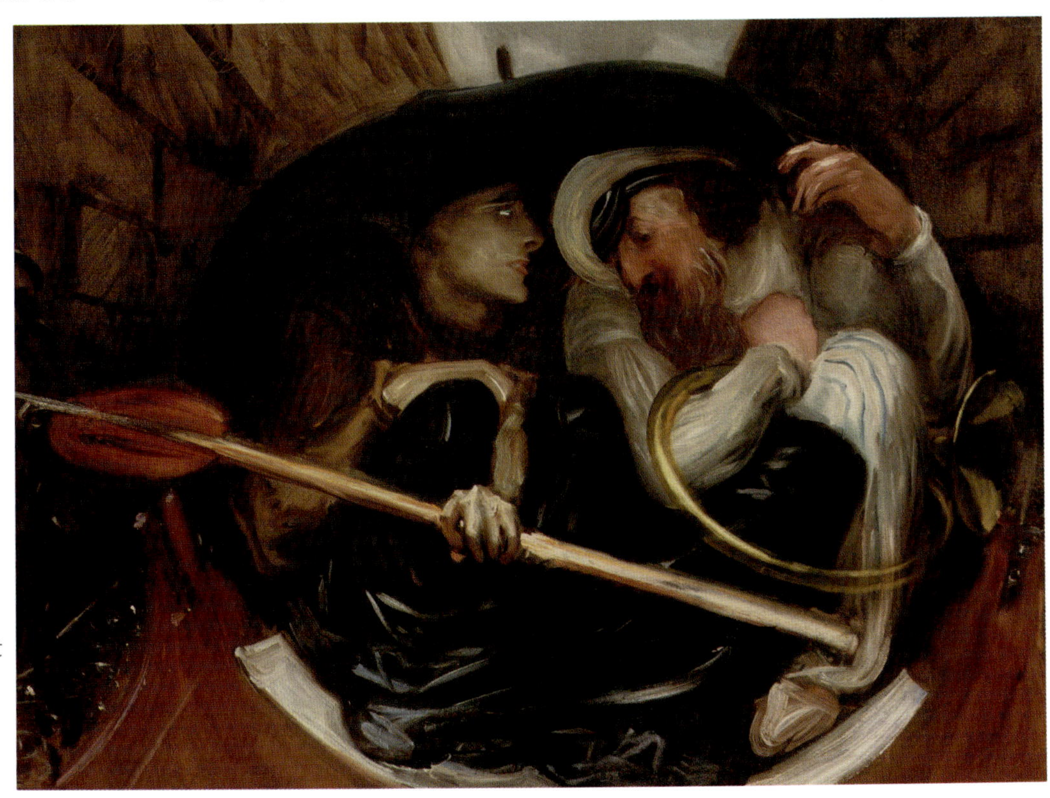

ELLEN TERRY

Although Sargent was now successful in both America and Britain, commissions were scarce during 1888. So he began working on a portrait of his choosing, of the actress Ellen Terry (1847–1928) in her current role of Lady Macbeth. He styled the portrait dramatically, featuring a pose that did not occur in Shakespeare's play.

Sargent's St Botolph's exhibition inspired great appreciation of his work among American art buyers. Despite having never lived in America, he was welcomed by both old and new friends and patrons, and after his St Botolph's triumph, he was immediately commissioned to paint two portraits of wealthy Americans. One was of Mrs Adrian Iselin, née Eleanora O'Donnell (1818–1905), who was shocked when he asked her to pose in her ordinary street clothes, with her walking stick, rather than in one of her sumptuous French ball gowns (see page 138).

CALCOT MILL

In May, Sargent left America for London, but on arrival, he discovered that his father had suffered a stroke. He immediately rented a house at Calcot Mill near Broadway, and arranged for his family to stay there, soon joining them and over the next few months only travelled back occasionally to his London studio. Vernon Lee, who also occasionally stayed with them, later wrote of the tenderness with which Sargent helped his father each evening. The time was short however; Fitzwilliam Sargent died in April 1889.

While at Calcot Mill, Sargent also invited Claude Monet to stay, and continued to seek his own interpretation of Impressionism, painting several views along the River Avon, often featuring his sisters. He also painted his friend George Henschel (1850–1934), a German-born British baritone, pianist, conductor and composer whom he had met in 1887. Henschel admired Sargent's talents as a painter and his extensive knowledge of music. Sargent completed his portrait

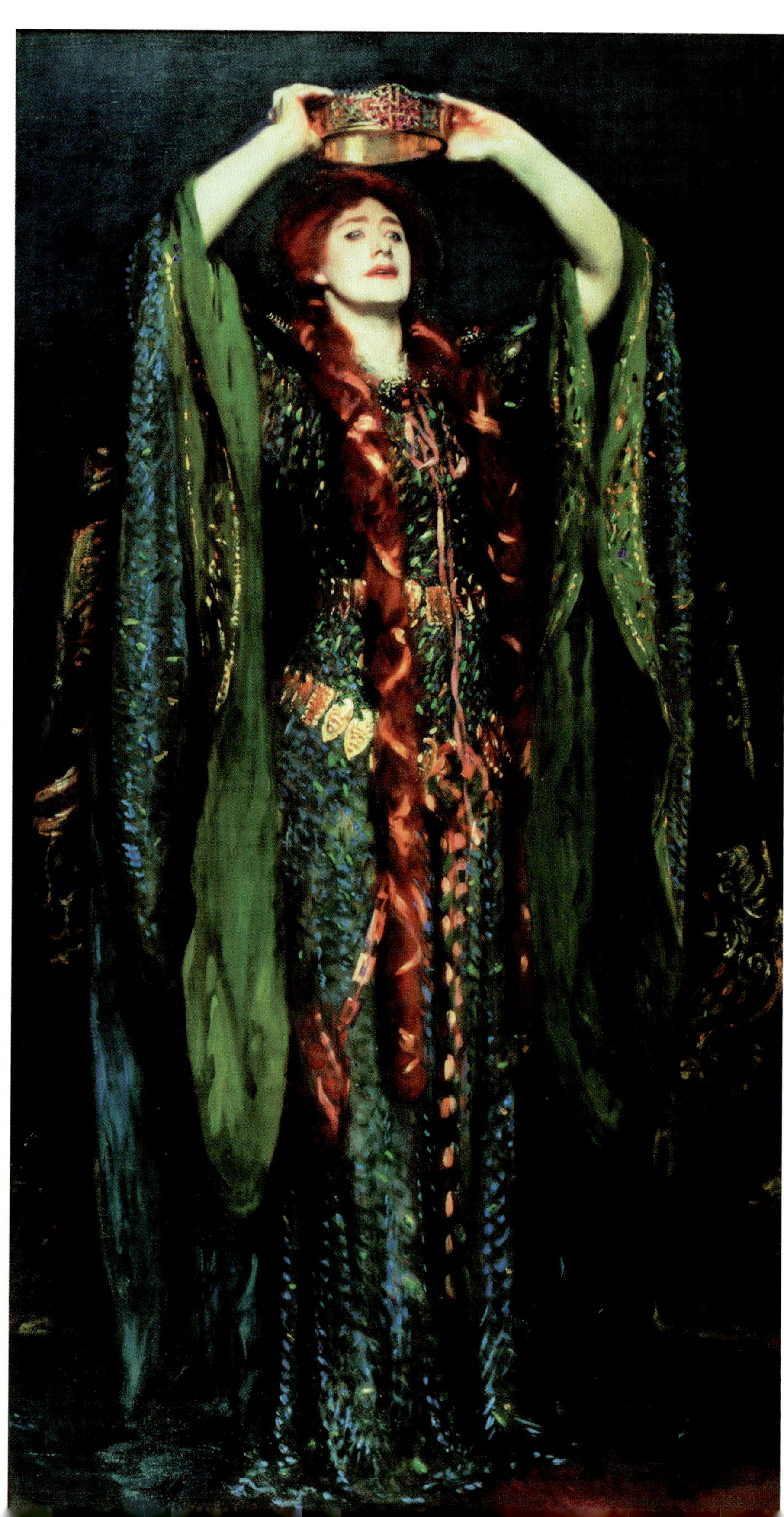

Right: The dramatic — and somewhat controversial — portrait of Ellen Terry as Lady Macbeth, 1889.

in five sittings, while Henschel stood and sang. The result is personal and affectionate, demonstrating the regard the two men felt for each other.

VILIFICATION AGAIN

At the opening performance of Macbeth in London in December 1888, Sargent was struck by Ellen Terry's appearance as Lady Macbeth. He persuaded her to sit for a portrait, and suggested the dramatic pose despite it not occurring in the production. Her exotic emerald green costume was designed by Alice Comyns Carr (1850–1927), the wife of Joseph Comyns Carr, director of the Grosvenor Gallery (see page 45). Alice wanted the dress to look: 'much like soft chain armour...and yet have something that would give the appearance of the scales of a serpent.' In green silk and blue tinsel, it was sewn all over with iridescent green beetle wings, with a Celtic patterned border decorated with rubies. Terry later wrote in her diary that she thought the portrait was 'magnificent,' but a review in the London-based literary magazine, *The Athenaeum*, scathingly proclaimed: '...the coarseness of her surroundings – down to the blue and green of her robes, layers of stage

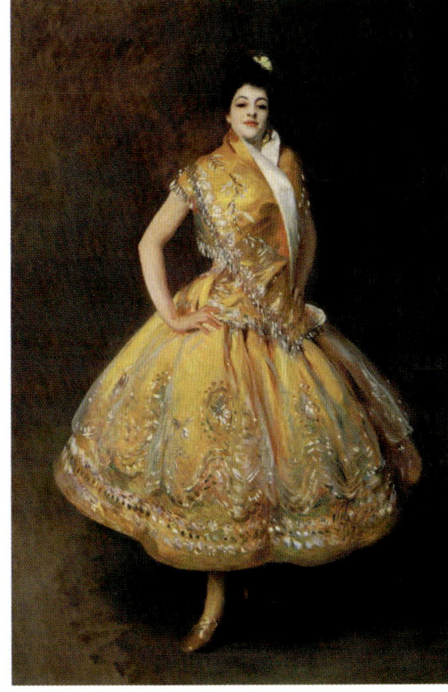

Above: The full-skirted yellow satin and lace costume suggests the twists and turns of Carmencita's dance, 1889.

Below left: Mrs F. Abington (1737–1815), after Joshua Reynolds (1723–92), c.1890.

Below right: Influenced by Velázquez and his own natural understanding of children, Sargent captures these two little girls with his characteristic loose brushwork.

paint on her face, lips contorted... the visitor will shudder. This painting is for the pit.' Similarly, another article in the London newspaper *The Saturday Review*, asserted: 'Miss Ellen Terry as Lady Macbeth enjoys the distinction... of being the best-hated picture of the year.'

CAPTIVATED BY DANCE

Sargent had always been captivated by dance and in the same year as Ellen Terry's portrait, he painted the dancer known as 'La Carmencita'. Carmen Daucet Moreno (1868–1910) was a Spanish-style dancer who first attracted attention at the 1889 Paris Exposition Universelle and then in America. Contemporary accounts described her as dancing like a 'writhing serpent.' Both Sargent and William Merritt Chase (1849–1916), one of New York's most fashionable painters, were transfixed by her and Sargent arranged for her to dance in some evening performances at Chase's New York studio where they both painted her. *The New York Times* journalist H. J. Brock wrote about how Sargent held her interest as he painted her: 'Sargent used to paint his nose red to rivet her childish interest upon himself, and when the red nose failed he would fascinate her by eating his cigar.'

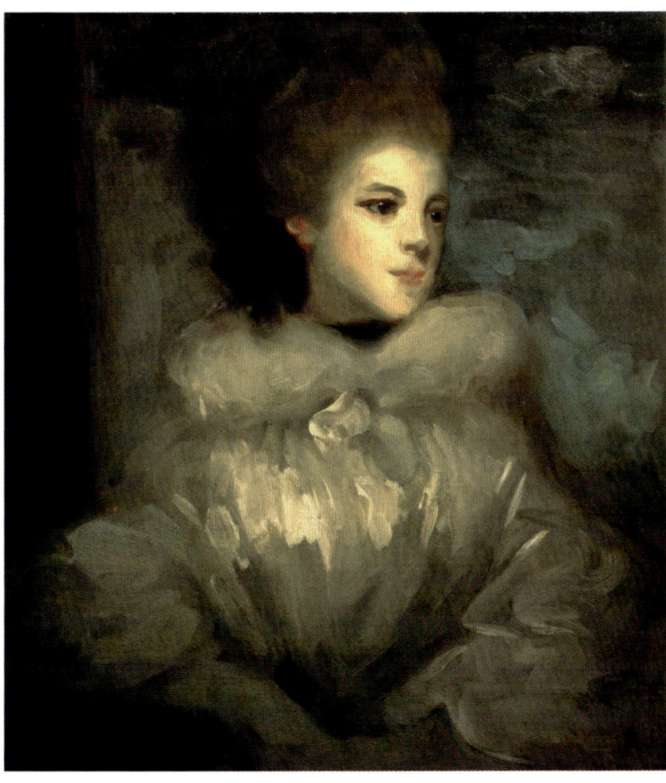

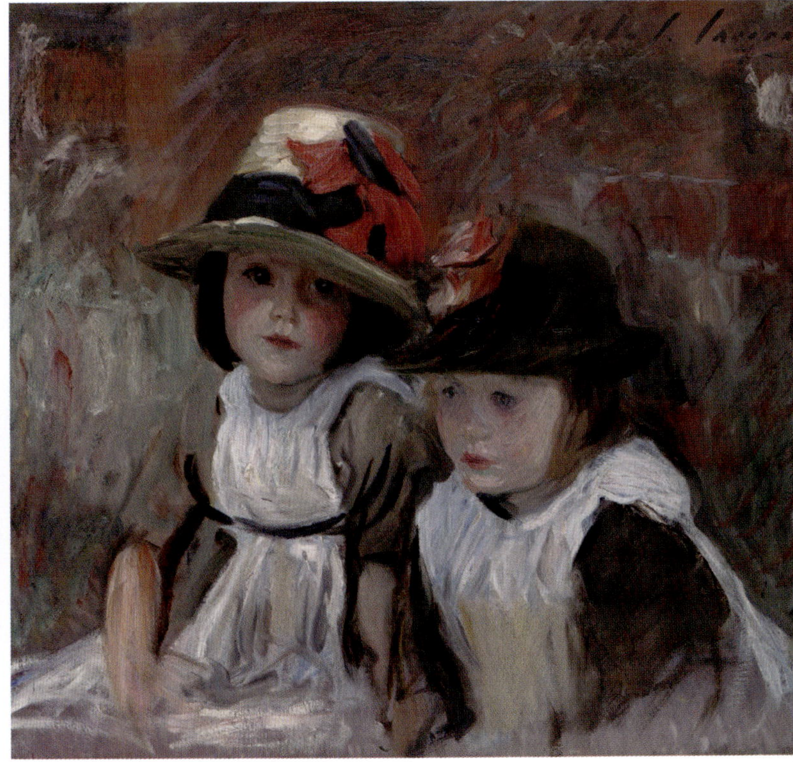

LANDSCAPES

Sargent's earliest work had been of landscapes, and he saw himself as a portraitist only to earn a living. His first years in England were dominated by his experiments with Impressionism, particularly through landscapes, in which he expresses his appreciation of the natural world and friendships.

Sargent's depictions of light-filled, colourful scenery were more vivid and dynamic than the landscapes themselves. Although his palette and portrayals of tone were fairly traditional, his brushstrokes were expressive and modern. Capturing a wide range of elements, from Renaissance architecture to fresh mountain scenery, tumbling rivers and rolling fields, the paintings were often embellished with colourful figures, from peasants working the land to friends relaxing together.

A REASSESSMENT OF HIS WORK

After absorbing the principles of Impressionism, Sargent's audacious style enabled him to capture form and light with a few deft strokes. As we know, shortly after his death, he became rather unfashionable; his work was perceived as old-fashioned in relation to emerging avant-garde art movements such as Post-Impressionism, Expressionism and Fauvism, for example. But gradually his work was reassessed and he is now recognized as an original artist with an accomplished and unique style. His landscapes were not depicting just the scenes he viewed before him; he judiciously selected aspects that he manipulated into compelling themes, viewed from unexpected angles and including interesting juxtapositions.

Perhaps more than with his other paintings, his landscapes can be read like an autobiography.

TEXTURE, PATTERN, COLOUR

Over many summers, Sargent holidayed in the Alps near Val d'Aosta and Simplon with his sister Violet's family, where he painted the landscape and often included his

Below: Walnut Tree at Sablons in Spring, *by Alfred Sisley (1839–99), 1883. Inspired by Sisley and other Impressionists, Sargent aimed to capture the freshness and freedom he found in their landscapes.*

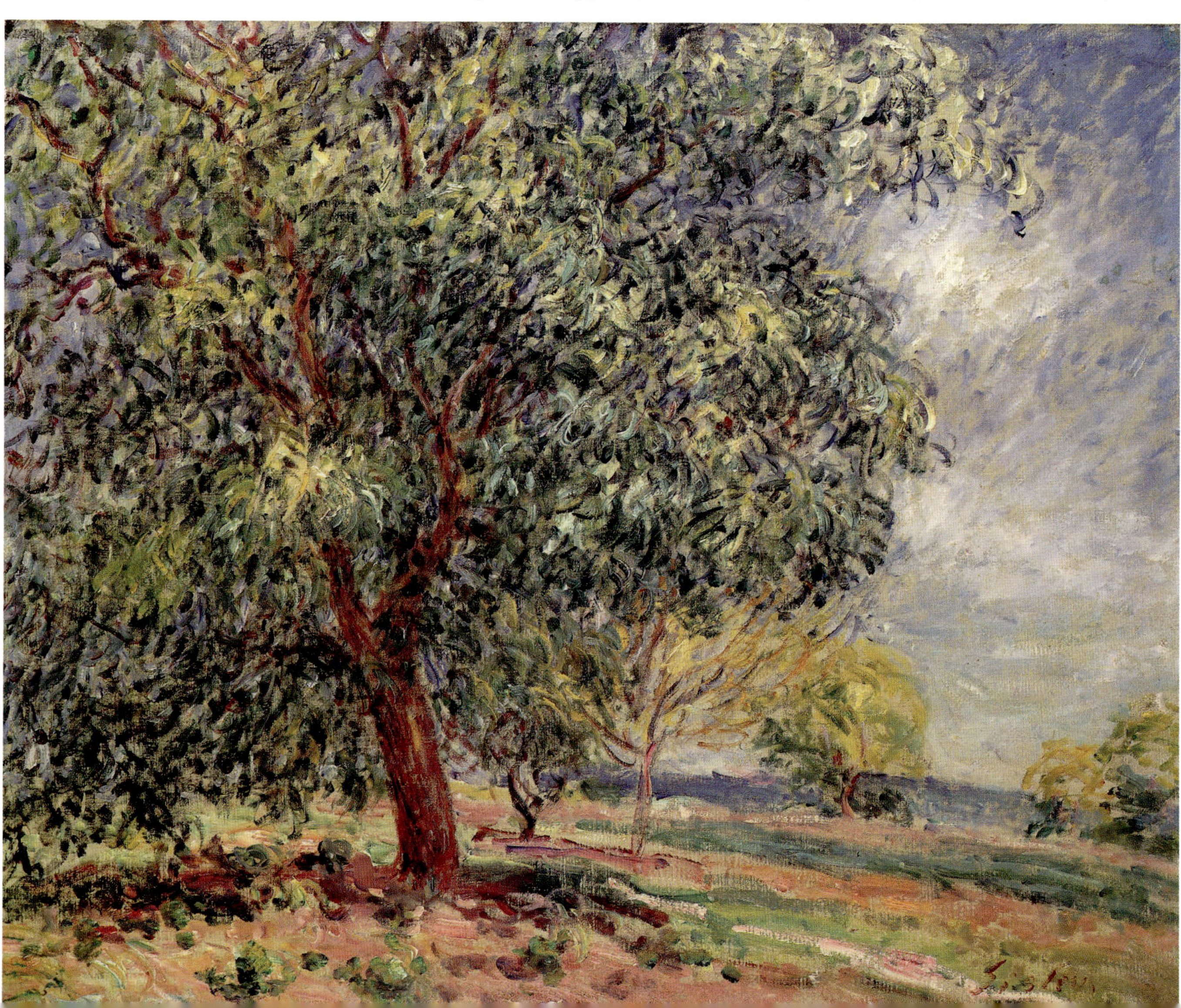

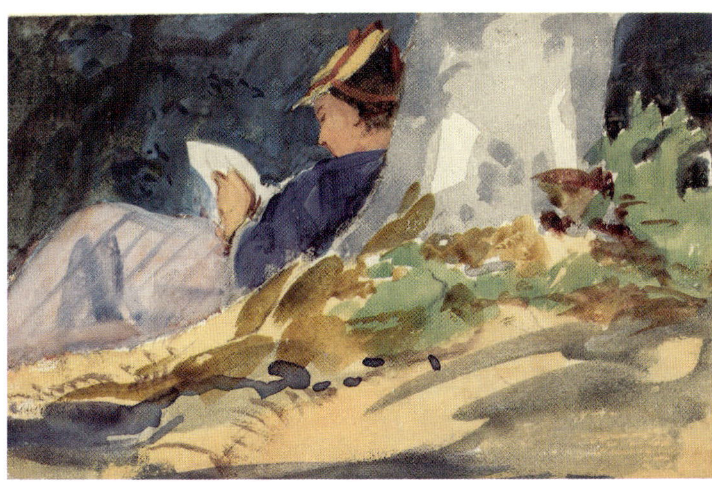

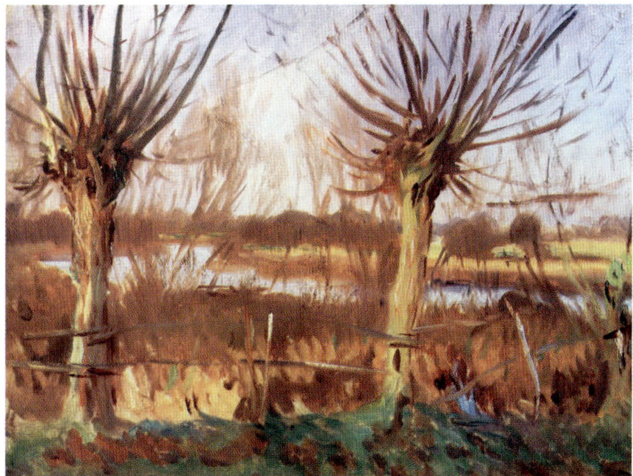

Above left: Resting, *c.1880–90. With a few quick, sketchy brushmarks Sargent captures a figure reading in repose against a tree*

Above right: Landscape with Trees, Calcot-on-the-Thames, *c.1888. A spontaneously painted landscape near Calcot Mill, where Sargent stayed with his family.*

Below: Pine Forest, *c.1907–08 Sargent was as accomplished with watercolour as in oils, employing a range of techniques.*

nieces, Rose-Marie (1893–1918) and Reine Ormond (1897–1971) and their friends. Rose-Marie in particular became one of his favourite models during his later years. He frequently depicted the young women reclining in open landscapes, often using watercolours in varied techniques, from dry brush to wet-into-wet, and from transparent washes to opaque gouache highlighhts, which allowed him to be especially expressive. He also dressed his models in Turkish costumes and cashmere shawls, contrasting the exotic patterns and textures of man-made fabrics with the colourful landscapes. Portraying these elegant creatures in close-up, these narrative-style landscapes were a departure from traditional landscapes and portraits. Classical landscapes frequently feature some figures, but these are usually small and secondary to the scene, while Sargent's figures are of equal significance, and his use of foreshortening and cropping are purposefully included to create a sense of rhythm and fluidity.

In his studies of brooks, waterfalls and rock formations, Sargent often took a high viewpoint and with swift brushwork, applied vibrant colours in strong contrasts; with buildings, he often painted from low or level viewpoints, employing a light touch to emphasize the play of light.

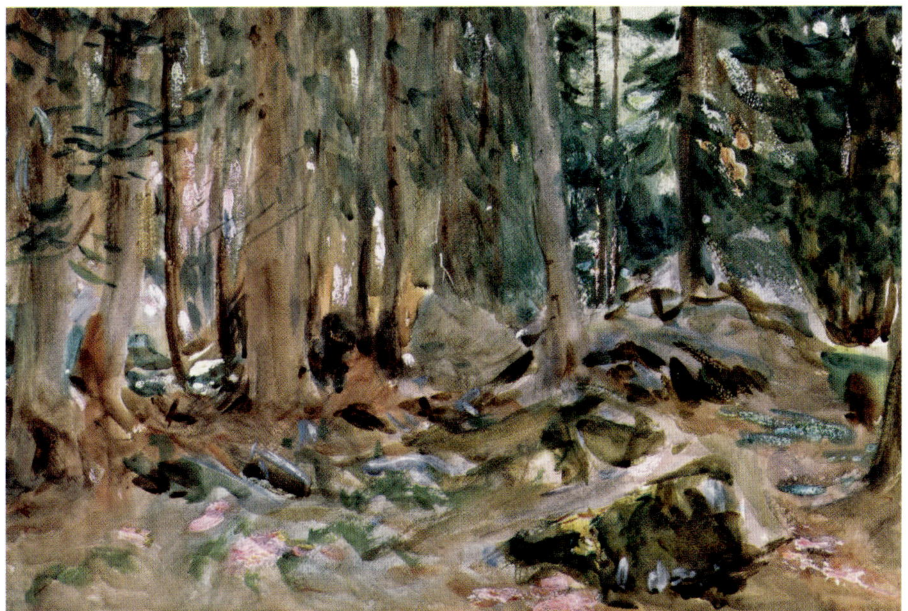

HOLIDAYING IN EUROPE

Over the latter part of the 19th century, Sargent's travels took on a pattern. He usually spent the summer in the Alps with Emily and Violet's family. In September, Sargent would often travel to Venice, and then to Italy or Spain. In Rome and Florence, he sketched and painted the parks, fountains and colonnades, including the Villa Borghese and the Boboli Gardens. Venice viewed from a gondola was one of his favourite themes, for the elegant, yet decaying buildings with the iridescent reflections in the surrounding water and contrasting shapes of bridges, alleyways and side streets.

AT FLADBURY

In the summer of 1889, Sargent rented the old Rectory with his mother and sisters at Fladbury village in the Cotswolds near Broadway. There he was visited by numerous friends, including his old friend Paul Helleu and his young wife, Alice (1870–1933). While there, he painted numerous outdoor landscapes, continuing his Impressionist experiments of painting en plein air, and featuring several of his female companions, including Violet, reclining and generally relaxing.

CONTRASTING CULTURES

Fascinated by different cultures, Sargent travelled widely to places where he could observe lives unfamiliar to him and which he perceived as exotic and exciting. This notion was universally fashionable at the time, with several elements of Eastern design emerging in the sinuous styles of Art Nouveau.

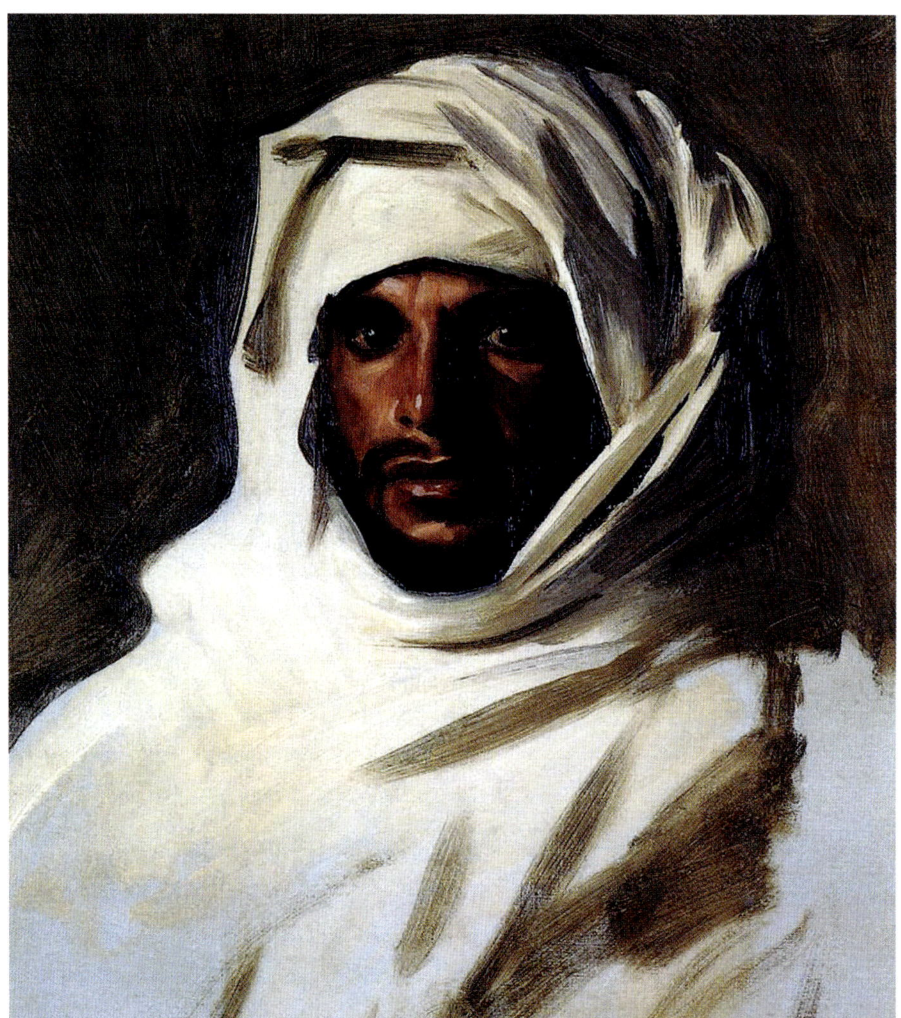

REVIVING REPUTATION

In June 1889, Sargent showed six paintings in the American section of the Exposition Universelle in Paris. The works, which included *La Carmencita* (see page 47), were so admired that the French government awarded him a medal and made him a Knight of the Legion of Honour, as Carolus-Duran had been honoured 17 years earlier.

His reputation was certainly reviving. Although by 1890, when he travelled back across the Atlantic, it was only his third visit to America, he remained there for nine months, establishing studios in New York and Boston, and painting approximately 40 portraits. In February, he exhibited again at the New York Union League Club, works including *Paul Helleu Sketching with his Wife* (see page 53), and *Morning Walk* (see page 134). He exhibited them next in Chicago and Philadelphia to mixed reviews. In May, he participated again in an exhibition at the Society of American Artists, New York.

PRESTIGIOUS APPOINTMENT

Sargent had made some hugely influential friends in the US, including Ned Boit, Isabella Stewart Gardner, the architects Stanford White (1853–1906) and Charles McKim (1847–1909), and the banker Charles Fairchild (1838–1910), who later managed his American financial affairs. These friendships led to several important portrait commissions, and in May 1890, he and Edwin Austin Abbey were approached about painting murals for the Boston Public Library

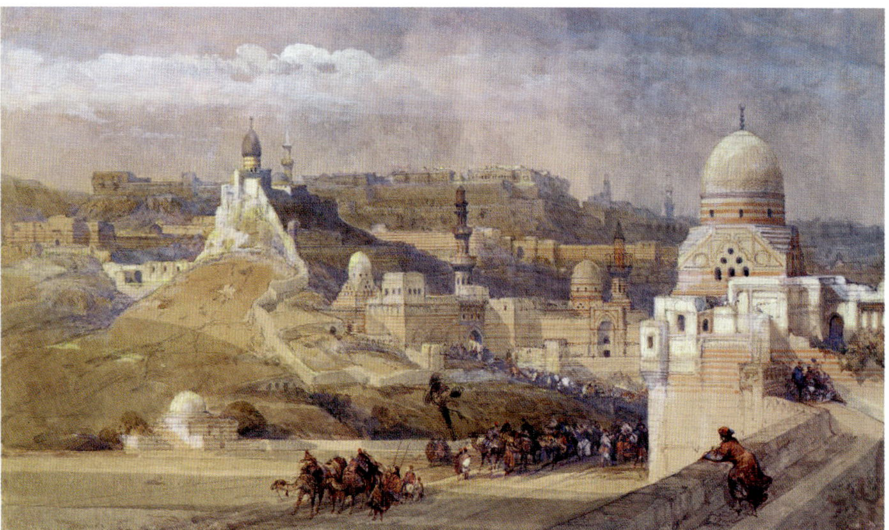

Above left: A Bedouin, *c.1891, intense and expressive; Sargent was fascinated with people he perceived as exotic.*

Left: Coloured lithograph, The Citadel of Cairo, Residence of Mehmet Ali, *1842–49 by David Roberts (1796–1864).*

that was under construction, designed by McKim. The new library was to be a grand structure in the style of great European public buildings, and the murals were to be similarly impressive. In November 1890, through the influence of White, McKim, and the sculptor Augustus Saint-Gaudens (1848–1907) whom Sargent had met in Paris in 1878, Sargent was officially appointed to paint a sequence of murals for the upper staircase of the Boston Public Library. The project subsequently occupied him for more than 30 years. Initially he thought he would make Spanish literature the theme, but he eventually chose to depict the history of religion.

EXTENDED VISIT ABROAD

To develop ideas for the murals, Sargent took an extended trip to North Africa, Egypt, Greece and Turkey with his mother and two sisters (Violet was not married until the following year). They went first to North Africa, then Egypt and then to the Middle East. Sargent left nothing to chance, extensively observing, drawing and painting, gathering source material, capturing visual details of colour, forms, light and atmosphere. They visited Alexandria, Cairo, Luxor, Thebes, Aswan and Philae, and while in Cairo, Sargent rented a studio where

he painted works such as *Pavement in Cairo*, *Egyptian Girl* and *Door of a Mosque*. Next, they journeyed up the Nile to Luxor. As always, Sargent sketched throughout their trip, including along the Nile, and the atmospheric interior of the Santa Sophia in Constantinople.

Non-Christian cultures had captivated Sargent for years. His Moroccan visit of 1880 had resulted in his successful Salon painting *Fumée d'Ambre Gris* (see page 112), and this visit once again stimulated his fascination for the different qualities of light, the clothing, architecture and people of these regions. His subsequent paintings show his enchantment with the patterns, shapes, colours and textures he encountered. Drapes and folds of fabrics, golden skin, semi-hidden faces and tessellated stone slabs were all captured in vibrant and atmospheric watercolours, oils and charcoal drawings.

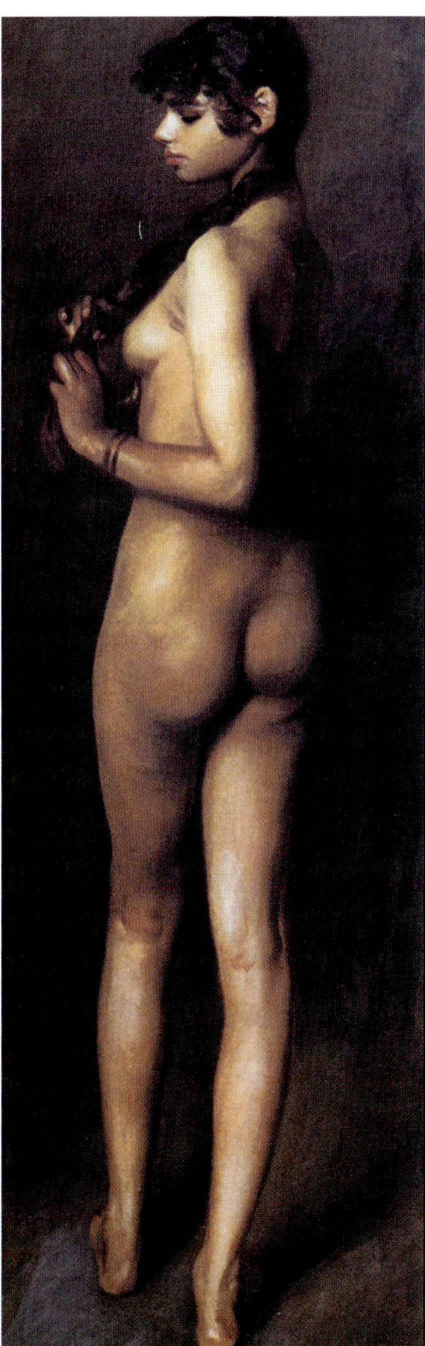

Right: Egyptian Girl, *1891, reflects Sargent's academic training, in the carefully modelled form and honey-coloured flesh tones.*

Below: Sargent painted this watercolour of Pavement, Cairo *in 1891, demonstrating his attention to detail and fascination for the patterns and tones of the location.*

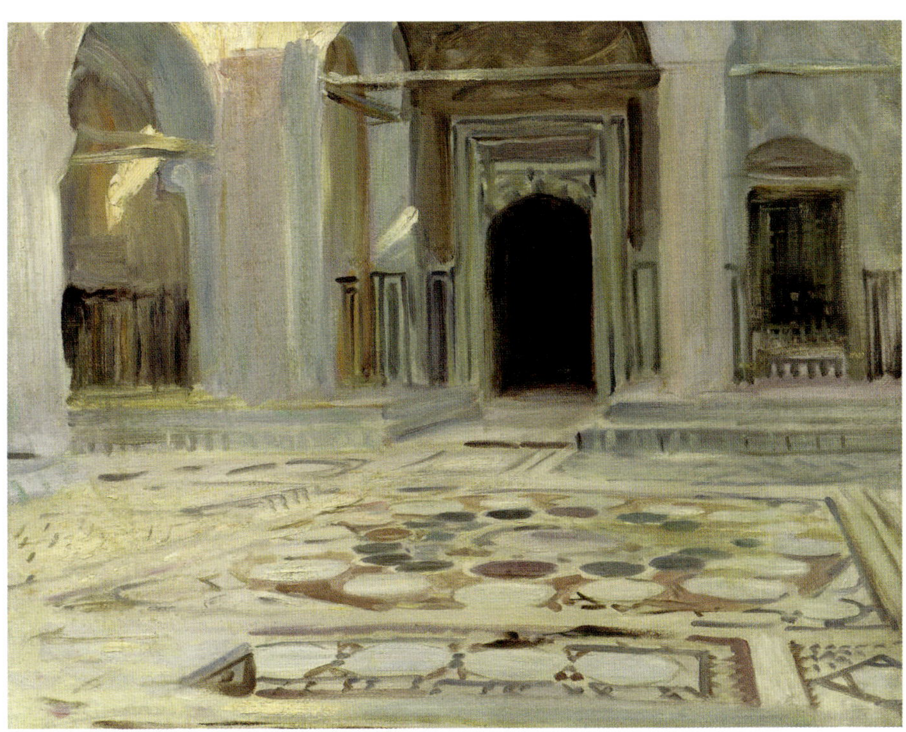

CONSOLIDATION

On Sargent's return to England in 1891, he exhibited *La Carmencita* at the Royal Academy, and a portrait at the Society of American Artists. That summer, he travelled to the Villa Ormond at San Remo, Italy, owned by Violet's fiancé's family, and then in July, to Paris, for Violet and Francis's wedding.

Back in London in the autumn, Sargent helped to move Emily and his mother to the highly respectable address of Carlyle Mansions, Cheyne Walk in Chelsea. It was his mother's first permanent home in 35 years. Meanwhile his friend Abbey had just established an extremely large studio at Morgan Hall in Fairford in Gloucestershire with his wife and mother-in-law. Away from both the London and Broadway artists, it was a tranquil, spacious setting, and Sargent joined him there in November where they began working on their individual Boston Library murals. Abbey had previously made enquiries to find some art students from Paris who might want to study under them, and he had chosen two young men: James Wall Finn (1866–1913) and Wilfrid de Glehn (1870–1951). Sargent stayed working there for several weeks and returned every year from 1891 to 1894, as he created the first section of his mural cycle for the Boston Library, and as Abbey worked on his own murals.

WORKING AND SOCIALIZING

De Glehn and Sargent became lifelong friends. He and Abbey also employed two regular models: Angelo Colarossi (1875–1949) and Nicola D'Inverno (1873–unknown). D'Inverno became Sargent's studio assistant and valet for the next 20 years. He later recalled Sargent's daily routine: 'His life was as orderly as that of a bishop. He awoke at 7, breakfasted at 8, then had a bath. At about 9am, he handled his correspondence and by 10 was in the studio. He would then work until one o'clock, take an hour for lunch, and painted from 2 or 2.30 to 5pm.' In 1896, the American landscape painter and art critic William Anderson Coffin (1855–1925) wrote: 'Sargent's studio is always a sociable place. Unlike many artists, the presence of visitors and companions does not disturb him when he is painting. He seems to work without obvious exertion even in his intensest activity. When models are resting, he fills up the gap by strumming on the piano or guitar.'

ESTABLISHING HIS CREDENTIALS

In the first months of 1892, Sargent continued to work on portraits and murals in Fairford, then in August, he travelled to Spain to visit his mother and Violet. The Musée du Luxembourg bought *La Carmencita* (see page 47), and he received a commission from Andrew Noel Agnew (1850–1928), a barrister who had inherited the baronetcy and estates of Lochnaw in

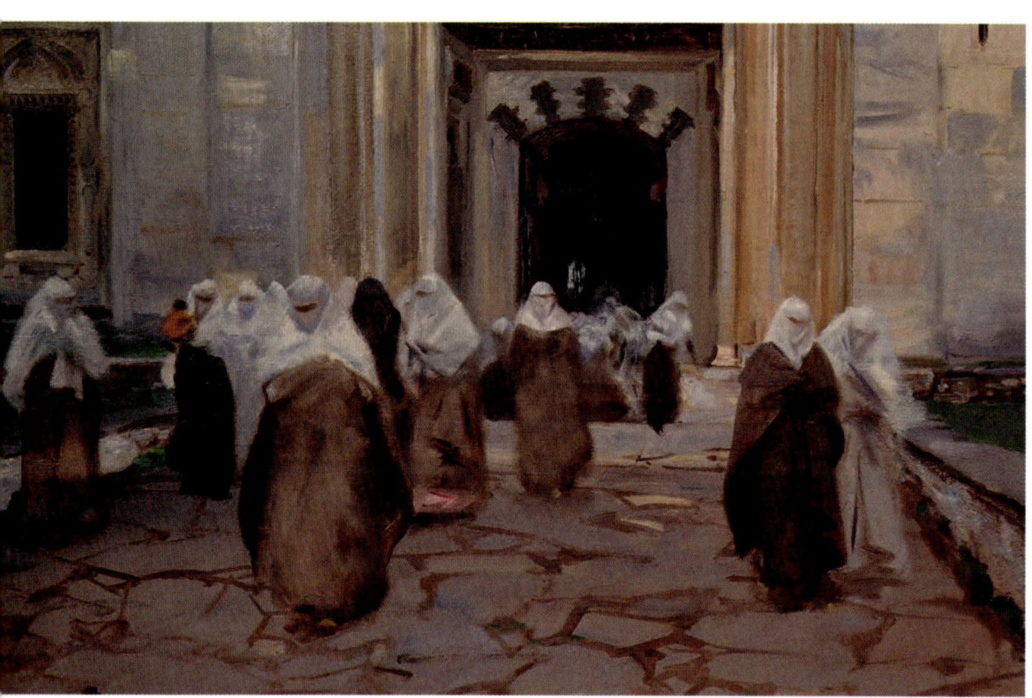

Above: During 1891, Sargent travelled to Egypt. Door of a Mosque *is one of a group of oil sketches he made there in Cairo's citadel complex.*

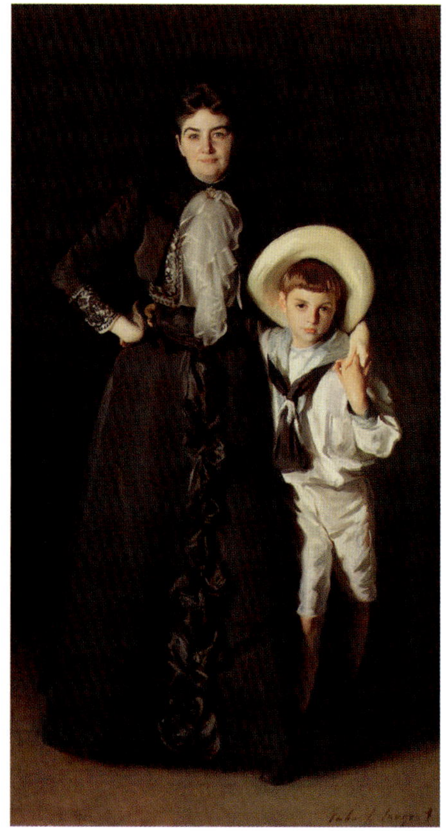

Right: Portrait of Mrs Edward L. Davis and her Son, Livingstone Davis, *1890 — one of the most important portraits that Sargent produced in America in 1890.*

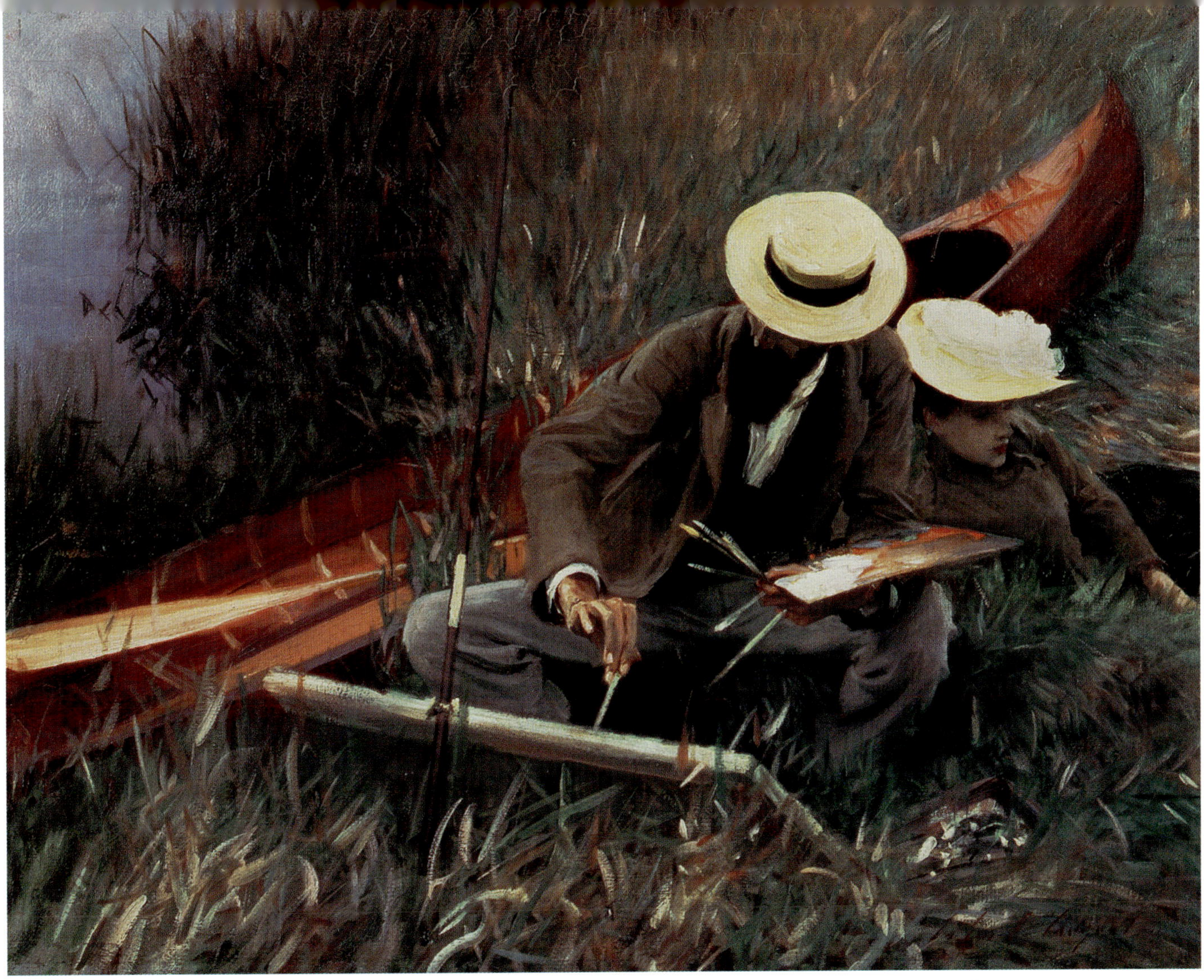

Galloway, Scotland, to paint a portrait of his young wife. Gertrude Vernon, Lady Agnew (1865–1932), was a pale-skinned, dark-haired beauty, and Sargent used expressive brushwork and a delicate palette to create a relaxed image of the young woman sitting in a chair, looking directly at the viewer. Serene and calm, she is smiling slightly, showing both confidence and vulnerability.

When he exhibited Gertrude's portrait the following year, the painting attracted wide acclaim, as exemplified in this excerpt from *The Times*: 'A masterpiece... not only a triumph of technique but the finest example of portraiture in the literal sense of the word, that has been seen here in a long while.' The portrait generated a rush of new commissions in Britain from the fashionable elite. At last, Sargent was truly established; he had become a celebrity and the favourite portraitist among both the British and American upper classes.

Above: One of Sargent's closest friends, this is Paul Helleu Sketching with his Wife, *painted by Sargent in 1889. It is one of his last Impressionist-influenced works (see also pages 98–99).*

Below: The direct gaze and relaxed pose of Lady Agnew of Lochnaw, with her contrasting, fashionable clothes, established her as a celebrated beauty and Sargent as an illustrious artist.

ABANDONMENT OF IMPRESSIONISM

In 1892, Sargent exhibited his painting *Paul Helleu Sketching with his Wife* at the New English Art Club in London, but despite Impressionism being more accepted in Britain by then, once again Sargent's Impressionist style received little public attention. At last, he decided that his experimentation with Impressionism simply did not appeal to the public, and he never exhibited another Impressionistic painting. He continued to paint some Impressionist-style landscapes for his own pleasure, but never again put them forward for public criticism.

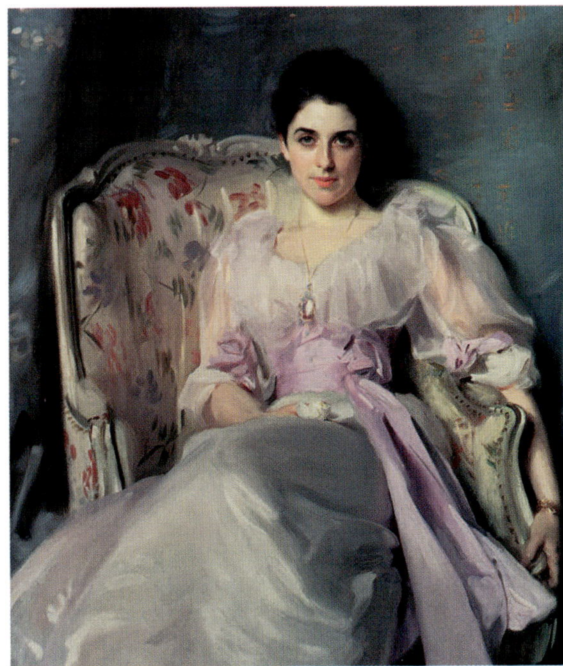

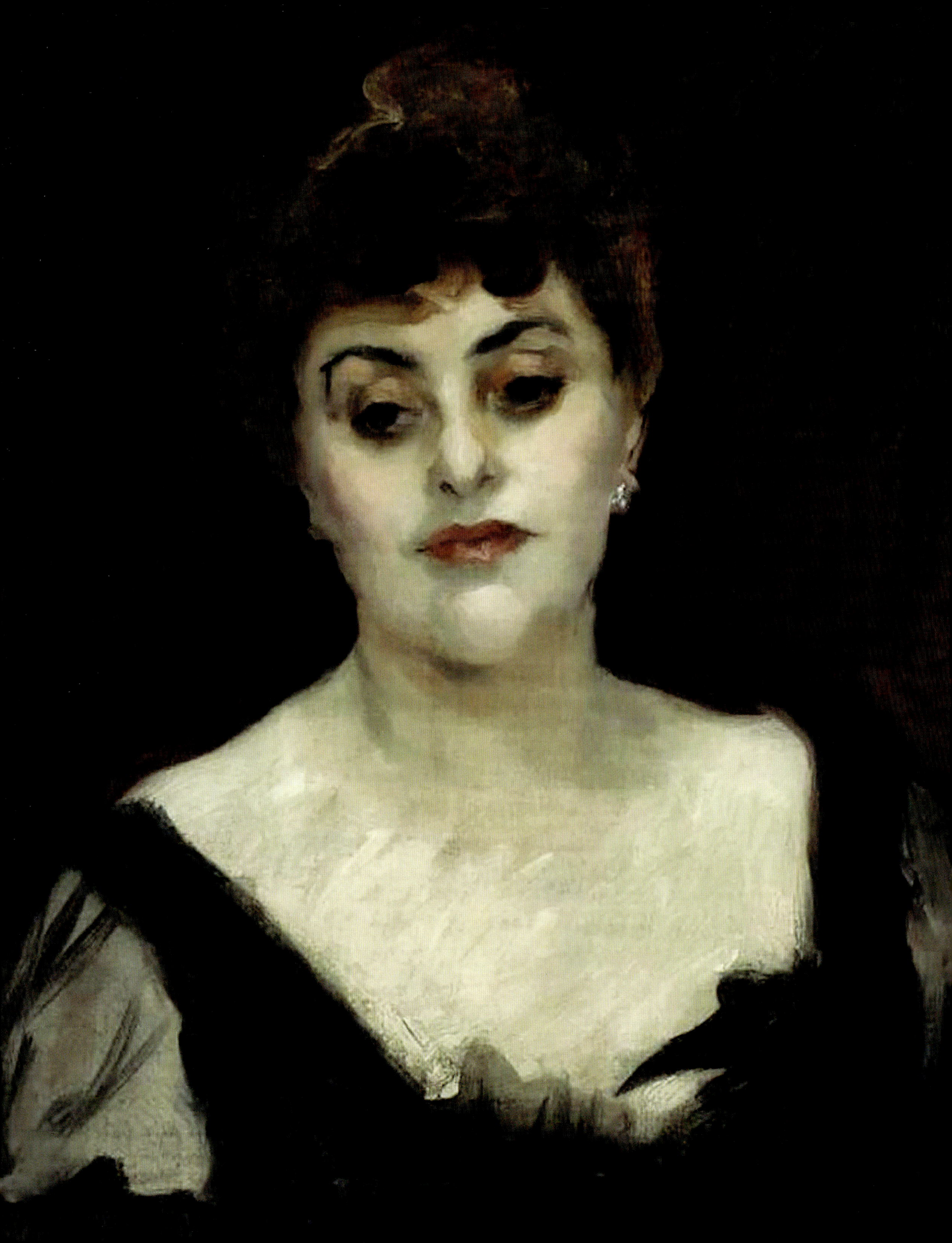

PAINTING EMINENCE

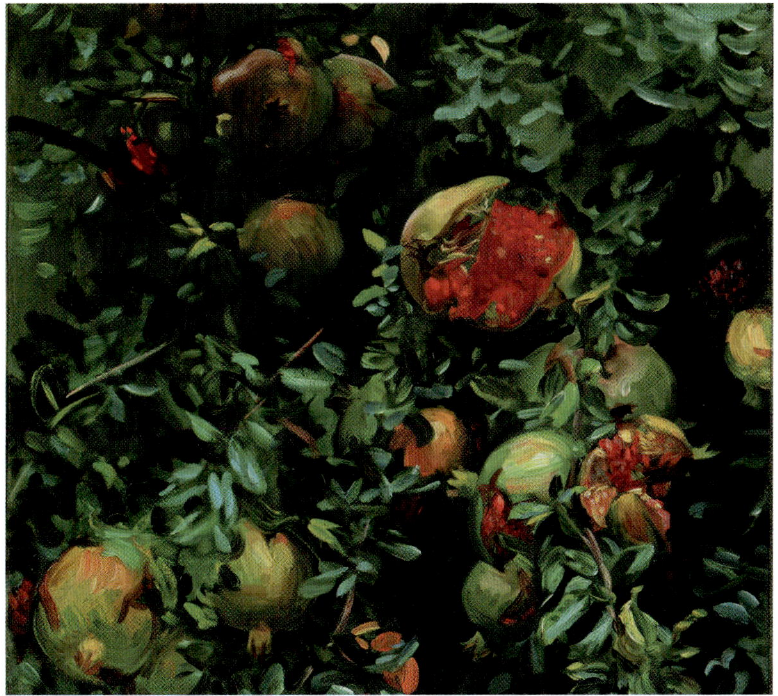

Sargent's renown as an accomplished portrait painter who could execute a commission with aplomb was now established across both sides of the Atlantic. Frequently compared to Velázquez, his rapid and spontaneous paint application, ability to capture the character of his sitters, and the versatility he exerted in his landscapes set him above many of the already successful artists of the day, as the scandals that had shadowed him in recent years were finally dispersing. In the light of this reappraisal, the recognition he had so long sought appeared in the commission for the Boston mural (see page 58), and accolades were awarded to him in America, France and Britain.

Above: Pomegranates, Majorca, c.1908 is an example of Sargent's versatility and acute sense of colour. The energetic, gestural brushwork is almost abstracted.

Left: Mrs Harry Vane Milbank, née Alice Sidonie Vandenburg was a recognized beauty and socialite who had divorced her first husband and who spent a great deal of time in both America and Britain. Sargent painted her portrait in 1884.

ROYAL ACADEMICIAN

In 1893, Sargent sent eight paintings to Chicago for the World Columbian Exposition, where he and Whistler were especially celebrated. The following January he was elected as an Associate of the Royal Academy in London; a sign that he was not only accepted by the people, but also by the establishment.

Two portrait commissions completed in 1892 brought Sargent particular acclaim: the portrait of Lady Agnew (see page 149), and the portrait of Mrs Hammersley, née Mary Frances Grant (c.1863–c.1902). The wife of a banker and a fashionable London hostess, Mrs Hammersley was admired for her poise and style. Sargent portrayed her on an elegant French sofa, her slender figure and relaxed expression demonstrating his ability to both flatter and capture an individual personality. The work displayed his skills to potential British patrons when it appeared at the New Gallery in London in 1893. The positive reviews it received there and at the Salon of the Société Nationale des Beaux-Arts in Paris in 1894, finally quelled the rumblings about *Madame X*. The two society portraits, of Mrs Hammersley and Lady Agnew, attracted further commissions of glamorous British women on both sides of the Atlantic. To American art lovers, he was the epitome of European style and panache. His art captured the spirit of the times and he became the leading portrait painter of the day. In the spring of 1893, Vernon Lee's friend Clementina 'Kit' Anstruther-Thomson (1857–1921) wrote to her: 'As to Mr Sargent, London is at his feet, Mrs Hammersley and Mrs Lewis are at the New Gallery, Lady Agnew at the Academy. There can be no two opinions this year. He has had a cracking success. Mrs Hammersley has just sat down on that peach coloured sofa for one minute – she will be up

Above right: Private View at the Royal Academy, *by William Powell Frith, 1881– 82, depicts visitors at the RA Summer Exhibition in 1881.*

Right: Self-portrait, *1892. With his body turned to the left, and his head turned to face viewers, Sargent retains his mystique.*

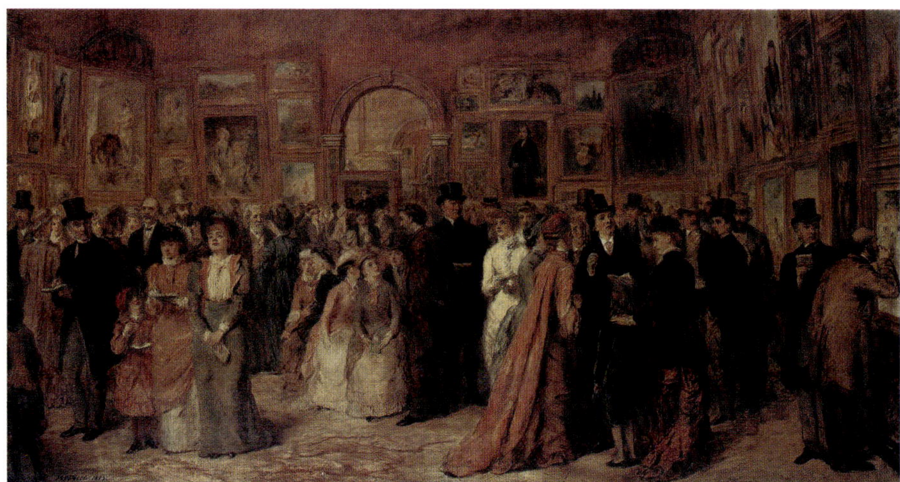

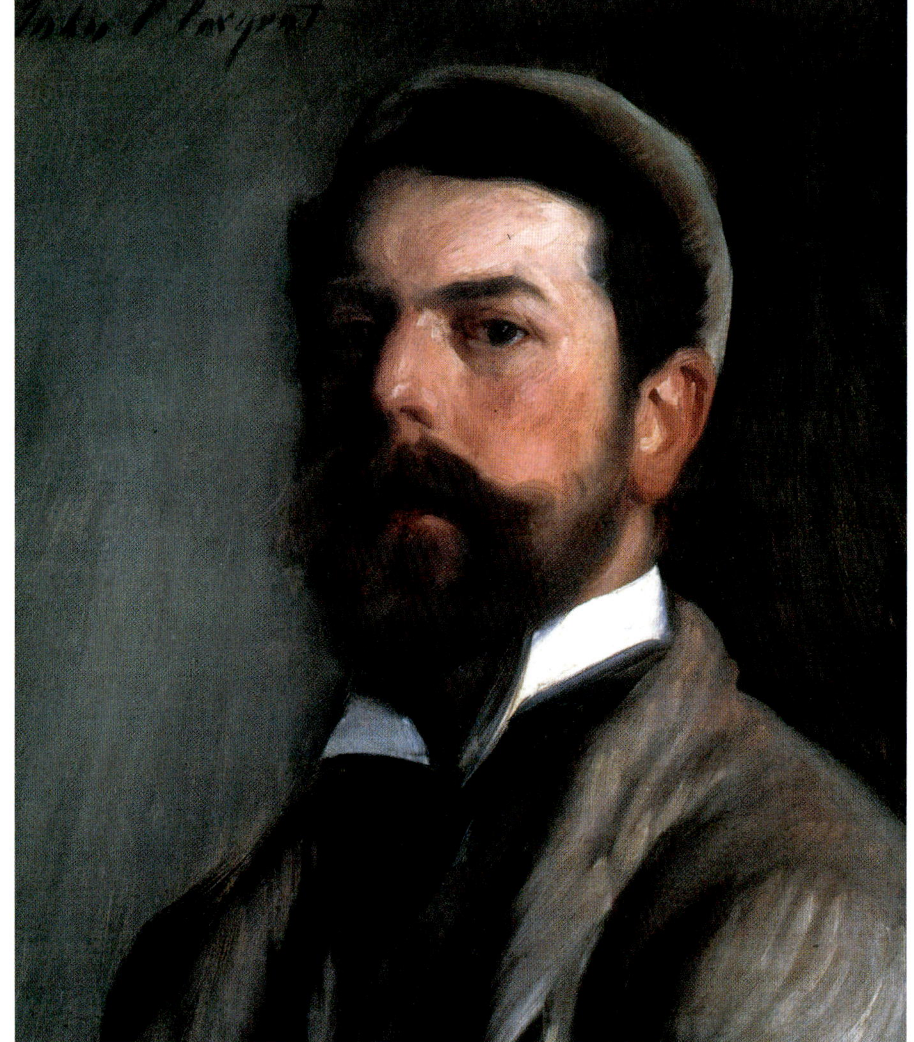

again fidgeting about the room in the next moment, but meanwhile, Mr Sargent has painted her!'

SUDDEN AND UNEXPECTED

The portraits of both Lady Agnew and Mrs Hammersley were almost universally admired. The *Sunday Review* described Lady Agnew as: 'Strange beauty, great art,' while a journalist for the *Art Journal* said it was better than everything else on the walls of the Academy, especially the work of contemporary portraitists with: 'their preference for dull brown tones.'

The success continued. In 1894, Sargent was awarded the Temple Gold Medal from the Pennsylvania Academy of Fine Arts. His rise to success in Britain was somewhat sudden, unexpected and in comparison with his previous efforts at the Paris Salon, relatively unplanned. Largely through the RA's president, Frederic Lord Leighton, in 1894, he became an Associate at the Royal Academy. It was an esteemed role, as he wrote to his cousin Ralph Curtis:

'My dear Ralph,
Thanks for your flourish of trumpets and waving of caps – If one lives in London, as I seem to be doing vaguely, I suppose it really counts for something to be an A.R.A. It remains to be proved; but I shall watch for the symptoms with interest. I have no end of letters and congratulation from Academicians, which would point to the fact of my having more of an affinity with the old fogies than I expected.'

From that time, his portrait commissions increased markedly. By 1897 (when he was made a full Academician), he complained that he was: 'having three sittings a day and hardly an interval between.' From an annual average of two to three British portrait commissions before 1893, he had six in 1894, and over 20 in 1898.

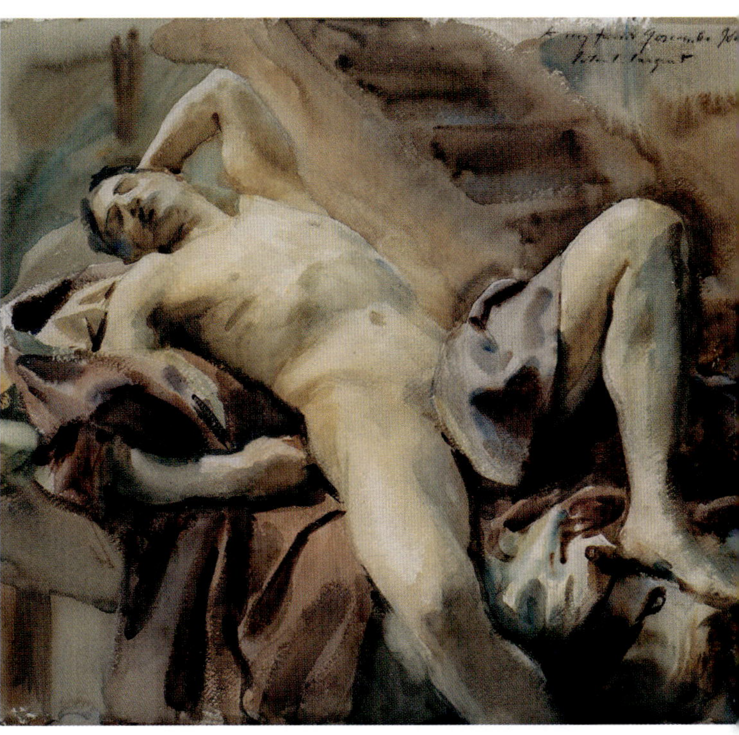

Right: Figure Study, *c.1900 – despite the beauty of many of Sargent's female portraits, he was equally appreciative of the masculine form.*

Below: Sargent's portrait of Mrs Hammersley in 1892 was one of the paintings that brought him immediate acclaim. (See also page 148.)

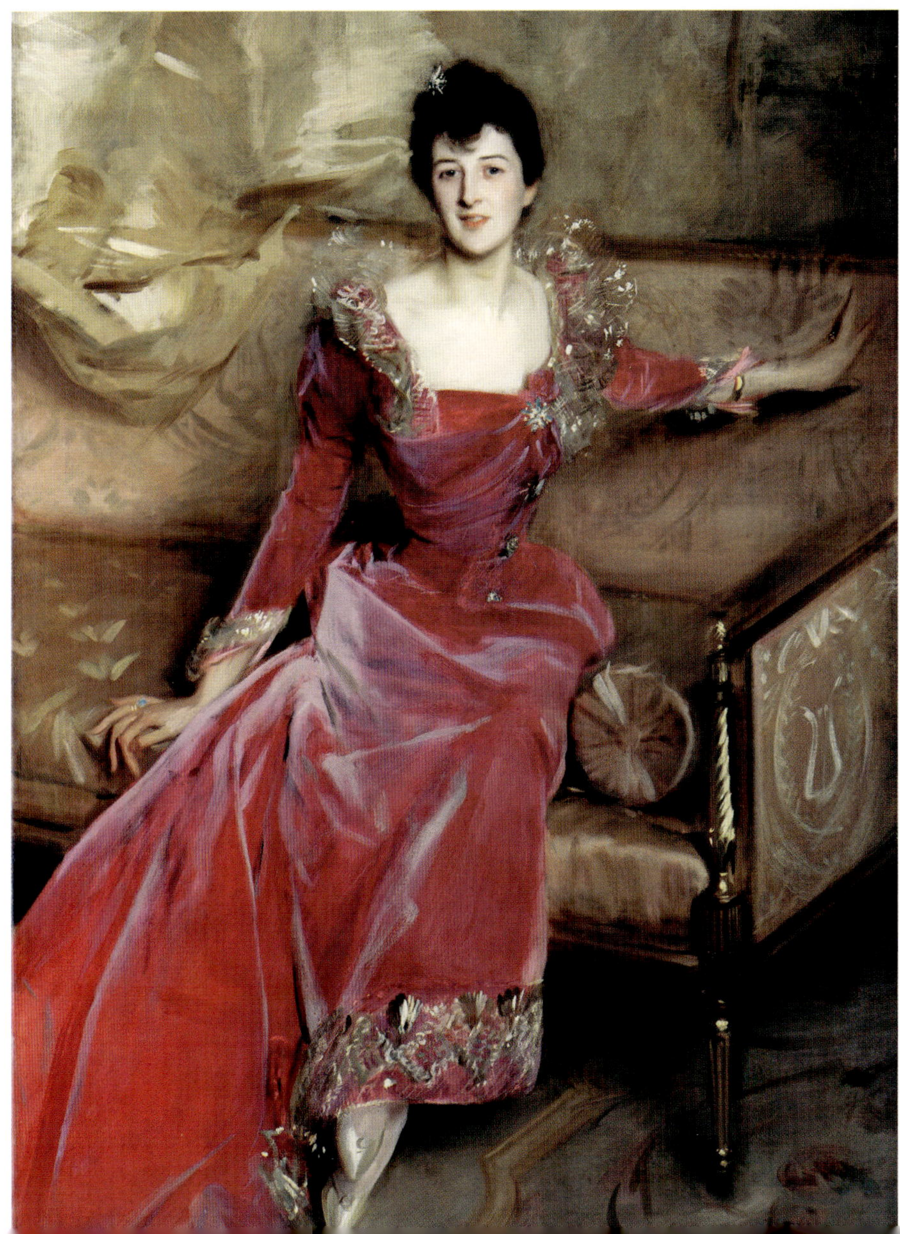

THE BOSTON MURAL

From the moment he was asked to paint the Boston mural, long before he received a written contract, Sargent began planning it. He hired and sketched several models and he had a miniature model made of the library's interior so he could try out compositions that would complement the architecture.

The series of murals was conceived as part of the celebrations of the library's status as the city's 'shrine of letters'. Sargent continued working on his mural plans when he was back in London, neglecting portrait commissions and instead constantly drawing models in different positions and costumes, trying out gestures and expressions. A number of his friends acted as models for the *Frieze of Prophets*, which he found amusing. He had included friends as characters in paintings before, and it appealed to his sense of humour.

THE NORTH WALL

Just before he was made an ARA (see page 57) in the spring of 1894, Sargent exhibited the completed mural that was to decorate the north wall of Boston Library, at the Royal Academy in London, before its installation in Boston. Influenced by Renaissance frescoes that he knew from Florence and during his extensive Italian travels, it was a complete departure from all his previous work. Stylized, dramatic and decorative, it preceded in many ways the glamour, exoticism and angularity of Art Deco, with biblical and pagan figures swathed in voluminous cloaks, sumptuous Egyptian costumes and exotic adornments. Later called the *Triumph of Religion*, the mural depicts the Israelites clustered together, flanked by their oppressors, the Egyptian Pharaoh and the King of Assyria. Below, a frieze depicts numerous Hebrew prophets, including Moses holding two stone tablets bearing the Ten Commandments. The image represents the Old Testament, in which the Israelites were oppressed and Moses led them to safety. Sargent also depicted pagan gods that the Jews turned to when Moses went up to Mount Sinai to speak to God. Embellished with gold and jewels, the deities include

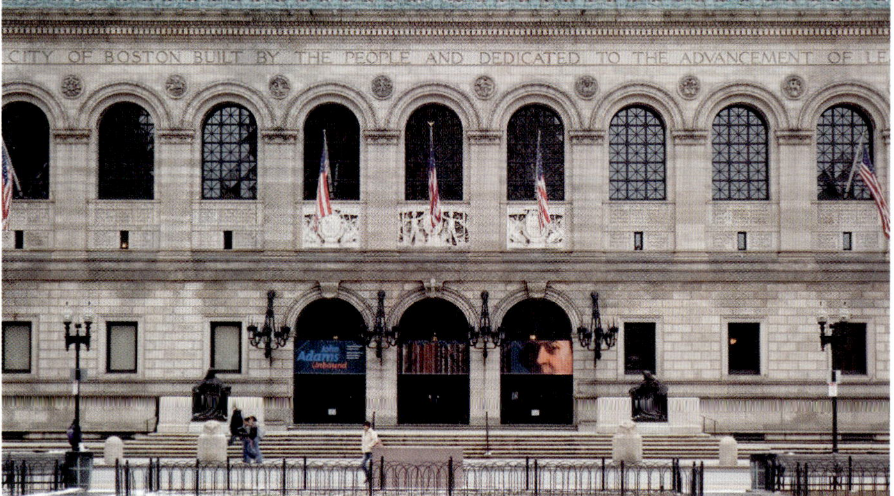

Above: The Italian Renaissance-style façade of the Boston Public Library.

Right: A preliminary study for a panel for the east wall over the staircase in the Boston Public Library.

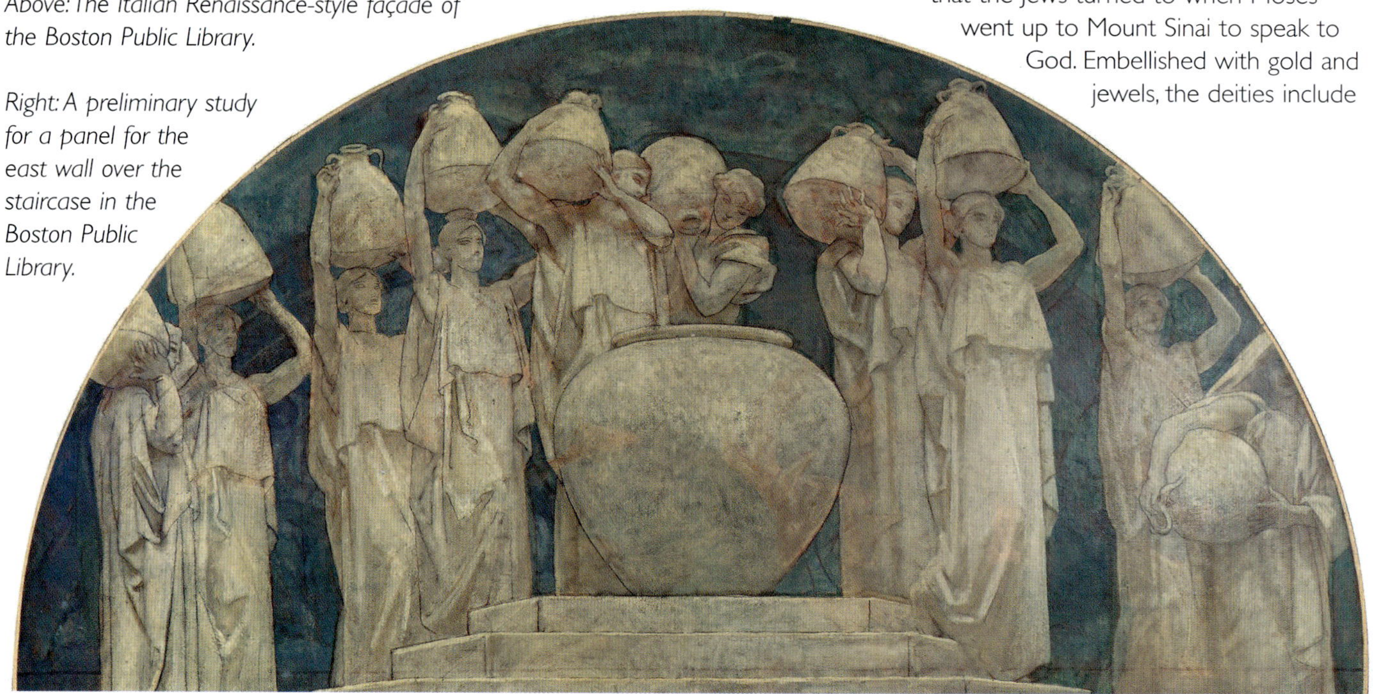

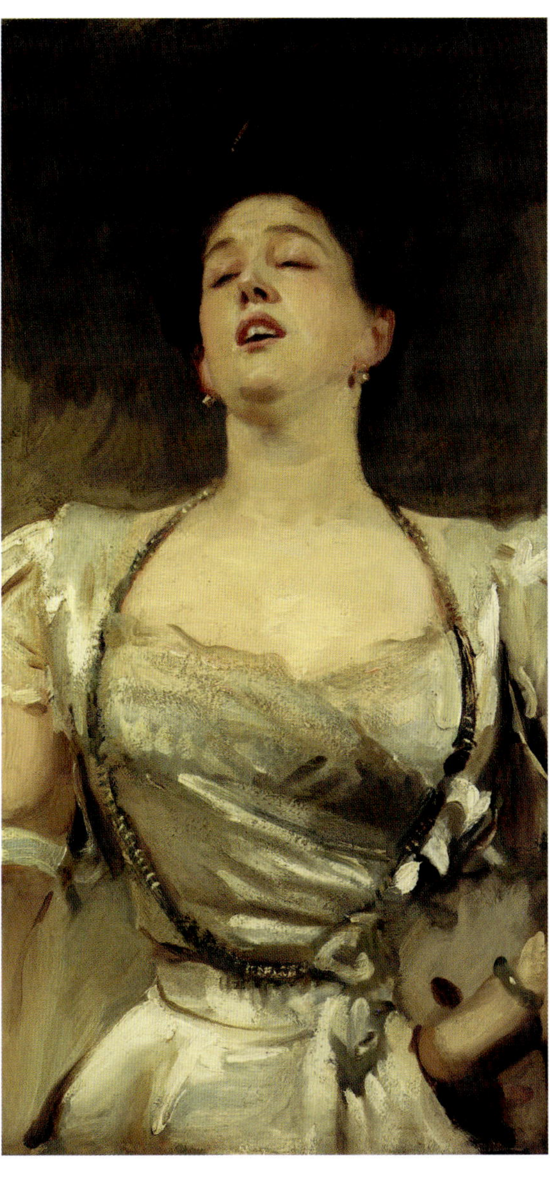

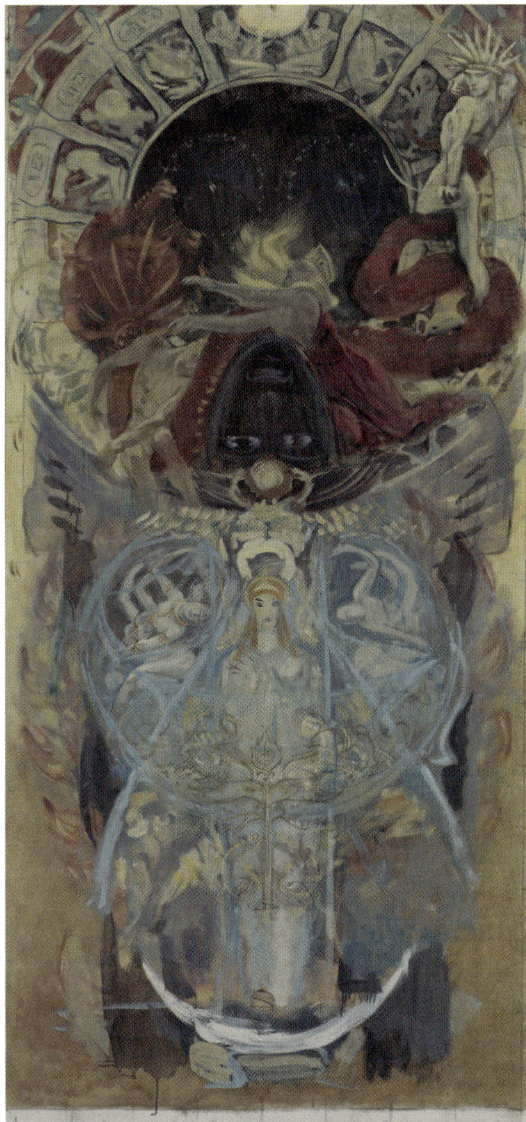

Far left: Mrs George Batten, *c.1897. Mabel Batten (c.1857–1915) was a talented amateur mezzo-soprano whom Sargent greatly admired.*

Left: This is one of Sargent's many studies for the Boston Public Library murals, depicting the Triumph of Religion.

Astarte, goddess of sensuality, Moloch, the god of material things, and Neith, the goddess of war and weaving. They appear both frightening and alluring, to convey how they seemed to the Israelites.

The smooth contours, subtle tonal contrasts and stylized forms of Sargent's mural style provoked mixed opinions. Writing for the *Saturday Review* a critic declared: 'We are too much startled to comprehend at once how the realistic painter of so many mundane portraits has suddenly become the illustrator of Ezekiel. Much study should be given to these extraordinary figures before a final verdict is submitted. It is enough to say that of their originality and impressiveness there can be no question.'

EXTENDING THE COMMISSION

In April 1895, Sargent travelled to Boston to oversee the mural's installation. Treating the interior as one giant canvas, he had created an extensive decoration, with many raised reliefs incorporated to catch the light, all fitting around architectural elements. The Trustees of the library were so delighted that they invited Sargent to extend his commission to the entire hall and began raising funds for the purpose. Sargent travelled back to London and took on a much larger studio at 12–14 The Avenue, Fulham Road. He kept this studio for 21 years.

The remaining murals took him almost another 30 years. Facing the north wall, he painted the 'Christian story' of the New Testament on the south wall, installing the main part of this in 1903. The *Frieze of Angels* on the south wall mirrors the *Frieze of Prophets* opposite. Above is the *Holy Trinity*, linked by a red robe entwined with golden lettering. In the centre is the *Crucifixion*, flanked by Adam and Eve, who hold cups beneath Christ's wounds to collect his blood. This section was fully completed in 1916, including the *Fifteen Mysteries of the Rosary*, and six smaller semi-circular lunettes, which include *Judgement*, featuring a set of embossed scales that weigh souls at the gates of Heaven. To the left is *The Passing of Souls into Heaven*, and to the right is *Hell*; comprising a green, soul-eating monster. Finally, in 1919, two panels depicting *Synagogue* and *Church* were fixed to the stair wall.

RECOGNITION AND TRAVEL

By the time the first Boston mural had been installed, Sargent's reputation was widely established. He painted the rich and the noble, art collectors and art dealers, bankers and statesmen, literary figures, actors, entertainers and his solicitor, the leading lawyer in London, Sir George Lewis (1833–1911).

FOREMOST PORTRAITIST

Through the 1890s, Sargent's portraits were made with expressive brushwork, capturing light and colour, and also individual personalities. Often using unexpected compositions, he experimented with aspects of Velázquez's approach, including a reduced palette, black on black and vigorous brushmarks. From the mid-1890s, he painted the likenesses of the most prominent figures, including the English poet and art critic Coventry Patmore (1823–96); the elegant Countess Clary Aldringen (1867–1943), (see page 155); the wife of the emissary to the Rothschilds and chairman of De Beers, Mrs Carl Meyer (1862/63–1930) with her children (see page 155); art collectors George Vanderbilt (1862–1914) and Henry G. Marquand; and the American landscape architect, Frederick Law Olmsted (1822–1903), (see page

152). Coventry Patmore described Sargent as: 'the greatest, not only of living English portrait painters, but of all English portrait painters.' Whereas a few years earlier, he had been consistently criticized, by the mid-1890s, general opinion had reversed. Admired for the individuality he portrayed, he became the foremost portraitist of the era. His 1896 portrait of Adèle Meyer for instance, with her daughter Elsie Charlotte (1885–1954) and son Frank Cecil (1886–1935), reflects her love of theatre and opera. With dramatic foreshortening, she is viewed from above, close to the picture plane. Extending her right arm back to her son, she looks up, at once creating a diagonal composition and a connection with viewers. The children look out of the canvas from behind their mother's opulent chair. In complete contrast with traditional style of family portraits, this

was received with great admiration when it was exhibited at the Royal Academy in 1897, along with the portrait of the four-year-old *Honourable Laura Lister* (1892–1965).

JEWISH SITTERS

During this period, particularly in Europe, Jews were frequently the subject of undisguised envy. Many had earned their fortunes rapidly and had risen to prominent positions in society. This success was viewed with resentment and prejudice by many, partly through anti-Semitic feelings, and partly through snobbishness about new wealth rather than old money. Perhaps because he was so widely travelled and socialized with many different nationalities, religions and cultures, Sargent did not share this prevalent anti-Semitism. Many of his sitters were Jewish, including the Meyer

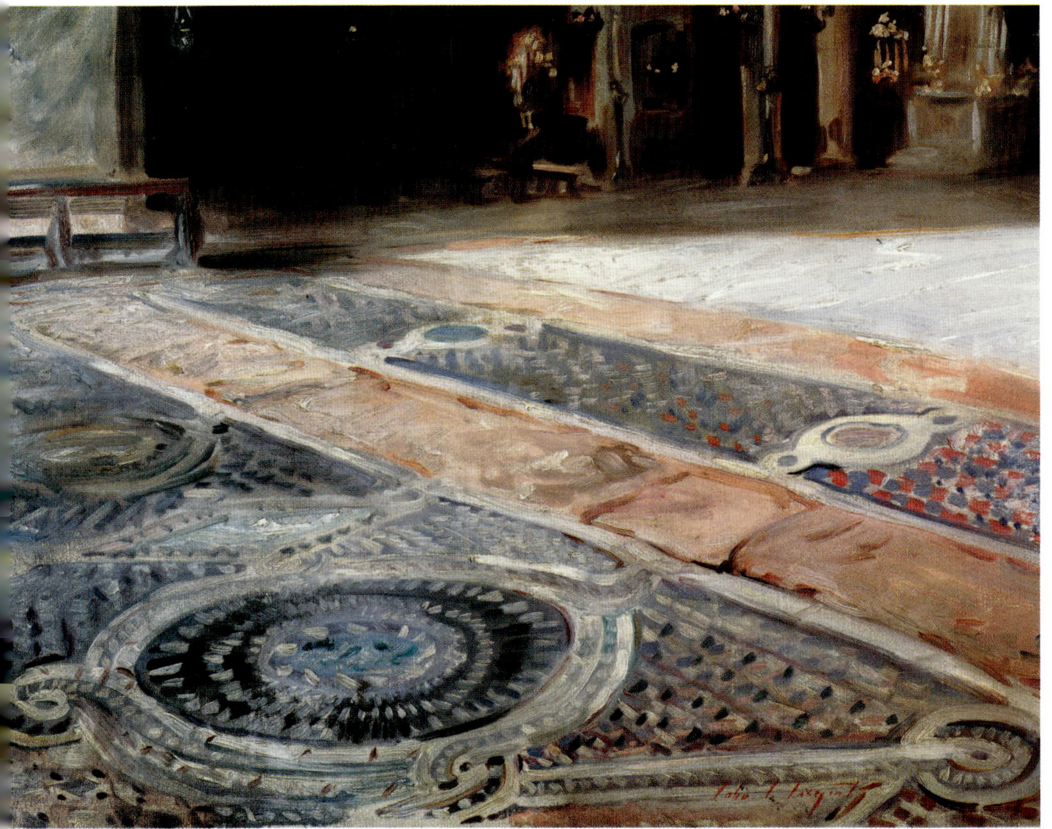

Above: With his brilliant handling of light, Sargent attracted wealthy patrons of all ages. This is Mrs Frederick Meade, 1893.

Left: Venetian Interior Pavement, 1898. Capturing the strong light on this Venetian Palazzo floor, Sargent picked out the subtle colours and exotic patterns of the tiles.

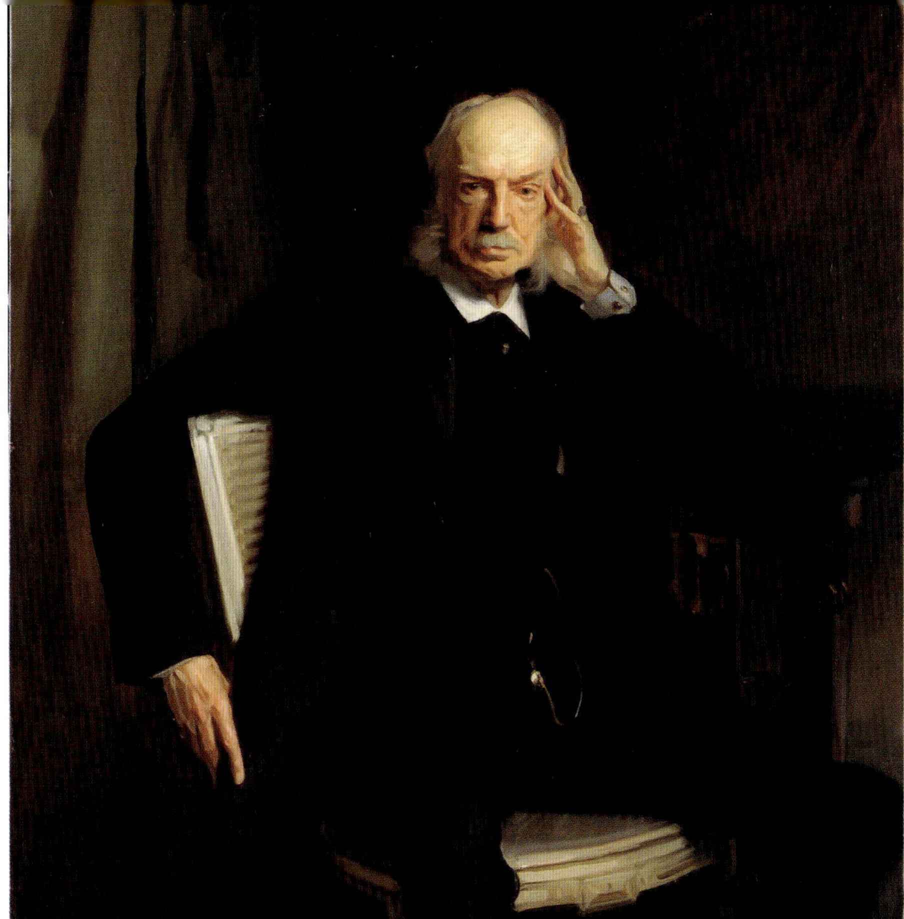

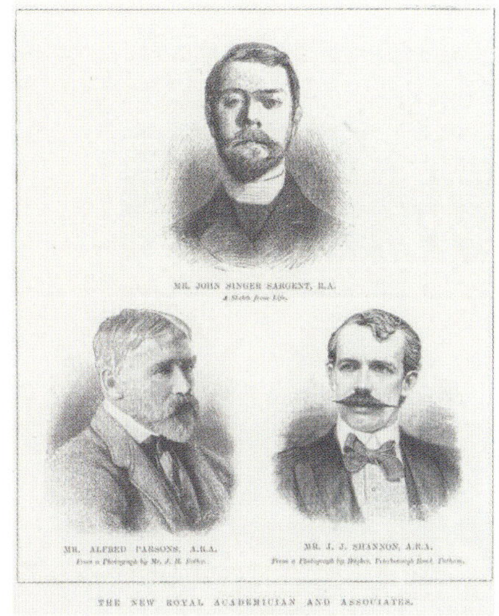

Left: Henry G. Marquand. *The trustees of New York's Metropolitan Museum commissioned this portrait of Marquand in February 1896, in recognition of his generosity while serving as the museum's president.*

Above: the Illustrated London News, *23 January 1897 – Sargent was made a full member of the RA in 1897.*

Below: In 1898 Sargent sketched the opulent mosaics at Ravenna, the seat of Byzantine Italy until the eighth century.

family, George Lewis and several of his American subjects, and many were also his friends. In 1898, he began painting the portrait of a prominent Bond Street art dealer, Asher Wertheimer (1844–1918) with his black poodle Noble. Wertheimer had built up a successful business specializing in French furniture, ceramics and paintings, and and the two men became close friends. After his own portrait, Wertheimer went on to commission Sargent with 12 further portraits of other members of his family. Yet critics freely censured his Jewish sitters. For instance, an American journalist commented about the portrait of *Mrs Carl Meyer and her Children* that: '\$10,000 was not much for a multi-millionaire Israelite to pay to secure social recognition for his family.'

MURAL RESEARCH

From January to March 1897, Sargent travelled to Sicily, Rome and Florence to seek ideas for his mural (see pages 58–59). He visited Palermo Cathedral, and studied the art and architecture of Florence and Rome. In Rome, he went to the Borgia Apartments in the Vatican, which had been decorated with paintings and frescoes between 1492 and 1494 by the Renaissance painter Pintoricchio (1454–1513). Sargent spent the summer of 1898 in Venice with the Curtis family at the Palazzo Barbaro.

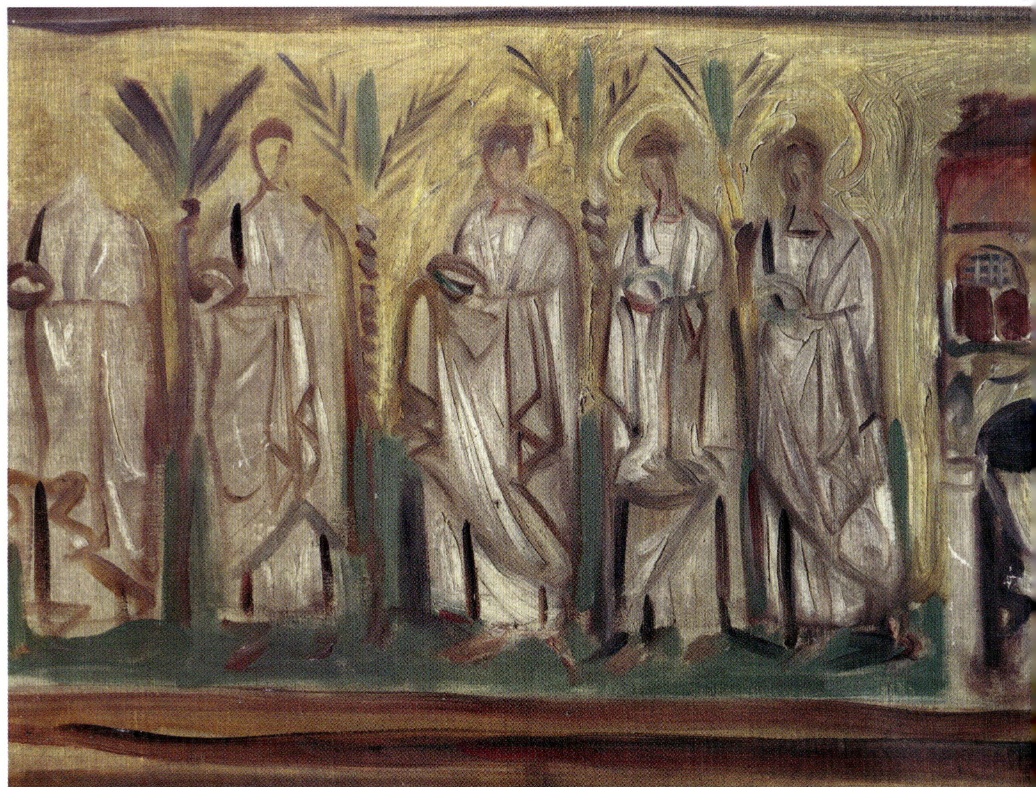

'SARGENTOLATRY'

Sargent painted the Boston murals intentionally to appeal to the general American public, but he created his portraits for the international market, to be exhibited in galleries and captivate wealthy aristocratic, political, intellectual and artistic patrons. Over his career, he produced more than 600 such portraits.

SICKERT'S ESSAY

Sargent's joining of the Establishment was seen as a betrayal by several progressive artists with whom he associated, especially Whistler, who scorned such official art institutions. In May 1910, Walter Sickert (1860–1942) – who had joined Sargent at the New English Art Club in 1888, and took control of it the following year – wrote an article he titled *Sargentolatry*, describing the fervour that bordered on idolatry over Sargent's portraits by critics and the public, especially in Britain. Following the Impressionists, Sickert was exploring methods of painting with colour, while Sargent focused less on colour and more on tonal contrasts, which Sickert and several others considered old-fashioned. Sickert wrote of the: 'prostration before [Sargent] and all his works' by the British art press and the effect this adulation had on other artists working at the time. Perceived as a trendsetter, a major influence on general tastes and the embodiment of a great master artist, Sargent's reputation was putting other artists in the shade, and although Sickert was not against his friend's success, he and other artists found it frustrating to be marginalized or ignored beneath Sargent's perceived brilliance:

'I doubt if anyone can be as much surprised and amused as Sargent himself... at the prostration before him and all works that has been the attitude of the English press for the last decade or so... It is a pitiful thing, and one of the best proofs of the nullity of art criticism in this country, that Sargent's painting is accepted, as it is, as the standard of art, the... high-water mark of modernity...'

He continued: *'...my lazy and ignorant critical colleagues have put me in the tiresome and odious position of appearing to attack an artist who has constantly given me real pleasure. I find myself forced to write grudgingly of a man whose great and rare qualities I cordially envy... he was the Magnetic Pole towards which the critical needles must all point... I can even remember seeing a poster in the street, issued by an exhibiting society, worded: 'Works by Mr. John Sargent and others'...Visitors would hurry in, ask the secretary which were Sargent's pictures, and, having inspected them, go out again.'*

Sickert ended with: *'The only person who has resolutely abstained from any complicity in the Sargent boom has been Mr Sargent himself.'*

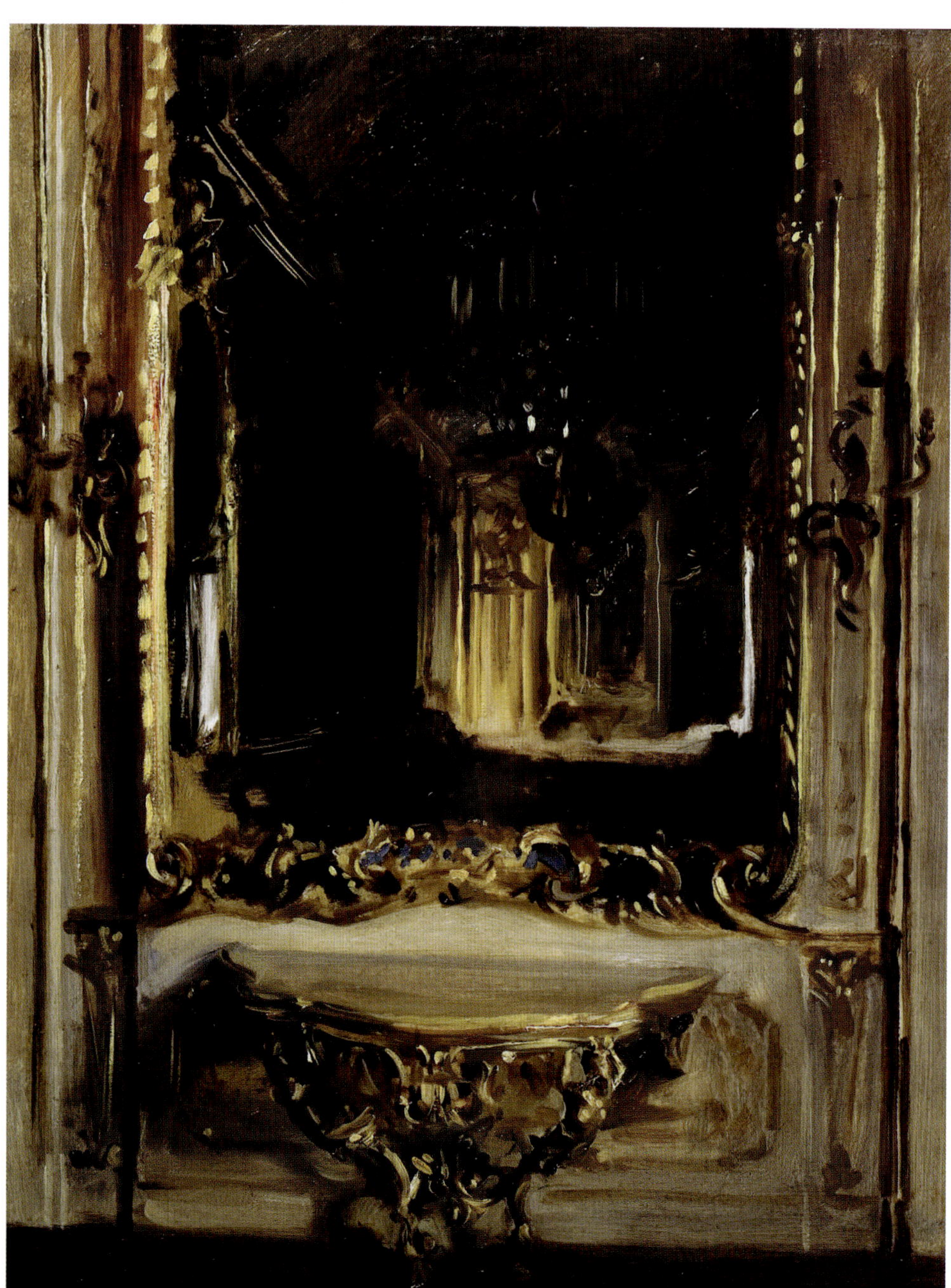

Left: Unusually painted in oil on wood, Sargent used fluid, dynamic brushstrokes to capture this Rococo mirror in 1898.

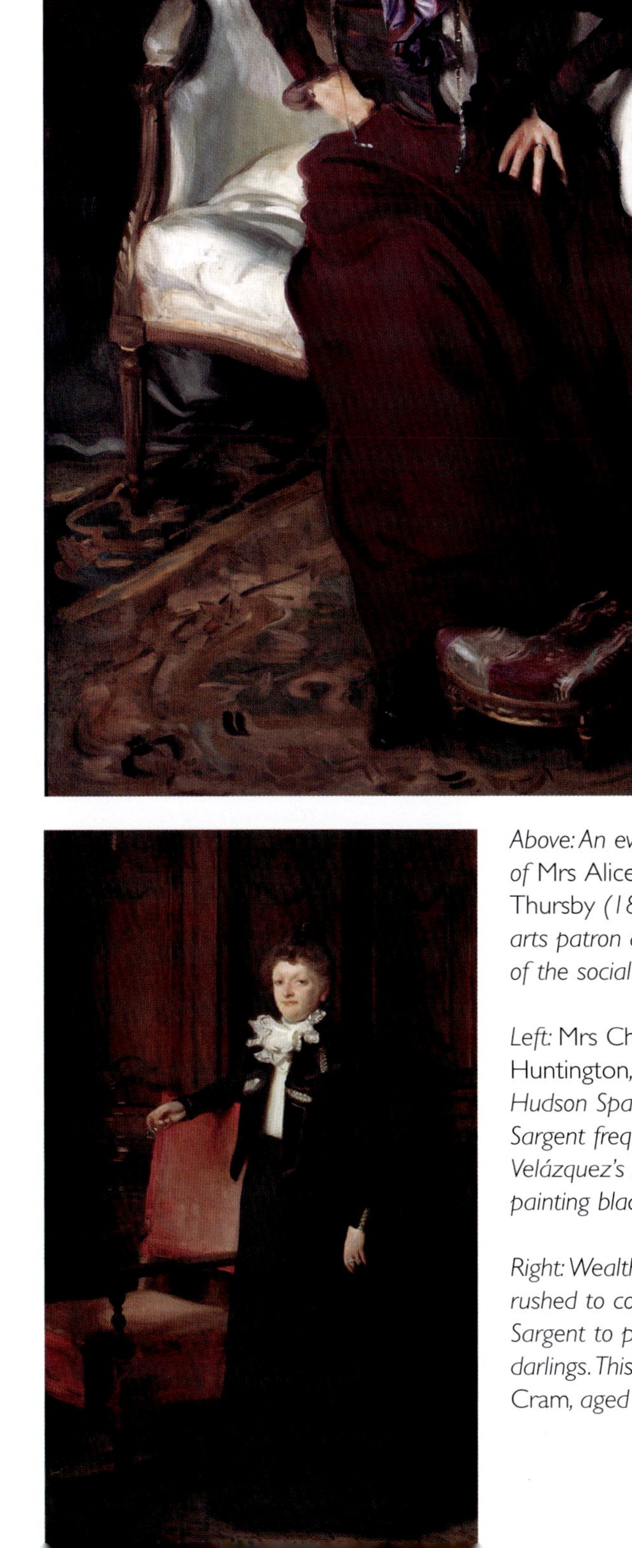

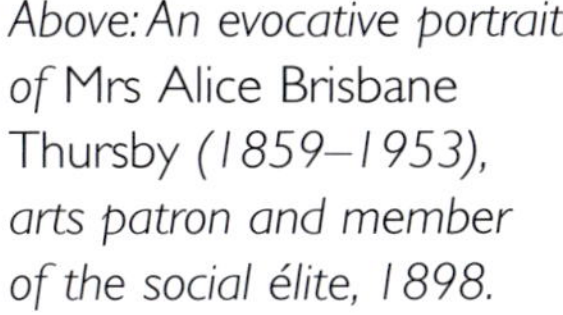

Above: An evocative portrait of Mrs Alice Brisbane Thursby (1859–1953), arts patron and member of the social élite, 1898.

Left: Mrs Charles Huntington, *née Jane Hudson Sparkes, 1898. Sargent frequently practised Velázquez's method of painting black on black.*

Right: Wealthy parents rushed to commission Sargent to paint their little darlings. This is Charlotte Cram, *aged seven.*

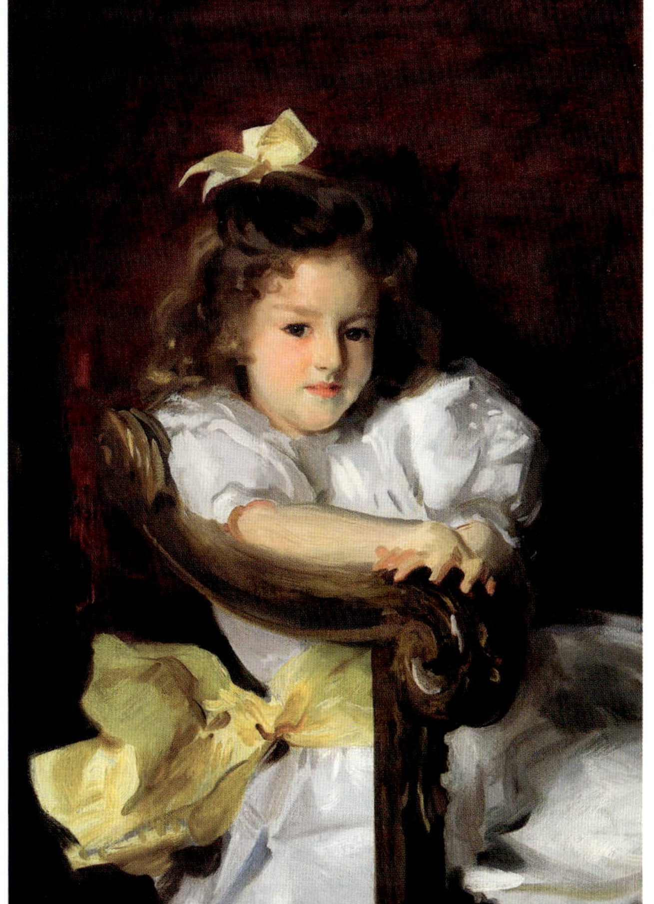

INFLUENTIAL PATRONS

Édouard and Marie Pailleron were among Sargent's earliest patrons (see page 32), and their backing was crucial in launching his career. Although the scandal of *Madame X* caused a hiatus for a few years, the steadfast patronage of well-connected individuals reinforced and sustained his prominence in the art world.

THE GRAND MANNER

Particularly during the 1890s, Sargent came to be relied upon by the extremely wealthy to continue in the portraiture traditions that followed the 'Grand Manner' of the 17th and 18th centuries. This is a grandiose, idealized style of painting, influenced by academia and ancient history. These 'Grand Manner' portraits – also known as swagger portraits – were commissioned to evoke a sense of power, importance and status. Usually full-length and life-sized, with the subjects dressed expensively and in poses and gestures often derived from ancient Roman or Italian Renaissance art, these portraits are theatrical and imposing, while still managing to express the subject's personality. Artists who were particularly recognized for the style included Sir Peter Paul Rubens (1577–1640), Van Dyck, Sir Joshua Reynolds (1723–92) and Thomas Gainsborough. In recognition of his fulfilment of this role, in 1902, Auguste Rodin described Sargent as 'the Van Dyck of our times' and by the 1890s, because of this, he had eclipsed all previously respected contemporary portraitists, including Sir Edward Burne-Jones (1833–98), Lord Frederic Leighton and Lawrence Alma-Tadema (1836–1912).

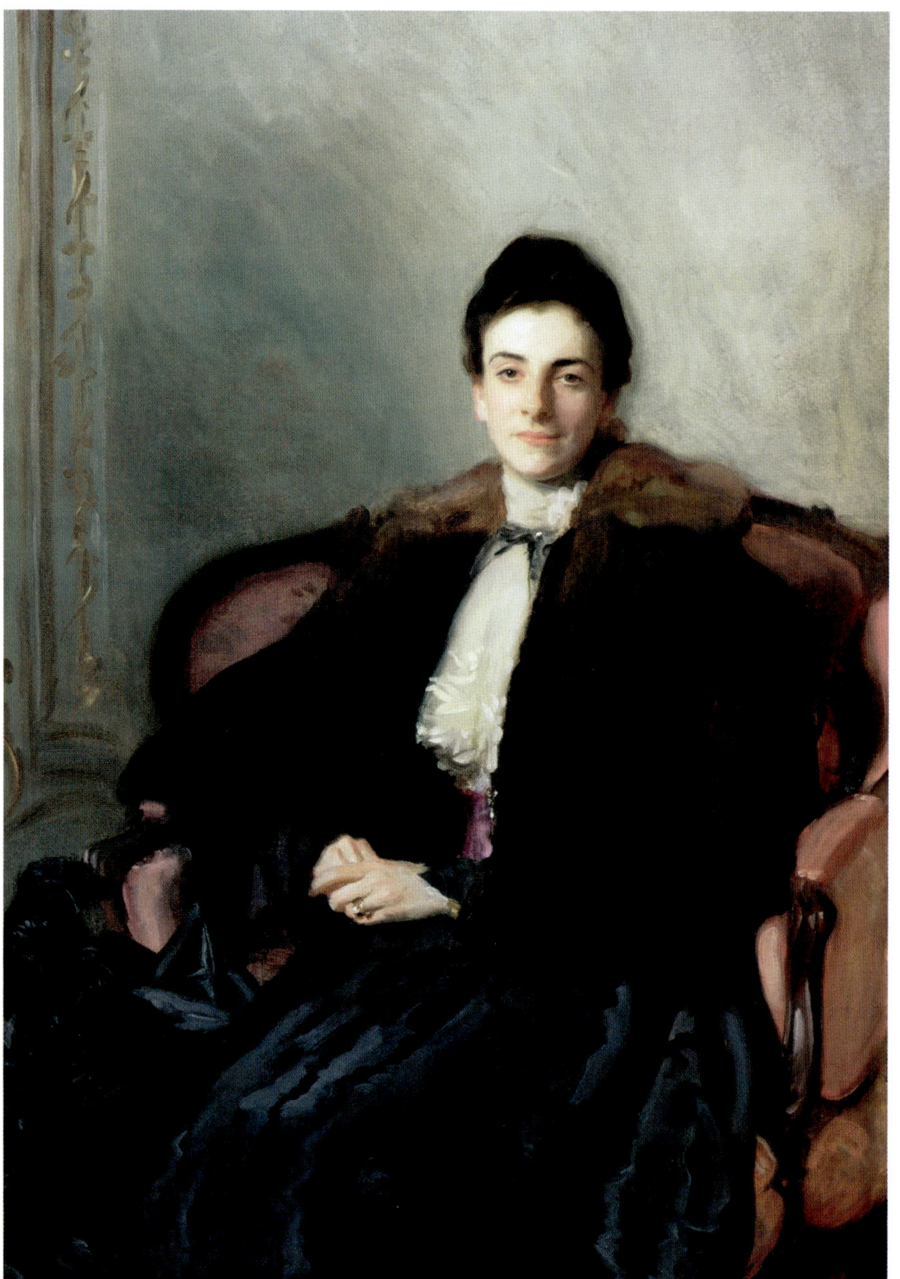

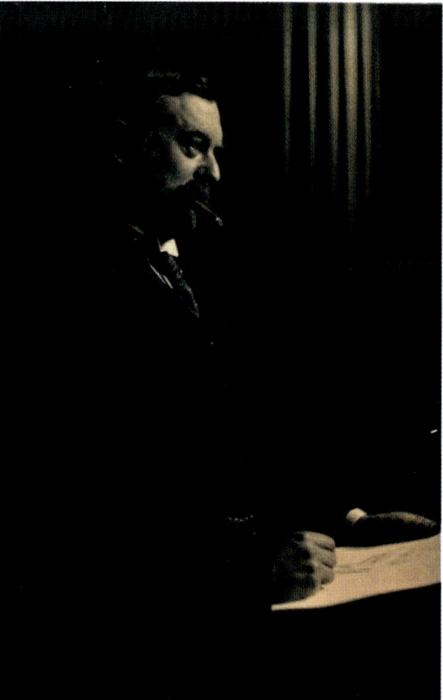

Above: Sargent drawing a portrait of the actress Ethel Barrymore (1879–1959), photographed in Boston in 1903.

Left: Mrs Harold Wilson, 1897, one of Sargent's eminent sitters of the 1890s.

FASHIONABLE PARTIES

During his first few years in England, Sargent had few patrons or portrait commissions, but he was introduced to British high society early on by Henry James and then by James's friend, socialite Margaret 'Daisy' Stuyvesant

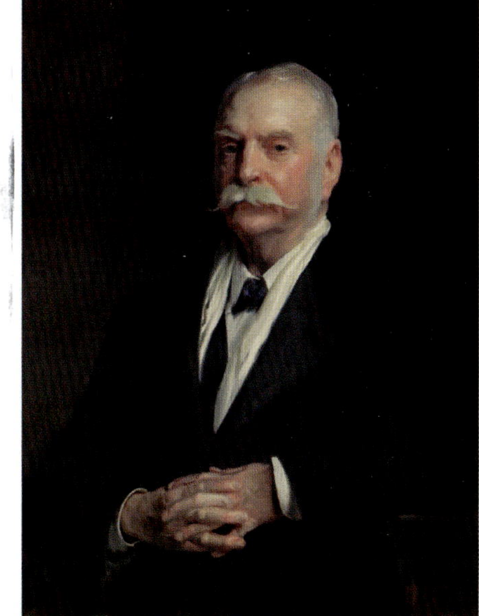

Above: Lord Airedale, Sir James Kitson *(1835–1911) was a British politician, a Member of Parliament and then a peer. Sargent painted his portrait in 1905.*

AESTHETICISM

The phrase 'art for art's sake' suggests that art has its own value and should be judged purely for its beauty, not for its subject or theme. The phrase first emerged in the early 19th century in France, partly as a reaction against the Romantic movement and initially written about by Théophile Gautier. The theme attracted support among other writers, especially Charles Baudelaire (1821–67). In 1873, the English critic, essayist and humanist Walter Pater (1839–94) published Studies in the History of the Renaissance, in which he used the phrase, and it became a doctrine for the British Aesthetic movement, which included many of Sargent's circle, including Whistler, Wilde, Burne-Jones, Lord Leighton and members of the 'Souls'. Also partly influenced by the Arts and Crafts movement and Pre-Raphaelite Brotherhood, Aestheticism blended different styles, including Classical and Japanese art, design and culture; it also challenged Victorian values and promoted artistic, sexual and political experimentation. Even fashion was influenced, with female Aesthetes abandoning corsets, instead wearing loose, flowing garments in subtle colours, modelled on medieval styles, and leaving their hair untied..

Rutherfurd White (see also page 38), who had recently moved to the US Embassy in London with her diplomat husband Henry White (1850–1927). The couple hosted many fashionable parties and there Sargent mixed with the upper classes, successful businessmen, performers, writers, artists and other prominent society figures, such as Oscar Wilde (1854–1900) and Sir Max Beerbohm (1872–1956). The Whites were part of the Souls; an elite association of individuals, including politicians and diplomats who were united in their social and political ambitions and also supported the Aesthetic movement. Further soirées and events were hosted by the politician Sir Philip Sassoon (1888–

1939) and his sister Sybil (1894–1989), and Sargent's solicitor George Lewis and his wife Lady Elizabeth Lewis (1844–1931) who was one of London's most illustrious hostesses (which helped reduce some anti-Semitism). Lewis had built an outstanding reputation in criminal litigation, particularly working for celebrities and the aristocracy, and he and Sargent became close friends. The socializing resulted in Sargent being inundated with commissions, and his list of patrons read like a 'who's who' of the period. His friend and biographer Charteris wrote: '...during these years, the nineties, it had ceased to be a question who would be painted by Sargent; the question was whom he would find time to paint.'

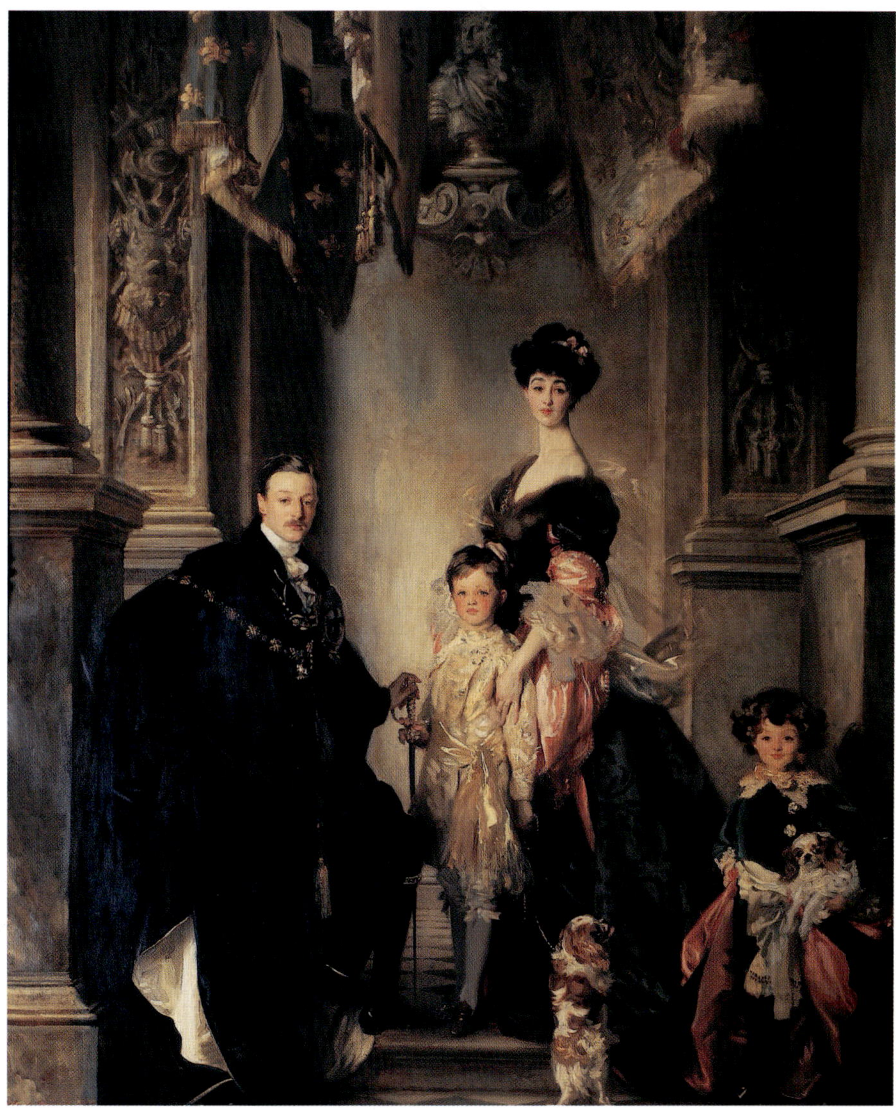

Above: The Spencer-Churchills, 9th Duke and Duchess of Marlborough and their two sons, *1905 (see also page 191).*

ARISTOCRATIC SOCIETY

From 1877, Tite Street, near the River Thames in London's Chelsea, was developed specifically as an artists' quarter. Whistler had a studio-house built there, which Sargent moved into in September 1886, signing the lease nine months later. Oscar Wilde also lived opposite with his wife and children.

TITE STREET

By the turn of the 20th century, Sargent's studio at number 33 Tite Street was too busy to accommodate the constant procession of illustrious individuals arriving to sit for their portraits, so he leased the house next door, had the dividing wall knocked through, and used that house (number 31) as his entrance. Whistler had originally decorated the large, airy rooms in a pared-down yellow Aesthetic style with judicious placements of fans

Below: The Sitwell Family, surrounded by heirlooms. Sir George wears riding boots despite rarely riding, and Lady Ida arranges flowers even though this was always done by the head gardener.

and porcelain, but Sargent filled it with the many treasures, antiques and props he had collected during his travels. He also hired a dressmaker to make curtains and cushions, and a florist to fill his vases and urns with azaleas and arum lilies.

Although many of his portraits appear to be painted in his privileged clients' homes, most were executed in Tite Street. In 1900, Sir George Sitwell (1860–1943) asked him to paint a portrait of his family at Renishaw Hall, their Derbyshire home. Sargent was too busy and disinclined to travel to and from Derbyshire for the painting, so he turned down the commission. But Sir George was desperate to convey an aspect of British life that he

feared was being eroded and made great efforts to persuade Sargent. Eventually, Sir George compromised. He sent some of his furnishings to Sargent in Tite Street so that elements of Renishaw Hall could be recreated, and the Sitwell family travelled to Sargent in London. Sir George wanted the work to emulate family portraits he owned of his antecedents, particularly one painted in 1787 by the American artist John Singleton Copley (1738–1815), so throughout the sittings, he advised and criticized Sargent as he worked. One point he insisted that Sargent observe was his daughter Edith's crooked nose. In the completed portrait, Edith's nose is straight, but Sir George's is somewhat misshapen.

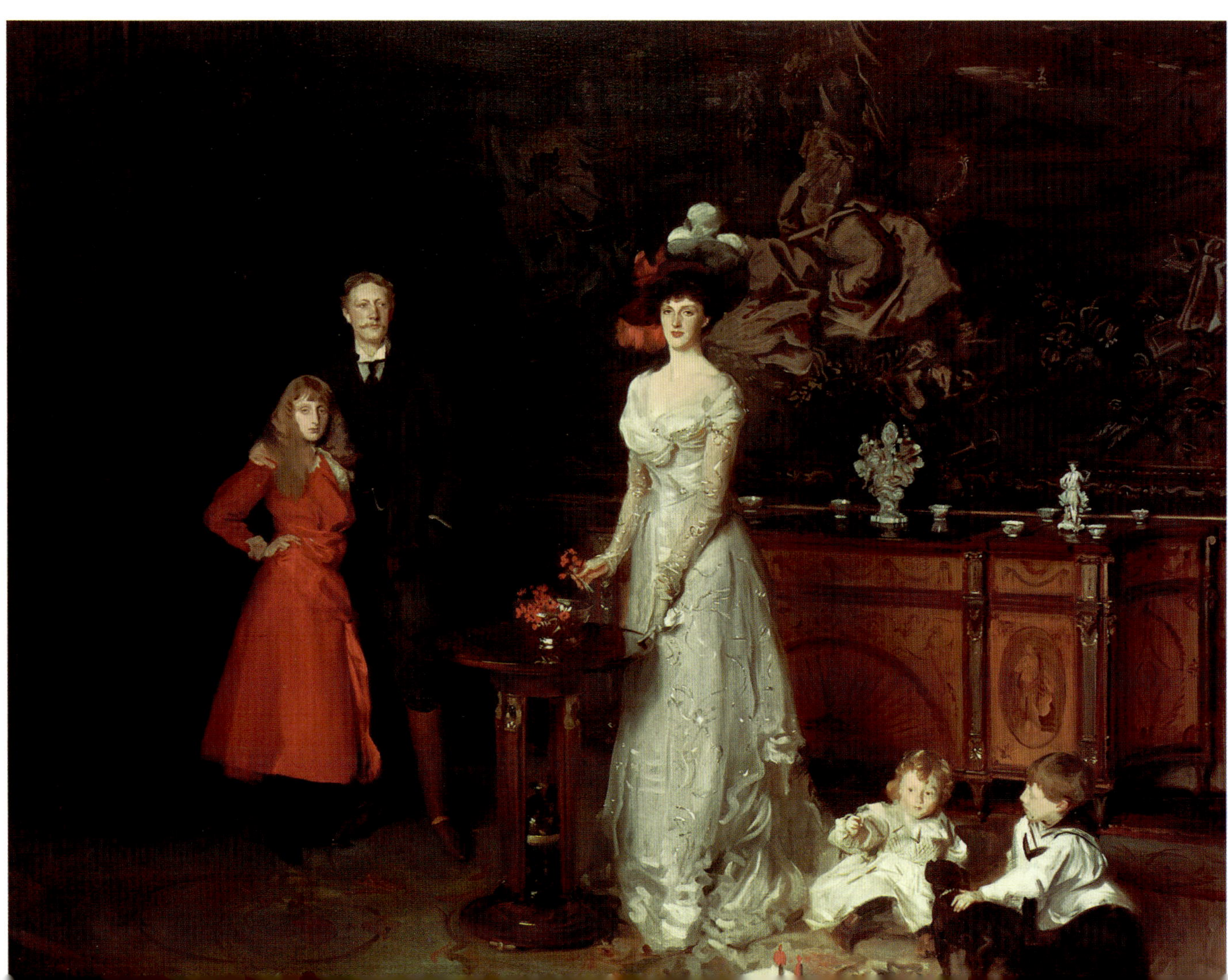

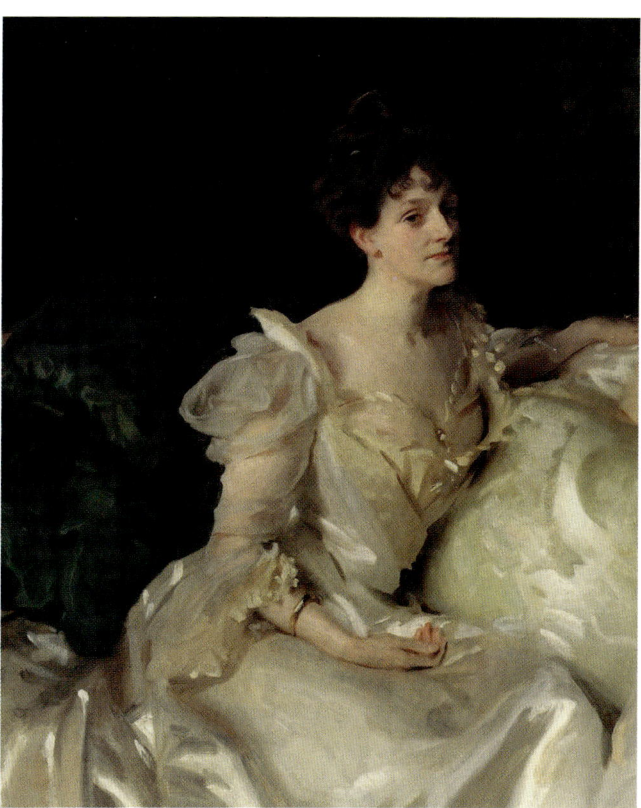

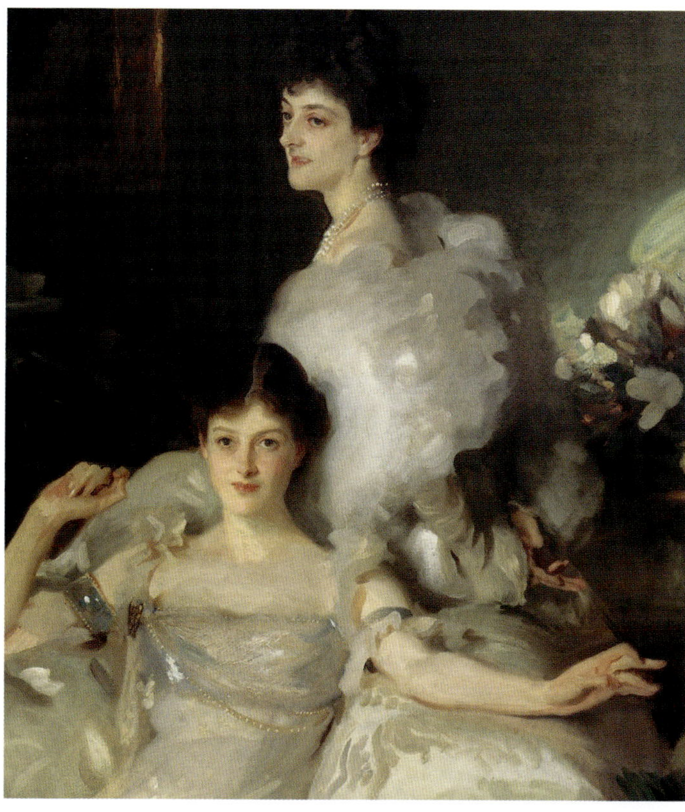

GILDED EXISTENCE

Although he never relished being a portraitist, Sargent tolerated the snobbishness of some of his upper class patrons as they paid him extremely well; in 1898, he was charging 1,000 guineas for a portrait. It was an artificial world, but he was versatile, adaptable and urbane. In 1899, he painted a portrait of the three Wyndham sisters, the daughters of the Honourable Percy Wyndham (1835–1911) and Madeline Caroline Frances Eden (1860–1920). They were beautiful, rich, and by then, all

Above left: Detail of The Wyndham Sisters, *1899. This is Mrs Adeane.*

Above right: another detail of The Wyndham Sisters. *Lady Elcho is behind and Mrs Tennant, the youngest sister, in front (see also page 160).*

married. They include Mary Constance, Lady Elcho (1862–1937), Madeline Adeane (1869–1941) and Pamela Tennant (1871–1928). Sargent portrayed them reclining languidly in the bottom half of a large composition beneath their mother's portrait painted in 1877 by George Frederick Watts (1817–1904). Their sumptuous white gowns, brocade sofa and white peonies create striking tonal and textural contrasts in the asymmetrical composition. Their slender figures are typical of Sargent's style at the time, echoing fashionable Art Nouveau styles and also aristocratic notions of elegance. At the Royal Academy's annual show in 1900, the painting was universally acclaimed. Reflecting the leisured, gilded existence of the late Victorian aristocracy, *The Times* hailed it as: 'the greatest picture of modern times,' while the Prince of Wales called it: 'The Three Graces.'

PREPARING FOR A PORTRAIT

At Tite Street, Sargent used numerous props and accessories in his portraits, including chairs, tables, fabrics, screens and even a piece of carved panelling taken from a Rococo interior. Before starting, he usually visited his sitters' homes and reviewed their wardrobes to choose what they should wear, and he occasionally viewed where the portrait would hang. Men generally had a minimum of eight sittings and women had at least ten.

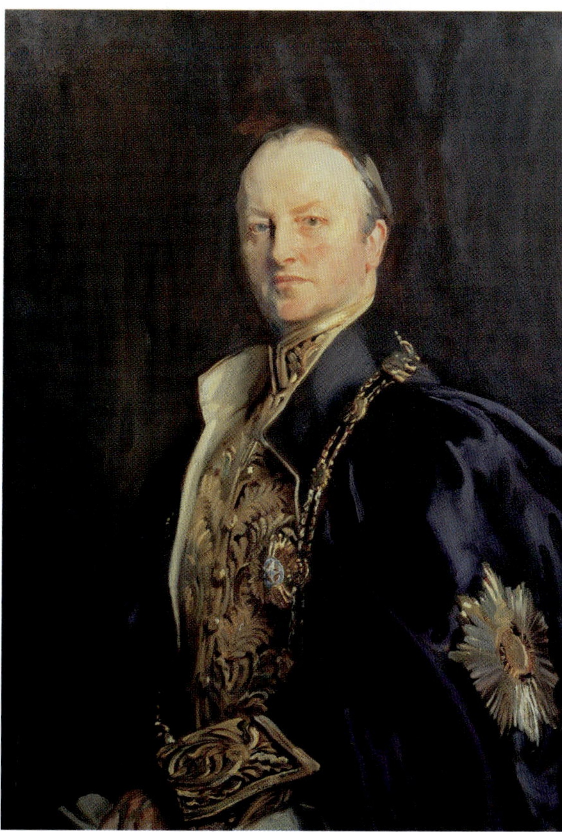

Above: Among Sargent's prestigious patrons was George Nathaniel Curzon, Marquess Curzon of Kedleston (1895–1925), who was a prominent politician as well as an administrator and explorer.

FURTHER TRAVELS

Despite the wide enthusiasm for his portraits, Sargent continued to doubt his own ability in producing what his patrons wanted, and felt increasingly uncomfortable with their vanity and demands. His escape was to travel with his mother, sisters and friends, sketching in charcoal, watercolour and oils wherever he went.

COMPLEX PERSONALITY

Sargent was often irritated when sitters made comments and suggestions as he painted their portraits, and about the preconceptions that were evolving about him. During a sitting in 1905, the American newspaper publisher Joseph Pulitzer (1847–1911) remarked that he had been told that Sargent exposed his sitters' 'inner weaknesses as well as their strengths.' Sargent replied: 'I paint what I see... I don't dig beneath the surface for things that don't appear before my eyes.' He developed a maxim: 'I chronicle, I do not judge' in the hope of silencing the unwanted opinions.

Sargent valued his privacy and shunned publicity. To strangers or acquaintances, he often seemed shy or brusque. Public occasions agitated him, and contrasting with his fluid, expressive paintings, he stammered awkwardly if having to speak in public. With friends he was spirited and witty, but reserved and quiet in large gatherings. In 1903, the art historian and critic John Charles van Dyke (1861–1931) met him on a transatlantic crossing and later remarked: 'He was a little shy, even with men, and more or less embarrassed by women, but everyone liked him, and of course, everyone admired him for

his work.' His friend, the English artist, writer and art collector W. Graham Robertson remarked that he was fond of society, but never 'seemed altogether at one with it.' He also commented: 'Sargent talked little and with an effort; why he went everywhere, night after night often puzzled me.'

Also generous and warm-hearted, Sargent often helped struggling artists and musicians, and patronized various important collections, exhibitions and galleries.

PARIS, SWITZERLAND AND ITALY

After a decade of working predominantly to commission, by 1900, Sargent began producing more informal and personal paintings and turning away some commissions. Now in his forties, he devoted more time to holidays which became integral to his art. He was also researching for his murals. Since becoming a full Academician in 1897, he had been more involved at the Royal Academy, regularly visiting and teaching at the RA schools, and advising galleries and museums about their collections and exhibitions.

In early 1900, he played host to Claude Monet who was staying at the Savoy Hotel in London, and painting views of the River Thames. In the spring, he met Monet again in Paris, and he also spent time with the artists Giovanni Boldini (1842–1931) and Augustus Saint-Gaudens (1848–1907). He exhibited three paintings at the Paris Exposition Universelle, for which he was awarded a medal of honour. While his house was being enlarged, he travelled

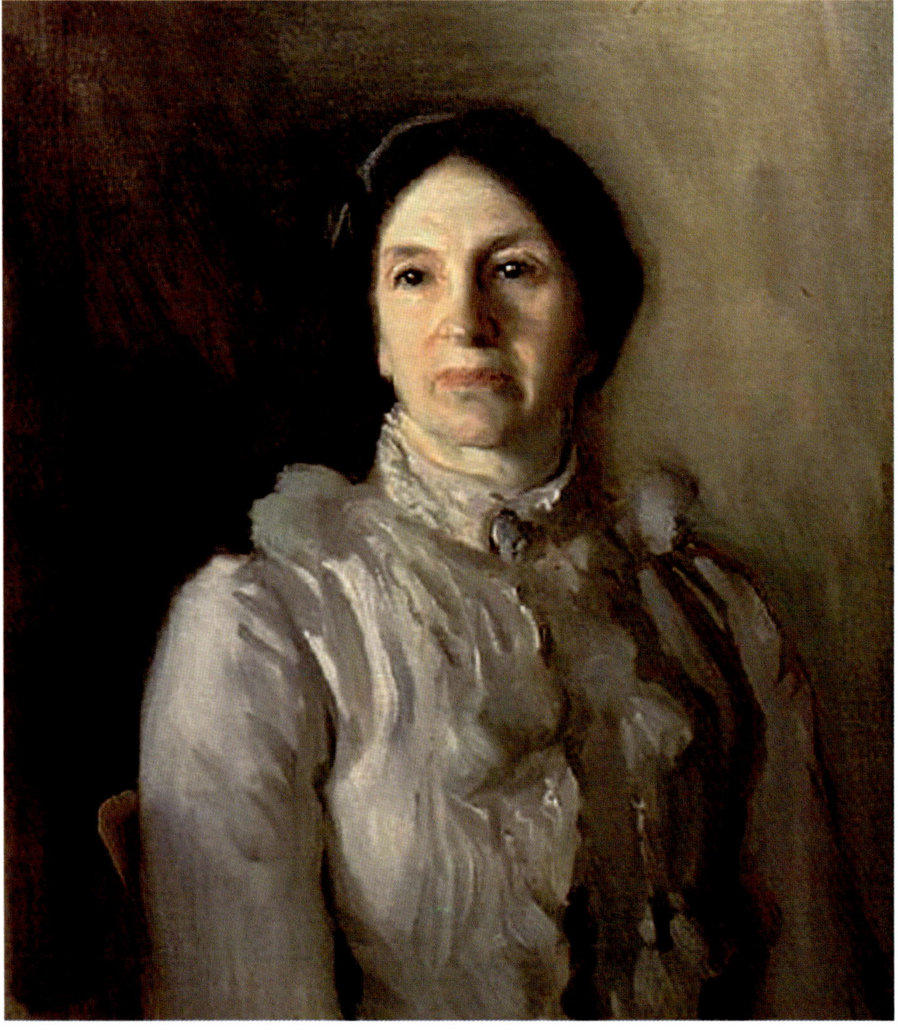

Left: Annie Adams (1834–1915) was an author, philanthropist and the hostess of an artistic and literary salon in Boston, where she entertained various well-known authors and artists.

to Switzerland and then Italy, where he spent time in Florence, Bologna, Genoa and Milan, but back in London, he discovered that the work on his houses in Tite Street was still not completed, so he stayed at the Reform Club in Pall Mall.

The following January and February, Monet returned to London and Sargent once again entertained him. In February 1901, Sargent invited Monet to watch Queen Victoria's funeral procession from a friend's house opposite Buckingham Palace, along with Whistler and James. Soon after, Sargent was asked to paint the coronation of Edward VII, but he declined; instead, his friend Edwin Austin Abbey took on the commission.

NORWAY AND SICILY

In the autumn of 1901, Sargent travelled to Norway with his friends the McCulloch family, who went there for the salmon fishing. George McCulloch (1848–1907) was a wealthy and important art collector with whom Sargent had struck up a friendship. His sketches show how relaxed he felt in their company in Norway, and he also painted a rather different commissioned portrait; *On His Holidays* is a portrait of George's son Alexander McCulloch (1887–1951) who later competed as a rower in the 1908 Olympics.

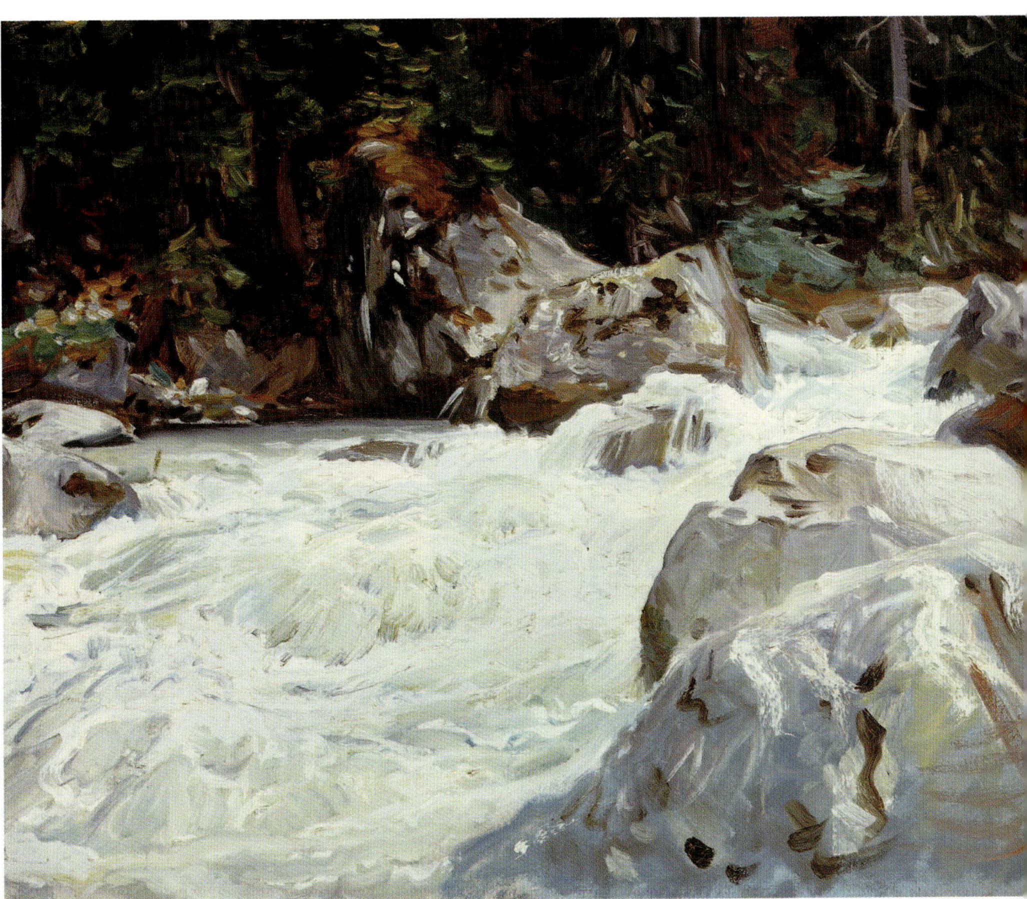

Above: A Torrent in Norway, *1901 — vigorous and dynamic, this demonstrates how liberated Sargent felt away from the constraints of portrait painting.*

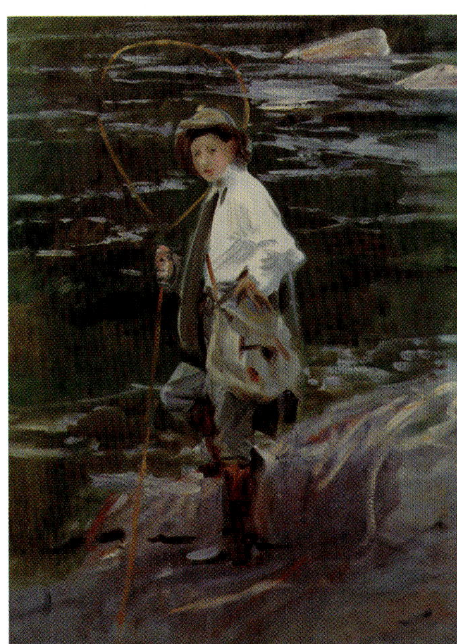

Above: Young Salmon Fisher, *1901 — another image of 14-year-old Alexander McCulloch on holiday in Norway.*

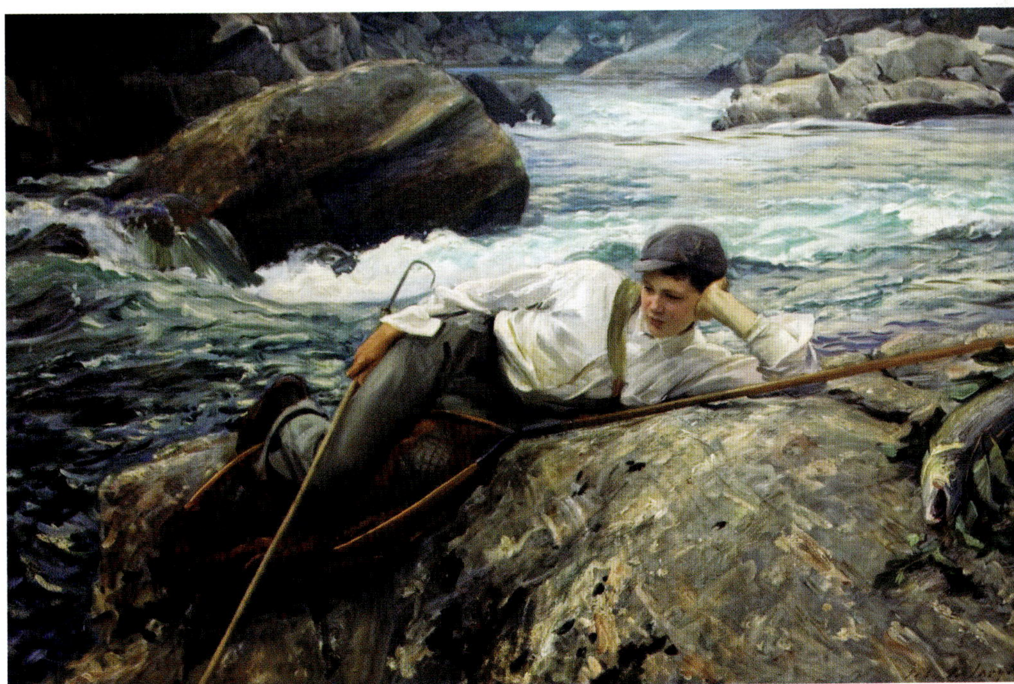

Above: On His Holidays, *1901–02: A poignant portrait of the schoolboy on holiday from Winchester College, Alexander is shown reclining precipitously above a swirling torrent.*

NEW VIEWPOINTS

Sargent's holidays after 1900 set a pattern that echoed his early years, when he and his family spent winters in Nice and Florence and summers in the Swiss Alps and the Austrian Tyrol. After a decade dominated by portraits and murals, travelling and painting landscapes offered him some respite.

From 1901, almost every summer and autumn until 1914, Sargent visited the Alps, Venice and parts of southern Europe and the Near East. He usually travelled with his mother and sisters or parties of friends. After first visiting the Holy Land in 1890 to research his murals, he continued when the project was extended. As a child, his mother had encouraged him to make drawings of places he visited and he had continued the practice all his life. From 1900, he drew and painted on

Below: Detail from Venetian Wine Shop, *1902, the interior of a local bistro that Sargent visited while staying with the Curtis family (see also page 170).*

location even more. A favourite place for this was Purtud, near Courmayeur, an isolated village high up in the Italian Alps near the French and Swiss borders. In 1902, he returned to Granada for three weeks and the following year, went to Madrid, Portugal, Purtud and the Val d'Aosta in Italy.

CLOSE FRIENDS

Although uncomfortable with strangers, Sargent had a large social circle with whom he was exceptionally close, including his sisters Emily and Violet, Violet's husband Francis and particularly one niece, Rose-Marie, plus his old friends James, Abbey, the Barnards, the Curtises, the Wertheimers, the Lewises, Isabella Stewart Gardner, and Vernon

Lee. Others included the Archbishop of Canterbury, Randall Thomas Davidson (1848–1930), the artists Alberto Falchetti (1878–1956), Charles Gere (1869–1957) and Henry Tonks (1862–1937) who was professor of fine art at London's University College, and Eliza Wedgwood (1859–1947). In 1895, he met Mary Hunter (1857–1933) and painted her portrait three years later. Generous and energetic, Mary was married to an exceptionally wealthy man, and was famous for her literary

Below: Another view of Venetian Wine Shop *(1902). Some figures were posed by Sargent's friends and he added the vibrant red to enliven the composition.*

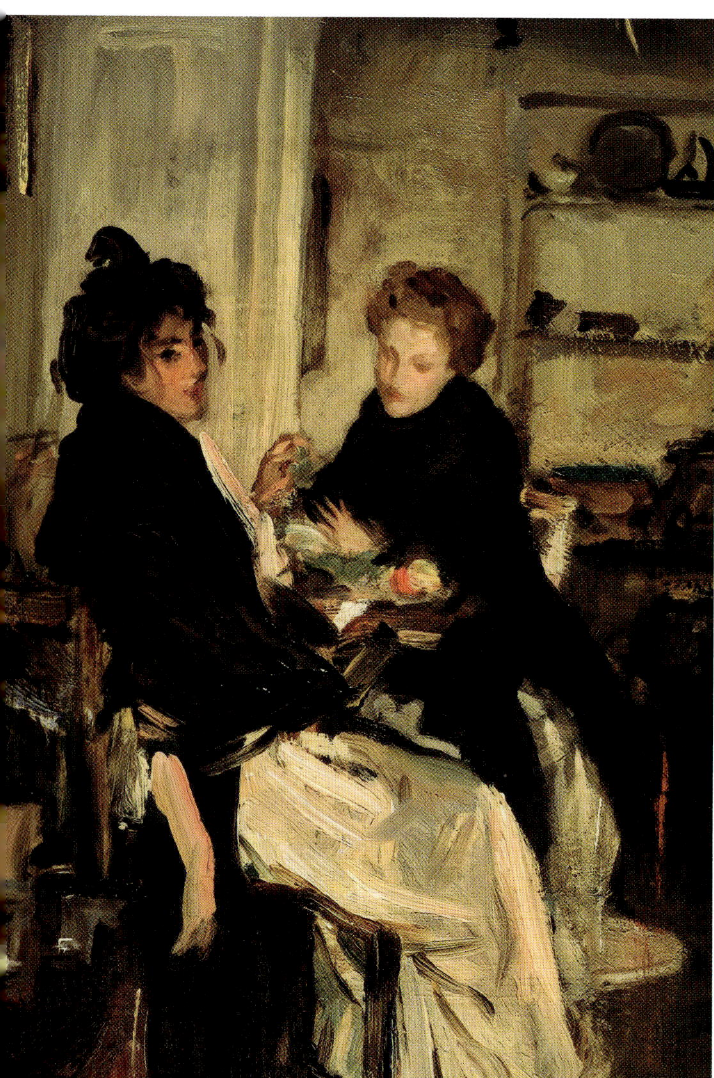

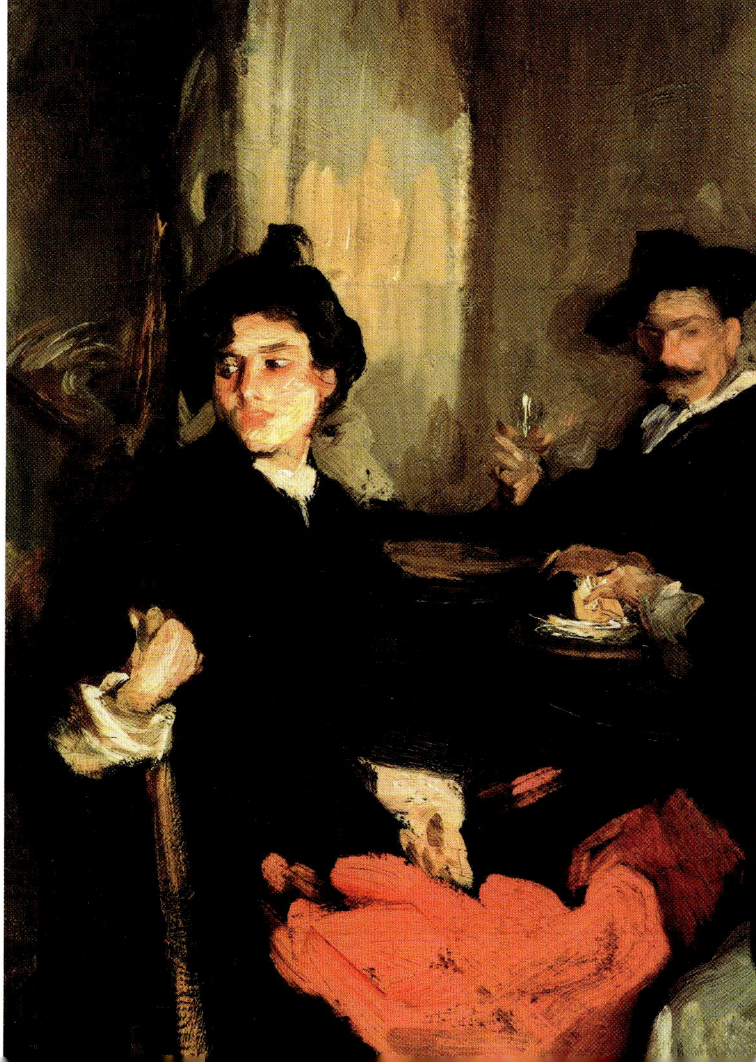

and artistic salons in London and house parties at Hill Hall in Epping. She became something of a confidante to Sargent. Her sister, Ethel Smyth (1858–1944), a musician and an active member of the Women's Suffrage Party also became a good friend. Other friends with whom Sargent travelled included Wilfrid de Glehn, the painter who had assisted him in 1890 on the Boston murals at the studio in Gloucestershire (see page 52), and the American artist Jane Erin Emmet (1873–1961) who married Wilfrid de Glehn in 1904.

RETURN TO VENICE

After 16 years, Sargent returned to Venice in 1898. The contrasts of colour and movement, of dark shadows and sparkling highlights always beguiled him. Initially he painted several interiors of the Palazzo Barbaro, owned by the Curtis family, and after 1900, he returned there nearly every year for over a decade, usually in late August or September and stayed until October. From that time, he began using the

Curtis gondola almost as a floating studio. From 1902, many of these works were painted in watercolour.

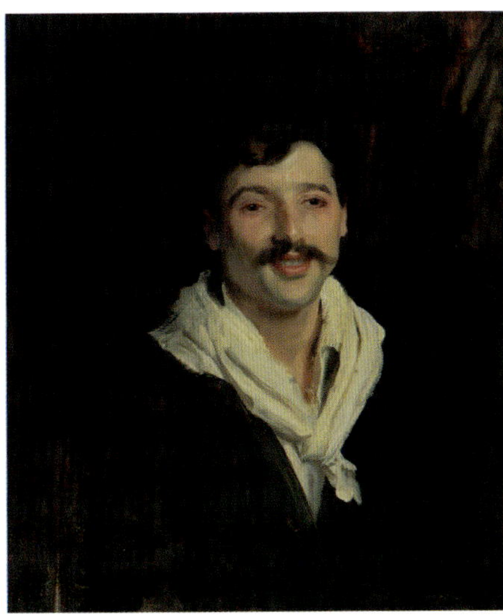

Above: Using a minimum of brushmarks Sargent captured An Italian Sailor.

Below: 1903, Sargent painted workers Bringing Down Marble from the Quarries to Carrara, *which was Michelangelo's favourite quarry.*

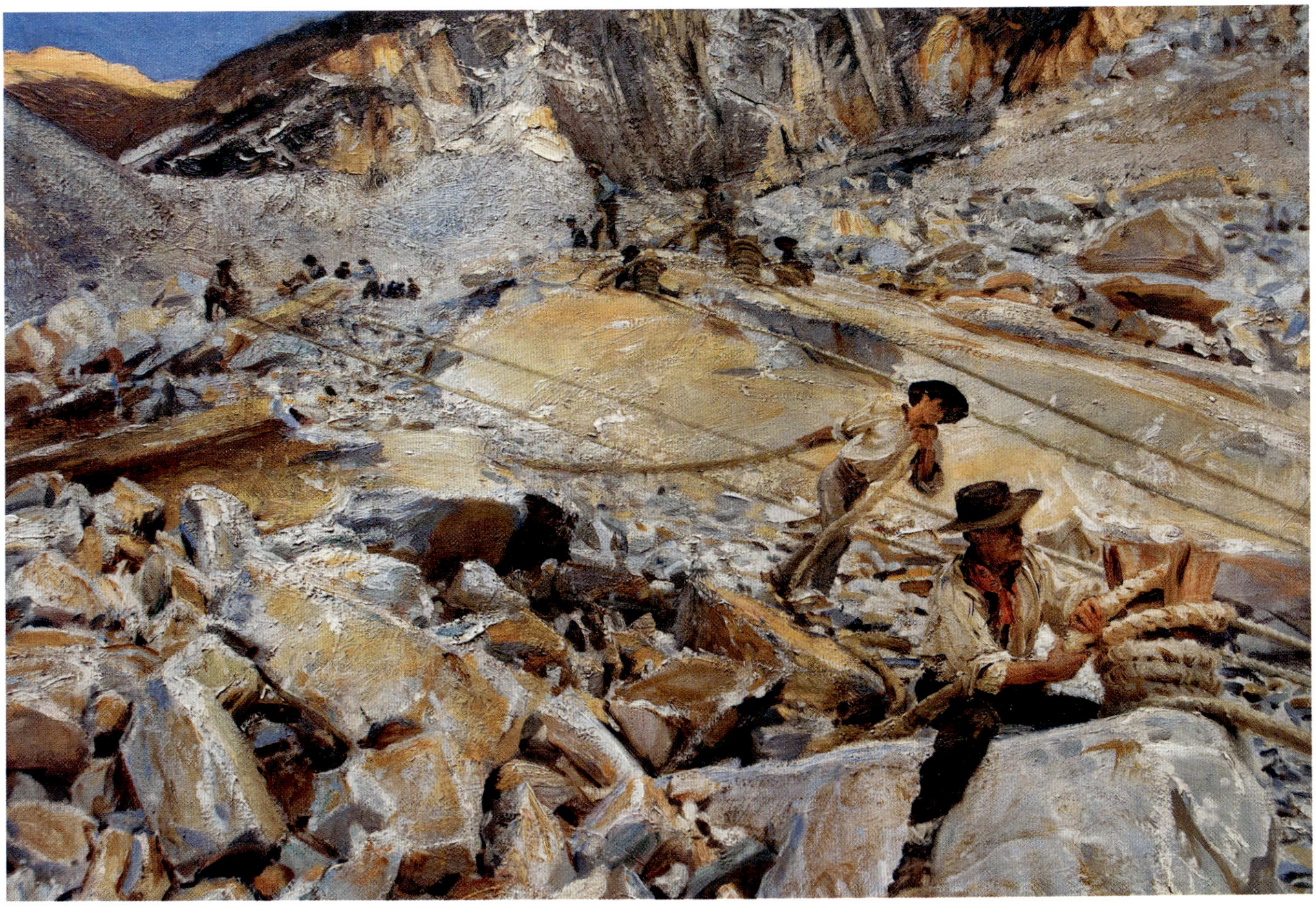

WATERCOLOURS

Sargent had worked in watercolour in his youth, but his use of it decreased as his fame grew and he worked predominantly in oils. In the 1870s and 1880s, he occasionally painted with watercolour, but from around 1902, his watercolour box became an essential part of his travelling equipment.

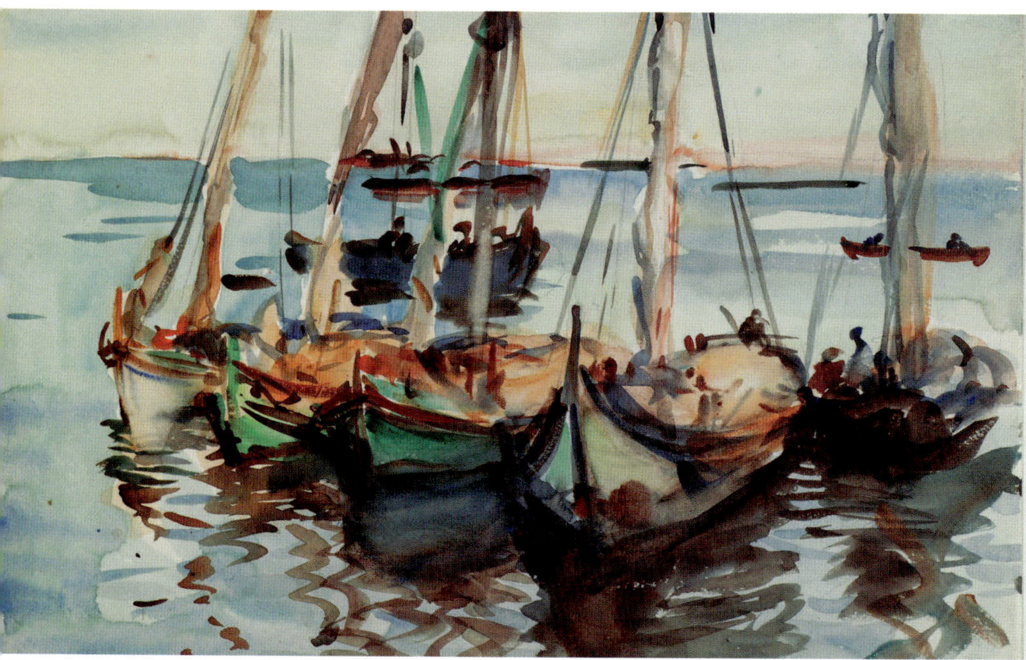

In 1892, Sargent had written a preface to the catalogue of an exhibition of paintings by the English artist Hercules Brabazon Brabazon (1821–1906) at the Goupil Gallery in London. He admired Brabazon's watercolour style that resembled Turner's. He wrote: 'Only after years of the contemplation of Nature can the process of selection become so sure an instinct; and a handling so spontaneous and so freed from the commonplaces of expression is final mastery, the result of long artistic training.' A decade later, Sargent seemed to follow his own words.

PALETTE AND METHODS

Using a brighter palette for watercolours than for his portraits, Sargent initially applied transparent washes, then added more intense colours and used either the white of the paper or Chinese white (gouache) for accents and highlights. His watercolour palette included: alizarin carmine, brown pink,

Above: Portuguese Boats, c.1903. Sargent painted with translucent watercolour and touches of gouache over graphite.

Below: Angels, Mosaic, Palatine Chapel, Palermo, 1897–1903, Sargent painted this watercolour while in Sicily, conveying the light and the radiating gold and mosaic figures on the domed ceiling.

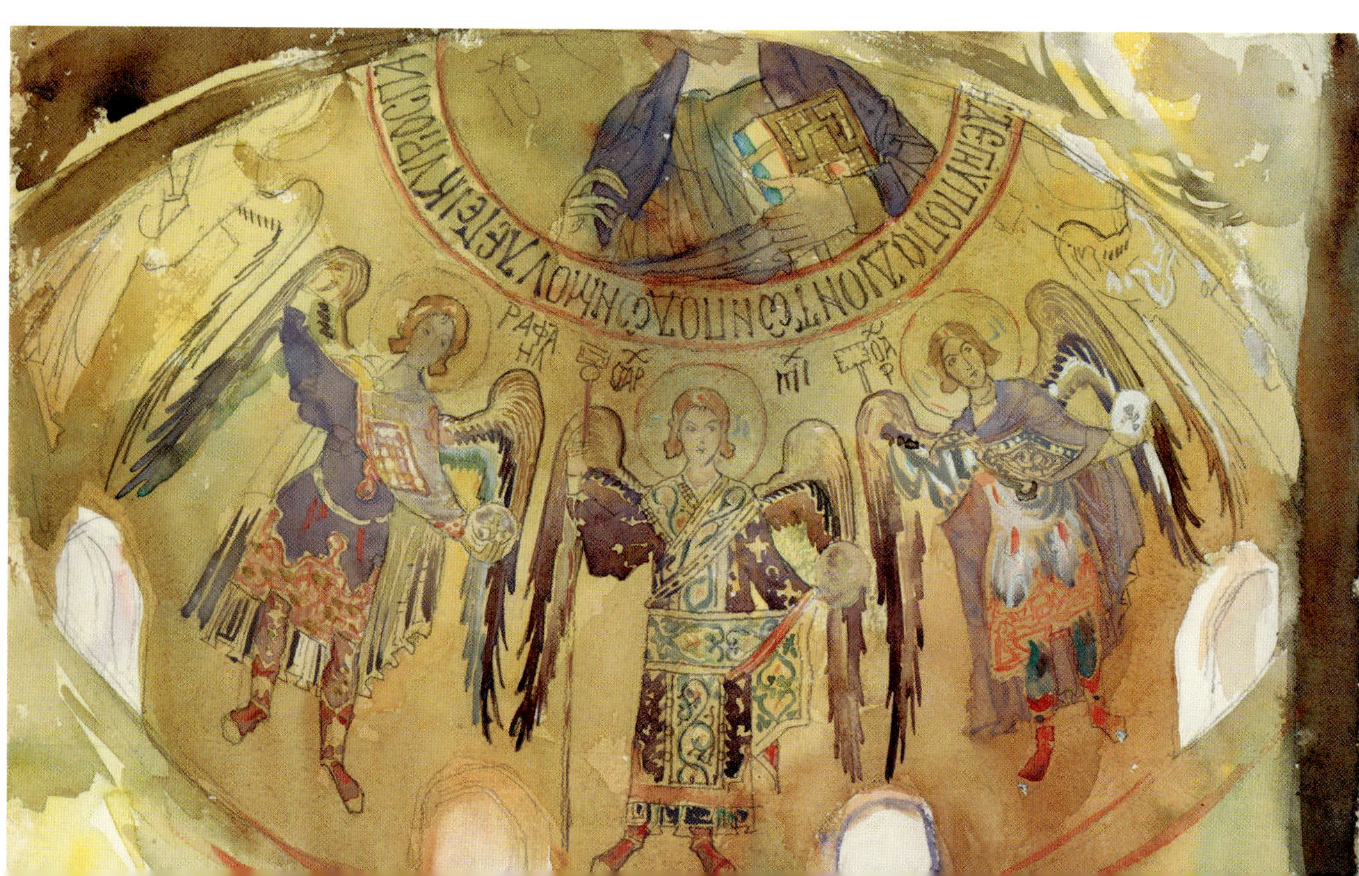

burnt sienna, cadmium yellow pale, chrome yellow, cobalt blue, gamboge, lamp black, rose madder, ultramarine, Vandyke brown, scarlet vermilion, deep vermilion and viridian. Ultramarine and Vandyke brown were his principal colours. At first he only used traditional watercolour techniques but by 1908, he also began applying less conventional methods, including wax resist, scraping out and scratching through, or applying blocking or masking agents to keep certain areas clear of paint. Disregarding contemporary taste for carefully composed landscapes, his bold, dense marks, loosely defined forms and unexpected viewpoints expressed the freedom he felt away from the restraints of commissioned portraits.

EXHIBITING HIS WATERCOLOURS

Despite enjoying the sense of liberation watercolours gave him, Sargent participated in only two major watercolour exhibitions in the United States during his lifetime, and both of these were at the urging of his friend and co-exhibitor Edward Darley Boit. The first exhibition of Sargent's watercolour paintings was held in New York and Boston in 1909, and it proved to be a sensation. Of the 86 works on display 83 were immediately purchased by the Brooklyn Museum.

The second exhibition in 1912, was equally acclaimed, 45 of the paintings were bought by the Museum of Fine Arts in Boston. In 1903, Sargent had his first solo exhibition in Europe, in London at the Carfax Gallery where he exhibited a selection of drawings, a group of oil studies, and for the first time, some of his watercolours as well. The following year, he joined the Royal Society of Painters in Water Colours in London, and from there he exhibited his watercolours regularly, participating in their summer and winter exhibitions. He also had two more exhibitions at the Carfax Gallery, where he exhibited watercolours in 1905 and 1908, and he also showed them occasionally at the New English Art Club.

COMPREHENSIVE CHRONICLE

Representing a journal of his travels from 1902, Sargent's watercolours convey the atmosphere of each location he visited, from the English countryside to Venice and the Tyrol, and from Corfu and the Middle East, to Maine and Florida. He painted more than 2,000 watercolours, setting up his easel wherever he was and painting what he saw in front of him. His images were vivid, fresh and expressive, whether of local people in the Middle East and North Africa at their daily tasks, or of his friends relaxing by fountains, in gardens or on mountainsides.

'Cultivate an ever-continuous power of observation. Wherever you are, be always ready to make slight notes of postures, groups and incidents. Store up in the mind without ceasing, a continuous stream of observations from which to make selections later. Above all things, get abroad, see the sunlight, and everything that is to be seen, the power of selection will follow.'

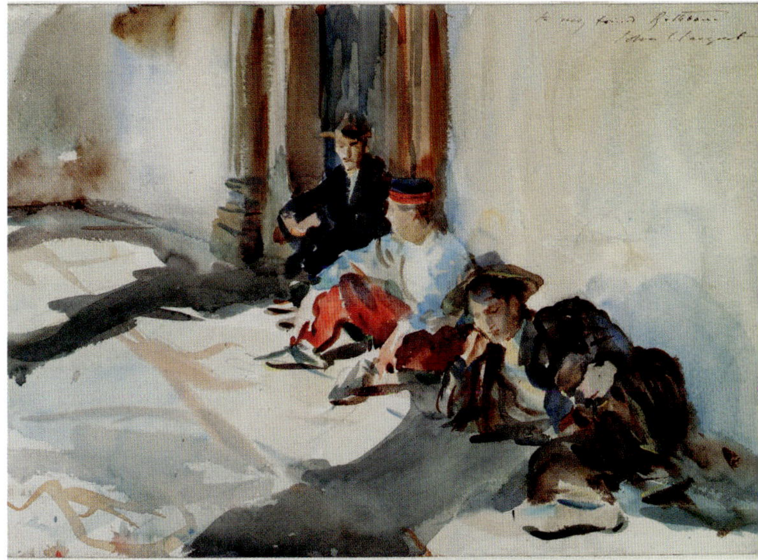

Right: Spanish Soldiers, *c.1903. Sargent sketched this loosely first, then applied both translucent and opaque watercolours.*

Below: Santiago de Compostela, *c.1903. A master of watercolour, Sargent allowed the white of his paper to act as highlights.*

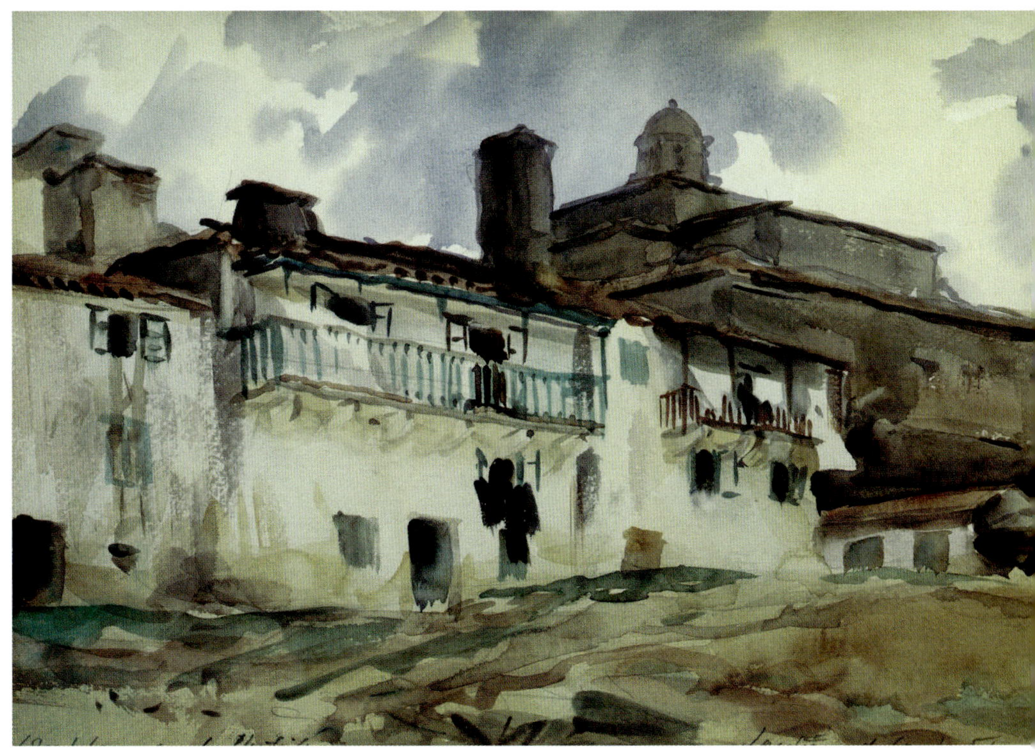

PORTRAIT PAINTING PROCESS

While in London between 1900 and 1907, Sargent produced approximately 25 portraits a year. In 1903, he took his second group of mural painting panels to Boston and remained in America for 18 weeks, where he completed 20 portraits, including one of President Roosevelt (1858–1919).

Sargent returned to America in 1903 to install his second instalment of mural panels in the Boston Public Library, and while he was in the States he found himself in constant demand for portrait commissions. His vivacious yet intimate style of portraiture contrasted with the more rigid, formal portraits produced by other artists, and continued to attract eminent clients. Several wealthy figures keenly awaited his visit so that they could commission him. Yet, Sargent was firm with all his sitters. They had to accept from the start that he told them what to wear and how to pose, and he decided on the composition, although if the portrait was for a specific location, he would agree to use a suitably dimensioned canvas.

PROBLEMS OF A PORTRAITIST

William Merritt Chase (1849–1916) was an American painter and teacher who began an art school that became the renowned Parsons School for Design. He was a great admirer of Sargent's work and in 1902, some of his students commissioned Sargent to paint his portrait, intending to give it to the Metropolitan Museum of Art in his honour. Sargent painted it at Tite Street, instructing Chase to wear his 'old blue studio coat,' rather than his preferred black frock coat. To raise the money to pay Sargent, Chase's students exhibited the portrait in New York, Philadelphia and Chicago.

Meanwhile, the federal government was seeking an artist to paint a portrait of President Roosevelt, presenting him as a distinguished, but personable statesman. Roosevelt decided that Sargent was the

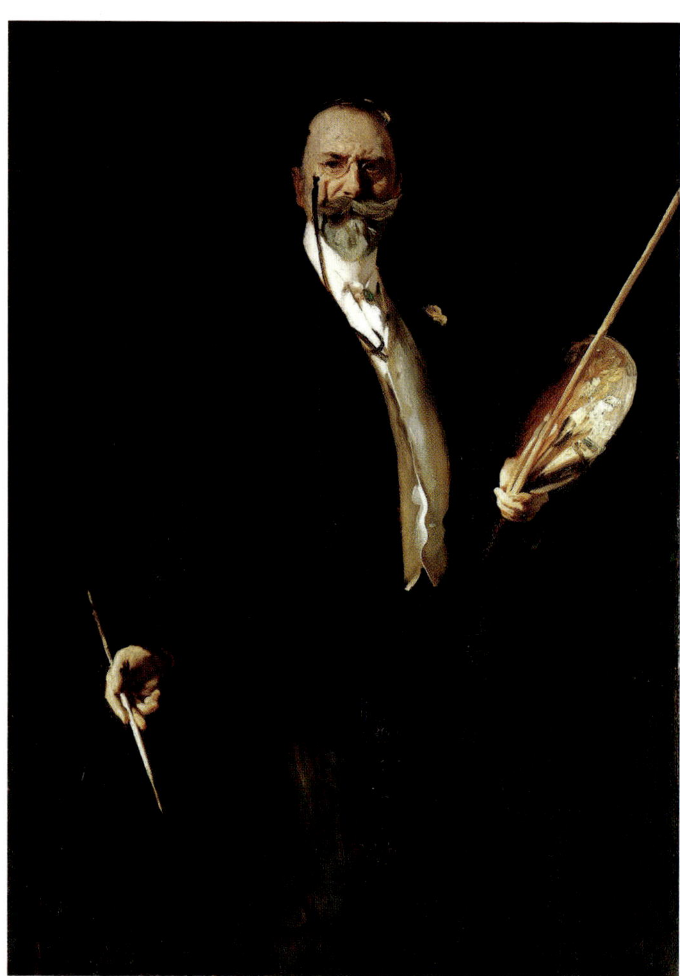

Above: Delighted with Sargent's portrait, William Merritt Chase's pupils exhibited it in New York, Philadelphia and Chicago (see also page 166).

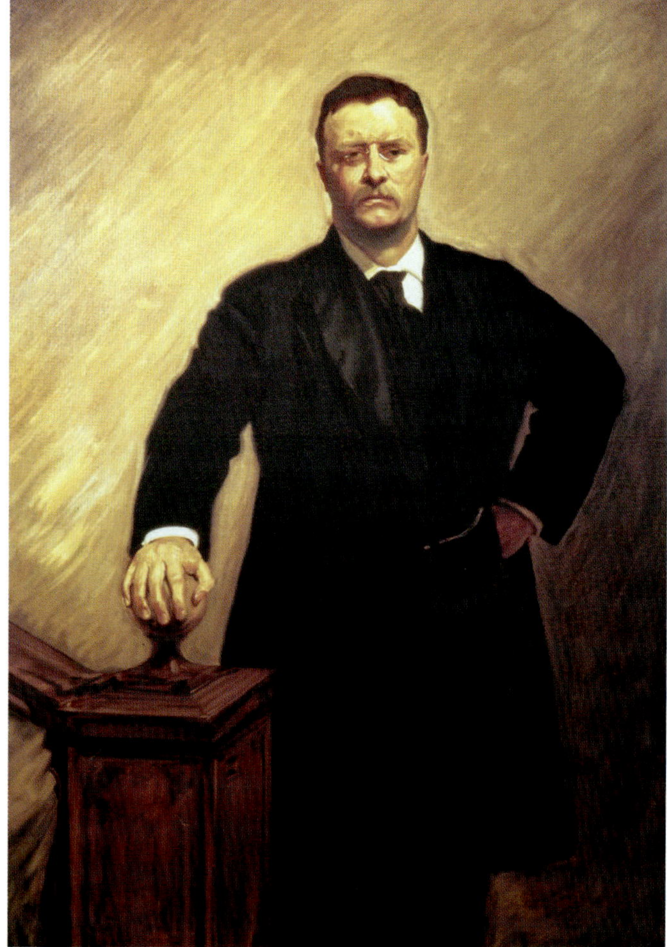

Above: Theodore Roosevelt, 1903, 26th President of the United States. Sargent captured his commanding presence (see also page 180).

only suitable artist and in February 1903, Sargent stayed at the White House for a week to undertake the task. It was not the most comfortable experience. Sargent found the President obstinate and Roosevelt was irritated by Sargent's insistence that nowhere on the first floor was a suitable location. As they went upstairs to look, Roosevelt commented that Sargent did not seem to know what he wanted and Sargent retorted that Roosevelt did not seem to know what was involved in painting a portrait. Furious, Roosevelt swung round, his hand on the newel post, booming: 'Oh don't I!' Sargent was delighted. He had found the pose and location he wanted. The President's schedule meant that he could only spare half an hour for Sargent each day, which was not enough. Still, the portrait was completed and when Roosevelt saw it, he was enchanted.

Not all his portraits worked as well. In January 1905, he began a portrait of Lady Sackville-West (1862–1936). After six weeks, the work was still not completed and Sargent said it was: 'Not good enough to sign.' Lady Sackville-West wrote to a friend that the portrait had: 'a horrid face...But

he wrote afterwards that he would do a drawing of me for Vita's birthday, for nothing!' Sargent completed the complementary charcoal portrait in an hour, and Lady Sackville-West described it as 'charming.'

SARGENT'S METHOD

Sargent's arresting compositions, often featuring cropping and angled light was enhanced by fluid, energetic and rhythmic brushwork. He began most portraits by quickly sketching a few charcoal lines. Then he wiped the canvas lightly with a rag so the lines were barely visible and rubbed a little turpentine-diluted paint over the canvas, picking out mid-tones in the

head, hair and clothing. Next he began painting properly, painting the head in one session and often placing his easel next to his sitter so he could see both the canvas and his subject together. He always started by painting the middle tones to establish values, as that was what Carolus-Duran had taught him. He explained to a friend: 'If you begin with the middle-tone and work up towards the darks, so that you deal last with your highest lights and darkest darks, you avoid false accents.'

Below: La Carmencita, 1905. Sargent preferred capturing the dancer naturally rather than posed (see also page 47).

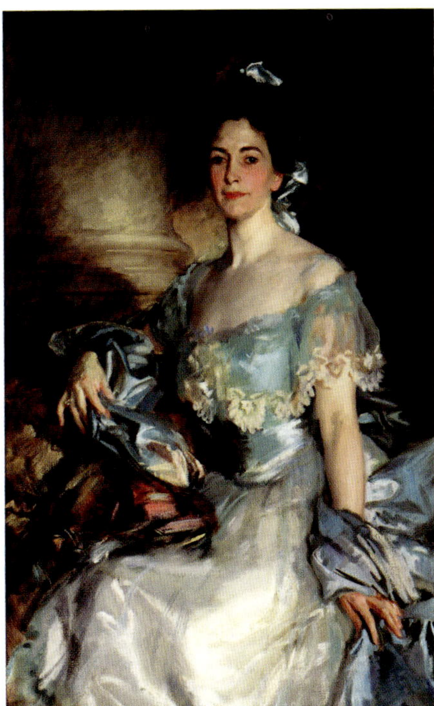

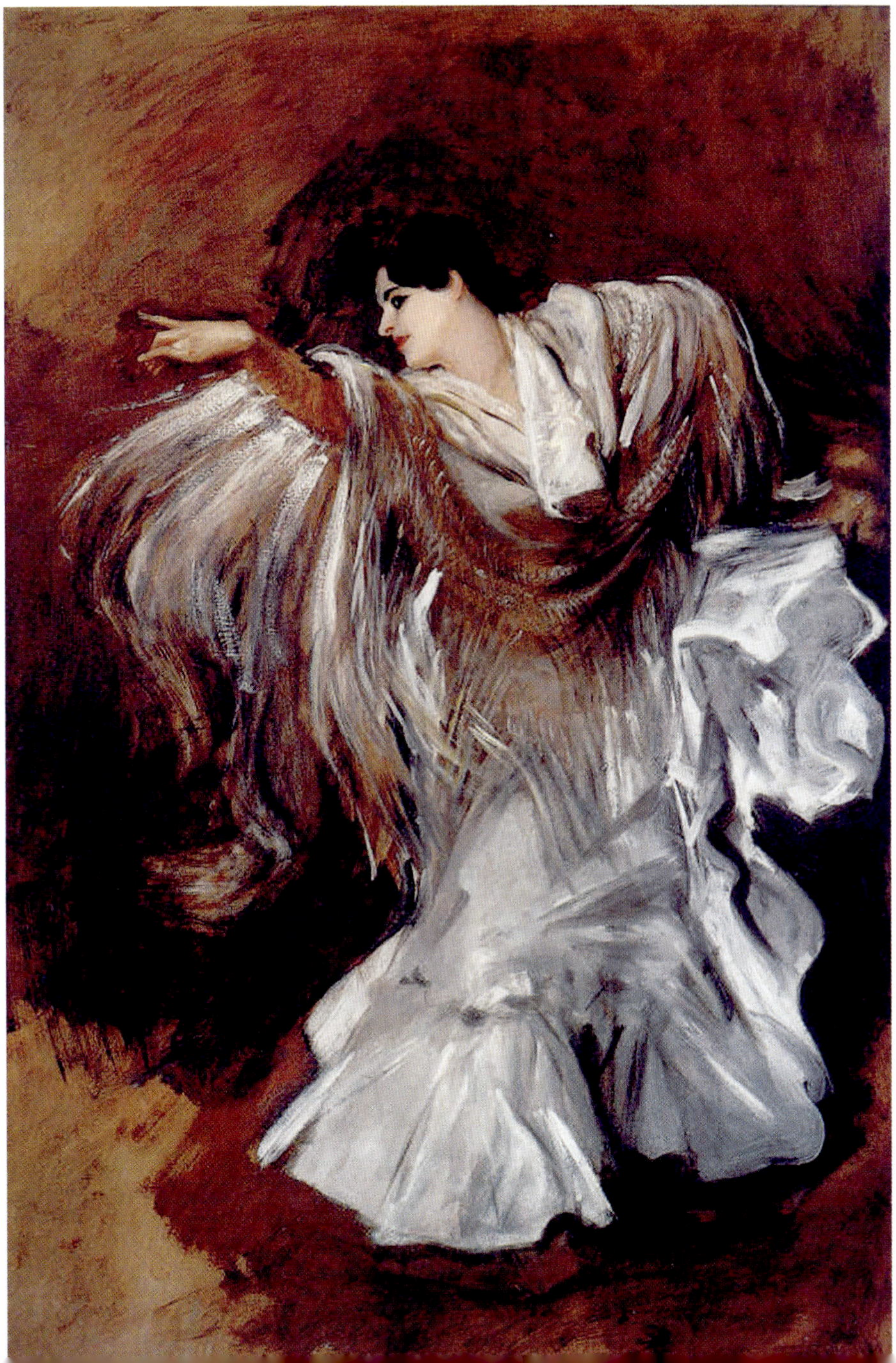

Above: Sargent painted this portrait of Mrs A. Lawrence Rotch (1867–1941) while he was in Boston.

GIVING UP PORTRAITURE

In the early years of the 20th century, Sargent's skills were in greater demand than ever and portrait commissions continued to increase. But his dislike of painting them became overwhelming. In 1907, at the age of 51 and at the peak of his success, he declared he was giving up portraiture.

In 1902, Sargent had shown eight portraits at the Royal Academy, including one he had painted of Thomas Lister (1854–1925), fourth Baron Ribblesdale that had not been commissioned, but he asked to paint. It portrays the quintessential tall, slender aristocrat wearing riding clothes (see page 168). Sargent had first met Ribblesdale, a trustee of the National Gallery at an Artists' Benevolent Fund dinner and in the summer of 1899, stayed at his house. Another of the portraits on display was of the Ladies Alexandra, Mary and Theodosia Acheson; the daughters of the fourth Earl of Gosford. It is believed that the work was commissioned by their grandmother, Louisa, Duchess of Devonshire. Also included at the RA exhibition was a portrait of Mary Hunter's three daughters; Kathleen, Cary Phyllis and Sylvia Hunter. Executed in Tite Street, it is another innovative composition, with the sisters sitting on a circular sofa, their full skirts creating a fan-shape, their pet dog Crack relaxing in the foreground. It was this portrait in particular that inspired Sargent's friend Rodin to declare he was: 'The Van Dyck of our time.' The flattering accolade was followed the next year with the publication of a book of black and white reproductions of several of his paintings, entitled *The Work of John S. Sargent, RA*, with the introduction written by writer, editor and suffragist Alice Meynell (1847–1922).

GALLERY SUCCESSES

By 1905, Sargent began complaining to his friends about the drudgery of executing commissioned portraits. He wrote to his friend Ralph Curtis about his dislike of the work, declaring that he hoped never to have to do another. He also commented to another friend, the French painter Jacques-Émile Blanche (1861–1942): 'What a nuisance having

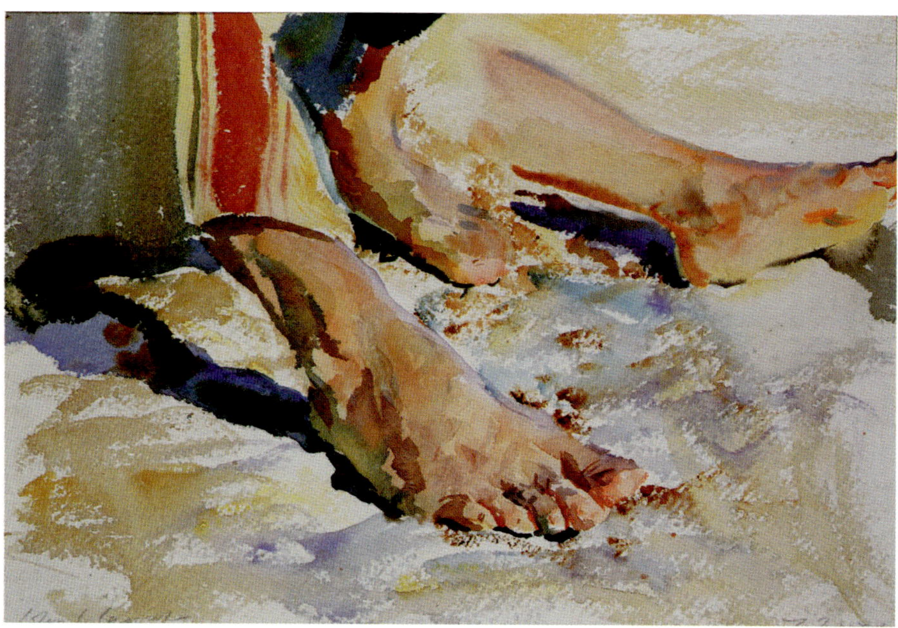

Above: While he was in Tiberias, Israel, researching material for his Boston Library murals, Sargent painted many watercolours like this purely for his own pleasure.

Below: This Study of a Hand demonstrates the detailed preparation and effort Sargent went to when capturing a likeness.

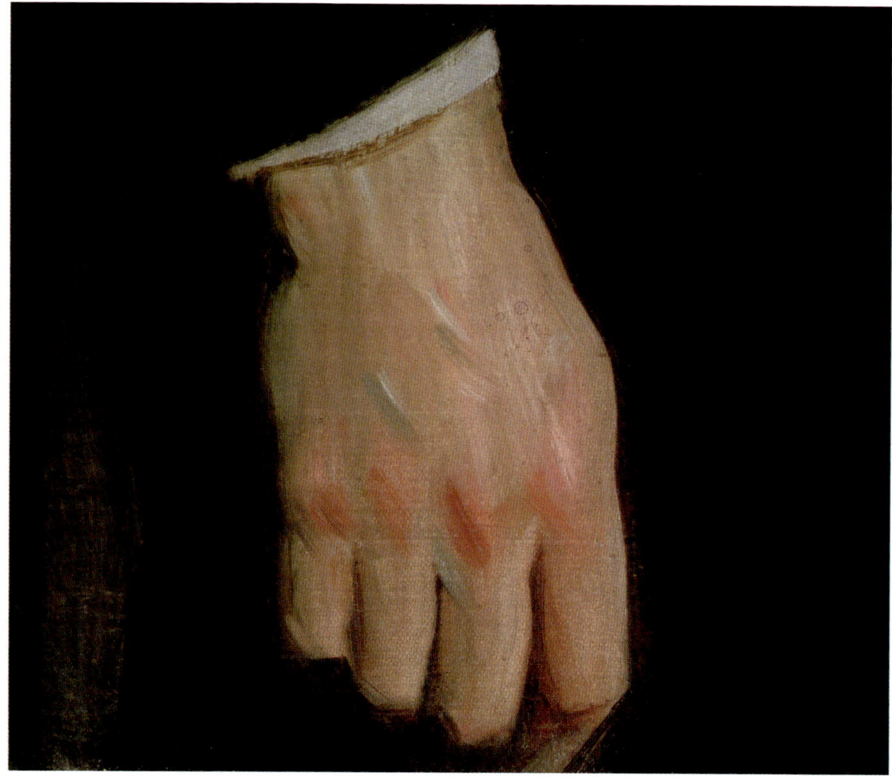

to entertain the sitter and look happy when one feels wretched.' That year he exhibited at the inaugural exhibition of the Albright Art Gallery in Buffalo, New York and showed 47 paintings at the Carfax Gallery in London, 44 of which were watercolours. Among the other paintings, he included *Madame X* for the first time since the scandal of 1884 (see pages 34–35). The following spring, the Museum of Fine Arts, Boston, bought his painting *An Artist in his Studio* for $1,000, the first non-portrait work by him to be purchased by an American museum (see page 187).

A CHANGE OF LIFE

In January 1906, Sargent was in the Middle East when the news of his mother's death reached him. He telegraphed his sisters asking them to delay the funeral until he returned, and wrote to a friend: 'Everything is dreadful except that her friends were good and that death itself came unsuspected and unrecognized.' He was back in England by the beginning of February 1906. The death of his mother was devastating. He had been particularly close to her throughout his entire life. It was she who encouraged him to paint, and who insisted that no matter how many sketches were started each day, one had to be finished; a discipline he adhered to. The shock and grief of his parent's death made him reconsider his own life and mortality. He decided to stop taking on new portrait commissions, declaring: 'Painting a portrait would be quite amusing if one were not forced to talk while working.' From 1907, he finished only those portraits he had already agreed to and a few he could not refuse, such as John D. Rockefeller (1839–1937) and some close friends like Sybil Sassoon, the Marchioness of Cholmondeley, and Henry James. He did, however, produce more than 600 charcoal portraits. In that same year, he painted his last self-portrait, for the Vasari Corridor that links the Uffizi Gallery with the Pitti Palace in Florence.

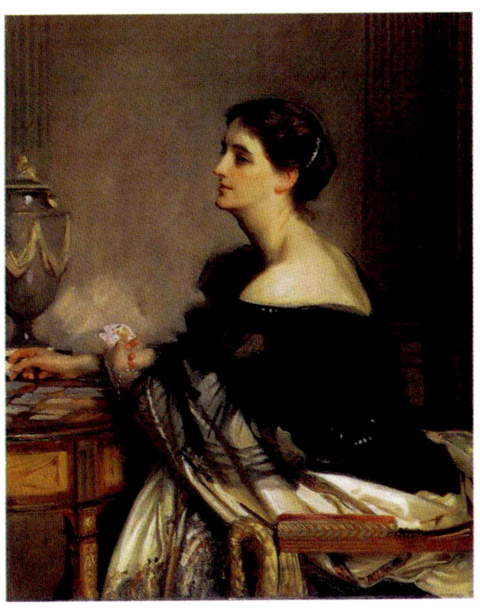

Above: In the year before he gave up portraiture, Sargent painted Sybil, Lady Eden, *mother of the future British Prime Minister, Anthony Eden.*

Below: Painted in 1908, while Sargent was in the Middle East, Melon Boats *is a dramatically cropped, vividly coloured depiction of a moment in time.*

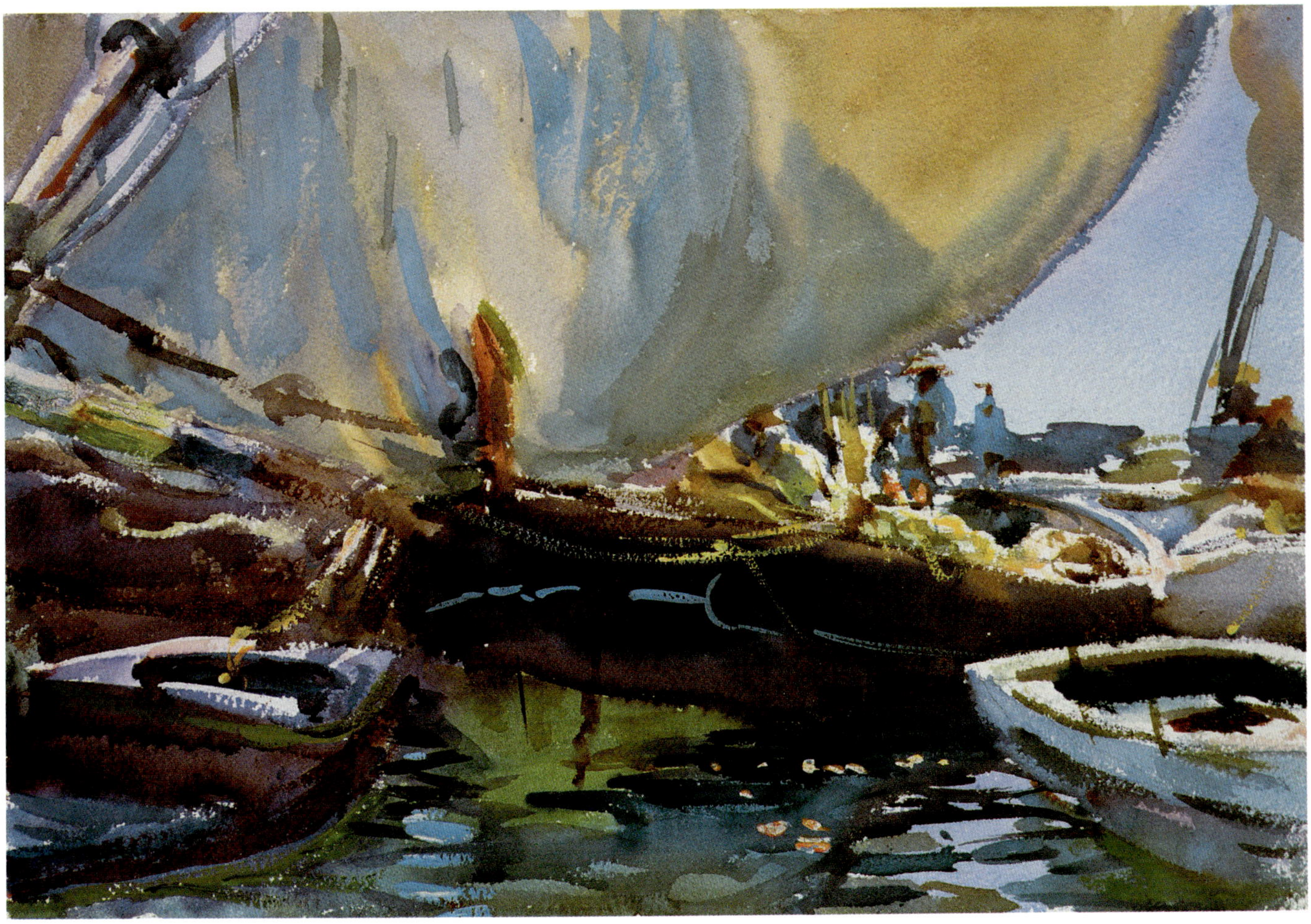

FAMILY AND FRIENDS

In the year in which he relinquished portrait painting, Sargent also declined a knighthood in England as it would have meant renouncing his American citizenship, which he was not prepared to do. That summer, he travelled to Purtud in the Aosta valley, where he painted his companions in exotic, oriental-style clothing.

LETTER TO THE PRIME MINISTER

When the British Prime Minister, Sir Henry Campbell Bannerman (1836–1908) offered Sargent a knighthood on the recommendation of King Edward VII, Sargent decided that he did not relish the honour as much as he enjoyed retaining his US citizenship. So he wrote the Prime Minister a short letter declining the honour:

'The Rt. Honble. Sir Henry Campbell Bannerman
[from] 31, Tite Street, Chelsea

Dear Sir Henry,
I deeply appreciate your willingness to propose my name for the high honour to which you refer, but I hold it as one to which I have no right to aspire as I am not one of His Majesty's Subjects but an American Citizen.
Believe me,
With very great respect,
John S. Sargent'

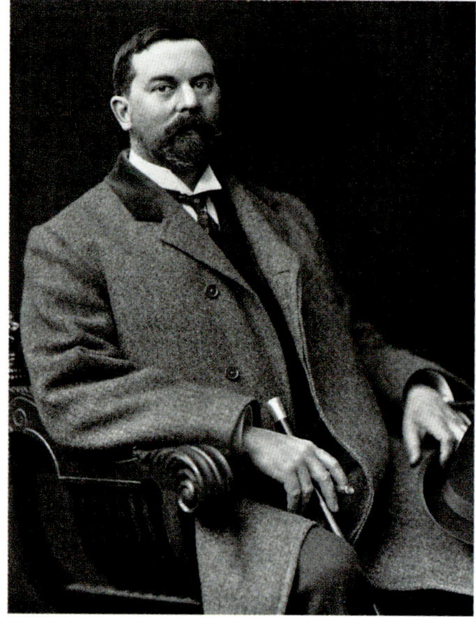

Above: A black and white photograph of Sargent taken in 1908.

Below: Dolce Far Niente, c.1907. Val d'Aosta in Italy became one of Sargent's favourite locations, and he spent part of several summers painting there.

COLOUR AND CONTRAST

That August, Sargent travelled to Purtud with Emily, Violet and her children, Jane and Wilfrid de Glehn, and Polly Barnard, who long ago had modelled for him in *Carnation, Lily, Lily, Rose* (see pages 40–41). Sargent loved Purtud almost as much as Venice, and produced some of his most bucolic paintings of his friends there, relaxing; painting, playing chess or simply sitting amid the beautiful landscape. He also made several watercolours of the streams that ran through the area. He began taking several cashmere shawls with him on these trips, specifically to paint the textures and colours and display their richness against the lush scenery. He became quite obsessed with making a feature of the women of his party wearing the shawls, and of catching the reflected elements in sparkling, flowing mountain streams. All friends and family members accompanying him on these holidays became used as models. That

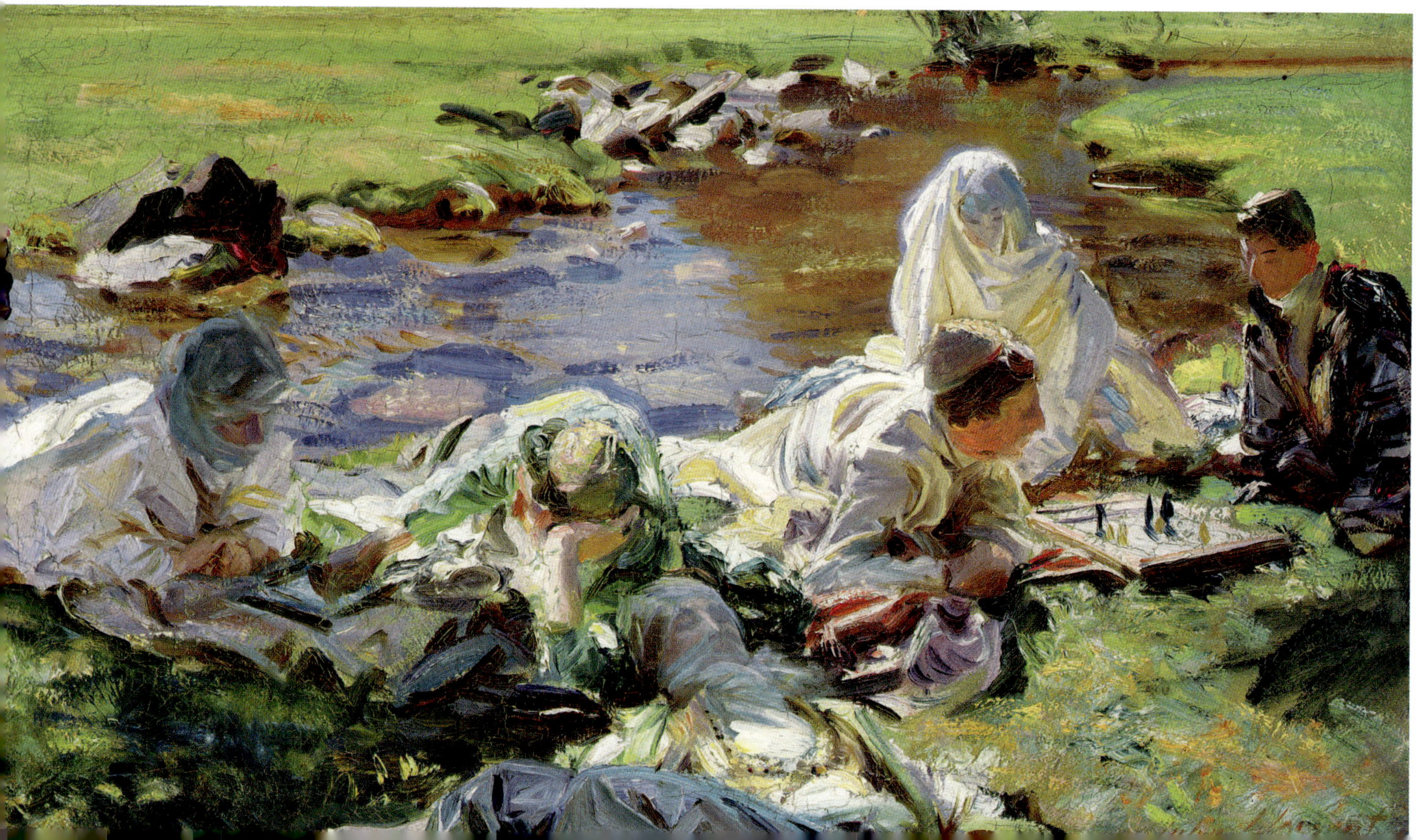

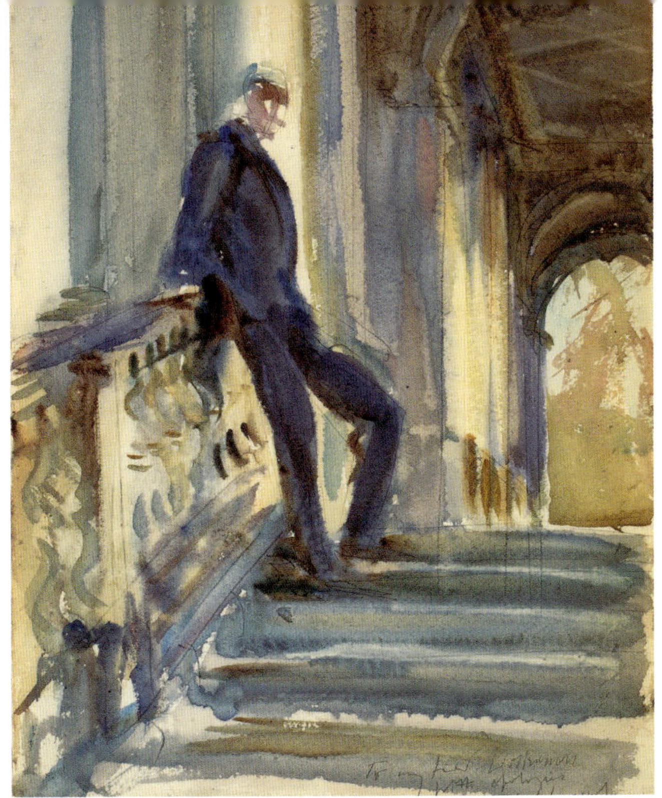

Left: Sir Neville Wilkinson on the Steps of a Palazzo, *1904–05. Sargent inscribed this 'To my friend Wilkenson [sic], with apologies'.*

Right: William Butler Yeats *(1865–1939) found Sargent 'good company', and this portrait of him, drawn for the frontispiece of his 1908* Collected Poems *'charming' and 'very flattering.'*

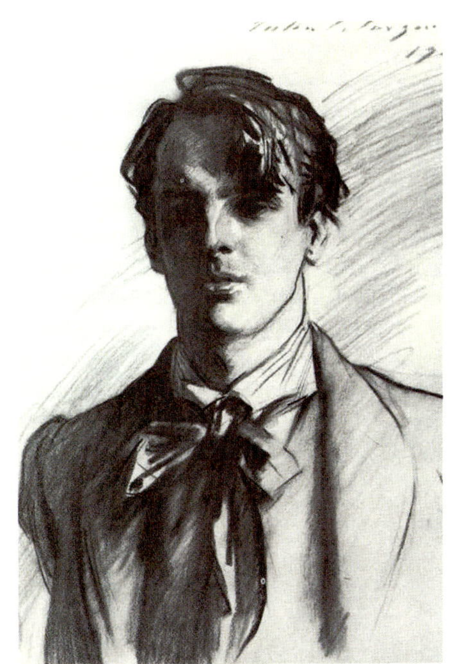

summer, he frequently painted his sister Violet and her two daughters, Reine and Rose-Marie, in paintings glowing with warmth and exuding a sense of calm recreation, such as *The Brook, The Game of Chess, A Siesta, Turkish Woman by a Stream* and *Lady in a Bonnet.*

The following month, he was in Venice staying at the Palazzo Barbaro, and then travelled with Emily and Eliza Wedgwood to Perugia and Narni, in Umbria, Italy. Once again, Jane and Wilfrid de Glen joined them and went with them to Frascati, and to Rome and its environs. While in Frascati, Italy, Sargent painted Jane and Wilfrid in *The Fountain, Villa Torlonia* (see page 205). His oils and watercolours of 1907 to 1908 featured ladies in cashmere shawls; from 1909 his models usually wore white dresses and held parasols. All emanate an exotic, indolent impression. His oil palette at this time included silver white, Naples yellow, yellow ochre, ochre dew (English red), red ochre, vermilion, ivory or coal black, and Prussian blue, from which he created a vibrant spectrum of colours.

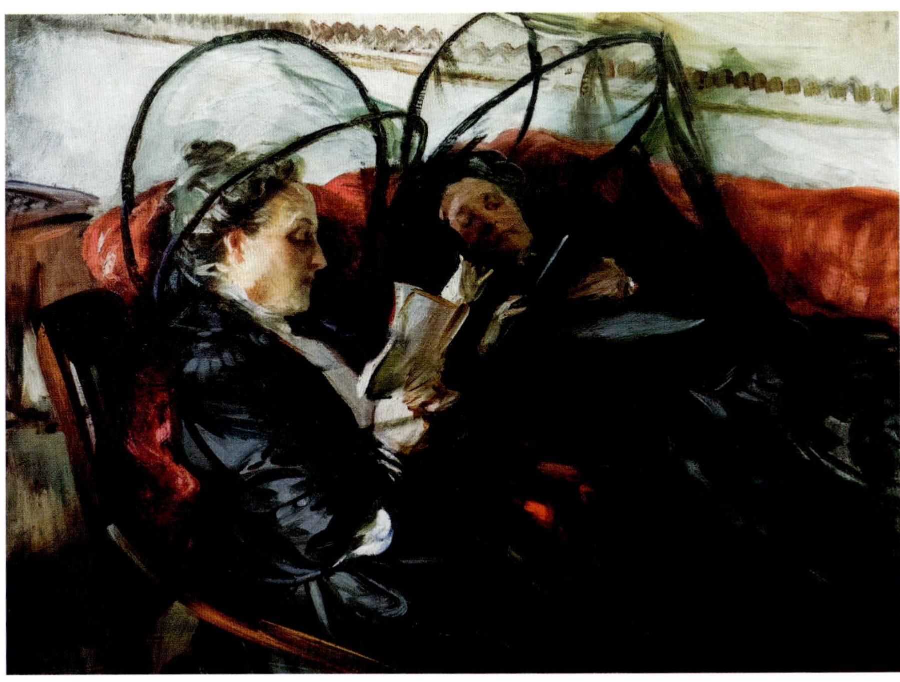

SARGENT'S PAINTING ADVICE

From 1897 to 1900, Sargent taught at the Royal Academy Schools. His advice gives technical insights into his own painting methods, such as: 'Painting is an interpretation of tone through the medium of colour drawn with a brush. Keep the planes free and simple. Always paint one thing into another, and not side by side, until they touch. The thicker your paint, the more your colour flows. Simplify, omit all but the most essential elements. You must clarify the values. The secret of painting is in the half tone of each plane, in economizing the accents and in the handling of the lights. You begin with the middle tones and work up from it...so that you deal last with your lightest lights and darkest darks, and avoid false accents. Paint in all the half tones and the generalized passages quite thick.'

Left: Mosquito Nets, *1908, painted in Valdemossa in Majorca. Eliza Wedgwood wrote of this unusual work: 'Sargent painted in oils such an amusing picture of Emily and me...[in] Emily's invention for keeping out mosquitoes.'*

RELAXED AND INFORMAL

One of the main reasons that Sargent was happiest abroad was his inherent shyness, which may seem odd considering the large number of friends with whom he travelled. But he was not comfortable with many aspects of his own celebrity, particularly when he was expected to present a public persona to the world.

As he felt relaxed abroad, Sargent loved to depict his friends similarly relaxing in beautiful surroundings, and often swathed in the costumes or accessories he provided. These were not meant to be replicas of indigenous costumes, but were intended to depict a general exotic appearance. Another favourite theme was of fellow artists painting. His first work in this theme was *Paul Helleu Sketching with his Wife*, 1889, (see page 53). In 1904 in Purtud, he painted *An Artist in His Studio* (see page 187), his friend Ambrogio Raffele (1845–1928) using a cramped hotel bedroom as a studio. To paint the scene, Sargent also had to squeeze into the small room with his paints and easel. Another painting of Raffele during the same holiday is the sketchy watercolour: *A Glacier Stream in the Alps*. Since the death of their mother, Sargent's sister Emily was his closest holiday companion and in 1908 in Majorca, he painted *Miss Wedgwood and Miss Sargent Sketching* showing Emily holding a paintbrush between her teeth while dipping another into a box of paints. Eliza sits companionably by her side.

THE ROYAL WATERCOLOUR SOCIETY

In 1904, Sargent had exhibited for the first time with the Royal Society of Painters in Water Colours, later the Royal Watercolour Society or RWS, and he was elected an associate member soon after. Four years later, he became a full member. The custom in art academies and societies was that once elected, full members donated a work of high standing, called their 'diploma work.' Sargent's diploma painting was the detailed *Bed of a Glacier Torrent* painted in Purtud in 1904. (*An Interior in Venice* of 1898 had been his diploma work for the Royal Academy.) By 1905, he had become as celebrated for his

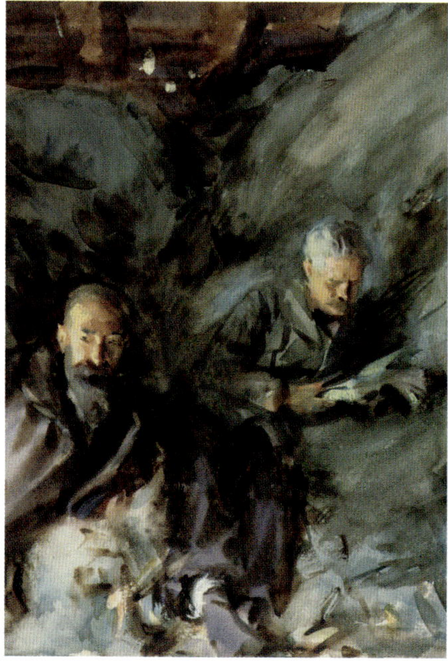

Above: In a Hayloft, 1904. *Depicted here are the Italian artists Ambrogio Raffele and Carlo Pollonera (1849–1923), who painted with Sargent in Purtud.*

Below: A Glacier Stream in the Alps, *c.1904 – with rapid brushwork, Sargent captured Raffele painting in Purtud.*

watercolours as for his portraits and like those, he used many original and unusual techniques.

A GREAT REALIST

In 1908 and 1909, Sargent travelled even more than usual. For instance, in August 1908, he stayed in Breuile, an Alpine region in north-west Italy, with his friends Polly Barnard, Dorothy Palmer (1880–1961), and the artist brothers Lawrence Alexander 'Peter' Harrison (1866–1937) and Leonard 'Ginx' Harrison (1870–1939). The following month he travelled with Emily and Eliza to Barcelona and Majorca, and in February 1909, he exhibited in New York in a two-man show with his old friend Ned Boit. Later that month, Vanity Fair published a caricature of him, dressed in evening clothes, holding a cigarette, titled 'A Great Realist.' Remaining in the United States, Sargent worked on the Boston Public Library vaults and lunettes during March and from August until November, he was in the Val d'Aosta and Venice, then Corfu, staying with the de Glehns, Emily

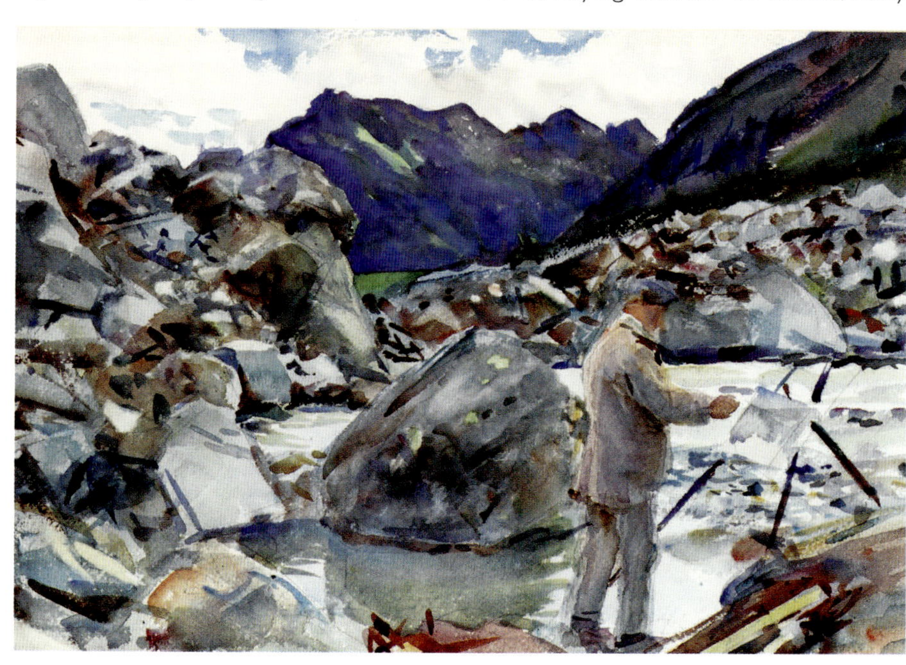

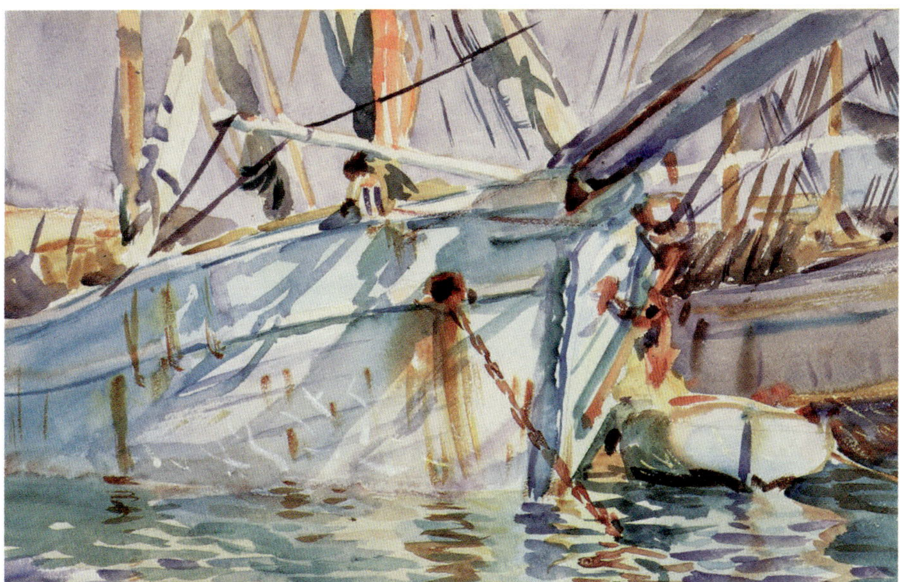

and Eliza. They stayed in the hotel St George in Corfu town for five days and then in a villa four miles away, where they discovered the Italianate gardens of the Villa Soteriotisa with its urns, terraces, orange trees and sea views. Sargent spent a great deal of time painting there.

Above: In a Levantine Port, c.1905–06. *Here Sargent is not so much exploring the location or the boats, but focusing on colour, reflected light and cast shadows.*

Below: Fascinated by the natural landscape of Corfu, Sargent painted zealously while staying there in 1909.

MORE AWARDS

In recognition of Sargent's outstanding achievements and great popularity, as well as the Chevalier of the Legion of Honour in France in 1889, which was elevated in 1896 to Officier, his status as Royal Academician, and the offer of a knighthood in Britain, he was also given various honorary doctorates from universities in the United States and Britain, and further honours from France and Belgium. In 1903, the University of Pennsylvania bestowed him with the degree of LLD. The next year, he was awarded the DCL from Oxford University. In 1909 he was conferred the LLD by Cambridge University, the French Order of Merit for distinguished service in art, and the Order of Leopold from Belgium. In 1916, he was granted both the LLD from Yale and the Doctor of Arts from Harvard Universities.

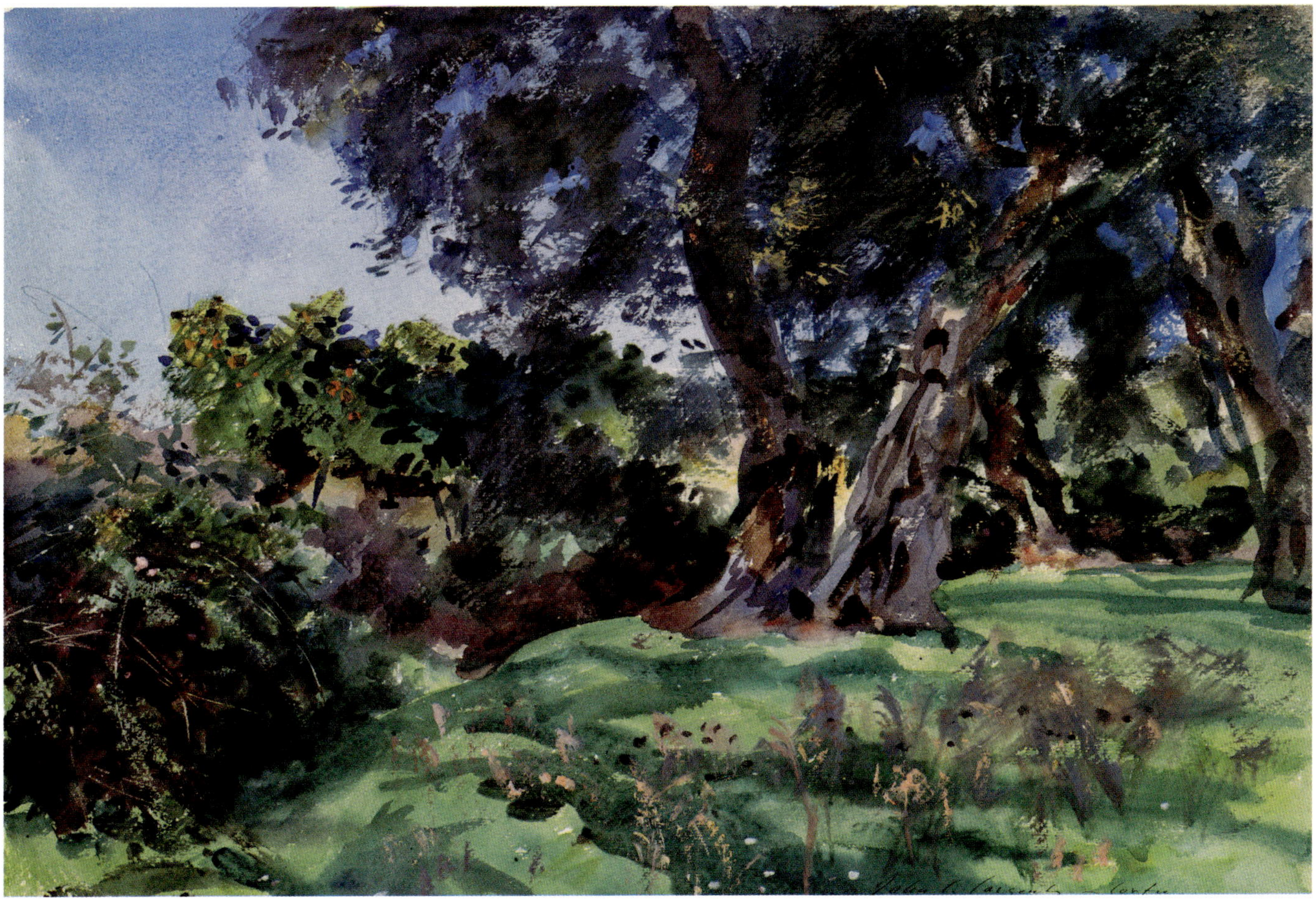

LIGHT AND SHADOWS

Watercolours enabled Sargent to be more expressive with colour and light than he had been with oils. Although he had a delicate touch with oils, his handling of watercolours was even lighter and more spontaneous, and he used them to evoke sparkling sunlight and the atmosphere of the scenes he painted.

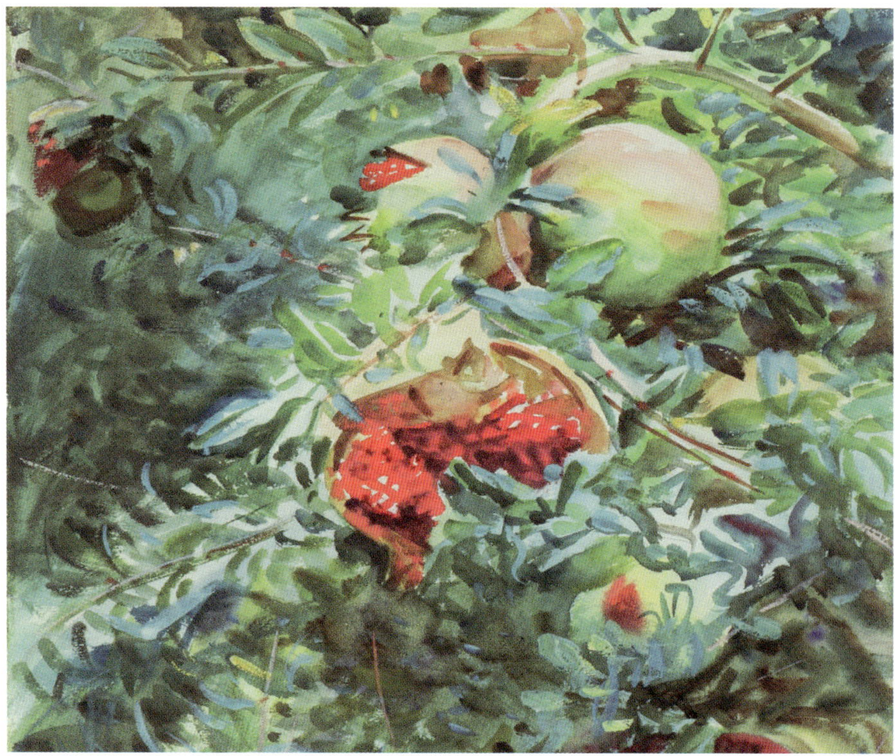

Above: Pomegranates, *1908. Inspired by the lush vegetation of Majorca, this close-up image contrasts bright red seeds against dense green foliage.*

Below: Landscape, Corfu, *1909. An Impressionistic watercolour painted en plein air of a path through the trees.*

IMPRESSIONIST INFLUENCE

Although in 1892, Sargent had relinquished all attempts at creating his own version of Impressionism, he nevertheless remained influenced by several ideas of the movement, and this became apparent in his watercolours, in such things as his rejection of black and his use of colours for highlights, shadows and reflections. He often used blue and mauve shadows on white for instance, while sunlight on white was frequently conveyed with amber, yellows and pinks. Using these soft or vibrant colours, he powerfully portrayed both direct and reflected light, creating a sense of light and airiness. Two paintings, an oil of 1888 and a watercolour of 1910, demonstrate his interest in Impressionistic concepts. The oil painting, *A Morning Walk*, is of his 18-year-old sister Violet and recalls Monet's paintings of 1775 and 1886, in its depiction of a young woman dressed in white, holding a parasol (see page 134). Like Monet's paintings, Sargent focuses on the effects of sunlight on the young woman. Twenty-two years later, he painted Violet's 17-year-old daughter, his niece Rose-Marie, in *The Cashmere Shawl* (see page 225). The young woman is, again, in a white dress, this time draped with a cashmere shawl. Both of these paintings celebrate and embrace light and shadows through colour to portray white, and both are graceful, ephemeral images of young women who look away from viewers, beyond the picture.

In 1909, Sargent was staying in the villa, Mon Repos, south of Corfu town, and painted a hut in the grounds. *Light and Shadows, Corfu* is typical of his interest in capturing the impression of light on objects and demonstrates his fascination with the ways in which shadows from the olive tree branches create patterned shapes on the plain white walls. As with most of his

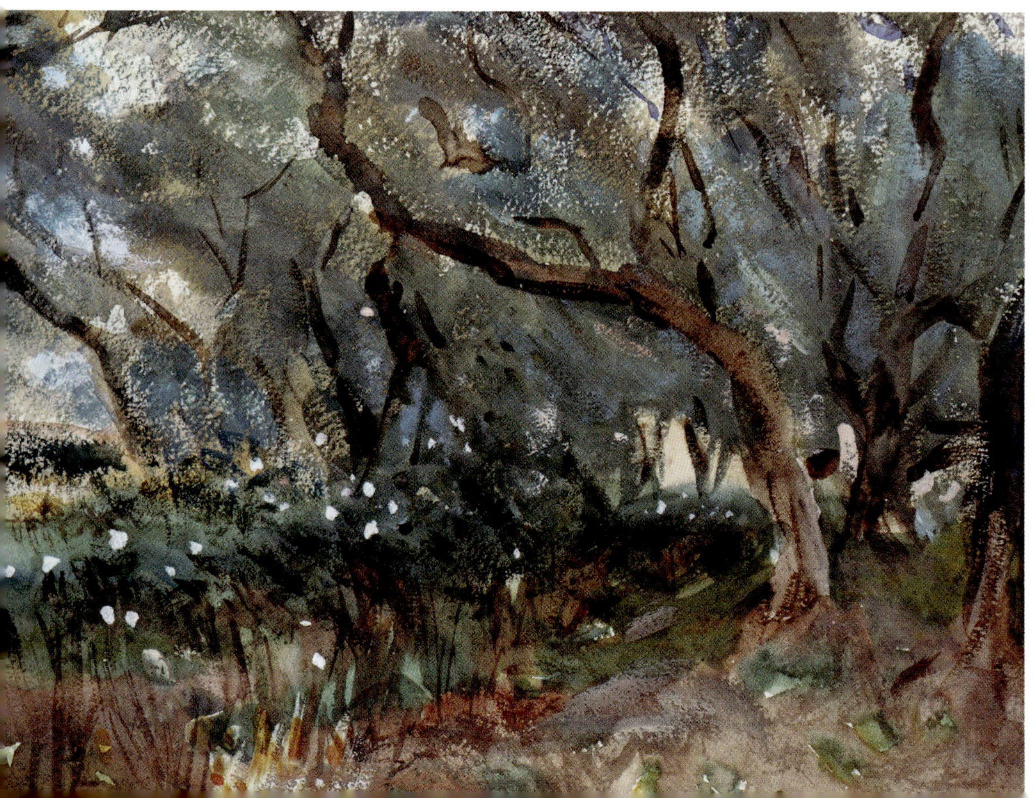

watercolours, his hues are jewel-bright, not natural, with amethyst and topaz shadows on the hut, emerald and sapphire on the doorway, bright blue on the roof, and mid-tones created with purples, pinks and yellows. The cropped, simplified composition creates an immediate and powerful impact.

GROUND AND SKY

Sargent admitted that expansive views and vast skies did not appeal to him, and this can be seen in many of his outdoor watercolours; skies and even grounds are often not visible or are minimized, as he focused on objects bathed in light and colour rather than broad panoramic views. He preferred to build up tapestry-like images of colours and textures across an entire work, emphasizing the decorative elements of his compositions and allowing his energetic, gestural brushwork to create more expressive forms of imagery than static pictures.

WHITE AND WATER

Throughout his career, Sargent often heightened the impact of his paintings with areas of white space – usually highlights – that draw the eye in and around the composition. But it was not until the 20th century that he began deliberately and frequently featuring actual white objects as a visual draw, including the hulls of boats, dresses, parasols, rocks, animals, buildings – and during World War I – tents. In watercolour, white was made either from the paper being allowed to show through or the use of opaque gouache, or he created it with soft colours, such as violet and peach. *Two White Dresses* of c.1909–11 (see page 86) was specifically a study of frothy white dresses. The models are actually his niece, Rose-Marie, painted twice.

During the 1880s, Sargent was fascinated by Monet's floating studio; later, his gondola in Venice, waterside locations in Majorca and his own floating boat-studio in Florida enabled him to depict the shimmer of light on water, demonstrating his continuing fascination with the ways sunlight defines shapes and space.

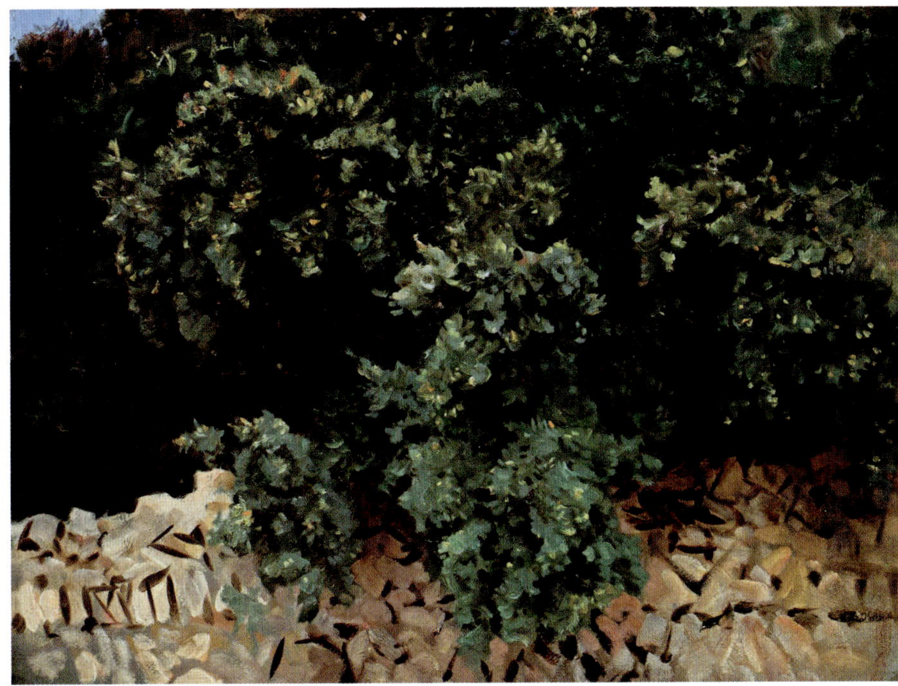

Above: Ilex Wood Majorca, *1908 – Sargent asserted that: 'enormous views and huge skies do not tempt me'.*

Below: Villa Torlonia, Frascati, *1907. Loose brushwork and tonal contrasts depict an elaborate stone fountain.*

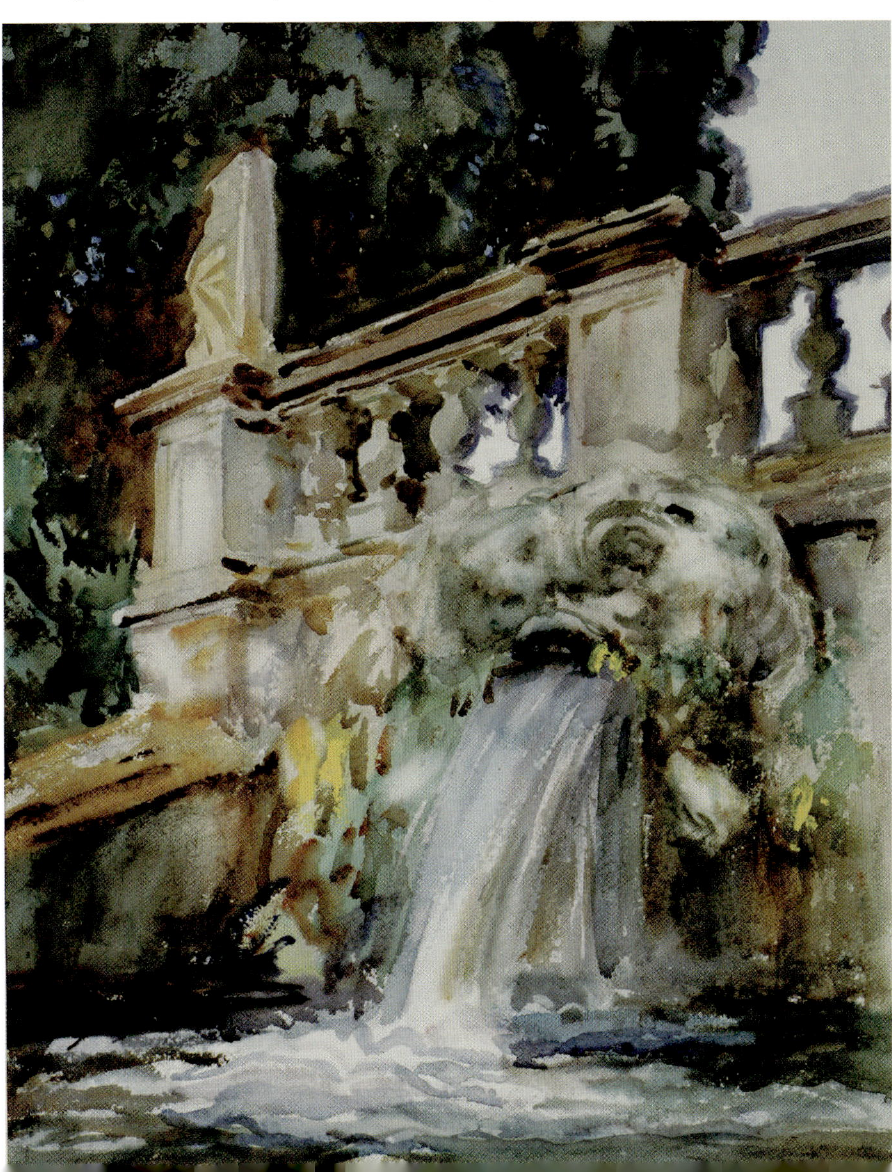

ITALY

Despite living in England and retaining his American citizenship, Sargent spent a great deal of time in the country of his birth. Whether in Venice, Purtud, Florence, Naples, Rome or Frascati, all his paintings of Italy demonstrate his inherent love of the country and appreciation of sensual beauty.

Sargent returned to some part of Italy every year and the paintings he produced there represent the scope of the country and its heritage, from ancient ruins to breathtaking scenery, including lakes, mountains, sculpture, fountains, gardens, rivers, streams, canals, hills, flowers and architecture. Yet even his more humble subjects, such as the interior of a wine cellar in Florence painted in about 1882, or leather wine bags hanging on a wall that he painted nearly 30 years later, or the workmen at the Carrara quarry (see page 71) of 1903, convey his affinity with the country and its people. In 1910, at the same time as painting the Florentine wine bags, he also painted a large watercolour of *Florence: Torre Galli*. This square composition portrays the

Right: Sargent used graphite, watercolour and gouache to paint the Statue of Vertumnus at Frascati *in 1907.*

Below: Painted in the Florentine Boboli gardens in 1907, this expresses Sargent's enjoyment of juxtaposing stone statues and lush greenery, light and shadow.

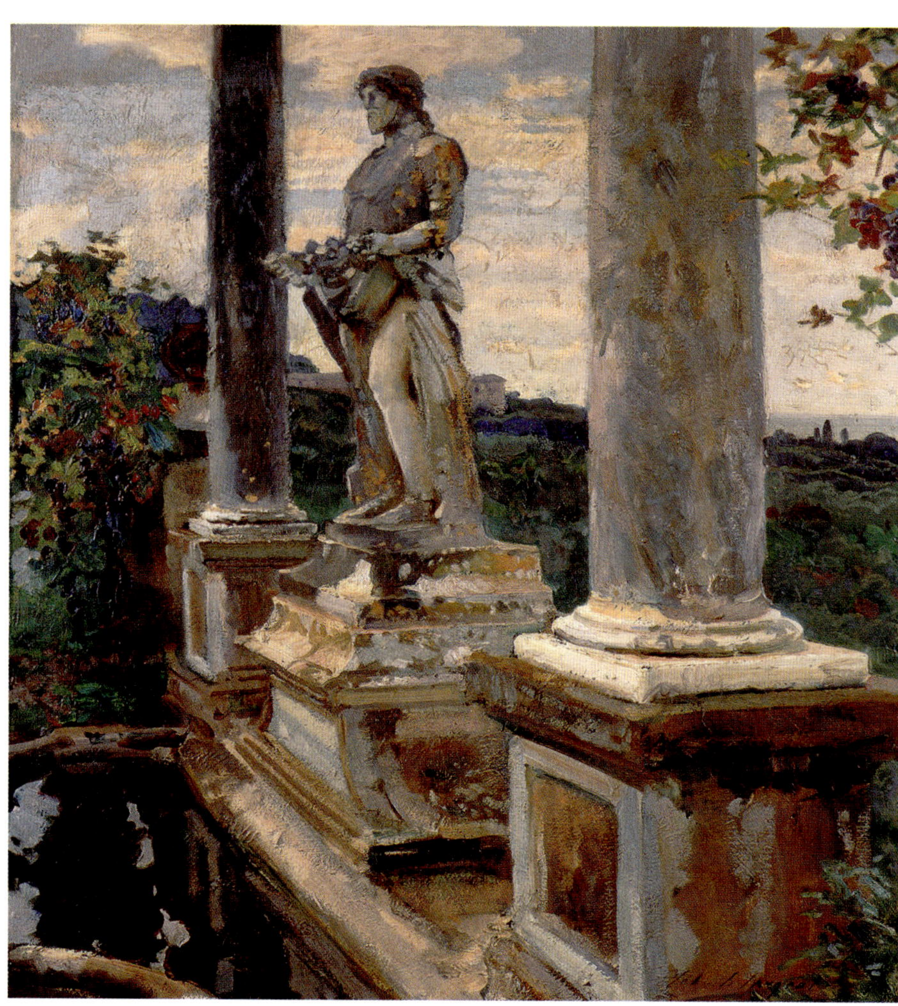

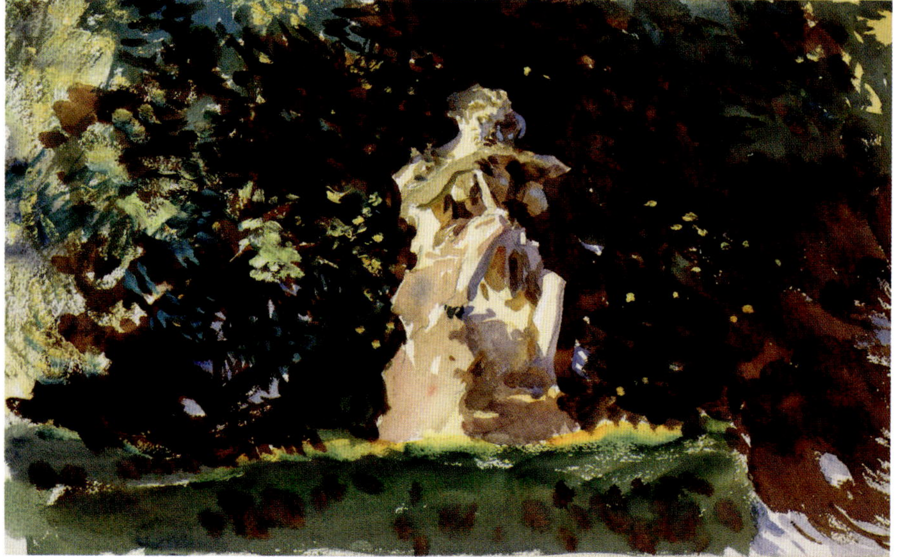

courtyard of the Castello di Torre Galli, originally built as a castle in the 15th century. It had been turned into a grand home in the 19th century and Sargent stayed there with fellow artists Jane and Wilfrid de Glehn, Sir William Blake Richmond (1842–1921) and his second wife, Lady Clara Richmond (dates unknown), and Emily and Eliza, having been lent it by his friend the Marchese Farinola.

Sargent's love of Italian architecture, light, vegetation and approach to life pervades his paintings, as can be seen especially in his Venetian works. While his depictions of Venetian architecture are often highlighted or bleached by the sun, his scenes of activity on the waterways are demonstrated through dramatic, intensely coloured shadows.

THE SIMPLON PASS
Naturally restless, Sargent never liked staying in one place for long. In 1909,

Right: With a light touch, Sargent captured this spontaneous, ethereal view In the Dolomites *in 1914.*

Below: The Palazzo Labia and San Geremia, *Venice, 1913, looking north west at the merging of the Grand Canal and the Cannaregio Canal.*

he travelled from Purtud to the Simplon Pass, where he had been before in 1904. The Simplon Pass links Switzerland and Italy, and Sargent and his party stayed at the Bellevue Hotel there in 1909, 1910 and 1911. On these extended visits, his friends came and went. Regulars were

Emily and Eliza, the Ormond family, the Harrisons, the Barnards, the de Glehns, Raffele, Davidson the Archbishop, and the artists Adrian Scott Stokes (1854–1935) and his wife Marianne (1855–1927). While he painted, Sargent's companions indulged in picnics, walking

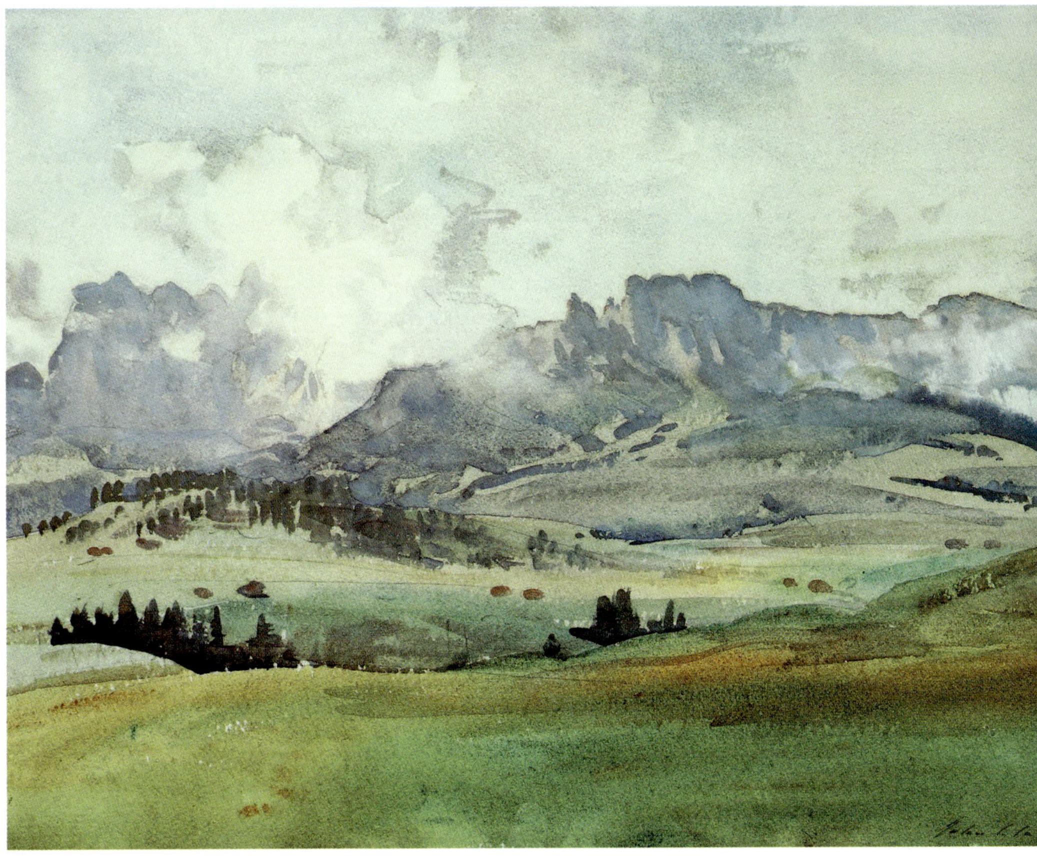

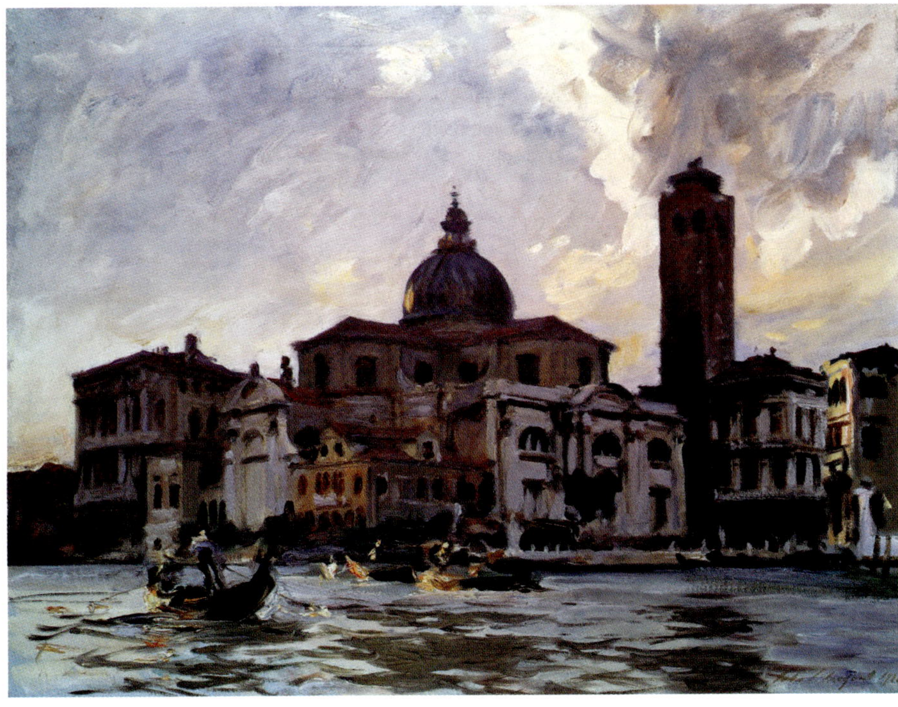

expeditions and games of chess or cricket. Adrian Stokes recalled his time away with Sargent: 'My recollections of him during our first happy stay on the Simplon Pass are still vivid. Though he most likely considered himself to be on holiday, his industry was constant. Whatever the weather was, he came down early – not extravagantly early – and I think the time was 8.30, when, if fine, he started out, accompanied by his often heavily laden manservant [Nicola d'Inverno], for one of the landscape subjects he had in progress, or to find a new one…When once settled and protected maybe by as many as three painting umbrellas – one to keep off a cold wind, another the sun, and a third some tiresome reflection – the rapidity and directness with which he worked was amazing…'

THE RIFT

Since the scandal of *Madame X* had dissipated, criticism of Sargent's work was minimal. He remained sought after and highly esteemed in America and England. Then, in the earliest years of the 20th century, the artist and art critic Roger Fry wrote a series of adverse appraisals of his work.

DISPARAGEMENT

Initially, Fry's criticism was more to do with his desire to shake up British sensibilities and enlighten artistic tastes than to do with Sargent's work specifically. He wanted to make gallery goers aware of the groundbreaking art that was being made in other parts of Europe, particularly in Paris. In 1900, he reviewed a group exhibition at the New Gallery in London and acknowledged Sargent's portrait of *Major-General Ian Hamilton* as a brilliant example of his work, but declared that in general, Sargent was a 'précis-writer of appearances' with 'no desire to transcend the mood of ordinary life' and that he missed 'fundamental traits of character' and 'important emotions' because he only painted external appearances. Three years later, in an unsigned review of Sargent's solo exhibition at the Carfax Gallery, he wrote that Sargent was 'our best practitioner in paint', but he could only be categorized with the 'professionals' and not the 'poets' – meaning that his work was slick and emotionless rather than thoughtful. He wrote that Sargent's Venetian sketches appeared to be painted by an 'ordinary tourist,' that his colour would appeal to 'the common man' and his gondoliers portrayed a 'vulgarly picturesque type.' He added that for all his painting skills, Sargent lacked imagination and 'finer perceptions and instincts.'

OTHER NEGATIVE VOICES

In 1905 in the magazine *Les Arts de la Vie*, Comte Robert de Montesquiou (1855–1921), who had been painted by Whistler and Boldini and was the model for Proust's character Baron de Charlus, reviewed *The Work of John S. Sargent, RA* from 1903. Apart from the portrait of Madame Pierre Gautreau, Montesquiou wrote that Sargent did not deserve his high status, and that Boldini was a better artist, as unlike Sargent, he used intelligence to convey

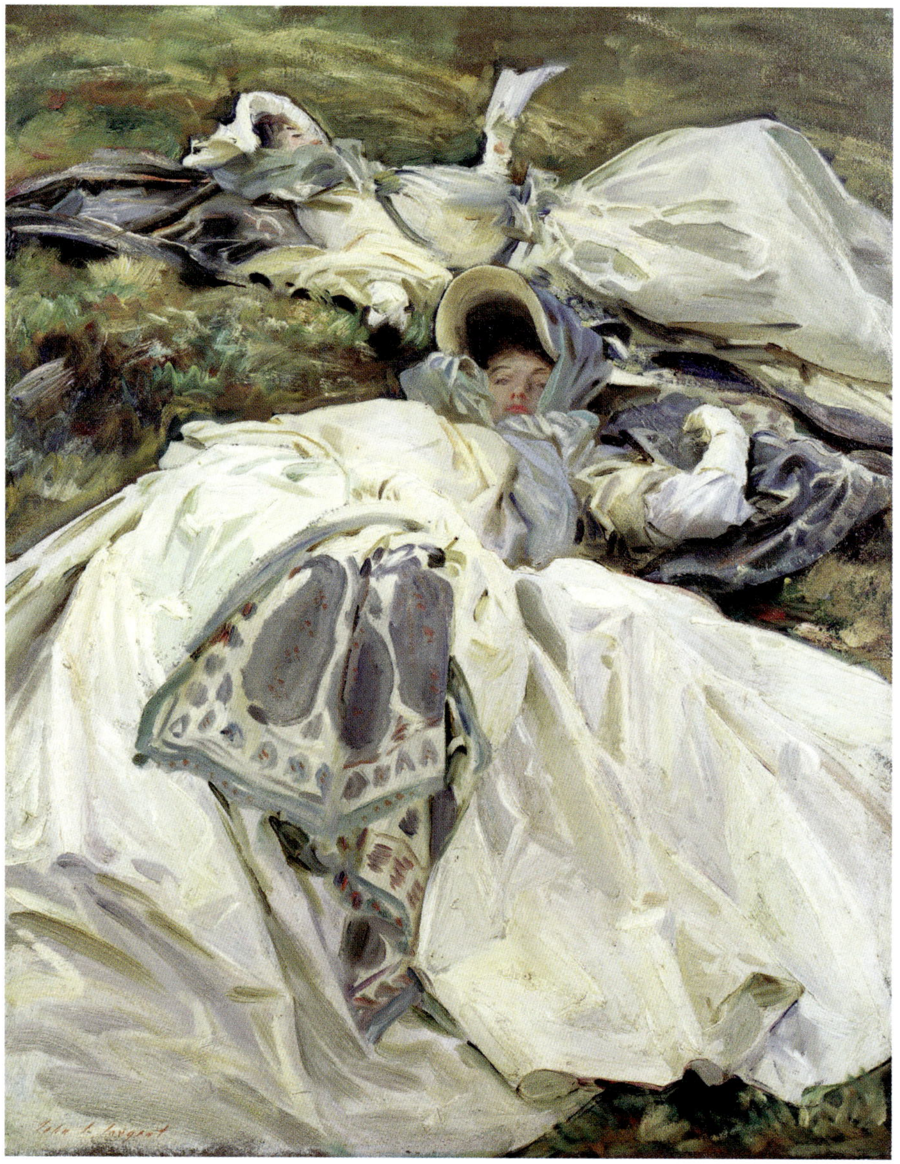

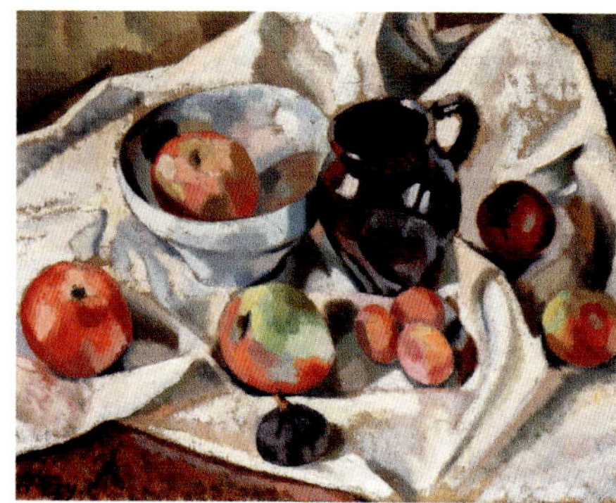

Above: Roger Fry's Still Life with Apples, Plums and a Jug, *of 1919, shows a dramatic change in his previously realistic style, and a response to Cézanne's art.*

Left: Two White Dresses, *c.1909–11, Sargent's use of paint was experimental, but does not explore inner feelings as many modern artists were doing.*

the character of his sitters. In 1910, Sickert wrote his essay *Sargentolatory* censuring the critics who were so reverent of Sargent. None of this had much of an effect on Sargent however. His enormous popularity meant that any criticism of him was quite insignificant. The wealthiest individuals still commissioned him, and the most esteemed galleries in America and England were buying his work.

THE DISAGREEMENT

Encouraged by the rest of the Bloomsbury Group, Fry decided to show several artists' work that he admired in an exhibition at the Grafton Galleries in London in November 1910. Although all had died relatively recently, these artists had broken new artistic ground. They included Paul Cézanne, Paul Gauguin, Vincent van Gogh (1853–1890) and Georges Seurat (1859–1891), and Fry named their work Post-Impressionism. He also included work by the Bloomsbury Group and Édouard Manet (whom Sargent also admired greatly), and so Fry called the exhibition *Manet and the Post-Impressionists*. It ran until January 1911.

Although criticism of the exhibition was intense, nonethelss over 25,000 attended. In an attempt to raise opinion of the art displayed, Fry wrote three articles for *The Nation,* an influential New York weekly journal. One article listed artists who supported the aims of Post-Impressionism, and included Sargent. Sargent responded in two open letters to *The Nation*, making clear his unfavourable opinions of Post-Impressionism. From then on, Fry became Sargent's greatest detractor. Even after Sargent's death, Fry continued censuring him, damaging his

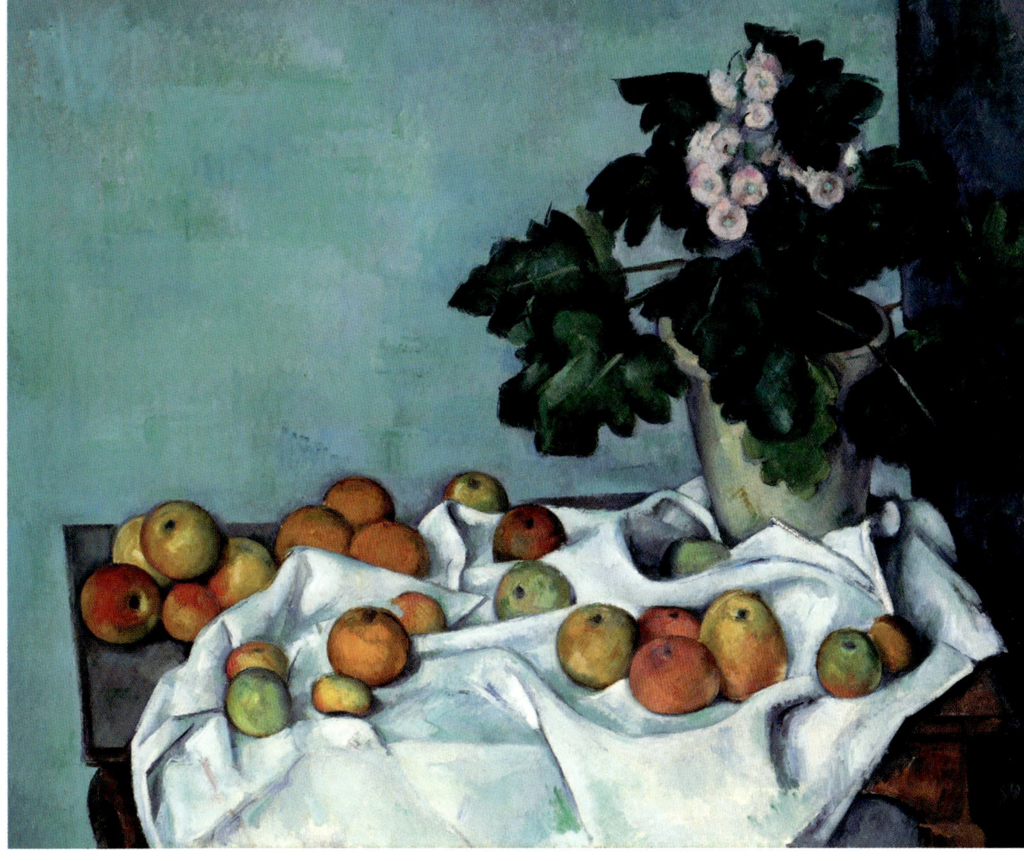

reputation for the next 50 years. His reaction to Sargent was fuelled in part by his anger that people did not accept Cézanne as a genius.

Above: Still Life with Apples and a Pot of Primroses, *1890, a still life painted by Paul Cézanne. The dynamic effect he creates was highly influential to Fry, among many others.*

Left: Matamoe or, Landscape with Peacocks. *In 1892 Paul Gauguin's bright, flat colours and symbolism were perceived by many as a lack of skill.*

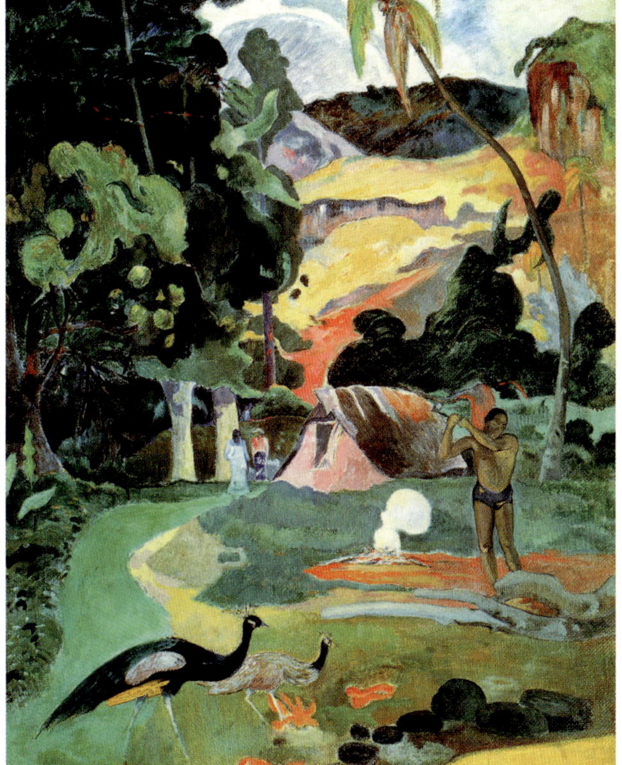
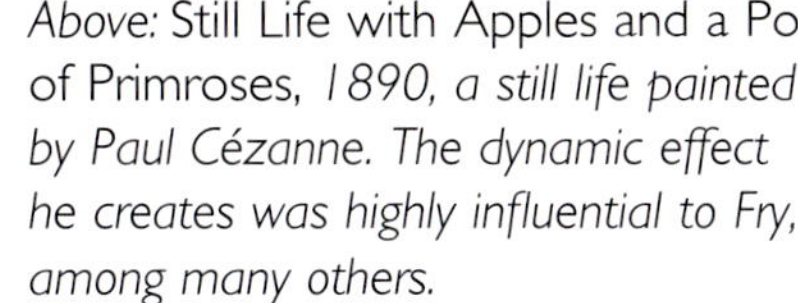

THE BLOOMSBURY GROUP

In 1905, a group of writers and intellectuals began meeting and sharing ideas at the London home of the artist Vanessa Bell (1879–1961) – who had been one of Sargent's pupils – and her writer sister Virginia Woolf (1882–1941). They became known as the Bloomsbury Group, and over the next 30 years, they produced some of the most important literature of the 20th century, and art that was recognized by avant-garde groups in Paris. Roger Fry was also part of the Bloomsbury Group.

PAINTING OBJECTIVELY

Meanwhile, Sargent continued painting and travelling, his work still greatly in demand. To fulfil the continued requests for his portraits, he now made them in charcoal, which he could produce quickly and were greatly admired. He seemed as oblivious to Fry's criticisms as he was to the impending threat of war.

FRIENDSHIP AND SUPPORT

If Sargent was affected by Fry's criticisms, he did not show it, and never once counter-attacked his opponent. Apart from his disparaging appraisal of Post-Impressionism in *The Nation*, neither did he usually criticize other artists. On the contrary, he was intensely supportive of many. For instance he had been particularly involved in helping to secure Manet's work for the French nation in 1889. When another friend, the Scottish painter Robert Brough (1872–1905) was fatally injured, Sargent rushed to his side. After Brough died, Sargent wrote an introduction in the catalogue for an exhibition of Brough's paintings: 'The developing of this natural gift into a perfectly supple and practised medium seems to be the direction in which his progress can best be traced when one follows it through the interesting series of portraits that are now gathered together in tribute to his memory.' In June 1911, he was in Munich with Adrian and Marianne Stokes when he received a letter from the wife of his old friend Edwin Austin Abbey. Abbey was dying, but some murals he had been working on were not finished. Sargent rushed back to England to his friend's bedside, and after Abbey had died, supervised the completion of his murals.

In April 1912, another good friend died, Frank D. Millet, with whom Sargent had stayed in Broadway in 1885, and where he had painted *Carnation, Lily, Lily, Rose* (see page 40). Millet had been travelling first class on the RMS Titanic's maiden voyage when it hit an iceberg and sank in the North Atlantic. Millet was one of the 1,517 who drowned. It was reported that he was last seen helping women and children into lifeboats.

PAINTING OBJECTIVELY

That summer, Sargent travelled to the French Alps with the Ormonds, staying in Abriès, Isère and the Dauphiné. The year before, he had stayed for weeks in a hut, devoid of all comforts, to paint the views around Carrara. Fascinated by boulder-strewn slopes, it appears he was as comfortable painting the Alps and rocky locations such as Carrara as he was depicting Baroque or Renaissance architecture. Unlike many more modern artists, he was not interested in representing his underlying feelings or any symbolism about these places, but concentrated all his powers instead on depicting objective realities. He told his friend Sir Edmund Gosse that: 'modern painters make mistakes in showing that they know too much about the substances they paint.'

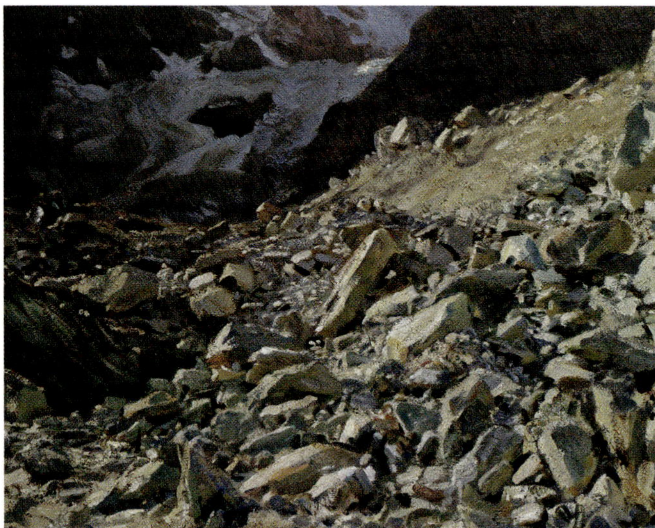

Left: The Moraine, *1908, oil on canvas. Intense observation enabled Sargent to create an objective image, with no sentimental interpretations.*

Below: Olives, Corfu *was probably painted by Sargent in 1909, when he was staying on the island and painted several images of olive trees.*

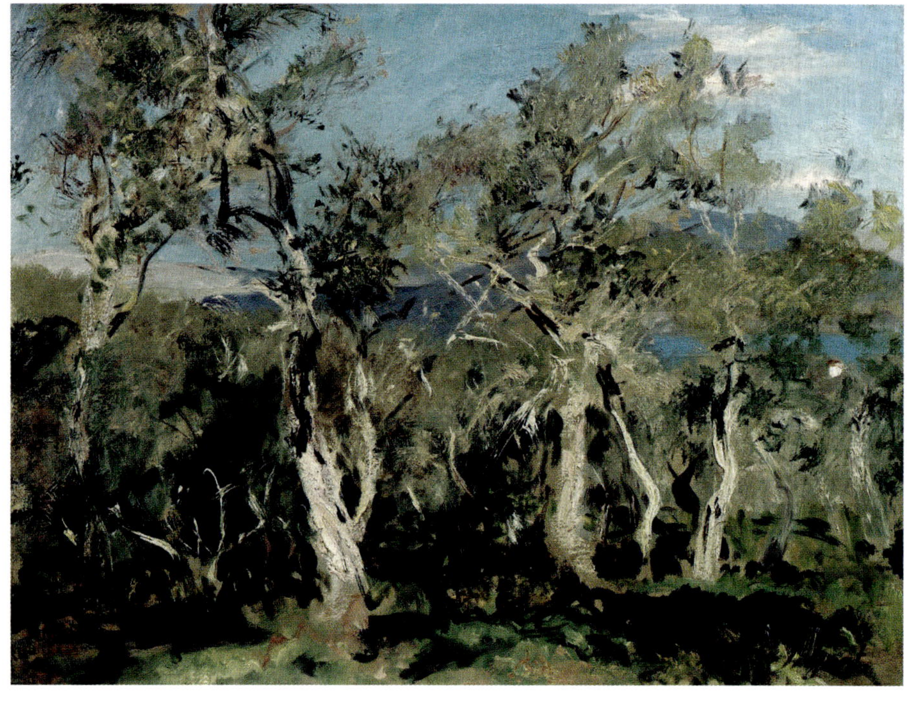

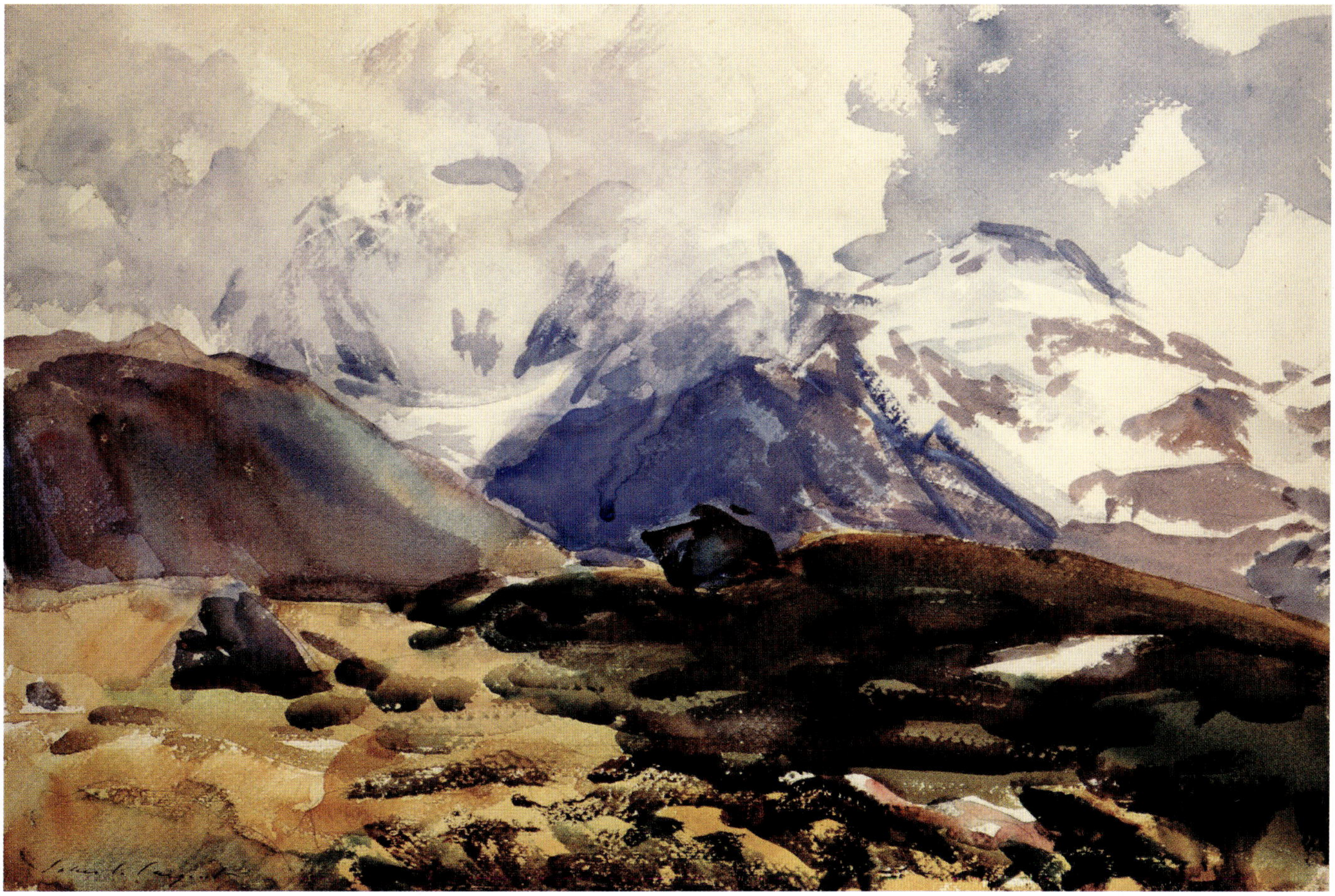

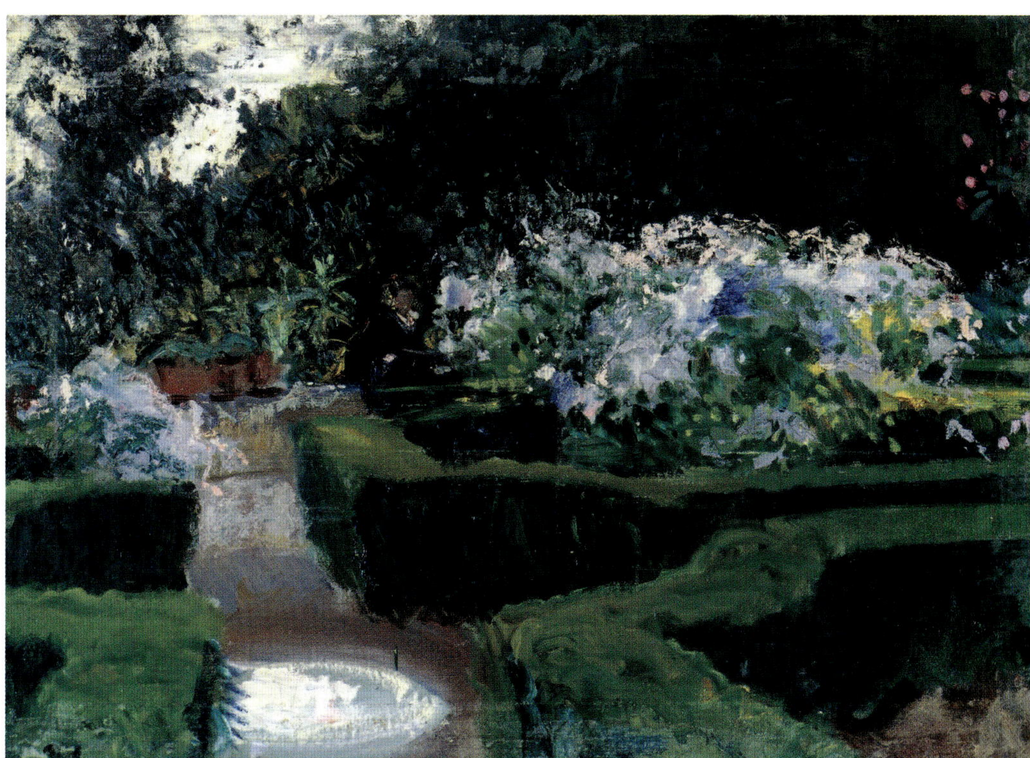

PAINTED DIARIES

From September to November, Sargent travelled to Spain with Emily and the de Glehns. They stayed in Seville and Granada and Sargent painted in and around the Alhambra, the fortified palace where the Moorish kings spent their last years before being expelled in 1492.

Moorish architecture fascinated him and he captured its elegant columns, arches and stonework. He also went to Corfu and Venice that year, and painted several scenes in oil and watercolour. His second cousin, Mary Newbold Patterson Hale later wrote: 'Other travellers wrote their diaries; he painted his.'

Above: The Simplon, *c.1910. In pencil and watercolour, Sargent focused on tonal contrasts and a sense of atmosphere.*

Below: Sargent painted Garden at Granada *in 1912, while he was staying in Spain with Emily and the de Glehns. This is part of the gardens of the Alhambra.*

MFA ACQUISITIONS

In the month before the sinking of the Titanic, Sargent had shared a second joint watercolour exhibition with his friend Edward Darley Boit in New York, after which, the Museum of Fine Arts in Boston (MFA) bought 45 of Sargent's watercolours and 38 of Boit's. This was a great accolade for both artists as in general, significant museums and galleries did not buy watercolours. Boit had also recently loaned Sargent's 1882 painting of his children (see page 120) to the MFA, and after their father's death, the Boit children gifted this painting to the museum.

HENRY JAMES

With their similar situations as Americans living in Europe and their mutual friends, Sargent and James are often compared, with Sargent's art perceived by many as an equivalent to James's writing. Since they had first met in Paris in 1884, James took an active role in Sargent's social and working life.

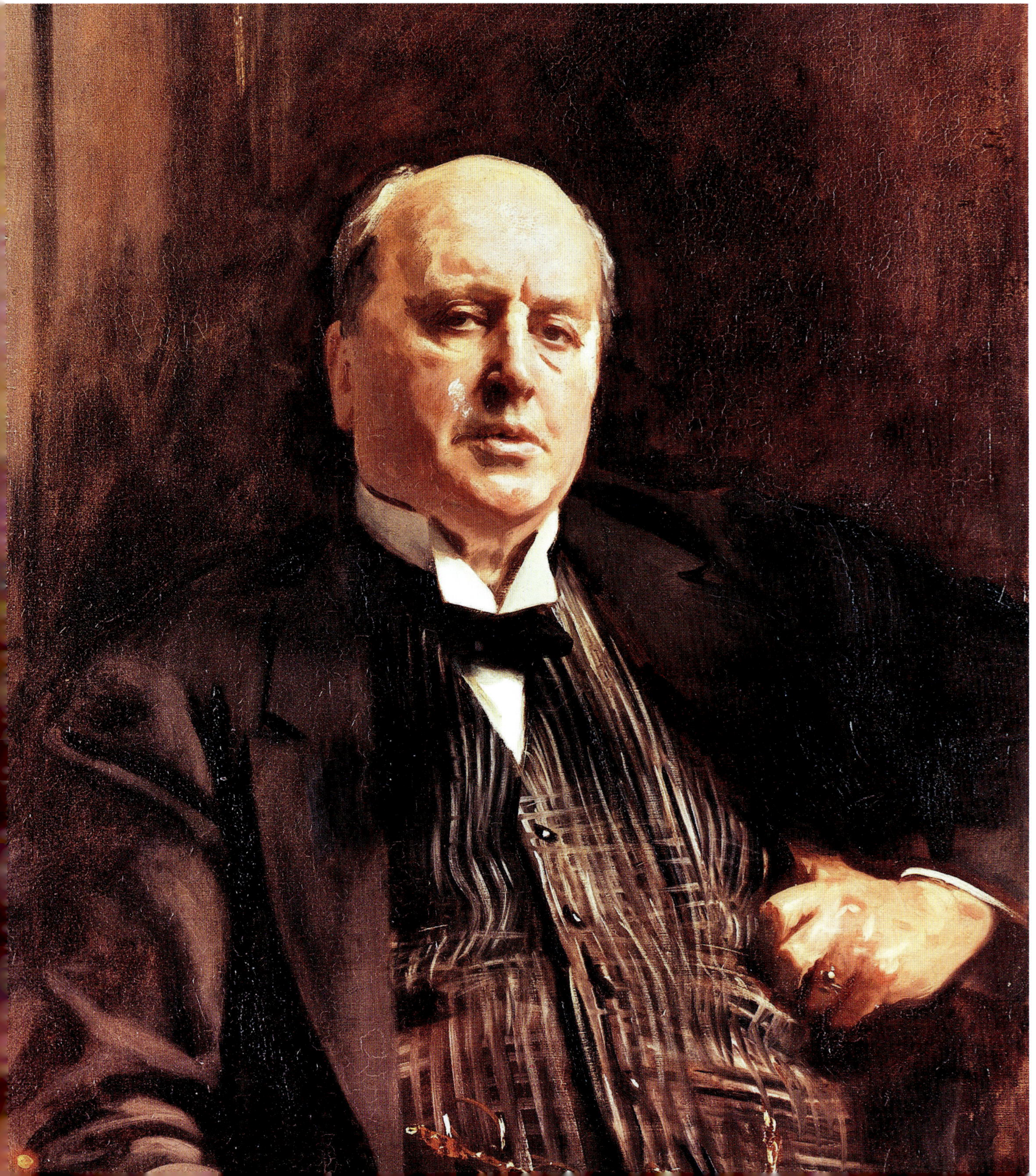

In October 1887, *Harper's New Monthly Magazine* featured a review by James of Sargent's work, which greatly increased Sargent's reputation (see page 43). The two men shared a wide circle of friends and acquaintances in Paris, England and America, and one of their mutual friends, W. Graham Robertson, recalled that Sargent and James were: 'real friends. They understood each other perfectly, and their points of view were in many ways identical.'

BIRTHDAY GIFTS

In 1886, Sargent had drawn a profile of James, and in 1911, he had made a second, unsuccessful charcoal drawing of him. Then in 1913, he was commissioned to paint a portrait of him by the novelist's English friends and admirers as a 70th birthday gift. Nearly 300 people formed a committee to raise money for the birthday. Everyone donated no more than £5 each, and with the money, they bought James a Charles II porringer and dish. The remainder was offered to Sargent for the portrait, but he would not accept payment for painting his great friend. Instead, the money was given to the British sculptor Francis Derwent Wood (1871–1926) to produce a bust of James as well. The sittings began on 8 May 1913 and on 18 June, James wrote to his brother William (1842–1910): 'One is almost full-face with one's left arm over the corner of one's chair back, and the hand brought round so that the thumb is caught in the arm-hole of one's waistcoat and said hand, therefore, with the fingers, a bit folded, entirely visible and 'treated.' A week later, he wrote to the Welsh novelist and short story writer Rhoda Broughton (1840–1920): 'It is now finished, parachevé (I sat for the last time a couple of days ago;) and is nothing less, evidently, than a very fine thing indeed, Sargent at his very best and poor old H. J. not at his worst, in short, a living, breathing likeness and a masterpiece of painting...' Over several days in December 1913, the committee members were

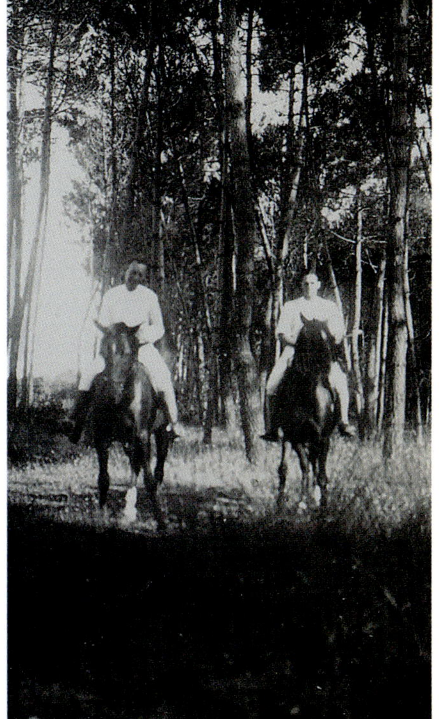

Top left: Photo of Sargent riding with a friend in a pine forest at Forte dei Marmi, near Lucca in Tuscany, Italy.

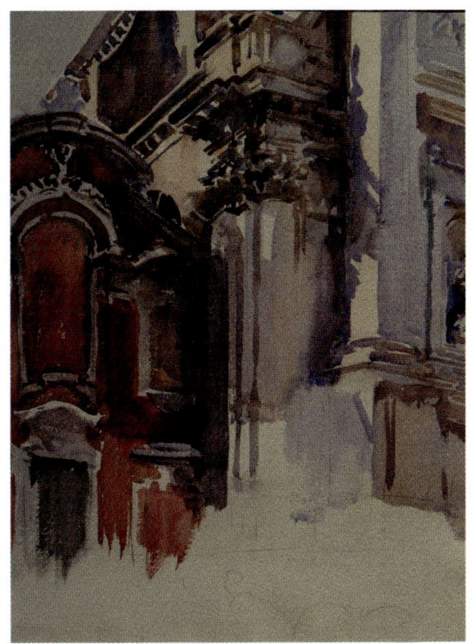

Left: Watercolour sketch for the oil painting of St Stae (see page 235), showing Sargent's method of layering tones – as used for his portrait of James.

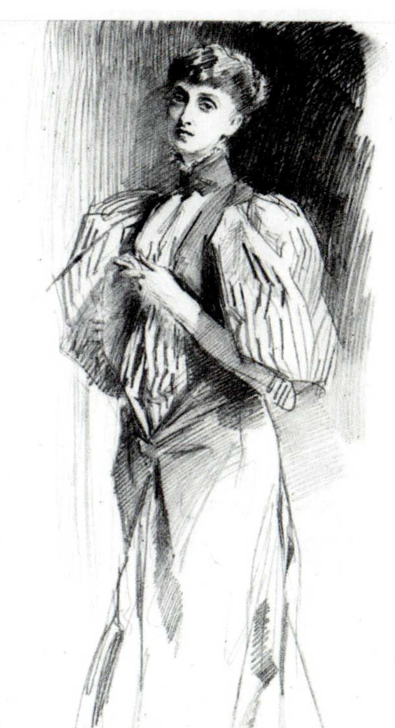

Left: Henry James – a natural, deftly painted 70th-birthday portrait of the novelist by his friend Sargent in 1913.

invited to a private view of the portrait in Tite Street. James was there on each occasion, so they could compare the painting with the man himself.

VOTES FOR WOMEN

The portrait was exhibited publicly during the Royal Academy's Summer Exhibition of 1914. Fry's vituperation was beginning to have an effect however, and reception of it was fairly subdued, but then, on 4 May, a suffragette, the elderly, widowed Mary Aldham (known by her maiden name of Wood) entered the gallery and hacked at it with a butcher's cleaver, crying 'Votes for women!' Uproar ensued and Wood later wrote to the Women's Social and Political Union: 'I have tried to destroy a valuable picture because I wish to show the public that they have no security for their property nor for their art treasures until women are given political freedom.'

Below left: An engraving of one of Sargent's drawings of his friend the writer and suffragist Alice Meynell, c.1913.

THE GILDED AGE

The Gilded Age was a time of unprecedented industrialization and urbanization, heralding the construction of transcontinental railways, innovations in science and technology, and business expansion. Miles of new railways made travel easier, and millions of rural Americans moved to the cities.

In 1873, the American authors Mark Twain (1835–1910) and Charles Dudley Warner (1829–1900) published a novel titled *The Gilded Age, a Tale of Today* that satirized greed and political corruption in post-Civil War America. It suggested that society had a superficial sheen of wealth and beauty, but that there was underlying corruption. The expression stuck.

CHANGING SOCIETY

The Gilded Age was a period of rapid economic growth roughly spanning the years between the late 1870s and the early 1900s. By 1900, what had been a predominantly agrarian society of small producers changed into an urban society dominated by industrial corporations. Nearly 40 percent of Americans now lived in cities. By the beginning of the 20th century, the modern American economy had emerged: income per head and industrial production exceeded that of any other country except Britain, and as American wages became much higher than most in Europe, especially for skilled workers, there was an influx of European immigrants. In 1913, the newly built Grand Central Station in New York reopened. It was the world's largest train station and it portrayed wealth and power, epitomizing US confidence.

DECADENCE AND CONFIDENCE

The early part of the Gilded Age roughly coincided with the mid-Victorian era in Britain and the Belle Époque in France; which was a time of decadence and confidence for many. The growing number of newly rich people created a strong demand for society portraits that emphasized the sitters' status, wealth and prestige, and with his often daring, beguiling style, Sargent became the first choice among numerous other highly skilled artists who made their livings as society portraitists.

After painting the portrait of James, in August 1913 (see page 90), Sargent went to Paris to attend the wedding of his niece, Rose-Marie and Robert André-Michel (1884–1914), a historian and art historian and the son of an art historian and critic André Michel (1853–1925). Tragically, just over a year after the wedding, at the beginning of World War I, Robert was to be killed in action. From Paris, Sargent continued to Venice where he stayed with the Curtises and then he spent some time in the Dolomites before returning to Venice. In September of 1913, he travelled to San Vigilio, Lake Garda, with Emily, Eliza and the de Glehns. He had no idea that this would be his last visit to Italy.

TROUBLES IN EUROPE

Meanwhile, European peace was fragile. In May 1913, the Balkan War had ended, but new trouble arose over the distribution of land, initiating a Second Balkan War. In June 1914, the heir to the Austrian throne, Archduke Franz Ferdinand and his wife were assassinated while visiting Sarajevo in Bosnia. Believing the assassin to be a Serbian nationalist, Austria-Hungary, with the backing of Germany, delivered an ultimatum to Serbia. Despite efforts made by major European powers to resolve the dispute, it ultimately led to World War I.

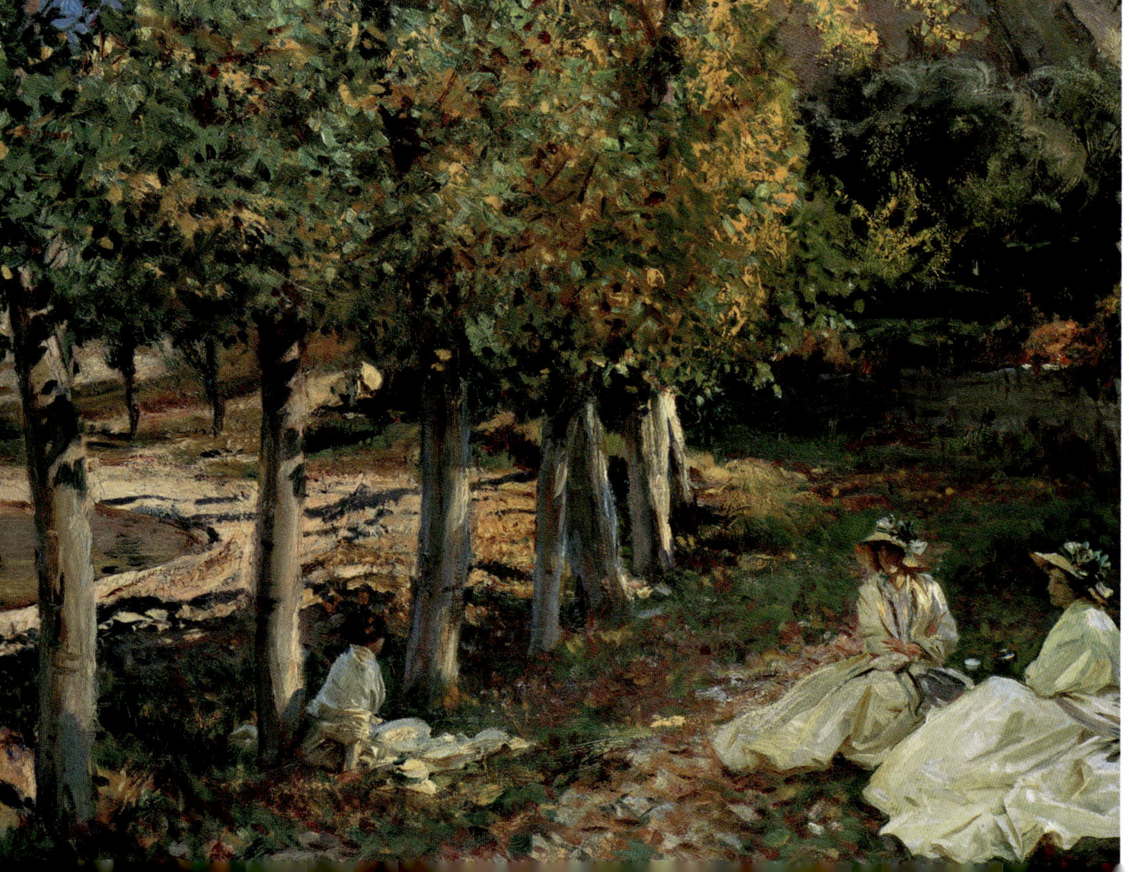

Left: Autumn Leaves, *Sargent, 1913. This sunlit view was painted long after Impressionism began, but Sargent remained influenced by many of its ideas.*

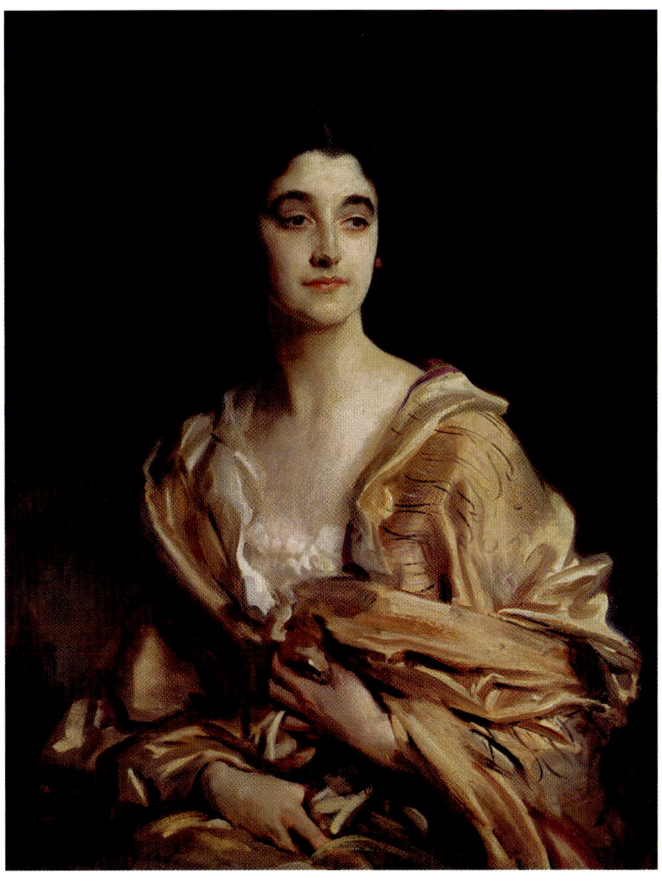

Above left: Sybil (née Sassoon), the Marchioness of Cholmondeley. Painted in 1913, this was one of Sargent's last oil portraits.

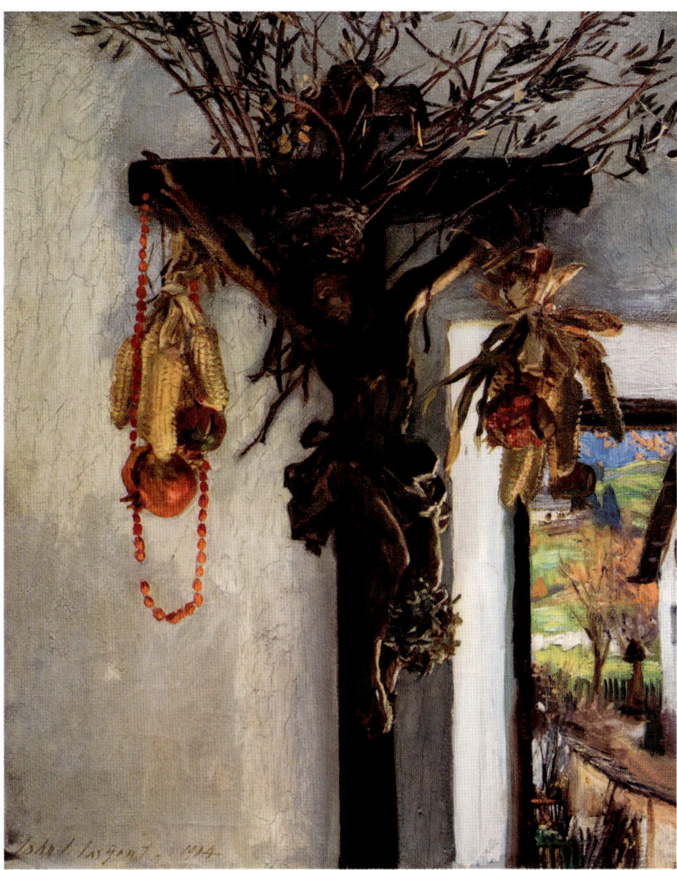

Above right: Still Life with Crucifix is one of two overtly Catholic images that Sargent painted in watercolour in the Tyrol during the autumn of 1914.

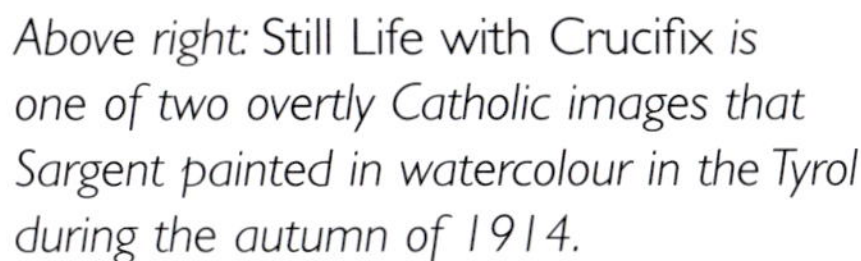

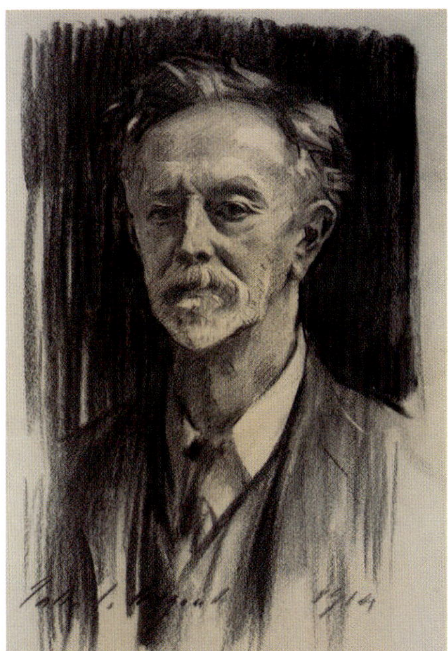

Above: Sir Walter Parratt (1841–1924), 1914, the organist of St George's Chapel, Windsor and Master of Music to Queen Victoria, Edward VII and George V.

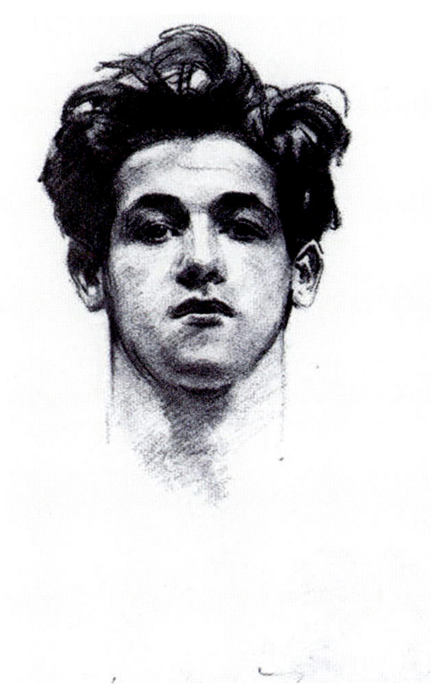

Above: This charcoal drawing of Olimpio Fusco, an Italian model, made in 1905–10, demonstrates Sargent's confidence in capturing proportions, tone and texture.

THE ARMORY SHOW

In 1913, an International Exhibition of Modern Art was organized by the Association of American Painters and Sculptors. It became called the Armory Show as it opened in New York City's 69th Regiment Armory and was the first large exhibition of modern art in America. The show travelled to the Art Institute of Chicago and then to the Copley Society of Art in Boston. Featuring approximately 1250 works of art by over 300 European and American artists, with examples of Cubism, Futurism, Fauvism and more, the exhibition introduced Americans to many European avant-garde developments and inspired American artists to experiment themselves. Some works, such as *Nude Descending a Staircase* by Marcel Duchamp (1887–1968), caused some shock and outrage, but essentially, it began changing many ideas about art, including the notion that Sargent's style might be a little outmoded.

THE GREAT WAR

Believing that artists should not even consider politics, Sargent ignored the threat of war and continued to travel. When World War I broke out in August 1914, he was in Austria with Adrian and Marianne Stokes. He was an American citizen, the Stokes were British and considered enemy aliens by the Germans.

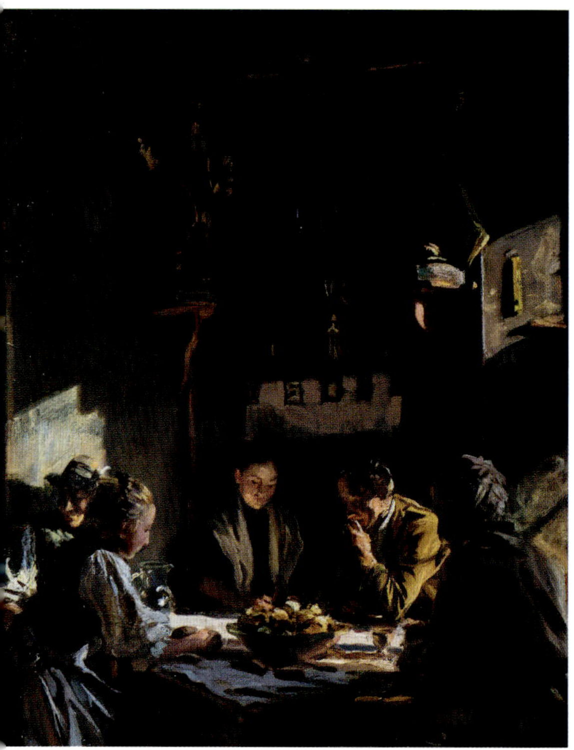

Sargent's party also included a neighbour of Emily's; Colonel Ernest Armstrong, a retired medical officer and amateur watercolourist, plus Sargent's valet and Marianne's maid. They were all forbidden to leave the country, Colonel Armstrong was taken as a prisoner of war, and their paintings were confiscated by the German authorities.

While they shared opinions on many things, Sargent and his friend Henry James differed enormously in their beliefs over the war. Before he had left for Austria, Sargent had refused to even consider the menacing situation, whereas James was preoccupied with it. Angry that the United States was not involved, in 1915, James became a British citizen.

Meanwhile, Sargent and his party were in a remote part of the Alps and when news reached them that war had been declared, Sargent's only anxiety

was for Emily who was in the north of France. As soon as he discovered she was safe, he relaxed and began painting again. At the beginning of October, Colonel Armstrong wrote to him appealing for help, and Sargent travelled to where he was imprisoned, taking an Austrian acquaintance, and managed to obtain Armstrong's release. By the end of November 1914, Sargent returned to England, where he discovered that Rose-Marie's husband, Robert André-Michel, had been killed at the Front.

STAYING IN AMERICA

Although Sargent now realised the seriousness of the war, he continued working. The Boston Public Library murals were only half finished and he had been asked to contribute to an exhibition in San Francisco to celebrate the opening of the Panama Canal. In February 1916, at the age of 72, James died. The following month, Sargent sailed for America. Because of the war, he remained for his longest stay there, and painted portraits of President Woodrow

Above: Painted in 1915 while Sargent was 'trapped' in Austria, Tyrolese Interior is darker than his more recent oil paintings.

Below: A Tent in the Rockies, 1916. Sargent's time in the Rockies reminded him of happier times in the Alps.

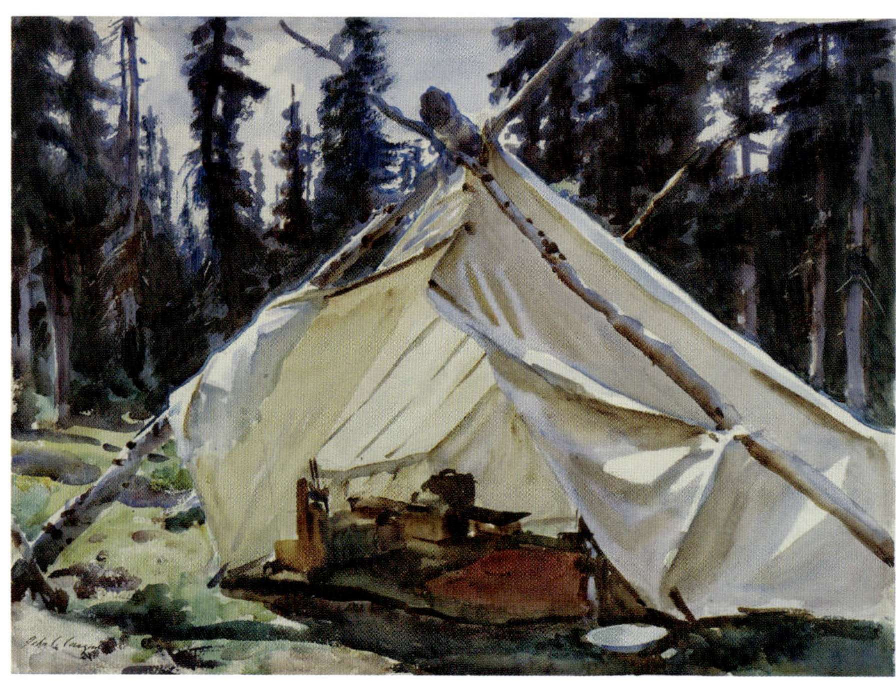

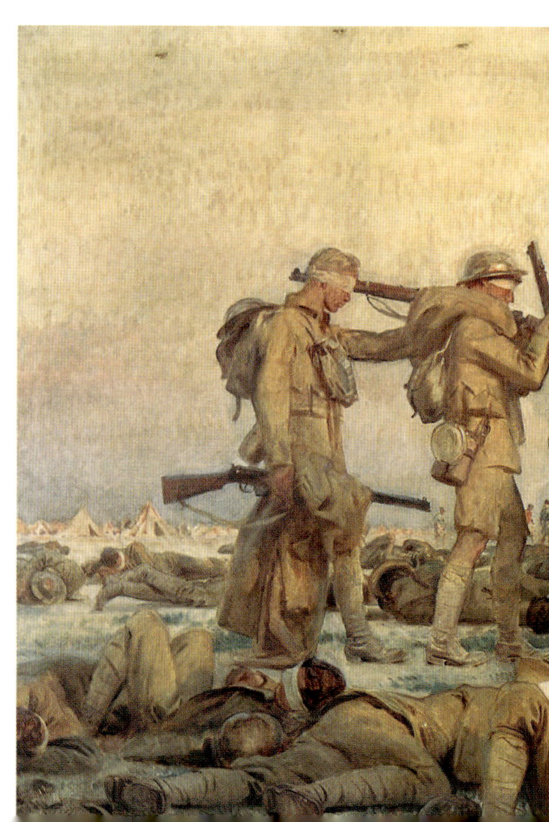

Wilson (1856–1924) and John D. Rockefeller. The trustees of the Museum of Fine Arts in Boston commissioned him to decorate the Rotunda of their new building, and he set up a studio there. That summer, he travelled to the Rocky Mountains of Canada, from where he wrote to Isabella Stewart Gardner: 'I am camping under the waterfall... It is magnificent when the sun shines which it did the first two days. I began a picture – that is, ten days ago – and since then it has been raining and snowing steadily– provisions and temper getting low – but I shall stick it out 'til the sun reappears... Your handkerchiefs are in constant use and still hold out in spite of a dripping nose and cold feet.'

The American businessman, art collector and philanthropist Charles Deering (1852–1927) had been friends with Sargent since 1876, and in March 1917, Sargent stayed with him in his mansion, the Villa Vizcaya in Miami. The following month, America entered the war against Germany.

EXPERIENCING ATROCITIES

In Paris in March 1918, Rose-Marie was attending a Good Friday service in the church of St Gervais when a German shell struck the building. She was killed instantly. Sargent returned to England as soon as he could, in May 1918, but soon after he arrived, accepted a commission from the British Government of official war artist. He was sent to the Western Front with his friend Henry Tonks, and stationed at Arras. After searching for a subject that would please the authorities, he witnessed a group of soldiers on the Arras-Louviers road, victims of mustard gas poisoning. Sargent's painting of the scene, *Gassed*, was named Picture of the Year at the Royal Academy in 1919.

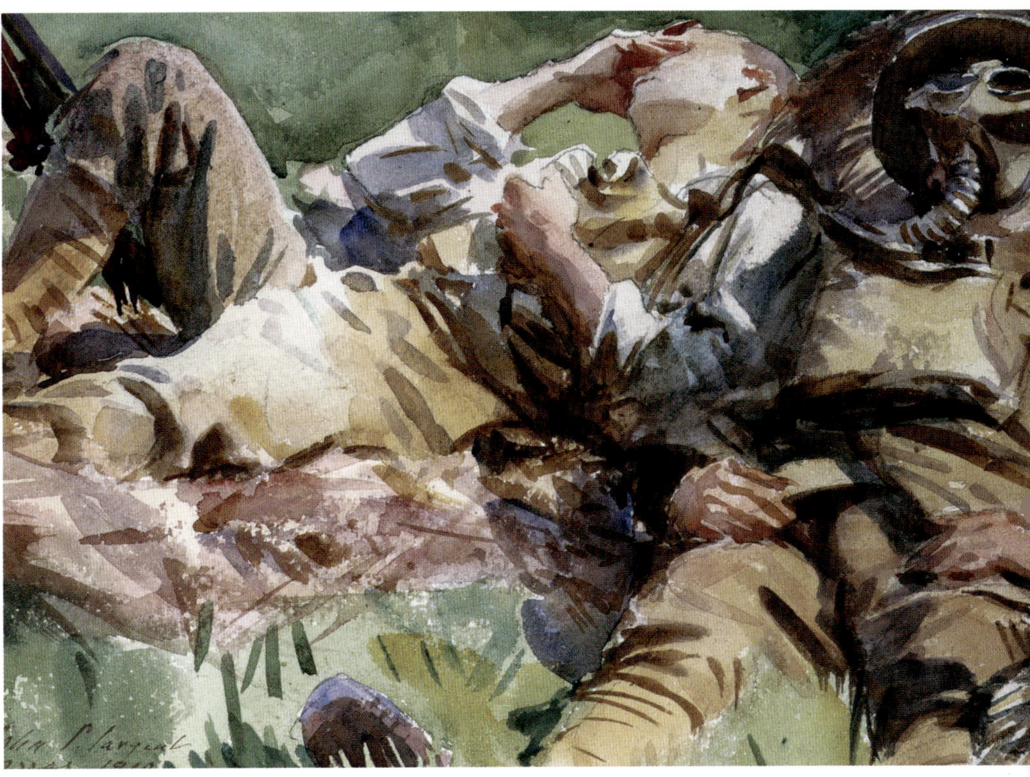

Above: A watercolour of Two Soldiers at Arras, *1918. Despite the fact that Sargent was 58 years old, he and Henry Tonks lived with the soldiers.*

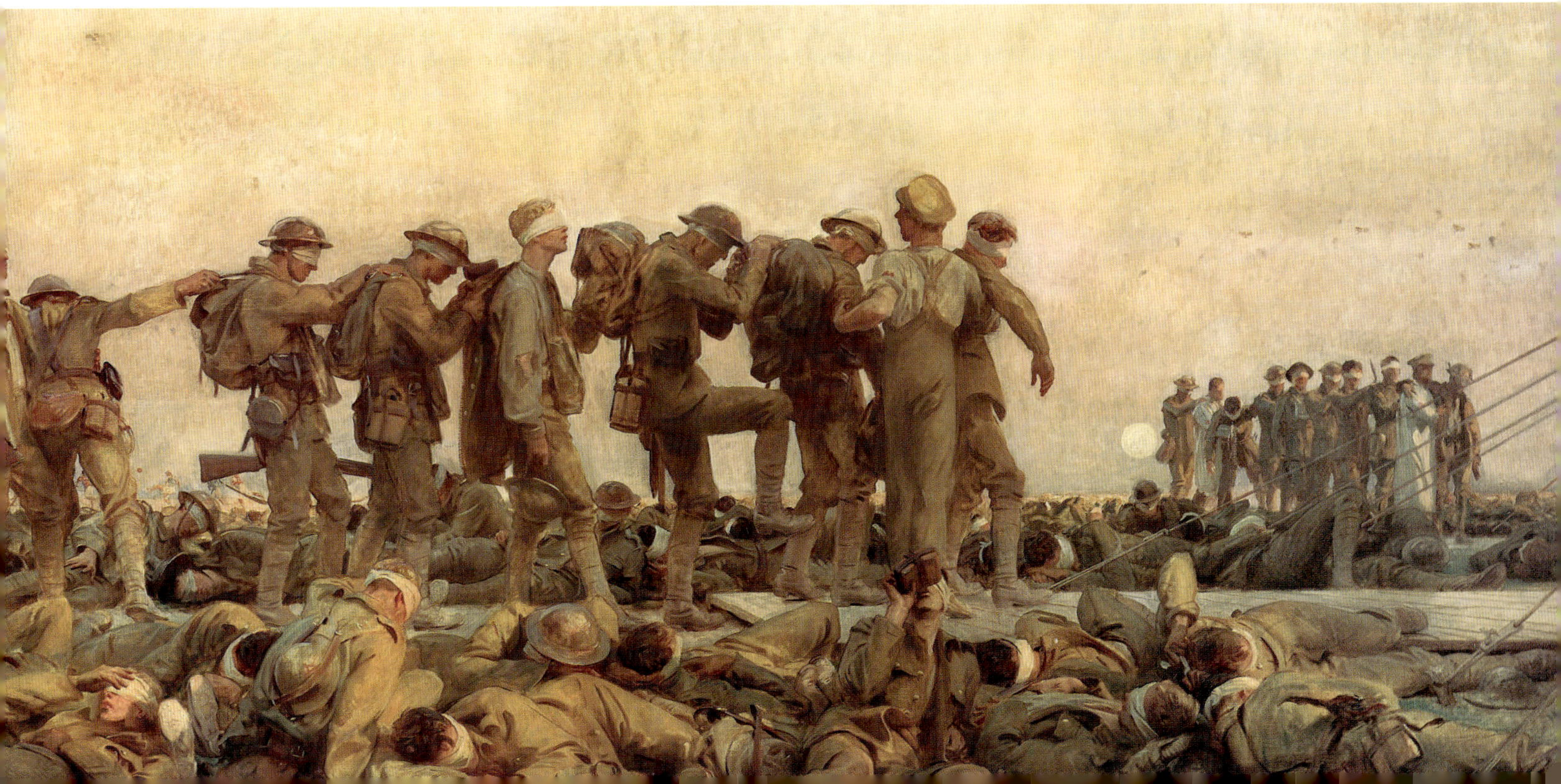

Below: Gassed, *1919 – blinded and retching from the the effects of mustard gas, a group of soldiers stumble toward a medical tent for new dressings. With a composition like a classical frieze, the horrors of the war are palpable.*

LAST YEARS

In 1919, Sargent was asked to accept the presidency of the Royal Academy, but with his acute fear of public speaking, he declined, explaining that he could not as he was still a working artist with many commitments. He also threatened to flee the country if elected against his wishes.

Despite deep feelings of loss, after the war, Sargent's life resumed. He continued travelling and living in and working from his studio on Tite Street, and worked on his large murals from another studio. He produced further important works, including the rest of the Boston Public Library murals, decorations for the Museum of Fine Arts in Boston (MFA), two large war memorials for the Widener Memorial Library at Harvard University and another war memorial for the National Portrait Gallery in London.

MEMORIALS AND MURALS

Sargent began making preparatory sketches for the war memorial for the National Gallery as soon as he accepted the commission. Depicting 22 full-length portraits, *General Officers of the Great War* was a monumental painting. Back in Boston in May 1919, he supervised the installation of his Library murals and worked on the Rotunda for the MFA. Like the Library, his Rotunda decoration was complex, featuring Neoclassical style paintings, reliefs and architectural ornaments. Impressed by the work,

the trustees of the museum asked him to extend the decorations over the staircase. He accepted and returned to America the following January, first visiting his friend Paul Helleu in New York and then returning to Boston. In 1922, he finished and delivered *General Officers of the Great War* to great acclaim (see page 253), delivered more MFA decorations and installed the two tall murals for the Widener Memorial Library that commemorate Harvard University's contribution to World War I and honour the dead.

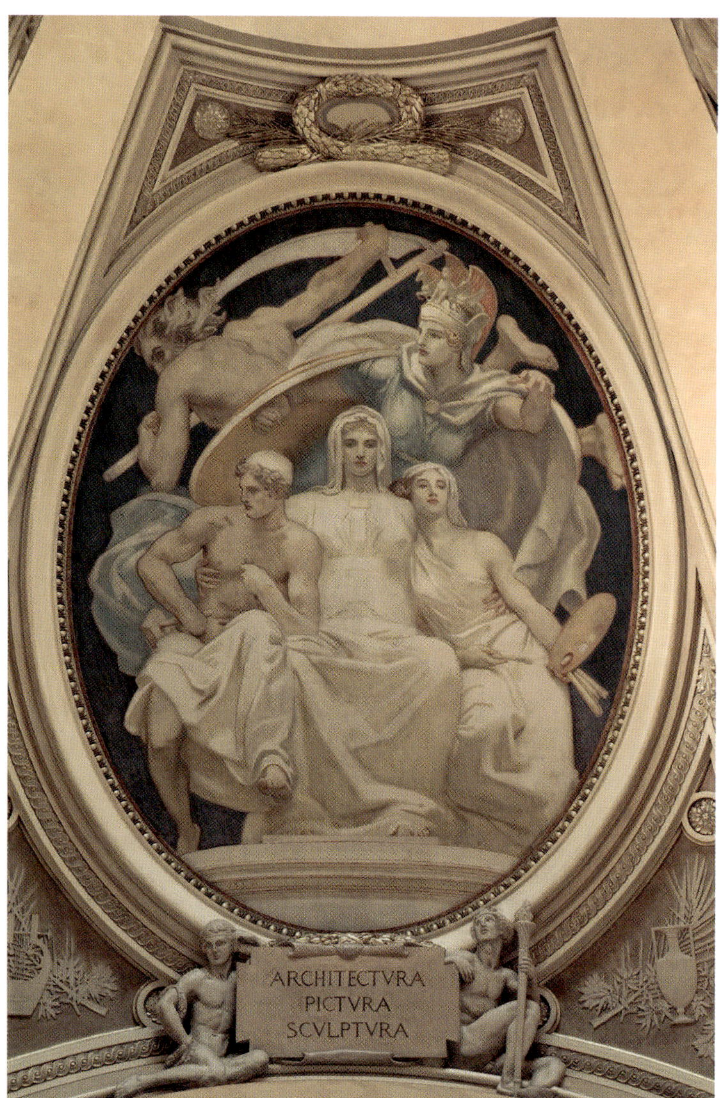

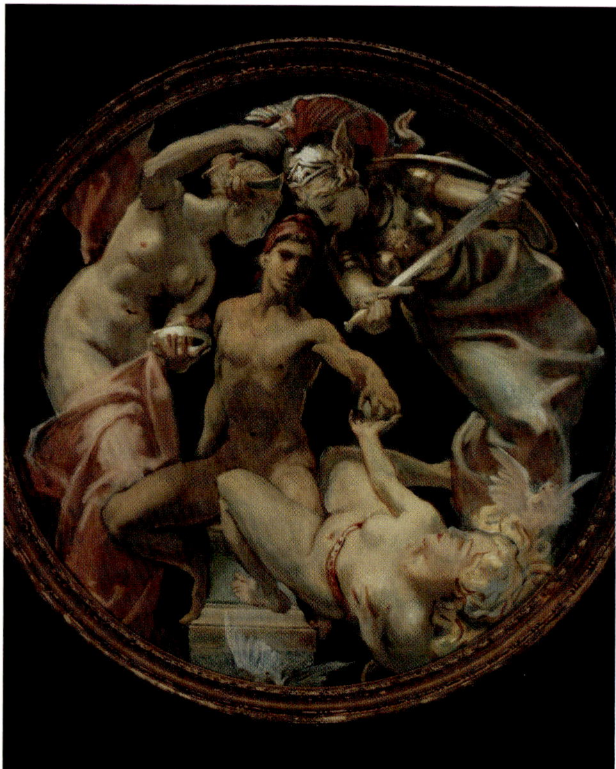

Left: Architecture, Painting and Sculpture Protected by Athena from the Ravages of Time, 1921 — One of Sargent's murals for the Museum of Fine Arts in Boston, his imaginative scheme used ideas from classical mythology to pay homage to the arts.

Above: The Judgement of Paris, 1920–22. A study for one of the murals for the Boston MFA. Images from Greek mythology were created to link the museum with the birthplace of Western civilization.

MURAL CONTROVERSY

The Boston Public Library murals represent the study and evolution of religion. Those unveiled in 1919 were intended to show similarities between Judaism and Christianity, yet caused controversy among Boston's Jewish community who believed that the painting *The Synagogue* perpetuated a biased image. In 1921, Sargent wrote to Charteris: 'I'm in hot water here with the Jews who resent my 'Synagogue' and want to have it removed.'

THE END

In 1923, Sargent exhibited at the inaugural exhibition of the Baltimore Museum of Art in Maryland, painted murals in his Boston studio and also a portrait of Harvard's president. In 1924, a major exhibition of his work was held at New York's Grand Central Art Galleries.

He completed his final panels for the MFA in April 1925; the night before his departure from London to supervise their installation, Emily gave a farewell dinner with Violet and close friends. One guest wrote that Sargent was: 'never in a better form, waving good night to us as he walked away from Emily's.' The next morning he was found at Tite Street, sitting up in bed, his reading lamp still burning, a book fallen from his hand. He had died of a heart attack aged 69.

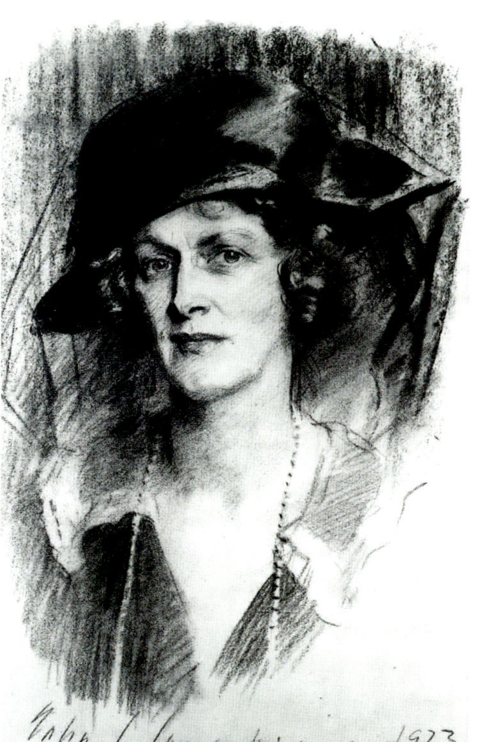

Right: Sargent's charcoal sketch of Nancy Astor; she was the first female Member of Parliament to take her seat.

Below: Sargent gave this charcoal portrait to Elizabeth Bowes-Lyons as a wedding present when she married Prince Albert, the Duke of York in April 1923.

SARGENT'S NUDES

Among some of Sargent's most expressive works are his sensual male nude studies. Most were made in preparation for the Boston murals, although not all can be dated. They have raised speculation about his sexual orientation, but nothing is conclusive. He had many close male and female friendships, but no sexual liaisons have ever surfaced. He was good friends with men who were either definitely or possibly homosexual, and his close friend Isabella Stewart Gardner surrounded herself with gay men. However, he also had many close heterosexual friends, and was friends with Jews during a time of rising anti-Semitism, but he was not Jewish. He did not paint as many nude females as males, but this may have been connected to his relationships with his mother, sisters and nieces. Even his relationship with his valet, d'Inverno was never speculated about during their time together; and as Sargent dismissed d'Inverno after he had a fight with another valet, it seems unlikely that their connection was intimate.

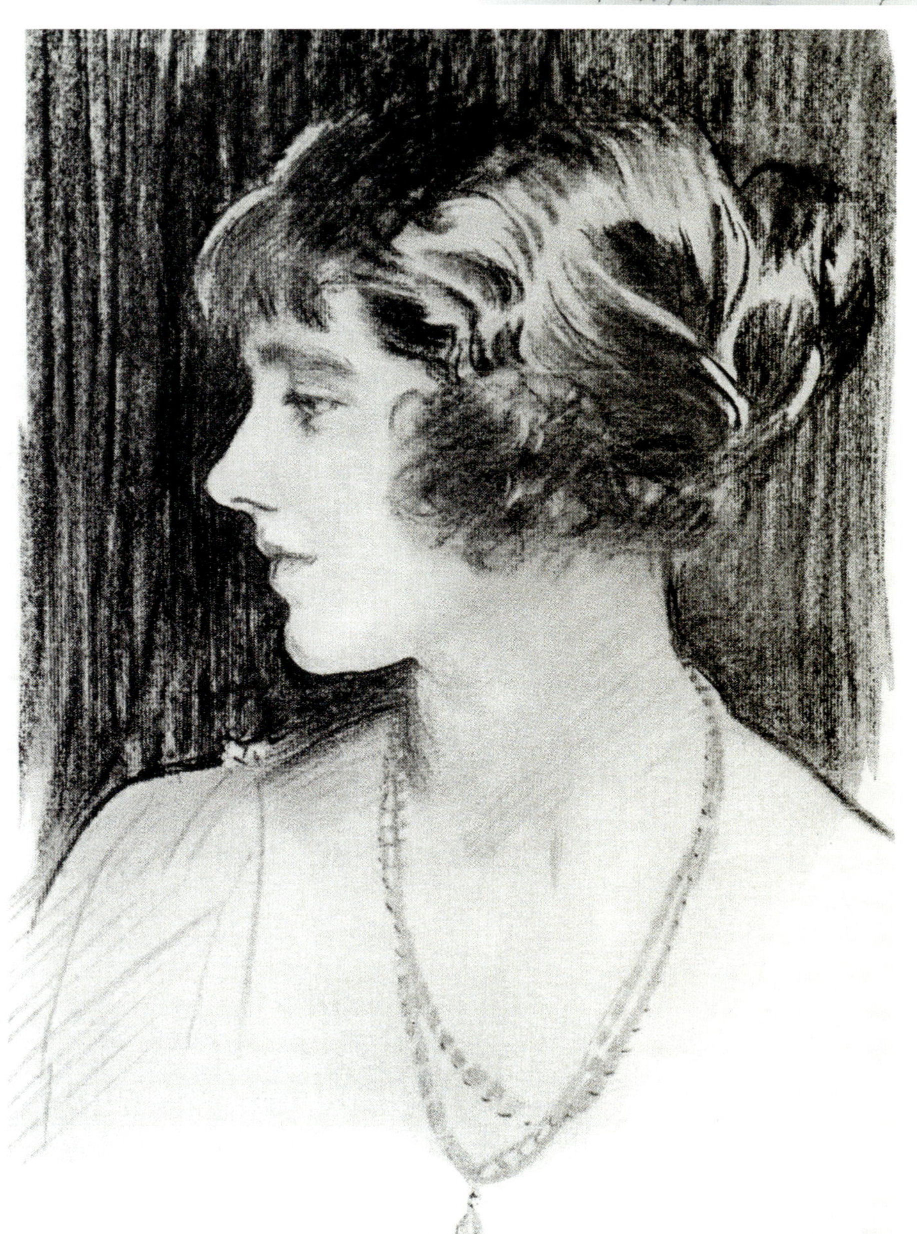

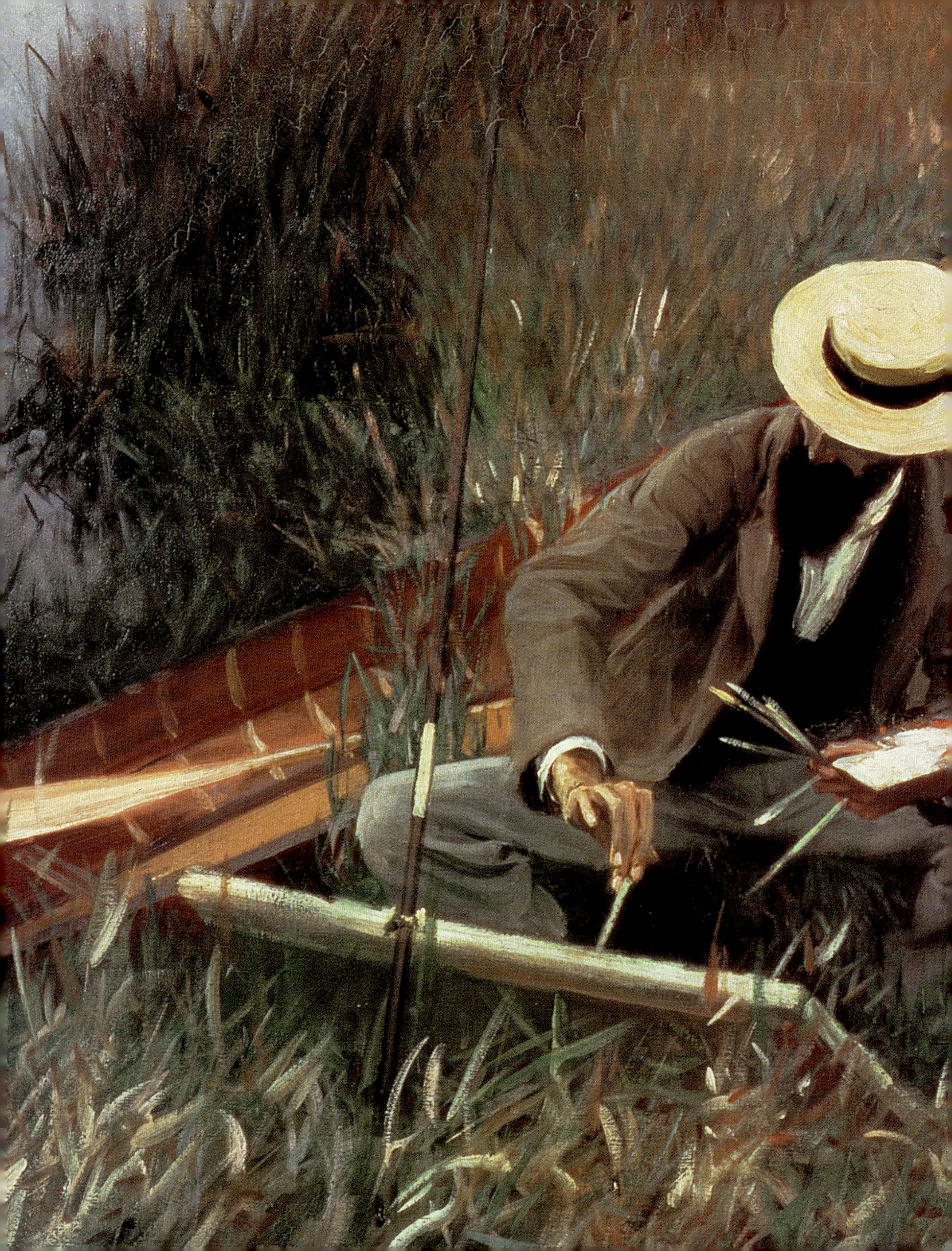

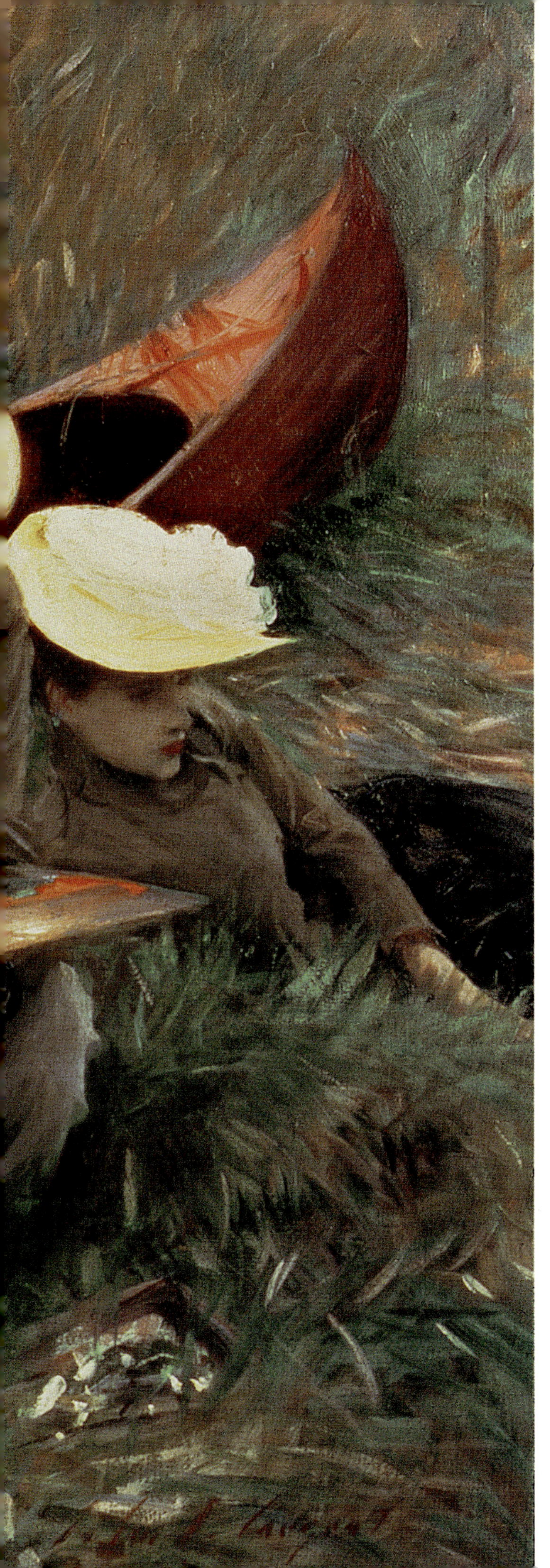

THE GALLERY

From his earliest years, Sargent had drawn and painted – and this passion continued undaunted throughout his life. Even though he drew on influences of other contemporary artists, his style and approach remained much the same during his career. For a long time, he was exceptionally sought after. By the turn of the 20th century, he was the most popular painter in Europe and America and in 1901, in recognition of this, he was asked to paint the coronation portrait of Edward VII. Although he declined, saying modestly that he was unfit for the task, he did accept commissions to paint hundreds of other aristocratic clients, and spent his spare time painting his friends and family, but most of all the world around him.

Left: Detail of Paul Helleu Sketching with his Wife *(see page 53), 1889, oil on canvas, 65.9 x 80.7cm (26¼ x 32¼in), Brooklyn Museum, New York, USA. Since Sargent had helped the 18-year-old Helleu out of his financial difficulties in 1878, they had remained close friends. In 1883, they travelled to the Netherlands together to study the work of Frans Hals. Helleu had married Alice Guérin three years before this painting was executed. Here, she was 19 and he was 30. Painted by the River Avon in England, Sargent was working in an Impressionistic style.*

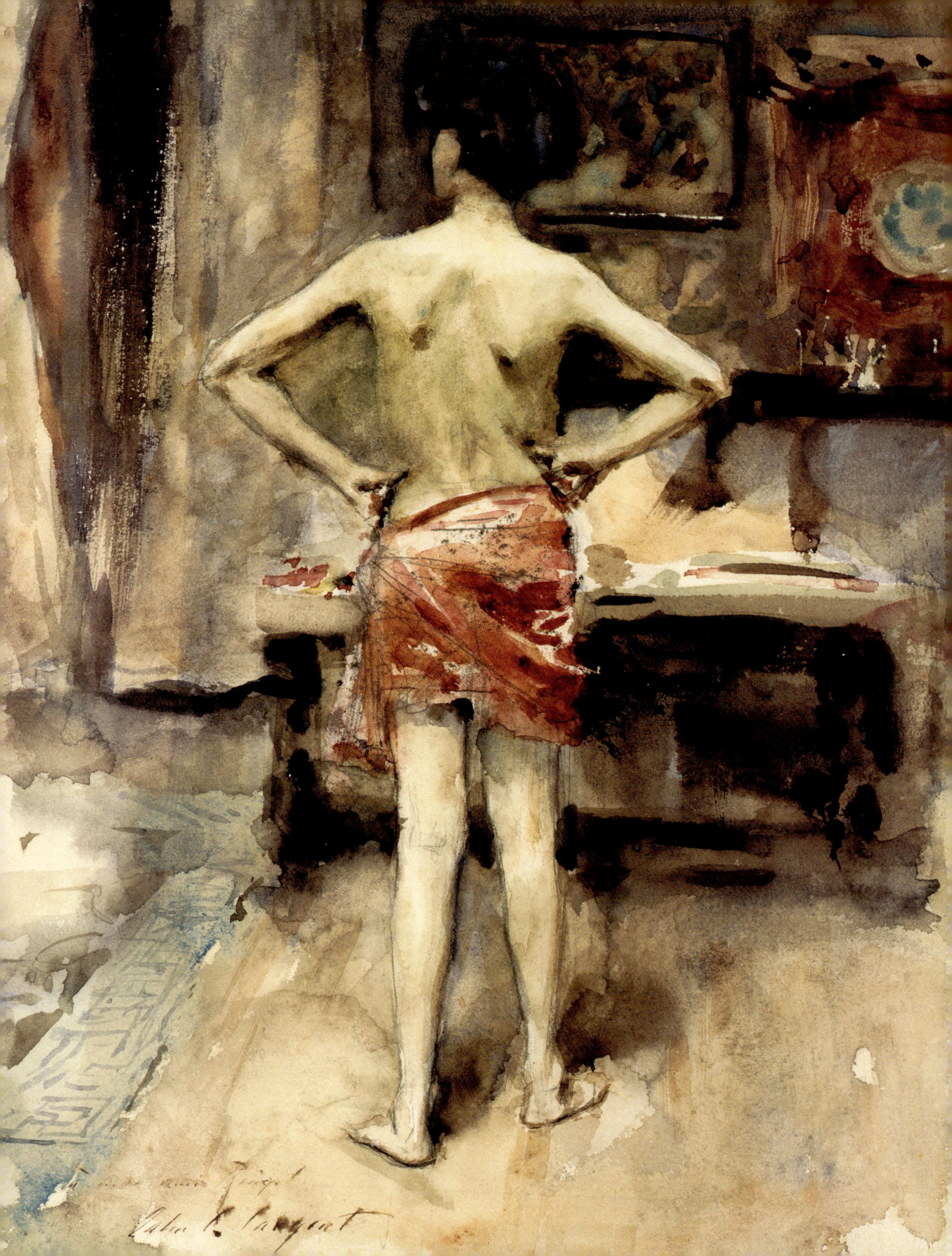

EARLY TALENTS

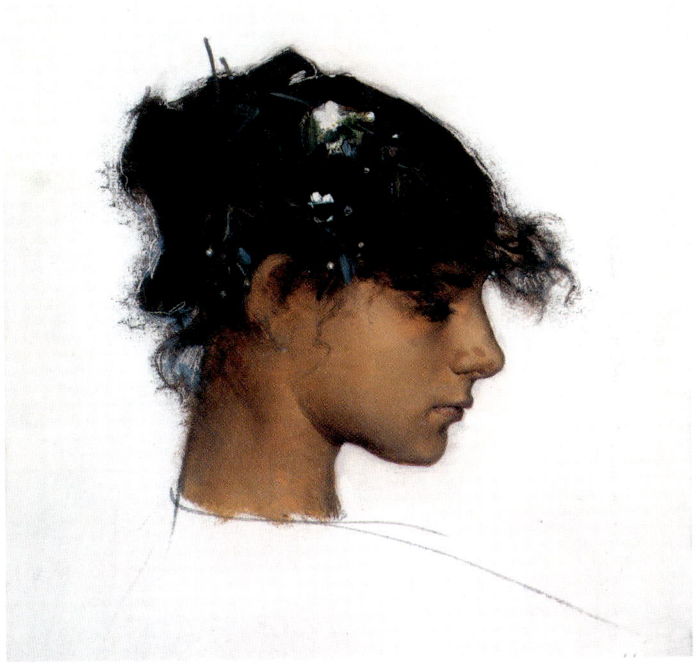

Recognized for his vibrant portraits and fresh and lively landscapes, Sargent modernized painting in many ways, updating traditions, using Impressionistic brushstrokes and original arrangements, partly developed through painting en plein air with his friend Monet. His compositions, light touch and fresh palette resulted in a distinctive approach that conveys immediacy and each sitter's personality and characteristics. As well as gaining ideas and methods from contemporary artists, he also learned a lot from several of the Old Masters, including Van Dyck and Velázquez.

Above: Rosina Ferrara, 1878, oil on canvas, 5 x 4cm (13 x 10¼ in), Private Collection.
Sixteen-year-old Rosina Ferrara came from a community of Anacapriote peasants and was introduced to Sargent in Capri when he was there, as he had been looking for a model. Rosina often modelled for local artists and Sargent was so captivated by her that he made several paintings of her including three profile studies of her head.

Left: The Model, c.1878–79, watercolour over graphite on paper, 29.2 x 22.8cm (11½ x 9in),
The Museum of Fine Arts, Houston, USA.

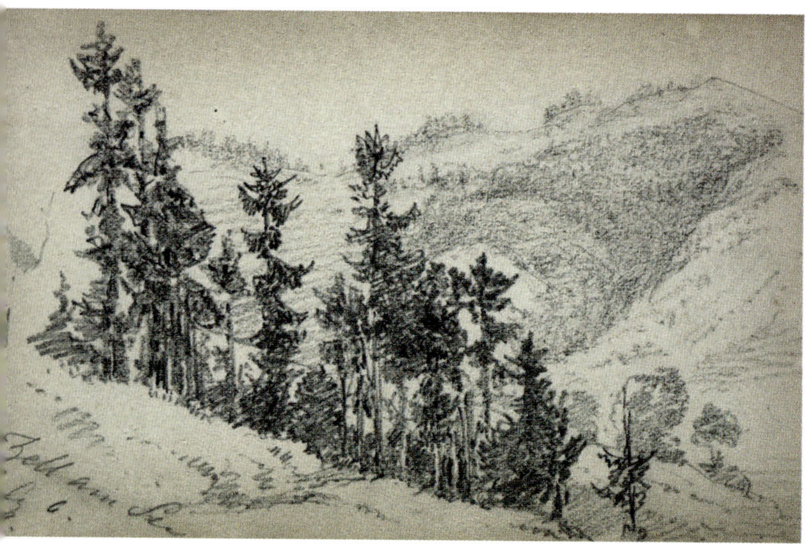

Alpine Landscape, Zell am See, Austria, c.1871, graphite on beige-grey wove paper, 10.3 x 17.2cm (4 x 6¾in), Harvard Art Museums, Massachusetts, USA

Drawn when Sargent was 15 and staying in the Alps with his family, this is one of many sketches he made in several sketchbooks soon after Violet had been born and just before they all moved to Dresden so he could go to school. From an early age, his mother had encouraged him to draw and paint what he saw, wherever he went. It was a discipline he retained throughout his life.

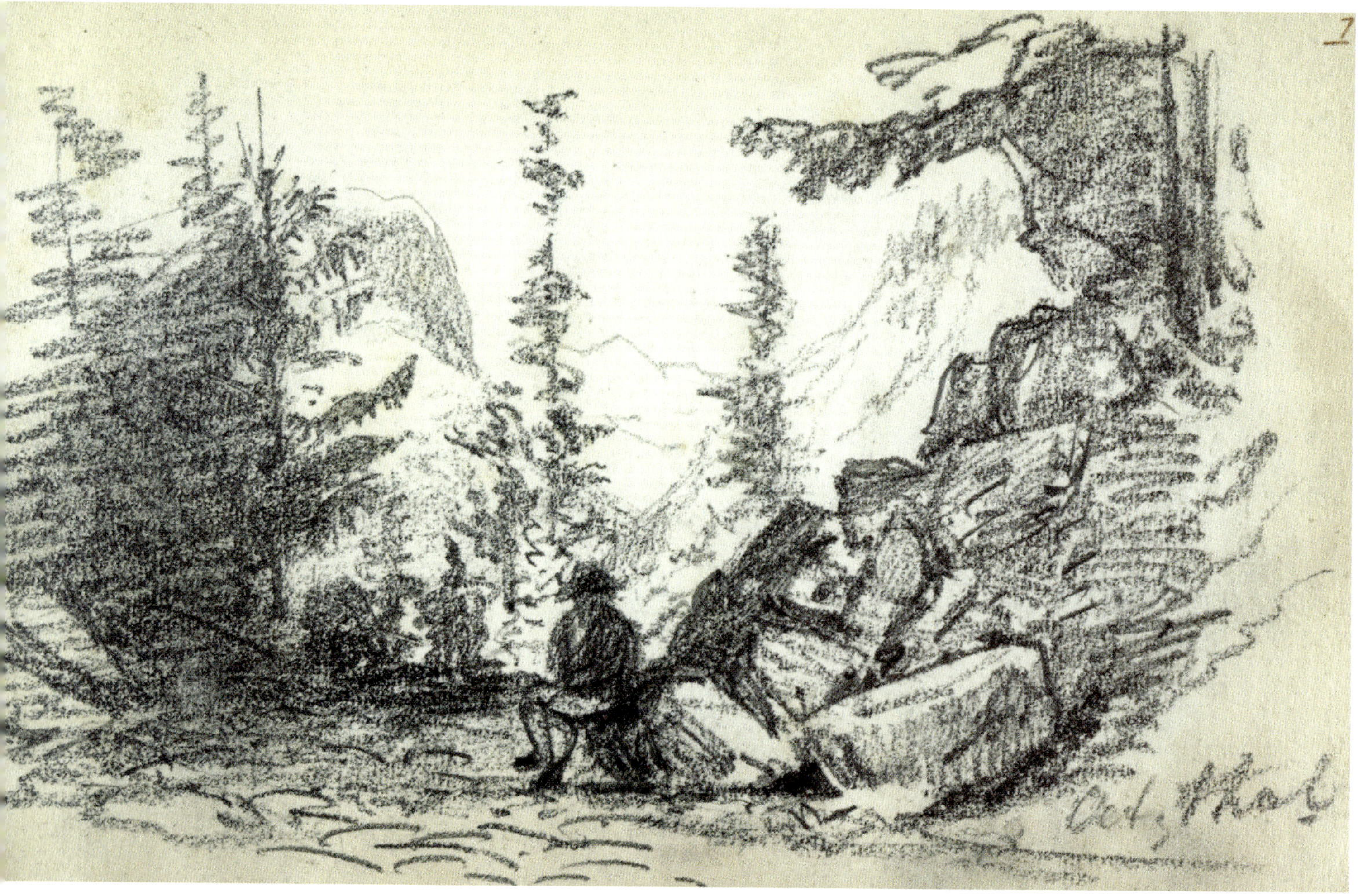

Alpine Landscape, Oetztal, Austria, 1871, graphite on darkened off-white wove paper, 17.2 x 10.3cm (6¾ x 4in), Harvard Art Museums, Massachusetts, USA

One of Sargent's sketchbooks from this period is filled with copies of classical statues from the plaster cast collection in the Albertinum museum in Dresden, plus copies of portraits by Rembrandt, animals and architectural details, and he filled another with many observational drawings of the sights he saw in the Austrian Alps. This is a view in Oetztal; a glaciated area of breathtaking beauty, the sketch shows his remarkable dexterity in drawing figures, objects and the natural world.

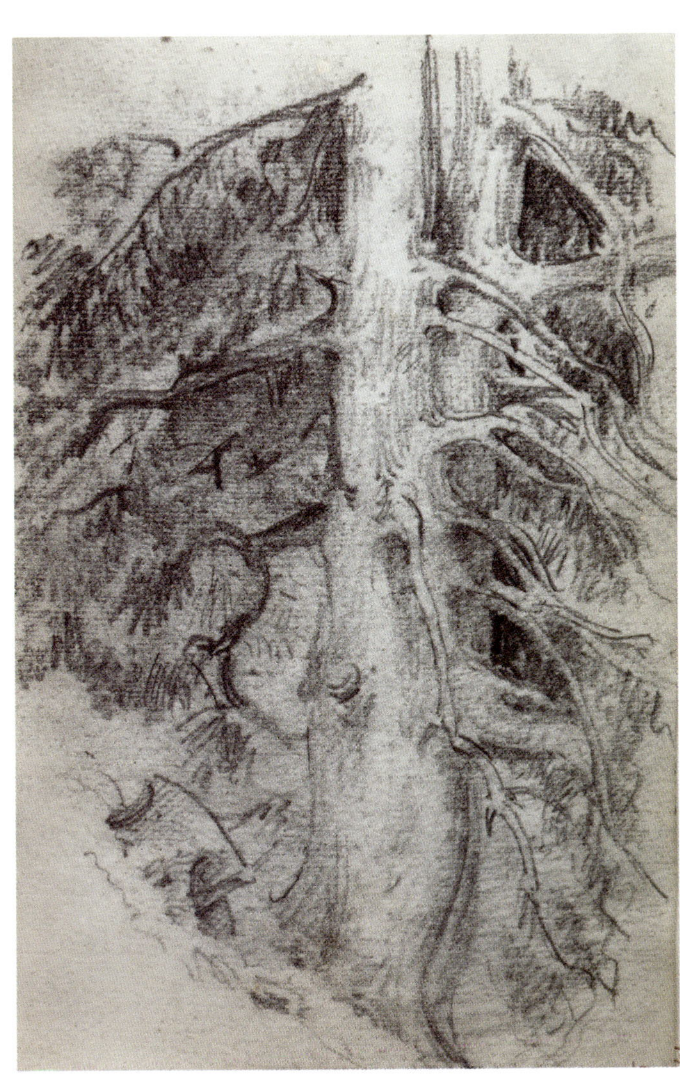

Study of a Tree, 1871–72, graphite on darkened off-white wove paper, 17.2 x 10.3cm (6¾ x 4in), Harvard Art Museums, Massachusetts, USA

Another extremely accomplished and sensitive drawing for a 15-year-old boy, this is also from Sargent's Tyrolean sketchbook. He developed such precocious skills partly through drawing wherever he went from a young age, following his mother's example, but mainly because of his inherent ability, which his mother recognized early on. He used a variety of techniques here, from broad, linear strokes, to refined tonal modelling.

Mountain Landscape with Trees, 1871–72, graphite on darkened off-white wove paper, 17.2 x 10.3cm (6¾ x 4in), Harvard Art Museums, Massachusetts, USA

In 1871, 15-year-old Sargent had already diligently copied the watercolours of German-American artist Carl Welsch and spent the summer of 1870 sketching in the Swiss Alps while on holiday. The following year, he produced the drawings on these pages while on holiday in the Tyrol. Charteris writes in Sargent's posthumous biography that it was Welsch who took him on that sketching trip.

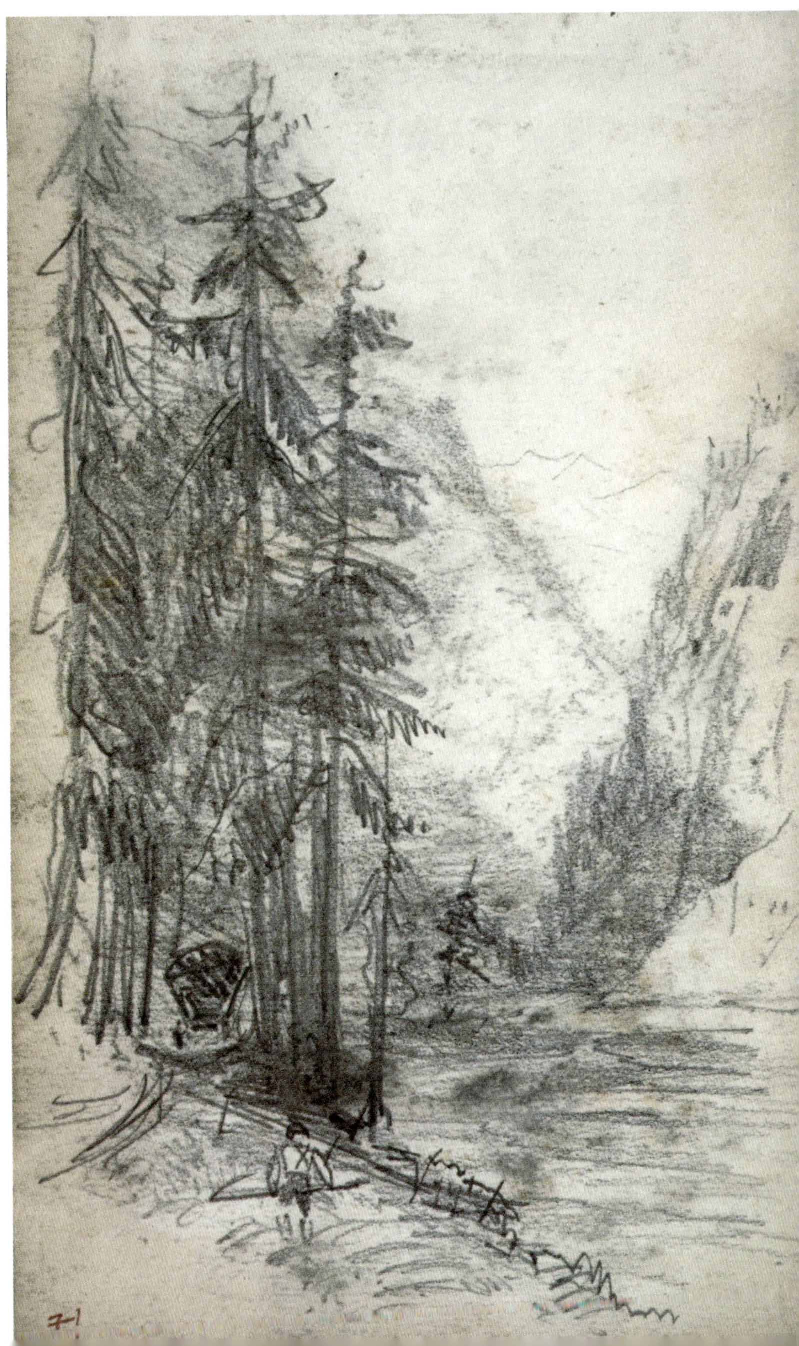

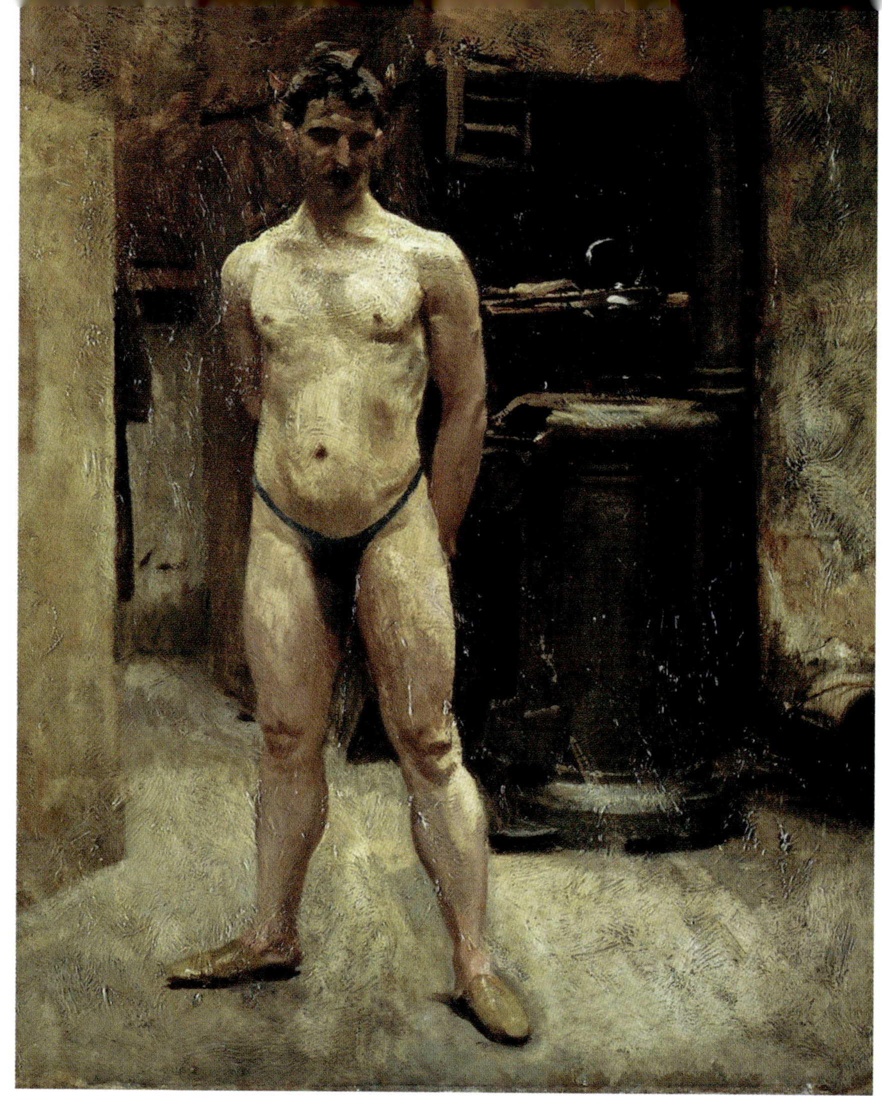

A Male Model in Front of a Stove, c.1875–80, oil on canvas, 71.1 x 55.9cm (28 x 22in), The Metropolitan Museum, New York, USA

By the time Sargent painted this, the Impressionists' first independent exhibition had closed and Sargent had been attending Carolus-Duran's studio for some months. He was also studying at the École des Beaux-Arts, at the life classes of Adolphe Yvon, and working in Léon Bonnat's studio. Under the influence of Carolus-Duran, in this work Sargent used what was described as a 'Spanish palette'.

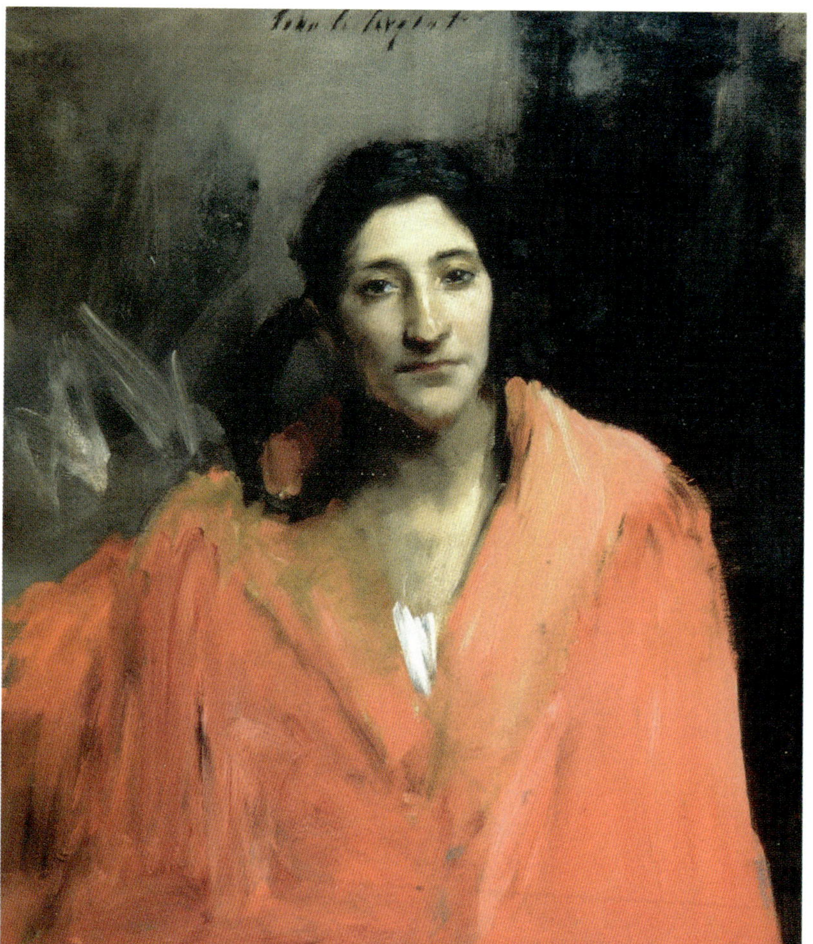

Gitana, 1876, oil on canvas, 73.7 x 60cm (29 x 23½in), The Metropolitan Museum, New York, USA

This dramatically rendered study is of a Spanish gypsy – a gitana – and demonstrates how Sargent had absorbed Carolus-Duran's teachings of the 'Spanish style,' chiefly inspired by Velázquez, including the use of a striking, sombre palette and strong chiaroscuro. The woman's dark hair and eyes are enhanced by her coral-coloured garment, and her gaze and stance shows how comfortable he was from early on in capturing people in relaxed moments.

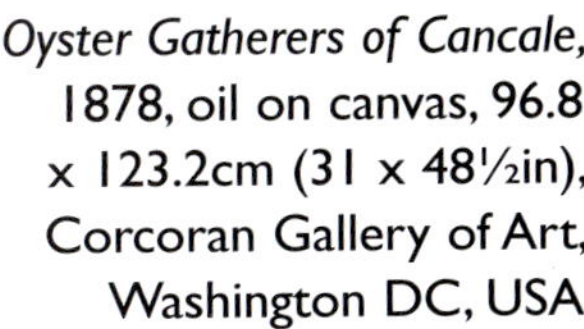

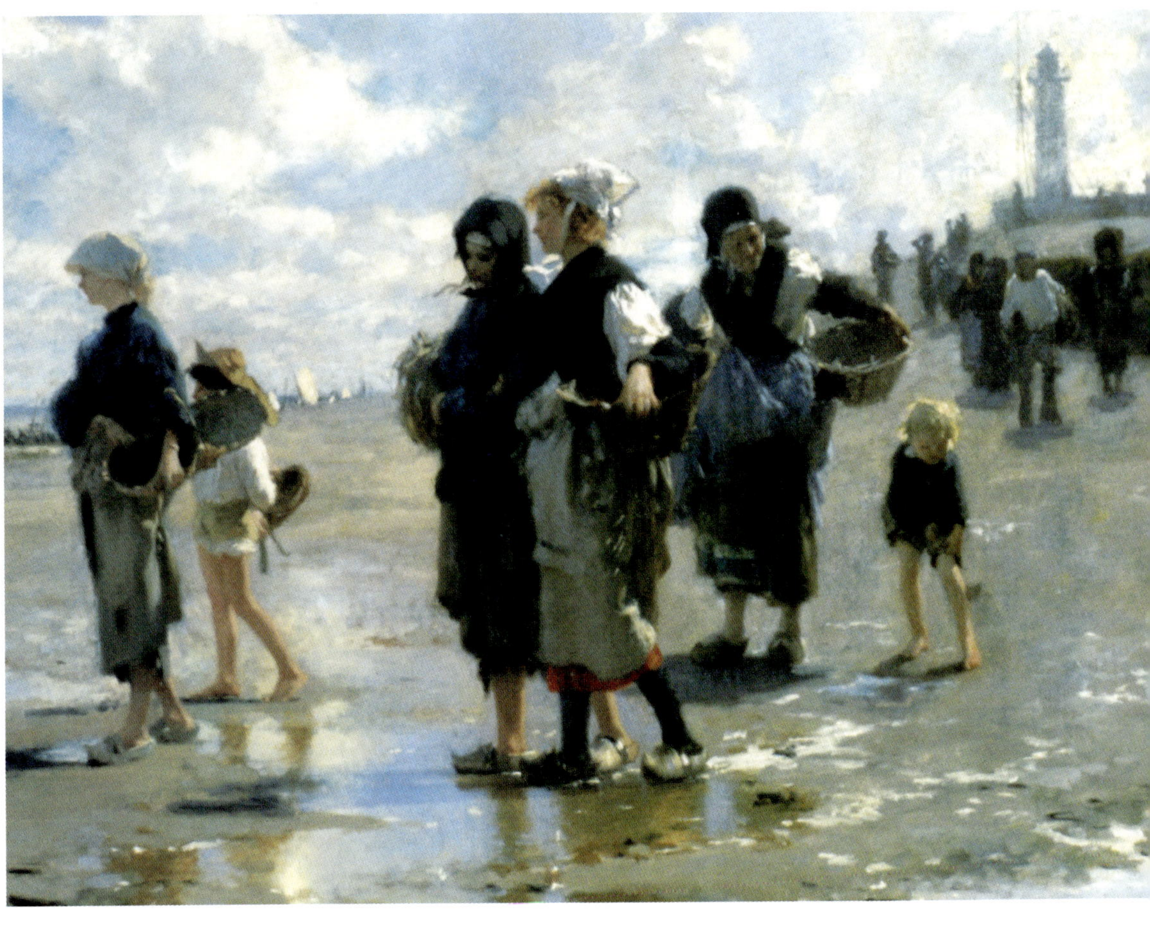

Oyster Gatherers of Cancale, 1878, oil on canvas, 96.8 x 123.2cm (31 x 48½in), Corcoran Gallery of Art, Washington DC, USA

In the summer of 1877, Sargent spent ten weeks on the Brittany coast, making drawings and oil sketches. Back in his Paris studio, he used the sketches to devise this composition. Early in 1878, he sent a sketch of the subject to the inaugural exhibition of the Society of American Artists in New York (see page 23). This finished work, which was twice the size of the sketch, was shown at the Paris Salon.

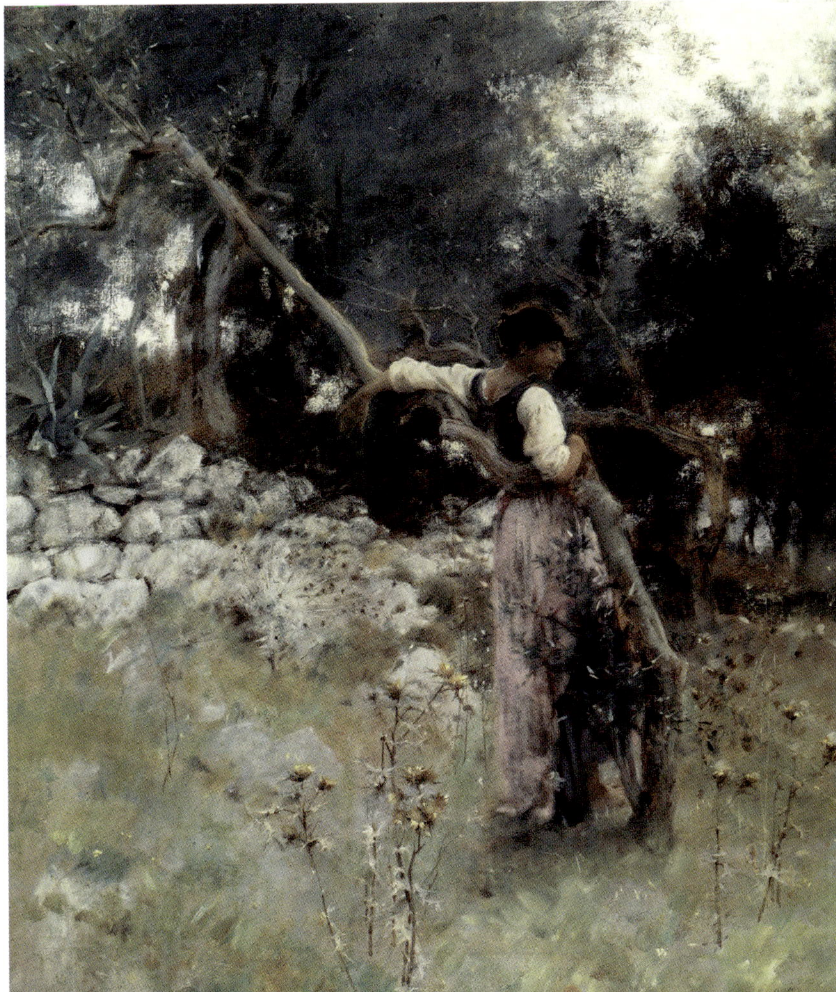

A Capriote, 1878, oil on canvas, 76.8 x 63.2cm (30¼ x 24¾in), Museum of Fine Arts, Boston, Massachusetts, USA

Travellers had been drawn to the beauty of Capri for many years when Sargent painted this. It was exhibited at the Society of American Artists in New York in March of 1879 and another version was exhibited at the Paris Salon that same year. While in Capri, Sargent was befriended by an English painter, Frank Hyde, who had a studio in the abandoned monastery of Santa Teresa. This is one of several paintings Sargent made of Rosina Ferrara in profile, seemingly inspired by the paintings of Jean-Baptiste-Camille Corot (1796–1875).

Rosina, 1878, oil on canvas, 35.2 x 17.2cm (13¾ x 6¾in), Private Collection

Throughout his career Sargent favoured dark-haired slender models and Rosina certainly fitted that description. Here, she is shown wearing the same clothing as in his painting of her dancing on the rooftops in Capri (see page 24). This was painted at twilight, the fading light illuminates the whiteness of her blouse, while the corset-like garment emphasizes her delicate and slender frame.

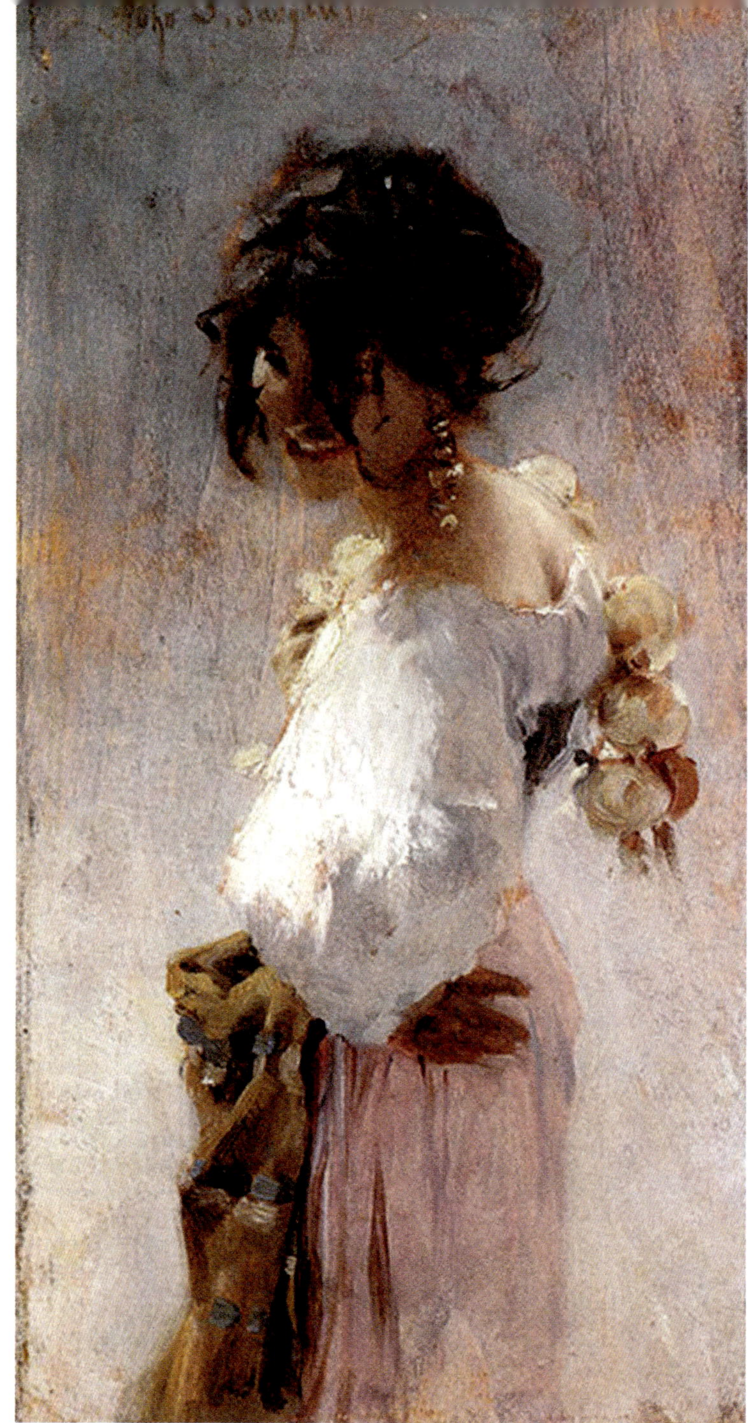

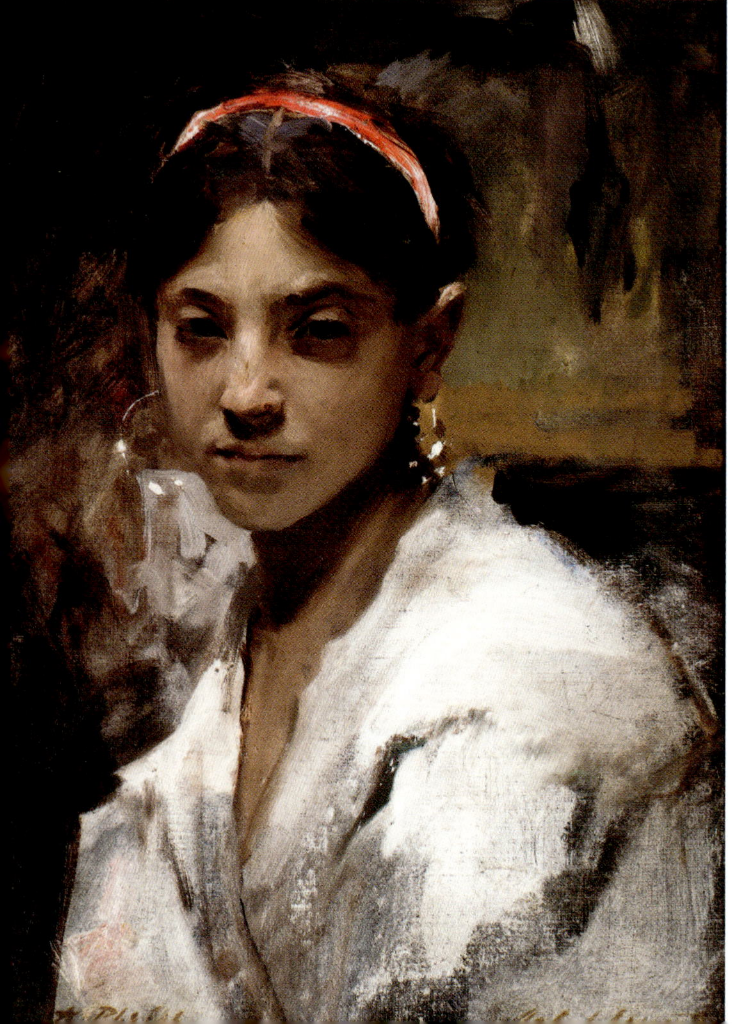

Head of a Capri Girl, 1878, oil on canvas, 43.2 x 30.5cm (17 x 12in), Private Collection

As well as the natural beauty of the landscape, Capri was also celebrated for the beauty of its people, its relaxed way of life, and its rich heritage left by ancient Phoenician, Greek and Roman settlers. At the time of Sargent's stay on Capri, several other artist friends were also visiting, which set a pattern for future convivial painting holidays there. This soft and haunting portrait reveals Sargent's confident portraiture skills.

A Summer Idyll, c.1877, oil
on canvas, 43.2 x 30.5cm
(16¼ x 28¼in), Brooklyn
Museum, New York, USA

In 1877, Sargent was 21
and had already attained
great success at the Paris
Salon. That summer, he
holidayed with his family
in Cancale on the Brittany
coast and probably painted
this languorous, richly
coloured image. Somewhat
vague, it shows three naked
boys relaxing at the end of
a summer's day. One boy is
blowing an aulos; an ancient
Greek wind instrument,
conjuring the impression of a
scene from Greek mythology.

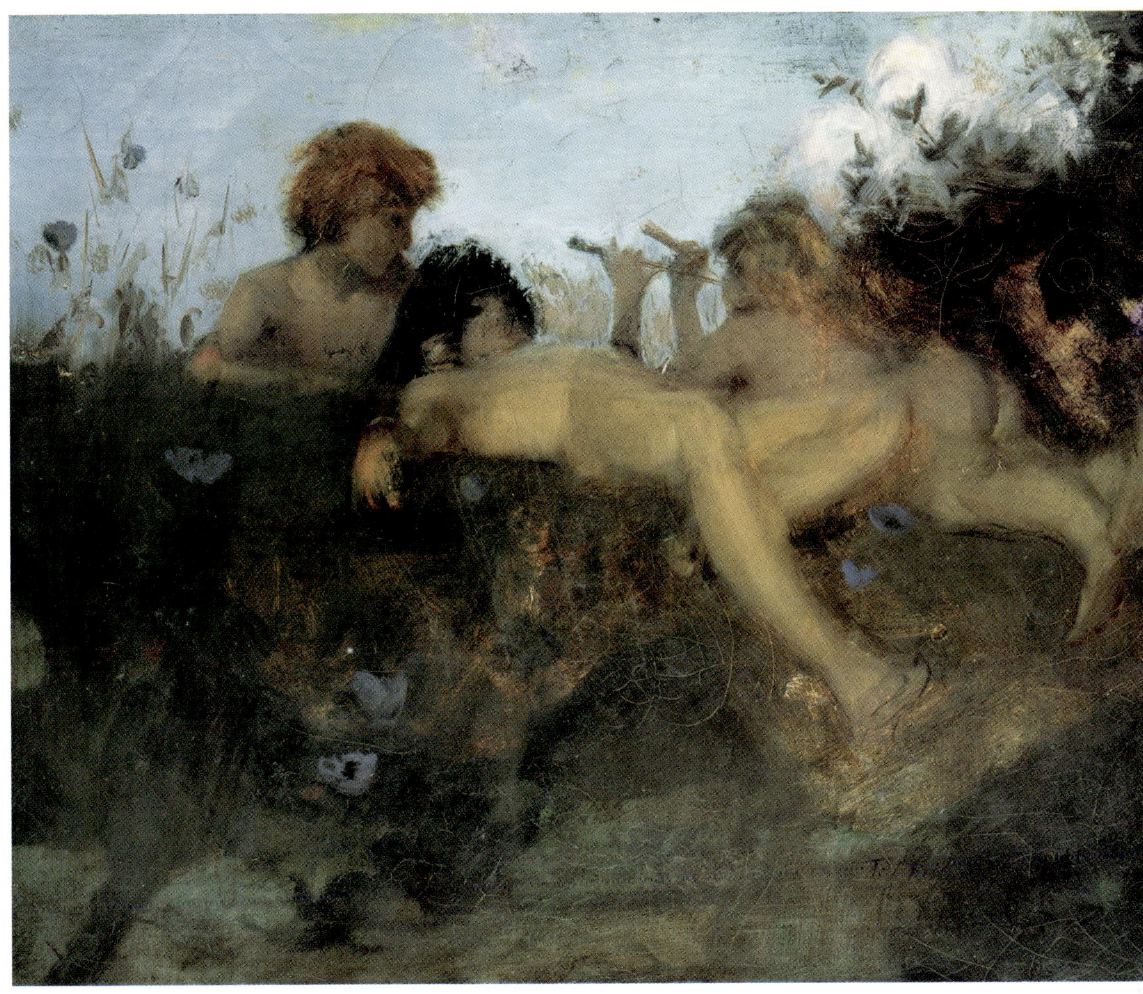

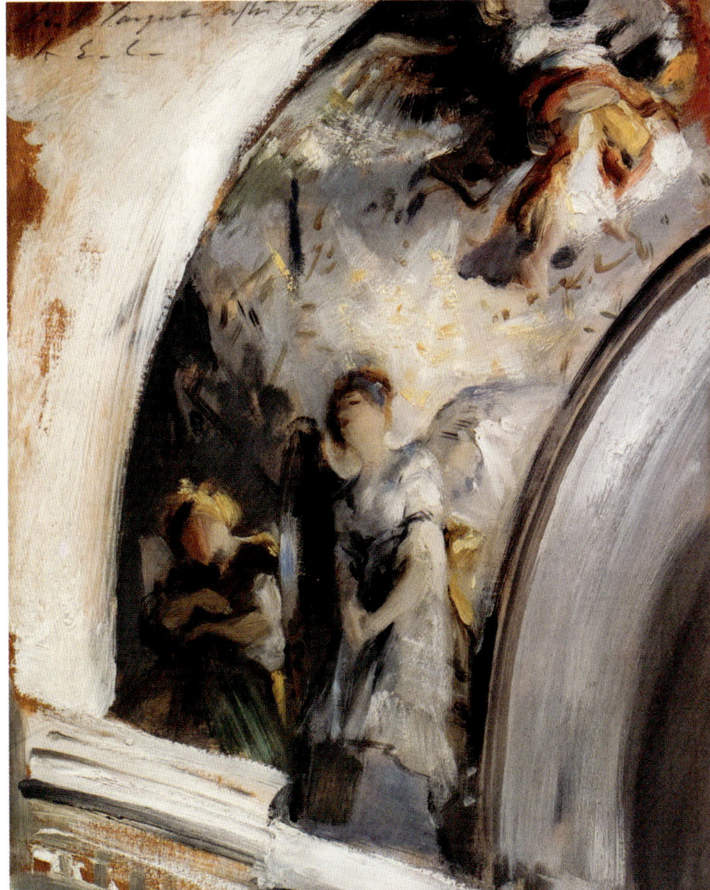

Angels in a Transept, Study
after Goya, 1879, oil on
panel, 34.6 x 26cm (13½ x
10¼in), Private Collection

Unlike most artists who
cease studying other artists
as they progress through
their careers, throughout his
life, Sargent continued to
make copies from the great
masters he admired. Whilst
retaining an Impressionistic
approach with light, quick
brushwork, his favoured
artists were always
Velázquez, then Goya,
Rembrandt and Manet,
which is why his palette
retained its intense tonal
contrasts.

Rehearsal of the Pasdeloup Orchestra at the Cirque d'Hiver, c.1879–80, oil on canvas, 57.1 x 46cm (22½ x 18in), Museum of Fine Arts, Boston, Massachusetts, USA

In the second half of the 19th century, Jules Etienne Pasdeloup (1819–87) conducted an orchestra in Paris for nearly 30 years. The orchestra rehearsed at the Cirque d'Hiver, and Sargent, a talented musician, often attended their concerts. This almost abstract work is one of his boldest experiments with Impressionist techniques. The monochrome palette, energetic brushwork and speedy marks convey the sound of the lively music.

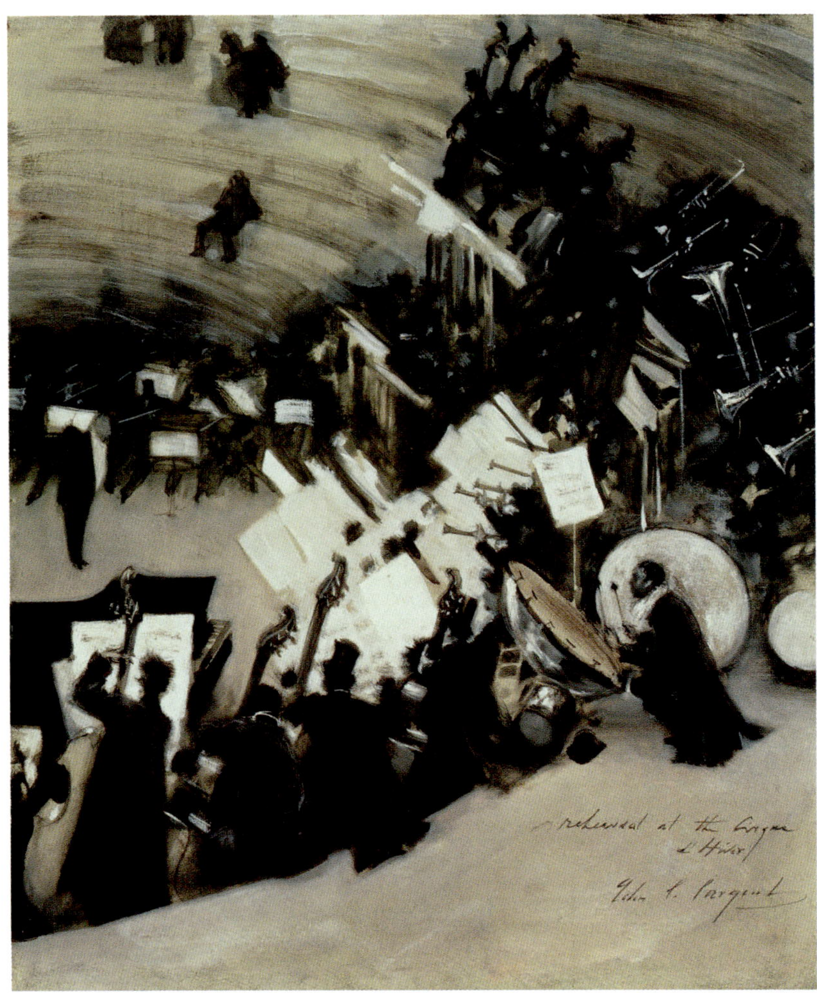

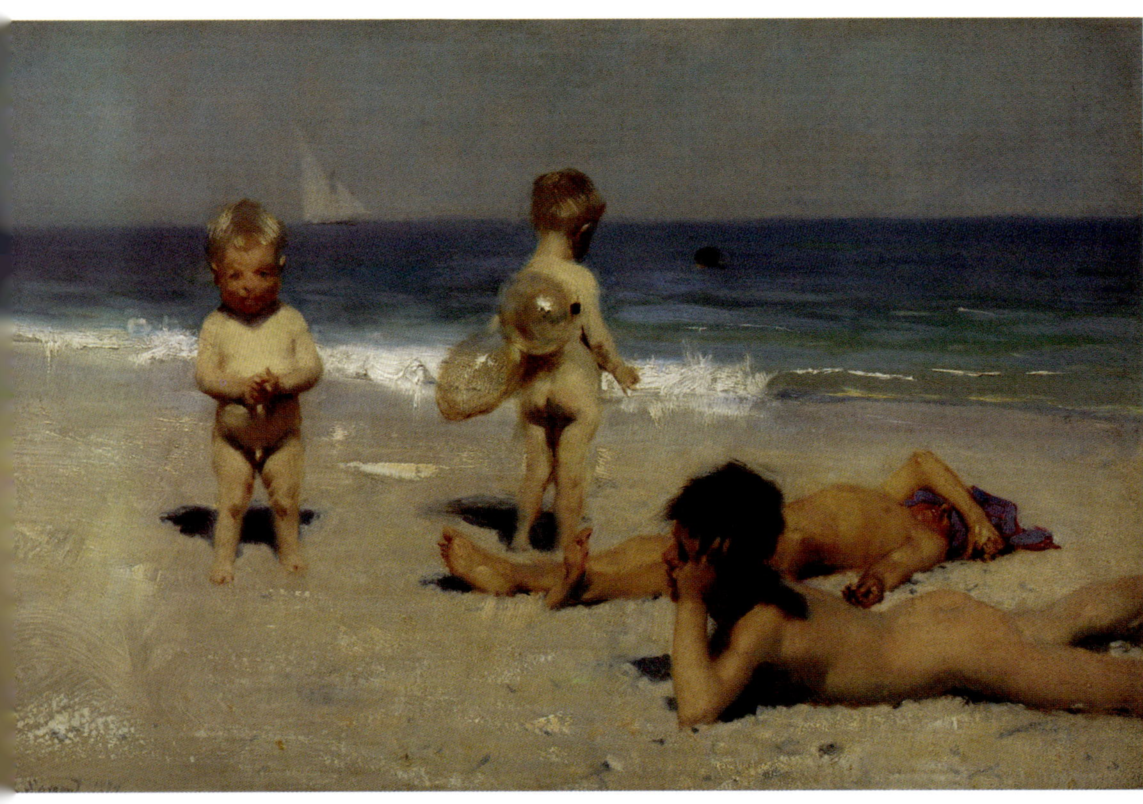

Neapolitan Children Bathing, 1879, oil on canvas, 26.8 x 41.1cm (10½ x 16¼in), The Clark Art Institute, Massachusetts, USA

Building up the composition from pencil sketches and oil studies, Sargent developed this charming work while visiting southern Italy. Little children relax on a hot beach. A small boy wearing an inflated device for swimming looks at the sea, where a swimmer's head can be seen. Two slightly older boys laze on the sand while a toddler stands and gazes. Thin washes of blue and green make up the water, with thicker frothy white describing the foamy waves breaking on soft sand.

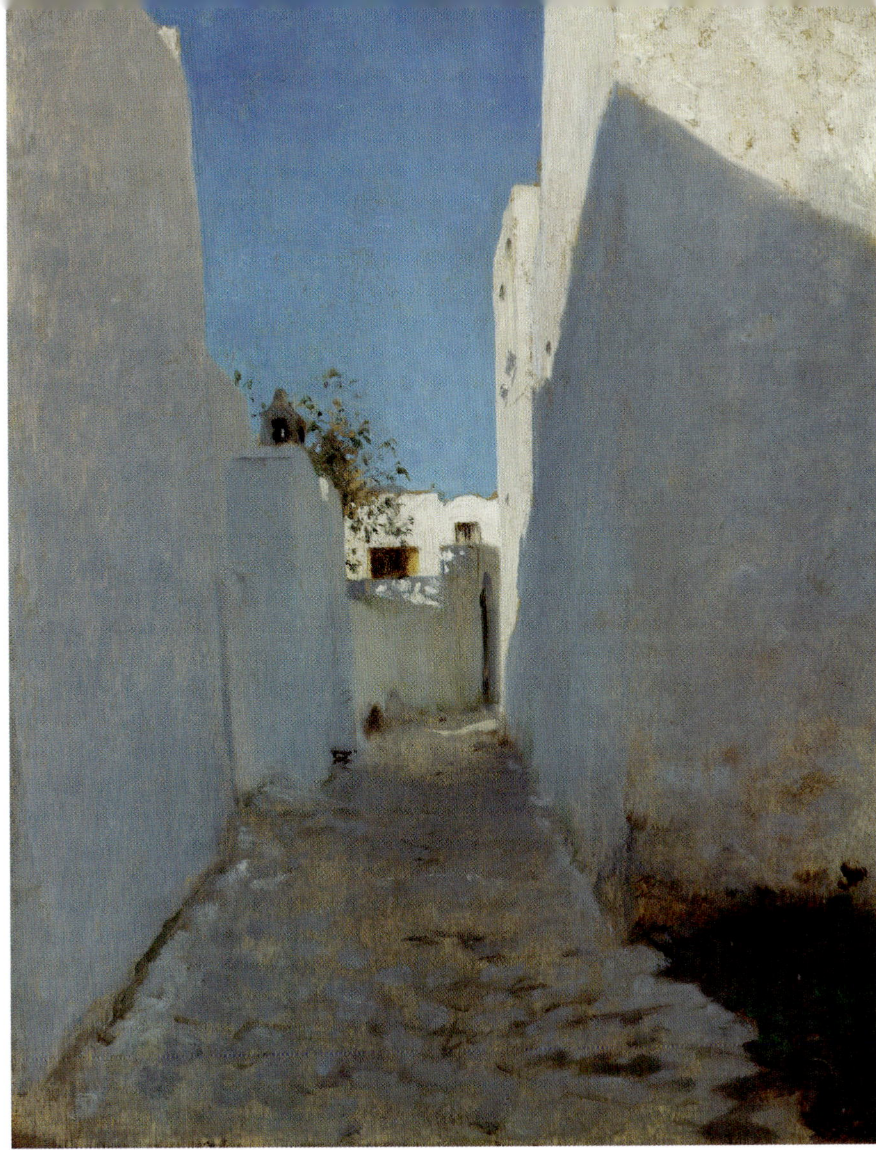

A Moroccan Street Scene,
1879–80, oil on wood, 34.9
x 26cm (13¾ x 10¼in),
Yale University Art Gallery,
Connecticut, USA

In January 1880, Sargent
travelled from Spain to
Morocco and stayed in
Tunis and Tangier. While
there, he produced at least
ten small oil paintings on
wood, including this image,
all of local scenes. Using an
X-shaped composition and a
restricted palette, he conveys
the sense of stillness and
heat, with just a glimpse of
blue sky and cool shadows
against the white walls.

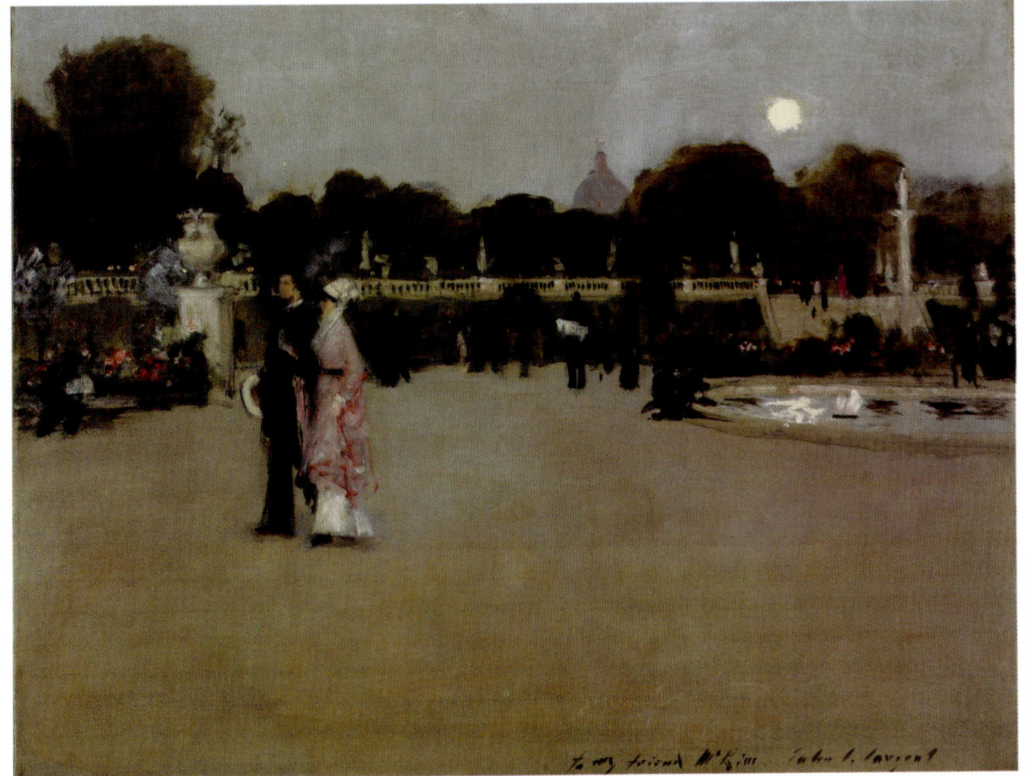

*Luxembourg Gardens at
Twilight,* 1879, oil on canvas,
73.7 x 92.7cm (29 x 36½in),
The Minneapolis Institute of
Arts, Minnesota, USA

Sargent had a studio
in Paris at the time he
painted this, not far from
the huge, formally laid out
Luxembourg Gardens.
Inspired by Whistler's
atmospheric paintings
of London parks, this
demonstrates Sargent's
interest in people and
various observed details,
such as the fashionable
couple strolling across
the park on the balmy
summer evening, and the
children sailing toy boats
on the pond.

Descent from the Cross after El Greco, c.1879, oil on canvas, 76 x 63.5cm (30 x 25in), Private Collection

In the autumn of 1879, Sargent went to Spain with two fellow artists, Charles-Edmond Daux (1855–1937) whom he had met in Capri and Eugène Boch (1855–1941) whom he had met at Bonnat's studio. While in Madrid, the friends copied artworks on display in the Museo del Prado. Sargent especially copied paintings by Velázquez and El Greco.

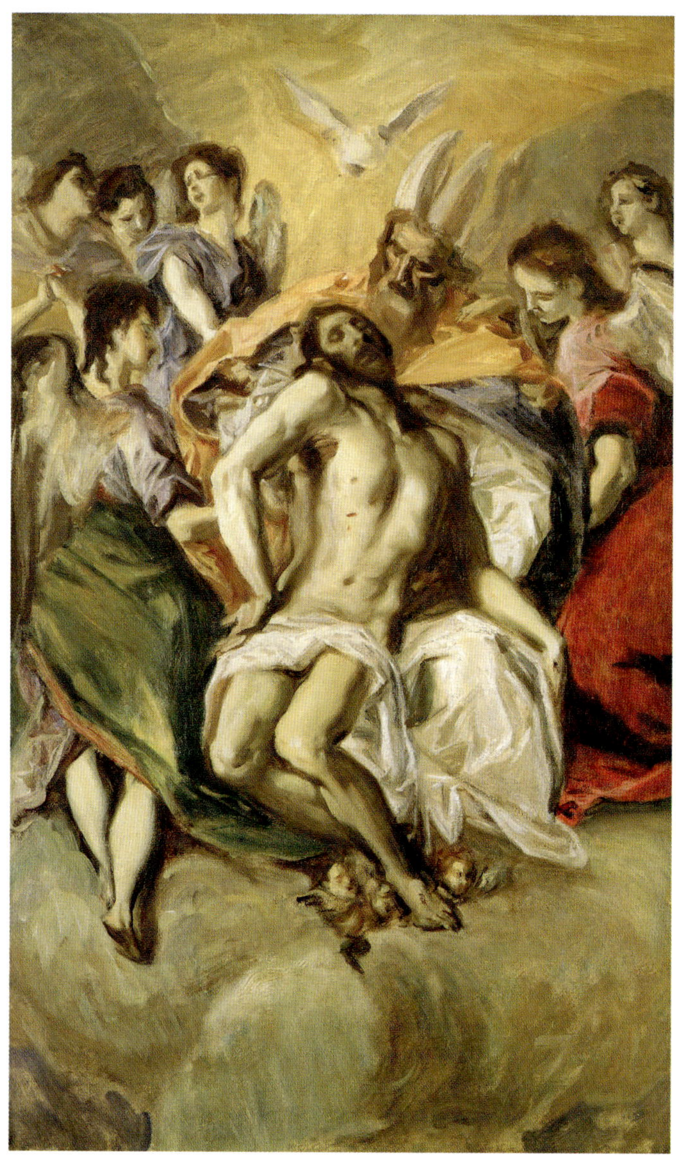

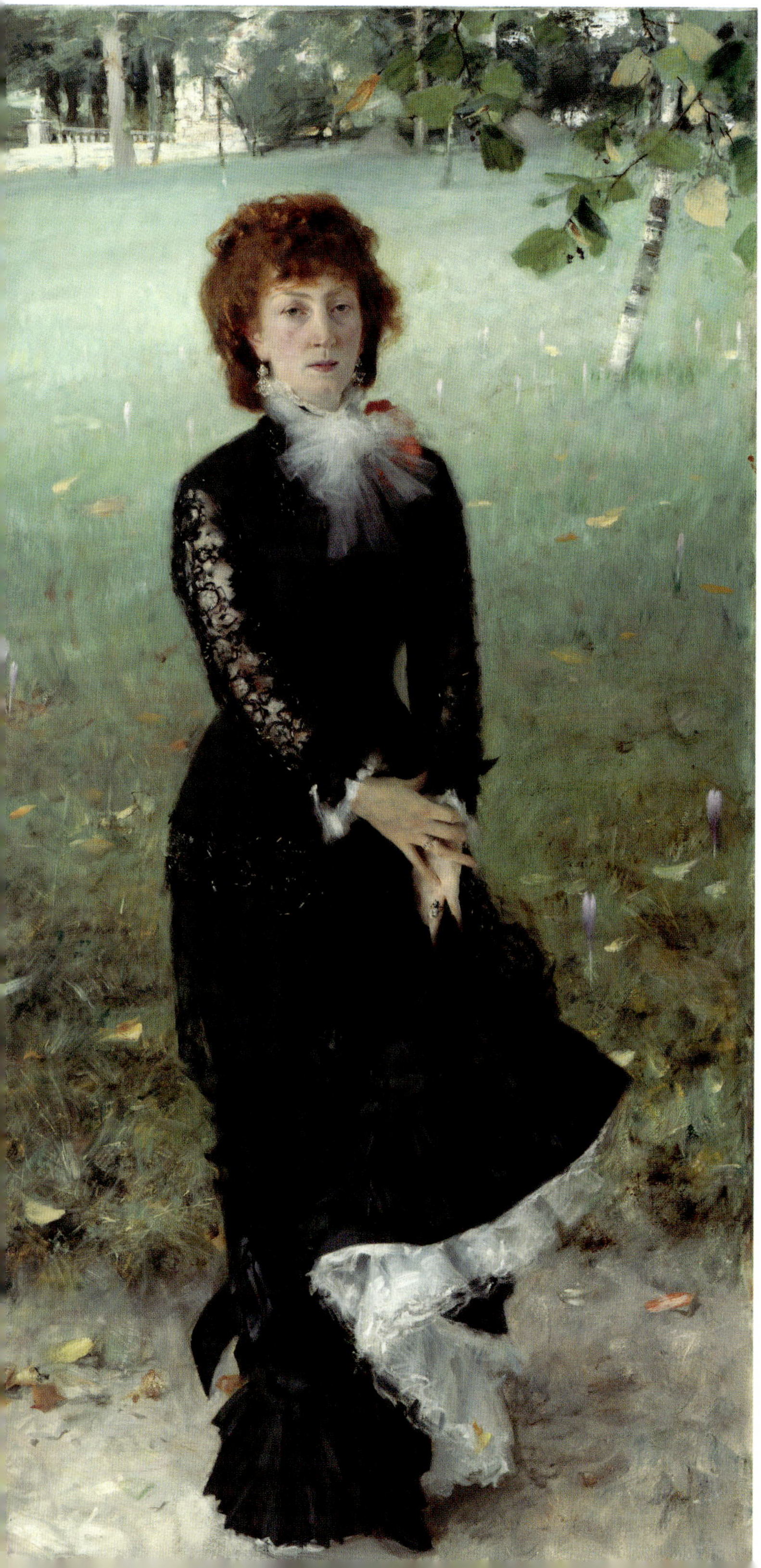

Marie Buloz Pailleron, 1879, oil on canvas, 211 x 104.5cm (83 x 41in), The Corcoran Gallery of Art, Washington DC, USA

The daughter of François Buloz (1803–77), an influential editor and the chief administrator of the Comédie-Française, Marie Pailleron was married to Édouard Pailleron. Sargent painted several members of the Pailleron family and became friends with the couple. This is a formal portrait with a twist: Marie is outside, and a tiny architectural element is cut off in the upper far left corner, creating a modern composition (see page 30).

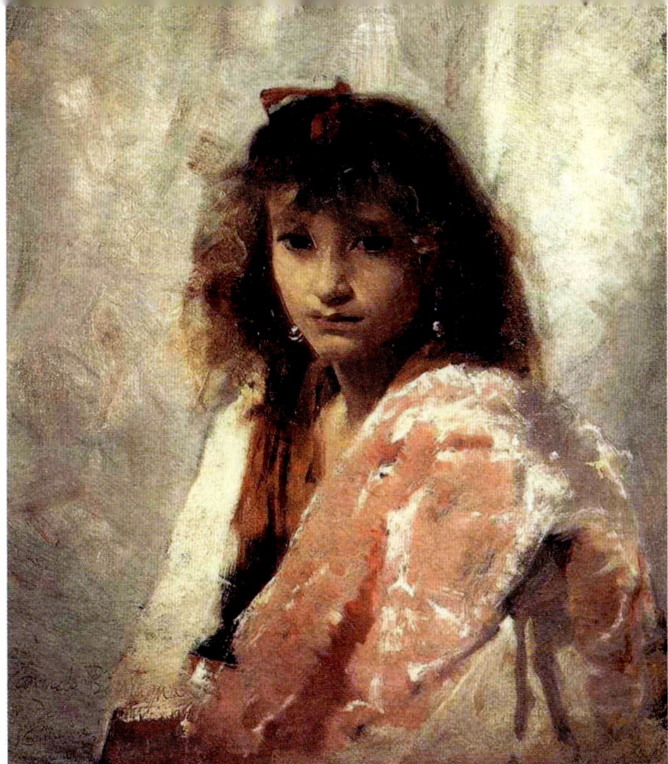

Carmela Bertagna, 1879, oil on canvas, 59.7 x 49.5cm (23½ x 19½in), Columbus Museum of Art, Ohio, USA

While staying in Spain during the September and October of 1879, Sargent was enchanted by the music, surroundings, culture and people. Using fluid brushwork and a limited palette, he captured this young señorita. The textures of the materials she is swathed in are created with thicker, freer marks, while her face is depicted in thinner, more detailed and smaller strokes.

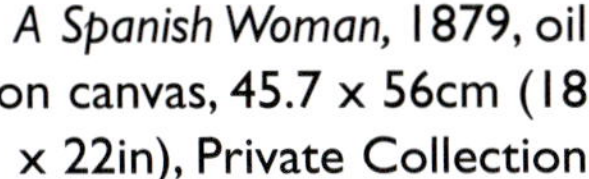

A Spanish Woman, 1879, oil on canvas, 45.7 x 56cm (18 x 22in), Private Collection

As with the above painting, Sargent was captivated by exotic, dark and sultry-looking individuals. This moody image captures the sense of inscrutability that enthralled him. The enduring influence of Carolus-Duran can be seen in his dark palette and strong chiaroscuro. Although entitled *A Spanish Woman*, the model was probably the Italian Gigia Viani (see page 118).

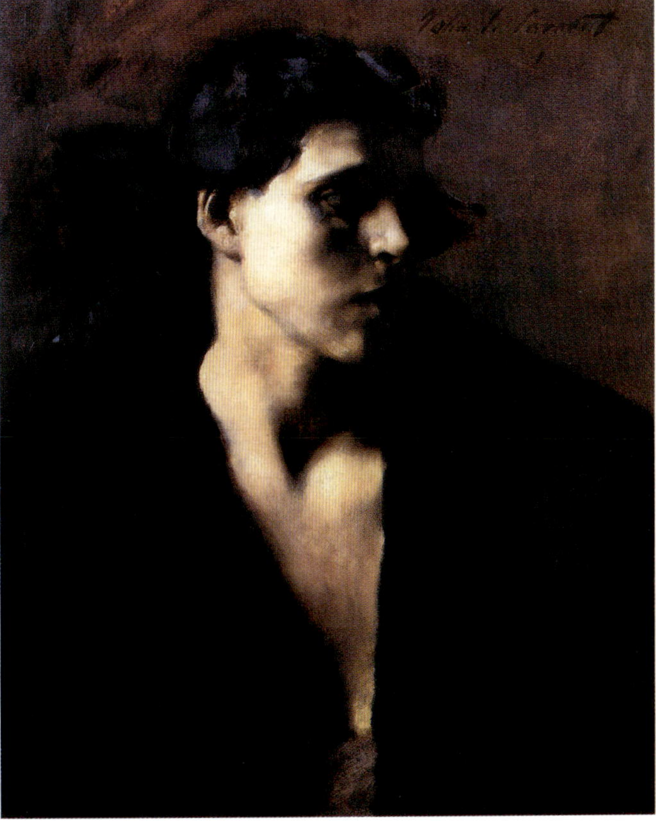

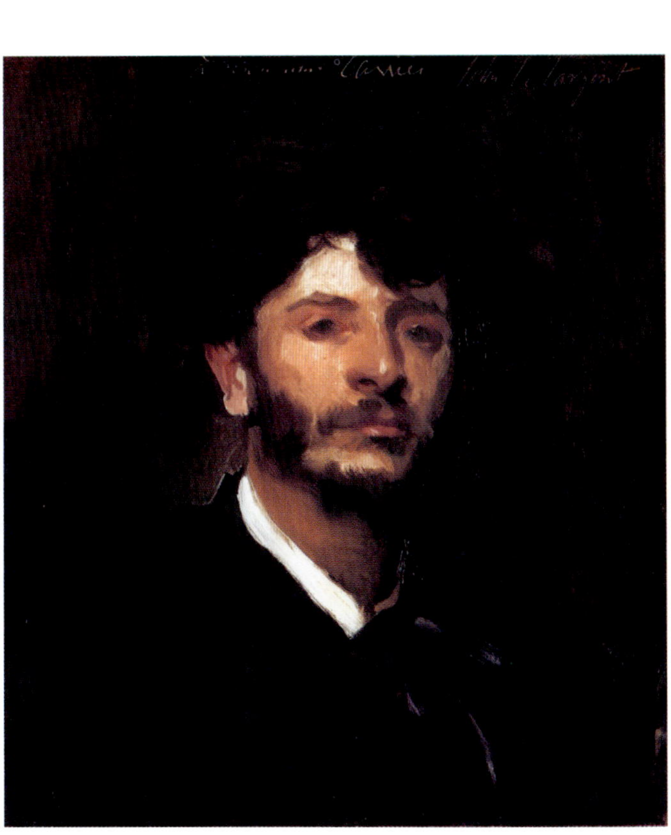

Joseph Marie Carriès, 1880, oil on canvas, 55.9 x 46.4 cm (22 x 18¼ in), Sheldon Memorial Art Gallery and Sculpture Garden, Nebraska, USA

Jean-Joseph Marie Carriès (1855–94) was a French sculptor, ceramist and miniaturist. After moving to Paris from Lyon in 1874, he met Sargent while they were both studying at the École des Beaux-Arts. Carriès first exhibited at the 1875 Paris Salon and attracted particular acclaim for his sculpted busts at the Salons of 1879 and 1881. Sargent painted his friend, applying impasto paint freely and rapidly.

Fumée d'Ambre Gris, 1880, oil on canvas, 139 x 90.6cm (54¾ x 35¾in), Clark Art Institute, Massachusetts, USA

Sargent made sketches for this oil painting during his visit to Tangiers in 1879 and completed the canvas later in his Paris studio, exhibiting it in the Salon the following year. Standing next to a tall Moroccan arch, a woman holds her veil over a silver incense burner to capture the perfumed smoke of ambergris. A waxy substance extracted from whales, ambergris was used in some religious rituals and was said to have aphrodisiac qualities. Orientalism was popular at the time; this scene combines several exotic ideas.

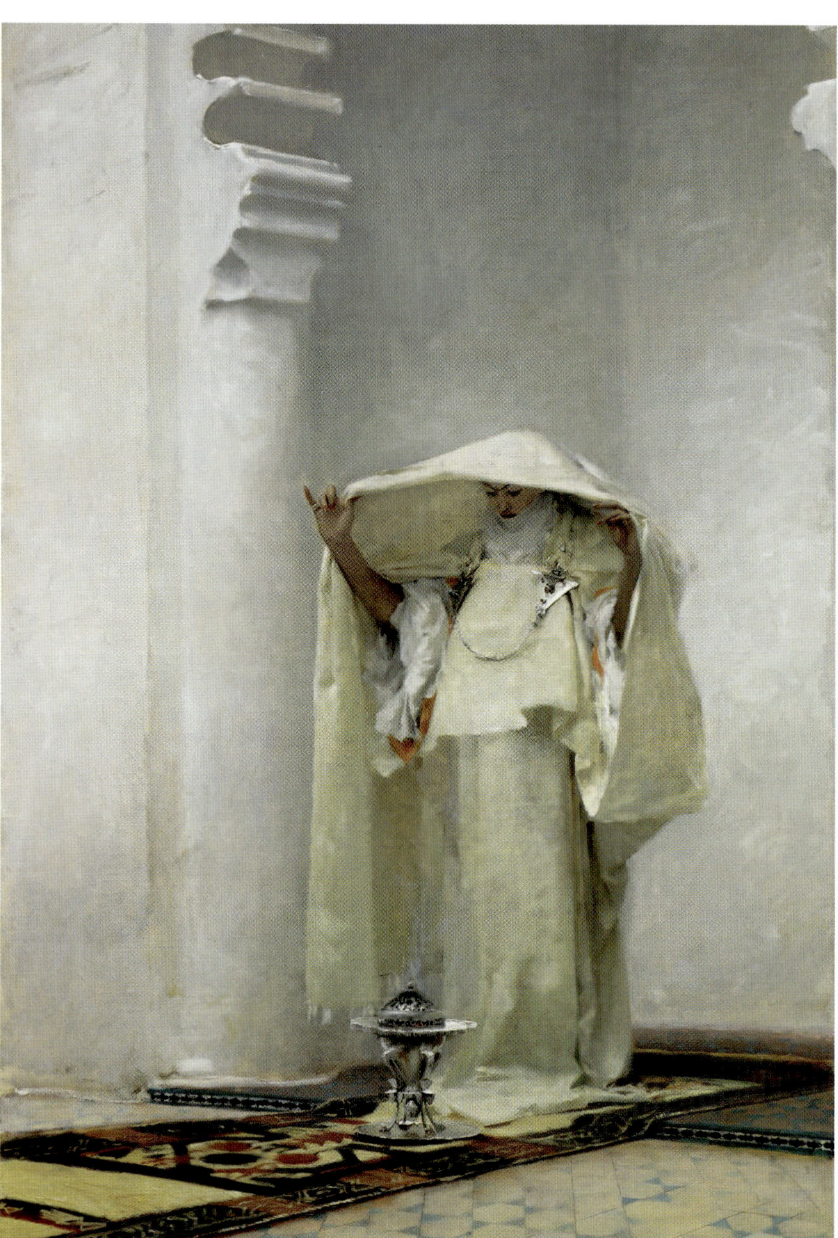

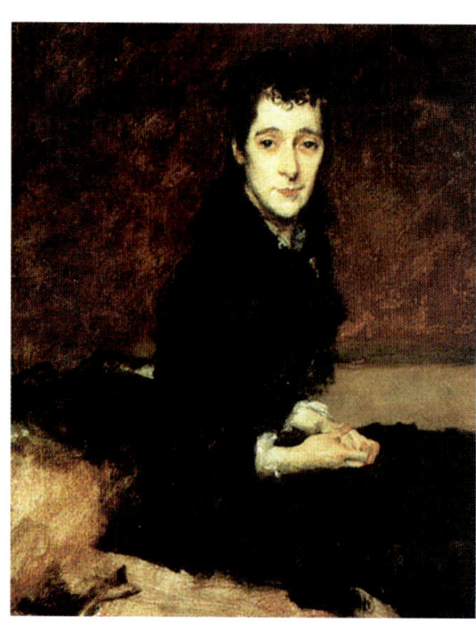

Mrs Charles Gifford Dyer (Mary Anthony), 1880, oil on canvas, 62.2 x 43.8cm (24½ x 17¼in), The Art Institute of Chicago, Illinois, USA

Mary Dyer (dates unknown) and her husband, Charles Gifford Dyer (1846–1912), were part of an expatriate community of American artists living in Europe in the late 19th century.

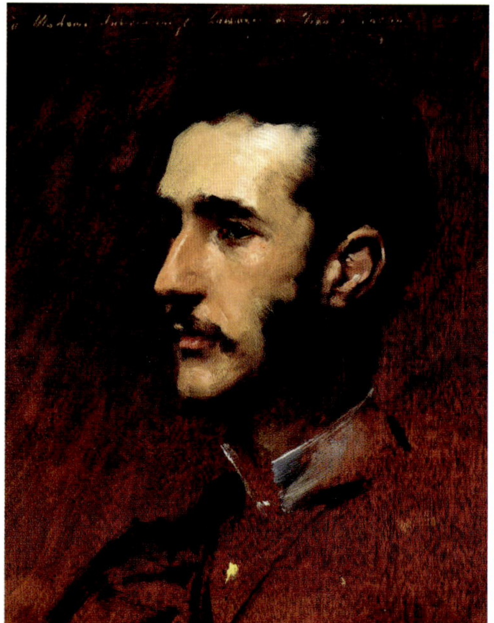

Ramón Subercaseaux, c.1880, oil on panel, 35.4 x 26.6cm (13¾ x 10½in), Saint Louis Art Museum, Missouri, USA

An unsigned painting of the author, diplomat and painter, Ramón Subercaseaux (1854–1937), who was the Chilean consul and one of Sargent's many friends. This pre-dates the full-length portrait of Subercaseaux's young wife that earned Sargent one of his first medals at the Salon in 1881.

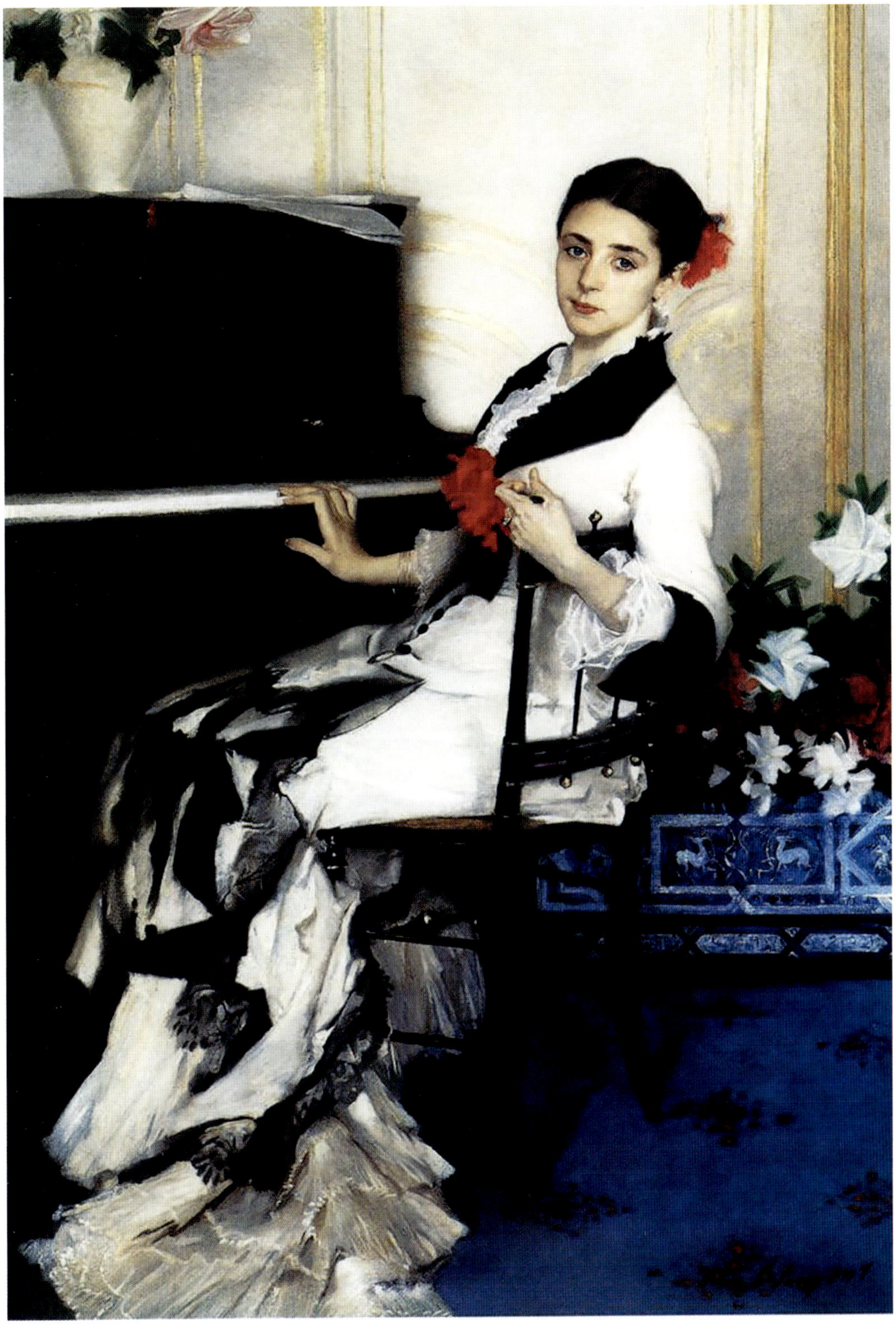

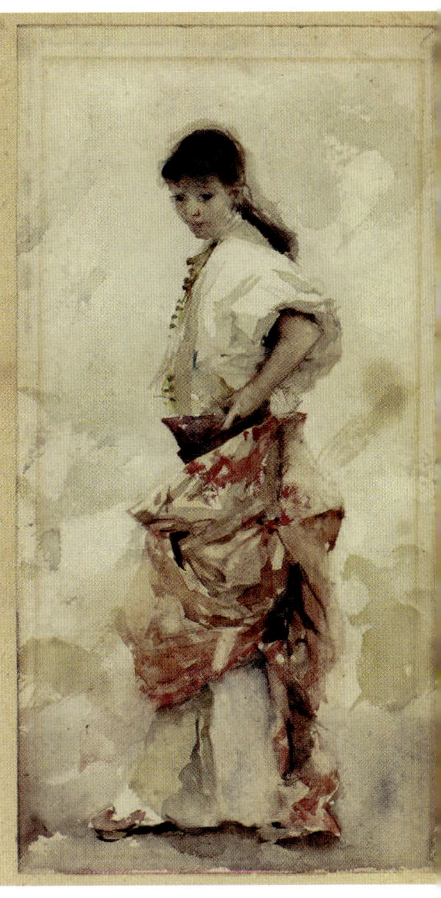

Girl in Spanish Costume,
before 1880, watercolour
on ivory wove paper, 32.9
x 16.5cm (13 x 6½in),
The Art Institute of Chicago,
Illinois, USA

The young, unidentified
Spanish girl seems poised
as if about to turn her
gentle movement into a
lively Spanish dance. The
image shows Sargent's
fascination with all things
Spanish, including the people,
colours, music and exoticism,
as well as his debt to the
Impressionists in capturing
a fleeting moment.

*Madame Ramón
Subercaseaux,* 1880, oil on
canvas, 165.1 x 109.9cm (65
× 43¼in), Private Collection

Newly married to the
Chilean consul and artist
Ramón Subercaseaux, Amalia
Subercaseaux (1860–1930)
was 20 when Sargent painted
her portrait seated at a
piano in the couple's elegant
residence on the Avenue du
Bois de Boulogne in Paris.
Amalia wrote in her diary: 'It
was in Paris during the Spring
of 1880 that Sargent painted
my portrait which won the
prize the following year [2nd
place at the Salon]... He ...
took great care of the effect
of each object and colour...'
Winning the second-class
medal meant that Sargent
could exhibit at future Salons
without submitting first to
the jury.

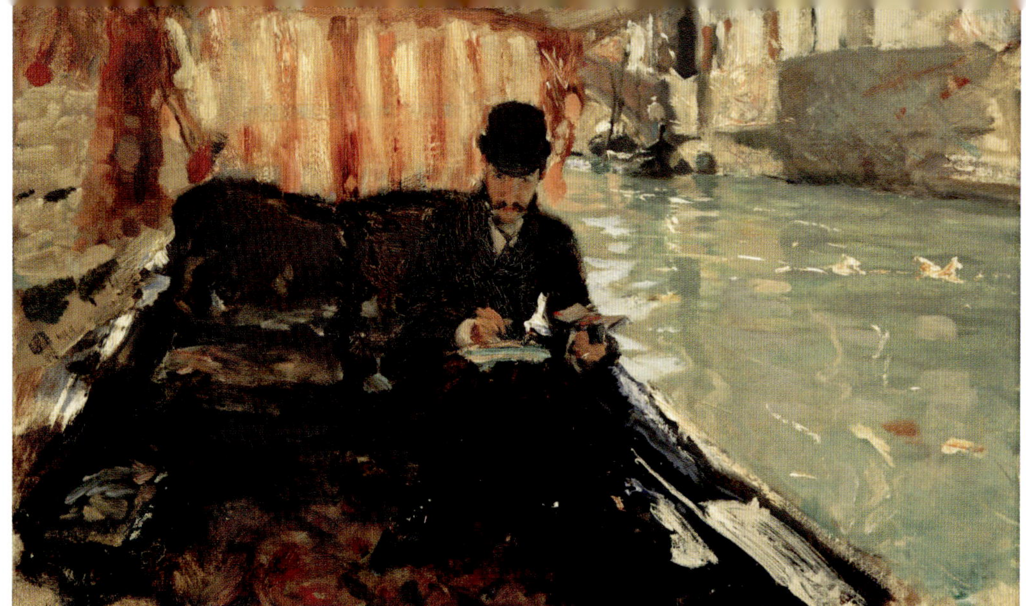

Ramón Subercaseaux in a Gondola, 1880, oil on canvas, 47 x 63.5cm (18½ x 25in), Dixon Gallery and Gardens, Tennessee, USA

Two years older than his friend Sargent, Ramón Subercaseaux had a successful career as a diplomat, which was only just starting when Sargent painted this. He had been in Paris since he was 20, in 1874, and he had recently married his beautiful bride Amalia Errazuriz y Urmeneta. They first met Sargent after the 1879 Salon when Subercaseaux commissioned a portrait of Amalia.

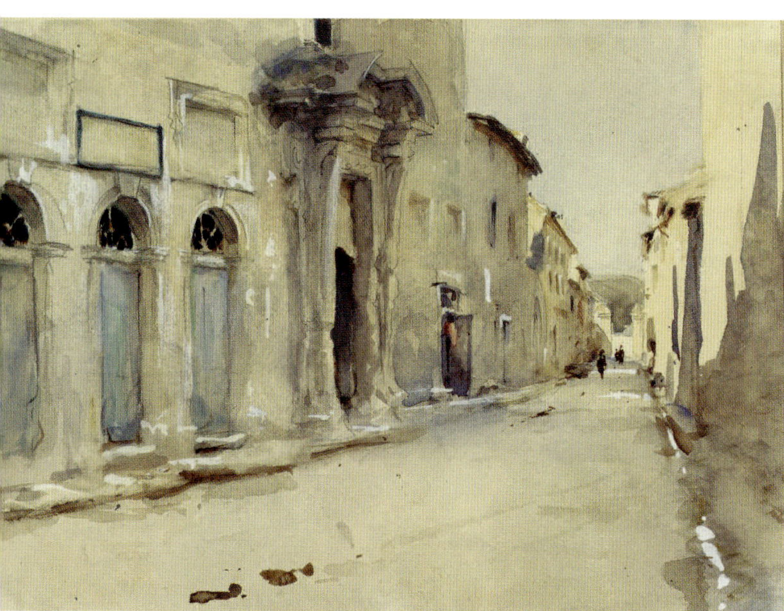

A Street in Spain, (see also page 30) c.1880, translucent and opaque watercolour over graphite on paper, 23.8 x 32.1cm (9¼ x 12¾in), Ashmolean Museum, Oxfordshire, UK

Sargent captured the sense of this almost-deserted Spanish street soon after leaving Carolus-Duran's studio, and still heavily under the influence of his tutor. The suggestion of figures can be seen at the shadowy end of the street, while he has picked out highlights with a brush loaded with diluted amounts of zinc white bodycolour, or gouache.

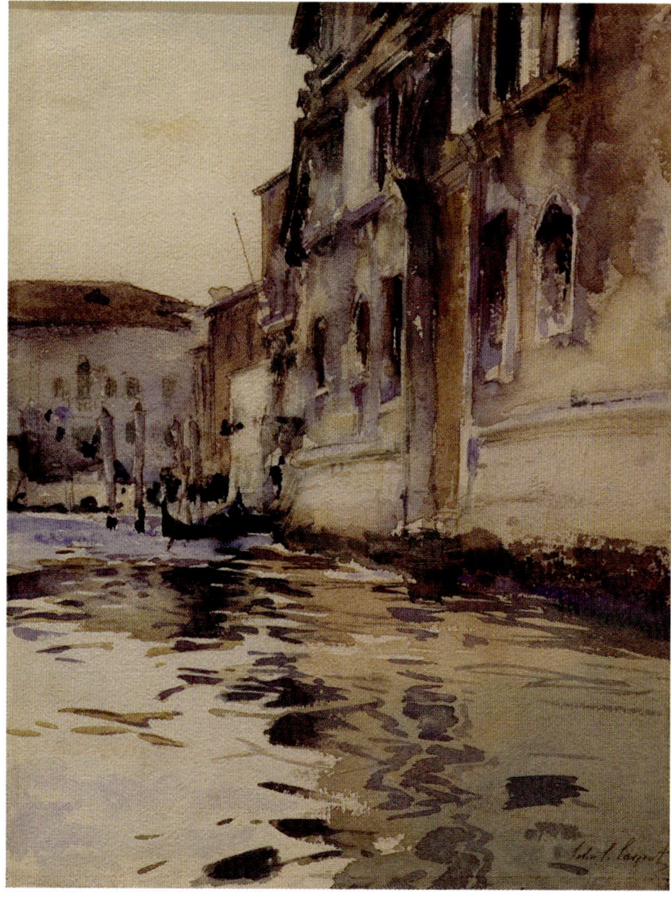

Venetian Canal, Palazzo Contarini degli Scrigni e Corfu, c.1880–81, watercolour on paper, 32.4 x 23cm (12¾ x 9in), Private Collection

While in Venice, Sargent met other artists who inspired him and while working from the studio in the Palazzo Rezzonico, he painted this view of the Palazzo Contarini with the Galleria dell'Accademia in the distance. With the complex composition, staccato, broken brushwork and his sombre palette of the time, this once again shows an influence of Velázquez.

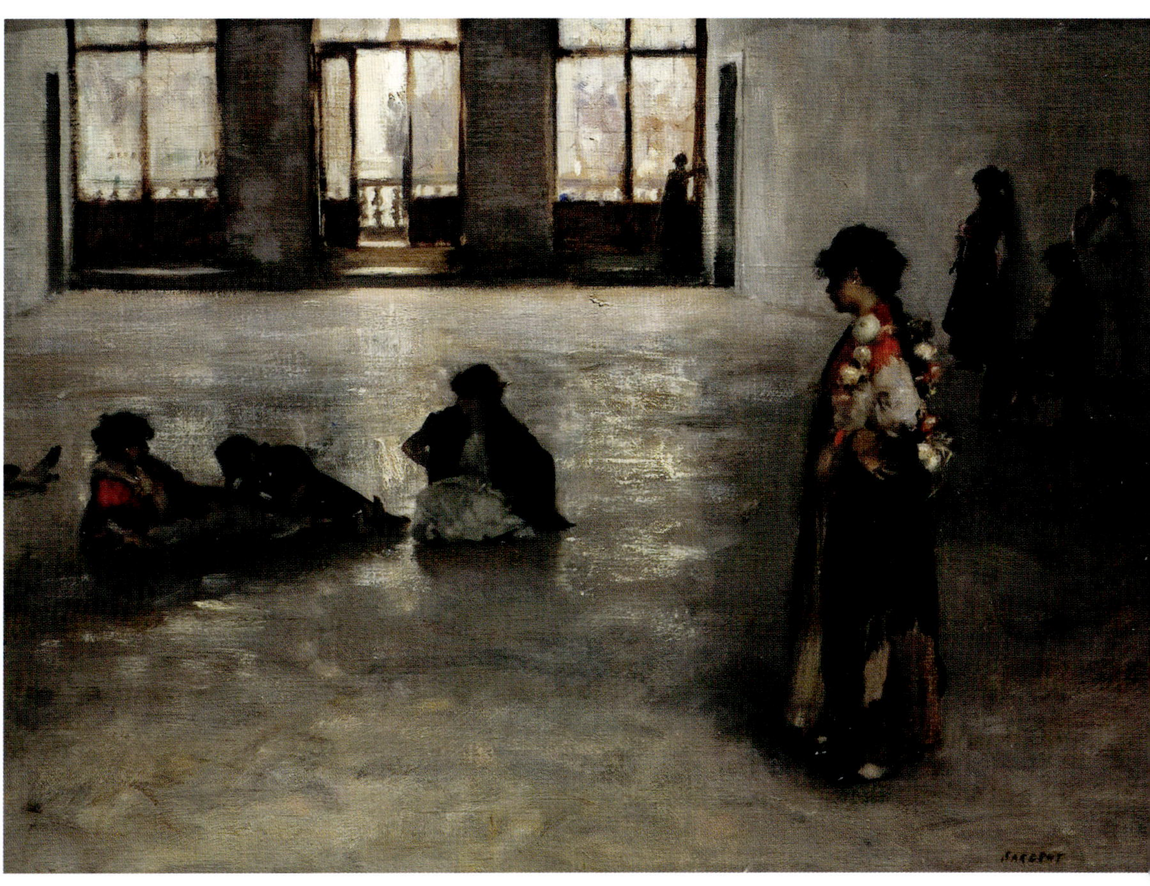

Venetian Women in the Palazzo Rezzonico, c.1880–81, oil on canvas, 45 x 63cm (17¾ x 2in), Private Collection

In the autumn of 1880, Sargent visited Venice with his family. With other artists there he set up a studio in the Palazzo Rezzonico; an old palace on the Grand Canal, where he stayed throughout the winter after his family had left. While there, he produced many sultry and expressive scenes like this, redolent with atmosphere. This shadowy interior features local figures who seemingly have not noticed the artist painting them.

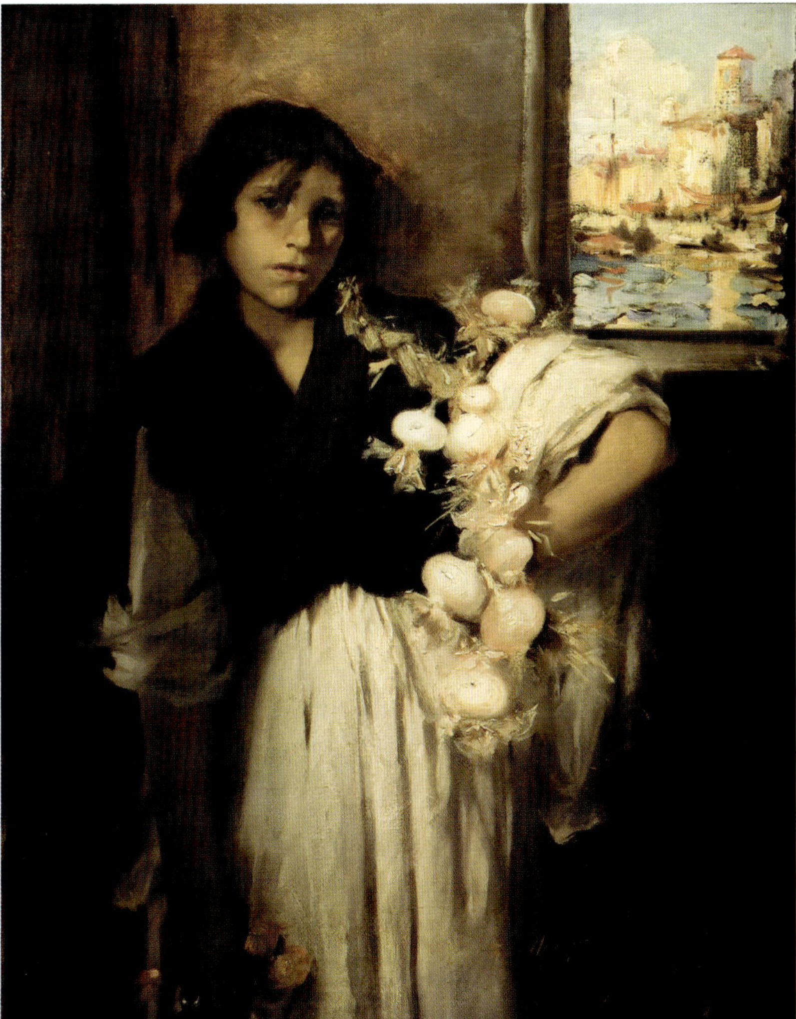

Venetian Onion Seller, c.1880–82, oil on canvas, 95 x 70cm (37½ x 27½in), Museo Thyssen-Bornemisza, Madrid, Spain

Still using his palette inspired primarily by Velázquez, this is another study of a local girl in the city of Venice. A three-quarter length portrait, this confident young onion seller has one hand on her hip and a large string of onions hanging over her shoulder. Her tanned skin contrasts with the white of her skirt and the onions. Sargent employs an unusual composition, featuring the main figure in sombre colours and cool shadows, with just a small window by her arm revealing the brilliant light and colours of Venice beyond.

Venetian Bead Stringers, 1880 or 1882, oil on canvas, 67 x 78.1cm (26½ x 30¾in), Albright-Knox Art Gallery, New York, USA

Glass beads made in Murano have been a big part of the tourist industry in Venice for many years. The process of stringing the beads has similarly been a long-standing mode of employment for many women over that time. Sargent was fascinated by the rhythmical procedure and the companionable fashion with which the women worked. In grey and black illuminated by patches of light, two of the women sit slumped in the gloom, sharing a tray of beads, while another stands tall and slender in front of them, wrapped in a shawl.

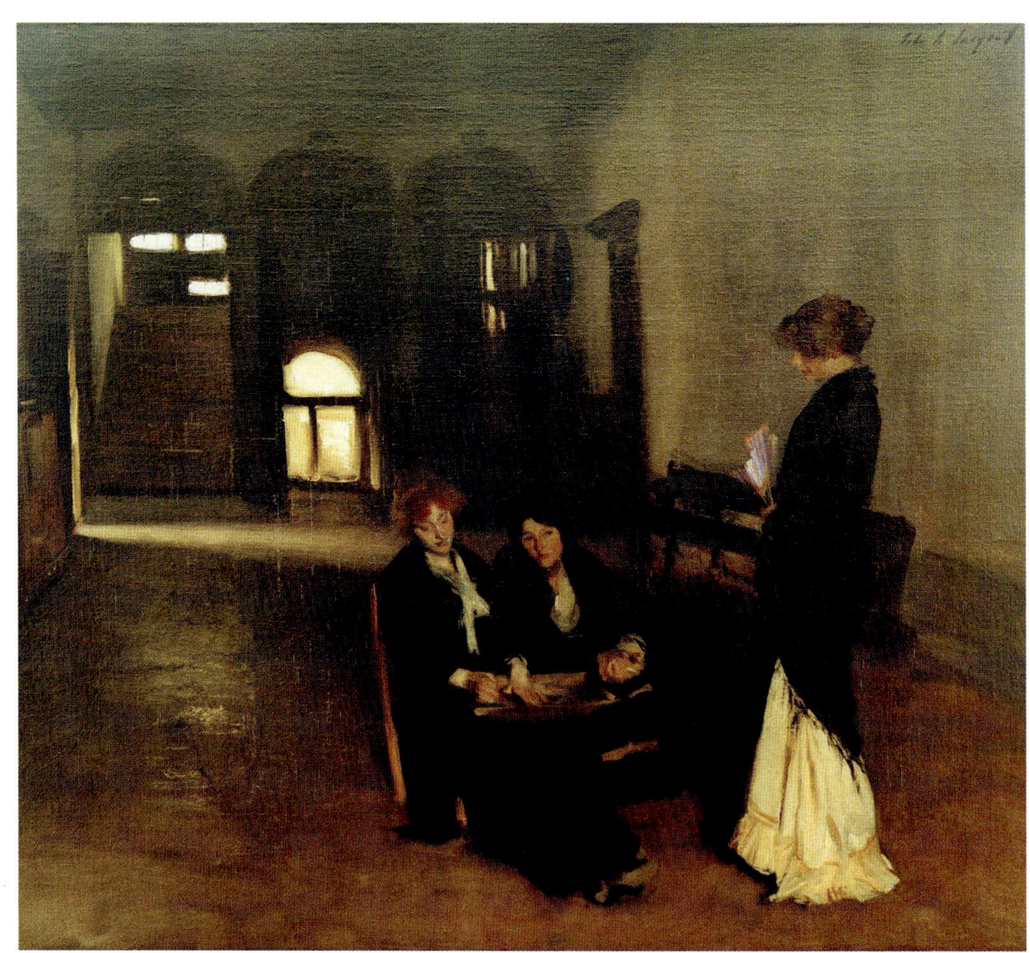

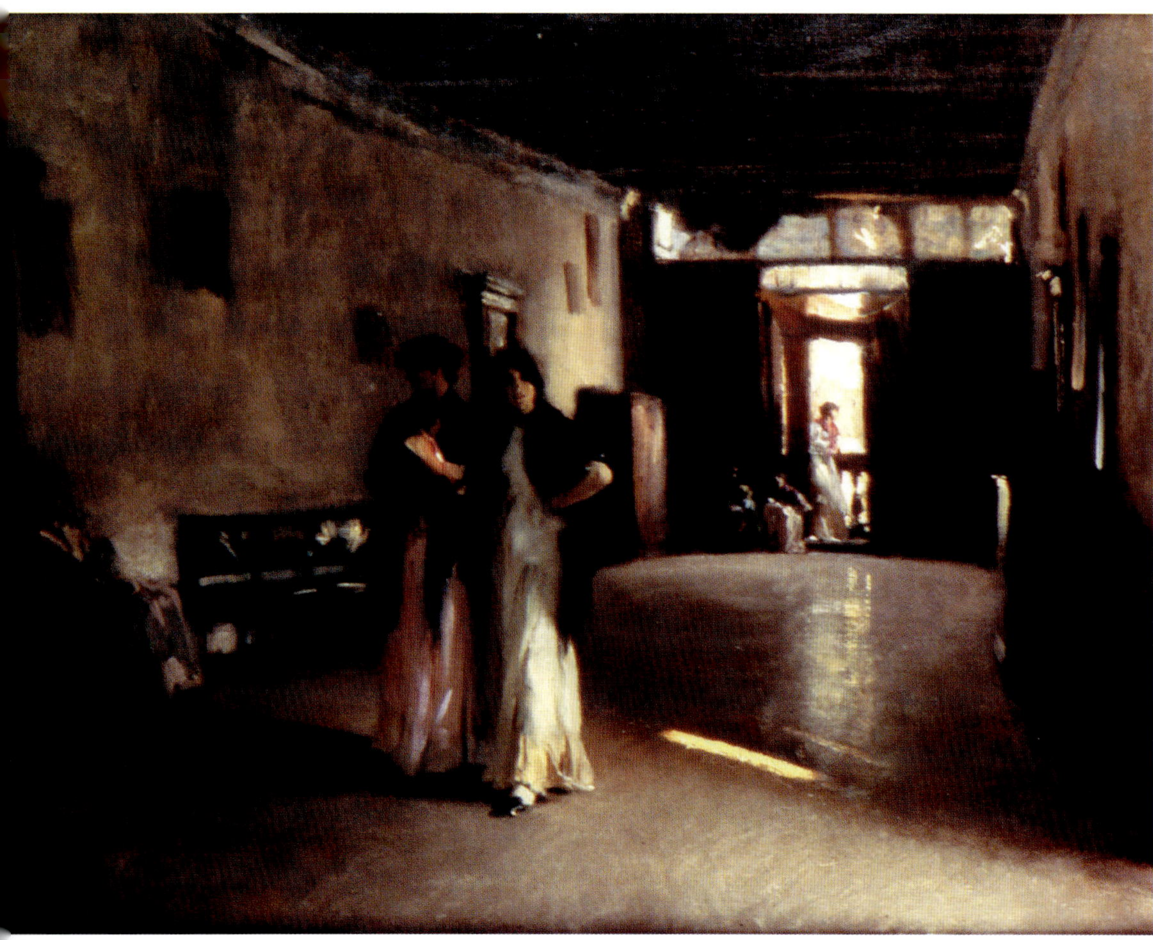

Venetian Interior, c.1880–82, oil on canvas, 68.3 x 86.8cm (26¾ x 34¼in), Carnegie Museum of Art, Pennsylvania, USA

In the autumn and winter of 1880 and 1881, Sargent spent time in Venice, which remained a popular destination for many artists because of its unique light and juxtaposition of ornate buildings against the sky and water. Yet at this time, Sargent concentrated more on interiors, especially the dark coolness of his friends' rather dilapidated Palazzo Rezzonico. Bright light can be seen on the balcony, while two elegant ladies stroll through the hall, and tiny patches of slanting sunlight illuminate the scene.

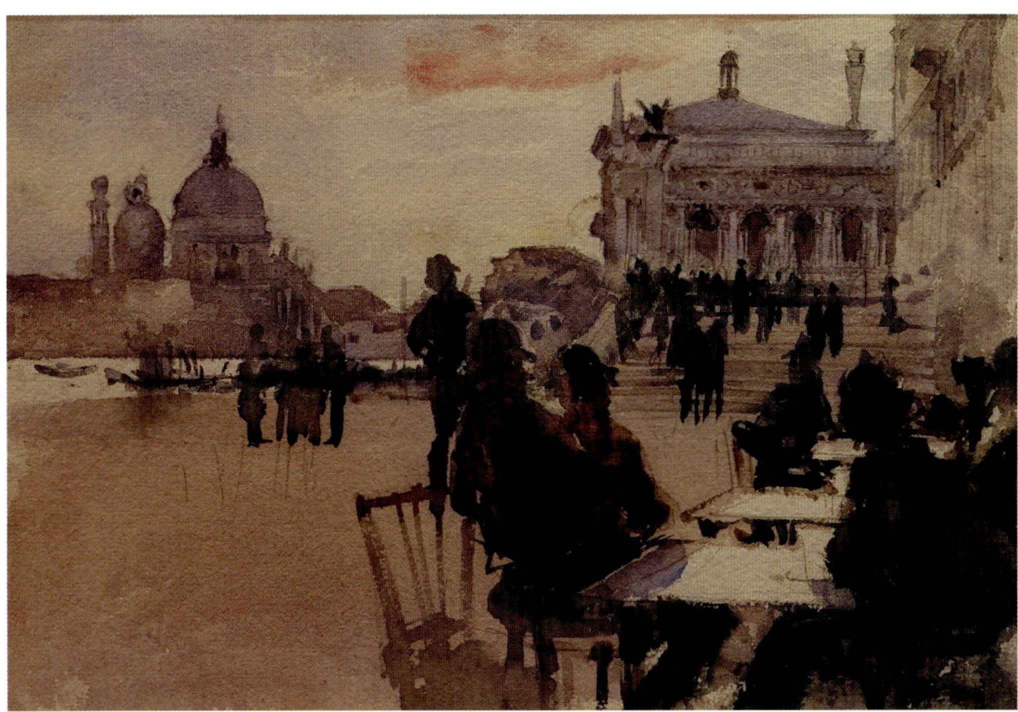

Café on the Riva degli Schiavoni, 1880–82, watercolour and graphite on paper, 24 x 34.3cm (9½ x 13½in), Private Collection

The paved quay that extends eastwards from the Piazzetta at San Marco in front of the Doge's Palace has always been a favourite promenade. The domed building across the canal is the Santa Maria della Salute, and the Libreria is straight ahead beyond the steps. Close by is the famous Café Oriental – which is now the site of the Hotel Danieli.

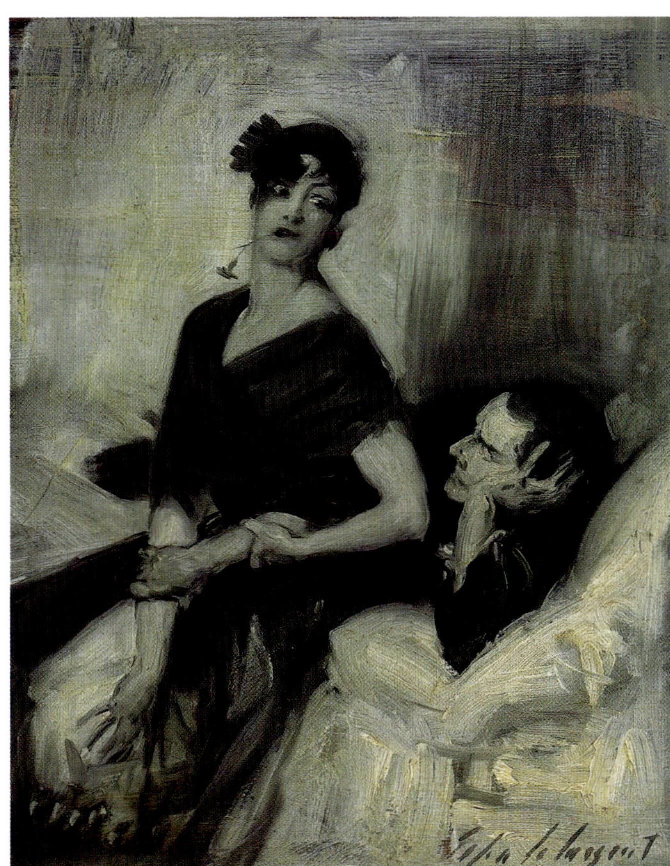

Man and Woman on a Bed, c.1880–82, oil on board, 28.6 x 22.2cm (11¼ x 8¾in), Private Collection

This monochromatic painting is one of three related studies of a man making advances on a woman. The other two images are pencil sketches, in which the woman's eyes are downcast as if she is shyly rejecting the man's unwanted advances; here, however, she bites a flower between her teeth and rolls her eyes angrily, suggesting her high-spirited confidence.

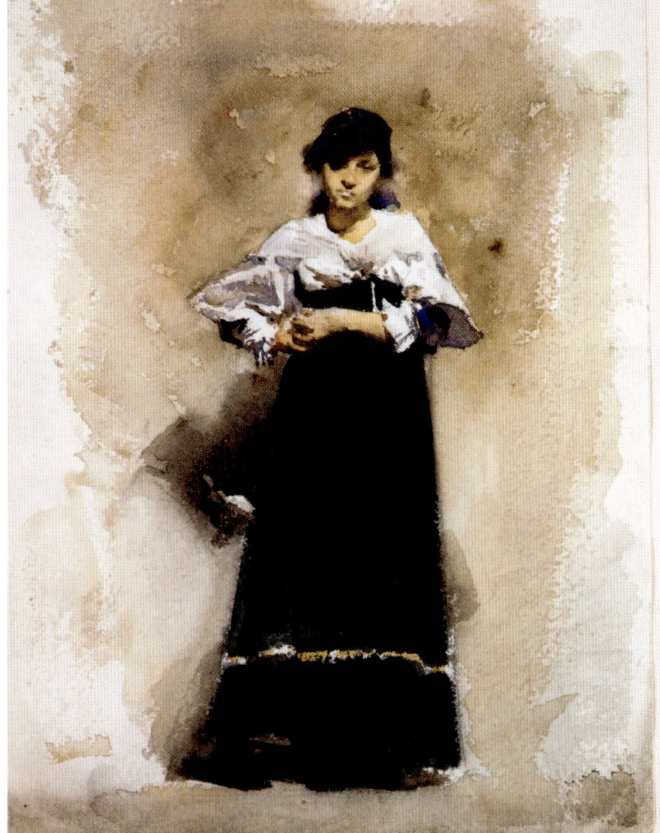

Young Woman in a Black Skirt, early 1880s, watercolour and graphite on white wove paper, 35.6 x 24.9cm (14 x 9¾in), The Metropolitan Museum, New York, USA

Standing proudly in her traditional Venetian peasant costume, this young woman looks back at Sargent as he rapidly captured her stance and clothing. The ruffled blouse, shawl and gathered long black skirt, combined with the girl's bold confidence, encapsulates his fascination with the exotic.

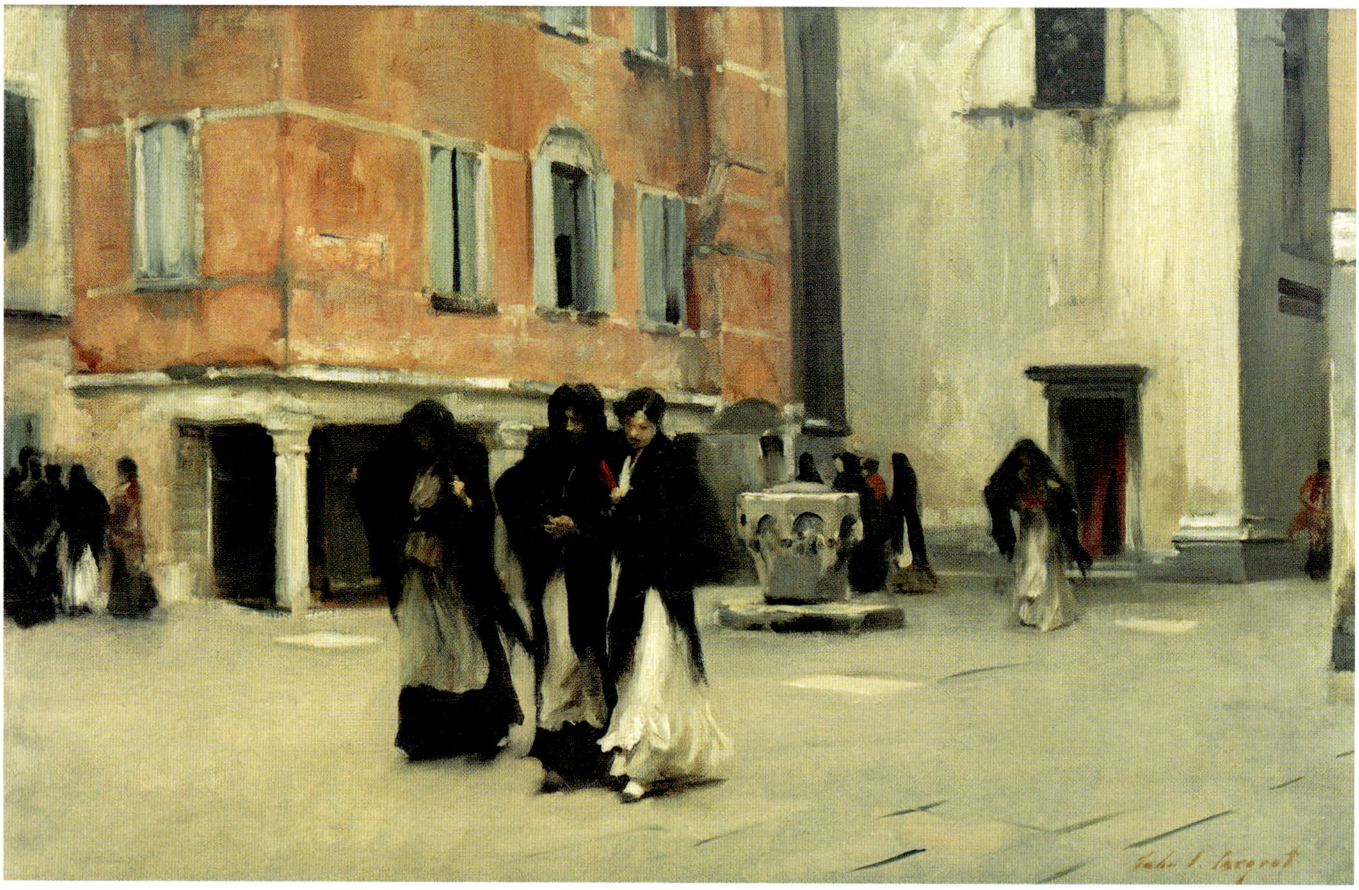

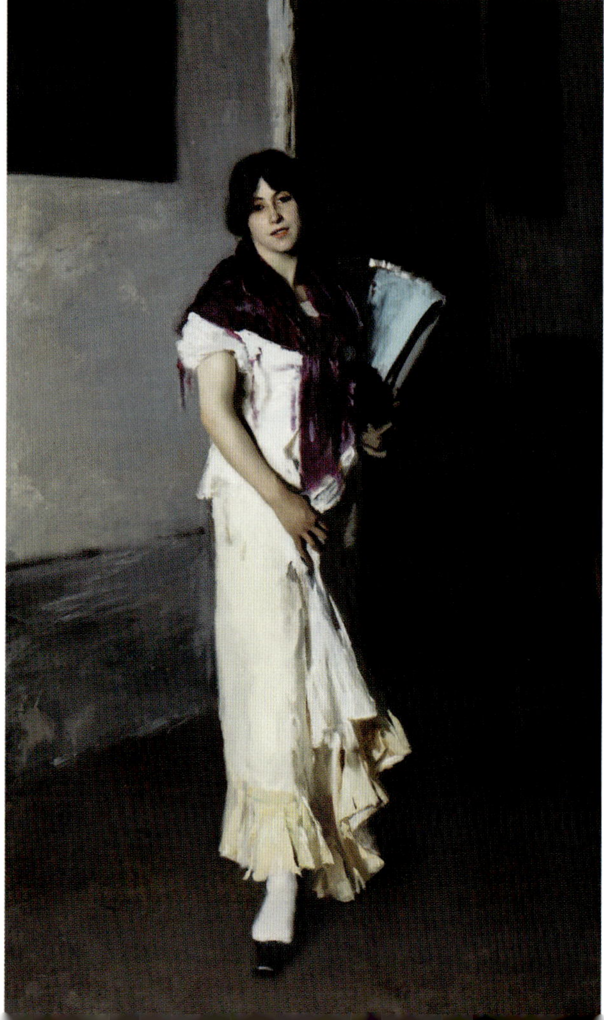

Leaving Church, Campo San Canciano, Venice, c.1882, oil on canvas, 59.9 x 85.1cm (22 x 33½in), National Gallery of Art, Washington DC, USA

One of many scenes that Sargent painted during his visits to Venice from 1880 to 1882. Avoiding the usual tourist spots Sargent instead explored the architecture and everyday life of the locals. Here, three women cross the Campo San Canciano as they leave church in the early morning light. It is probable that Sargent was staying in the square at the time as he described its old fountain in a letter to a friend.

Venetian Girl with Fan, 1882, oil on canvas, 238.1 x 133.4cm (93¾ x 52½in), Cincinnati Art Museum, Ohio, USA

This is a Venetian model called Gigia Viani, whom Sargent used for many of his Venetian paintings. Several of his artist friends also painted her. This large-scale work, however, is less of a Venetian scene and more of a portrait, as Sargent intended to submit it to the Paris Salon. In the end though the painting was not finished in time and he submitted other works to the Salon instead.

Campo Sant'Agnese, Venice,
1882, oil on canvas, 45.7
× 65.1cm (18 × 25¾in),
Davis Museum and Cultural
Centre, Massachusetts, USA

Sargent loved the
atmospheric old squares of
Venice, unchanged through
the years, steeped in history
and strongly portraying a
sense of a grander past.
This is the Campo Sant'
Agnese with the former
monastery of the Gesuati
(now the Istituto Artigianelli)
in front of him. Except for
the prominent Renaissance
well-head with black buckets
scattered beside it, the square
appears quite deserted.

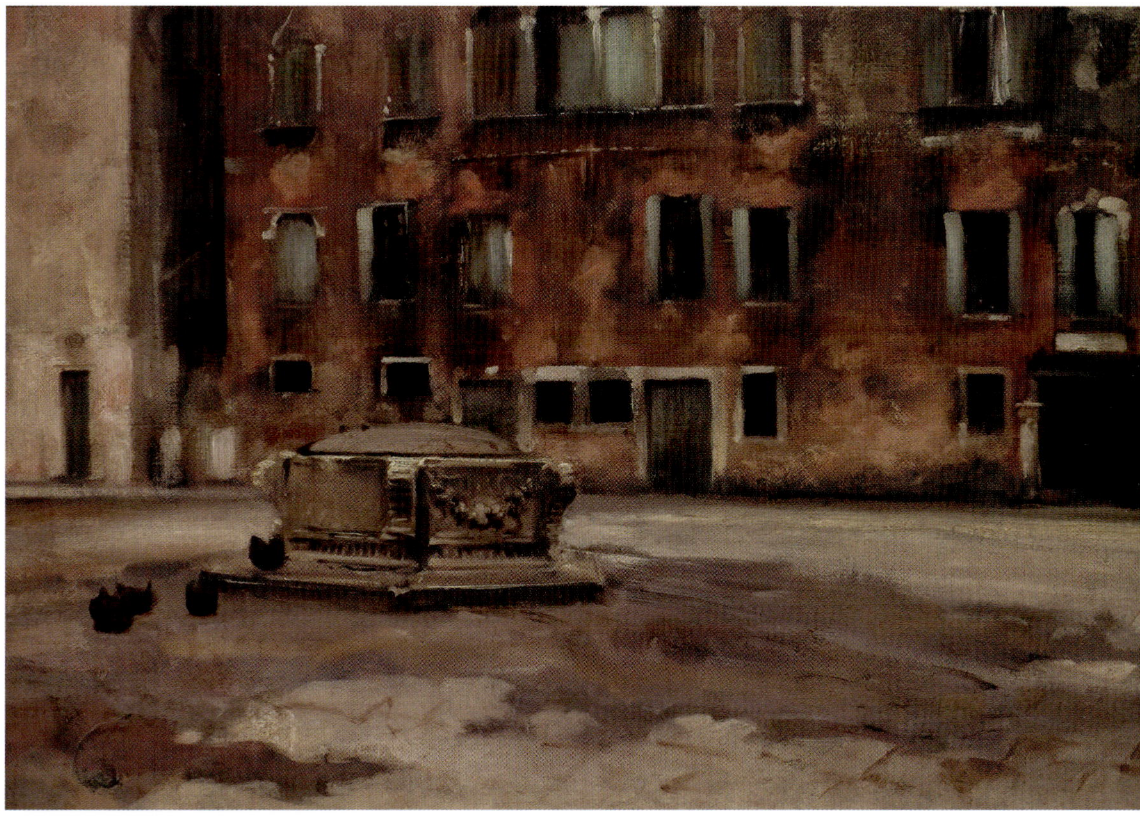

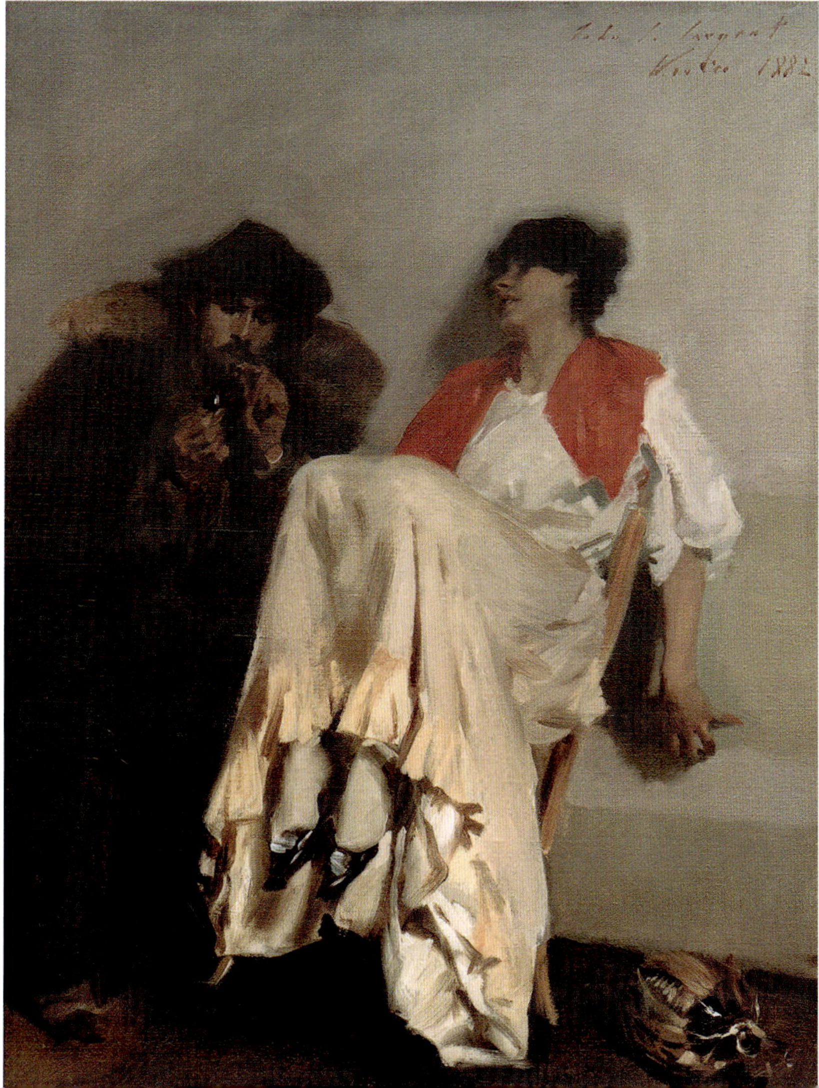

The Sulphur Match, Venice,
1882, oil on canvas, 58.4
× 41.3cm (23 × 16¼in),
Private Collection

A scene of intimacy between
a man and a young woman.
He is in darkness, partially
obscured, lighting a cigarette,
while she flirtatiously tilts
her chair back, in so doing,
hooking her heels on the
chair and revealing her
ankles; a provocative sight at
the time. An empty bottle
of wine is discarded on the
floor with a broken glass,
symbolizing her loss of
virtue.

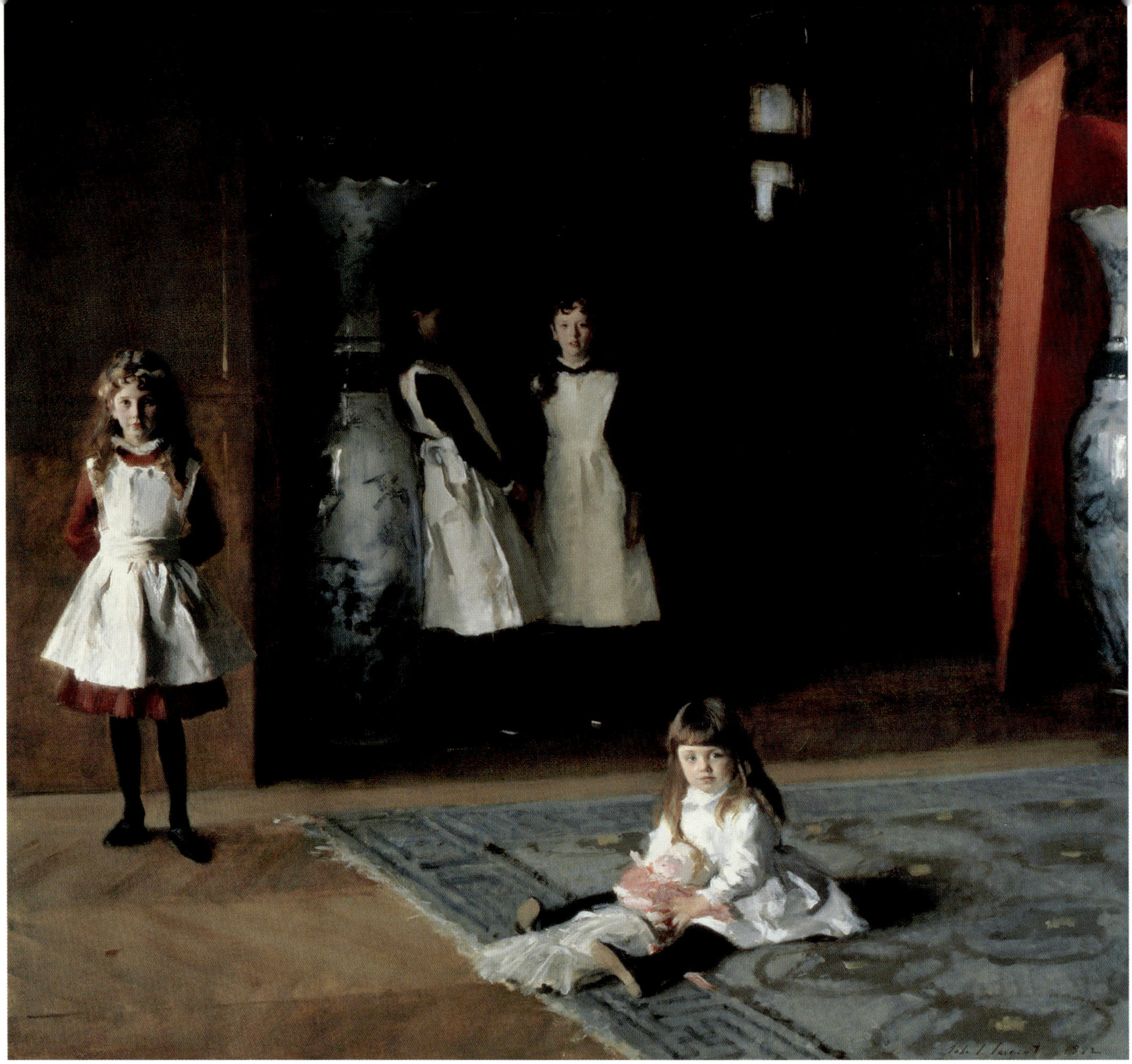

The Daughters of Edward Darley Boit, 1882, oil on canvas, 221.9 x 222.6cm (87¼ x 87¾in), Museum of Fine Arts, Boston, Massachusetts, USA

Painted in Paris in the autumn of 1882, these are the daughters of Sargent's close friends, Ned and Isa Boit. Ned was from Boston, a Harvard-trained lawyer who instead pursued a career as a painter, while Isa was a vivacious heiress who preferred Europe to America. Set in their luxurious apartment in Paris, this is an in-part shadowy and enigmatic portrait of their four daughters: Mary Louisa (eight), Florence (14), Jane (12) and Julia (four). The work is a demonstration of Sargent's mastery at painting different light conditions. The two tall Japanese vases were prized family possessions.

Detail of Sargent's
The Daughters of Edward Darley Boit, 1882 (right)

This is Julia, the youngest of the Boit daughters, who is four years old and the only figure who fully engages with viewers of the painting, while her older sisters progressively recede into the shadows.

Exhibiting it at the gallery of the French dealer Georges Petit in December 1882, Sargent called the work *Portraits of Children.* Overall, reviews were positive, but when he exhibited it again the following spring at the Salon, several critics were troubled by the ambiguities of the composition.

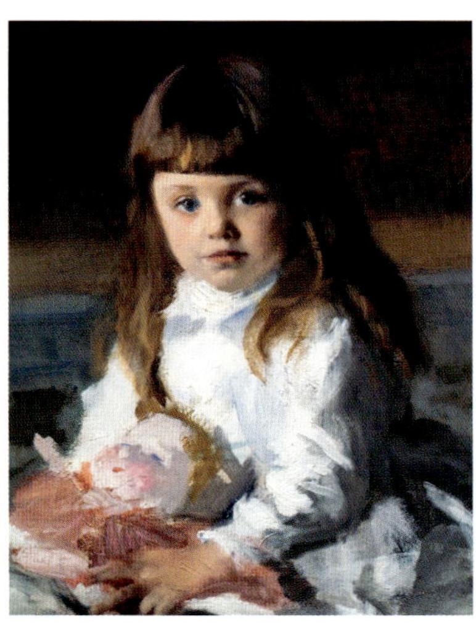

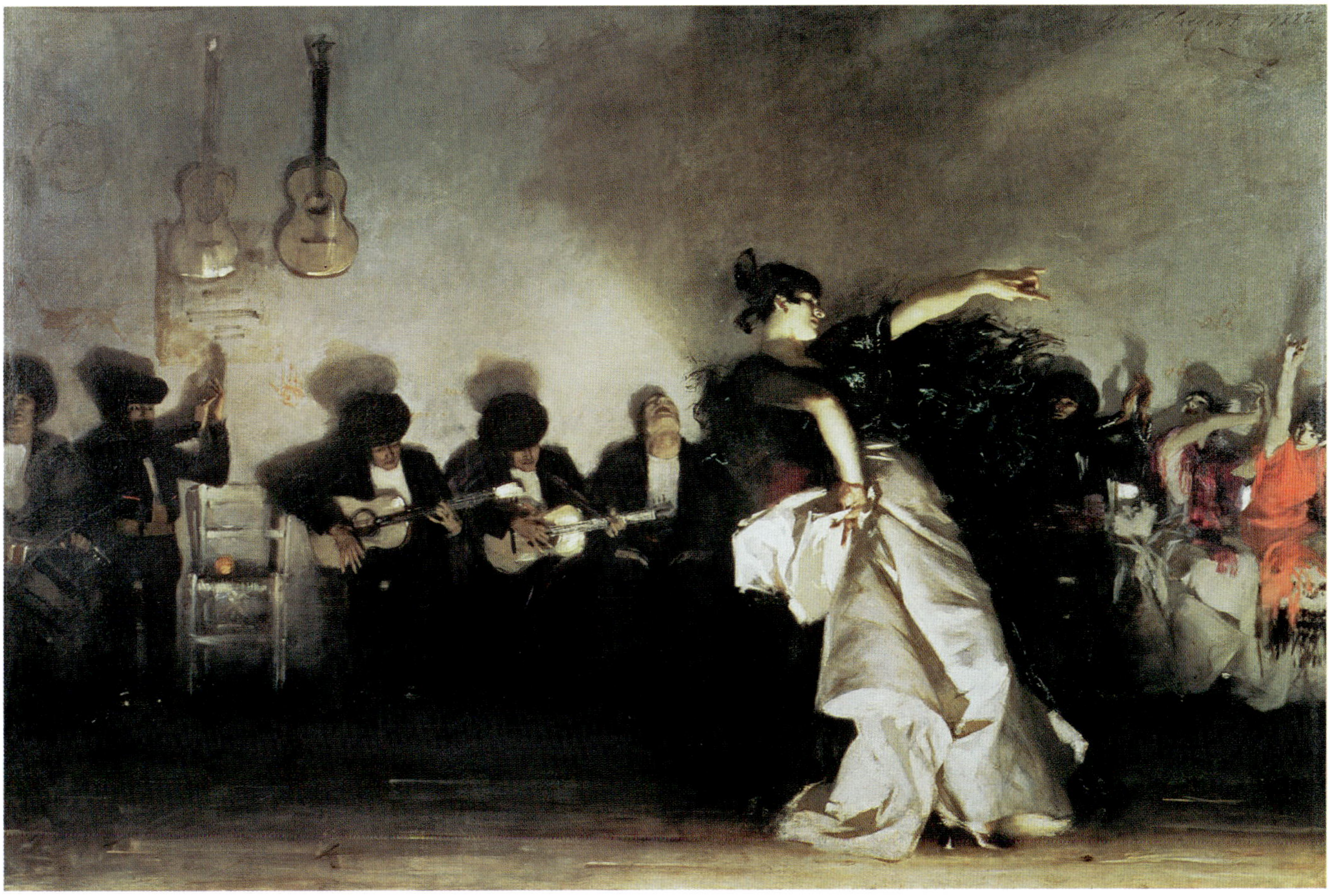

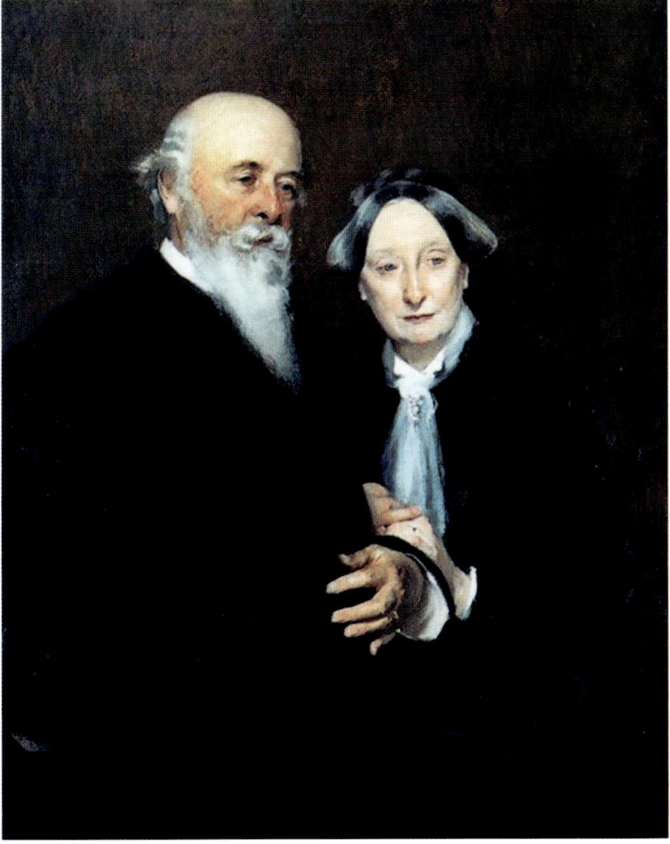

El Jaleo, 1882, oil on canvas, 232 x 348cm (93¼ 138½in), Isabella Stewart Gardner Museum, Boston, Massachusetts, USA

Sargent loved Spanish music and this monumental and dynamic masterpiece celebrates the flamenco. Tall shadows are cast on the rear wall, the dancer flicks her dress like a matador's cape, a man throws his head back to sing, and musicians strum their guitars and clap syncopated rhythms. *El Jaleo* was painted in Sargent's Paris studio after his Spanish trip during the autumn and winter of 1879–80. He submitted it to the Salon in 1892 (see also page 29).

Mr and Mrs John White Field, 1882, oil on canvas, 113.9 x 81.3cm (44¾ x 32in), Pennsylvania Academy of Fine Arts, Philadelphia, USA

Wealthy John White Field and his wife Eliza Peters mixed in an international social circle that included noted writers and artists of the period. Also passionate art collectors, the couple commissioned Sargent as he was well known for his elegant and reserved depictions of his upper class sitters. Sargent also captured the couple's closeness with their clasped hands and their heads tilting slightly towards each other.

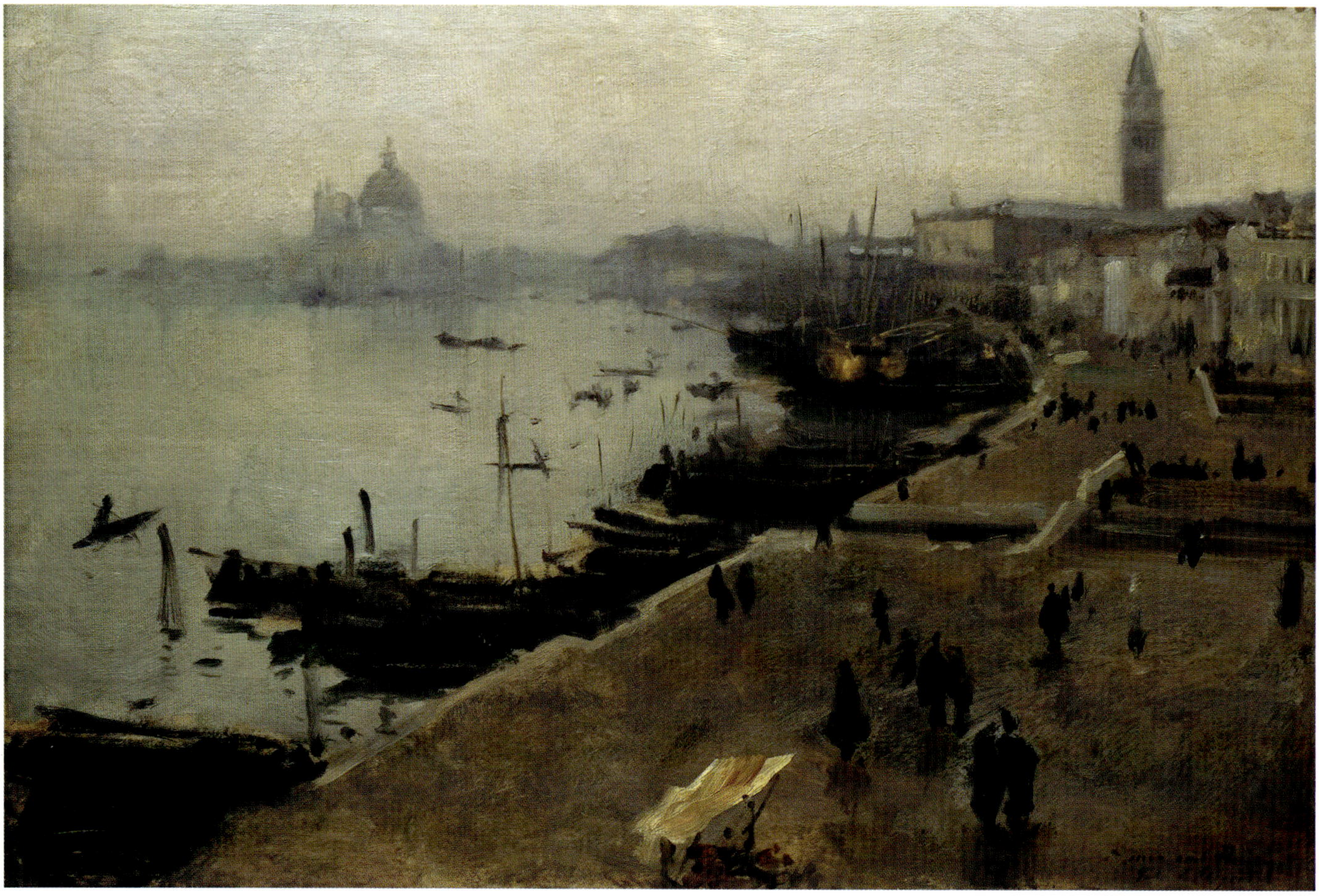

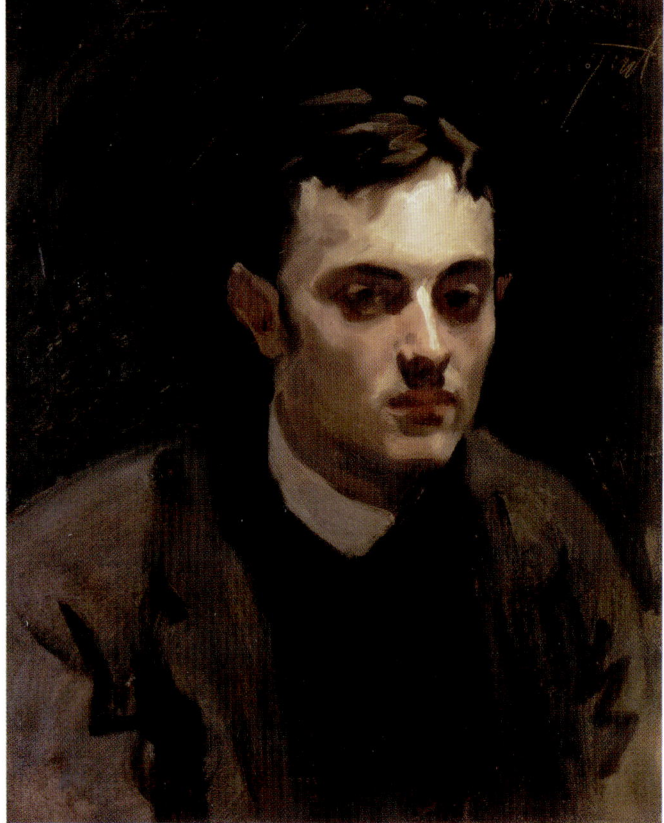

Venice in Grey Weather, c.1882, oil on canvas, 50.8 x 68.6cm (20 x 27in), Private Collection

The only panoramic cityscape that Sargent painted in Venice during the early 1880s, this is from a high viewpoint of the curving Riva degli Schiavoni, looking towards the Doge's Palace, with the Campanile and the Santa Maria della Salute ahead. The palette is practically monochrome, and Sargent's light handling creates a misty luminosity, possibly influenced by Whistler who had spent 15 months living in Venice recently, producing many atmospheric views of it.

Albert de Belleroche, 1882, oil on canvas, 61 x 45.7cm (24 x 18in), Private Collection

Although Albert de Belleroche (1864–1944) was a founder member of the Salon d'Automne who also exhibited with the Impressionists, and studied with Carolus-Duran in Paris, the two artists did not meet until 1882 when Belleroche briefly joined Carolus-Duran's atelier, but from the time they did, they became lifelong friends even though there was an eight-year age gap between them. This is one of three oil portraits of Belleroche painted by Sargent.

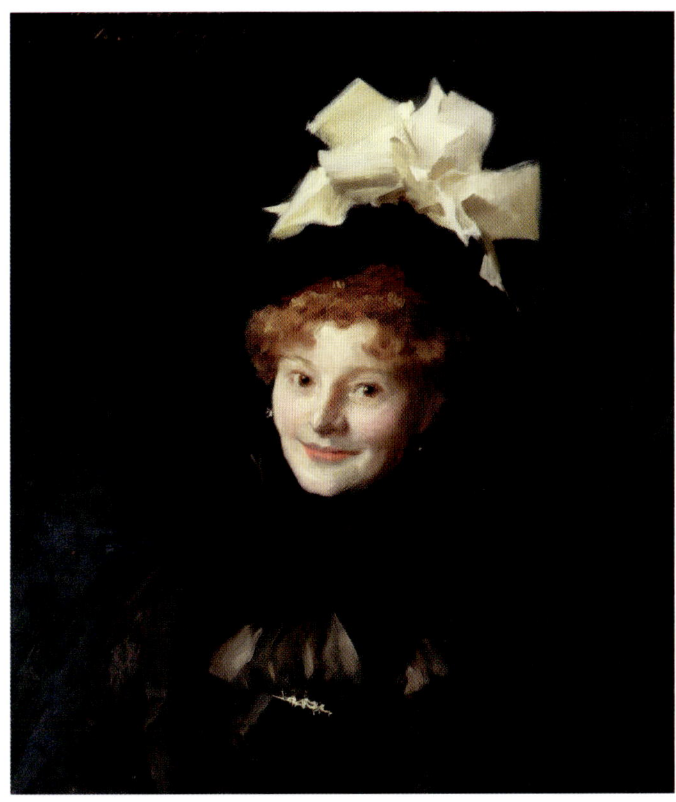

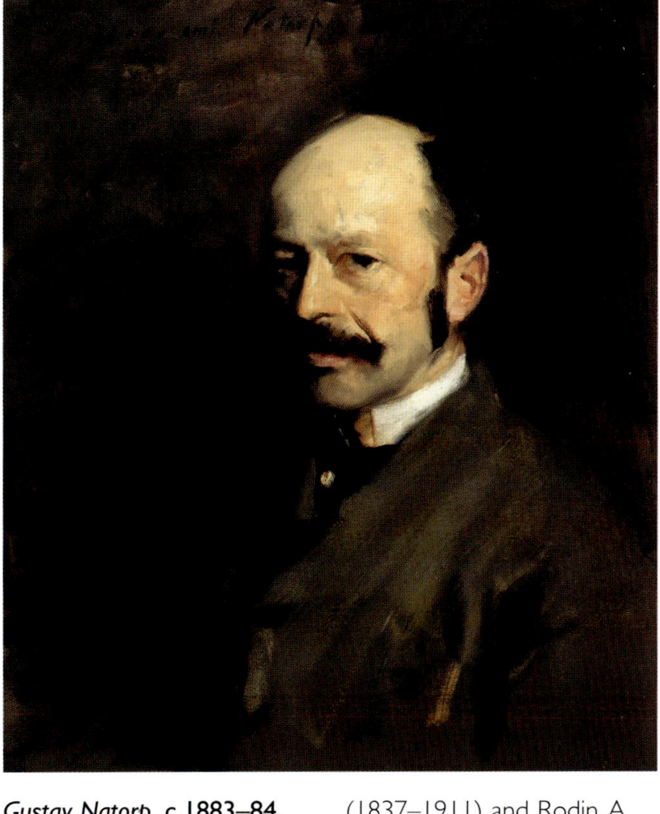

Madame Escudier, c.1883, oil on canvas, 73 x 59.7cm (28¾ x 23½in), The Sterling and Francine Clark Art Institute, Massachusetts, USA

An informal portrait of Louise Lefèvre Escudier, the wife of a Parisian lawyer. Her head is tilted as she smiles mischievously at the artist, her vibrant red hair highlighted by the deep blue background. Sargent painted at least two portraits of her, and this emphasizes his confident, free brushstrokes learned from the Impressionists and powerful tonal contrasts inspired by Velázquez.

Gustav Natorp, c.1883–84, oil on canvas, 63.2 x 50.2cm (24¾ x 19¾in), Allen Memorial Art Museum, Oberlin College, Ohio, USA

Hamburg-born sculptor Gustav Natorp (1836–1908) moved to Paris to study with Alphonse Legros (1837–1911) and Rodin. A mutual friend of Sargent and Tom and Frances Vickers, he advised the Vickers that Sargent would be the best artist to paint a portrait of their three daughters (see page 124). At the top of this portrait, Sargent wrote 'To my friend Natorp.'

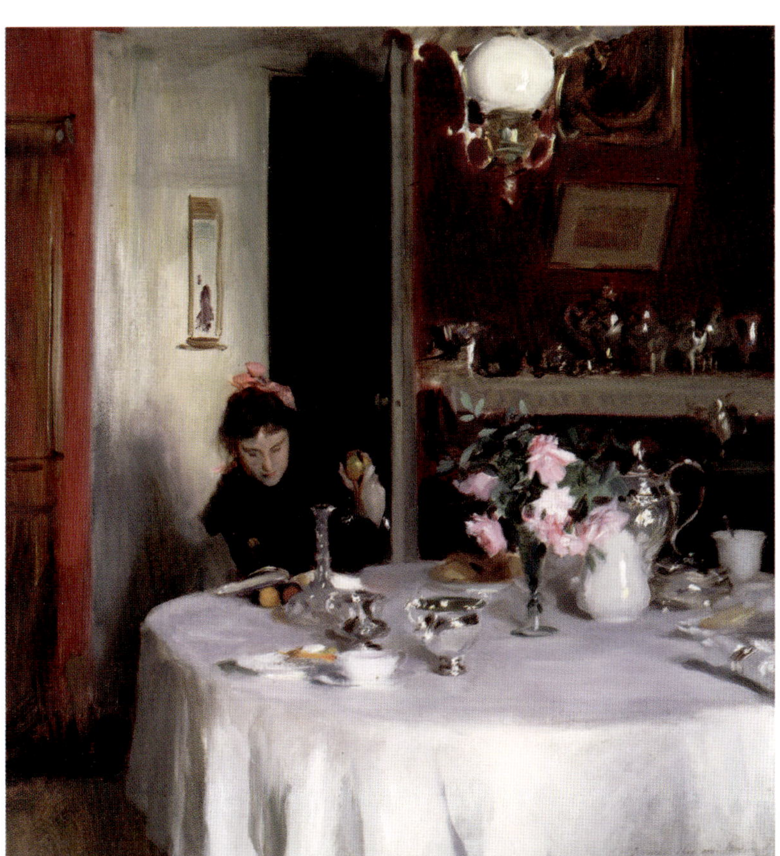

The Breakfast Table, 1884, oil on canvas, 54 x 45cm (21¼ x 17¾in), Fogg Art Museum, Boston, Massachusetts, USA

Sargent's younger sister Violet peels an orange whilst reading at the breakfast table. The snowy white linen tablecloth and shining silver tableware presents her comfortable lifestyle. It is the interior of an apartment that the Sargent family rented in the South of France in the summer of 1883, even though he painted it in Paris. The cropped composition, loose brushwork and thin paint show an influence of Degas and Manet.

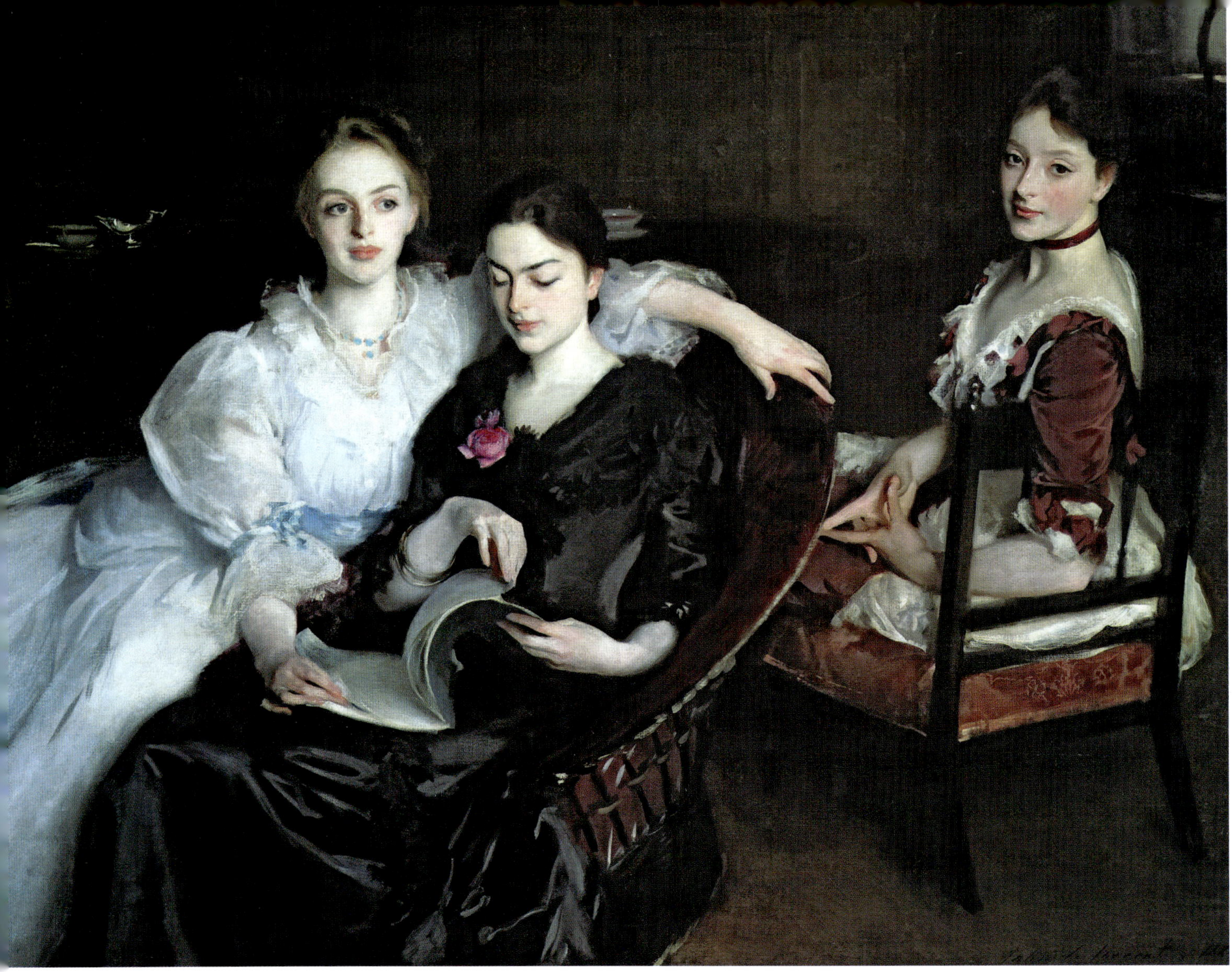

The Misses Vickers (see also pages 38–39), 1884, oil on canvas, 137.8 x 182.9cm (54¼ x 72in), Sheffield Galleries and Museums Trust, Yorkshire, UK

The three daughters of Tom and Frances Vickers: Evelyn (18) on the left, Mabel (21) in the centre and Mildred (19) on the right. Somewhat surprisingly given the young ladies' appealing looks, Sargent wrote to his friend Vernon Lee: 'I am to paint...three ugly young women at Sheffield.' The portrait composition is original and complex, but it was criticized at the Salon of 1885 and at the Royal Academy the following year. It was perceived as contrived and confusing.

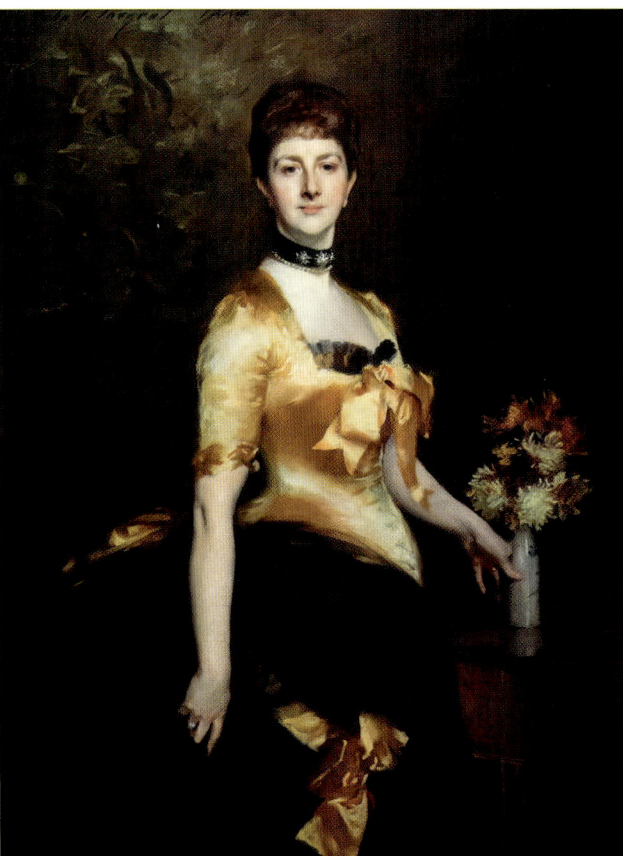

Edith, Lady Playfair (Edith Russell), 1884, oil on canvas, 152 x 98.4cm (59¾ x 38¾in), Museum of Fine Art, Boston, Massachusetts, USA

Even though at least one contemporary critic was scathing about this portrait, it shows an elegant woman in a graceful pose, standing in profile, turning to look beyond the canvas, wearing gold silk and holding a bouquet of carnations. Reviews were at odds with each other, as another wrote: 'Mr Sargent's brilliant Lady Playfair, so vivacious in pose, so charming in expression... so sparkling and delightful in effect.'

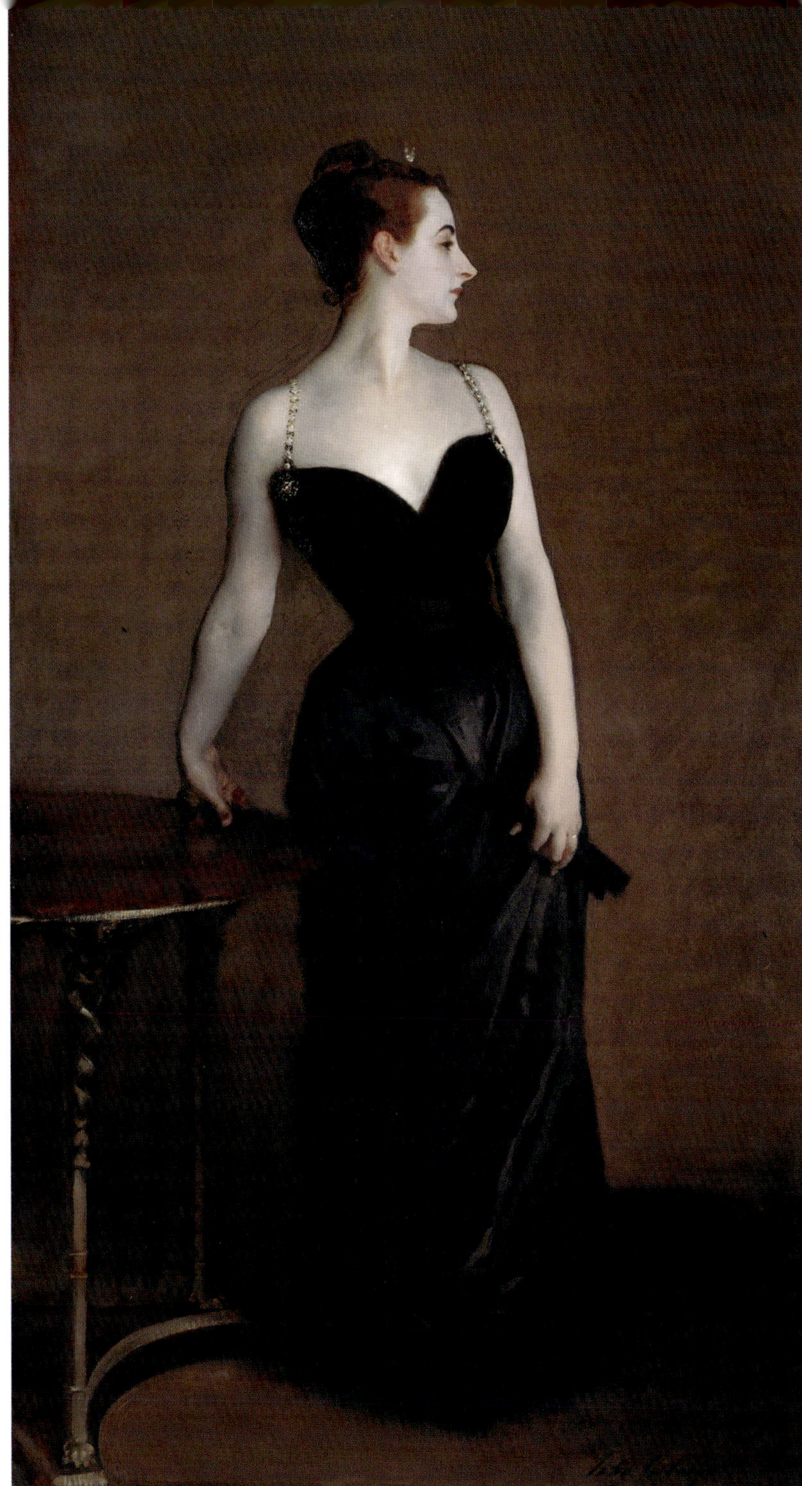

Study of Madame Gautreau,
c.1884, oil on canvas,
206.4 x 107.9cm
(81¼ x 42½in), Tate,
London, UK

Sargent's unfinished
copy of Madame X
(started while he was
still working on the main
painting) shows how

he originally painted
the finished work: with
Virginie's shoulder strap
falling down, which caused
a furore. The painting
scandalized Paris when
it was first exhibited,
damaging Sargent's
reputation so badly that
he moved to Britain the
following year.

Madame X, 1884, oil on
canvas, 208.6 x 109.9cm
(82¼ x 43¼in), The
Metropolitan Museum,
New York, USA

Sargent painted his portrait
of the celebrated beauty
Virginie Gautreau at her
summer home in Brittany in
1883. When exhibited at the
Paris Salon of 1884 as *Portrait
de Mme XXX* the painting
created one of the biggest
art scandals of the late 19th
century. Virginie stands in
an unconventional pose
for a woman of the period,
confident and bold, turning
her profile almost haughtily.
Sargent had emphasized her
daring personal style, and
shown the right strap of
her gown slipping from her
shoulder. He later repainted
the strap, but it changed his
career (see also page 35).

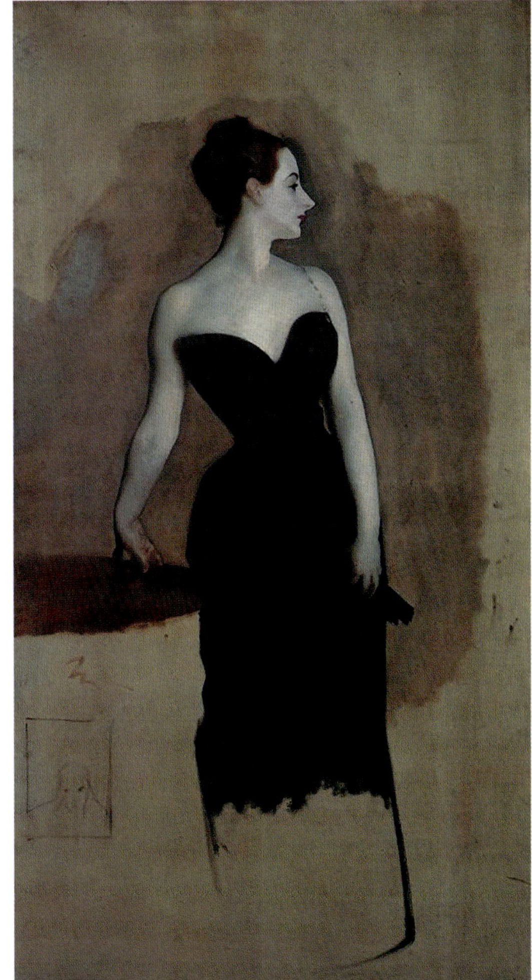

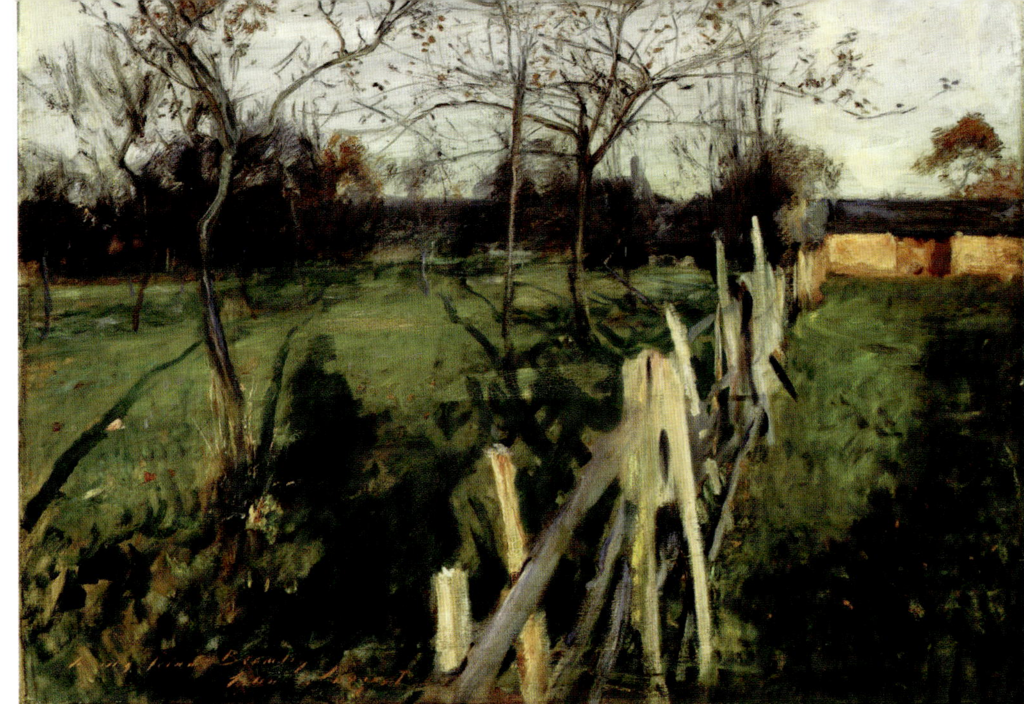

Home Fields, c.1885, oil on canvas, 73 x 96.5cm (28¾ x 38in), Detroit Institute of Arts, Michigan, USA

When Sargent first moved to Britain he mixed with a group of artists, including several American expatriates. That summer, they lived in the village of Broadway in the Cotswolds, together. Overlooking the Vale of Evesham. It was the perfect place to paint Impressionistic scenes en plein air like this, using a bright palette.

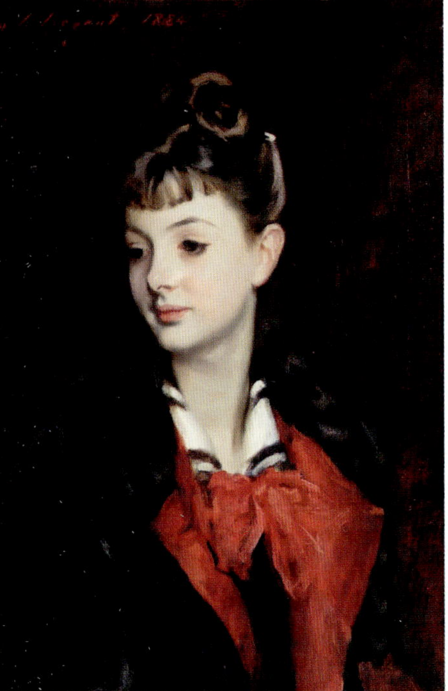

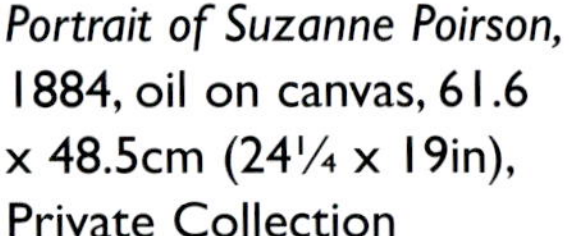

Portrait of Suzanne Poirson, 1884, oil on canvas, 61.6 x 48.5cm (24¼ x 19in), Private Collection

A portrait of the beautiful and composed 13-year-old girl, Suzanne Poirson (1871–1926), this work brought Sargent great acclaim. She was the daughter of Paul Poirson (1836–95) who owned the studio in Paris that Sargent had been using for the past year, and it is conjectured that Sargent painted this and a portrait of Suzanne's mother (right) in lieu of rent. The embodiment of elegance, the portrait follows the Grand Manner style of portraiture that was highly admired.

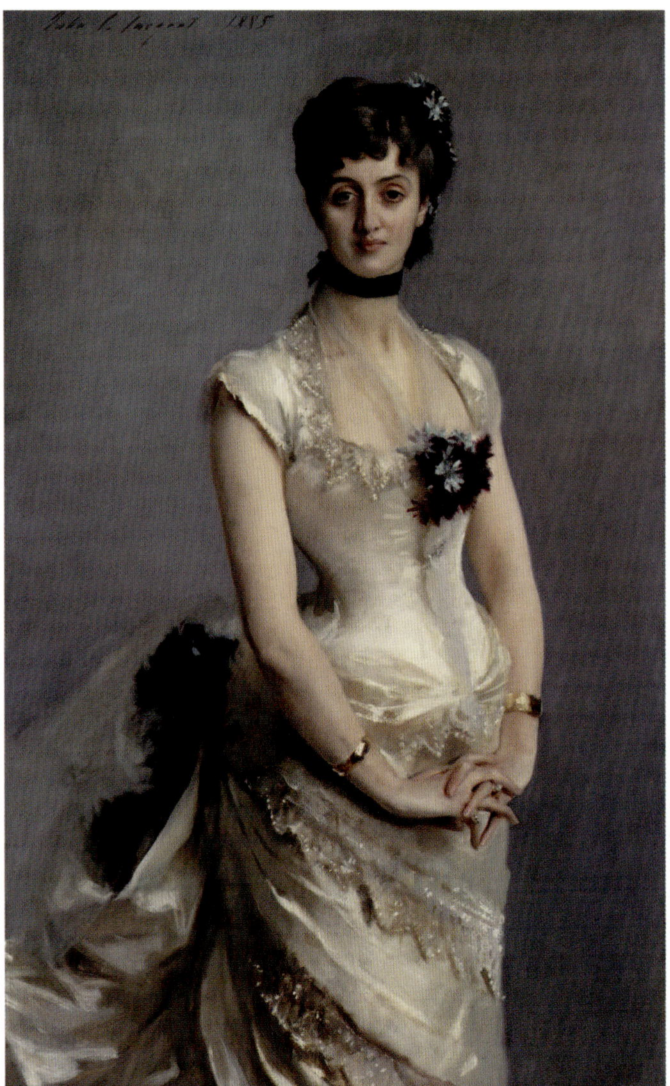

Madame Paul Poirson, 1885, oil on canvas, 152.4 x 86.4cm (60 x 34in), The Detroit Institute of Arts, Michigan, USA

The mother of Suzanne (far left), and wife of the artist Paul Poirson, this elegant woman is Seymourina Poirson (1846–1931), the illegitimate daughter of the 4th Marquess of Hertford. As part of the elite society, she dressed in the height of fashion, here in a corseted satin evening gown, trimmed with voile, lace and artificial flowers. Sargent's portrait style was described as being 'instinctively refined,' which made him highly sought after in wealthy circles.

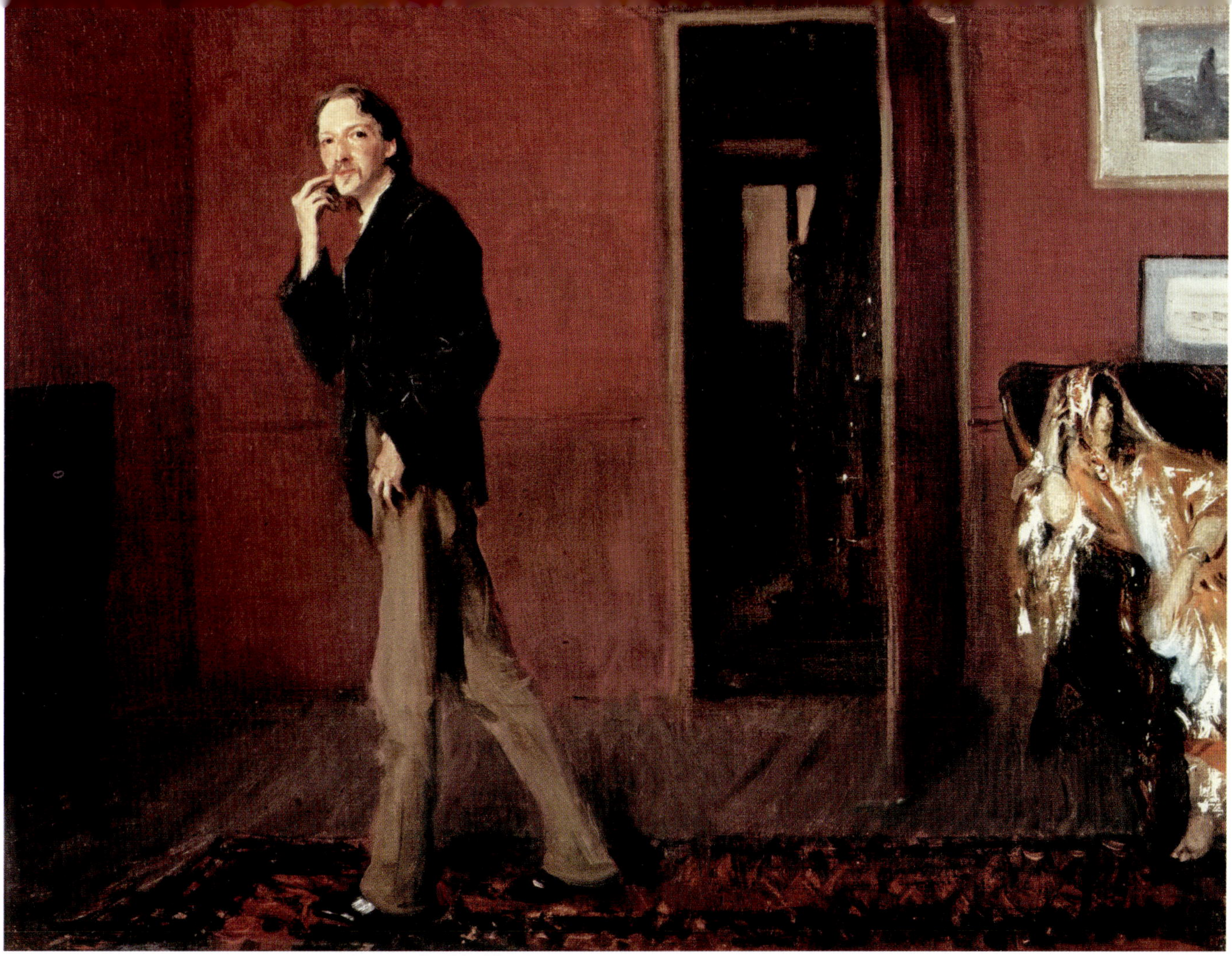

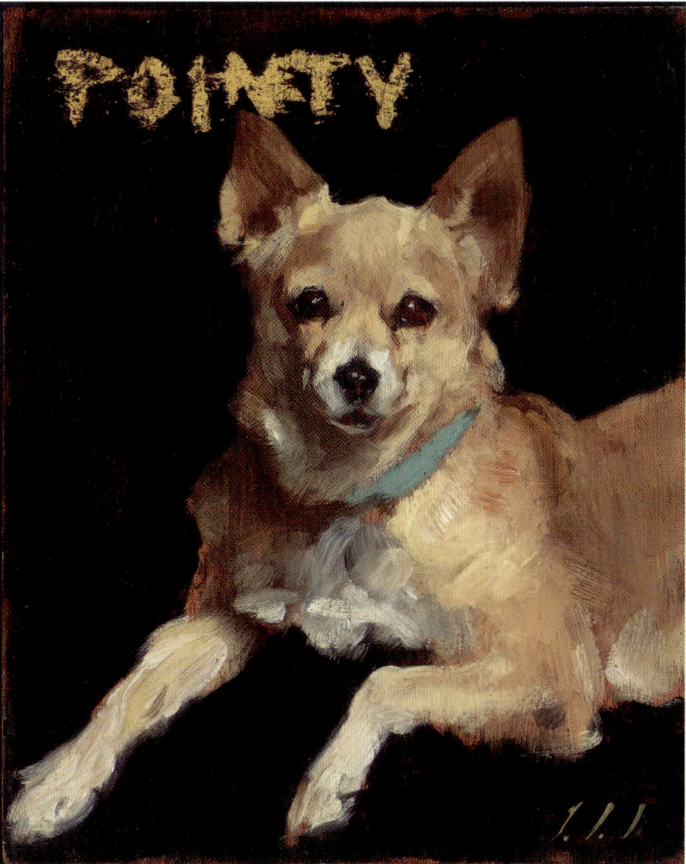

Robert Louis Stevenson and His Wife, 1885, oil on canvas, 52.1 x 62.2cm (20½ x 24½in), Private Collection

Sargent had known Robert Louis Stevenson for over ten years, as his cousin, Robert Alan Mowbray Stevenson (1847–1900) had studied at Carolus-Duran's studio with him. Sargent made three portraits of Stevenson, this was the second, painted at Stevenson's house in Dorset in the year before his book, *The Strange Case of Dr Jekyll and Mr Hyde* was published. In a captured moment, Sargent portrays Stevenson pacing and talking, an open door between him and his wife, who lounges in an exotic gold costume (see also pages 39 and 132).

Pointy (Portrait of Louise Burckhardt's dog), 1885, oil on canvas, 27.3 x 21.6cm (10¾ x 8½in), Private Collection

Sargent's close friend Louise Burckhardt (1862–92) owned Pointy, a little dog that accompanied her everywhere. Because he and Louise were so close, rumours spread that they were having an affair, and there was talk of an engagement, but this never happened. Sargent was close to the whole Burckhardt family and painted them all, so this charming little portrait was probably his joke – no family member was left out.

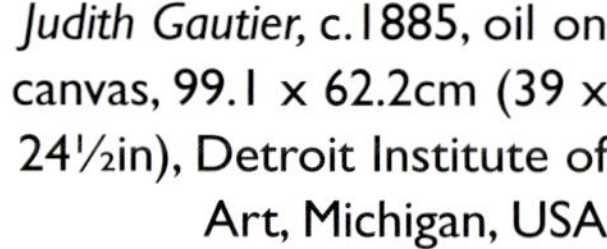

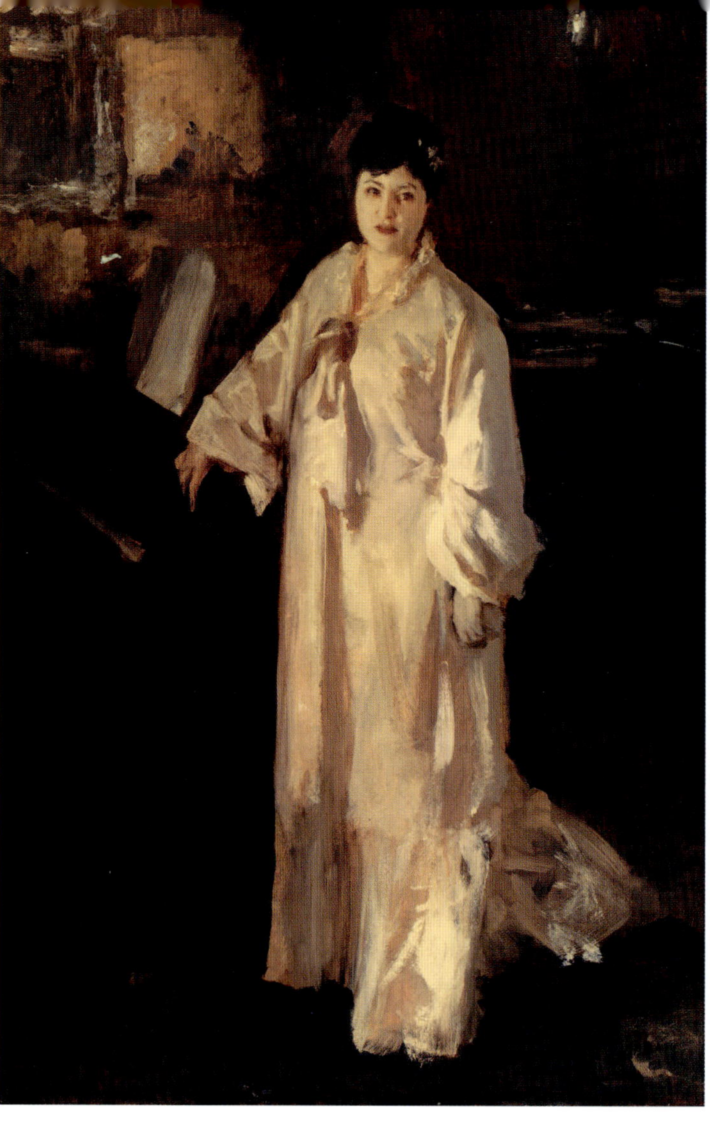

Judith Gautier, c.1885, oil on canvas, 99.1 x 62.2cm (39 x 24½in), Detroit Institute of Art, Michigan, USA

Novelist and poet Judith Gautier (1845–1917) was the daughter of the well-known art critic Théophile Gautier and his Italian mistress, Ernesta Grisi. After separating from her husband, the poet Catulle Mendès (1841–1909) she had a brief affair with the German composer Richard Wagner (1813—83). She also translated Japanese and Chinese poetry, and her admiration of those cultures can be seen in her distinctive mode of dress.

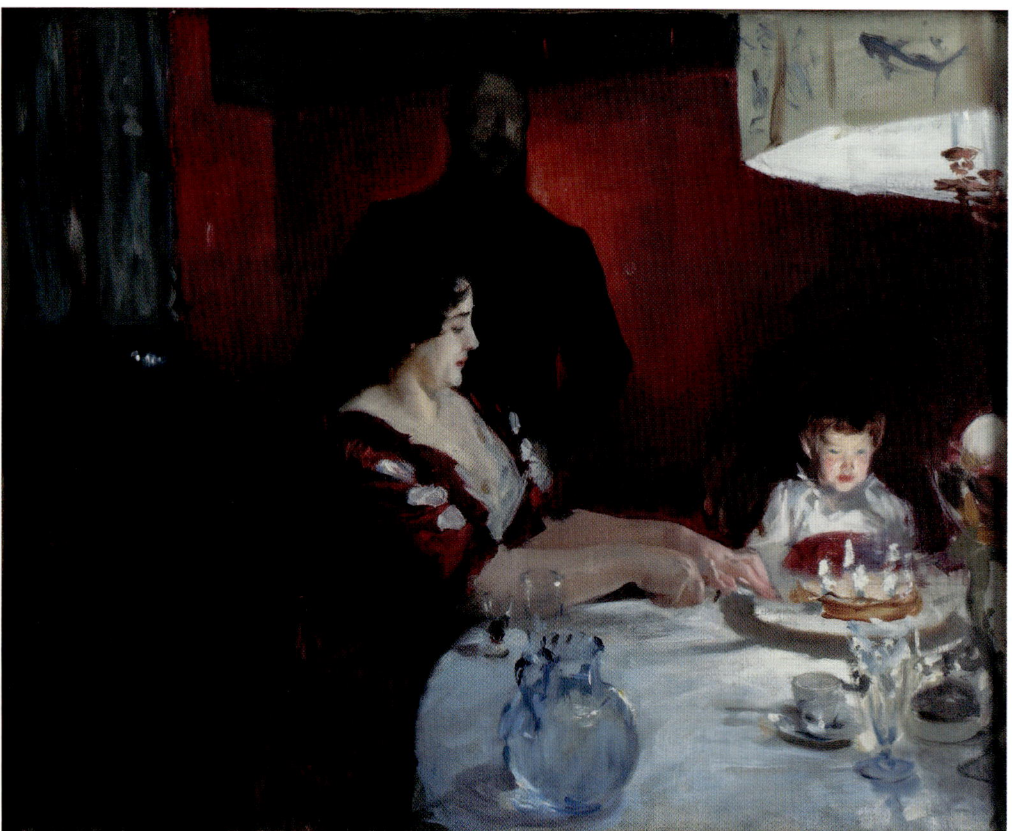

The Birthday Party, c.1885, oil on canvas, 60.9 x 73.7cm (24 x 29in), The Minneapolis Institute of Art, Minnesota, USA

Sargent's friends, the painter Albert Besnard (1849–1934) and his wife, the sculptor Charlotte Dubray (1855–1931) are celebrating their son Robert's birthday around a table. In an engagingly intimate scene, the little boy's happy face is illuminated by the glow of candles on his cake and overhead lamp. Attended to by his doting mother wearing a deep crimson gown, his father stands close by.

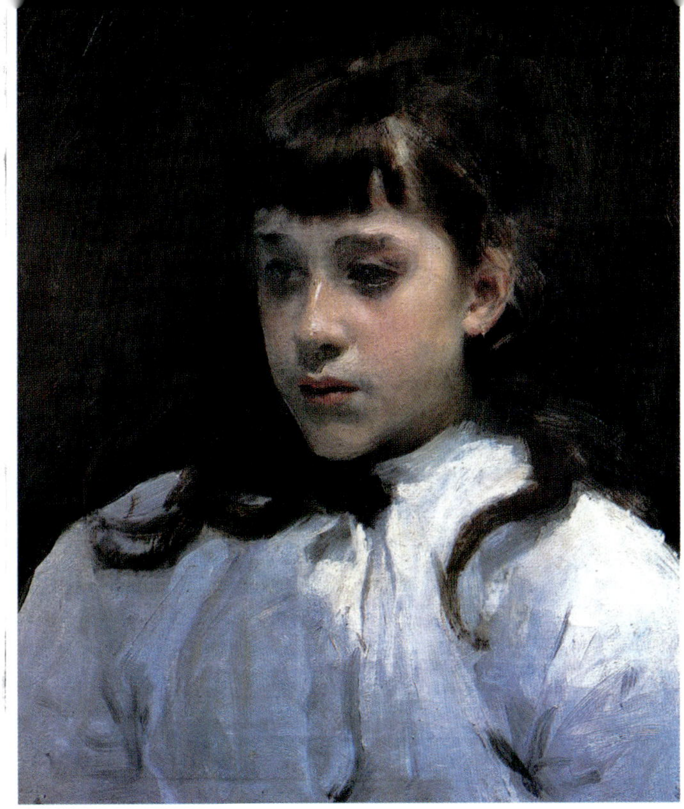

Young Girl in White Muslin Blouse, 1885, oil on canvas, 48.9 x 38.1cm (19¼ x 15in), Private Collection

Sir Lawrence Alma-Tadema (1836–1912) was one of the most revered artists of the period. Sargent was of the younger generation, but although the two knew each other, and their social circles meant that they often saw each other, particularly around Kensington and Chelsea and at London galleries, they were not close friends. This is a painting by Sargent of Anna Alma-Tadema (1867–1943), Sir Lawrence's daughter who later became a painter, a suffragette, and one of Sargent's good friends.

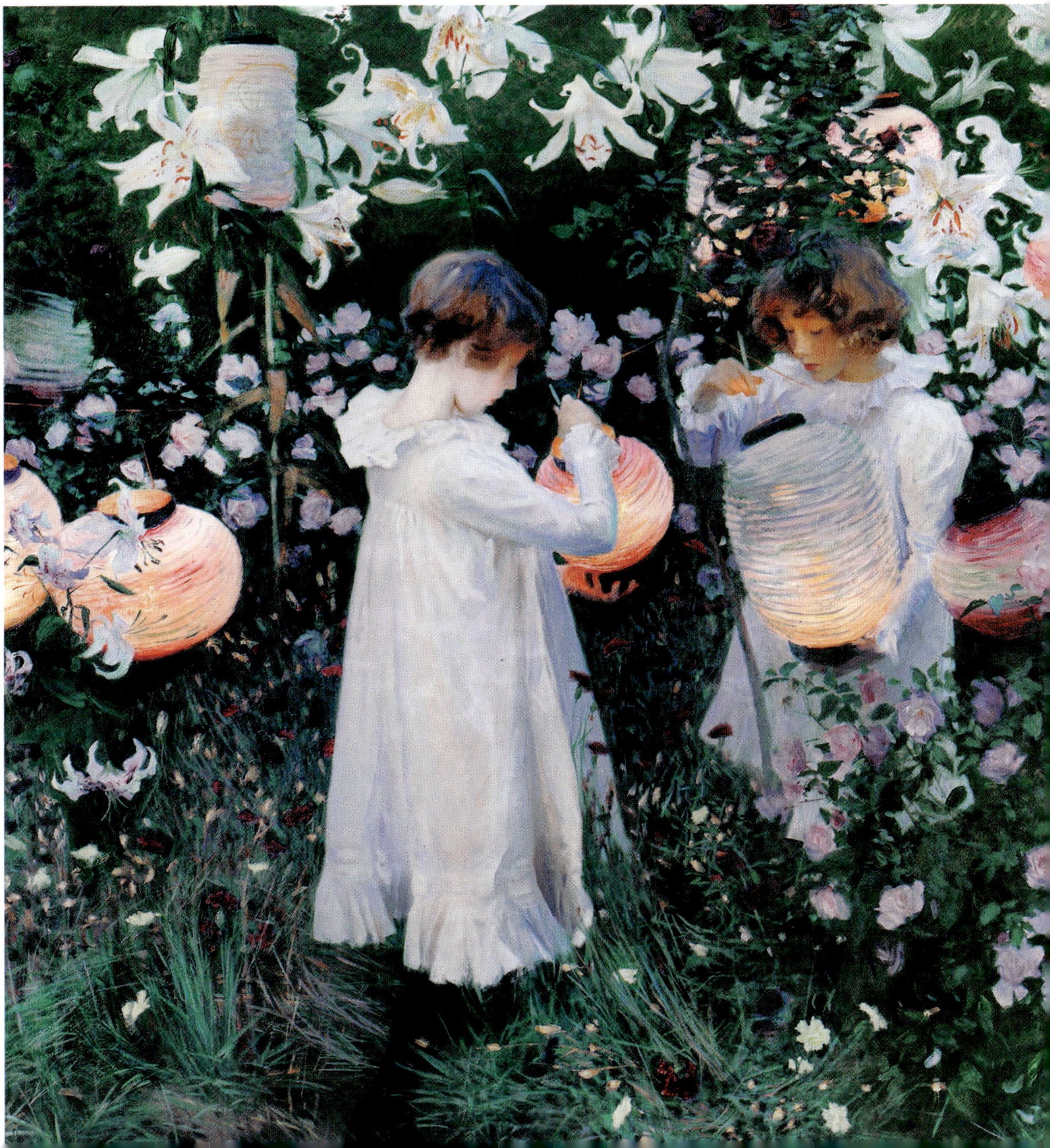

Carnation, Lily, Lily, Rose, 1885–86, oil on canvas, 174 x 153.7cm (68½ x 60½in), Tate, London, UK

Inspired by a scene he witnessed on a boating trip on the Thames with his friend and fellow artist Edwin Austin Abbey, Sargent began this painting while staying with the Millet family at Broadway in Worcestershire, England. Carefully planned, he made several sketches for the work before starting, and it took him weeks to achieve what he had in mind. It was one of the few figure paintings he completed en plein air (see also page 40).

Mrs Frank Millet, 1885–86, oil on canvas, 87.3 x 67.3cm (34¼ x 26½in), Private Collection

After sustaining a bad head wound while diving from a weir on a boat trip with his friend Abbey, Sargent was welcomed into the home of Frank and Lily Millet. Their kindness was reciprocated with devotion from Sargent and in gratitude, he painted pictures of their garden, their children and of them. This portrait is inscribed 'to my friend Mrs Millet.'

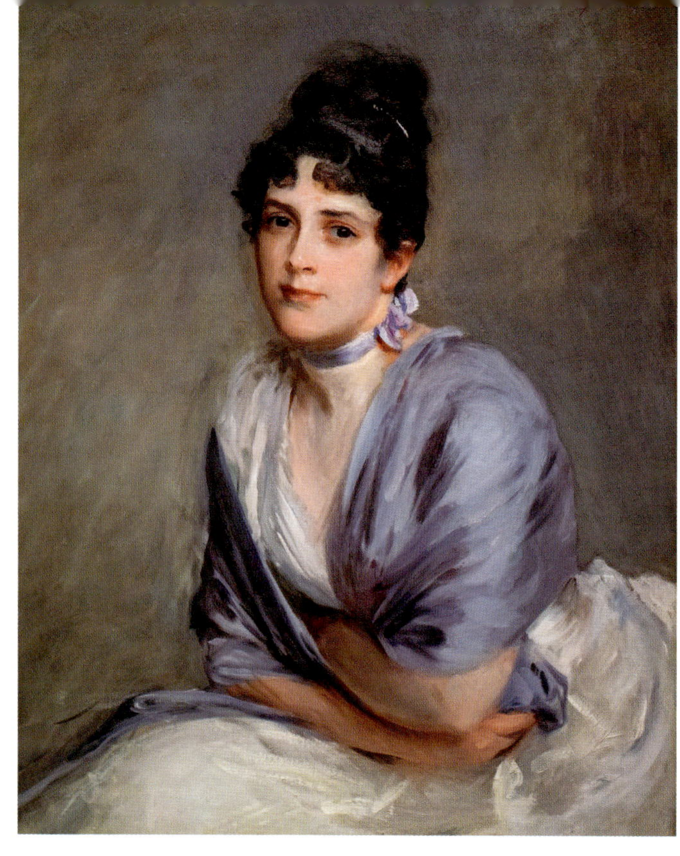

Violet Sargent, 1886, oil on canvas, 55.9 x 69.9cm (22 x 27½in), Private Collection

Sargent's youngest sister Violet became his muse. After studying at the Accademia delle Belle Arti, she married Francis Ormond and went on to have six children. Sargent had painted her since she was a child and as her daughters grew up, he sketched and painted them too. He was exceptionally close to both his sisters and nieces throughout his life.

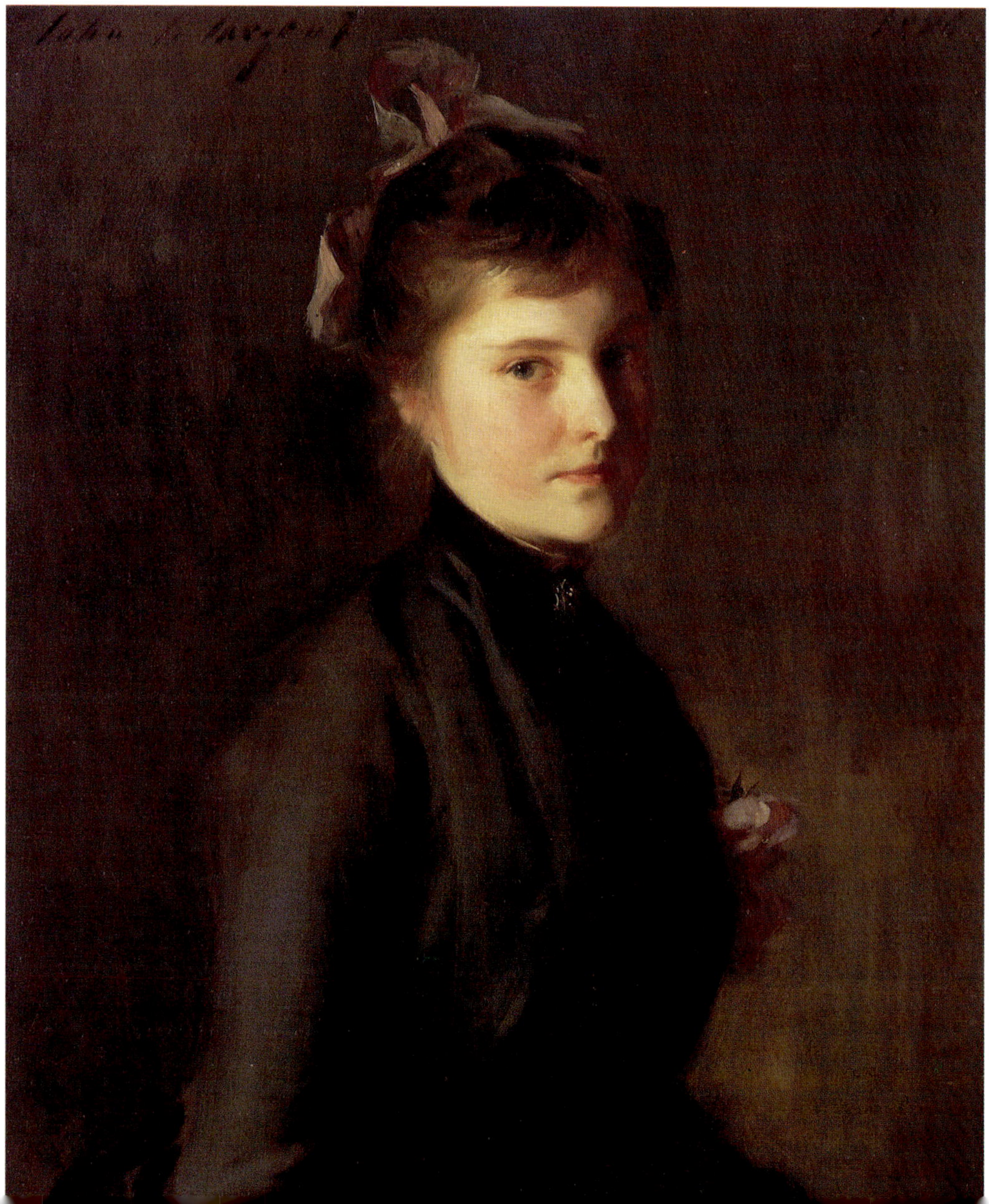

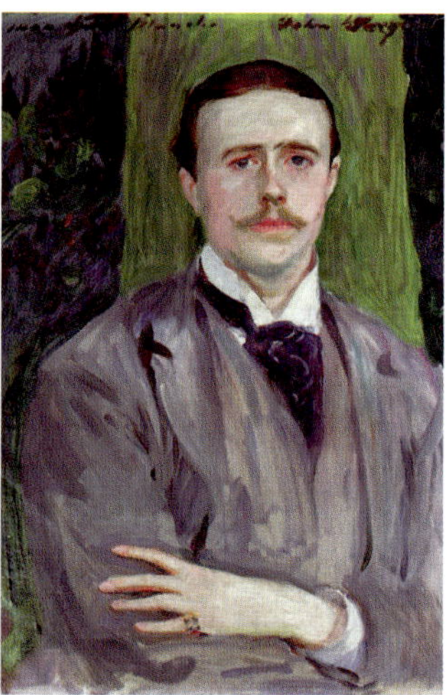

Portrait of Jacques-Émile Blanche, c.1886, oil on canvas, 81.9 x 48.9cm (32¼ x 19¼in), Musée des Beaux Arts, Normandy, France

An established portraitist, Jacques-Émile Blanche painted many distinguished writers, artists and musicians. He lived near Dieppe and often visited England, where he mixed in the same circles as Sargent. When Sargent decided he had had enough of painting portraits, Blanche was one of the first friends he told.

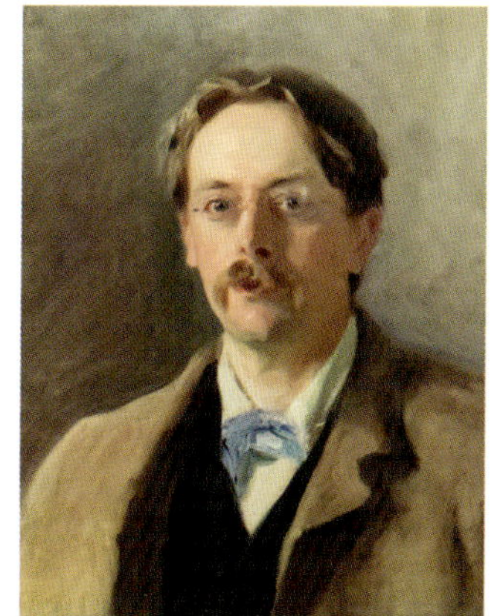

Sir Edmund William Gosse,
1886, oil on canvas,
54.6 x 44.5cm (21½ x
17½in), National Portrait
Gallery, London, UK

Gosse and Sargent first met
in 1885 at Broadway. That
summer was idyllic, with
the large gathering of artists
and writers filling their days
with painting, writing, tennis,
parties, boating jaunts, music,
conversation and theatrical
entertainments. Sargent
gave this portrait to another
mutual Broadway friend, the
painter Alfred Parsons.

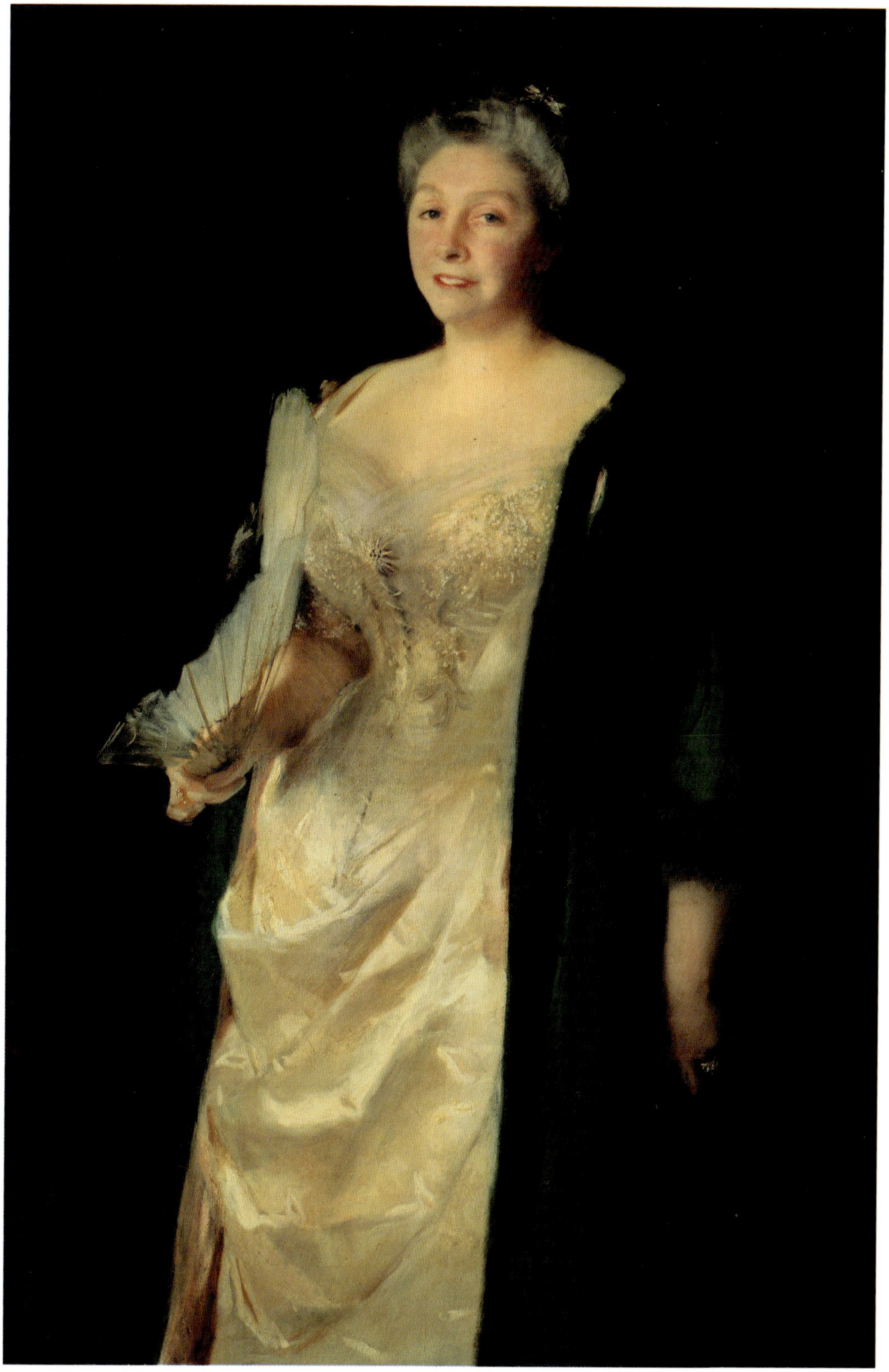

Mrs William Playfair, 1887,
oil on canvas, 153.7 x
99.1cm (60½ x 39in),
Huntington Library, Art
Collections and Botanical
Gardens, California, USA

This was exhibited to great
acclaim at the Royal Academy
in 1887 and the Paris Salon in
1888. Mrs Playfair (née Emily
Kitson, 1841–1916) wears
a shimmering yellow satin
gown and fur-lined green
velvet coat. She was the wife
of England's most eminent
obstetrician and they had
five children. Here, Sargent
captured her in a relaxed,
happy and natural pose,
unusual for a formal portrait.

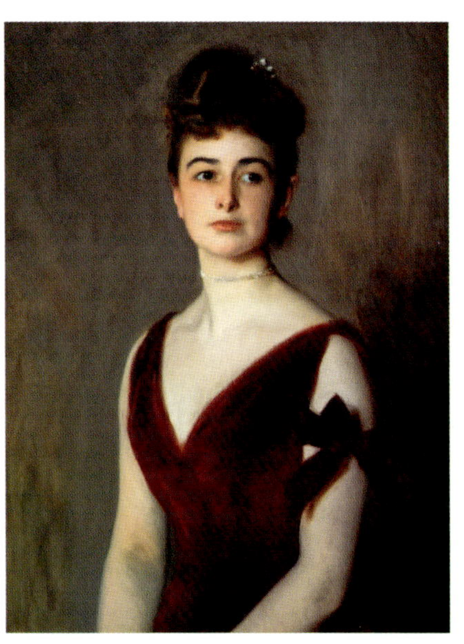

Mrs Charles E. Inches (Louise Pomeroy), 1887, oil on canvas, 86.4 x 60.6cm (34 x 23¾in), Museum of Fine Arts, Boston, Massachusetts, USA

In 1887, Sargent stayed in Boston with his friends Ned and Isa Boit. Charles Inches was Ned's first cousin, so he probably suggested this portrait. At age 22, Louise Pomeroy (1861–1933) had married Dr Inches who was 20 years her senior. She was recognized for her beauty and as a great society hostess. Here Louise was pregnant with her third child. She is dressed in a ruby red evening gown with detachable panels to accommodate pregnancies.

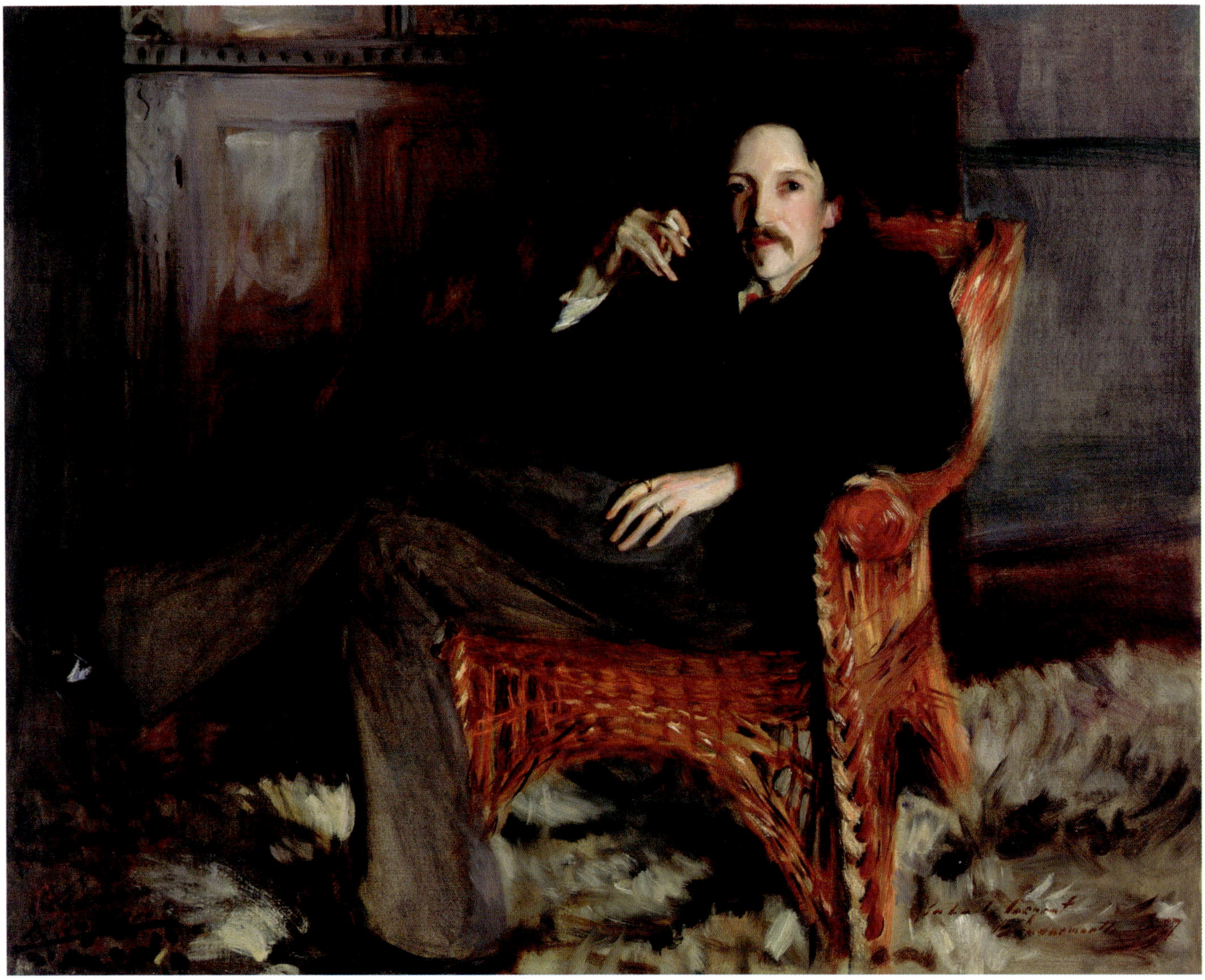

Robert Louis Stevenson, 1887, oil on canvas, 51 x 61.8cm (20 x 24¼in), Taft Museum of Art, Ohio, USA

This is the third and final portrait that Sargent executed of his friend Robert Louis Stevenson, commissioned by the Boston banker Charles Fairchild (1842–1924) as a gift for his wife. It is an informal image of the famous writer in his armchair, chatting to his friend the famous artist. Amid a sombre palette, Stevenson holds a glowing cigarette in his elegant and creative hands.

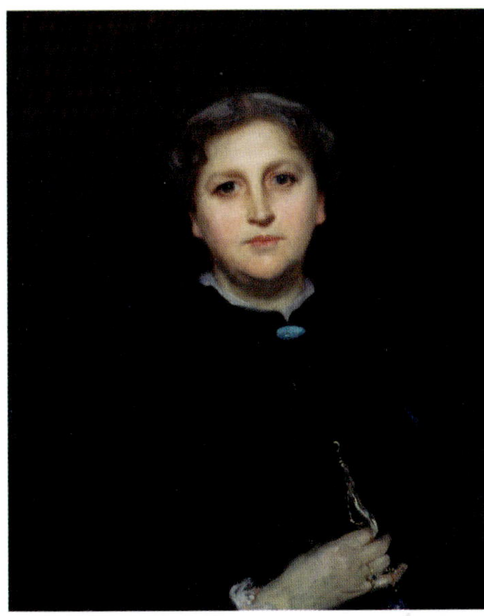

Portrait of Mrs Raphael Pumpelly, 1887, oil on canvas, 39.3 x 35cm (15½ x 13¾in), Berkshire Museum, Massachusetts, USA

In America during 1887, Sargent painted Mrs Pumpelly (née Eliza Shepard 1840–1915) at her home in Newport, Rhode Island, while he was staying with his friends, Admiral and Mrs Goodrich. Eliza was married to the American geologist and explorer Raphael Pumpelly (1837–1923). Sargent's technique of black on black, with the face seeming to emerge from within the canvas, follows the Spanish tradition.

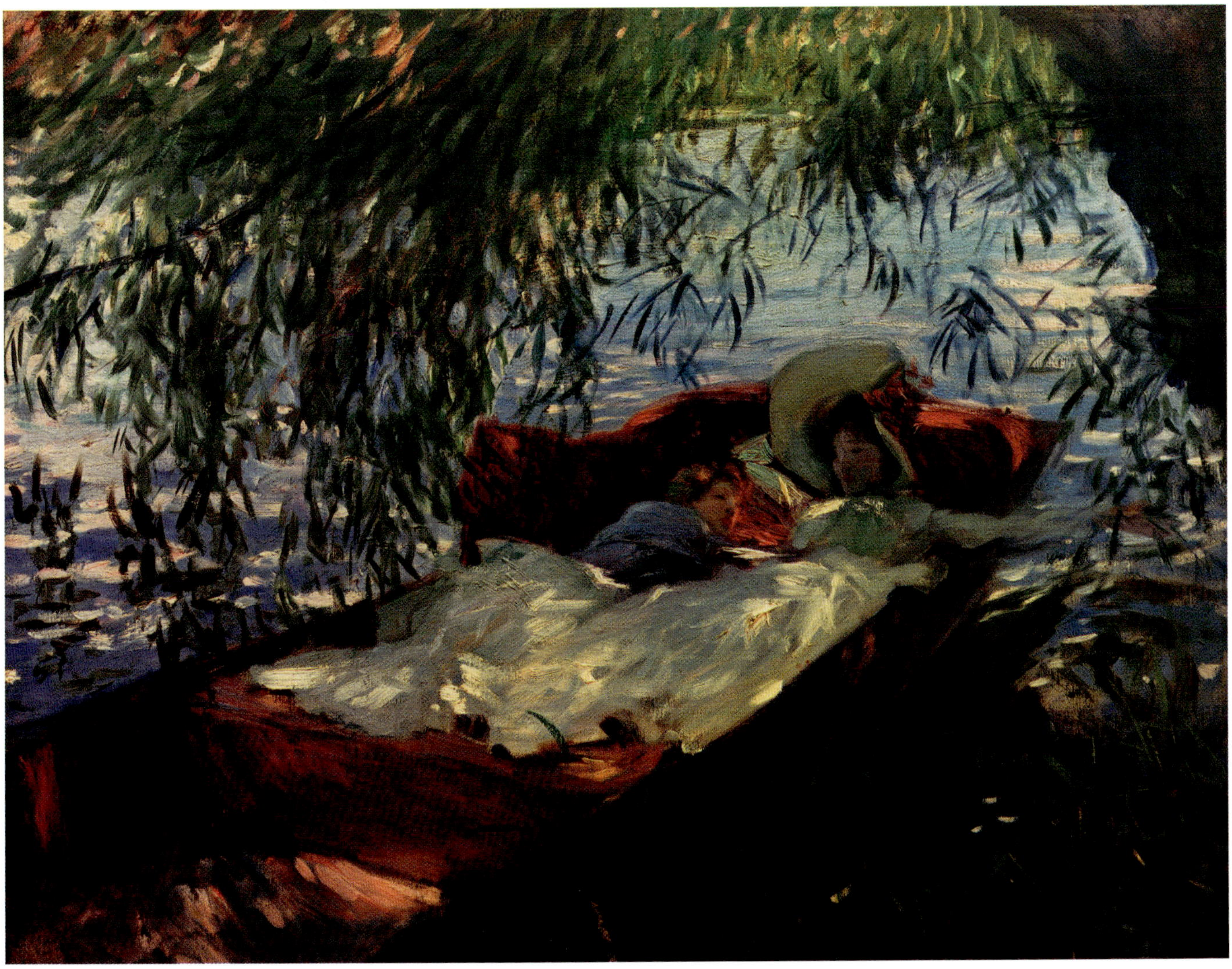

A Lady and a Little Boy Asleep in a Punt under the Willows, 1887, oil on canvas, 55.9 × 68.6cm (22 x 27in), Museu Calouste Gulbenkian, Lisbon, Portugal

Apart from his portraits, during the second half of the 1880s Sargent was working in an Impressionist phase. This was painted at Henley-on-Thames, when he was spending time with his friends Robert and Helen Harrison. Painted en plein air, he portrayed two dozing figures under a willow tree, lulled by the water gently rocking their punt. With quick brushstrokes conveying the sparkling summer light and rippling water this could have been created by one of his Impressionist friends.

The Late Major E. C. Harrison as a Boy, 1887, oil on canvas, 178 x 84cm (70 x 33in), Southampton City Art Gallery, Hampshire, UK

Sargent often stayed with his friends Helen and Robert Harrison at Shiplake Court, in Henley-on-Thames. There he built a floating studio like Monet's. This is their son Cecil Harrison standing in his sailor suit, looking beyond the canvas. Early in World War I, Cecil enlisted and rose to the rank of Major, but was tragically killed in 1915. The title of this work was bestowed after that.

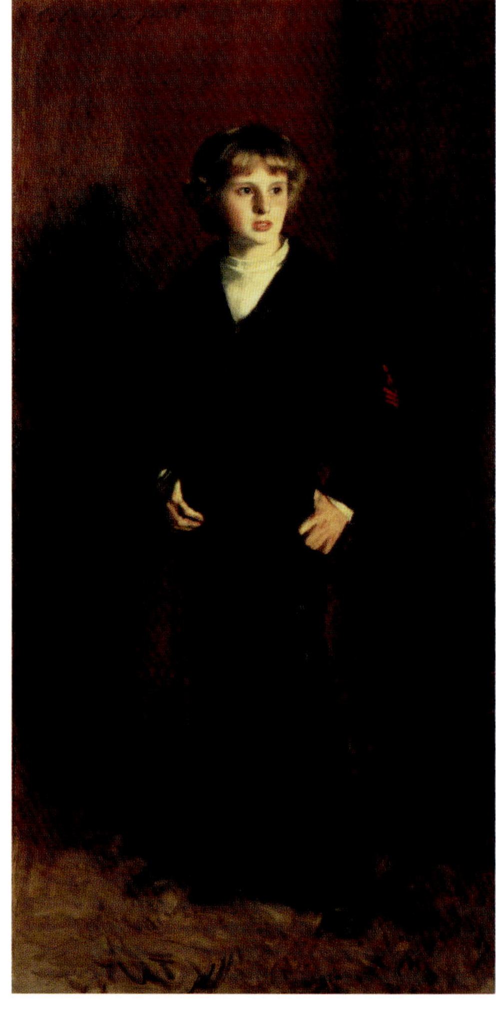

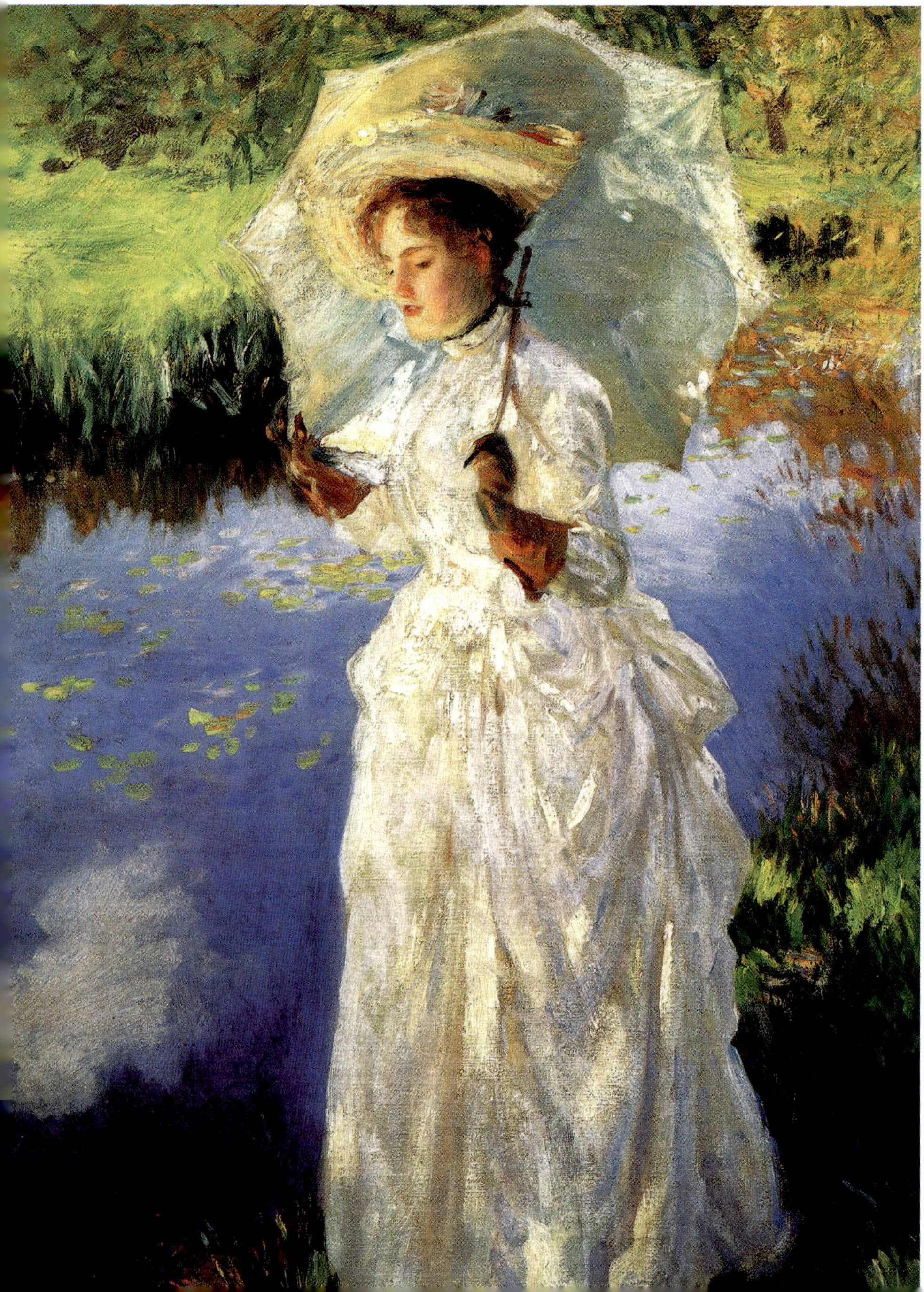

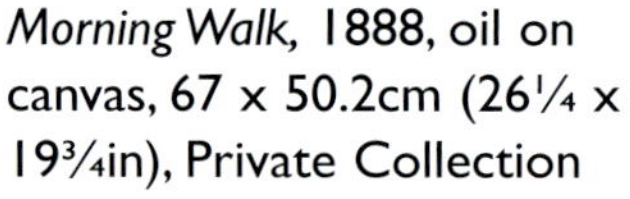

Morning Walk, 1888, oil on canvas, 67 x 50.2cm (26¼ x 19¾in), Private Collection

After visiting Monet at Giverny in 1887, Sargent became more focused on painting in an Impressionist style. Closely resembling paintings that Monet produced of his future stepdaughter, Suzanne Hoschedé, dressed in white and holding a parasol, Sargent painted his 18-year-old sister Violet, strolling near Calcot Mill where they were staying in Oxfordshire. Also wearing white and carrying a parasol, Violet is painted with broken, sketchy marks in vivid colours.

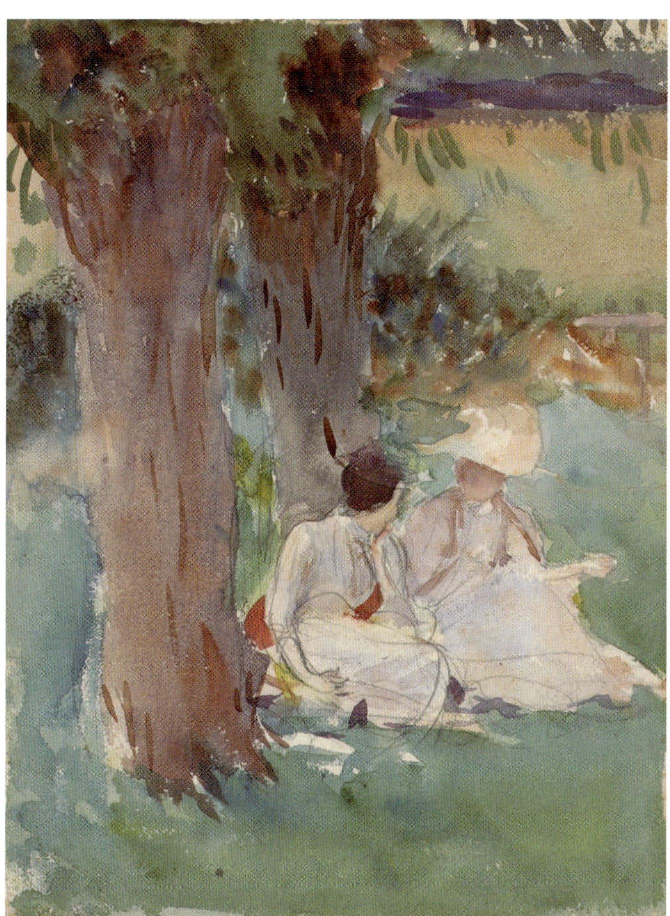

Under the Willows, 1888, watercolour and graphite on paper, 35.6 x 23.8cm (14 x 9½in), Private Collection

Inspired by his recent stay with Monet, and by Monet's reciprocal sojourn with him, while he and his family stayed at Calcot Mill, Sargent often went out painting, with family and friends. He produced some of his most Impressionistic works during this time. This is a rare early watercolour of Violet and Flora Priestley (1859–1936); a friend of Sargent's since the early 1880s when she had studied art in Paris.

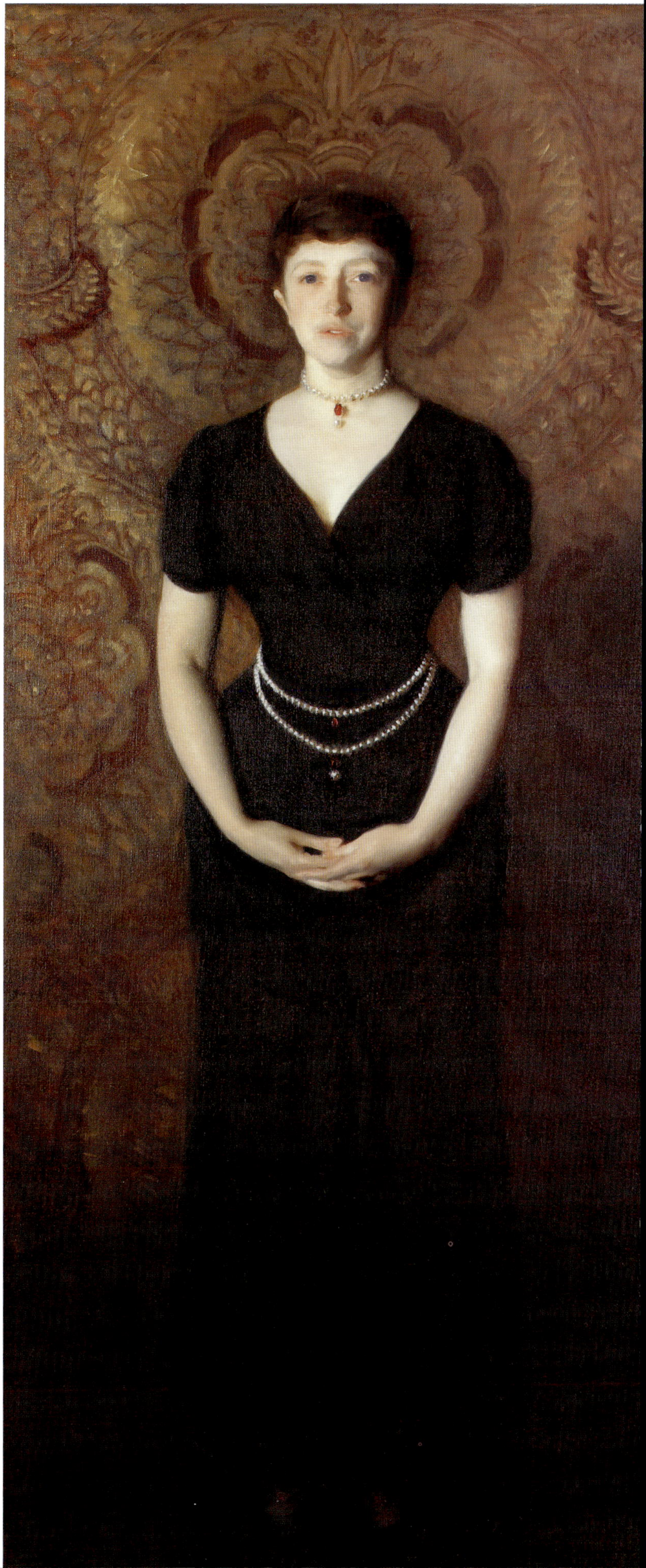

Mrs Isabella Stewart Gardner, 1888, oil on canvas, 190 x 80cm (74¾ x 31½in), Isabella Stewart Gardner Museum, Boston, Massachusetts, USA

Enthralled by *Madame X* (see pages 35 and 125), Sargent's friend Isabella Stewart Gardner wanted him to make her look as alluring. Sargent agreed that she could wear black, although the dress is more demure and she wears a long string of pearls to accentuate her waist and hips (see also page 44). The portrait was exhibited to great acclaim at Boston's St Botolph Club. Henry James described Isabella as a 'Byzantine Madonna' and another writer humorously called it 'Woman: An Enigma.'

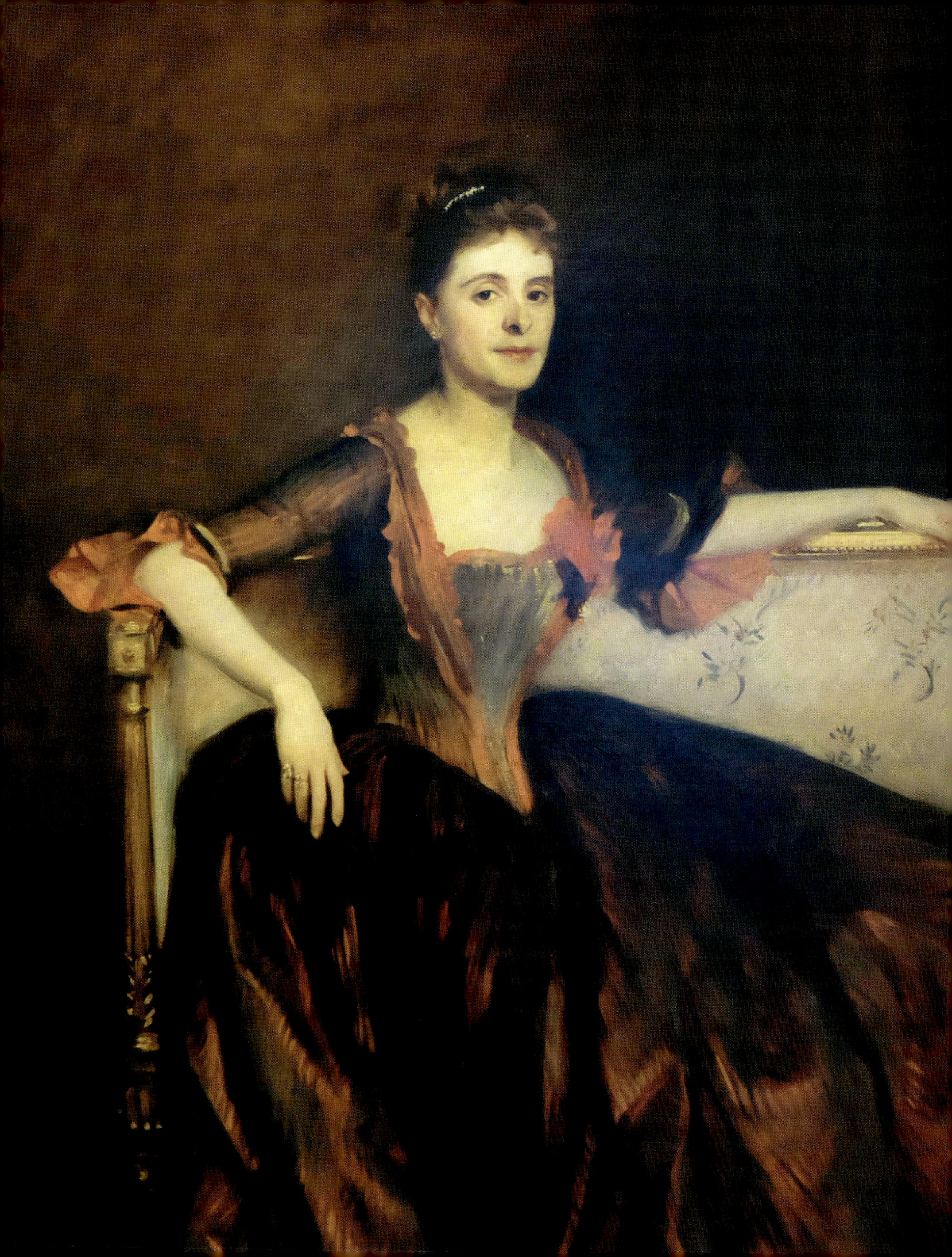

CAPTURING CHARACTER

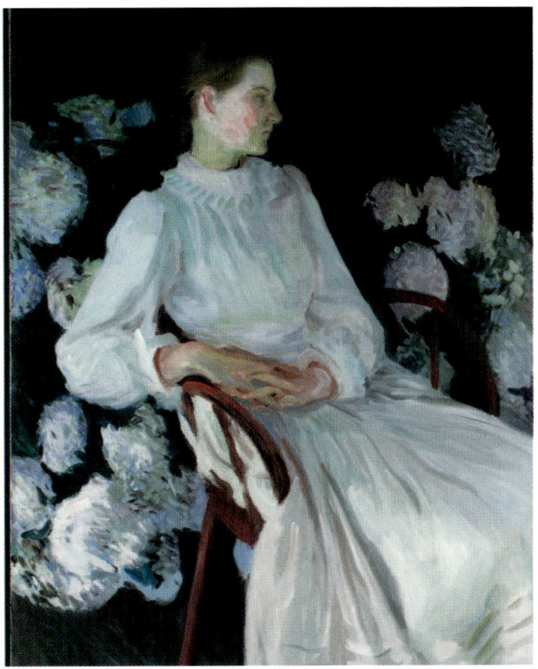

As the 19th century drew to a close, Sargent's reputation soared. No longer overshadowed by the scandal of Madame X, he became the most sought after portraitist in Britain and America and, financially secure, he relaxed and established long, warm friendships with many of his sitters. He began to move on from his Impressionistic style, but always retained the loose and fluid brushstrokes he so admired for capturing a sense of spontaneity, and as he painted ever more portraits, his confidence emerged on his canvases with expressive, accomplished images of unusual compositions that captured character as much as physical appearances.

Left: Mrs Thomas Lincoln Manson Jr, 1891, oil on canvas, 112.4 x 142.2cm (44¼ x 56in), Honolulu Museum of Art, Hawaii, USA.

Above: Katherine Chase Pratt, 1890, oil on canvas, 101.6 x 76.5cm (40 x 30in), Worcester Art Museum, Massachusetts, USA. One of two three-quarter-length portrait sketches of Katherine Chase Pratt (1875–1942), she is depicted surrounded by flowers and wearing a white dress. Sargent met and painted this thoughtful young woman six years before she married. She later gave up the trappings of materialism and became an evangelistic missionary and had quite a tragic life, as her husband and three young sons died prematurely.

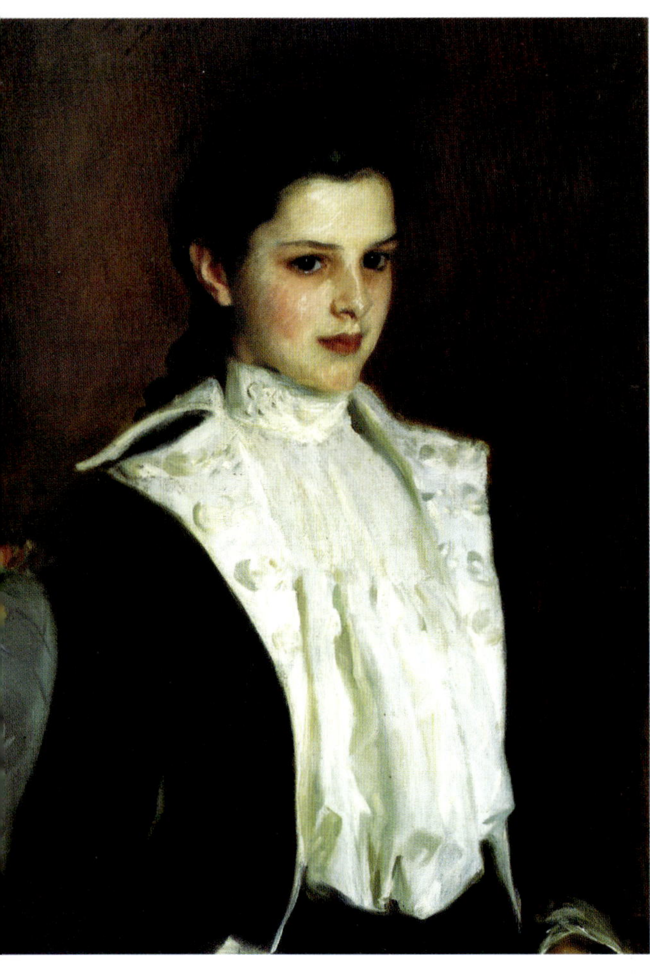

Eleanora O'Donnell Iselin (Mrs. Adrian Iselin), 1888, oil on canvas, 153.7 x 93cm (60½ x 36½in), National Gallery of Art, Washington DC, USA

The extremely prosperous Eleanora O'Donnell Iselin (1821–97) and her husband Adrian Iselin greatly supported cultural institutions in New York City. This portrait (see also page 46) was commissioned by Eleanora's two daughters and as Sargent arrived to begin, Eleonora greeted him with a maid laden with numerous ballgowns for him to choose from. She was not pleased when he asserted that she should remain exactly as she was, in the same position and her day clothes.

Alice Vanderbilt Shepard, 1888, oil on canvas, 76.5 x 55.9cm (30 x 22in), Amon Carter Museum, Texas, USA

Called Angela by her extremely wealthy family as they thought she was so sweet-natured and beautiful, Alice Vanderbilt Shepard Morris (1874–1950), was 13 years old here. Unusually, Sargent had not actually been commissioned to paint her, but he asked her parents if he could. He captured her white ruffled clothing with free, loose brushwork and her face with thinner, more delicately applied marks.

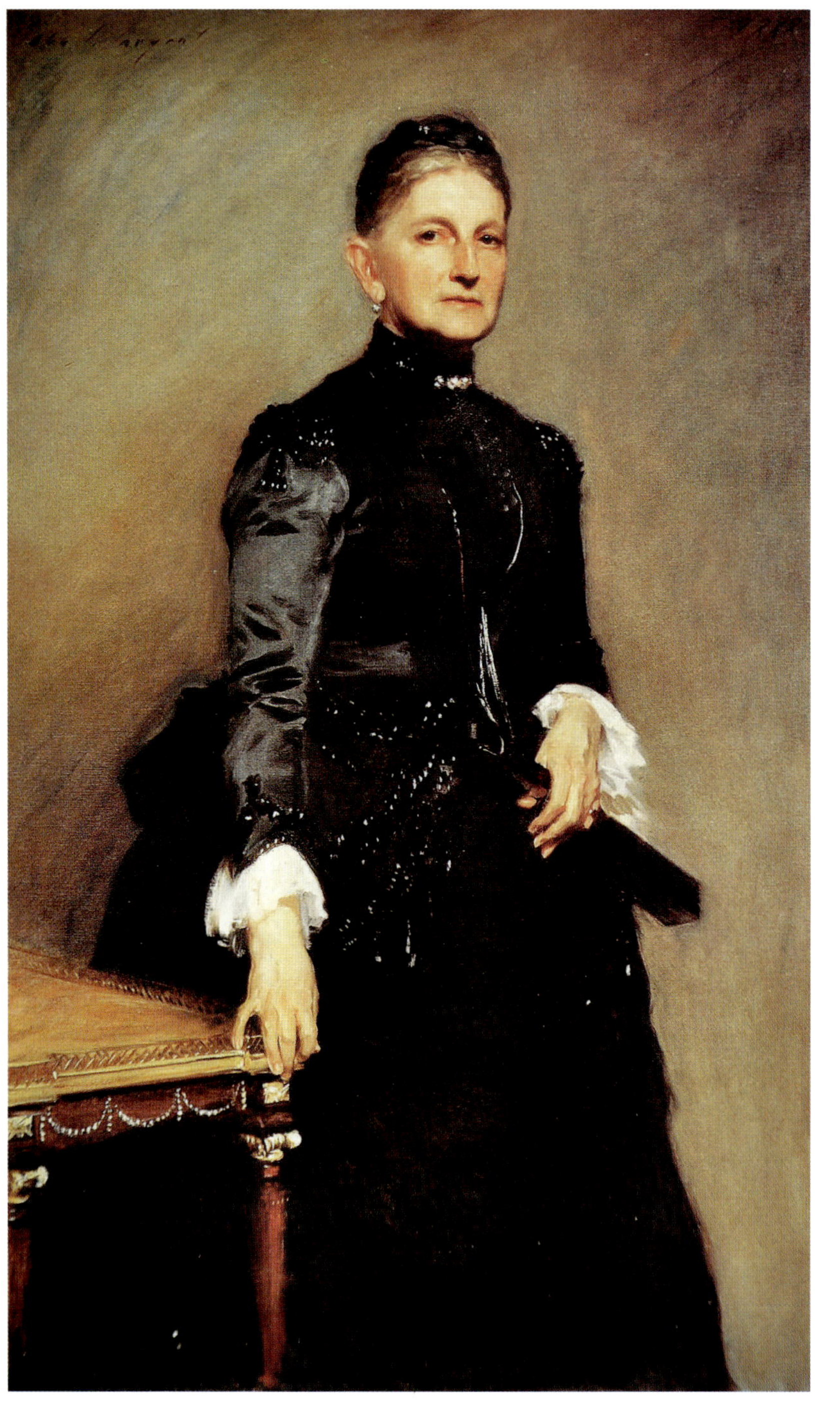

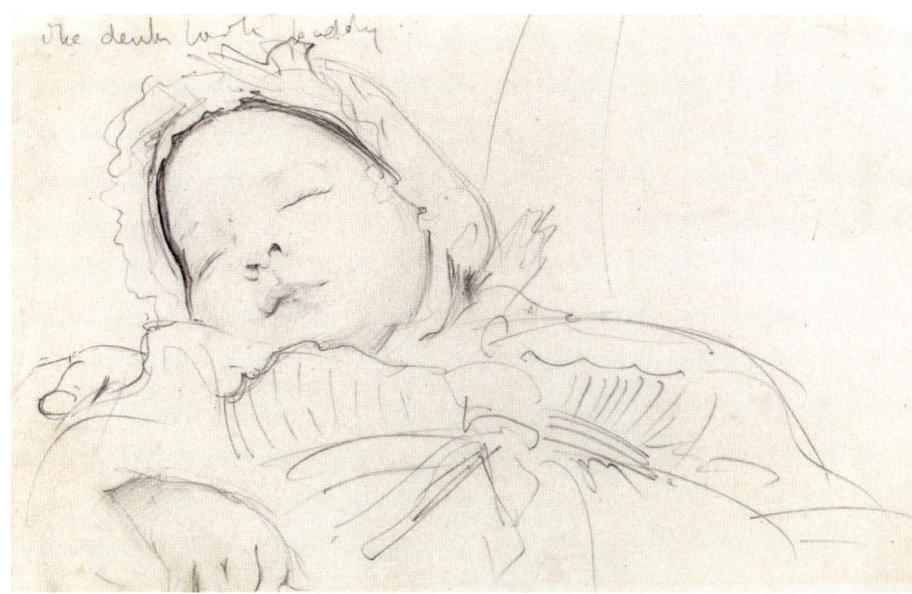

Jack Millet as a Baby, 1888, graphite on paper, 23.5 x 14cm (9¼ x 5½in), Fitzwilliam Museum, Cambridge, UK

Jack or John Millet (1888–1976) was the youngest surviving child in the Millet family, with whom Sargent stayed at their home in Broadway from 1885 to 1886. Jack's elder two siblings were Kate and Laurence. Sargent made this sketch of the baby when he visited the Millets soon after Jack's birth.

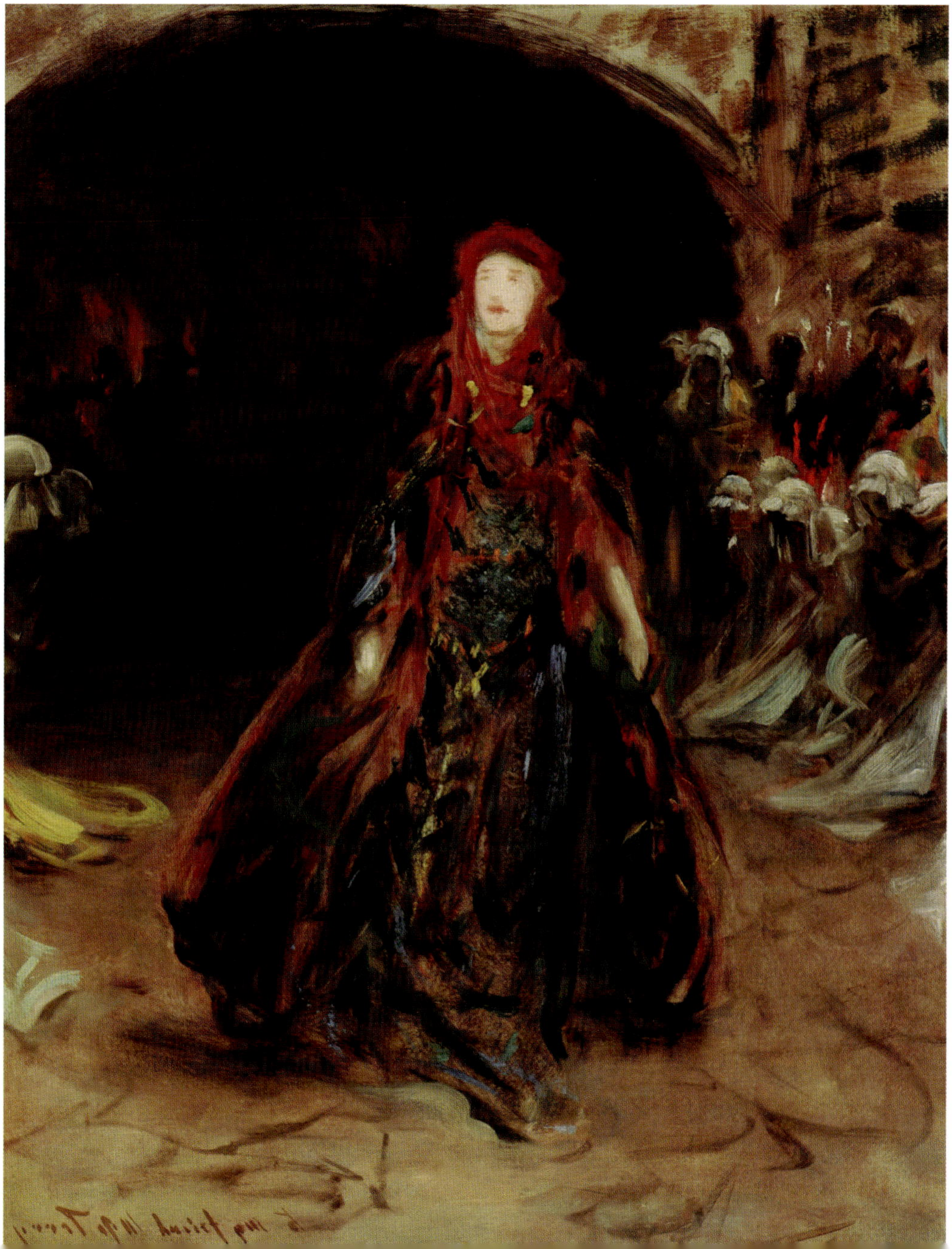

Dame Ellen Terry as Lady Macbeth, 1888, oil on canvas, 54.8 x 41.4cm (21½ x 16¼in), Smallhythe Place, Kent, UK

Dame Ellen Terry first played Lady Macbeth in Henry Irving's production of William Shakespeare's Macbeth in December 1888. Sargent was in the audience on the first night and was so taken with her performance that he determined to paint her in her spectacular green costume. This is a sketch, not the portrait that was received with such mixed reviews (see page 46). Instead this composition depicts her sweeping out of Macbeth's castle by torchlight.

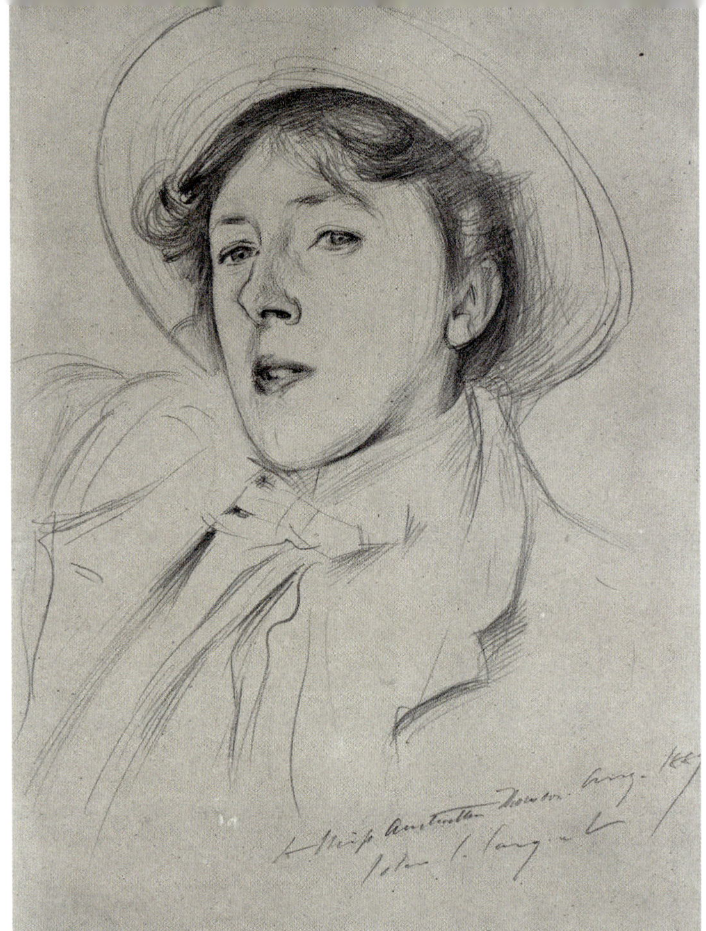

Portrait of Vernon Lee, 1889, graphite on pale buff paper, 33.7 x 22.8cm (13¼ x 9in), Ashmolean Museum, Oxford, UK

One of two drawings Sargent made in the same year of his childhood friend Vernon Lee. This shows the author of books on the Italian Renaissance as a sensitive, intelligent young woman. Although she called herself Vernon Lee, Sargent inscribed a painted portrait he made of her after these drawings 'to my friend Violet'. Reduced lines and minimal shading express the elusiveness of her personality.

Gabriel Fauré, 1889, oil on canvas, 61 x 54.6cm (24 x 21½in), Musée de la Musique, Paris, France

Highly influential, the music of the French composer, organist, pianist and teacher, Gabriel Urbain Fauré is often described as a link between Romanticism and Modernism. His most notable scores include *Pavane, Après un Rêve* and *Clair de la Lune*. He and Sargent greatly admired each other and were also good friends. Sargent painted this while visiting Fauré when he was in Paris in 1889 for the Universal Exhibition.

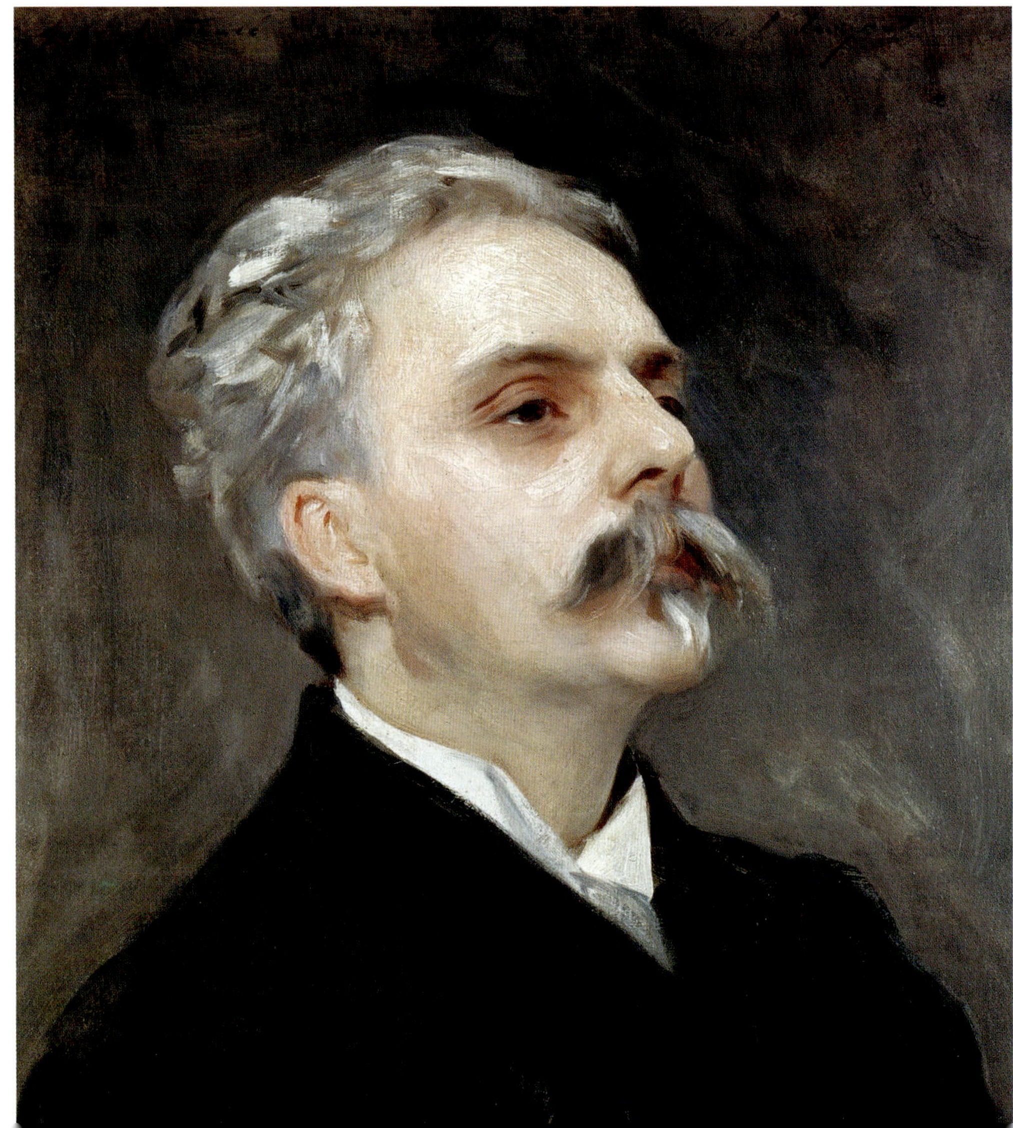

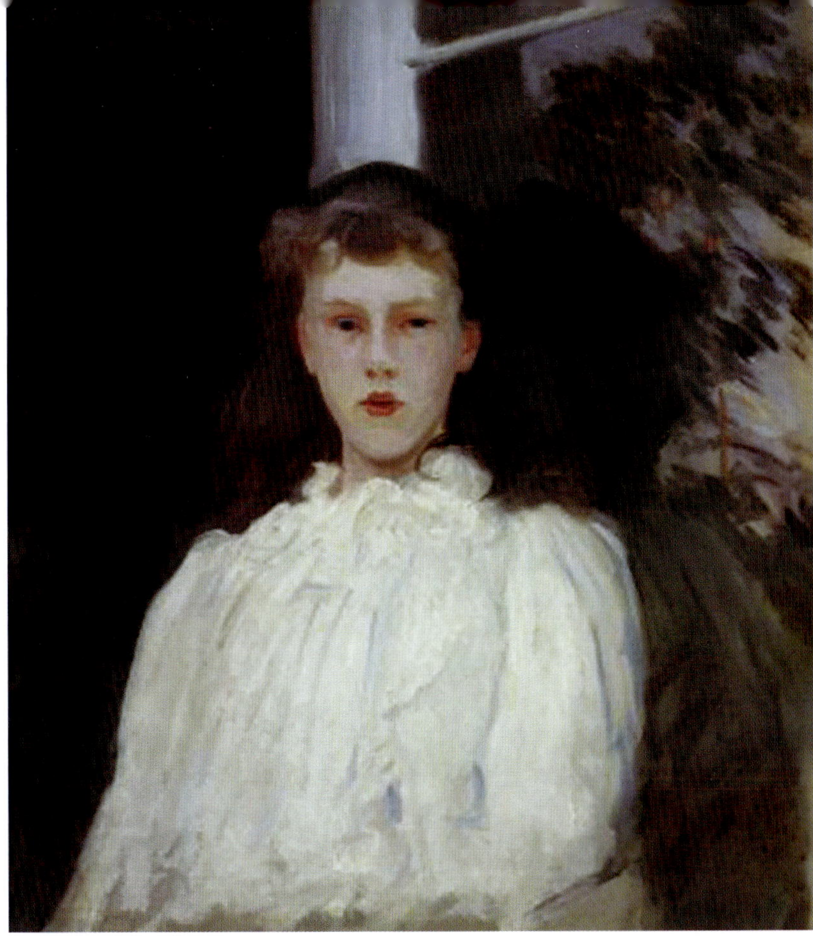

Polly Barnard (aka Girl in White Muslin), 1889, oil on canvas, 82 x 68cm (32¼ x 26¾in), Private Collection

Sargent had a remarkable ability to make and retain lifelong friends among a fairly diverse range of people. Most of his friends came from comfortable backgrounds, but they varied in ages and interests, including successful men and women, and the children of his friends who grew up to become a part of his social circle. Polly Barnard was one of these. This was painted four years after she posed for *Carnation, Lily, Lily, Rose* (see page 129).

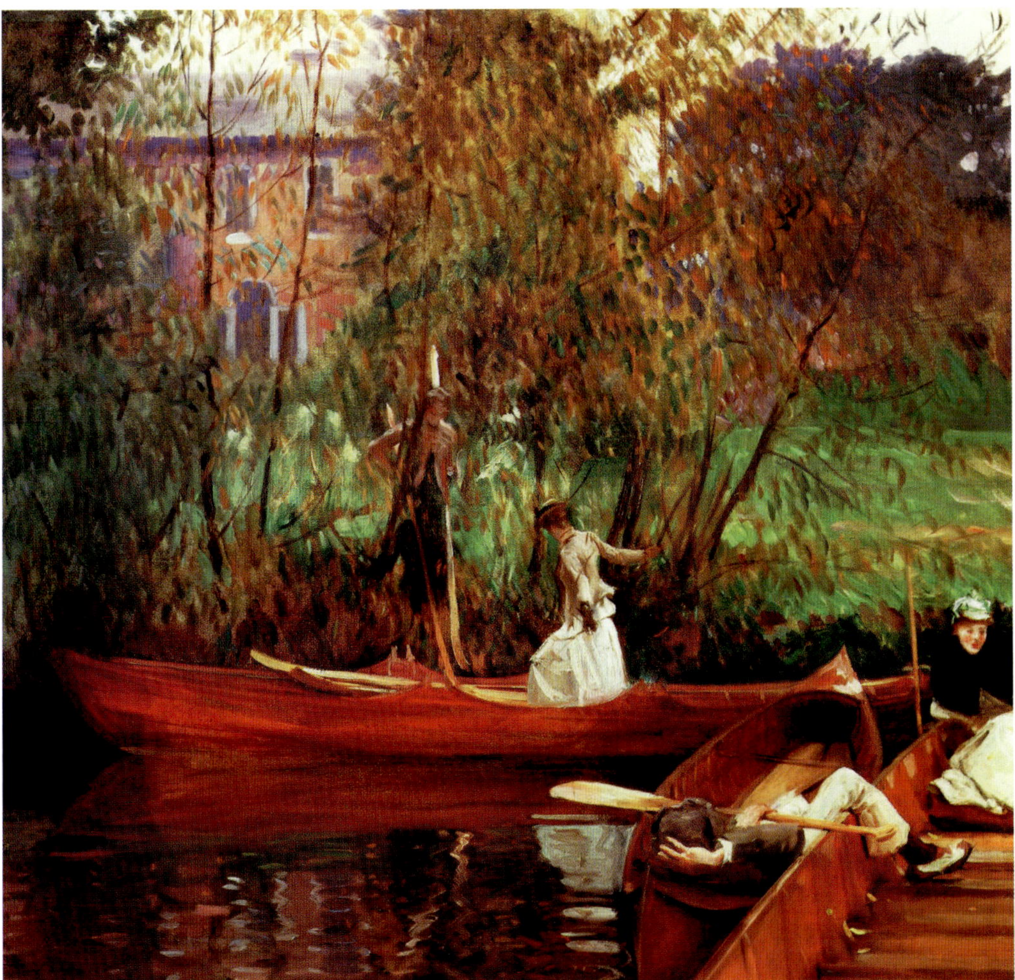

A Boating Party, c.1889, oil on canvas, 88.3 x 91.4cm (34¾ x 36in), Rhode Island School of Design, Rhode Island, USA

During a late summer holiday on the River Avon with his sister Violet and friends Paul and Alice Helleu, Sargent created this Impressionistic scene. In a characteristically unusual composition, he applies broken brushstrokes to convey the figures, boats and reflections. Cropped edges show the influence of photography and artists like Degas, as well as his delight in the individuality of his friends – such as Helleu holding on to his hat while anchoring his boat to land with a casually flung leg.

Lady Fishing: Mrs Ormond,
1889, oil on canvas,
184.8 x 97.8cm (72¾ x
38½in), Tate, London, UK

Aiming to recapture the
happy summer he spent
at Broadway during the
summers of 1888 and 1889
respectively, Sargent rented
Calcot Mill near Reading and
Fladbury Rectory beside the
River Avon in England. At
Fladbury in 1889, he painted
this of Violet standing on the
river bank holding a long
fishing rod, although he did
not complete the work.

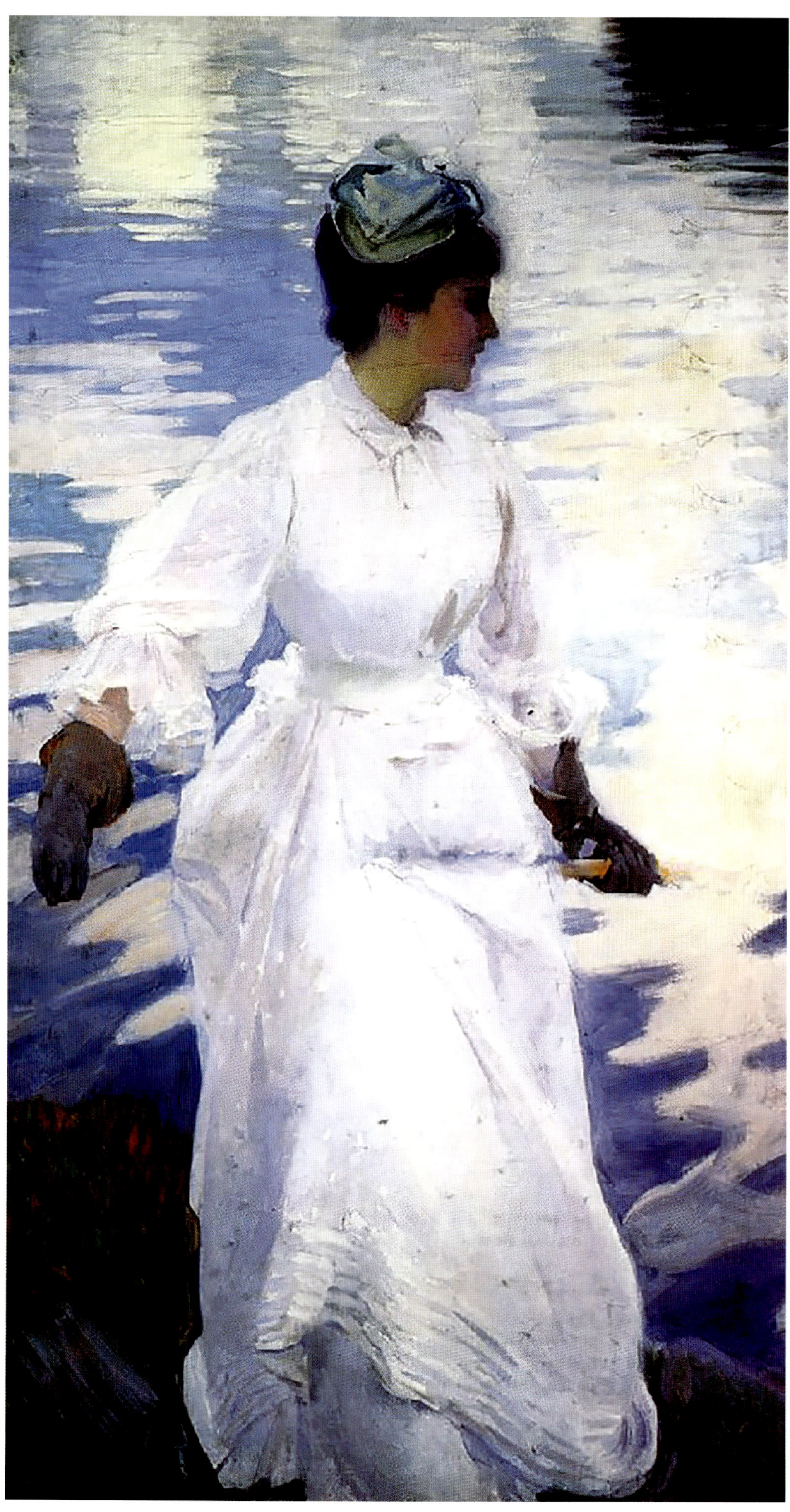

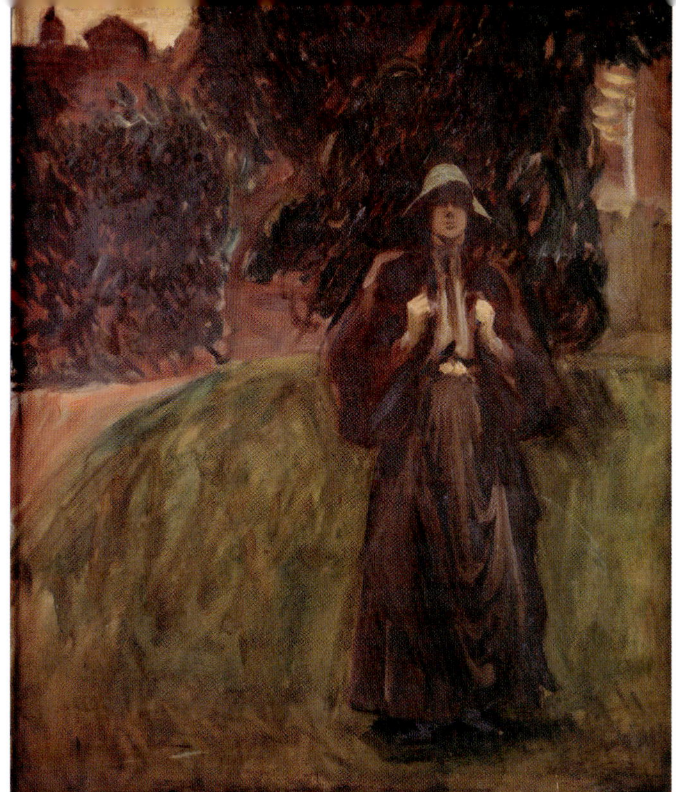

Portrait of Miss Clementina Anstruther-Thomson, c.1889, oil on canvas, 106.7 x 74cm (42 x 29¼in), Private Collection

This three-quarter-length portrait of Kit Anstruther-Thomson was painted by Sargent when she and

Vernon Lee visited him at Fladbury. Standing outdoors with a confident and energetic stance Sargent shows her ready for action, dressed in a walking suit and hat. She and Vernon shocked many people in their circle for being open about their lesbian relationship.

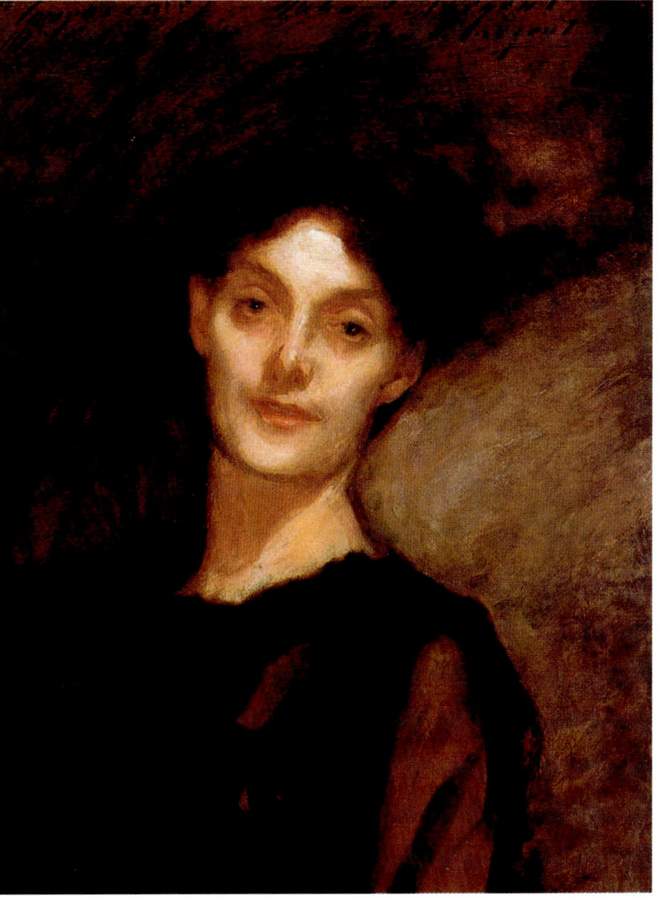

Mrs J. Comyns Carr, 1889, oil on canvas, 64.5 x 50.5cm (25½ x 19¾in), Speed Art Museum Louisville, Kentucky, USA

Alice Vansittart Comyns Carr, née Strettell, was married to Sargent's art critic friend

Joseph Comyns Carr. A costume designer, she was involved with the aesthetic dress movement that favoured flowing garments rather than tight corsets. This soft and candid painting is captured with a minimum of vigorous brushstrokes.

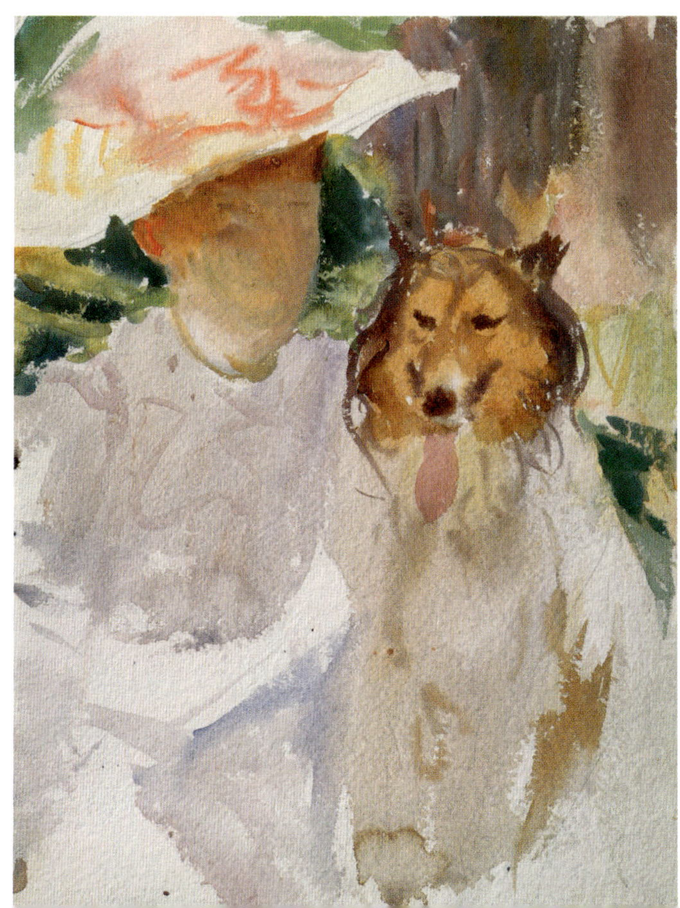

Woman with Collie, after 1890, watercolour, gouache and graphite on white wove paper, 35.4 x 25.2cm (14 x 10in), The Metropolitan Museum, New York, USA

This unfinished painting is possibly of Sargent's friend Margaret Stuyvesant Rutherfurd White – or Daisy as he and all her other friends called her (see pages 38 and 64–65).

Before he abandoned the painting, Sargent had completed more of the dog than the woman, which creates a lively and slightly amusing image. Soft fur is suggested with dynamic, fluid brushmarks, and diluted, transparent paint creates the pink floral hat and featureless face. Despite this lack of detail, the painting conveys a relaxed, happy and affectionate scene.

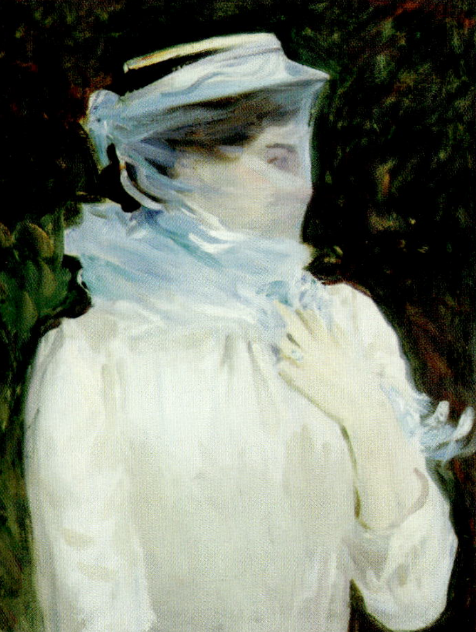

Sally Fairchild with Blue Veil,
c.1890, oil on canvas, 76.2
x 64.8cm (30 x 25½in),
Private Collection

In December 1889, Sargent
and Violet stayed in the
US with their friends the
Fairchilds. Charles Fairchild
had commissioned Sargent's
last portrait of Robert Louis
Stevenson as a gift to his
wife Elizabeth (see page
132). From then on, he
managed Sargent's American
finances. Sargent had painted
Elizabeth in 1887 and in
1890, he painted their
daughter Sally with her
veil over her face.

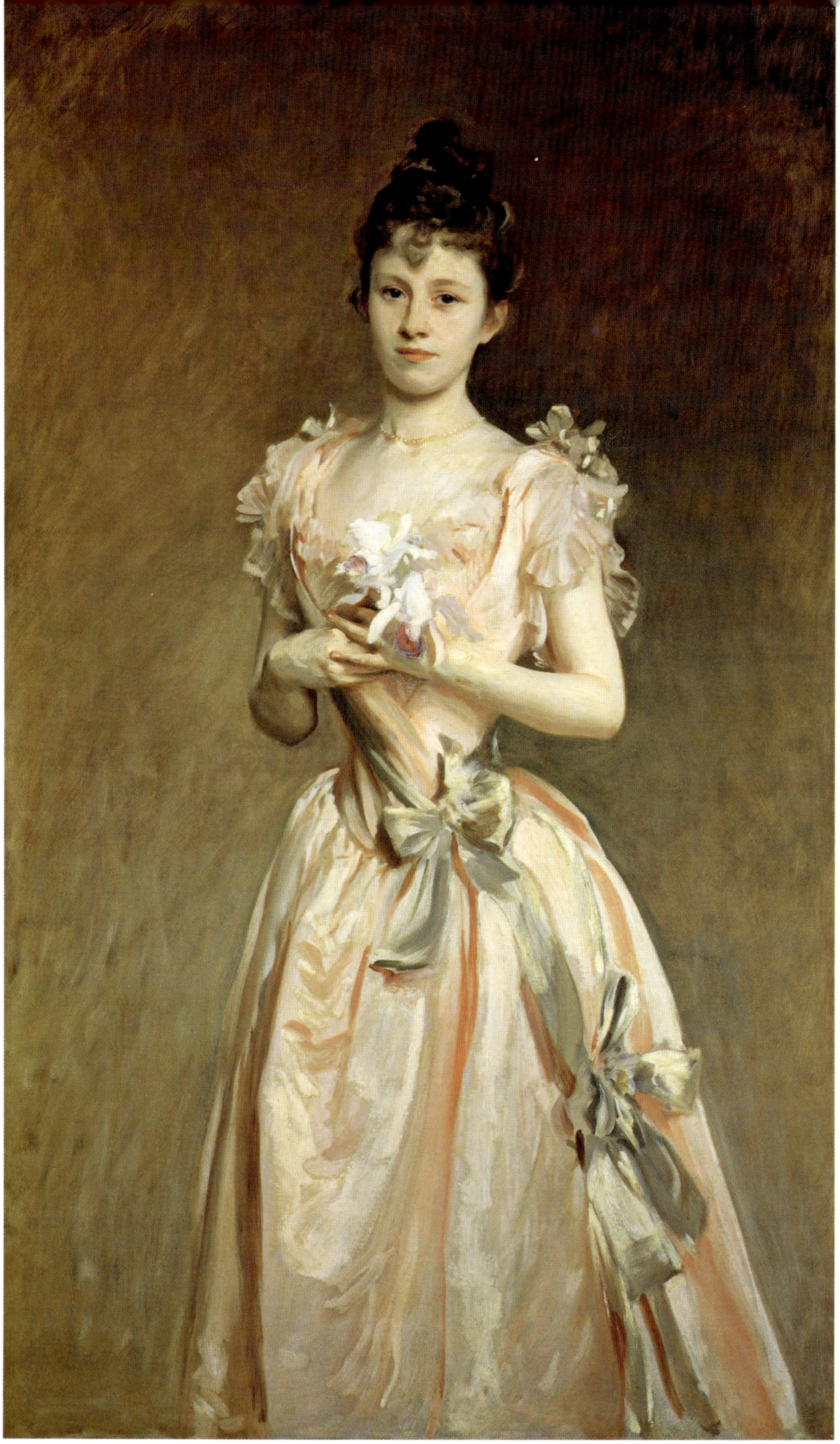

Miss Grace Woodhouse,
1890, oil on canvas, 162.9 x
94cm (64 x 37in), National
Gallery of Art, Washington
DC, USA

Evoking innocence and the
bloom of youth, Sargent
painted his sitter wearing
a peach satin gown in the
latest fashion, with ribbons
and pearls, and holding a
posy of flowers; a typical
young lady about to go to
her first ball. He worked
with his usual technique of
painting the clothing with
loose, bravura brushstrokes,
and thinner, more detailed
brushwork on the face.

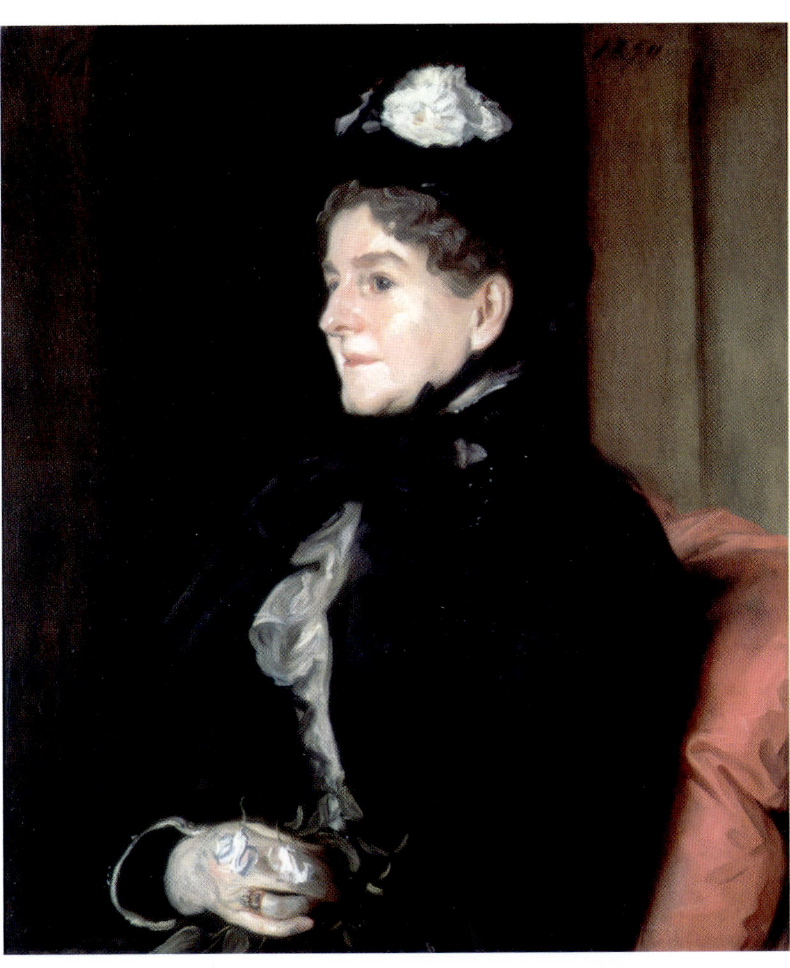

Mrs Alexander Hamilton Bullock, 1890, oil on canvas, 76.2 x 64cm (30 x 24¼in), Worcester Art Museum, Massachusetts, USA

During Sargent's stay in the US for nine months in 1890, he painted approximately 40 portraits, of which this was one. Elivira Hazard (1824–94) was the daughter of a prosperous Connecticut merchant and the widow of Alexander Hamilton Bullock (1816–82), an American lawyer, politician and businessman from Massachusetts.

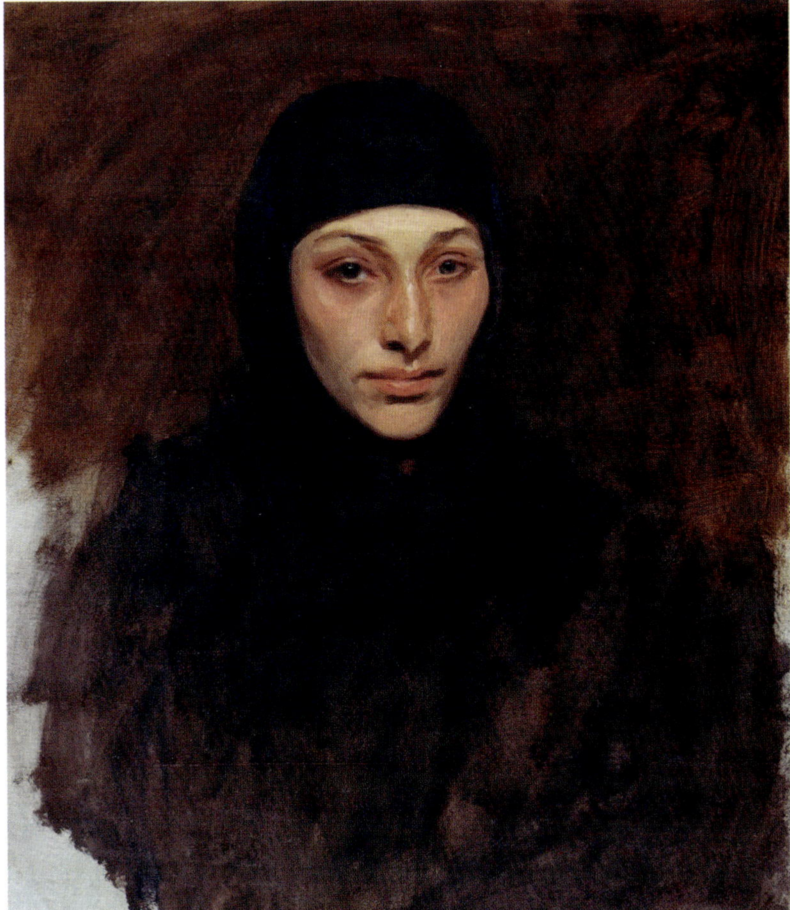

Egyptian Woman, 1890–91, oil on canvas, 64.8 x 53.3cm (25½ x 21in), The Metropolitan Museum, New York, USA

As soon as he was asked to create murals for Boston Public Library, Sargent decided to depict the origins of Western religion, and duly visited Egypt, Greece and Turkey to gather visual information. He perceived many elements of these countries and the people as particularly exotic and alluring as can be seen in this enigmatic portrait of an Egyptian woman.

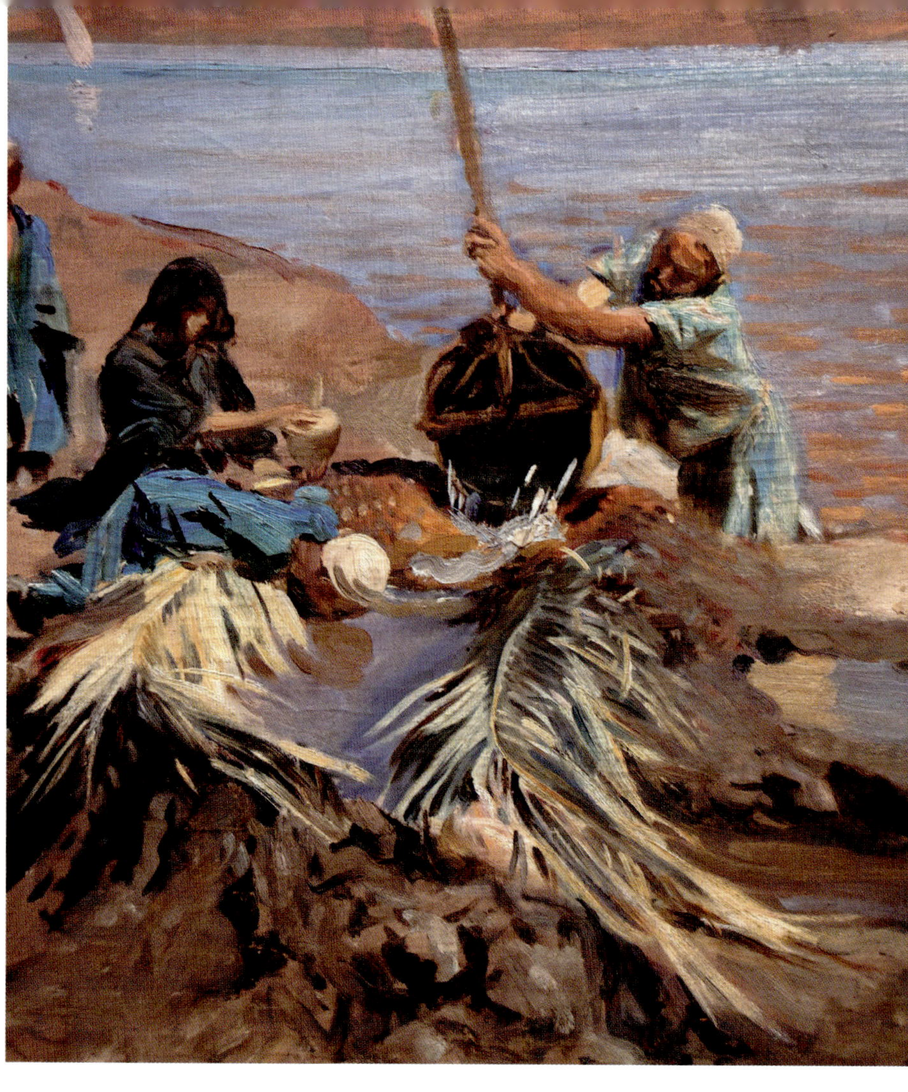

Egyptians Raising Water from the Nile, 1890–91, oil on canvas, 63.5 x 53.3cm (25 x 21in), The Metropolitan Museum, New York, USA

Sargent made this sketch while researching his theme of the history of Western religion. This is an Egyptian man using an irrigation device called a shaduf to fill a ditch. Next to him, others drink the water and wait to fill their containers. Convinced that this sort of occurrence had continued since biblical times, Sargent considered it relevant to his historical imagery.

Cliffs at Deir el Bahri, Egypt, 1890–91, oil on canvas, 34.9 x 62.9cm (13¾ x 24¾in), The Metropolitan Museum, New York, USA

Thought to represent the cliffs at Deir el Bahri on the west bank of the Nile opposite the city of Luxor in Egypt. This is an unfinished painting that Sargent made during his trip to Egypt in 1890 to 1891. Deir el Bahri is a complex of mortuary temples and tombs, part of the Theban Necropolis. The painting is simply an atmospheric suggestion of the view.

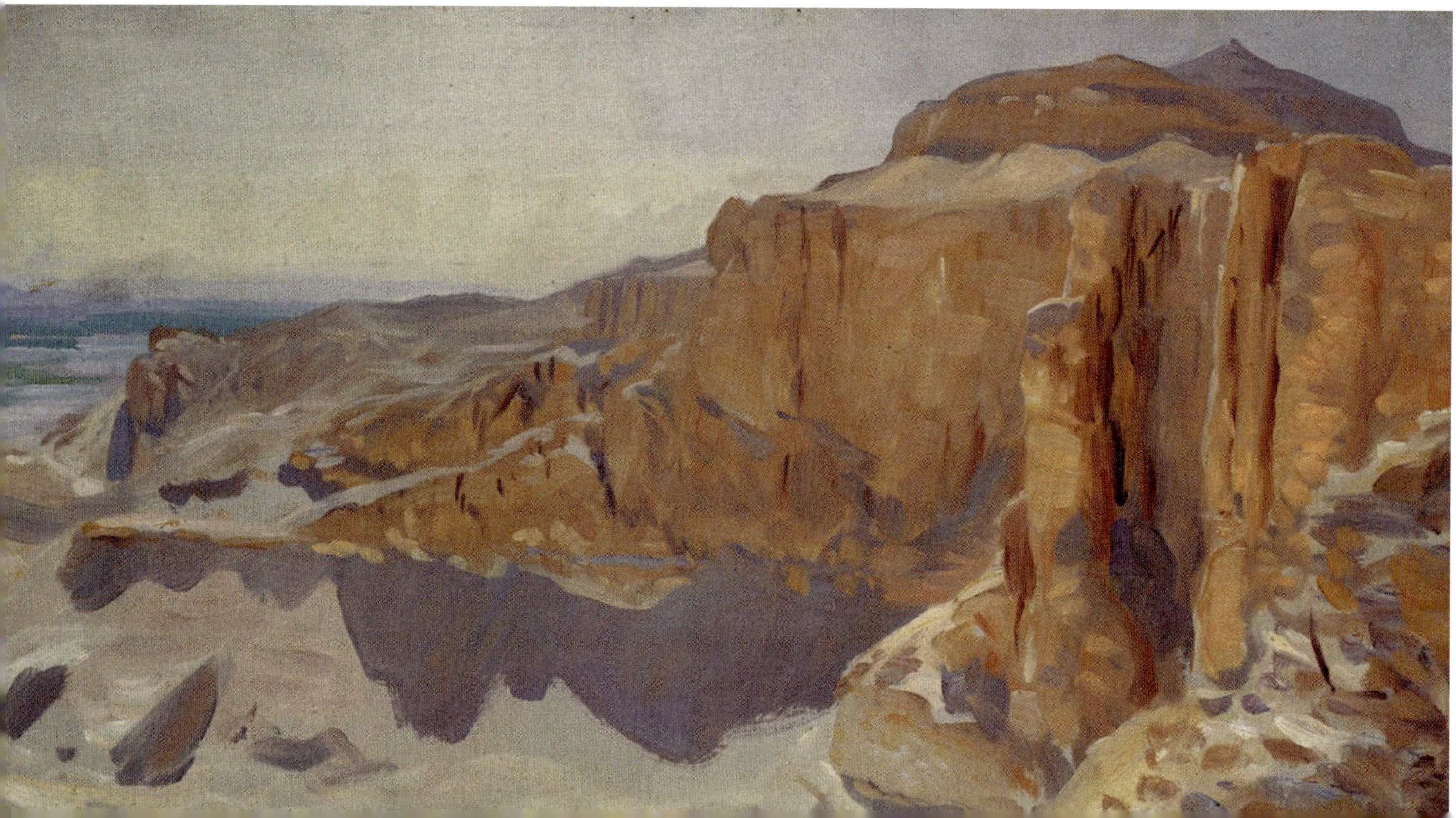

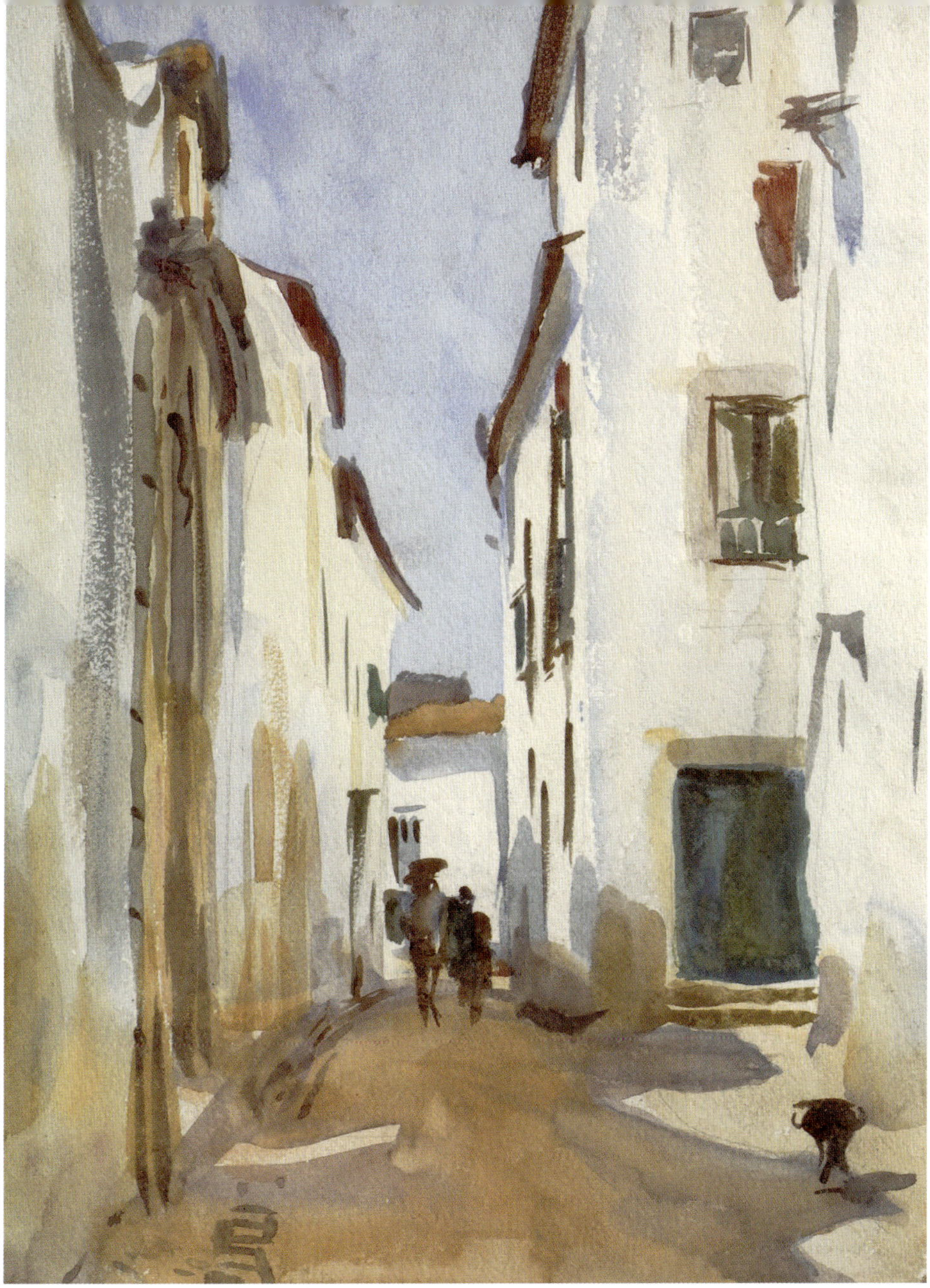

Street in a Mediterranean Town, c.1891, watercolour over graphite on paper, 35.5 x 25.2cm (14 x 10in), The Clark Art Institute, Massachusetts, USA

An atmospheric watercolour depicting a swelteringly hot summer's day, possibly somewhere in Greece, this is an example of Sargent's move towards freer, more expressive imagery using watercolours rather than oils. At the time, paintings were expected to be carefully and precisely executed, but his confident, bold marks and loosely defined forms grabbed attention and portrayed the immediacy of the moment.

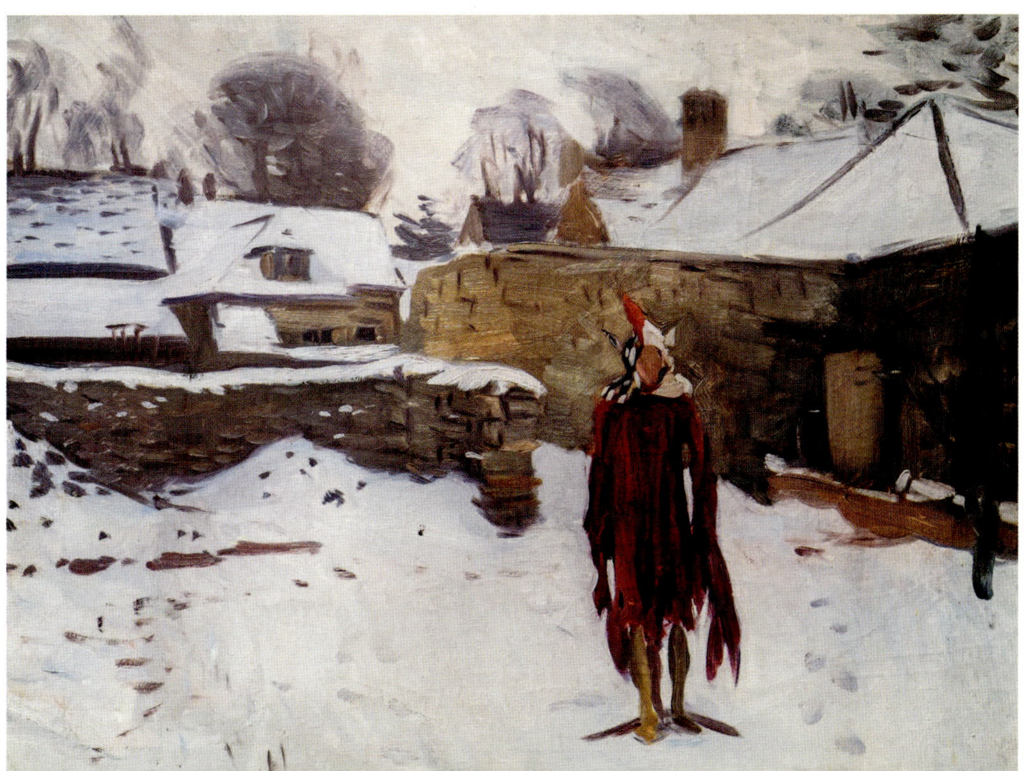

Mannequin in the Snow, 1891–93, oil on canvas, 63.5 x 76.2cm (25 x 30in), The Metropolitan Museum, New York, USA

At times over the years 1891 to 1894, Sargent shared a large studio at Morgan Hall in Fairford in Gloucestershire with his friend Abbey. As a break from their mural painting, they put this mannequin in the snow and painted oil sketches of it from the window. Sargent's painting evokes a rather sinister looking scene featuring the lifeless dummy.

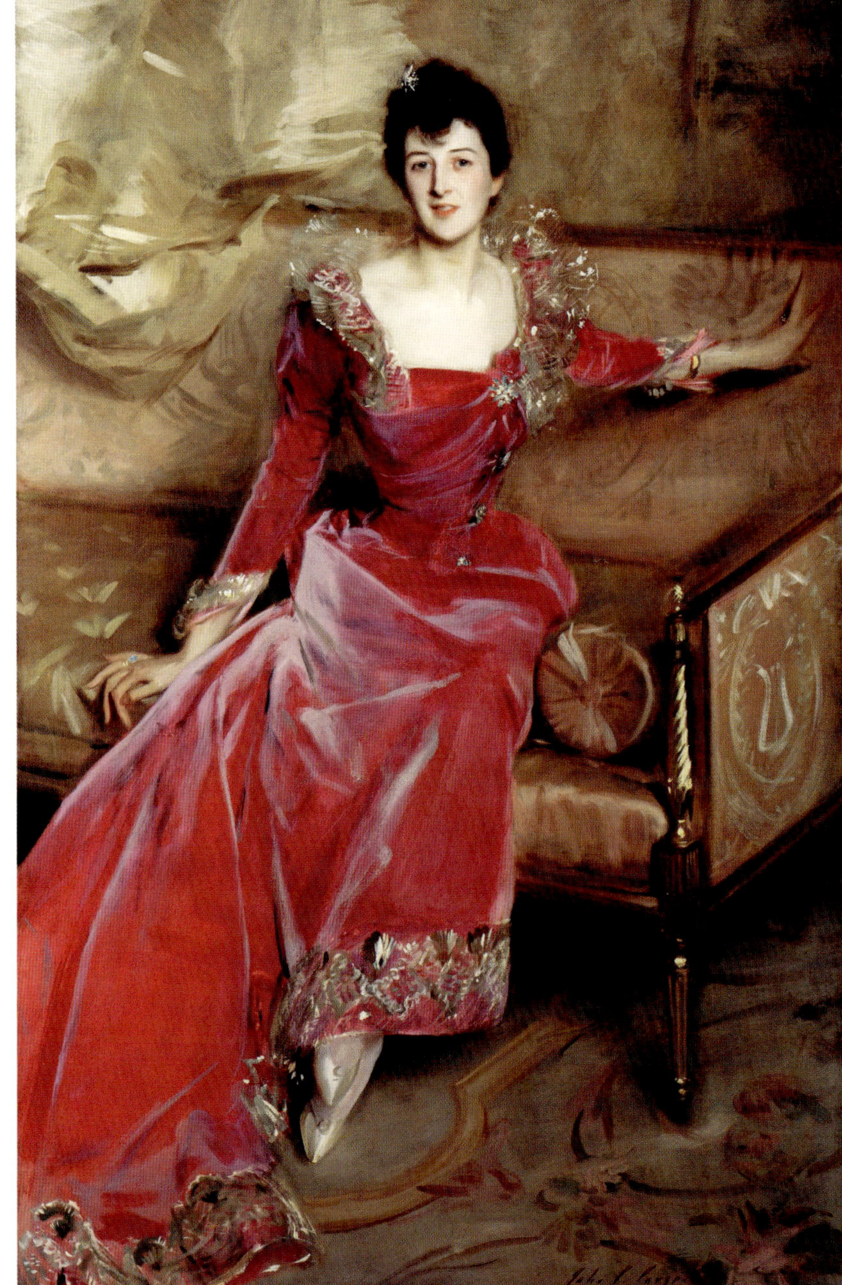

Mrs Hugh Hammersley, 1892, oil on canvas, 205.7 x 115.6cm (81 x 45½in), The Metropolitan Museum, New York, USA

Mary Hammersley wears an expensive gold-trimmed silk-velvet dress as she perches lightly on her lavish sofa, half smiling and seemingly about to jump up (see detail on page 57). Together with the portrait of *Lady Agnew of Lochnaw* (right), this dazzling work overcame any lingering negativity about Sargent's scandalous portrait, *Madame X* (see page 35). It set Sargent firmly at the top of his profession, able to command almost any price for his portraits.

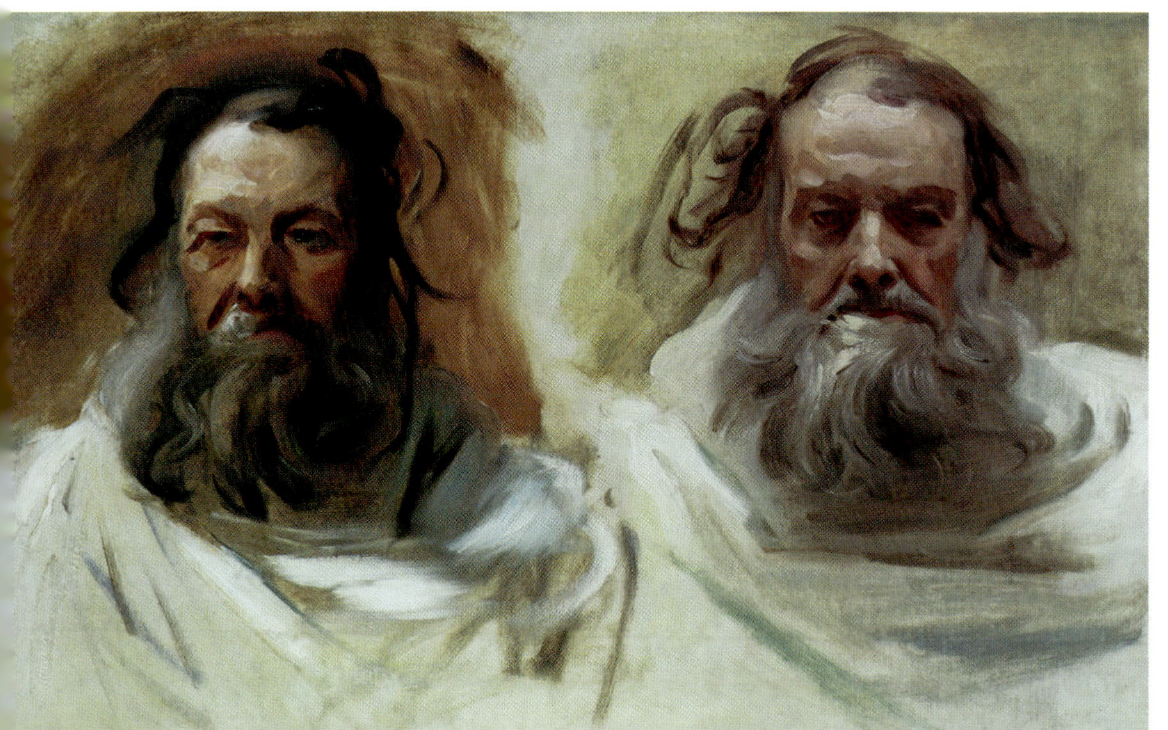

Study of Two Heads: The Prophets, c.1892, oil on canvas, 59 x 87cm (23¼ x 34¼in), Private Collection

This loose, expressive study is undated, but it is believed to have been painted by Sargent in preparation for his Boston murals. Recorded from life in an expressive, uncontrived style, the two faces depict two Hebrew prophets and helped to inform his final version of prophets from the Old Testament in his portrayal of the Triumph of Religion in his murals.

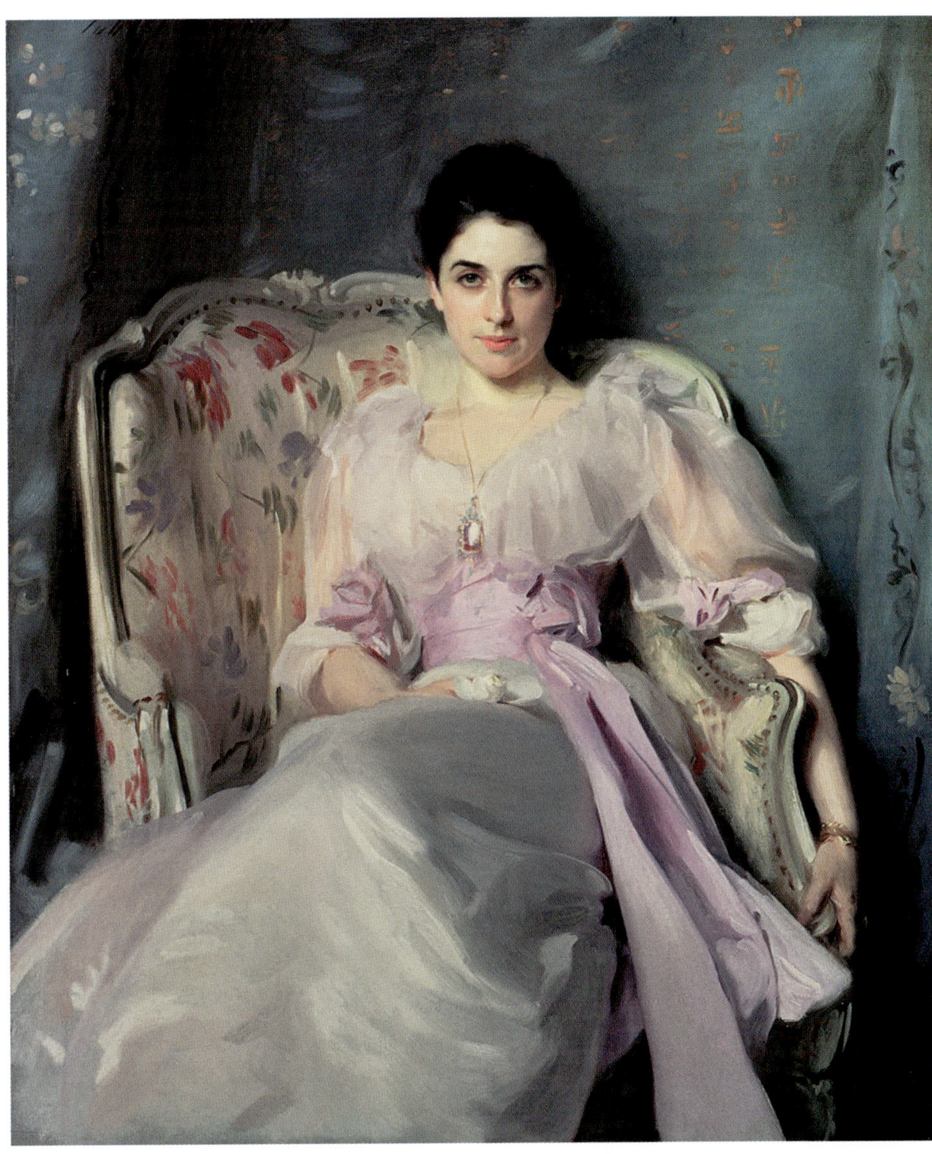

Lady Agnew of Lochnaw, c.1892–93, oil on canvas, 124.5 x 99.7cm (49 x 39¼in), National Galleries of Scotland, Edinburgh, UK

One of the first of Sargent's portraits that convinced critics that he could combine technical artistry with an expression of underlying character, this portrait of Gertrude Vernon, the wife of Lord Andrew Noel Agnew of Lochnaw, 15 years younger than her husband, received overwhelming praise. With its subtle harmonies and slightly impasto brushwork, the portrait was described by many as a masterpiece.

Elizabeth Winthrop Chanler (Mrs John Jay Chapman), 1893, oil on canvas, 125.4 x 102.9cm (49¼ x 40½in), Smithsonian American Art Museum, Washington DC, USA

Sargent declared that his 26-year-old sitter had 'the face of the Madonna and the eyes of a child.' When she was a child, Bessie Chanler's mother died, so she helped to bring up her seven younger siblings. Sargent painted this in London, conveying a mix of serenity and tension in her character. Her relaxed pose and sumptuous surroundings suggest calmness and wealth, while her direct gaze is wary.

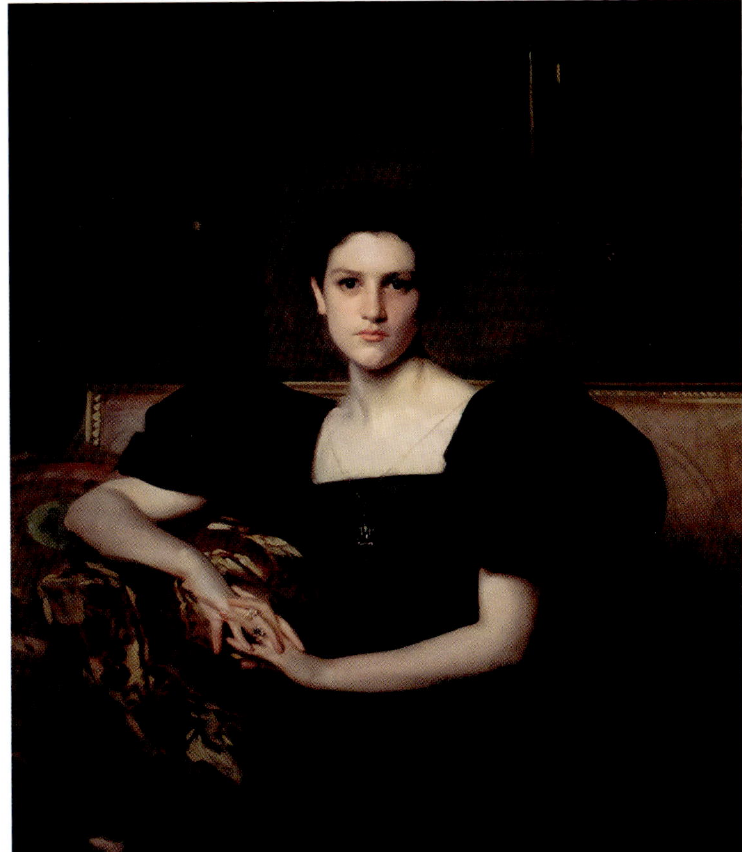

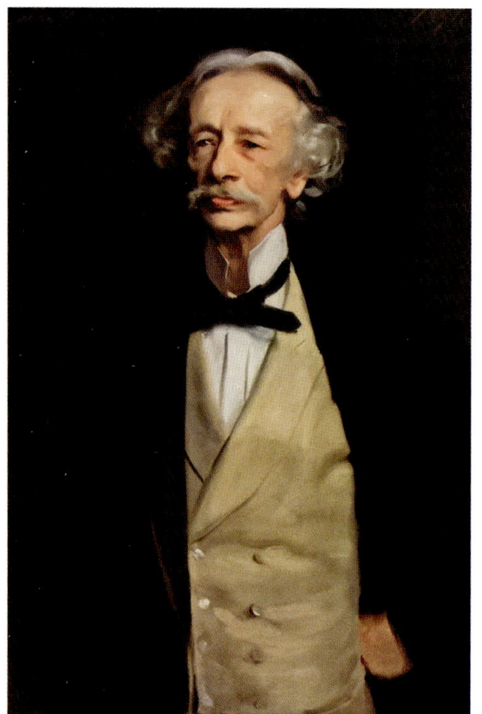

Coventry Kersey Deighton Patmore, 1894, oil on canvas, 91.4 x 61cm (36 x 24in), National Portrait Gallery, London, UK

Sargent painted this two years before the death of the sitter, the poet and writer, Coventry Patmore (1823–96). He was a deeply religious man who among many other things, wrote poetry praising married love. He was also man of extremely strong opinions, who fell out with all of his closest friends, including the poets Tennyson and Rossetti. The portrait exudes a sense of determination, character and thoughtfulness.

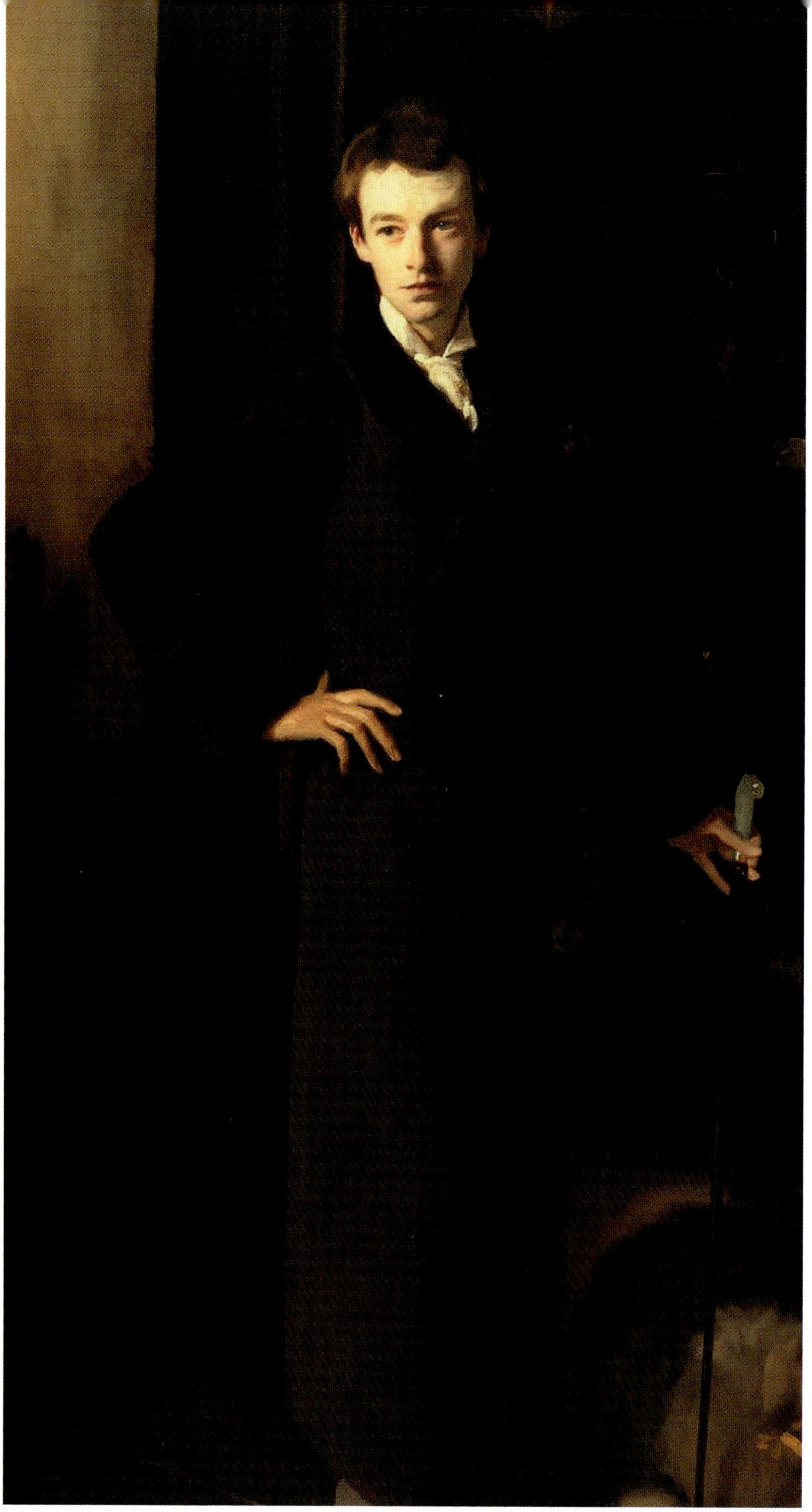

W. Graham Robertson, 1894, oil on canvas, 230.5 x 118.7cm (90¾ x 46¾in), Tate, London, UK

An elegant, slender, pale-skinned young man, this was Sargent's close friend, the gifted illustrator Walford Graham Robertson. Despite his protestations that it was too hot for his long coat in the summer, Sargent insisted that he wear it; and that Robertson's pet poodle, Mouton, was also included. To Sargent's amusement, Mouton bit him several times while he was trying to paint.

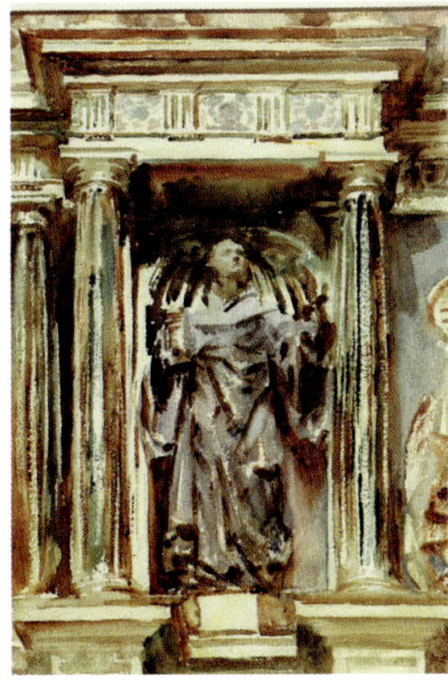

In a Church at Granada,
c.1895, watercolour, 53.3 x
34.cm (21 x 13½in), Private
Collection

While in Spain during the
late summer of 1895, Sargent
copied several works of art
by artists he admired, but
also spent time in churches,
painting and drawing art
around him. He never
stopped learning or gathering
materials for his murals. This
was painted in the Church
of Los Jerónimos in Granada,
along with several other
watercolours.

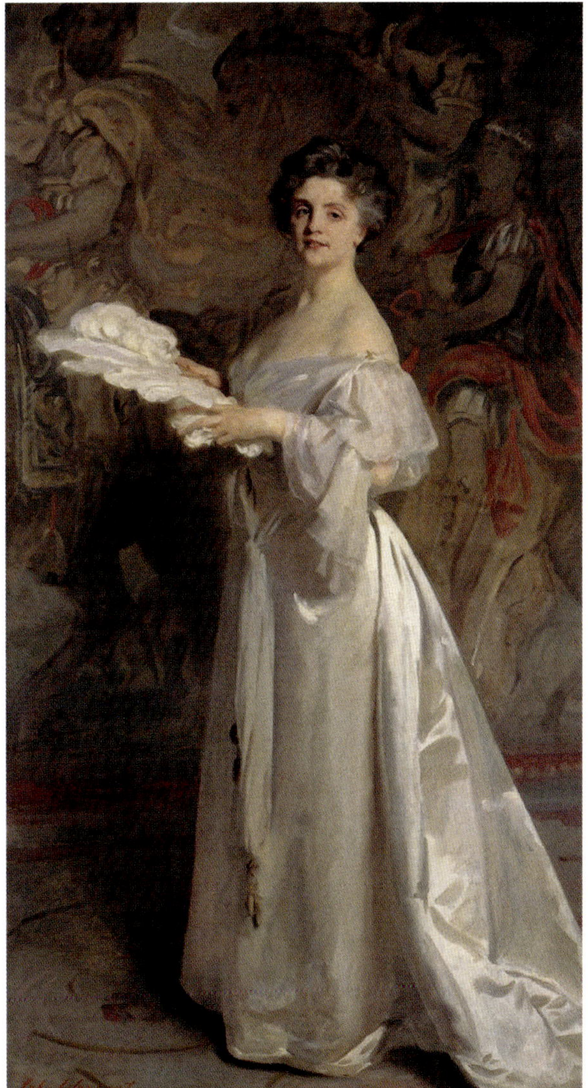

Ada Rehan, 1894–95, oil on
canvas, 236.2 x 127.3cm (93
x 50in), The Metropolitan
Museum, New York, USA

Born Delia Crehan in Ireland,
Ada Rehan (1860–1916)
grew up in Brooklyn, New
York. From the age of 14,
she followed her elder
sisters on to the stage but
when she was mistakenly
billed as Ada C. Rehan, the
name stuck. She became the
leading lady in the company
of Augustin Daly. Sargent was
commissioned to paint this
work by an admirer, and he
chose to present her in the
18th-century Grand Manner
of portraiture.

*Study of a Young Man
Drawing,* 1895, transfer
lithograph, 32.1 x 49.9cm
(12½ x 19½in), The
Metropolitan Museum,
New York, USA

In October 1895, the Palais
des Beaux-Arts marked the
centenary of the invention
of lithography by Aloys
Senefelder (1771–1834)
with an exhibition. The
British printer Frederick
Goulding (1842–1909) had
developed an improved
transfer paper for lithography,
and he encouraged Sargent
and others to participate.
Sargent's lithograph is filled
with contrasts, depicting a
young man drawing as strong
light falls across his form.

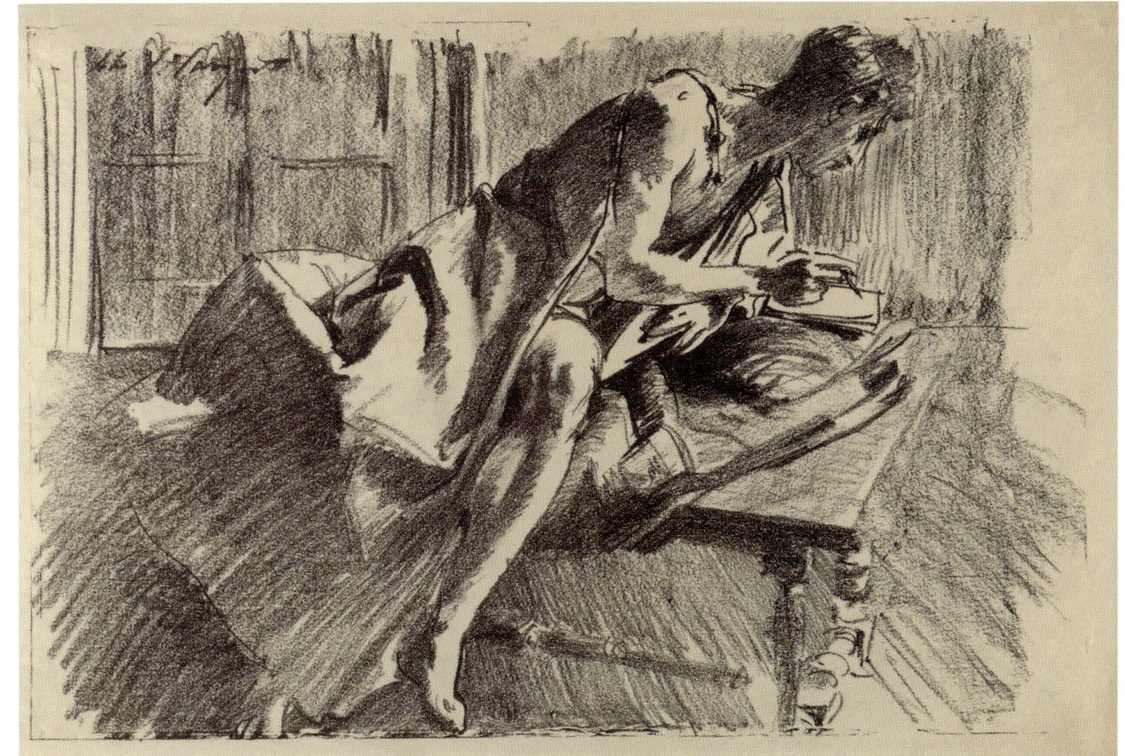

Helen Sears, 1895, oil on canvas, 167.3 x 91.4cm (65¾ x 36in), Museum of Fine Arts, Boston, Massachusetts, USA

Art collector, art patron, painter and photographer Sarah Choate Sears (1858–1935) commissioned this portrait of her daughter Helen (1889–1966) from her friend Sargent. In her cream dress, set against red, this is one of two portraits Sargent completed of little Helen that year, from a high viewpoint to emphasize her size and innocence. However, when he saw Sarah's photograph of Helen, in the same outfit, he despaired of his own work.

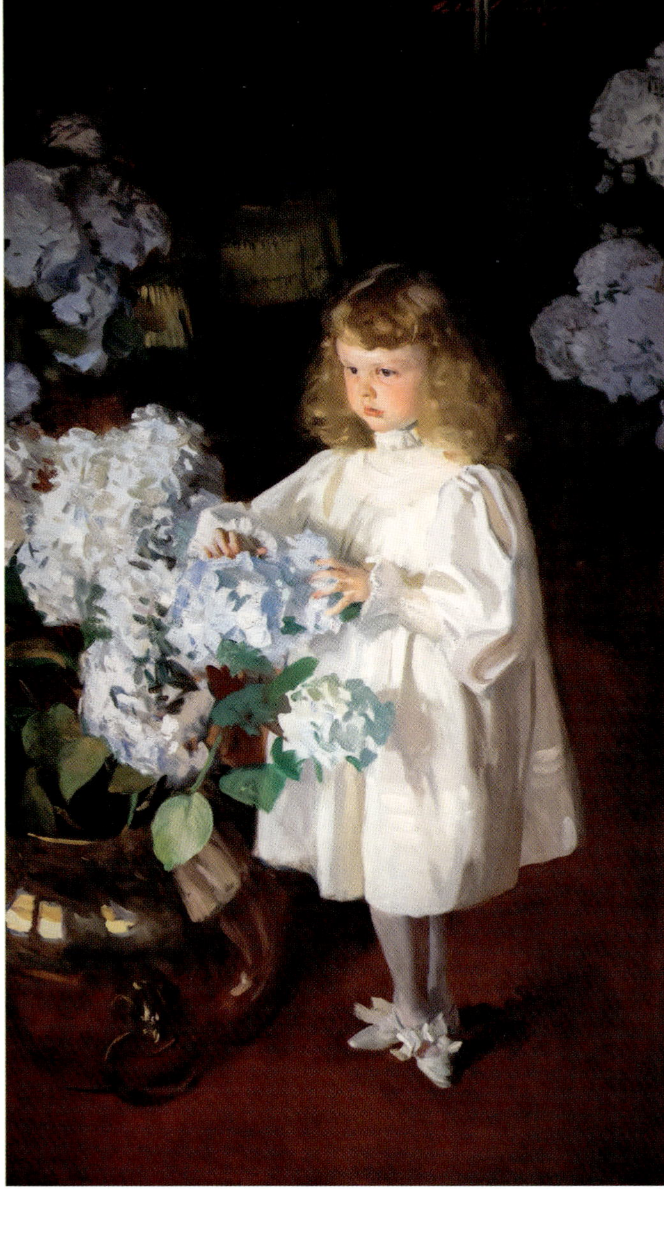

Frederick Law Olmsted, 1895, oil on canvas, 232.1 x 154.3cm (91½ x 60¾in), Biltmore House, North Carolina, USA

The great American landscape architect Frederick Law Olmsted (1822–1903) stands in the gardens he designed for the Vanderbilt mansion, Biltmore House in Asheville, North Carolina. Sargent posed him amid dogwood, rhododendrons and mountain lauren, but the light caused him problems, so he created a studio in an unfinished part of the mansion and completed the portrait there.

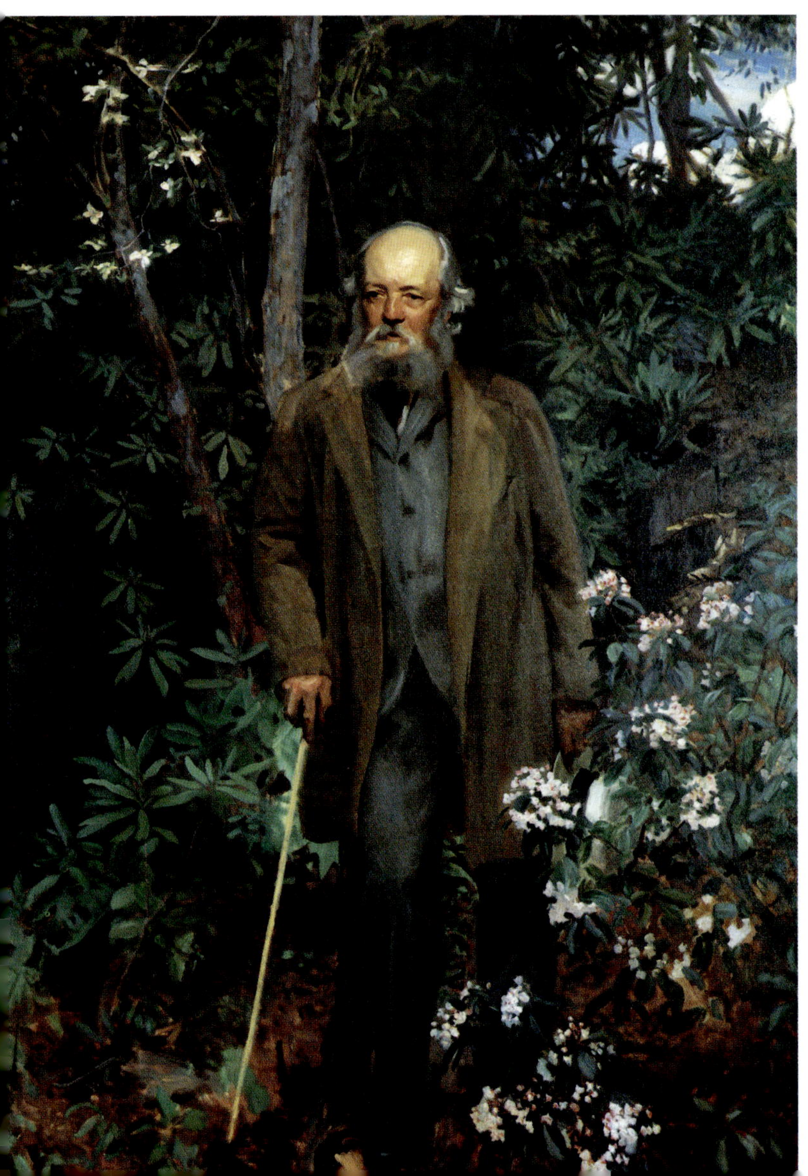

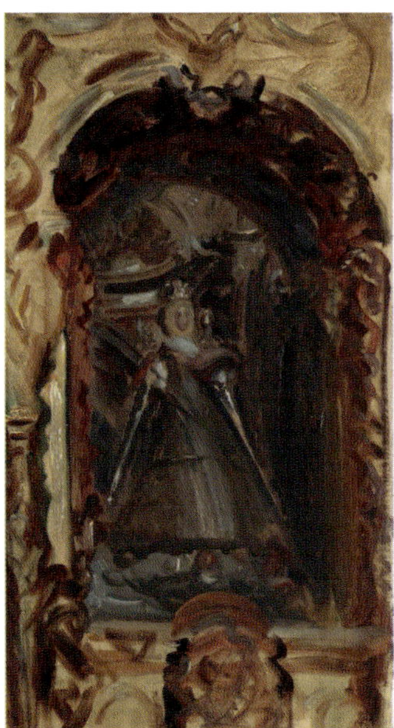

A Spanish Madonna, c.1895, oil on canvas, 46.4 x 27.3cm (18¼ x 10¾in), Saint Louis Art Museum, Missouri, USA

After his first phase of the Boston Library murals had been unveiled, Sargent travelled to Spain in June 1895, where he copied works by his favourite artists, including El Greco. He also made more sketches of details he observed, partly for his own pleasure but mainly to be stored as research, and possibly for use later on in his next phase of murals.

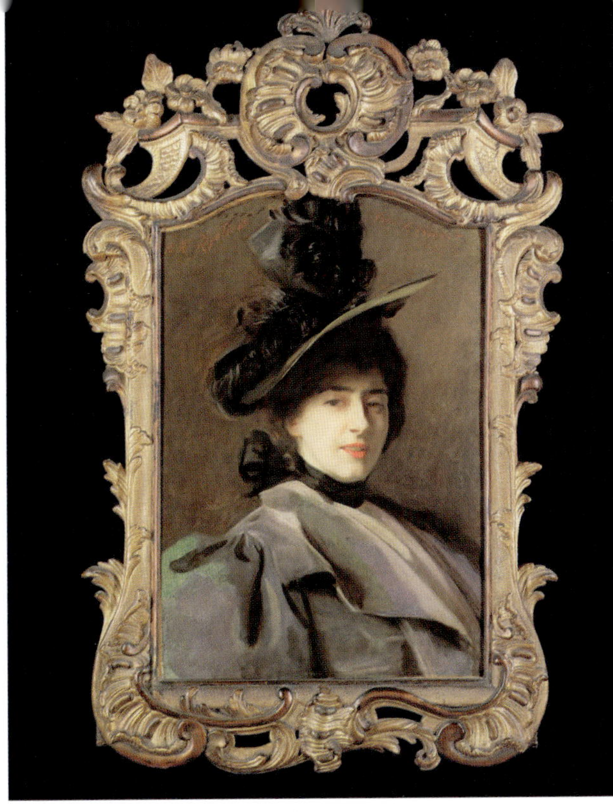

Portrait of Madame Flora Reyntiens, c.1895, oil on canvas, 74 x 49cm (29 x 19¼in), The Tuscaloosa Museum of Art, Alabama, USA

At first glance this portrait appears to have been painted rapidly with bold brushwork. However, friends who observed Sargent's painting methods record that as he began he would paint carefully and slowly, gradually working with more freedom. As he neared completion, he would stand back to analyze his work so far, then apply final strokes with spontaneity and freedom. Madame Reyntiens confidently looks back at the viewer, the warmth of her skin tones and lips contrasting with the muted monochrome outfit.

Study of a Young Man, Seated, c.1895, lithograph, 29.8 x 21.cm (11¾ x 8½in), The Metropolitan Museum, New York, USA

In October 1895, to mark the centenary of the invention of lithography by Aloys Senefelder (1771–1834), a large exhibition at the Palais des Beaux-Arts in Paris was held. Sargent created six lithographs, which later moved on to the Rembrandt Gallery in London. Demonstrating his understanding of tone, he left some areas of the paper white and scratched highlights across other areas, creating a subtle interplay of darks and lights.

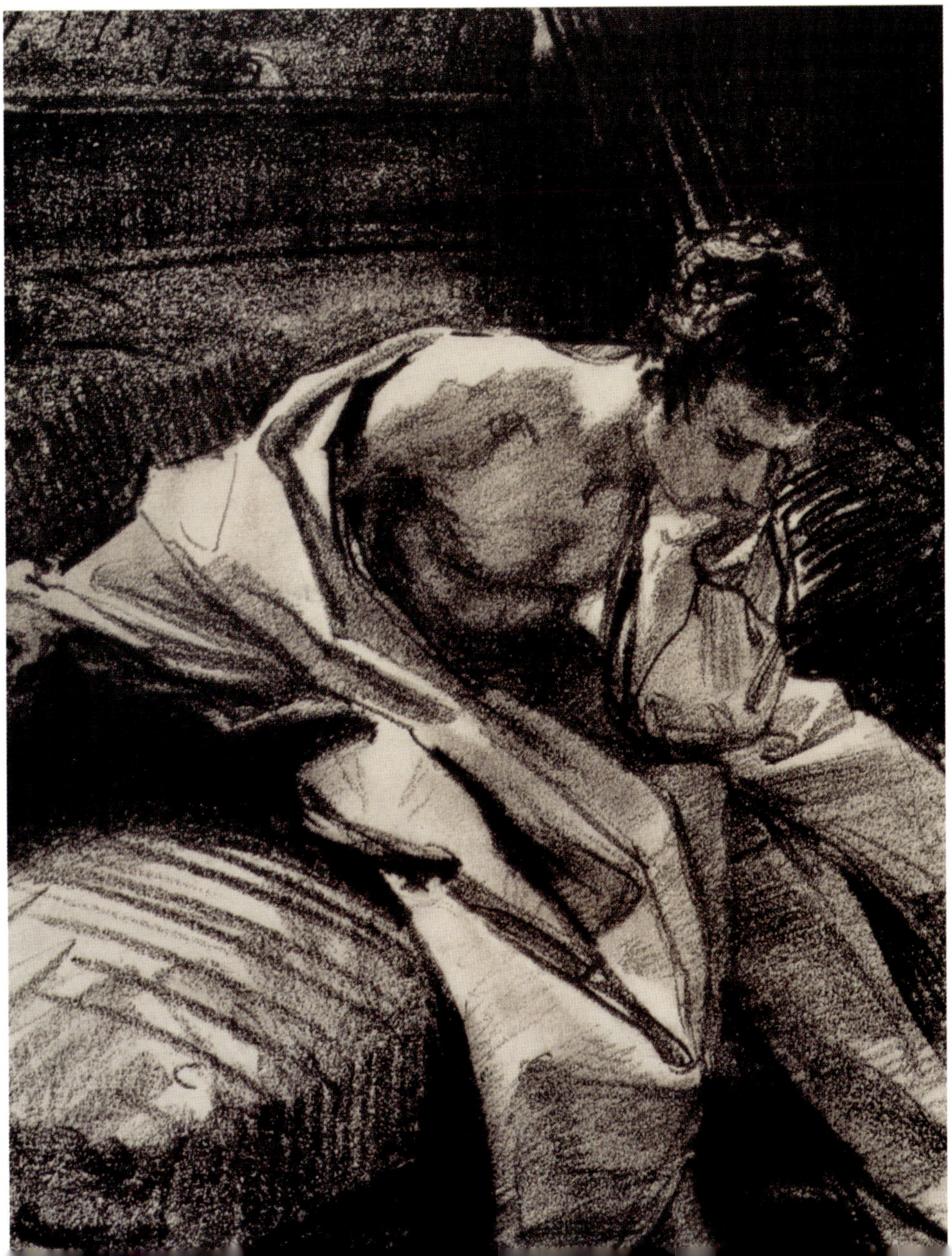

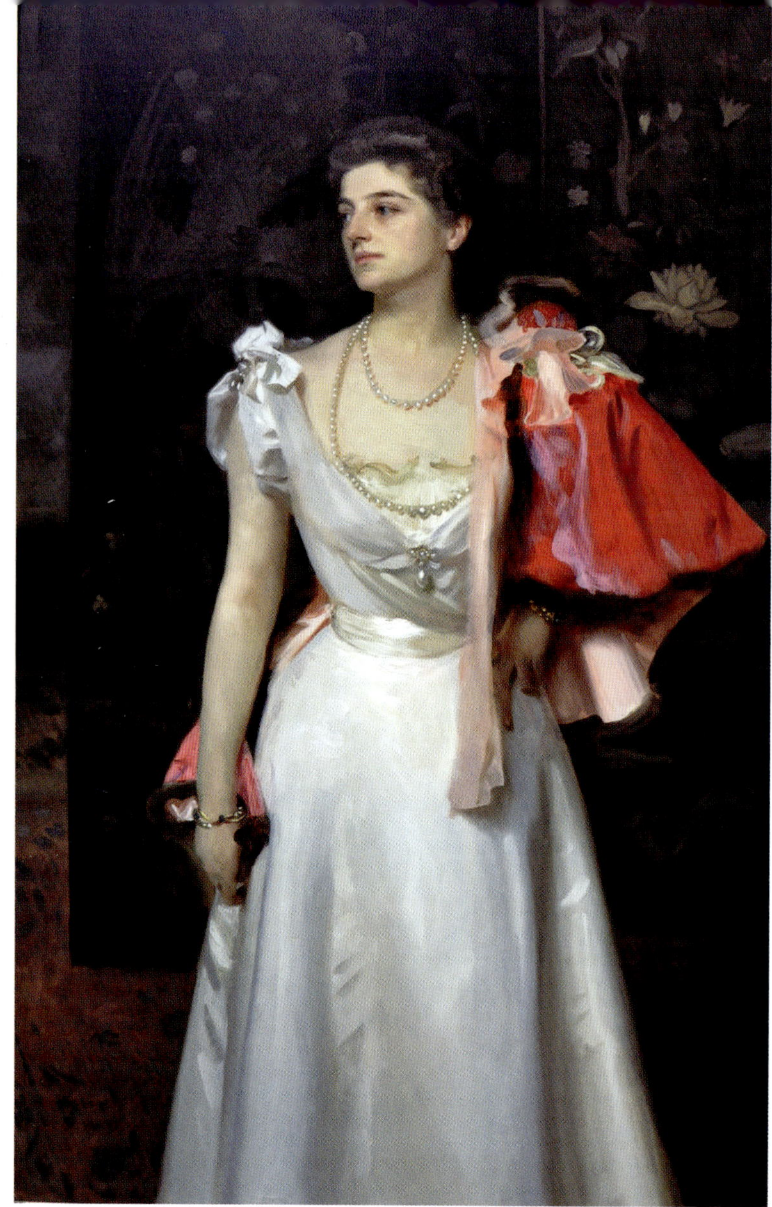

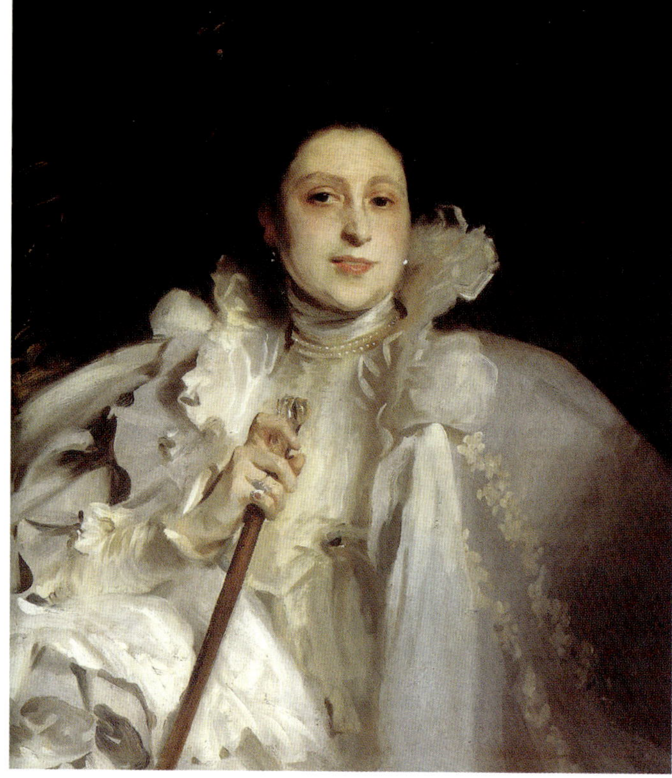

Countess Laura Spinola Nunez del Castillo, 1896, oil on canvas, 87 x 71.7cm (34¼ x 28¼in), Private Collection

Sargent has portrayed the dark-haired Countess Spinola draped in a flowing white cape, with pearls at her neck and in her ears, holding an expensive, silver-topped cane. She has been captured with Sargent's perceptive eye and with a combination of both loose and careful brushmarks. At some point, Sargent condensed the composition, heightening the drama by cropping the image.

Princess Sophie Illarionovna Demidoff, c.1895–96, oil on canvas, 167 x 97cm (65¾ x 38¼in). Toledo Museum of Art, Ohio, USA

In 1893, a celebrated beauty and fashion leader, Sophie Illarionovna (1871–1953) married Russian diplomat Count Elim Pavlovich Demidov, 3rd Prince of San Donato (1868–1943). Sargent painted her portrait in London, where her husband worked for the Russian Embassy. Standing in front of one of Sargent's props, a Chinese lacquer screen, the elegant young woman's white silk dress contrasts richly with her burnt orange cape.

Madonna and Child with Saints, 1895–1915, watercolour and graphite on off-white wove paper, 33.2 x 24.6cm (13 x 9¾in), The Metropolitan Museum, New York, USA

While exploring and gathering visual information for the Boston murals, Sargent studied the art and architecture of medieval and Renaissance Europe extensively. This sketch of the Madonna and Child with Saints is copied from an unidentified artist.

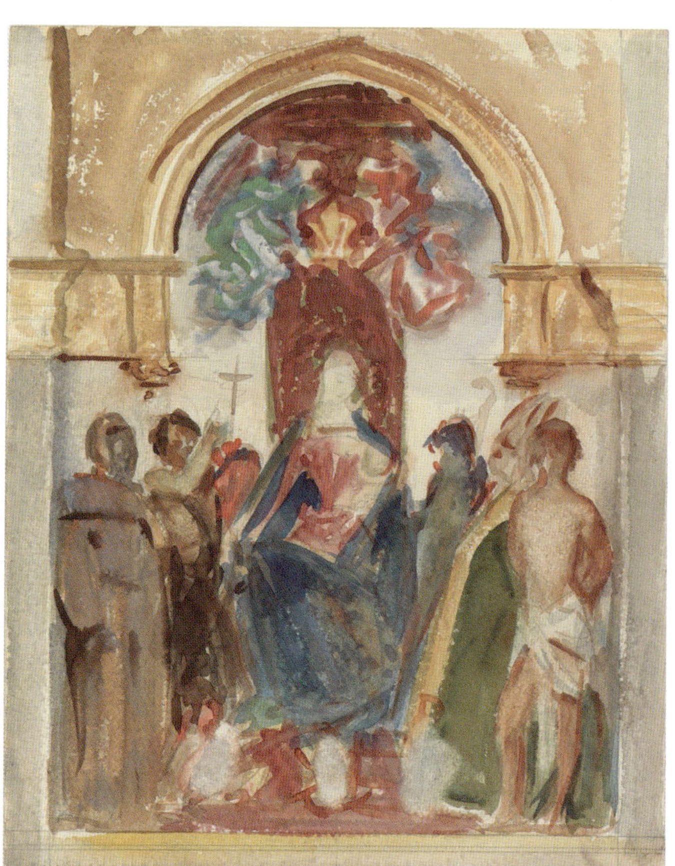

Mrs Carl Meyer and Her Children, 1896, oil on canvas, 201.4 x 134cm (79¼ x 52¾in), Tate, London, UK

Painted during the summer that year, this dramatically foreshortened portrait of Adèle Meyer with her daughter Elsie and son Frank overtly show the family's wealth and theatricality. The opulence of the surroundings is matched by the clothing; Mrs Meyer's peach satin skirt, which occupies half the picture space, has her tiny shoes peeping out from beneath. Her children nestle between gilded wood panelling and the Louis XV sofa.

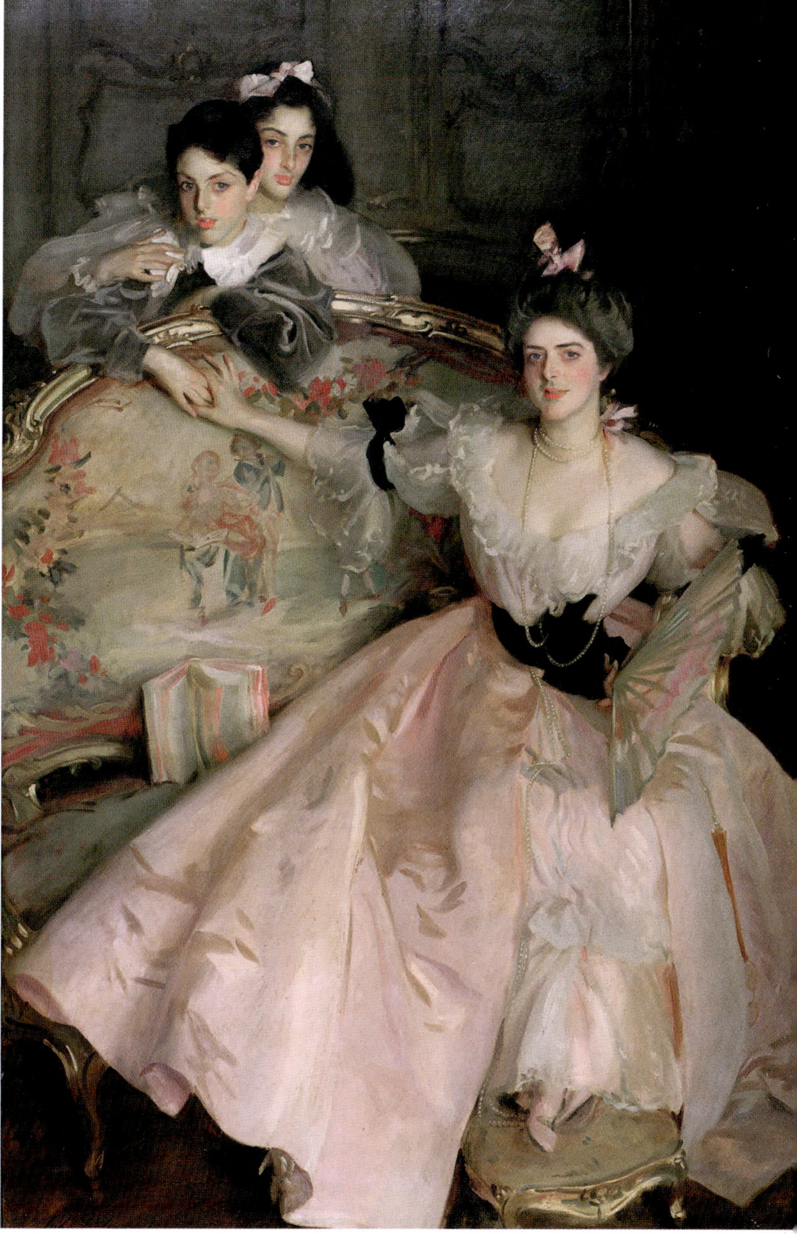

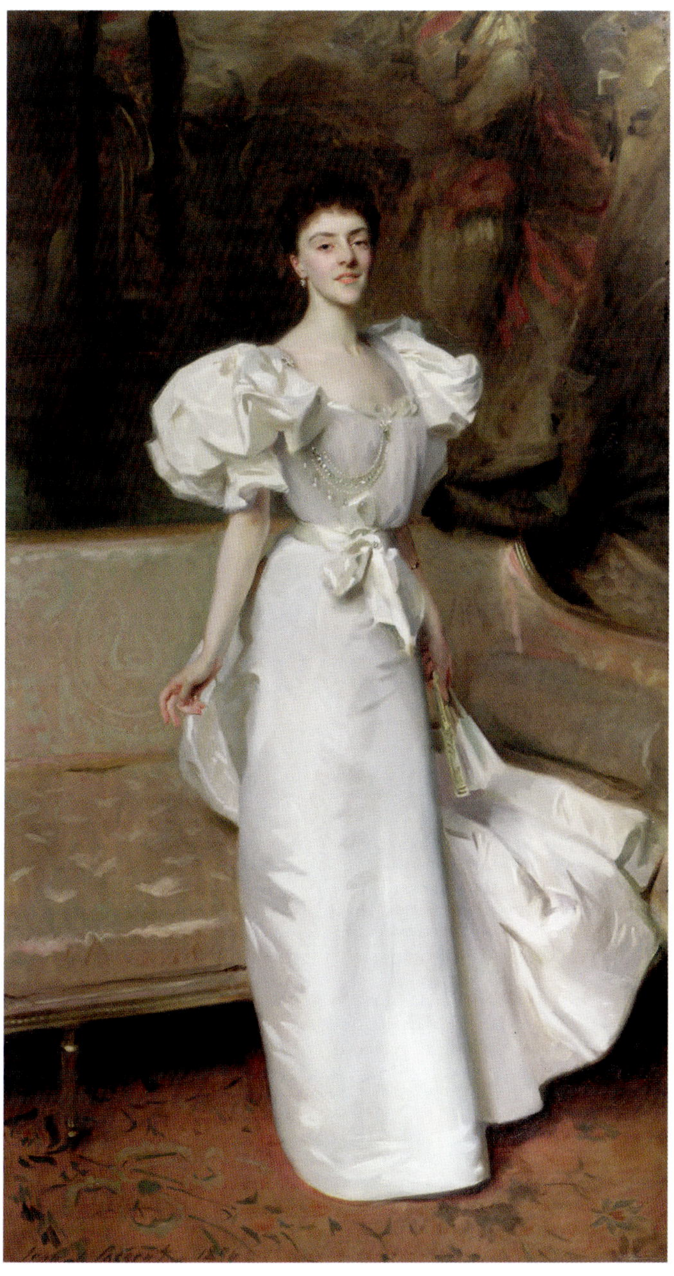

Portrait of the Countess of Clary Aldringen, 1896, oil on canvas, 225.6 x 121.9cm (88¾ x 48in), Private Collection

Thérèse (née Kinsky), Countess Clary-Aldringen (1867–1943), was a member of the aristocratic Polish Radziwill family, the wife of Prince Siegfried von Clary-Aldringen. She was an elegant and graceful young woman and the mother of three children. This was painted in what became known as Sargent's 'swagger' portrait period when he painted rich and titled sitters with flamboyance.

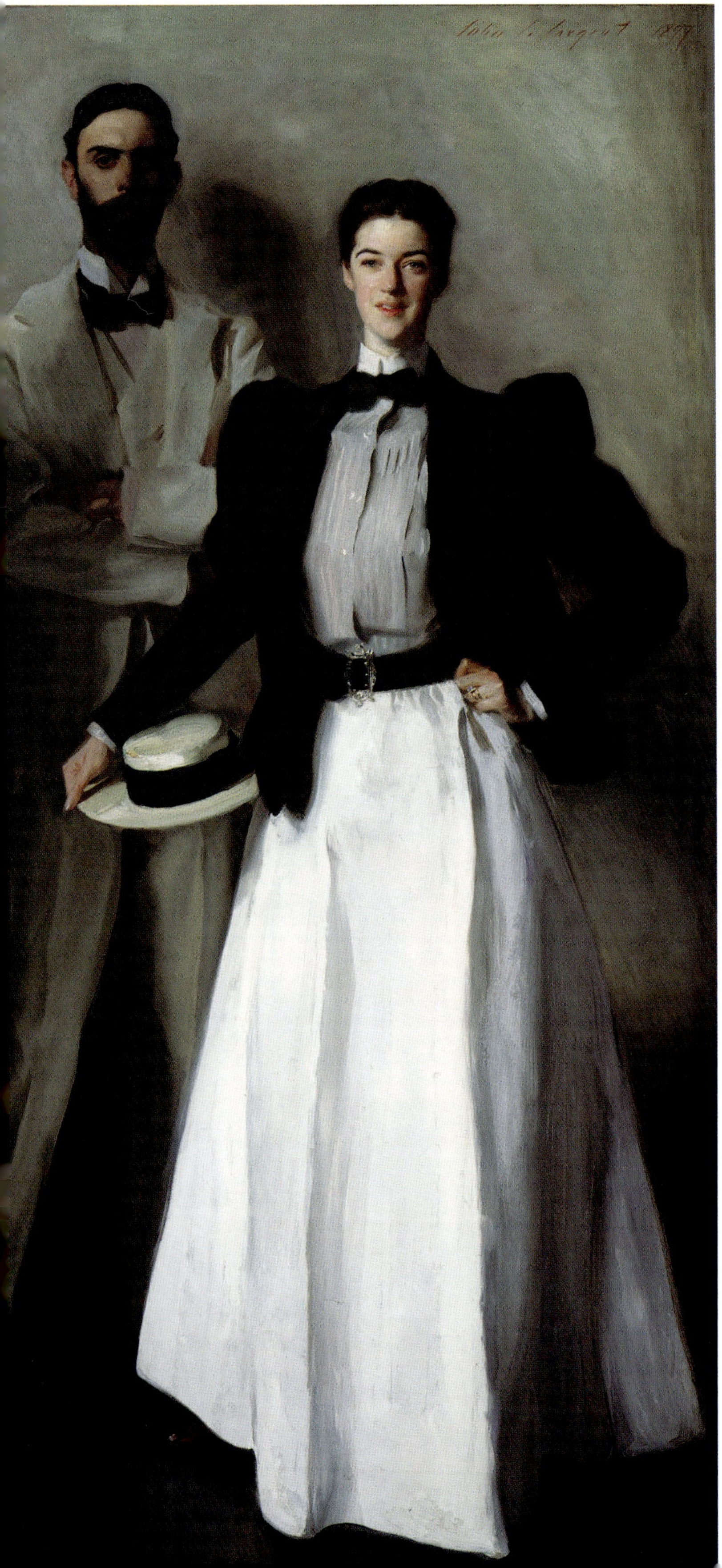

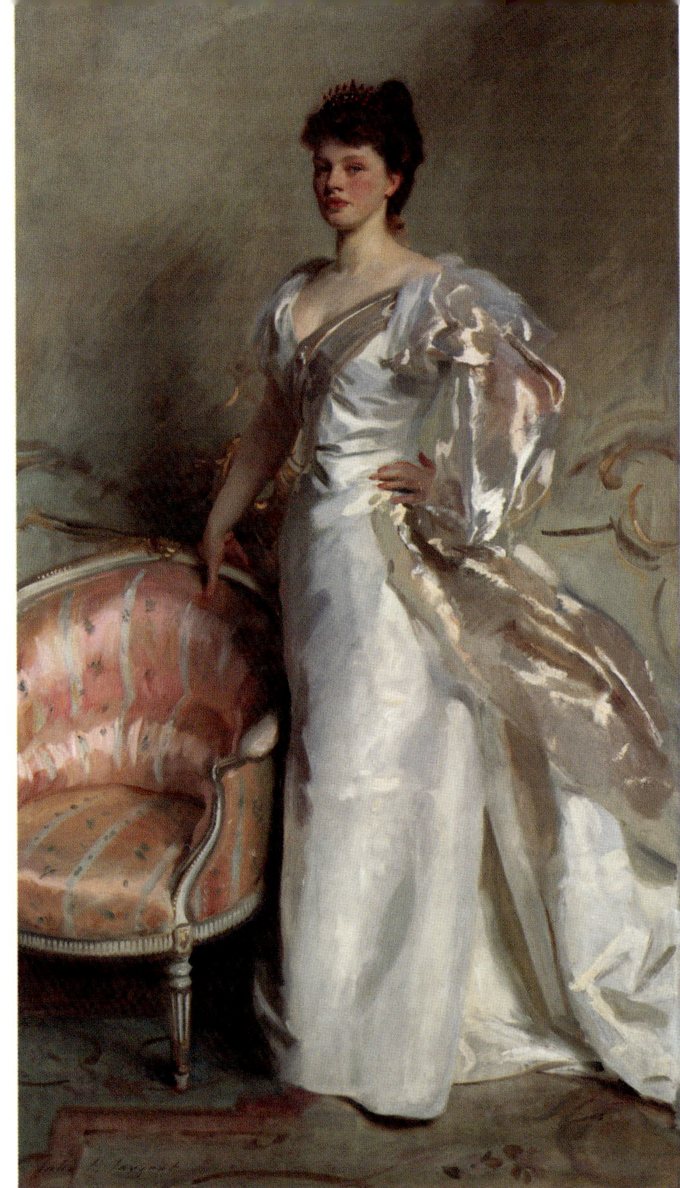

***Mrs George Swinton
(Elizabeth Ebsworth), 1897,
oil on canvas, 231 x 124cm
(90¾ x 48¾in), The Art
Institute of Chicago, IL, USA***

Elizabeth 'Elsie' Ebsworth
(1874–1966) was the
fashionable and sophisticated
wife of Scottish politician
George Swinton, who
was also an accomplished
amateur singer. With
his characteristic fluid
brushwork, Sargent has
emphasized her striking
looks, upright stance and
stylish clothes. In 1906,
Elsie horrified her upper
class family by becoming a
professional singer.

**Mr and Mrs Isaac Newton
Phelps Stokes, 1897, oil on
canvas, 214 x 101cm (84¼
x 39¾in), The Metropolitan
Museum, New York, USA**

While Isaac Newton Phelps
Stokes (1867–1944) was
studying architecture in Paris,
Sargent painted this double
portrait of him and his
wife, Edith Minturn Stokes
(1867–1937) as a wedding
gift from one of their friends.
He had first intended to paint
Edith alone in an evening
gown, but abandoned the
idea, preferring to depict her
in her day clothes with her
husband standing behind her.

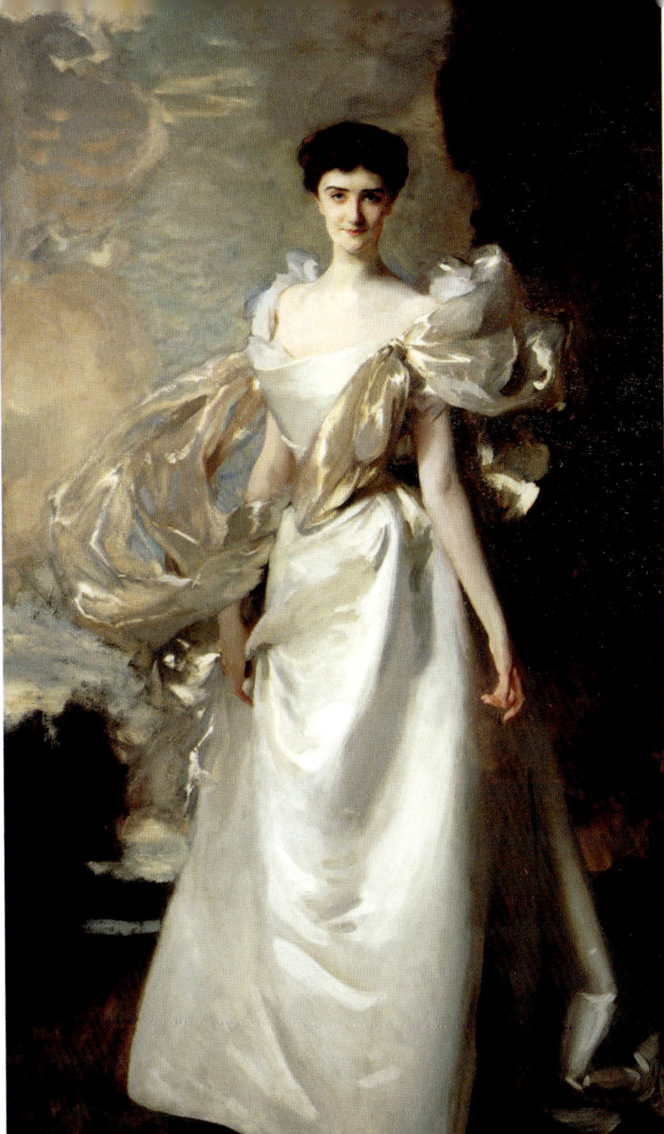

Portrait of Lisa Colt Curtis, 1898, oil on canvas, 219.3 x 104.8cm (86¼ x 41¼in), Cleveland Museum of Art, Ohio, USA

Sargent painted this portrait as a wedding gift for his distant cousin Ralph Wormeley Curtis — who was also his close friend — and his new wife Lisa de Wolfe Colt, who was an heir to the Colt firearms fortune. He conveys the young bride in flattering soft focus, in her fashionable, tightly corseted satin dress, standing as if she is welcoming guests into her grand Venetian home.

Daisy Leiter, 1898, oil on canvas, 228.6 x 119.4cm (90 x 47in), Kenwood House, London, UK

Daughter of wealthy American businessman, Levi Z. Leiter, Daisy would later become Margaret Hyde, 19th Countess of Suffolk. Five years after Sargent painted this, Daisy was visiting her sister Mary and her husband, George Curzon, who were Vicereine and Viceroy of India. There she met and fell in love with one of Curzon's aides de camp, Henry Howard, 19th Earl of Suffolk and 12th Earl of Berkshire. Much later, she became a helicopter enthusiast, flying from her Cornish home to her suite at the Ritz.

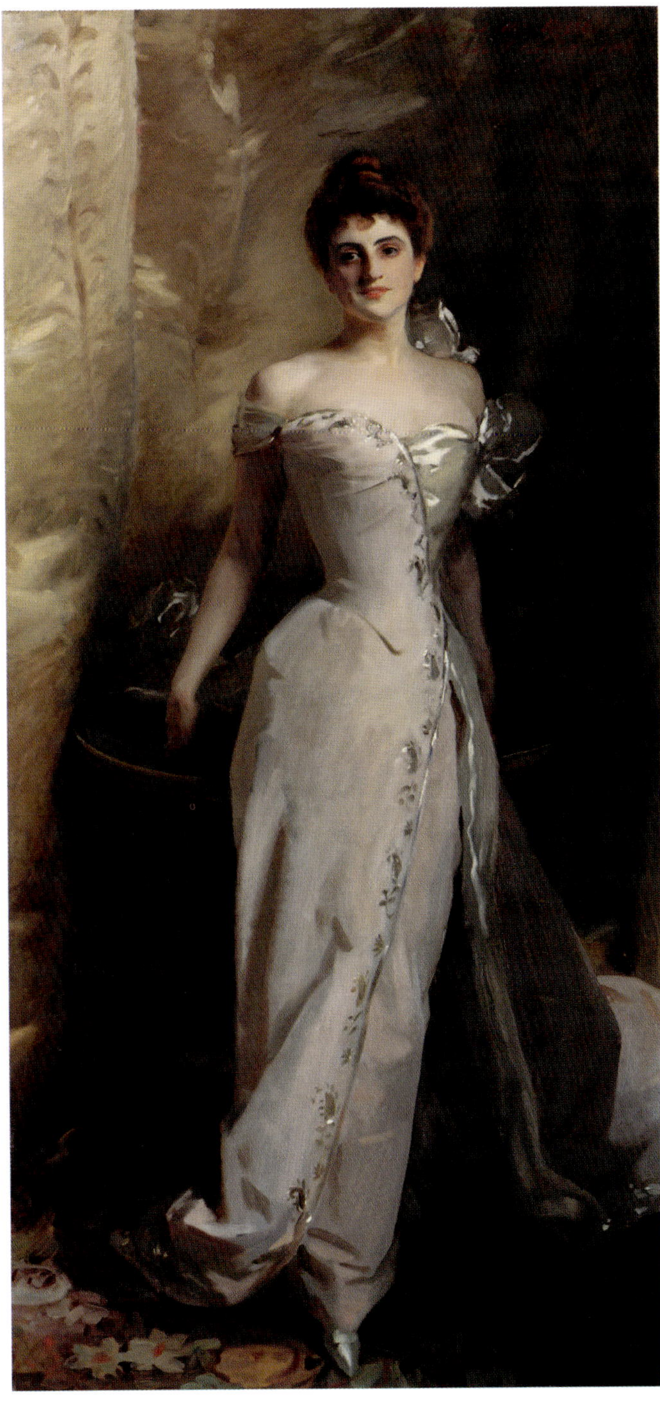

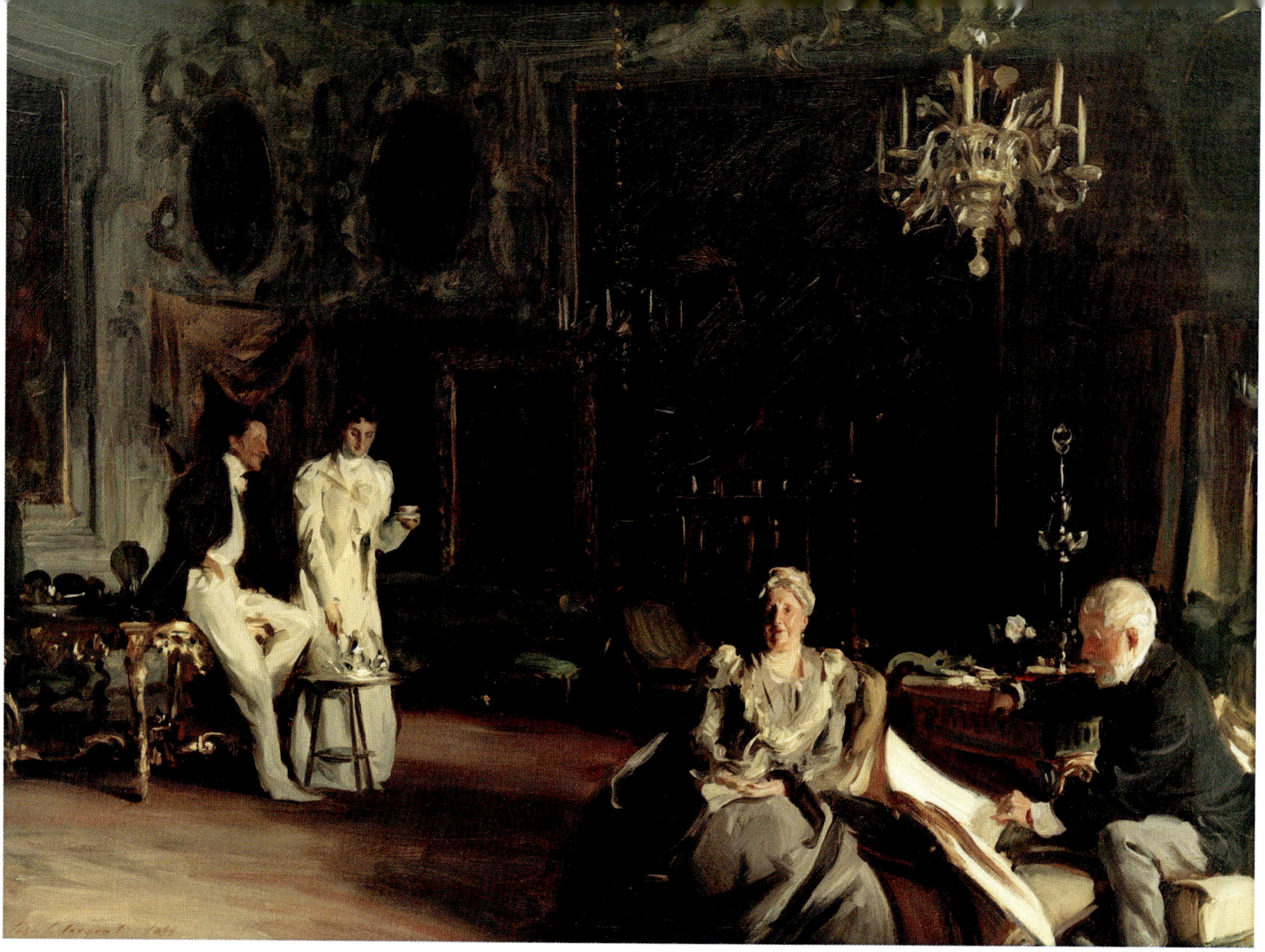

An Interior in Venice, 1898,
oil on canvas, 63.5 x 78.7cm
(25 x 31in), The Royal
Academy, London, UK

With dark, indistinct areas,
this depicts the grand
drawing room of Palazzo
Barbaro on the Grand
Canal where Sargent stayed
with the Curtis family
when he was in Venice.
The younger man on the
left in the background is
Ralph with his new wife
Lisa. The other figures are
Ralph's parents. Apparently
unaware of each other, the
two couples are separated
by a patch of carpet, bathed
in the shimmering light from
outside.

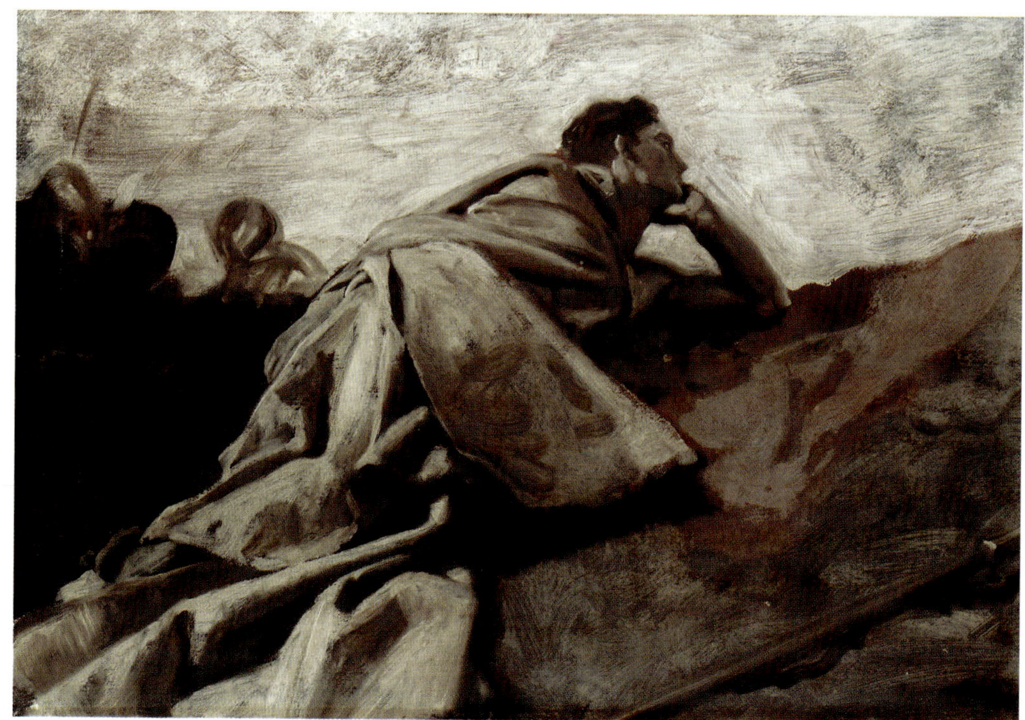

David in Saul's Camp,
undated, oil en grisaille on
canvas, 44.5 x 64.1cm (17½
x 25¼in), Private Collection

Although undated, this was
probably executed in 1899
because in 1900, Sargent sent
it to his solo exhibition put on
by the Boston Art Students'
Association at Copley Hall. It
formed part of his research
for his Boston Library murals.
Also in 1900, the painting was
written about in an in-depth
two-part essay on Sargent's
work (see also page 189).

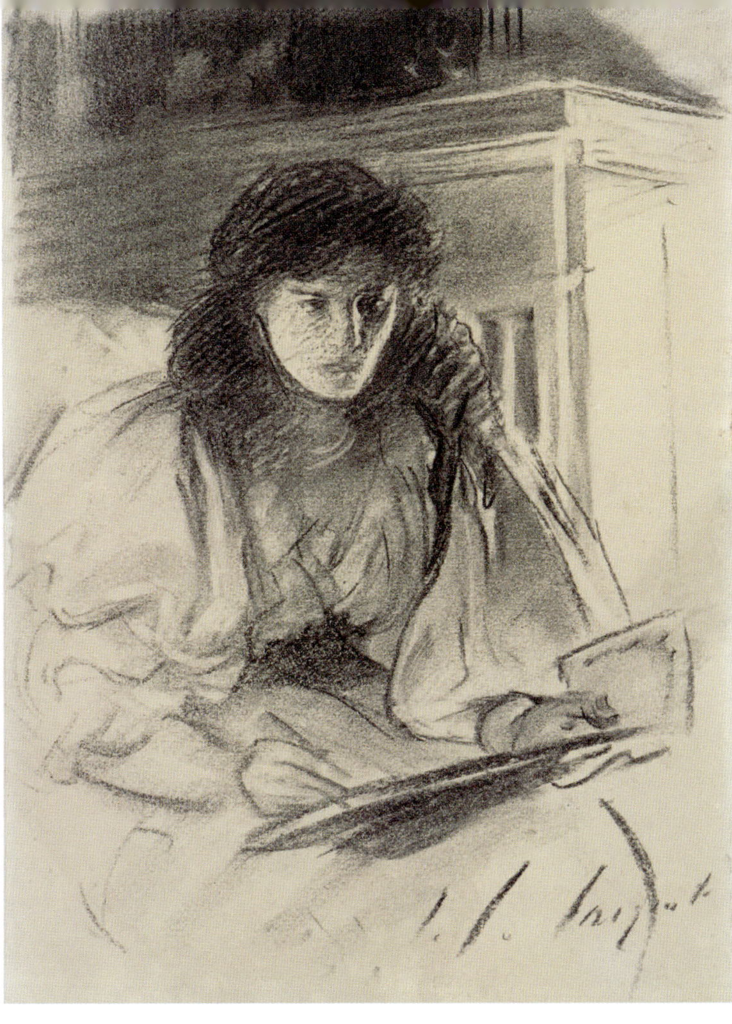

Miss Anstruther Thomson,
1899, charcoal on paper,
34.4 x 23.5cm (13½ x
9¼in), Dublin City Gallery,
Dublin, Republic of Ireland

In July 1889, Sargent
had visited the Universal
Exhibition in Paris with his
mother and sisters. They
returned to the vicarage at
Fladbury where they were
visited by their friends Kit
Anstruther-Thomson and
Vernon Lee. From the
1890s, the two women lived
together for six months each
year in Florence. In 1897
they jointly wrote *Beauty and
Ugliness and other Studies in
Psychological Aesthetics* which
appeared in the journal
Contemporary Review.

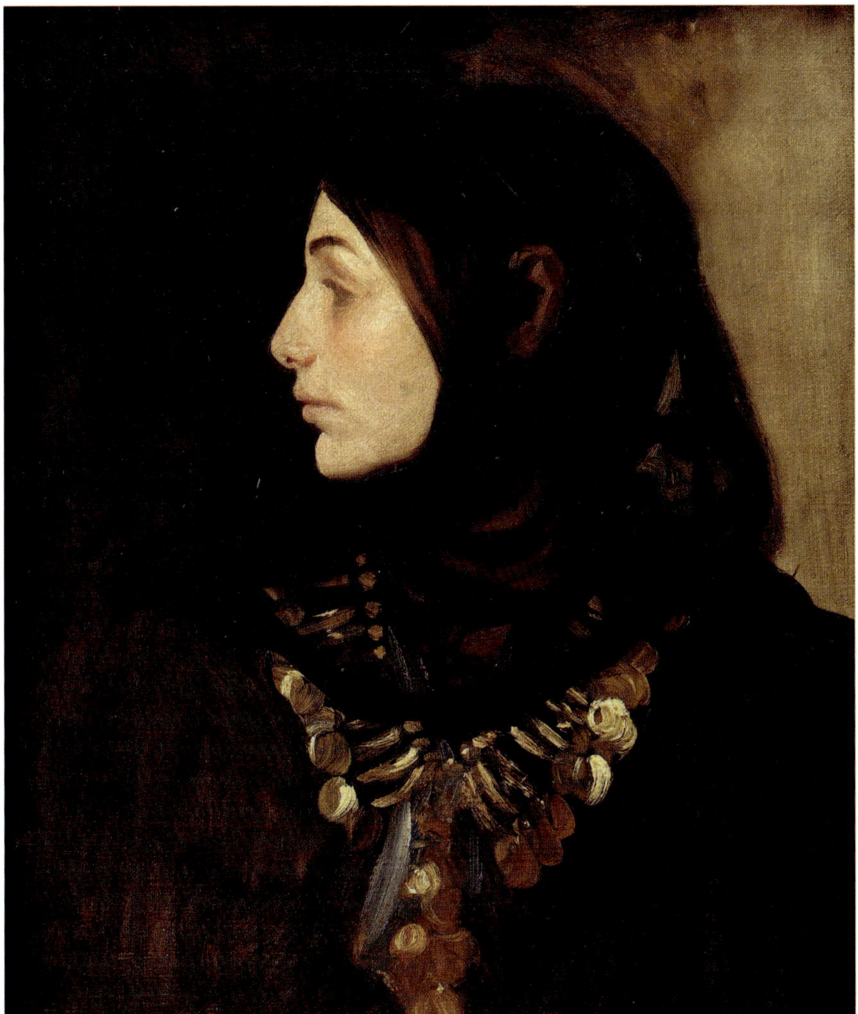

The Fellah Woman, 1899,
oil on canvas, 56 x 45.9cm
(22 x 18in), Private
Collection

Deriving from the Arabic
word for ploughman, the
term 'fellah' referred to a
farmer, agricultural labourer
or peasant in the Middle
East and North Africa. This
woman wears the traditional
simple cotton robe called a
galabieh with heavy golden
jewellery. Although this
is a sketch, Sargent has
clearly enjoyed depicting
the contrast of metal on
translucent fabric and the
young woman's glowing skin.

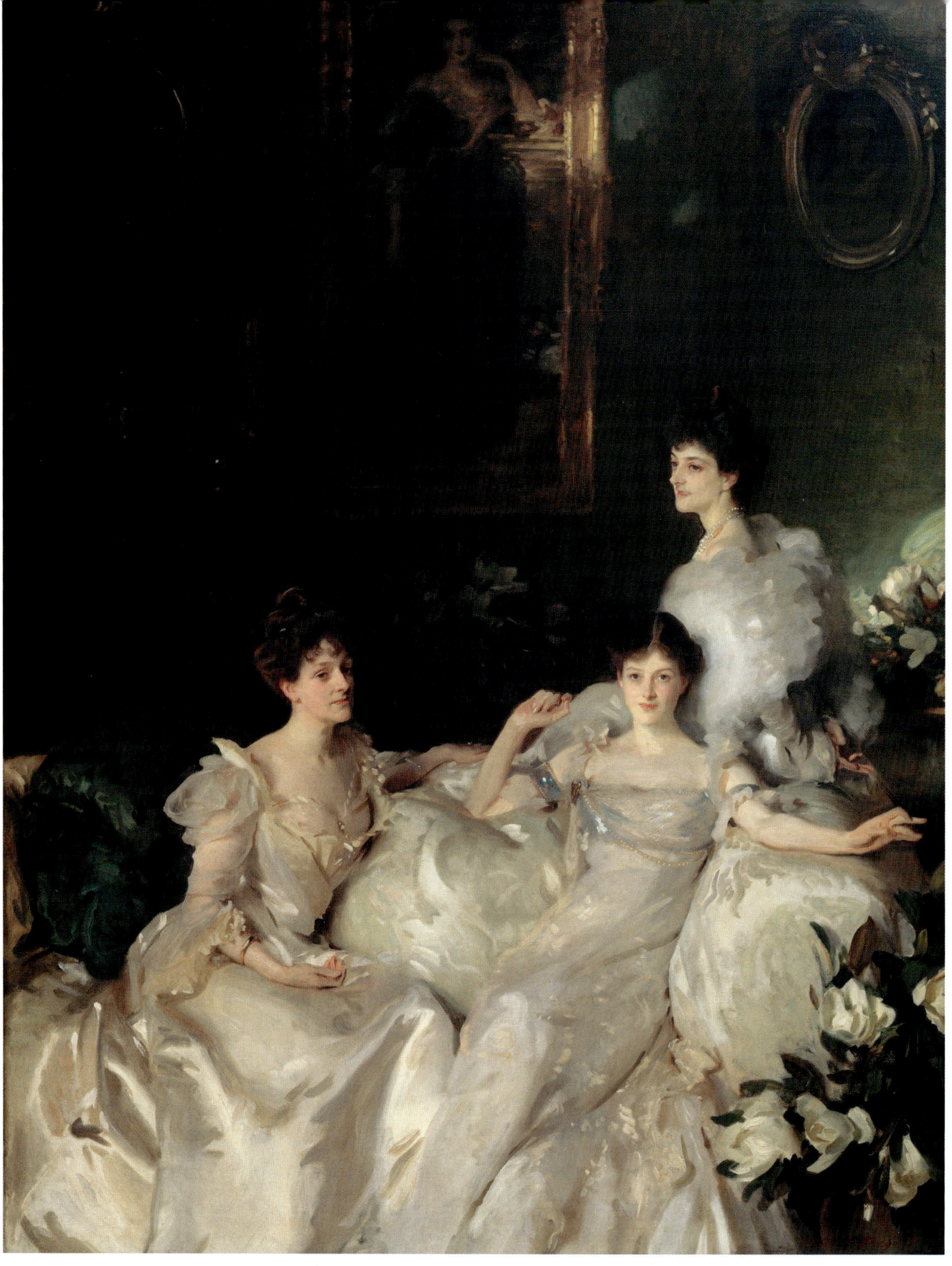

The Wyndham Sisters, 1899, oil on canvas, 292.1 x 213.7cm (115 x 84¼in), The Metropolitan Museum, New York, USA

Sargent's portrait of three fashionable sisters, epitomizing the contemporary idea of sophistication, was an outstanding success when it was exhibited at the Royal Academy. The composition is diagonally divided between the dark background and the shimmering whites and pinks of the young women and their dresses in the foreground, creating a spectacular contrast (see details on page 67).

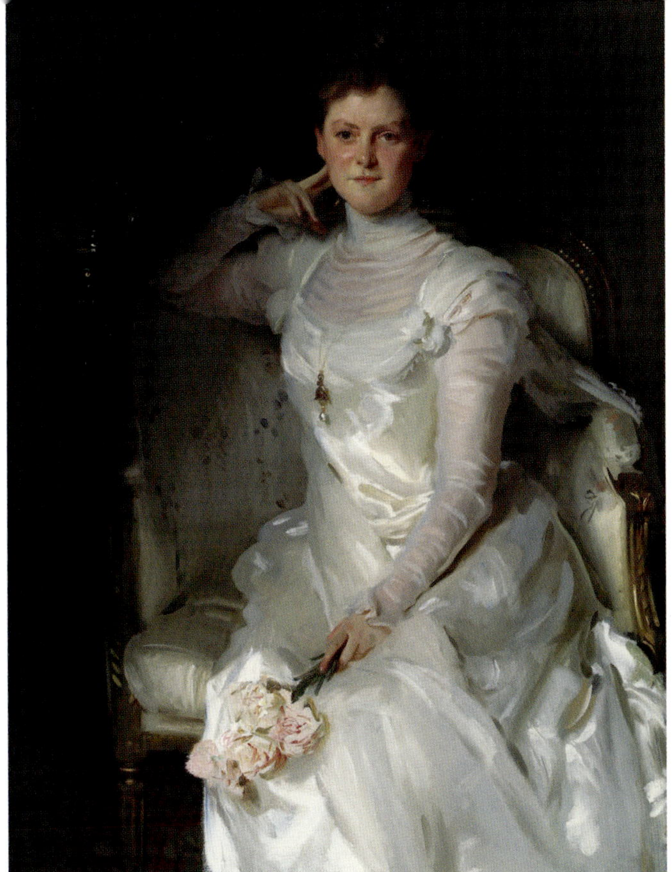

Mrs Joshua Montgomery Sears, 1899, oil on canvas, 47.6 x 96.8cm (18¾ x 38in), Museum of Fine Arts, Houston, Texas, USA

Sarah Choate Sears was a long-standing friend of Sargent's. After painting her daughter Helen (see page 152), he painted her, capturing her astute gaze and upright stance. Her satin dress enabled him to demonstrate his skill at rendering the shining white fabric, with free marks of lilac, blue and pink. These expressive, confident strokes capture the likeness with minimal means.

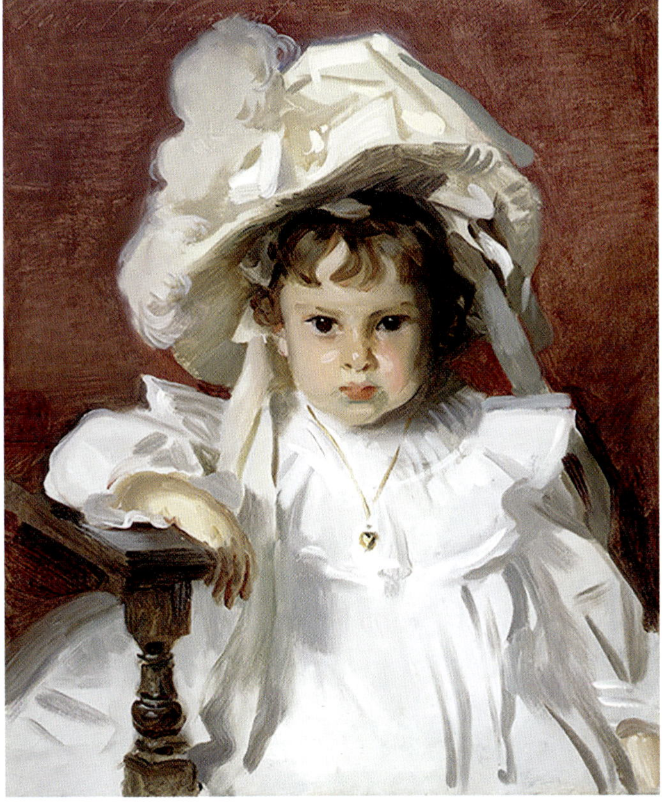

Dorothy, 1900, oil on canvas, 61.3 x 50.2cm (24¼ x 19¾in), Dallas Museum of Art, Texas, USA

Little is known about this young sitter. She was Dorothy Williamson, either the daughter or granddaughter of George Millar Williamson (1849–1921) of New York, one of Sargent's first American patrons. Sargent painted this in his Tite Street studio in London and showed it in 1901 at the Society of American Artists in New York. The vigorous, painterly brushwork describing the ornately dressed little girl creates an arresting, immediate image.

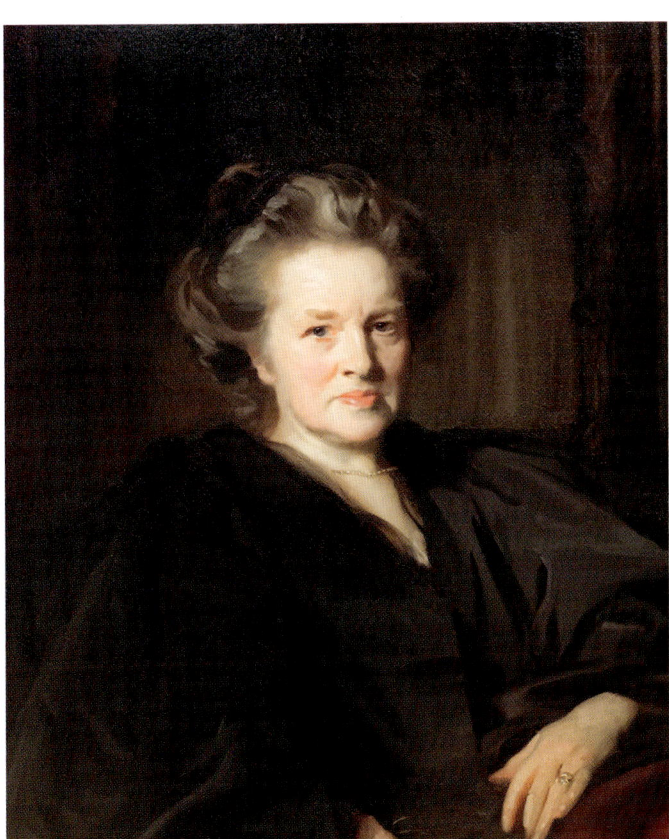

Elizabeth Garrett Anderson, 1900, oil on canvas, 83.8 x 66cm (33 x 26in), The National Portrait Gallery, London, UK

At 64 years old, the English physician and feminist, Elizabeth Garrett Anderson (1836–1917) was about to retire as dean of the London School of Medicine for Women. Elizabeth had requested to be painted in her MD gown, but Sargent wanted some jewellery, so she added a cheap pearl necklace. She was also irritated by Sargent's depiction of her hands. He covered one with her gown, but showed the other as tapering and artistic rather than her practical surgeon's hand.

Portrait of a Woman, after 1900, chalk on paper, 58.4 x 44.5cm (23 x 17½in), Museum of Fine Arts Houston, Texas, USA

Consuelo Iznaga (1853–1909) was a Cuban-American heiress, the eldest daughter of four children of a wealthy Cuban diplomat. Through her marriage to the Irish aristocrat and politician, George Victor Drogo Montagu, Viscount Mandeville (1853–92), she became the Duchess of Manchester. A great society hostess, this is one of two portraits Sargent produced of her, showing her warmth and an element of self-consciousness.

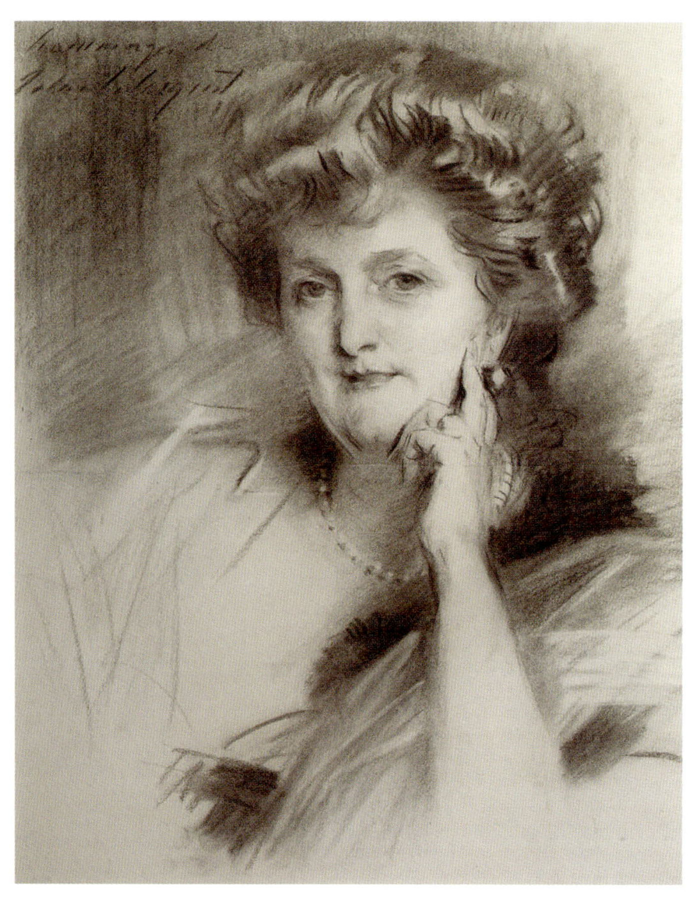

Portrait of Robert Brough, c.1900, oil on canvas, 64.1 x 44.5cm (25¼ x 17½in), **Private Collection**

Robert Brough (1872–1905) was a Scottish painter, who, after entering the Royal Scottish Academy, was awarded the Stuart prize for figure painting, the Chalmers painting bursary, and the Maclame-Walters medal for composition. He then went to Paris where he studied for two years and returned to Aberdeen in 1894, when he worked as a portrait painter and political cartoonist. Sargent executed his portrait with vigorous, swift marks, creating a face that is a profound psychological study.

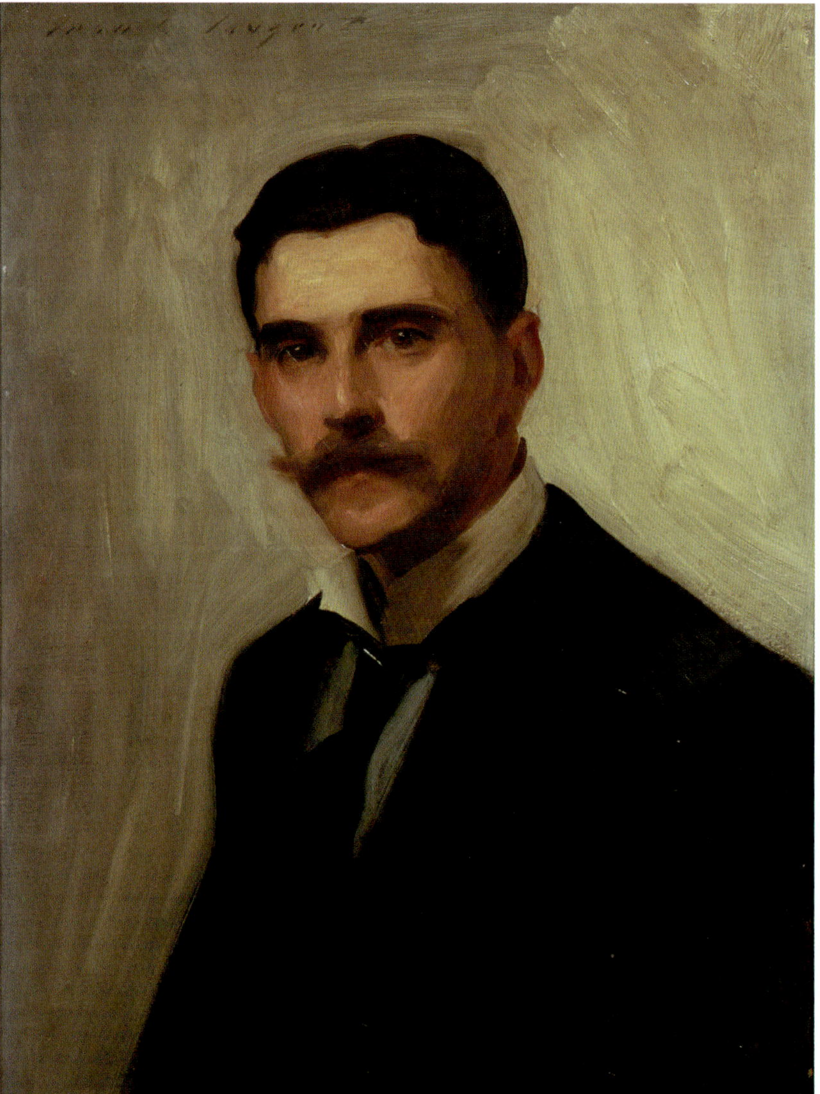

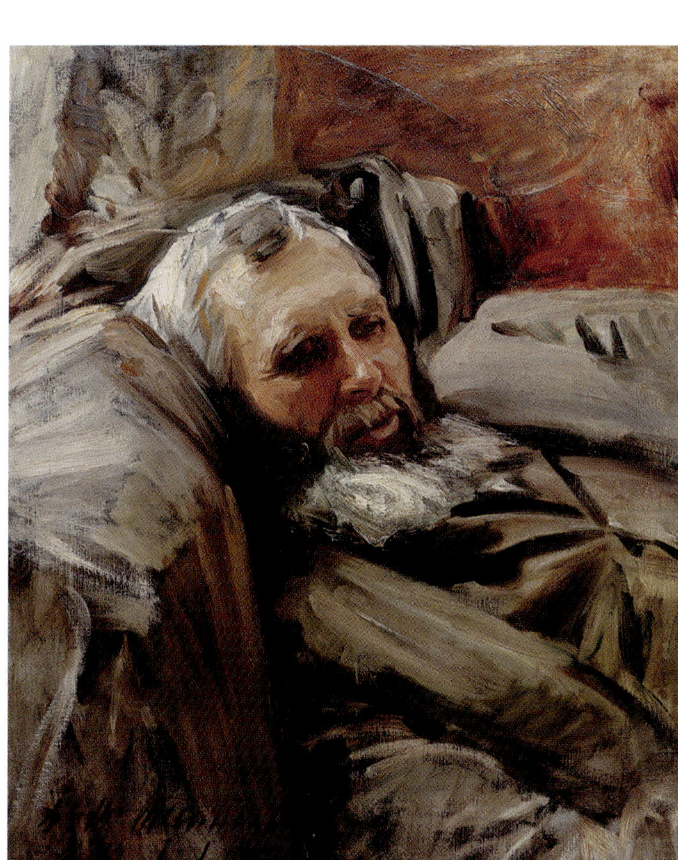

Hercules Brabazon Brabazon, 1900, oil on canvas, 56.5 x 40.6cm (22¼ x 16in), National Museum of Wales, Cardiff, Wales

Sargent was close friends with watercolourist Hercules Brabazon Brabazon (1821–1906), and Brabazon in turn was often mentioned as an influence on Sargent's watercolours. Although 30 years older than Sargent, the two artists had a lot in common, including their views on art, their love of music and their frequent travels. An indication of the affection with which Sargent held Brabazon; he kept this painting in his possession for the rest of his life.

George McCulloch, 1901, 69.8 x 54.6cm (27½ x 21½in), Boston Athenaeum, Massachusetts, USA

After making his fortune in silver ore in Australia, Scotsman George McCulloch (1848–1907) moved to London to live as a gentleman of leisure and to collect art. Sargent painted this portrait of his friend when the two men were on a fishing trip together in Scotland. Although he appears to be lost in reverie, McCulloch's face is full of character and his spirited expression is modelled with consummate skill.

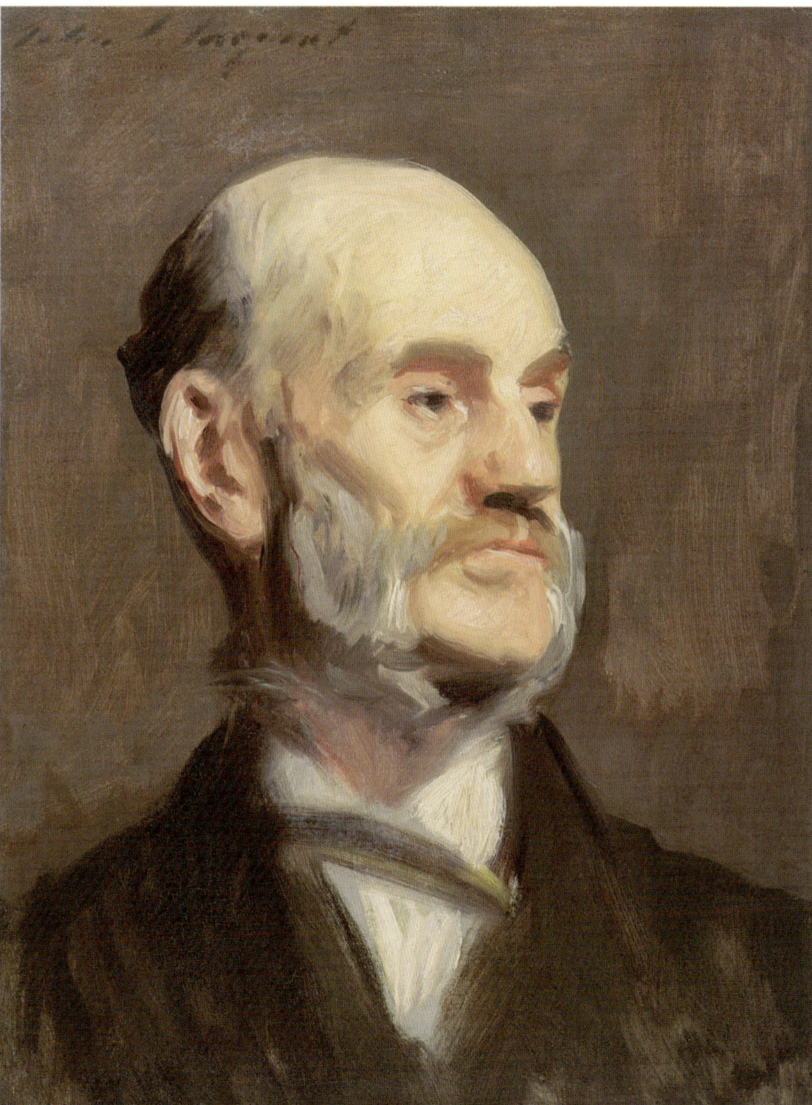

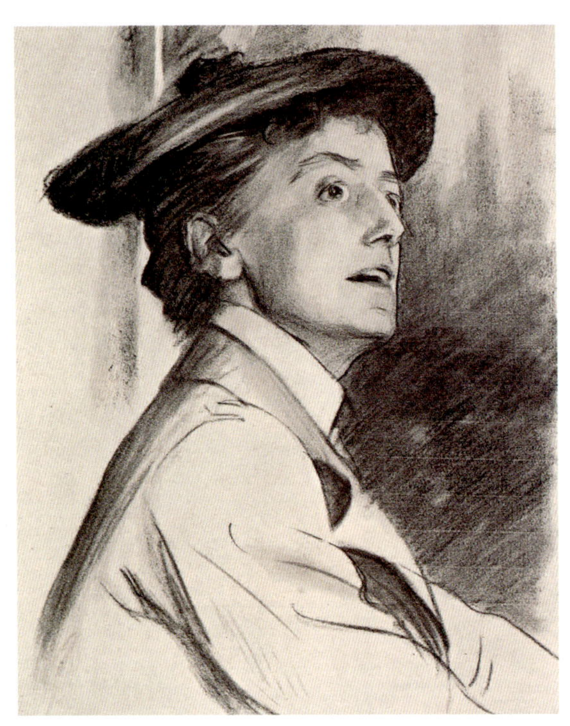

Ethel Mary Smyth, 1901, black chalk on paper, 59.7 x 46cm (23½ x 18in), The National Portrait Gallery, London, UK

Sister to Sargent's close friend Mary Hunter, Dame Ethel Mary Smyth also became his close friend. A composer, writer and suffragist, she eventually became deaf and turned her creativity to writing, producing ten highly successful, largely autobiographical books between 1919 and 1940. Sargent's production of charcoal portraits, like his watercolours, increased after the turn of the 20th century.

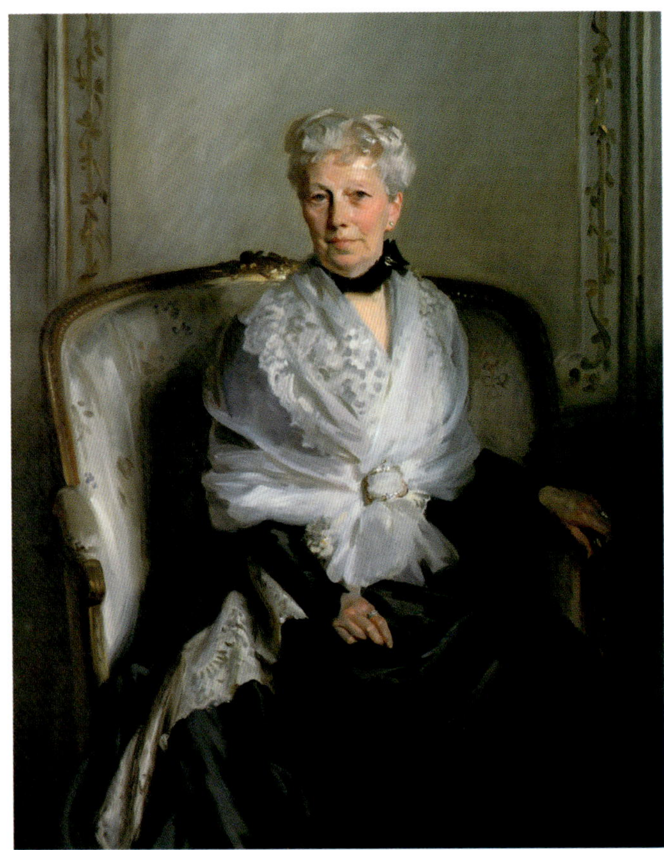

Mrs Edward Goetz, 1901, oil on canvas, 146 x 105.4cm (57½ x 41½in), Brigham Young University Museum of Art, Utah, USA

An amateur pianist and composer, Mrs Goetz sits upright and dignified, a lace shawl around her shoulders. Sargent's loose brushstrokes capture the transparency of her shawl, the sheen of her soft velvet skirt, and glinting metal of her buckle and ring. Mrs Goetz held a regular musical salon at her home at Hyde Park Terrace, London. She died soon after this portrait was completed.

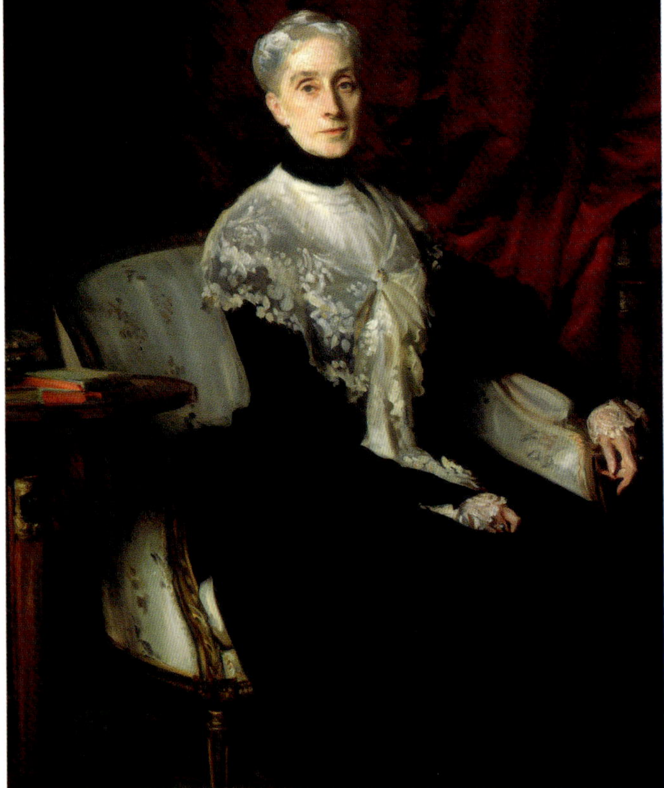

Ellen Peabody Endicott (Mrs William Crowninshield Endicott), 1901, oil on canvas, 162.9 x 114.3cm (64 x 45in), National Gallery of Art, Washington DC, USA

A prominent society hostess in Boston and Salem, Ellen Peabody Endicott (1833–1927) married William Crowninshield Endicott (1826–1900), who served on the Supreme Court of Massachusetts and was President Grover Cleveland's secretary of war for five years. Here Sargent has painted her portrait in heavy black mourning clothes.

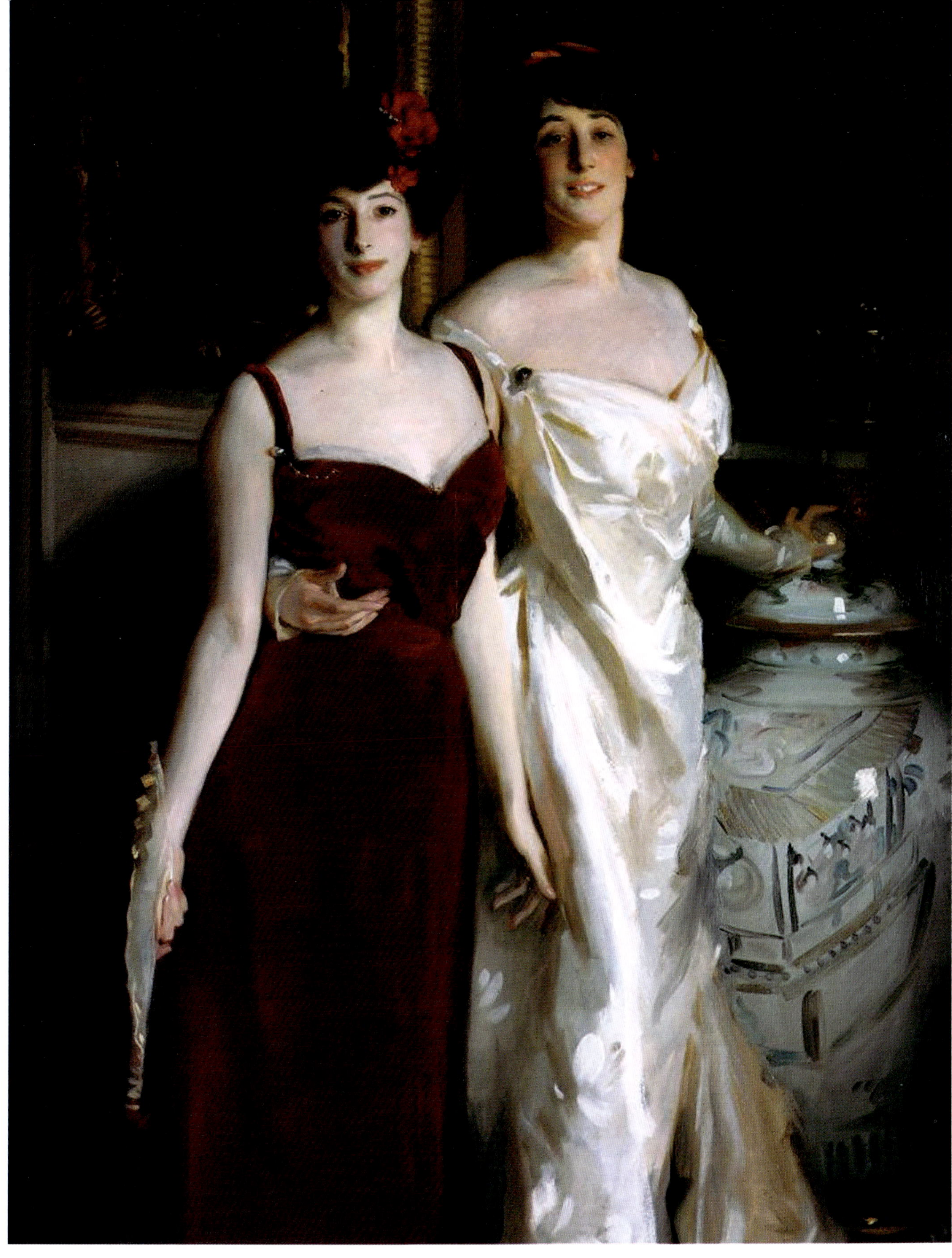

Ena and Betty, Daughters of Asher and Mrs Wertheimer, 1901, oil on canvas, 185.4 x 130.8cm (73 x 51½in), Tate, London, UK

These are the two eldest daughters of the art dealer Asher Wertheimer whom Sargent had painted in 1898. Elizabeth (Betty) (1877–1953) on the left and Helena (Ena) (1874–1935) were intelligent, lively and vivacious. Enjoying their warmth and charm, Sargent befriended the family and became especially close to Ena. The textures of the dresses are contrasted: Betty's red velvet against Ena's white damask.

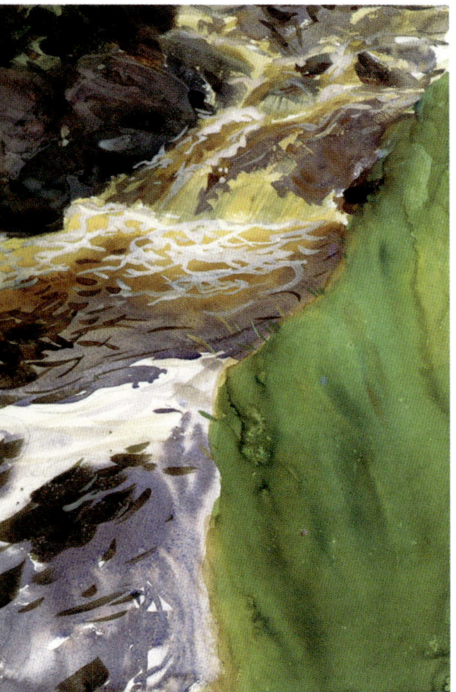

Rushing Water, 1901–08, translucent and opaque watercolour and graphite on paper, 35.6 x 25.2cm (14 x 10in), The Metropolitan Museum, New York, USA

Although best known for his portraits, after the turn of the 20th century Sargent began engaging increasingly with watercolour, experimenting and inventing new ways of working, demonstrating his eye for composition, colour and detail as he captured the beauty he saw about him. Far above portrait painting, watercolours gave him enormous pleasure, and he became one of the greatest watercolourists of his generation.

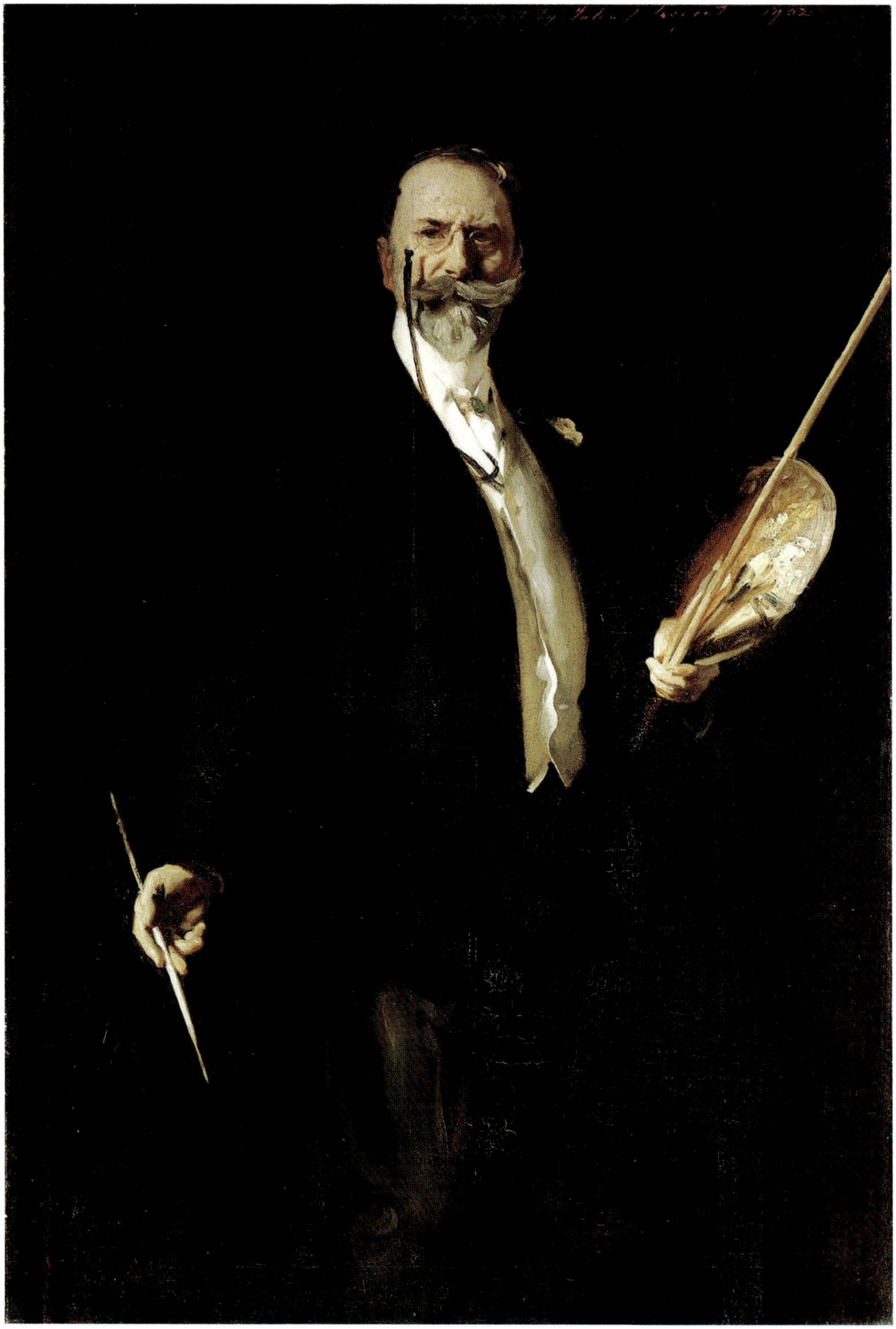

William Merritt Chase, 1902, oil on canvas, 158.8 x 105.1cm (62½ x 41½in), The Metropolitan Museum, New York, USA

An artist and motivational American art teacher, William Merritt Chase (1849–1916) met Sargent in 1881 in Europe and they became good friends. A group of Merritt's students commissioned this portrait, which Sargent painted in his Tite Street studio. Chase stands with his palette and brush in his hands, as if he is about to paint, presenting to the viewer a mixture of flamboyant artist and society gent (see also page 74).

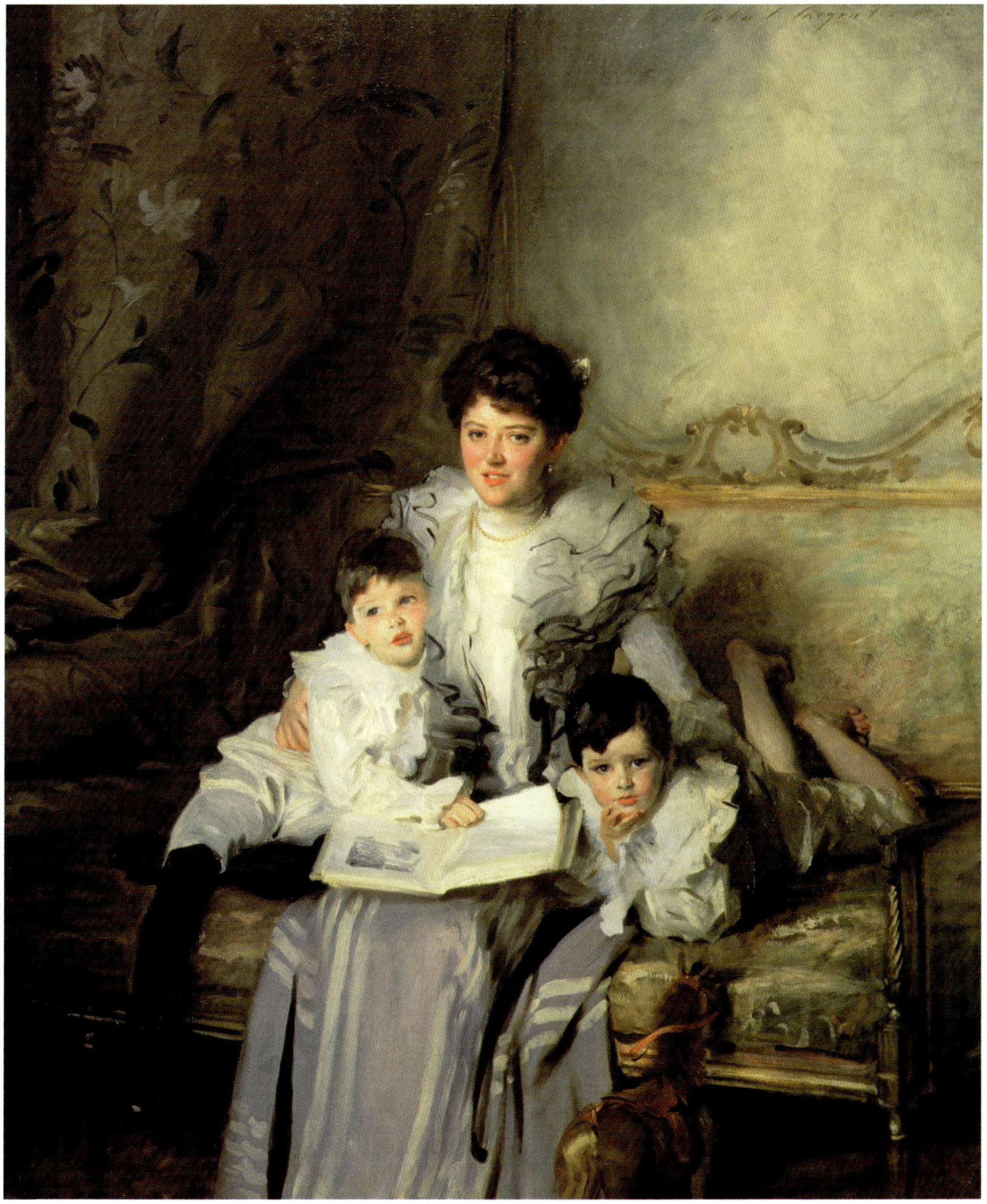

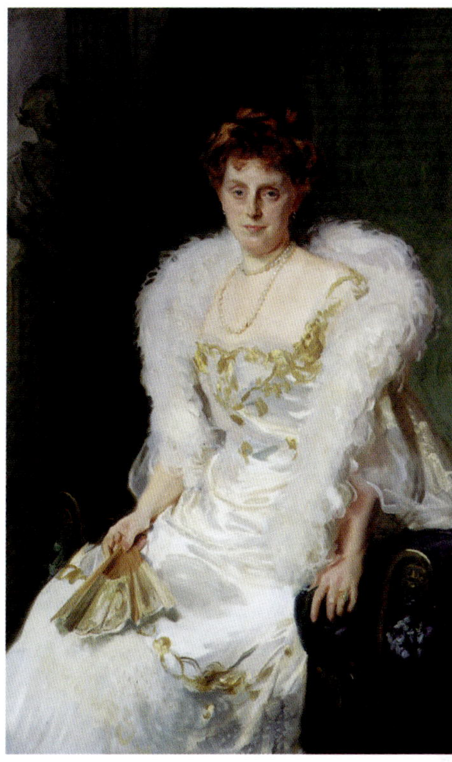

Portrait of Mrs Charles Beatty Alexander, 1902, oil on canvas, 147 x 96.5cm (58 x 38in), Private Collection

Holding her fan and dressed in a white satin gown with gold accoutrements and a white feather boa, this three-quarter-length portrait of Mrs Charles Beatty Alexander, née Harriet Crocker (1859–1935) presents her in sumptuous surroundings. As usual, Sargent has applied expressive, painterly marks to describe her clothing, and thinner, more detailed marks for the rendering of her face.

Mrs Knowles and Her Children, 1902, oil on canvas, 182.9 x 151.1cm (72 x 59½in), Butler Institute of American Art, Ohio, USA

Mrs Arthur Knowles, née Mildred Clare Buchanan, sits with her two little boys: seven-year-old John Buchanan and five-year-old Richard Arthur Lees. As with most of his portraits of this period, it was painted in Tite Street. Despite Mildred's fashionable grey outfit with soft ruffles around the collar and the boys' Pierrot costumes, the image is timeless; of a mother trying to amuse her children to keep them still.

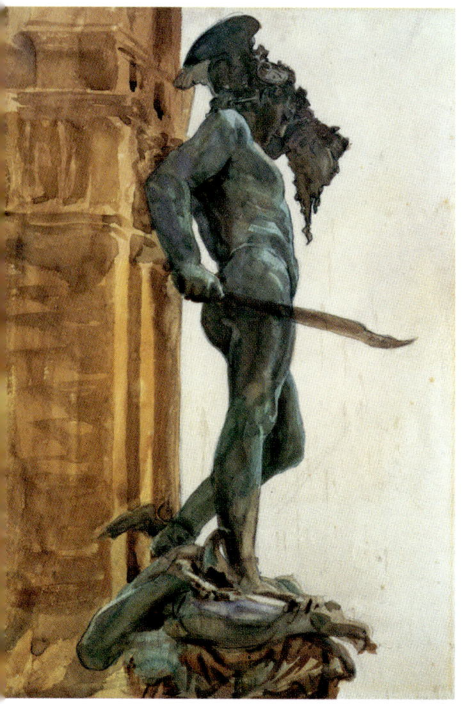

Perseus, c.1902, watercolour over graphite on paper, 37.5 x 26.7cm (14¾ x 10½in), Private Collection

This is Sargent's rendition of the 1545 bronze sculpture of Perseus by the polymath Benvenuto Cellini (1500–71) that stands in the Loggia dei Lanzi of the Piazza della Signoria in Florence. In his winged sandals, holding a sword in his right hand and the head of Medusa aloft in his left, Perseus looks down so he will not be turned to stone by the gorgon.

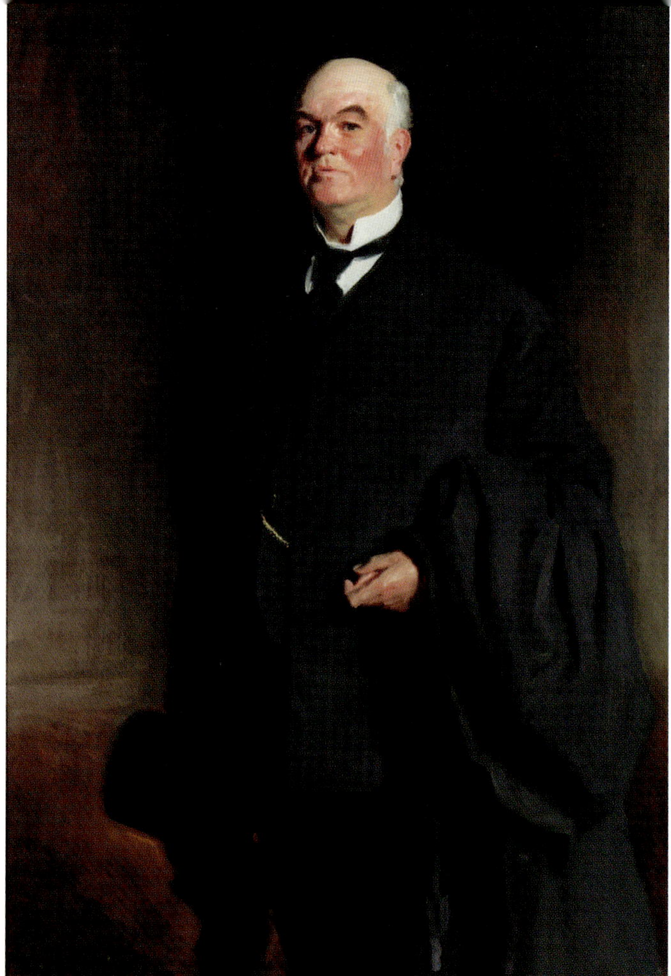

Above: *Henry Richardson,* 1902, oil on canvas, 147.7 x 97.7cm (58 x 38½in), Laing Art Gallery, Newcastle-upon-Tyne, UK

Painted to commemorate the sitter's 33 years of service with the Ashington Coal Company in Northumberland, Sargent painted the portrait in London. He returned to his earlier successful approach inspired by the Spanish artists he so admired, of dark clothing and background to emphasize and focus attention on the subject's face. The man of business stands, portmanteau in one hand, full-length coat slung over his other arm, his starched white collar and gold chain indicating his successful status in society.

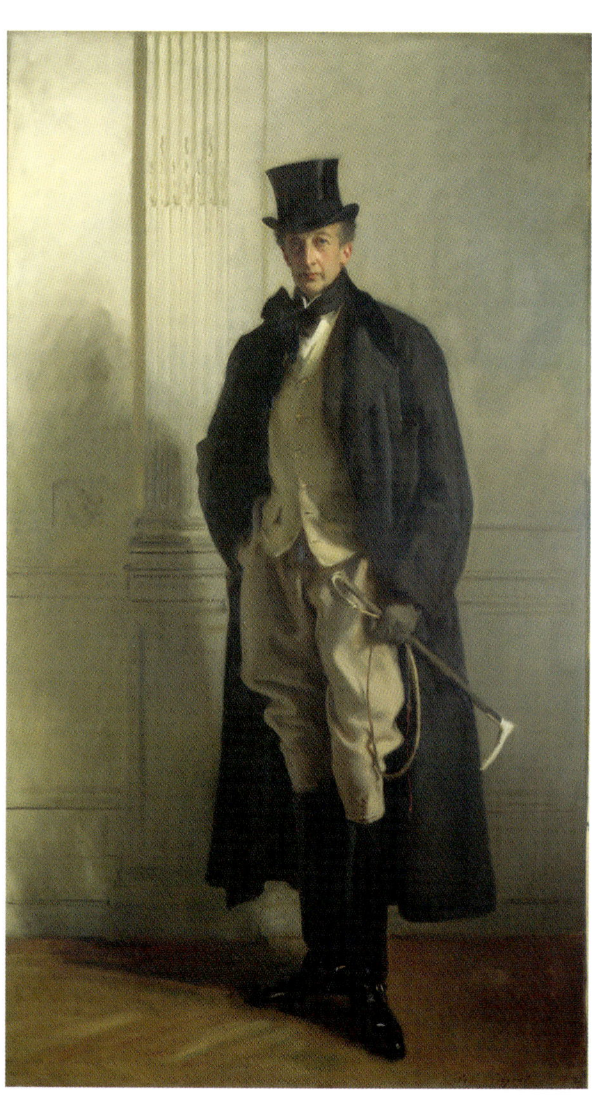

Lord Ribblesdale, 1902, oil on canvas, 258.4 x 143.5cm (101¾ x 56½in), The National Gallery, London, UK

Debonair and suave, Thomas Lister (1854–1925), 4th Baron Ribblesdale was a Liberal Whip in the House of Lords and a Trustee of the National Gallery. His unmistakably aristocratic air inspired Edward VII's nickname for him: 'the Ancestor.' After witnessing him give an after-dinner speech for the Artists' Benevolent Fund, Sargent asked to paint this portrait. Thomas Lister is also said to be the model for George Bernard Shaw's Professor Higgins in Pygmalion.

Evelyn Baring, 1902, oil on canvas, 148.8 x 98.4cm (58½ x 38¾in), The National Portrait Gallery, London, UK

Evelyn Baring, the 1st Earl of Cromer (1841–1917) was an administrator and diplomat who ruled in Egypt as British agent and Consul General for 24 years, profoundly influencing the country's development. Sargent has painted him at his desk in a corner of his Wimpole Street study in front of his leather-bound state papers. Although he is white-haired, his authority and power are quietly conveyed.

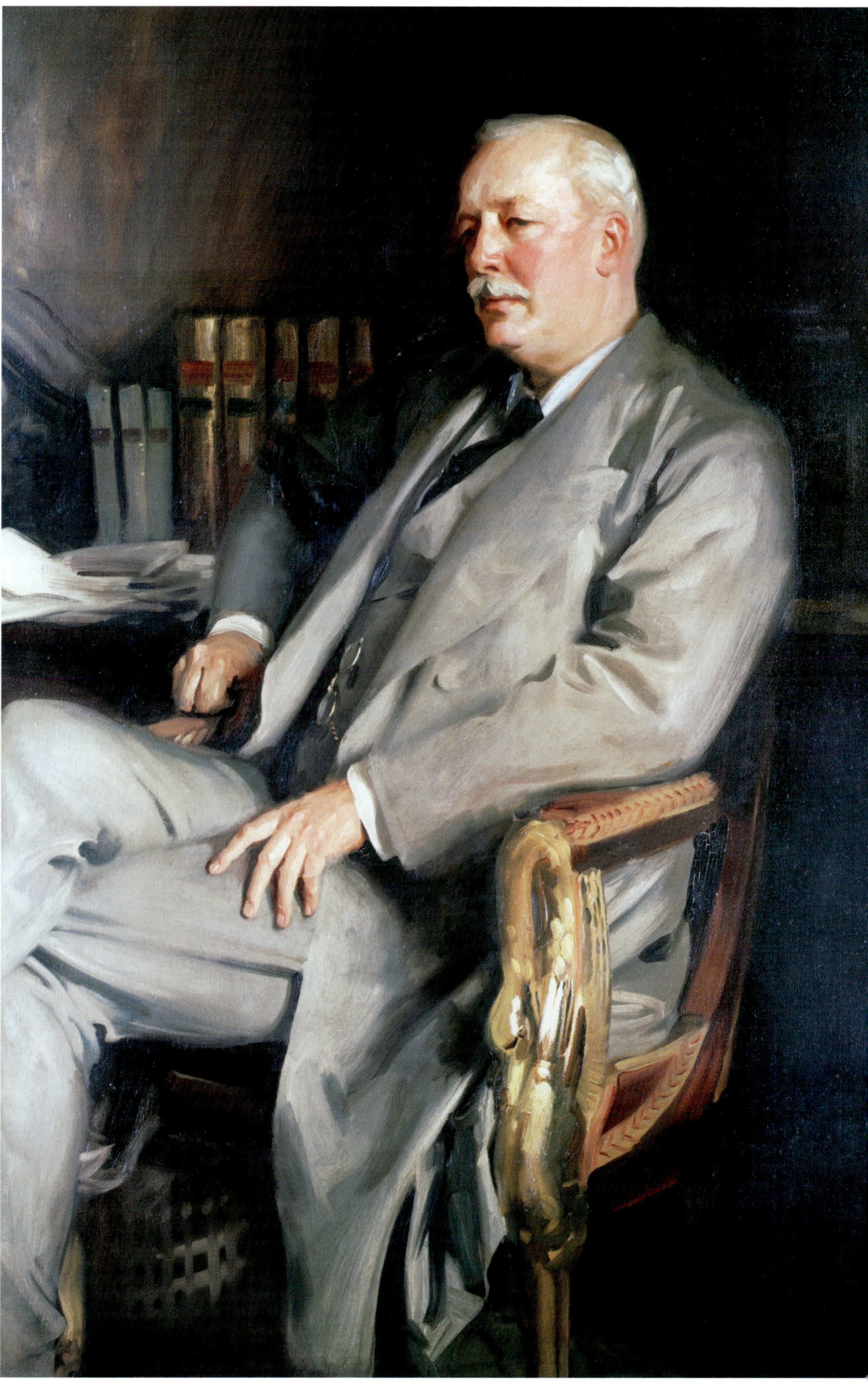

Mary Crowninshield Endicott Chamberlain (Mrs Joseph Chamberlain), 1902, oil on canvas, 150.5 x 83.8cm (59¼ x 33in), National Gallery of Art, Washington DC, USA

Swathed in white and pale blue satin, this is Mary Crowninshield Endicott Chamberlain (1864–1957), daughter of Ellen (see page 164). She holds her fan in long, satin evening gloves, her hair piled high emitting a sense of nobility and rank. Sargent's unique painting process and particular skill meant that he created some almost abstract areas alongside the details.

Below: *Venetian Wineshop,* 1902, oil on canvas, 69.8 x 53.3cm (27½ x 21in), Private Collection

A throwback to his genre scenes, Sargent painted the interior of a local bistro while staying with the Curtis family at the Palazzo Barbaro (see details on page 70). Some of the figures were modelled by his friends. A young Venetian woman turns in her chair to look over her shoulder at a second woman, seated on the left. The quiet woman in the corner, providing a counterpoint to this action, is his friend Jane de Glehn.

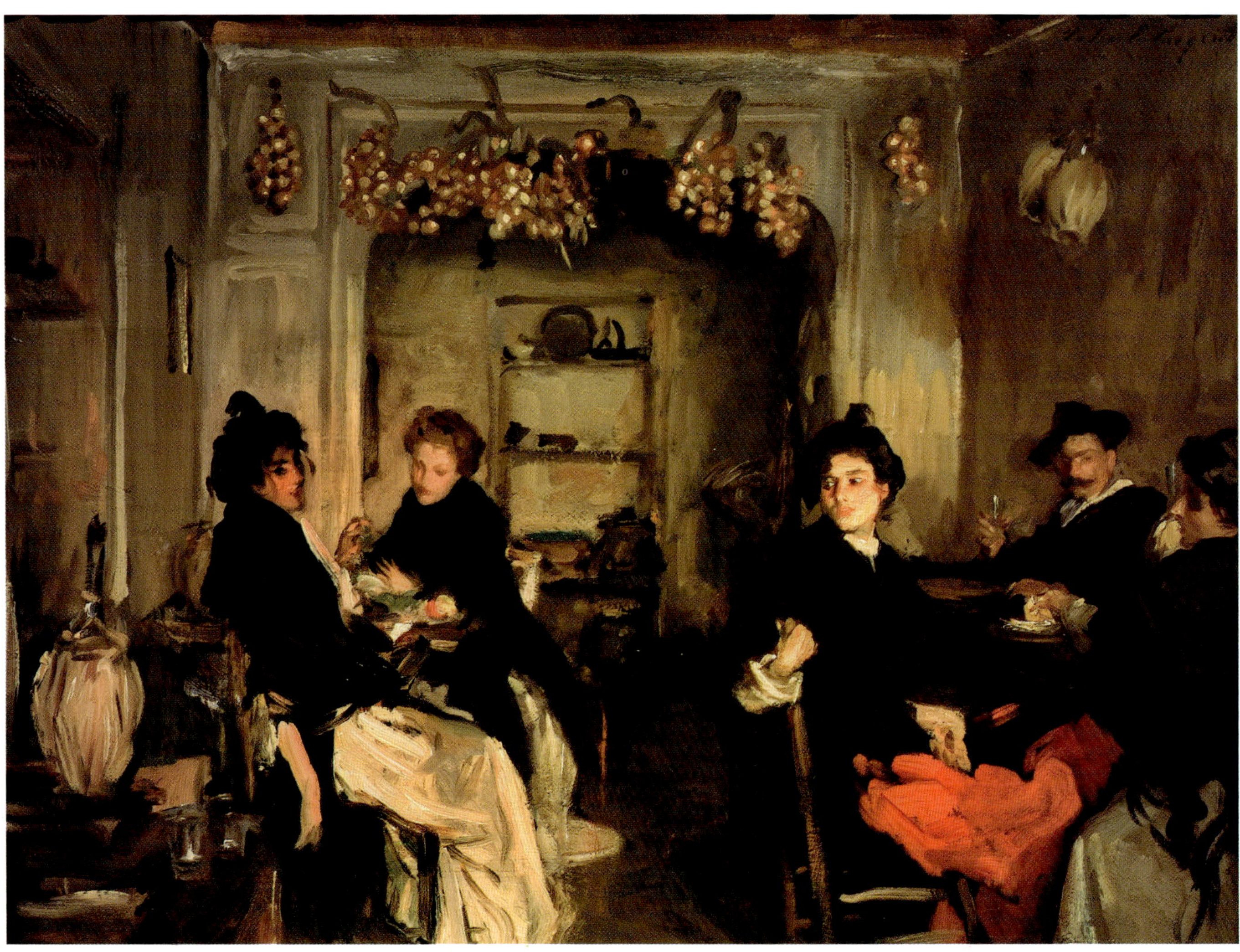

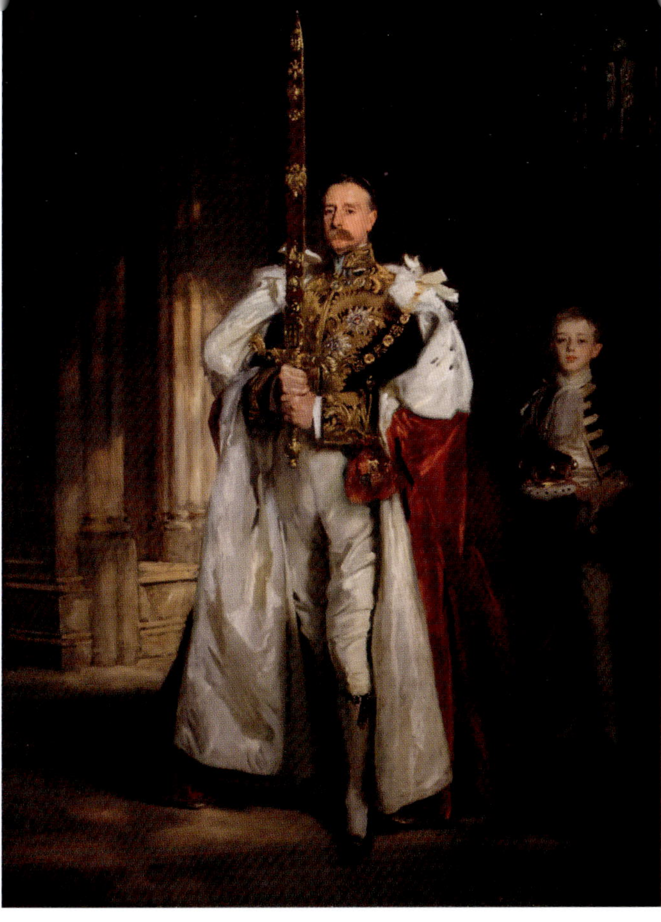

Charles Stewart, Sixth Marquess of Londonderry, Carrying the Great Sword of State at the Coronation of King Edward VII, August, 1902, and Mr. W. C. Beaumont, His Page on that Occasion, 1904, oil on canvas, 287 x 195.6cm (113 x 77in), Museum of Fine Arts, Boston, USA

Although Sargent had declined the official commission to paint the coronation of Edward VII in 1902, he captured the pageantry of the event in this portrait of Charles Stewart Vane-Tempest-Stewart (1852–1915), 5th Marquess of Londonderry, who held the Great Sword of State in the procession. Stewart's nephew Wentworth Henry Canning Beaumont (1890–1956) served as his page for the occasion, holding his train and coronet.

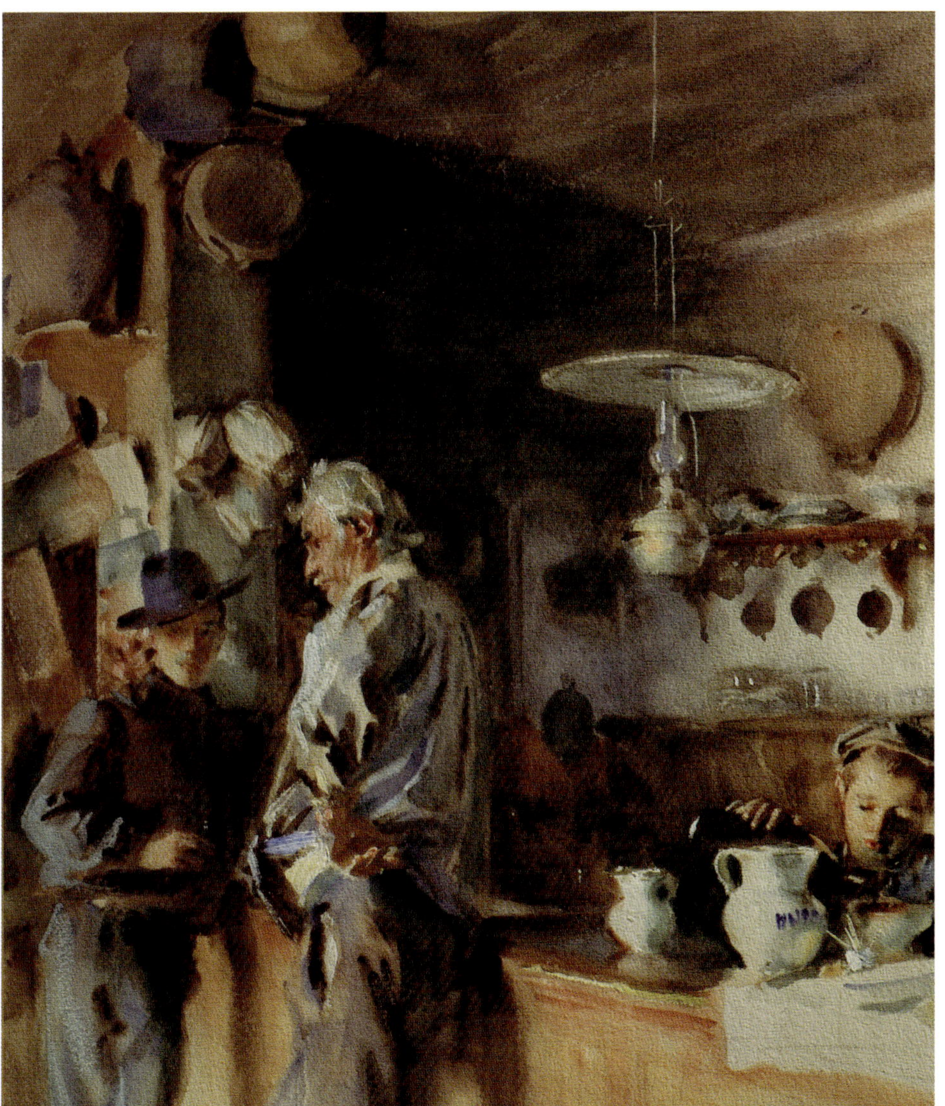

Venetian Interior (A Spanish Interior, The Wine Shop), 1902–03, watercolour, 57.2 x 45.7cm (22½ x 18in), Private Collection

Also known as *A Spanish Interior* or *The Wineshop*, this watercolour was probably painted at the same time as *Venetian Wineshop* (left). A young man and an older man lean casually against a bar inside a wineshop. A young boy behind the bar is carefully pouring wine. In the distilled light, with fluid marks, the three figures convey individuality.

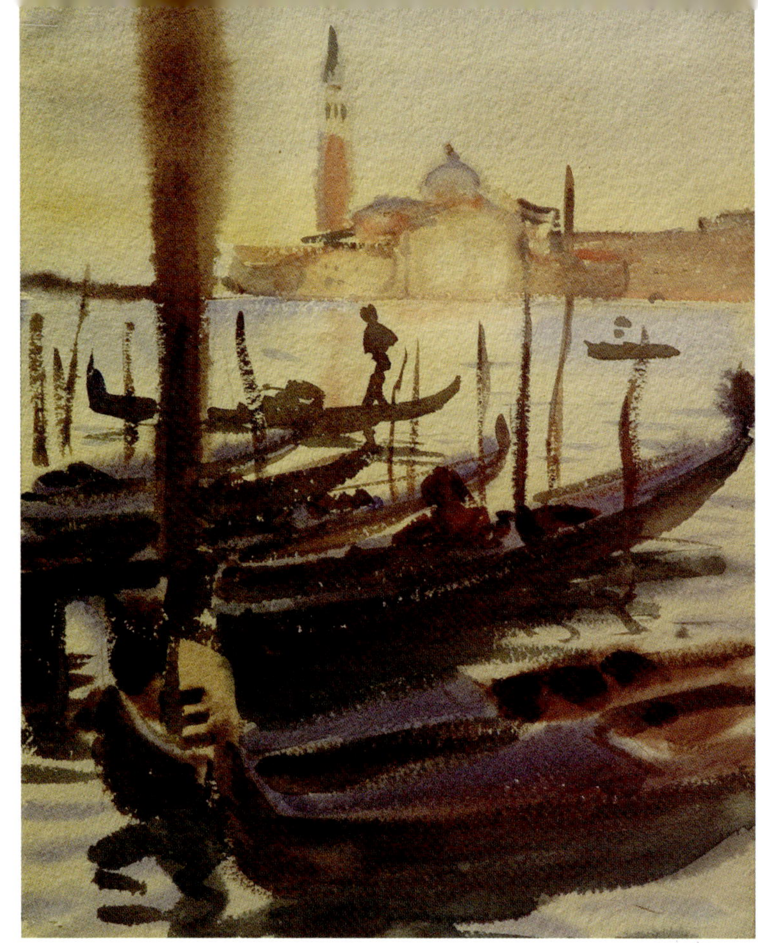

Gondolas in Front of San Giorgio Maggiore, 1902–03, watercolour on paper, 58.4 x 43.1cm (23 x 17in), Private Collection

Sargent's interest here is the water, the atmosphere and the light – particularly the dramatic contrast of the gondolas in silhouetted shadow against the golden early evening light. Additionally, he enjoyed painting the patterns of the shapes of the gondolas, and the masts and spars projecting across the sky and water. Using flowing diluted colour, he also portrays the Church of San Giorgio Maggiore in the misty background.

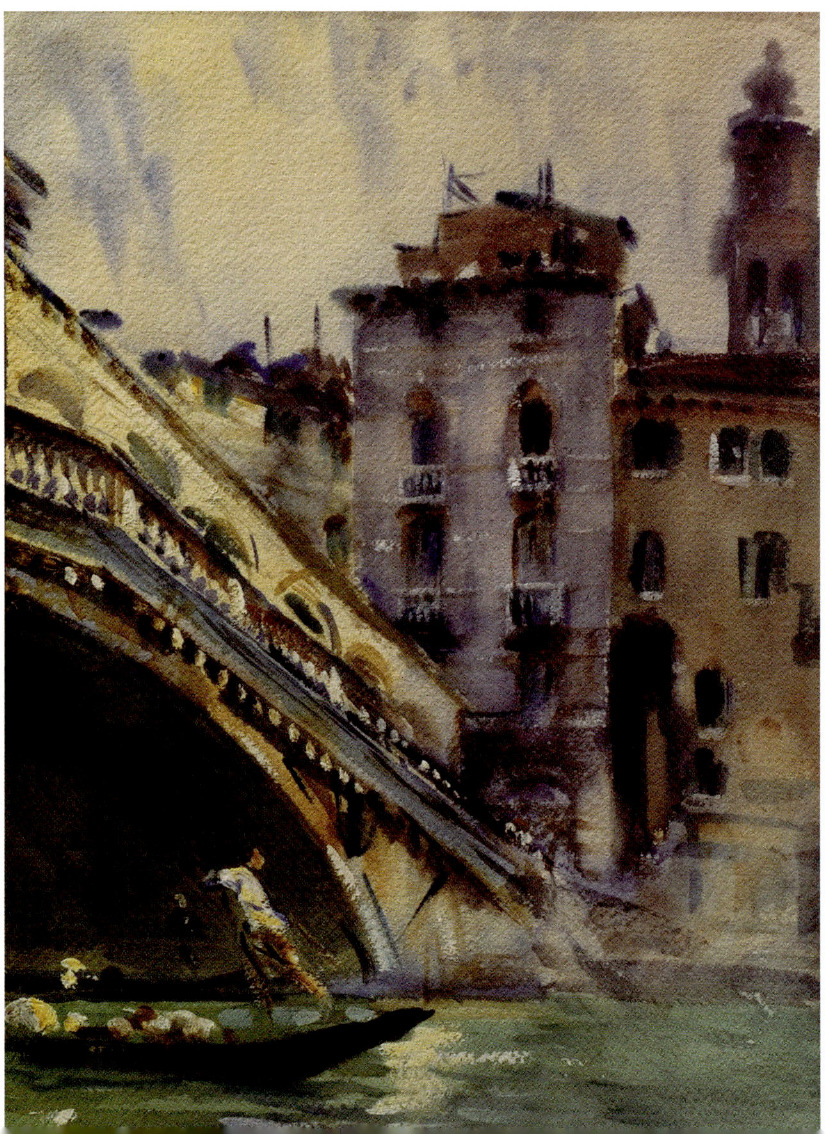

The Rialto, Venice, 1902–04, translucent and opaque watercolour over graphite on paper, 49.5 x 34.3cm (19½ x 13½in), Private Collection

Here, the dark span of the Rialto Bridge is highlighted with sections of sunlight. Painted from Sargent's gondola, it is level with another gondola being vigorously rowed by an energetic gondolier, just passing under the bridge. Sargent painted three versions of this view at different times, changing each slightly. The Rialto is one of the most iconic images of Venice, but Sargent's view, in dramatic close-up, alters its perspective so strongly that it is almost unrecognizable.

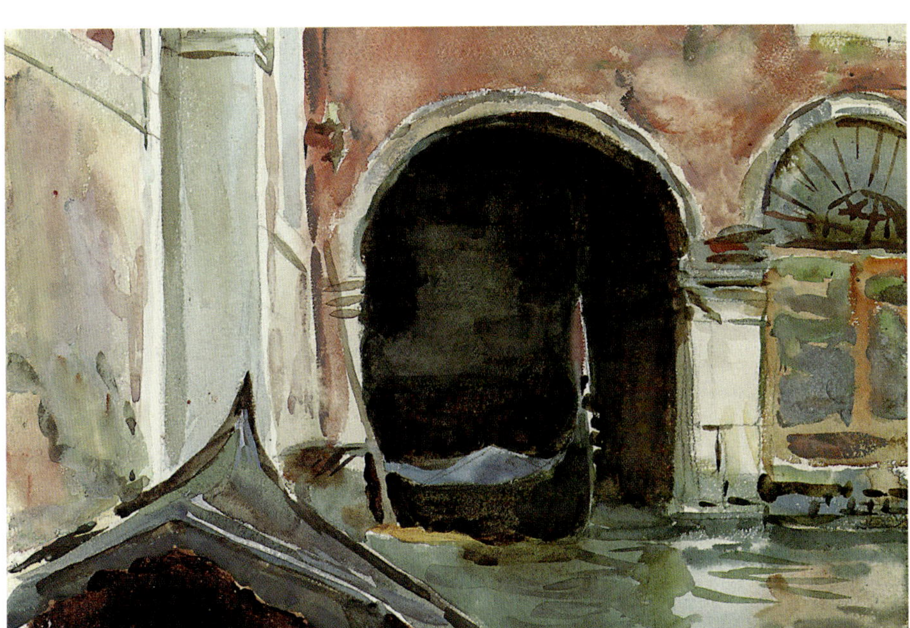

Venetian Canal, c.1902–04, watercolour over graphite on paper, 25.4 x 35.6cm (10 x 14in), Private Collection

Always captivated by Venice, Sargent stayed there for part of almost every year between 1898 and 1913 and painted 150 works during that time. Most, like this, were in watercolour. This is painted from a gondola, close to the water with a view of a large, dark archway rising up ahead, beyond that the canal. The sombre palette evokes the grey, rainy day.

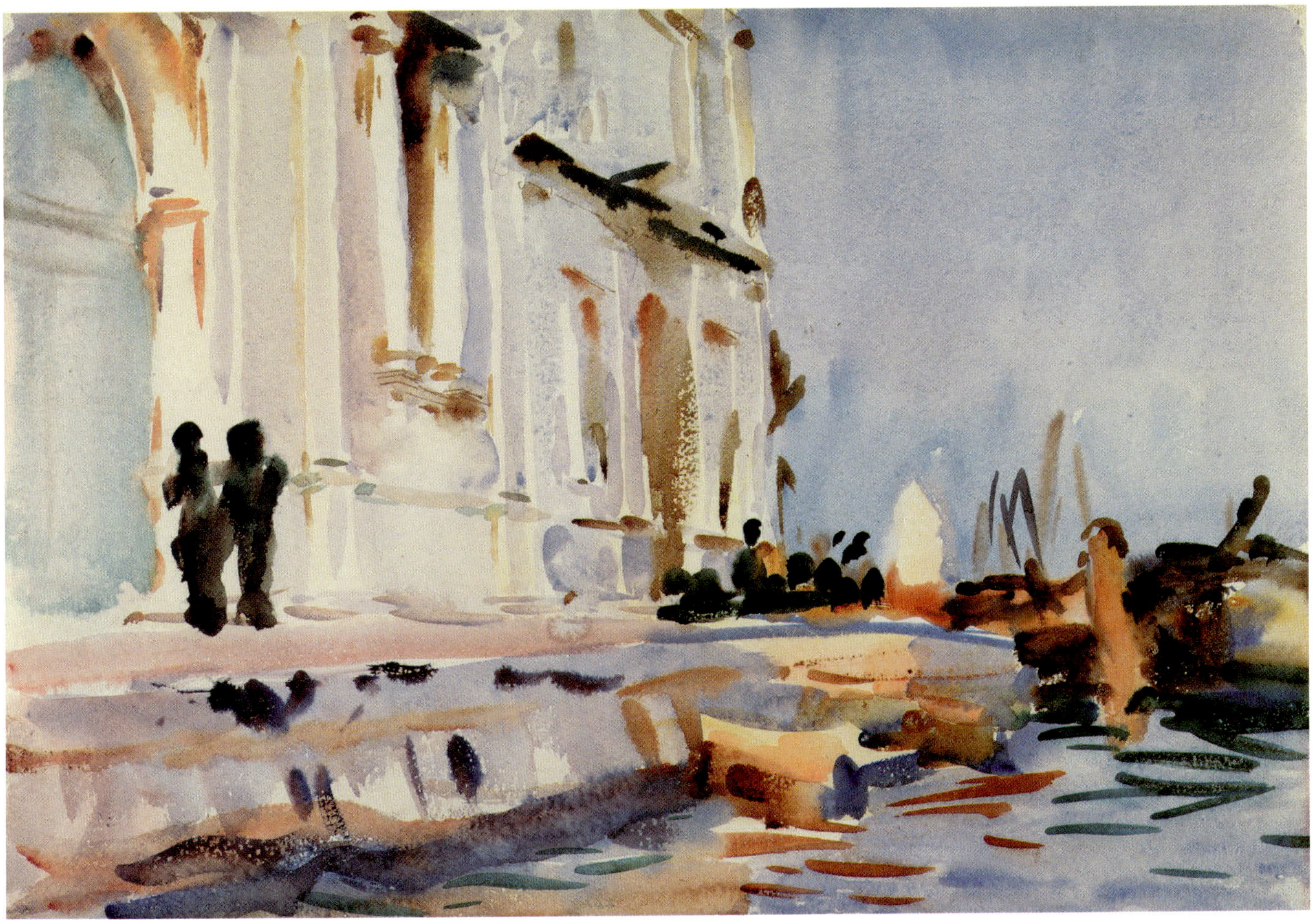

All' Ave Maria, c.1902–04, translucent and opaque watercolour on paper, 25.4 x 35.7cm (10 x 14in), Brooklyn Museum, New York, USA

Referring to vespers, or early evening prayer, this sketchy watercolour with its abridged brushmarks portrays the church and school of Santo Spirito, with adjacent buildings that face the promenade on the peaceful waterfront promenade, the Zattere. Painted wet-into-wet with no preparatory drawing, rich, liquid colours bleed into each other. In some places, Sargent wiped paint from the paper to soften those areas; other brushmarks are clearly delineated.

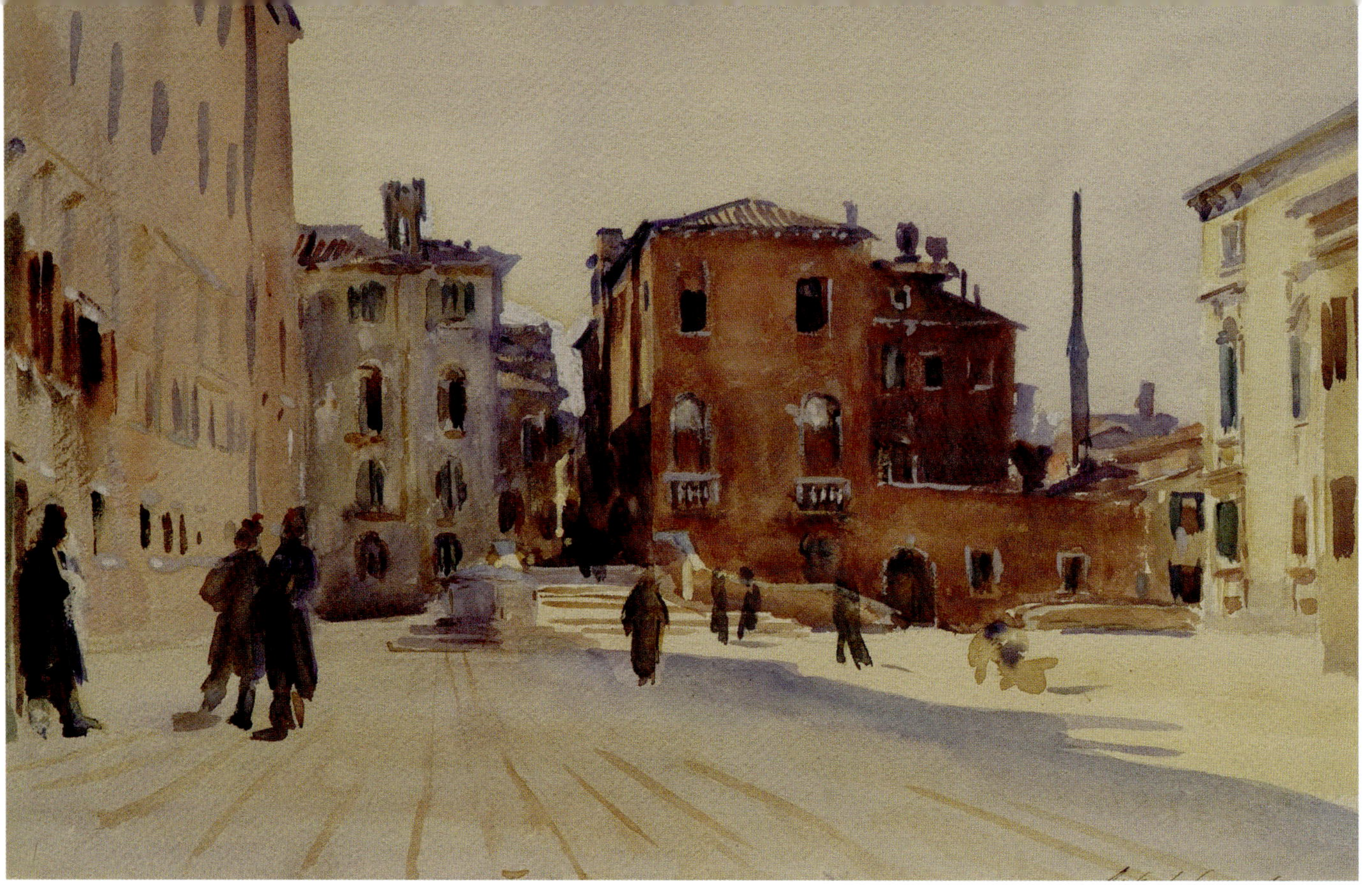

Campo dei Gesuiti, c.1902–
04, watercolour on paper,
34.9 × 50.2cm (13¾ ×
19¾in), Private Collection

One of a small number of
scenes of everyday Venetian
life that Sargent painted
during his later visits to
Venice, this is of the Campo
dei Gesuiti in the northern
area of the city. He sat in the
square, the shadow of the
Baroque church stretching
over and in front of him,
while he painted the sun
shining on the buildings and
figures walking through or
standing in the square.

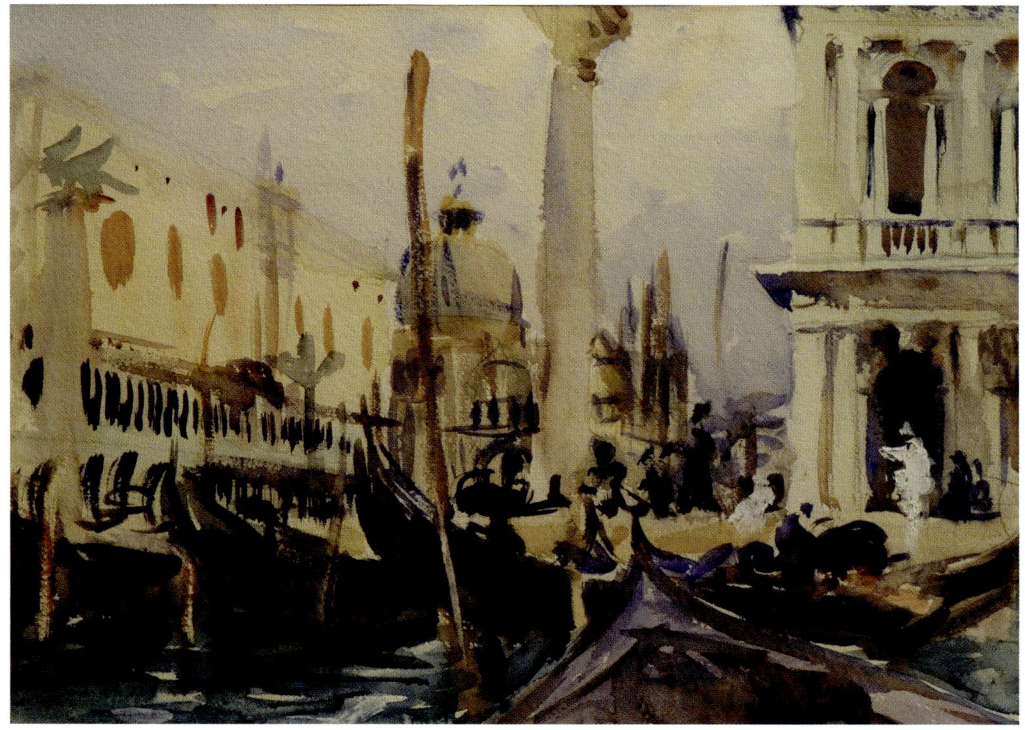

The Piazzetta with Gondolas,
1902–04, oil on cardboard,
with body colour over
graphite on paper, 24.5
x 34.9cm (9¾ x 13¾in),
Private Collection

A close-up view from a
gondola in front of the
Old Library with St Mark's
column in the middle
distance. This is one of
two paintings of the same
view, but both are entirely
different. This rapidly-worked
oil sketch sets the gondolas
in silhouette while the other
painting – a watercolour
– is light and colourful. As
Sargent moved away from
what he perceived as the
limits of portraiture, he
spent more time capturing
images that allowed him the
freedom of more dramatic
viewpoints and unusual
executions.

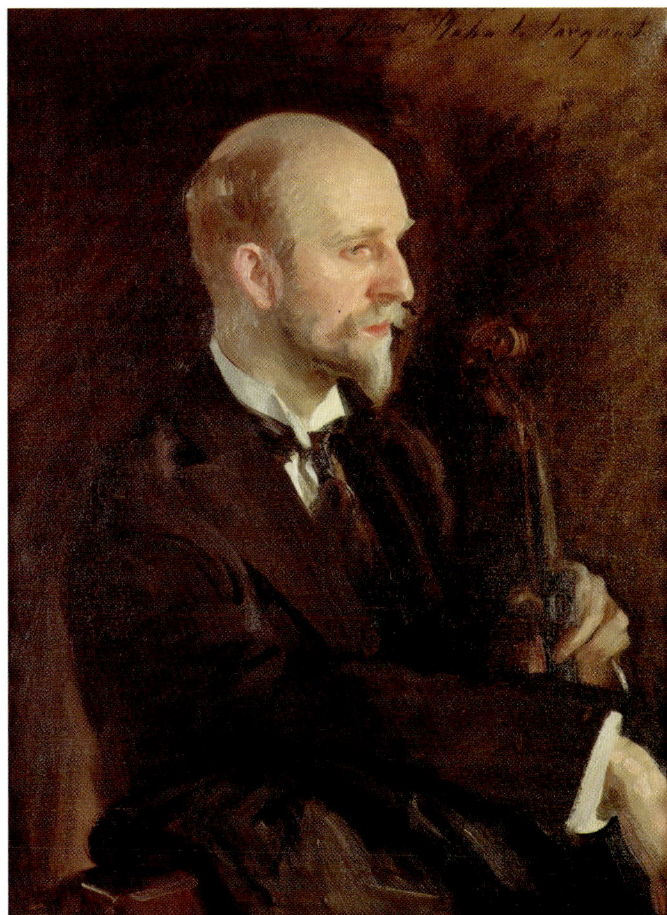

Portrait of Charles Martin Loeffler, 1903, oil on canvas, 87 x 62cm (34¼ x 24½in), Isabella Stewart Gardner Museum, Boston, Massachusetts, USA

Composer and violinist Charles Loeffler (1861–1935) was a close friend of Sargent and Isabella Stewart Gardner. Sargent painted this portrait in less than three hours and gave it to Isabella on 10th April 1903 as a birthday present. It is a fresh and spontaneous image of the French-born musician who had lived in the US since 1881. He had been joint first violinist of the Boston Symphony Orchestra, but left that position in order to devote himself to composing.

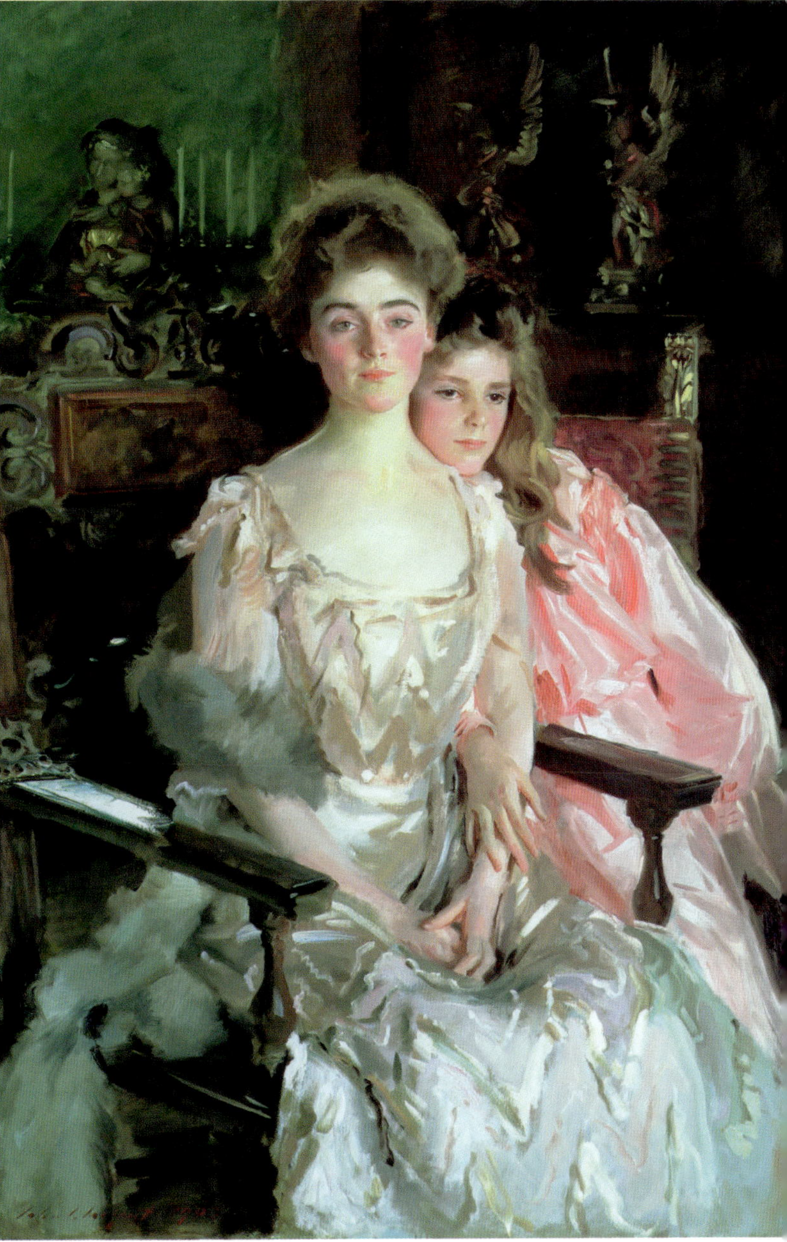

Mrs Fiske Warren (Gretchen Osgood) and her Daughter Rachel, 1903, oil on canvas, 152.4 x 102.55cm (60 x 40½in), Museum of Fine Arts, Boston, Massachusetts, USA

A member of a prominent Boston family and an accomplished poet, Gretchen Warren (1871–1961) posed for Sargent with her eldest daughter at Isabella Stewart Gardner's mansion, Fenway Court in Boston, where Sargent had set up a temporary studio. Emphasizing the serene beauty of his sitters, he used sweeping brushstrokes for their softly coloured and textured dresses. As usual, he has captured the most natural position, with the daughter, slightly bored and self-conscious, nestling her chin into her mother.

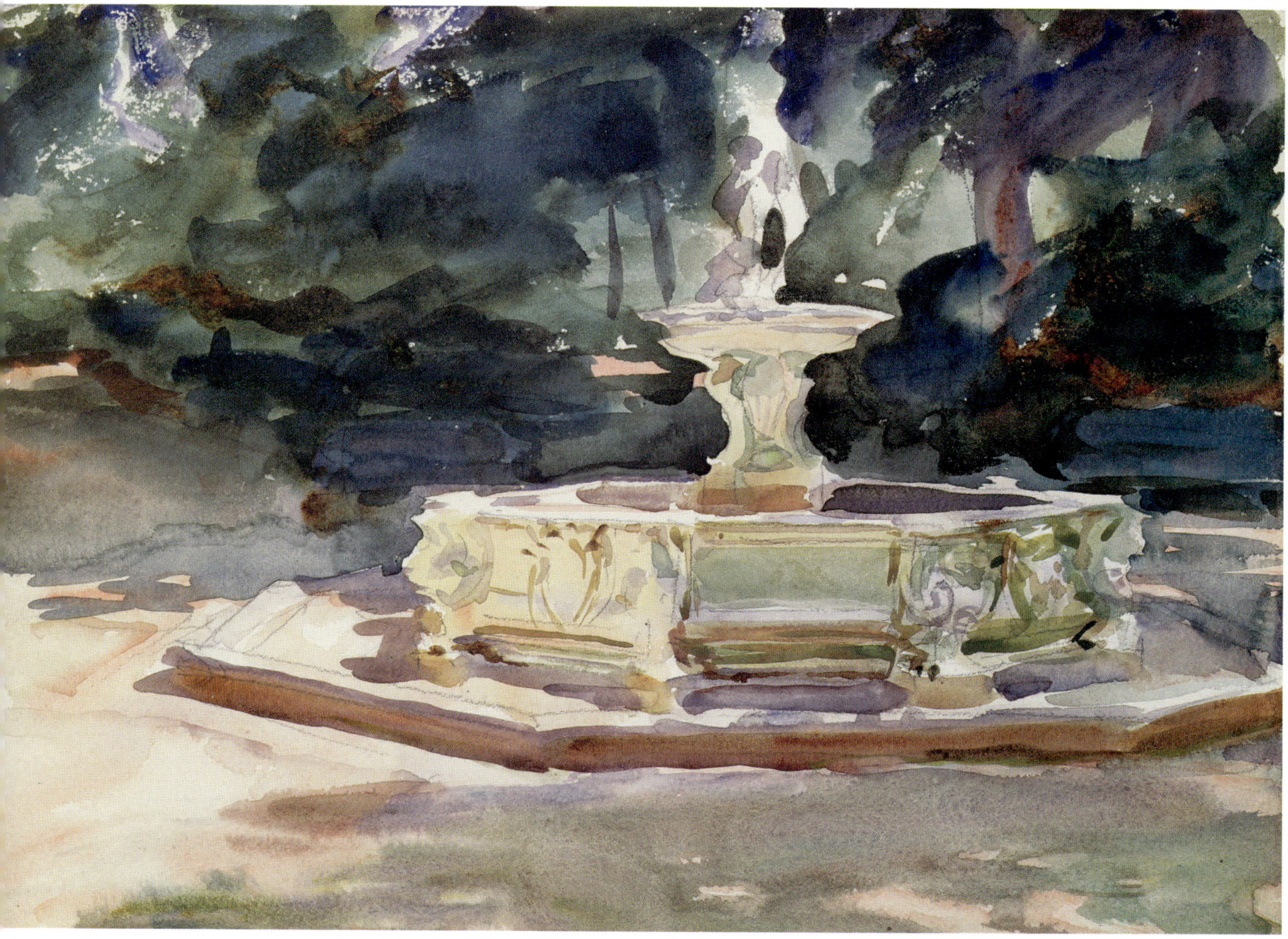

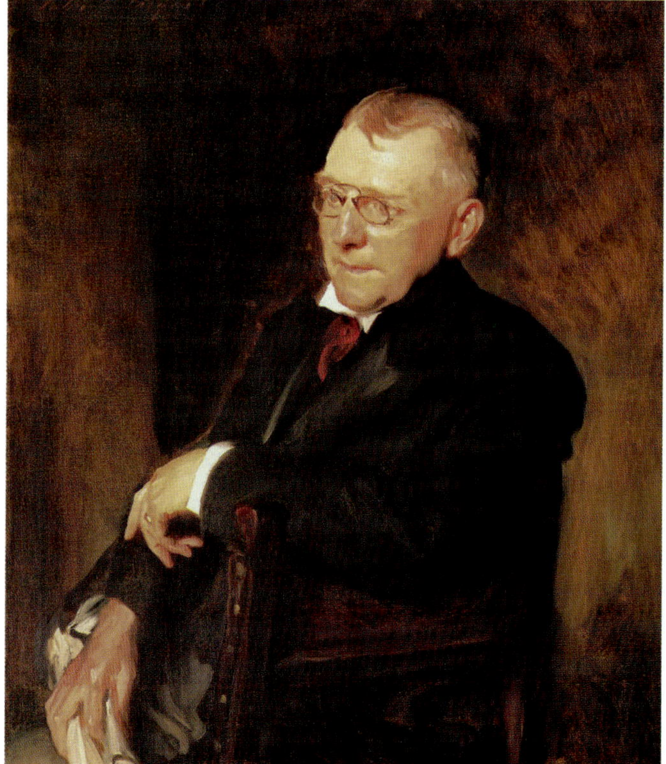

Aranjuez, c.1903,
watercolour on paper,
25.4 x 35.7cm (10 x 14in),
Brooklyn Museum, New
York, USA

After painting this, Sargent
produced many more images
depicting stone garden
features in verdant settings.
This was painted in the Jardín
de la Isla at the Royal Palace
of Aranjuez near Madrid,
one of several old, neglected
formal gardens that he
visited in Portugal and Spain
in 1902 and 1903. Using the
white of the paper for the
sunlit highlights, he captured
the small fountain and
sculpture of the mythological
figure Triptolemus, amid the
greenery of the garden.

*Portrait of James Whitcomb
Riley*, 1903, oil on canvas,
91½ x 77½cm (36 x 30½in),
Indianapolis Museum of Art,
Indiana, USA

Sargent's portrait shows
the American author and
poet, James Whitcomb
Riley (1849–1916) looking
thoughtful, holding a book to
indicate his profession. This
portrait was commissioned
by the Art Association of
Indianapolis (forerunner of
the Indianapolis Museum of
Art) and paid for with funds
raised at an 1898 benefit
performance, in which
Whitcomb Riley read his
own poetry. The painting
received mixed reviews
among Riley's friends.

Leonard Wood, 1903, oil on canvas, 76.5 x 63.8cm (30¼ x 25¼in), The National Portrait Gallery, London, UK

During the Spanish-American War (from April to August 1898), military officer Leonard Wood (1860–1927) together with his friend Theodore Roosevelt, founded the First Volunteer Cavalry Regiment that became known as the Rough Riders. Wood continued to make numerous effective changes in the US and Sargent, as one of his admirers, asked to paint his portrait.

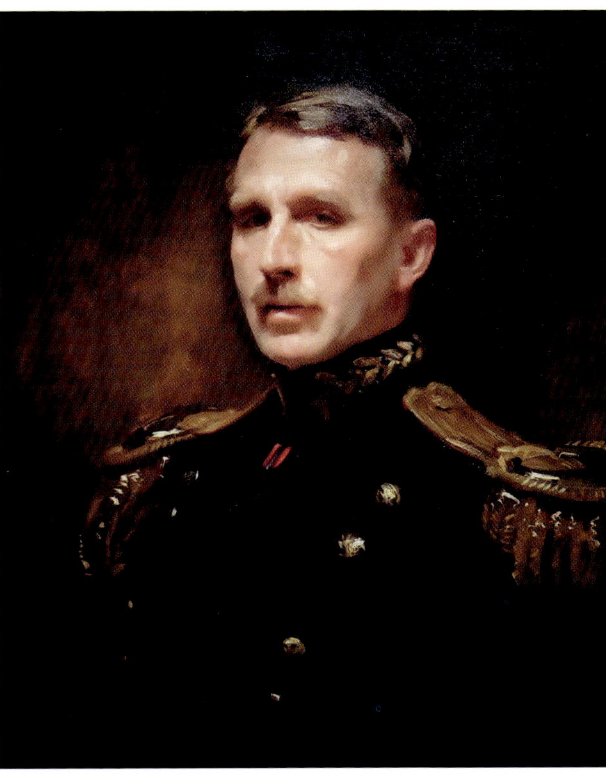

Below: *Stable at Cuenca*, 1903, oil on canvas, 57.2 x 72.1cm (22½ x 28½in), Smithsonian American Art Museum, Washington DC, USA

The Spanish city of Cuenca was built by the Moors. Nestling in the mountains, the walled old town, steep cobbled streets and medieval castle ruins appealed to Sargent. The biblical appearance of this genre scene was a deliberate reference to art of the past. However, unlike a precise Renaissance painting, Sargent's work is suggestive, with rapid marks capturing the impression of the stable.

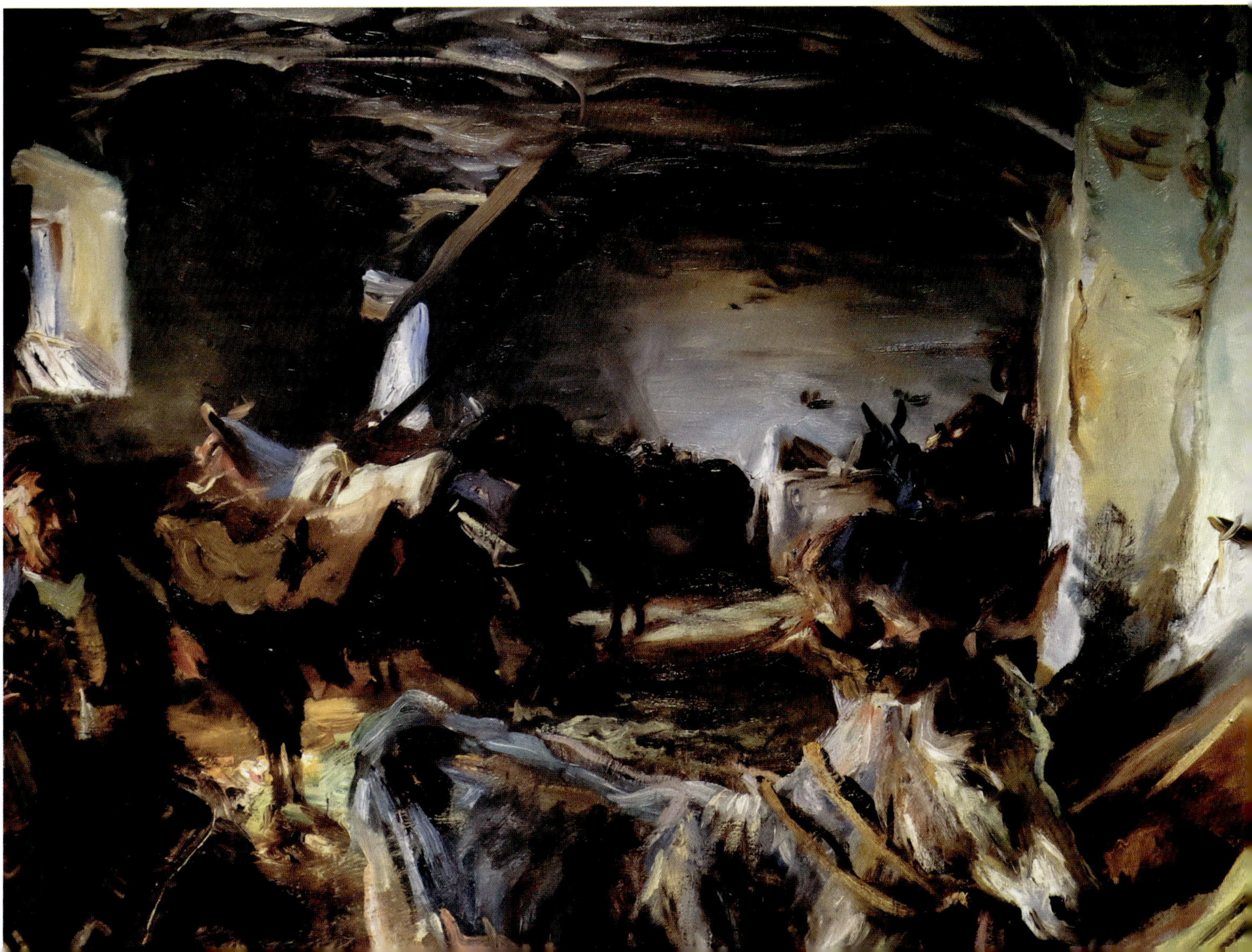

Portrait of Ramalho Ortigão, undated, charcoal on paper, 5.9 x 3.8cm (15 x 9¾in), Private Collection

Sargent met José Duarte Ramalho Ortigão (1836–1915), a Portuguese journalist and later a diplomat, through a mutual friend, the artist Columbano Bordalo Pinheiro (1857–1929). Ortigão also taught French and worked as a literary critic and like Sargent, travelled widely throughout his life. With light, deft strokes of his charcoal, Sargent has captured details, but most of all the sensitivity in this intelligent man's face.

On the Canal, 1903, watercolour on paper, 49.5 x 34.3cm (19½ x 13½in), Petit Palais, Paris, France

Two gondoliers steer their vessels in unison, past the Baroque and Renaissance palaces that line the canal. The low viewpoint creates drama; the eyeline is level with the gondolas, meaning that viewers have to look up at the buildings beyond. With fluid, mainly translucent colour, Sargent used ultramarine for his darkest tones and the white of the paper to create sparkling highlights.

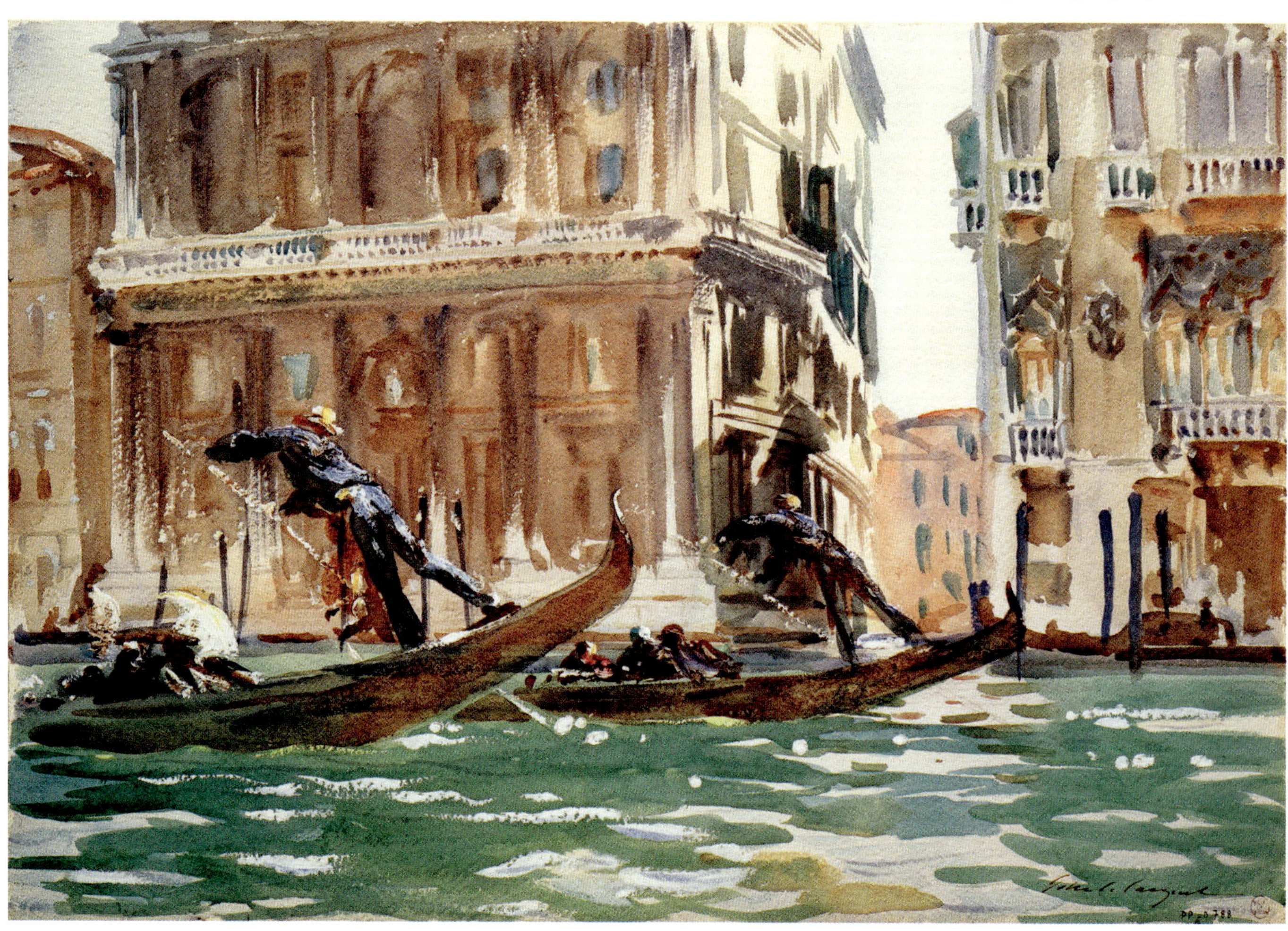

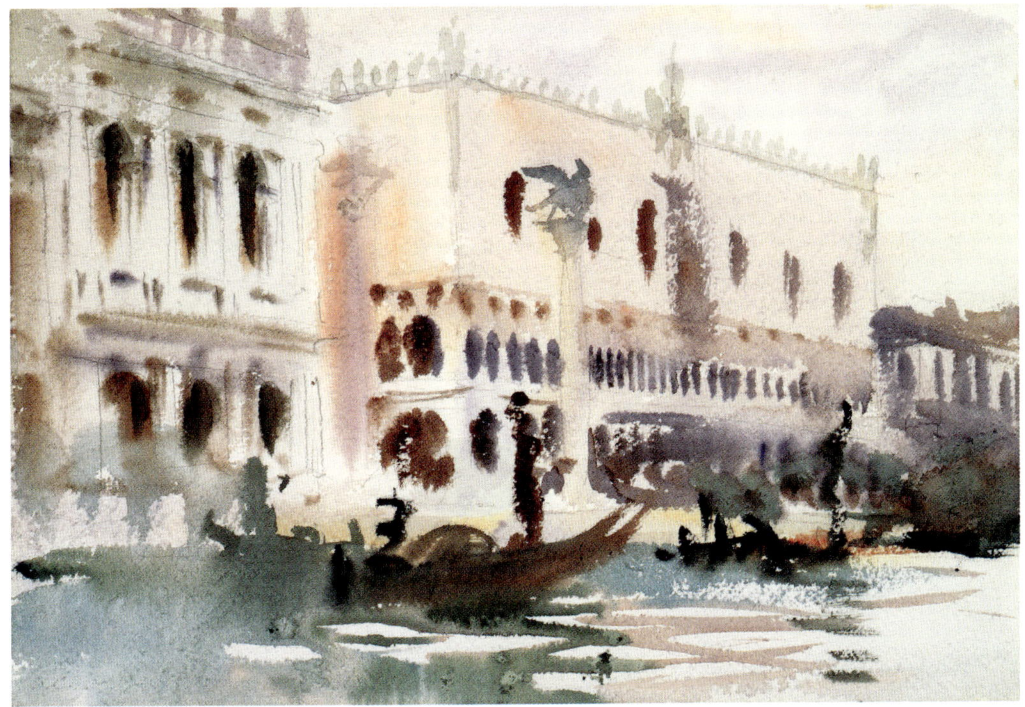

From the Gondola, c.1903, translucent and opaque watercolour over graphite on paper, 25.4 x 35.5cm (10 x 14in), Brooklyn Museum, New York, USA

Sargent's watercolour application always included some zinc white opaque watercolour to add emphasis to highlights. This fairly suffused image recalls aspects of paintings by Turner or Whistler, painted from a gondola in the Grand Canal on the approach to the Doge's palace.

Spirito Santo, Zattere, c.1903, watercolour over graphite on paper, 25.4 x 35.6cm (10 x 14in), Private Collection

Sargent painted five watercolours of this church, each similar in composition, but at different times of day. This work shows Sargent's remarkable control of the medium and his ability to work extremely quickly in order to capture the essence of the view. As well as evoking atmosphere, he depicted the most significant buildings in Venice, following the traditions of so many artists before him.

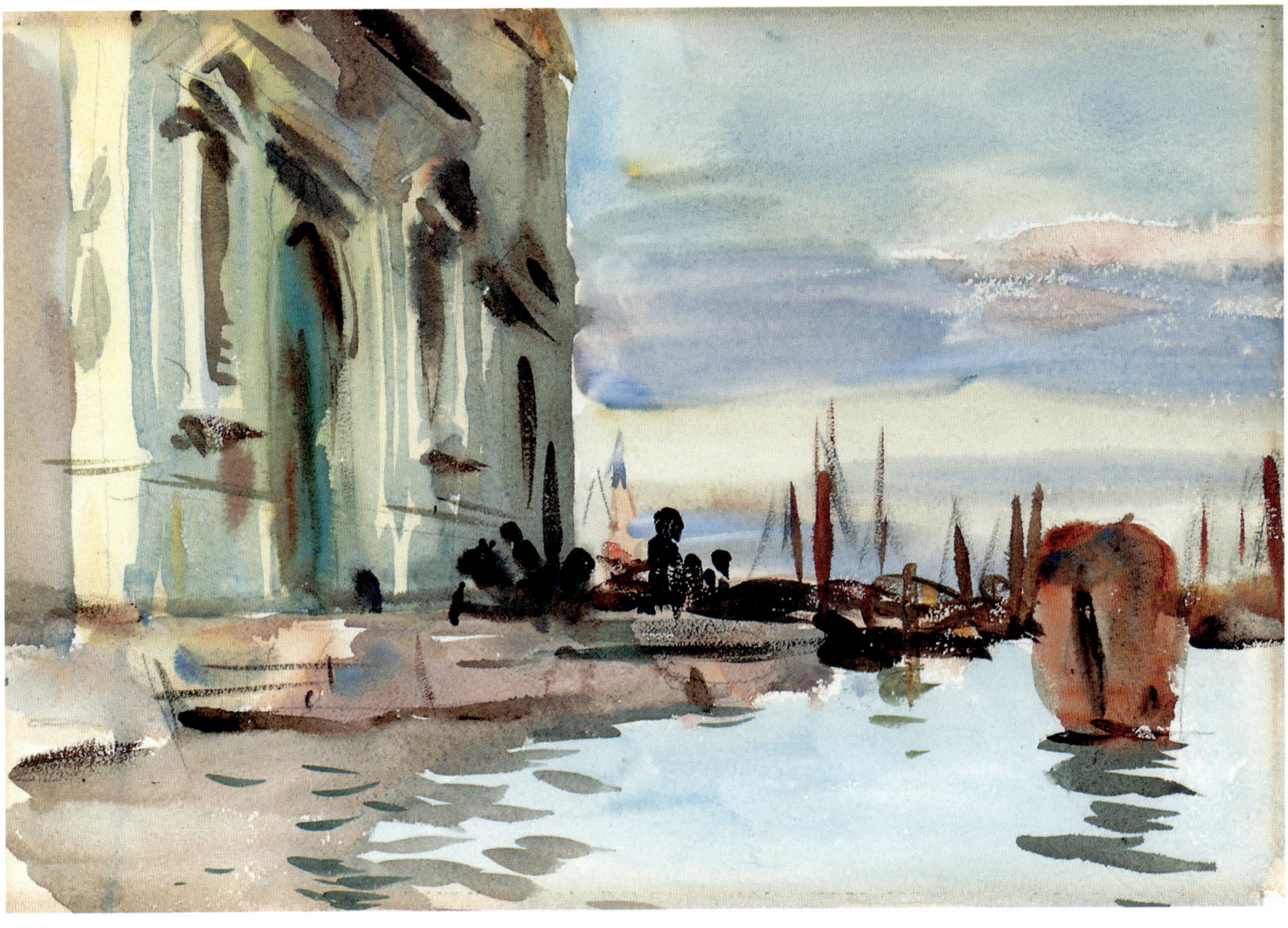

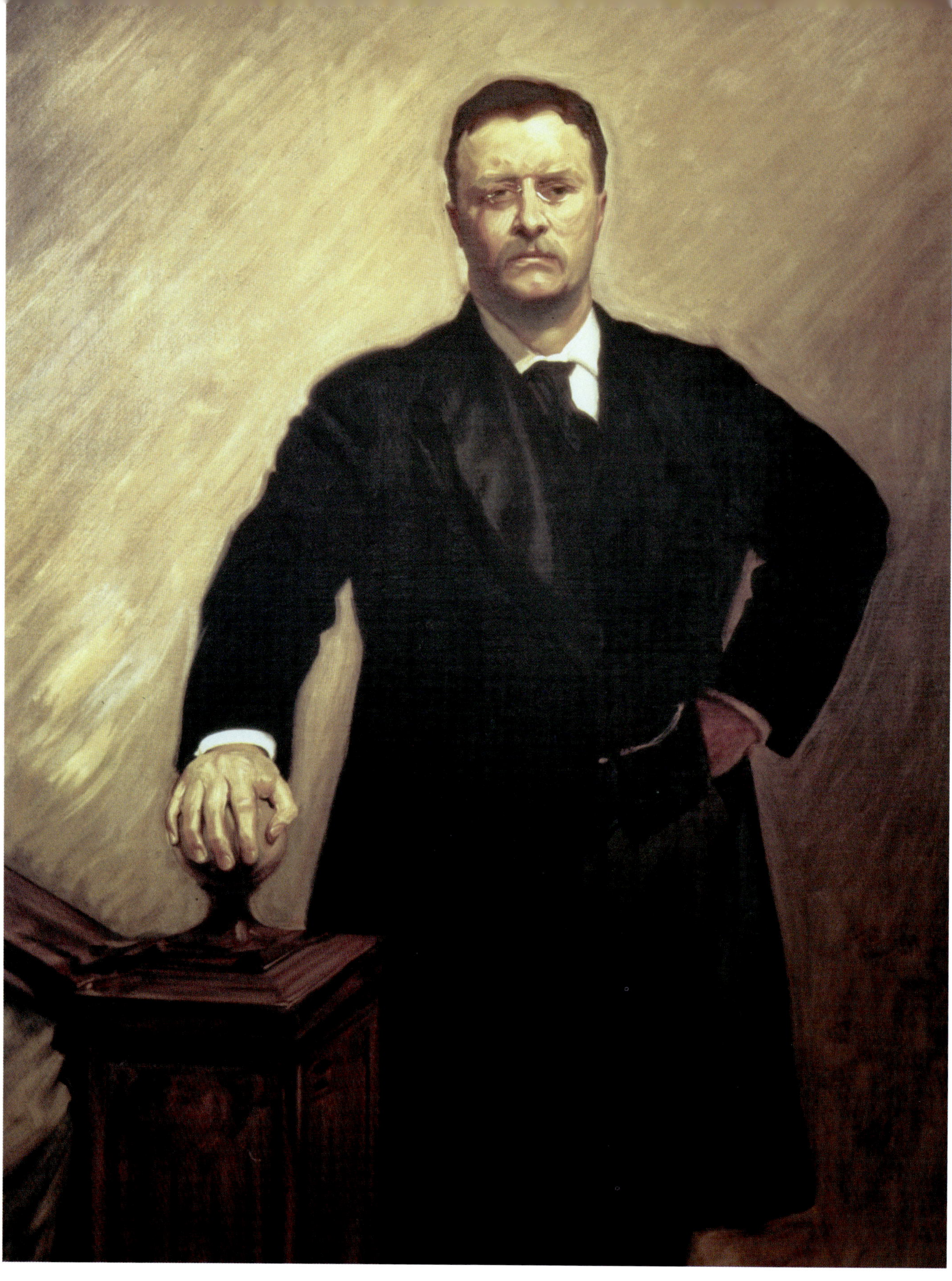

President Theodore Roosevelt,
1903, oil on canvas,
148.6 x 102.8cm (58½ x
40½in), The White House,
Washington DC, USA

Despite their personality
clashes, the President
declared: 'I like his picture
enormously.' it was hung in
the White House Entrance

Hall as Roosevelt's official
portrait. A critic observed:
'Mr Sargent has portrayed
more than the outer man...
He has pictured with the

President's features his
energy, his alertness, his
aggressiveness and his
unyielding disposition.'
(See also page 74.)

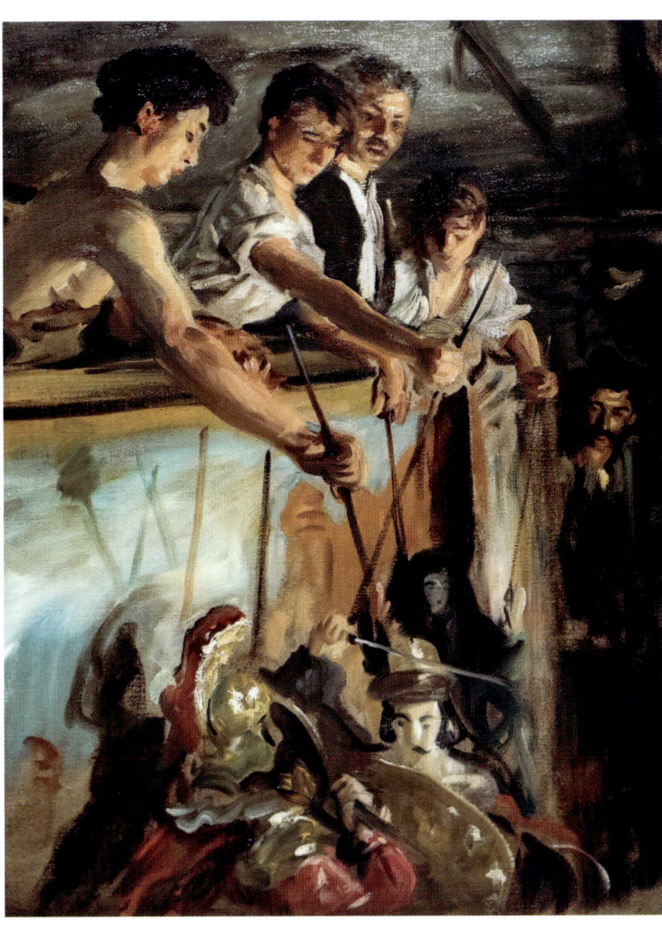

Behind the Curtain (Marionettes), 1903, oil on canvas, 73.7 x 53cm (29 x 20¾in), Private Collection

At the end of January 1903, Sargent travelled from London for a four-month stay in America. He painted this in Philadelphia during his last days there. It is backstage at a Sicilian marionette theatre and the dynamic composition evokes tension and a sense of complexity. The moving puppets are rendered with an expressive application of thick impasto. Sargent created the work for his own interests and experimentation.

The Bridge of Sighs, c.1903–04, translucent and opaque watercolour over graphite and underdrawing on paper, 25.4 x 35.6cm (10 x 14in), Brooklyn Museum, New York, USA

Using multiple techniques to portray the effects of light in his work, Sargent applied white impasto in areas, such as the gondoliers and their passengers. He also created light effects by using the white paper. Highlights were also created by dry scraping in certain judicious areas. This work has been painted with a palette that consisted mainly of ultramarine and ochre.

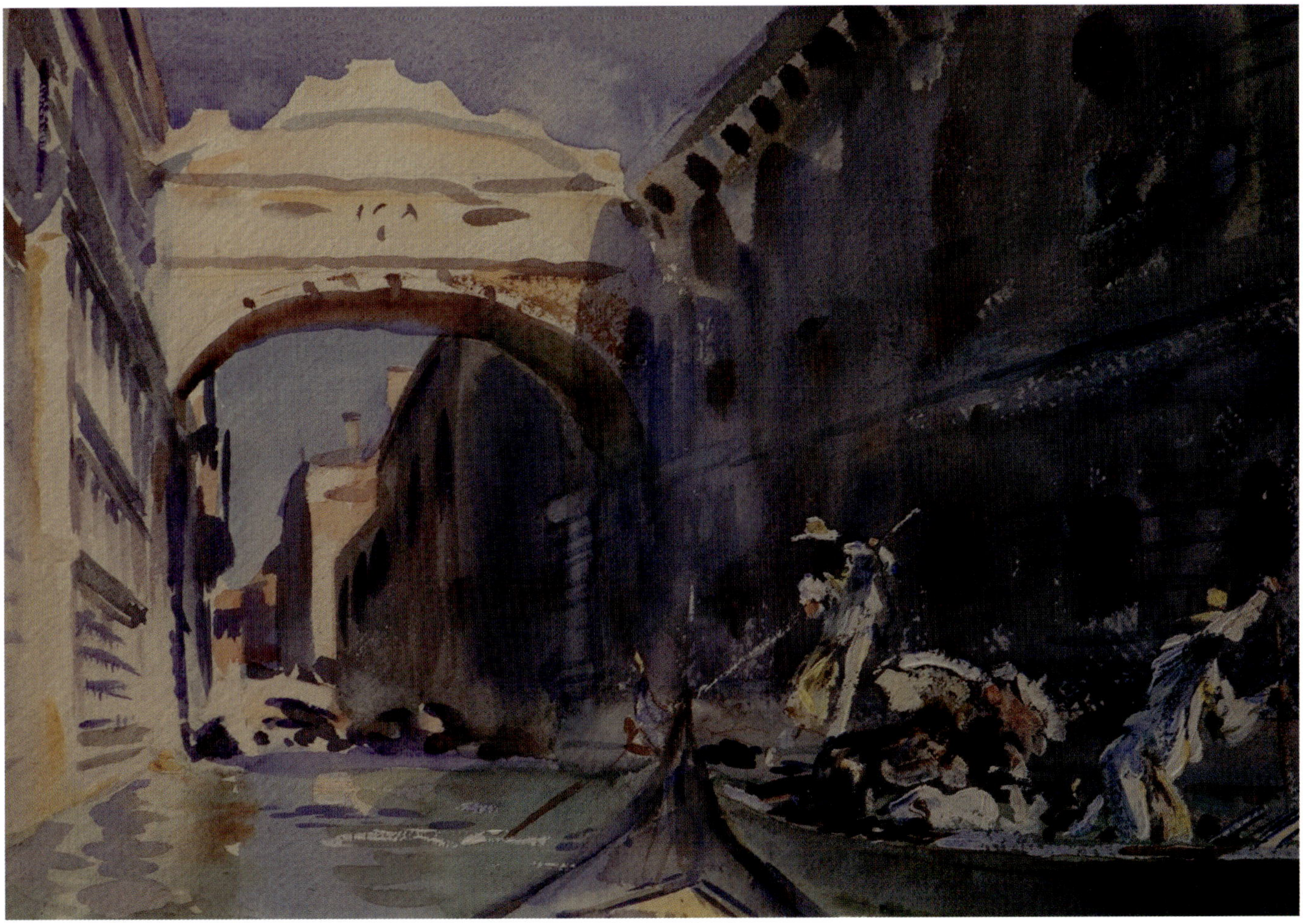

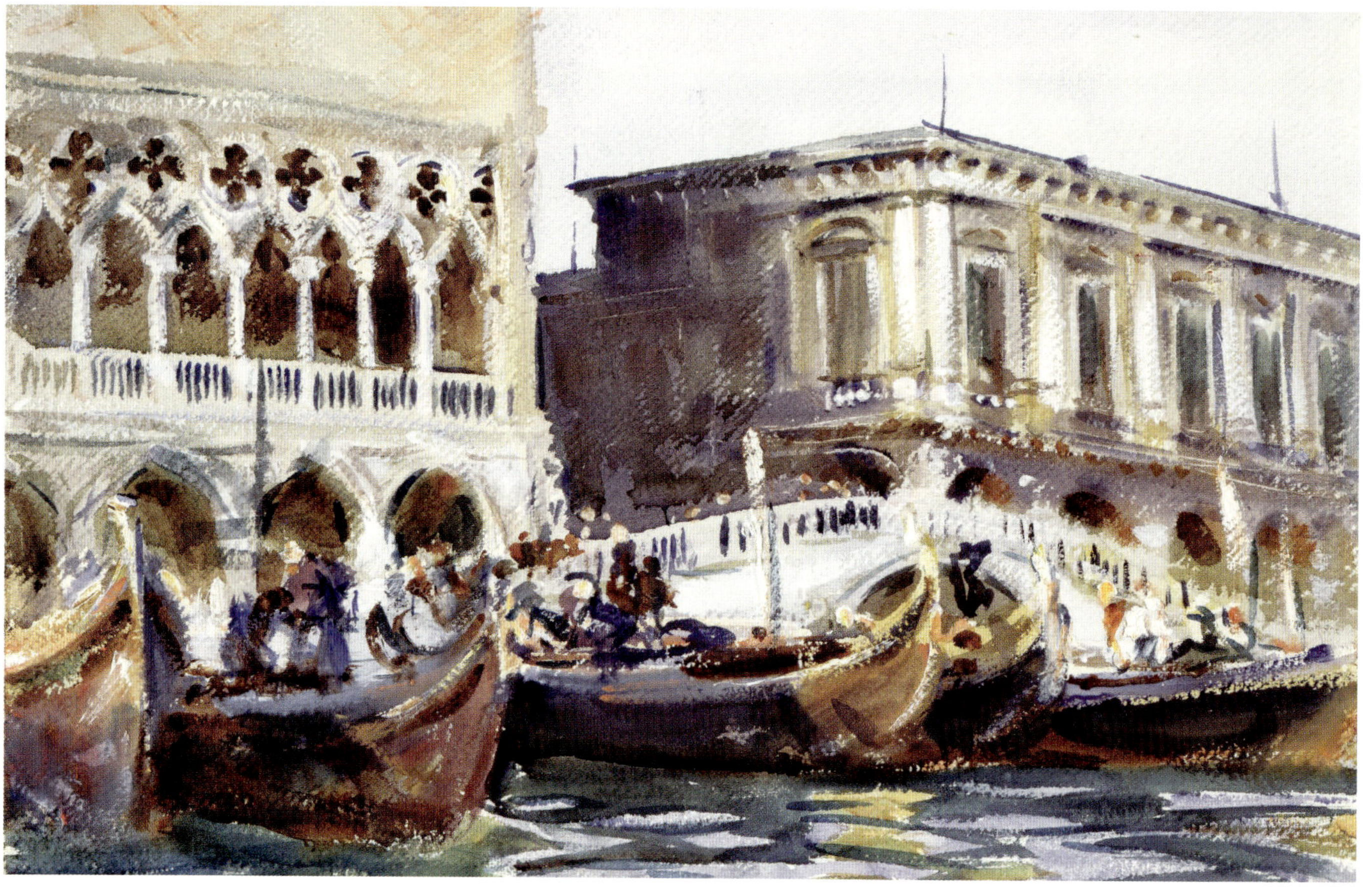

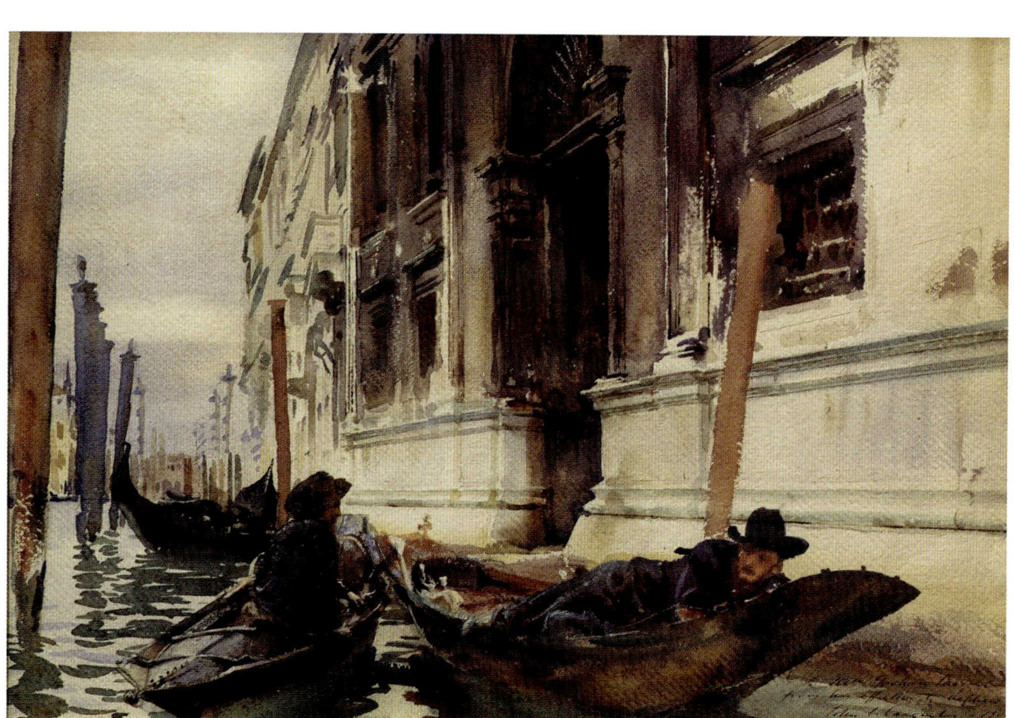

La Riva, c.1903–04, watercolour over graphite on paper, 35.6 x 50.9cm (14 x 20in), Brooklyn Museum, New York, USA

Simultaneously, Sargent painted two almost identical watercolours of this view. (see page 179). Painted from his gondola, he looked across the deep blue water of the lagoon, past moored gondolas and up to the Doge's Palace and the prison. Strong tonal contrasts and reflections project the unique atmosphere, with fairly dry and rapid brushwork, in translucent and opaque watercolours.

Gondoliers' Siesta, 1904, watercolour on paper, 50.8 x 35.6cm (20 x 14in), Private Collection

During September and October 1904, Sargent stayed in Venice where he continued to paint his surroundings with a fresh approach, creating a sense of immediacy and using his exceptional technical abilities. He spent much of the time painting and sketching outdoors, using rich colours to capture the autumn light. As with several of his Venetian views of this period, he painted directly from his gondola, so is almost level with the water.

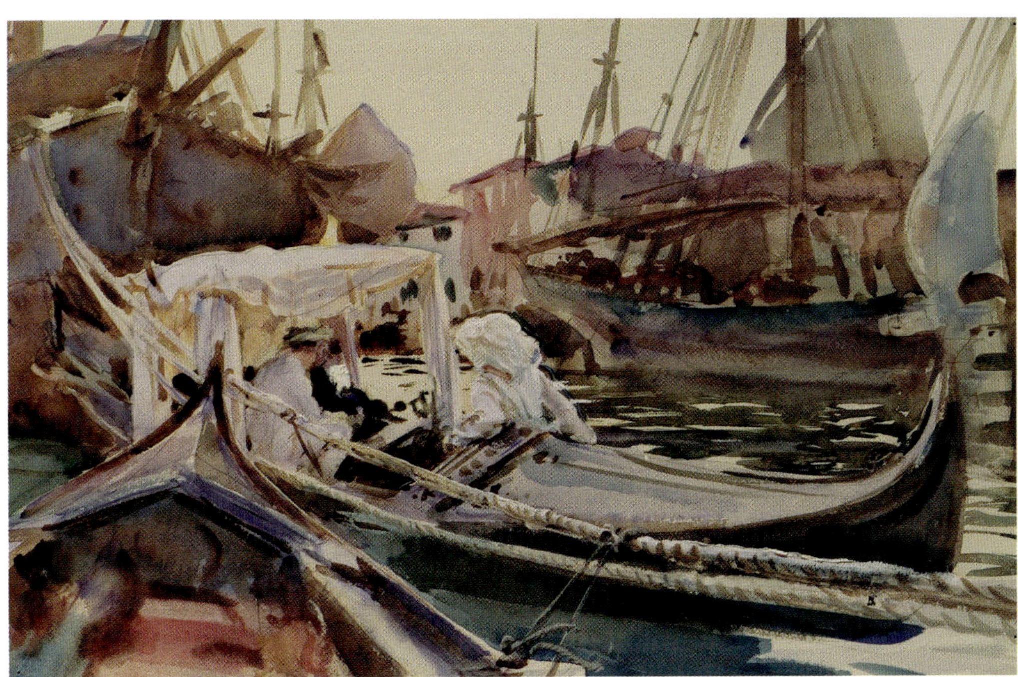

Sketching on the Giudecca, c.1904, watercolour over graphite on paper, 35.6 x 52.7cm (14 x 20¾in), Private Collection

Sargent followed Monet's idea of painting from a 'studio boat' by painting from a gondola when he was in Venice. (The Curtis family owned a gondola that he used when staying with them.) But Monet was inspired by Sargent when he visited the city eight years after this was painted; he was enraptured by the light, sky and the combination of water and ornate architecture.

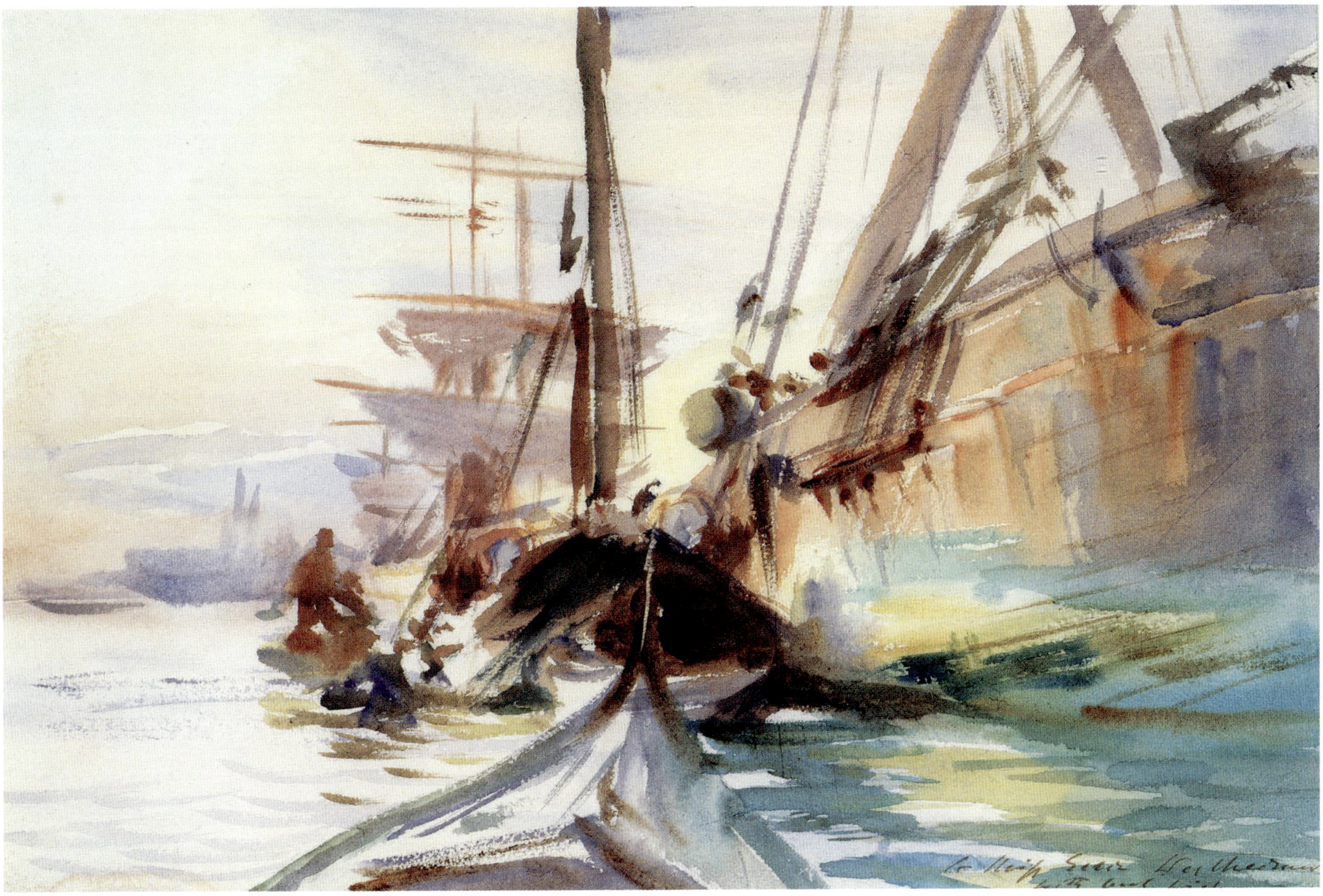

Unloading Boats in Venice, 1904, watercolour on paper, 25.4 x 35.3cm (10 x 14in), Private Collection

Sargent always arrived in Venice laden with his painting materials, and spent his time there painting en plein air. Reluctant to sell these personal works, he preferred to give them as gifts to his friends. He gave this to his friend Essie Wertheimer as a wedding gift. It is a rapidly painted, atmospheric image, created with fluid, mainly translucent colour, using the white of the paper to create sparkling highlights.

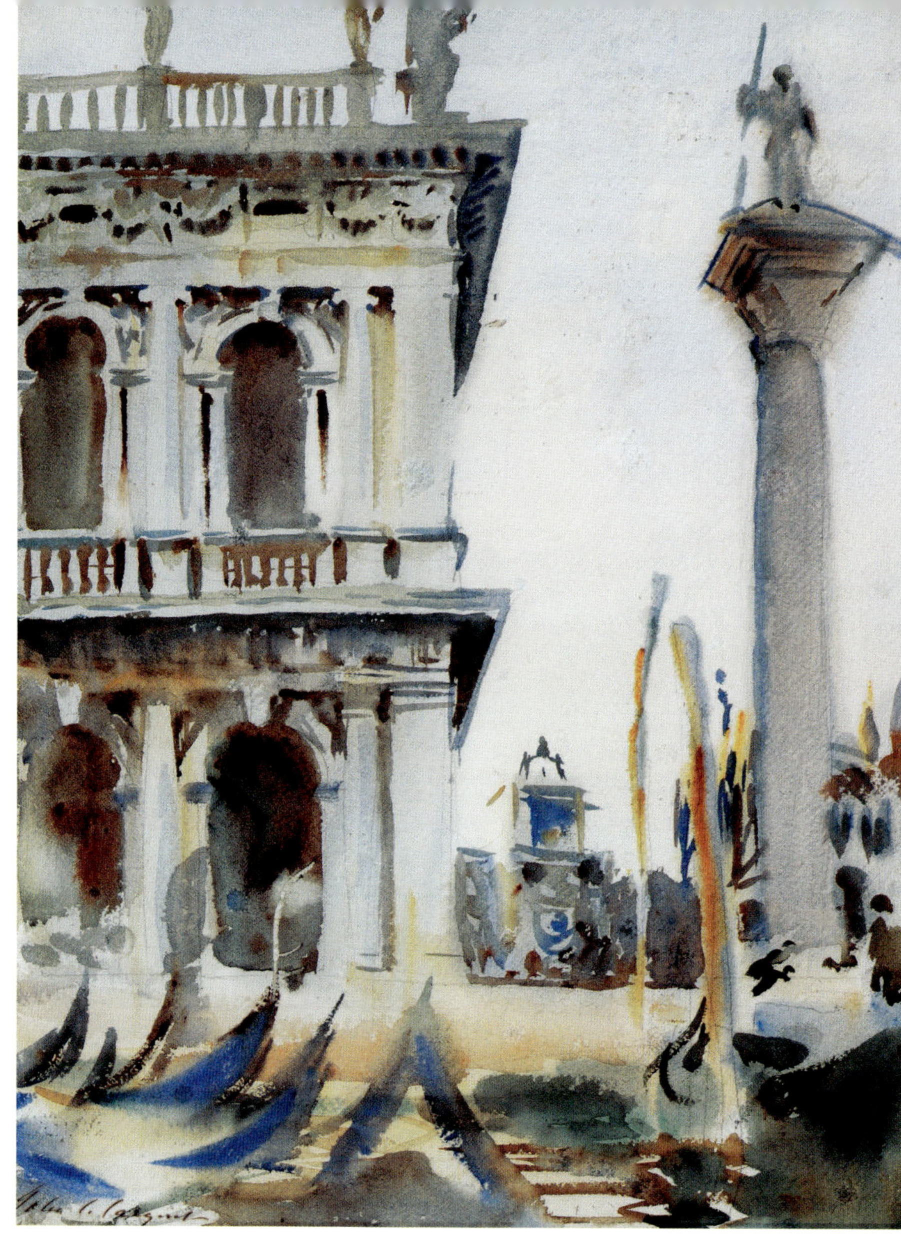

The Calle della Rosa with the Monte di Pietà, c.1904, watercolour over graphite on paper, 30.6 x 45.8cm (12 x 18in), The National Gallery of Art, Washington DC, USA

In dramatic perspective and low viewpoint, this scene represents a complete departure from Sargent's portraits where he was compelled to consider other people's wishes and opinions; this was clearly painted for his own pleasure. Using strong contrasts and quick, confident brushstrokes, he creates a sense of the gondola rocking gently as it nears its mooring.

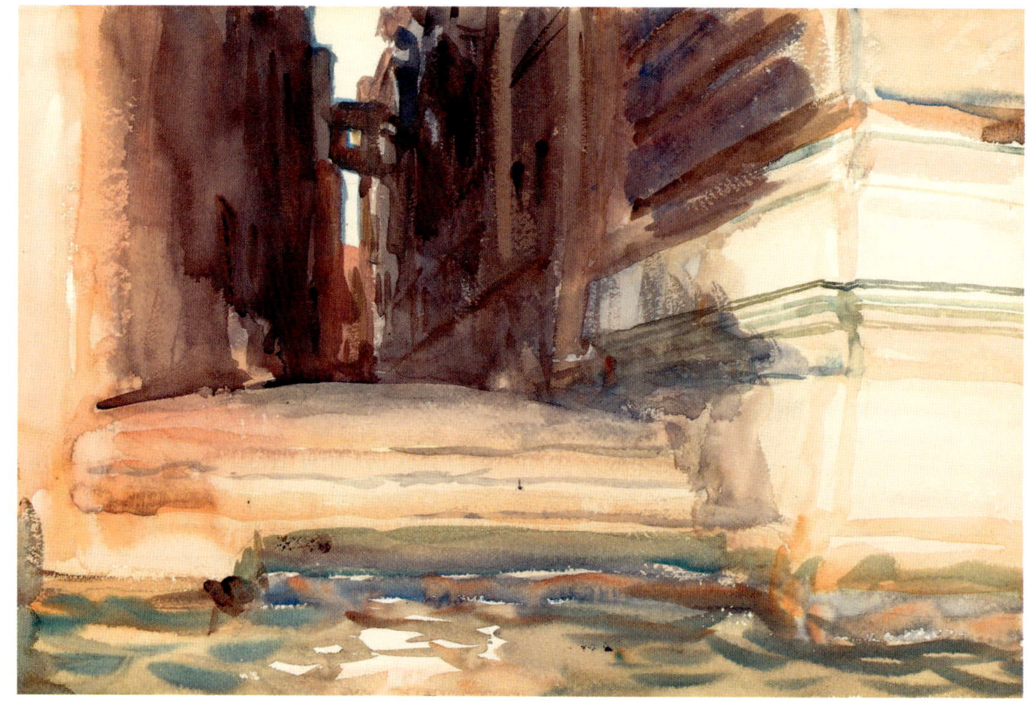

The Corner of the Libreria, with the Column of St. Theodore, Venice, 1904, translucent and opaque watercolour over graphite on paper, 49 x 34.3cm (19¼ x 13½in), Private Collection

Looking up from his gondola, Sargent depicts the open end of the Piazzetta that leads off St Mark's Square, with its large granite column bearing a statue of Saint Theodore, who was the patron saint of Venice before Saint Mark. The 'libreria' is the Biblioteca Nazionale Marciana; the imposing Renaissance building on the edge of the square, this aspect faces the lagoon.

Portrait of Lady Helen Vincent, Viscountess d'Abernon, 1904, oil on canvas, 158.8 x 108cm (62½ x 42½in), Birmingham Museum of Art, Birmingham, UK

In 1890, the beautiful daughter of an Earl, Helen Venetia Duncombe Vincent, Vicountess D'Abernon (1866–1954) married a handsome financier and diplomat, Sir Edgar Vincent (1857–1941). She soon after became a celebrated London hostess, socialite, diarist and a member of 'The Souls,' a salon of eminent intellectuals and statesmen, including Edith Wharton (1862–1937) and Henry James. Sargent painted her at her home on the Grand Canal, the Palazzo Giustiniani. The Grand Canal can be seen through the balustrade in the lower-left corner. As ever, Sargent celebrates physical beauty and his admiration of confident, intelligent females.

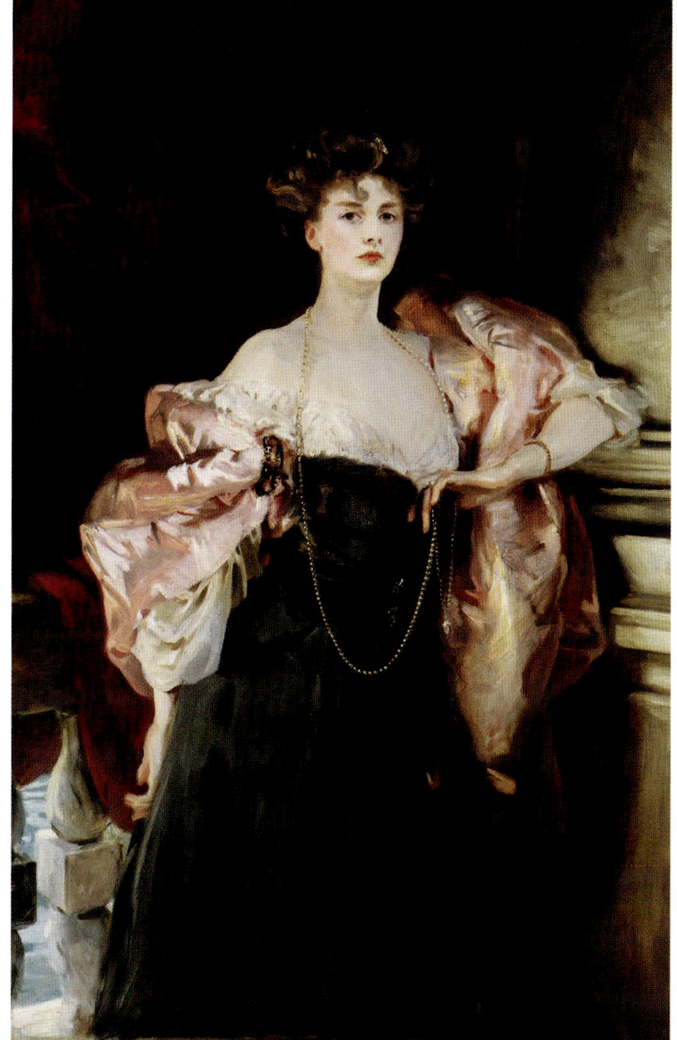

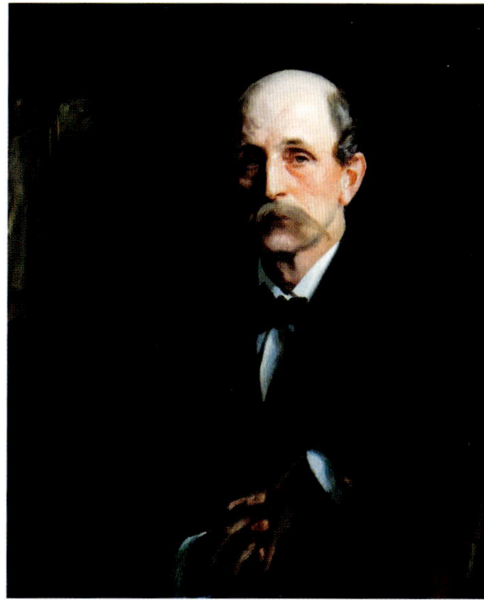

General Charles J. Paine, 1904, oil on canvas, 86.7 x 72.7cm (34 x 28½in), Museum of Fine Arts, Boston, Massachusetts, USA

General Charles Jackson Paine (1833–1916) was a railway executive, a general during the American Civil War and a yachtsman who won America's Cup races three times. Sargent painted the serious, highly respected gentleman in black on black.

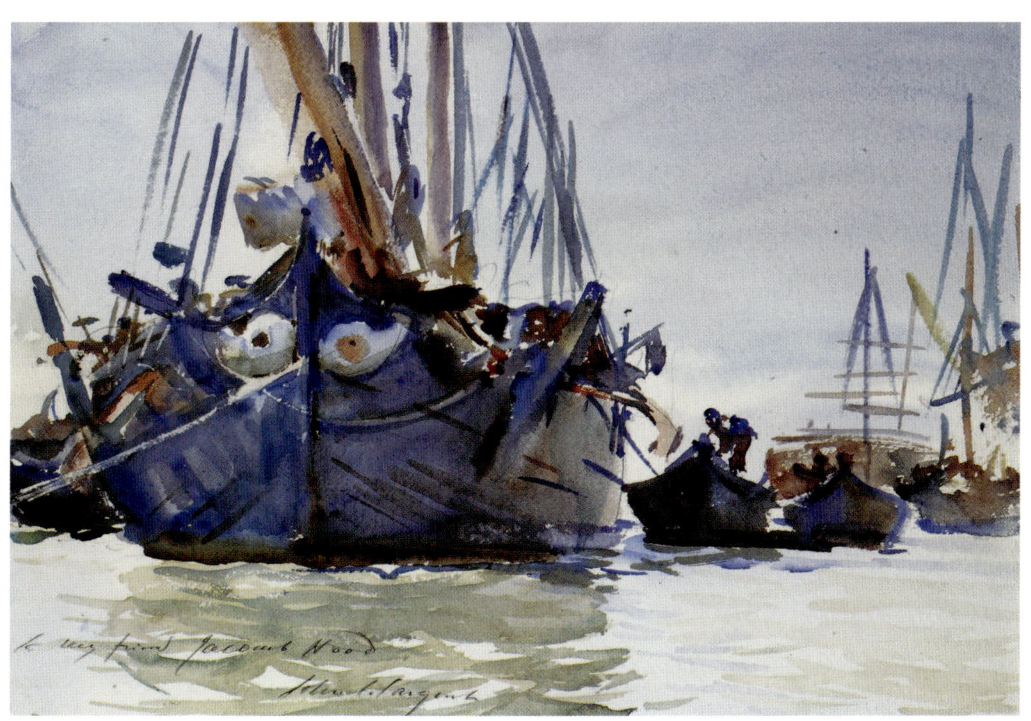

Italian Sailing Vessels at Anchor, c.1904, watercolour and graphite on paper, 35.2 x 50.3cm (13¾ x 19¾in), Private Collection

Leaving plenty of white paper showing through the richly-coloured translucent paint, Sargent expertly builds an impression of solid objects almost silhouetted against a bright, clear sky. Some elements of the rigging of the fishing boats drape and cross each other. With his light touch and understanding of blending, Sargent has made a fairly complex composition appear simple.

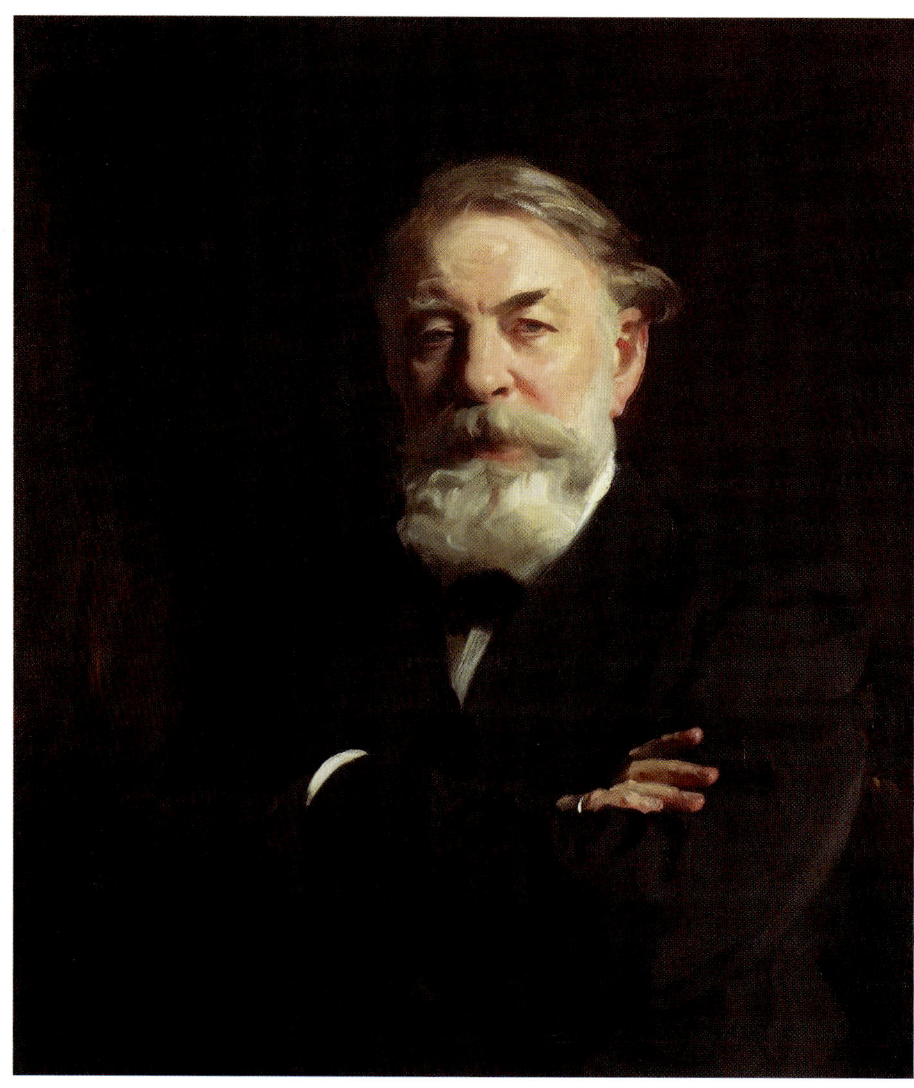

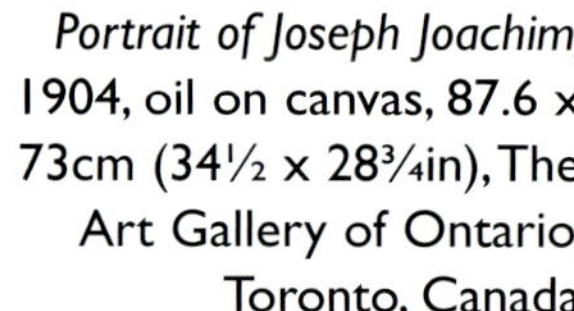

Portrait of Joseph Joachim, 1904, oil on canvas, 87.6 x 73cm (34½ x 28¾in), The Art Gallery of Ontario, Toronto, Canada

As a fairly accomplished musician himself, Sargent was particularly drawn to other musicians and Slovakian-born Joseph Joachim (1831–1907) is generally regarded as one of the finest violinists of his generation. His huge talents were first heard publicly when he was eight years old when he was sent to study in Vienna. Sargent created a powerful portrait expressing Joachim's strong presence.

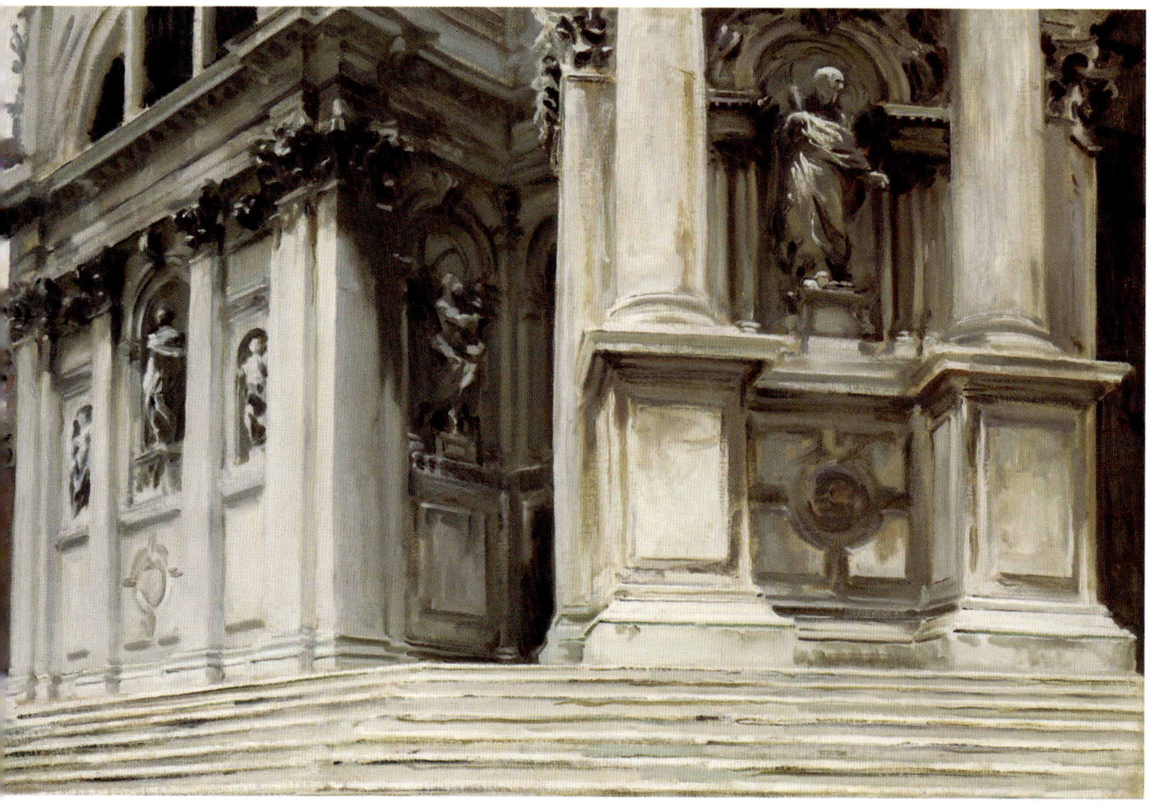

Santa Maria della Salute, Venice, 1904, transparent and opaque watercolour over graphite on paper, 46.2 x 58.4cm (18¼ x 23in), Brooklyn Museum, New York, USA

One of the most iconic buildings of Venice, the Santa Maria della Salute appears in several of Sargent's paintings, but never directly from the front or showing its entire façade. His Venetian views are created as snapshots, as it were; taken from various viewpoints, presenting the ambience of the place, its history and its contrasts. Here, his underdrawing is precisely rendered in careful straight lines overpainted with more rapidly applied washes.

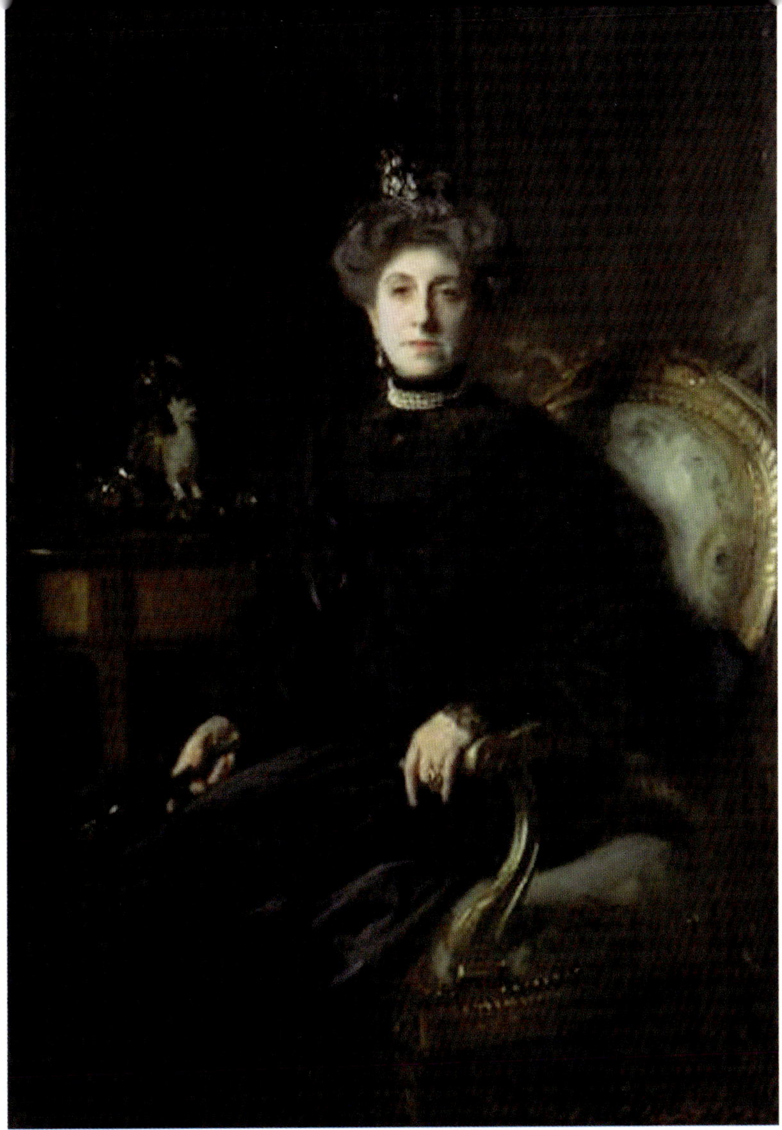

Mrs Wertheimer, 1904, oil on canvas, 163.2 x 107.9cm (64¼ x 42½in), Tate, London, UK

Sargent dined weekly with the Wertheimer family in London. Asher Wertheimer was a prominent art dealer and Mrs Wertheimer (née Flora Joseph) was the daughter of another successful art dealer. Because she did not like the first painting he had made of her in 1898, to celebrate the couple's silver wedding anniversary, six years later, Sargent painted this second portrait of her, which everyone admired.

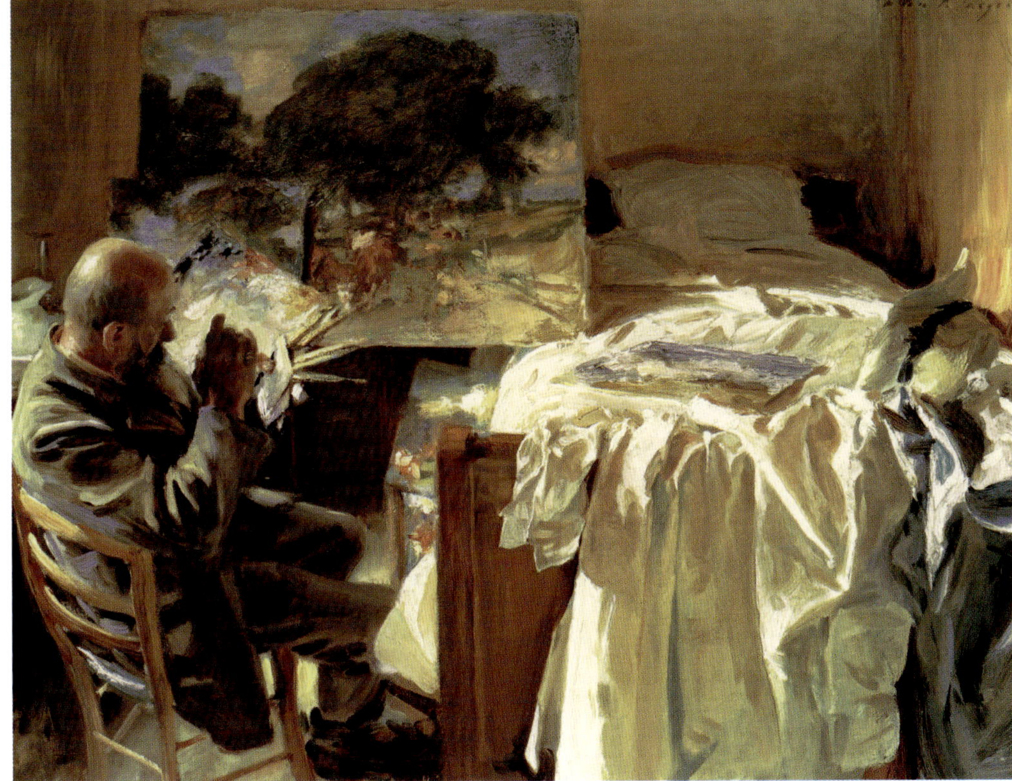

An Artist in his Studio, 1904, oil on canvas, 56.2 x 72.1cm (22 x 28¼in), Museum of Fine Arts, Boston, Massachusetts, USA

While staying at Purtud in the Italian Alps, Sargent's friend, the artist Ambroglio Raffele, used his hotel room as a studio. Sargent painted Raffele here, working on a landscape. With smaller sketches around him, Raffele holds a palette and several brushes, and perhaps a photograph of the view he is the process of painting. Using his accomplished loose brushwork, Sargent captured the clutter and disorder of the room, such as Raffele's straw hat and shirt tossed on his unmade bed.

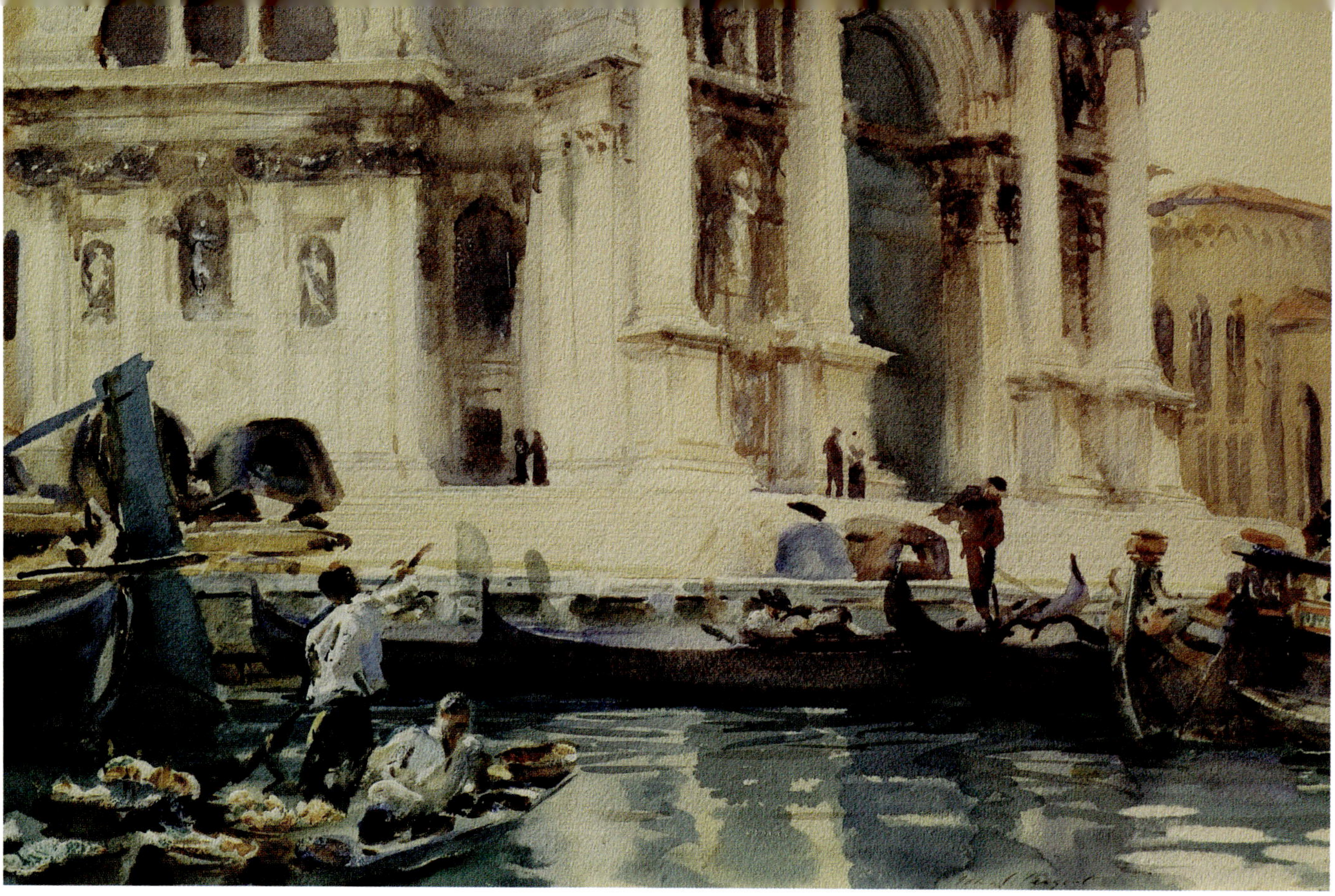

On the Steps of the Salute,
c.1904–06, watercolour
on paper, 35.6 x 52.7cm (14
x 20¾in), Private Collection

Sargent painted a total of 12 watercolours and three oils of of the Basilica della Salute on the Grand Canal. As with many of his Venetian paintings from this period, he painted directly from his gondola, never tiring of the play of light and colour on the Baroque façade in front of him. He found watercolour eminently practical, using water diretly from the canal and softening edges with a sponge dipped into the canal.

Doorway of a Venetian Palace,
c.1904–09, watercolour
on paper, 58.4 x 45.7cm
(23 x 18in), Westmoreland
Museum of American Art,
Philadelphia, USA

Employing a palette of predominantly ochre and ultramarine, Sargent applied minimal marks to convey the bright sunlight bleaching out areas of the façades of this Venetian palazzo and vivid reflections in the swirling water lapping around its steps and mooring posts. As with most of his views of Venice at this time, he painted this from his gondola, hence the low viewpoint.

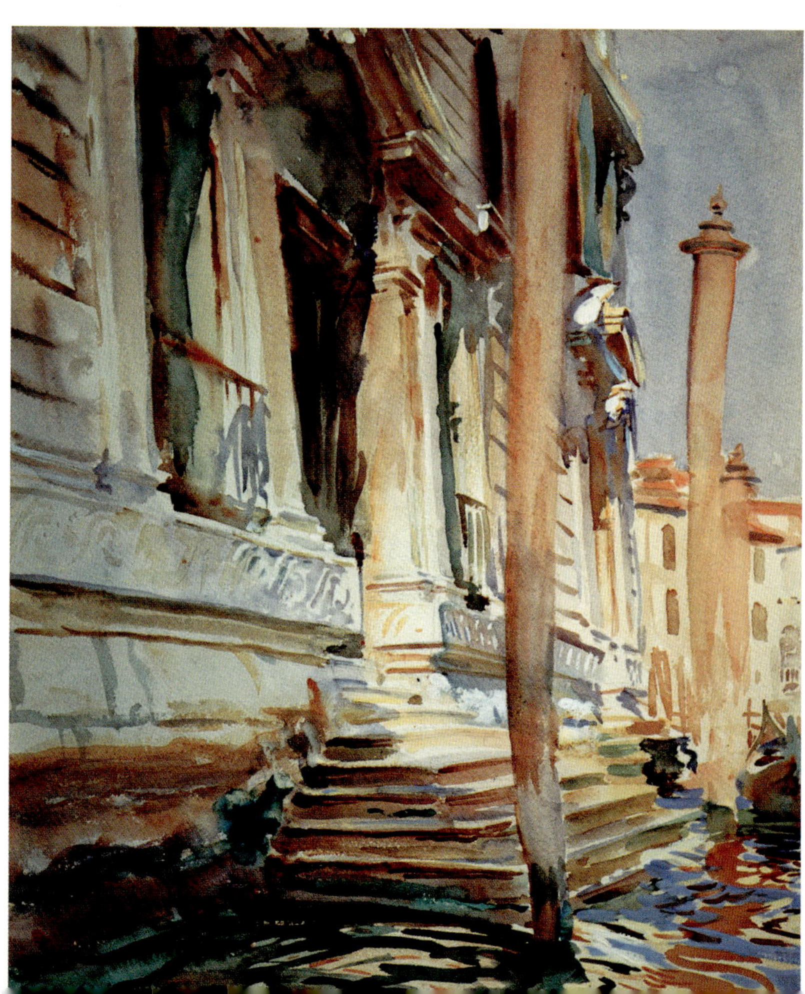

Reclining Figures, David in Saul's Camp, c.1905, charcoal on paper, 47.5 x 62cm (18¾ x 24½in), Museum of Fine Arts, Boston, Massachusetts, USA

Possibly made during Sargent's visit to Syria and Palestine in November 1905, to research ideas for his Boston Public Library Murals, this drawing relates to the grisaille painting on page 158. It illustrates the Old Testament story of King Saul putting David in charge of his army after the boy had killed Goliath. However, when David proved his courage and strength, he became more popular than the king, arousing Saul's jealousy.

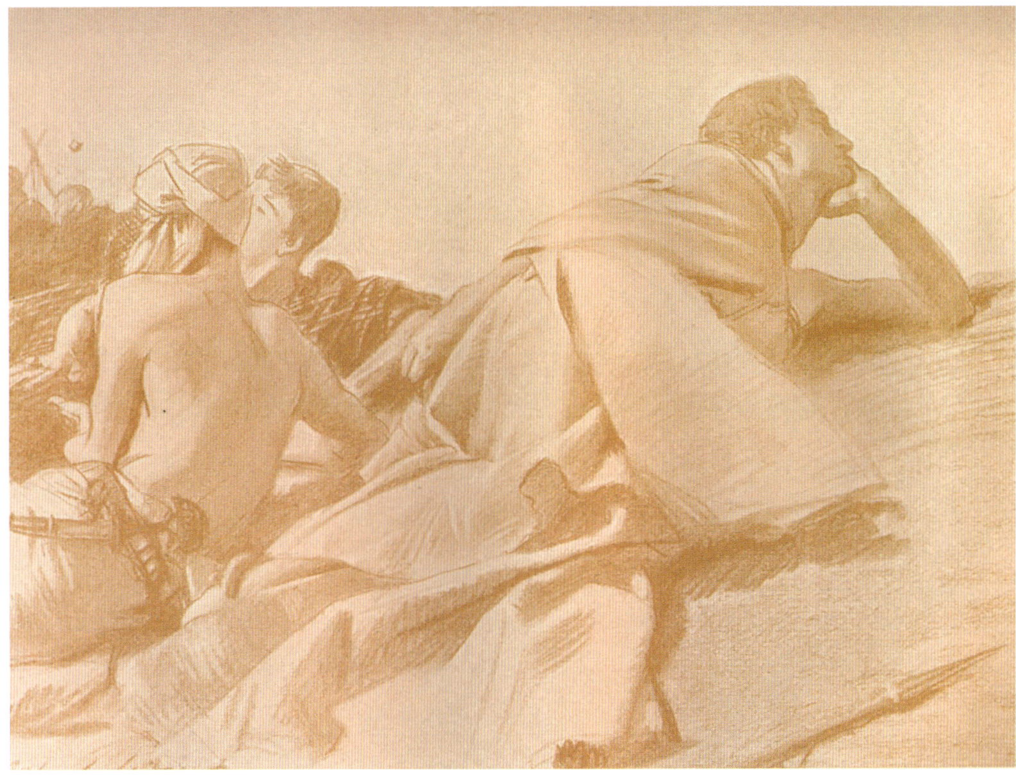

Padre Sebastiano, 1905, oil on canvas, 56.5 x 71.1cm (22¼ x 28in), The Metropolitan Museum, New York, USA

Father Sebastiano was a young priest whom Violet met while they were on holiday in the Italian Alps, and the painting is a departure from Sargent's usual type of portrait. The young priest was fascinated by nature and Sargent painted him as he pauses for a moment to consider while making notes about the alpine plants he had collected, and that are strewn all over the table in his hotel room.

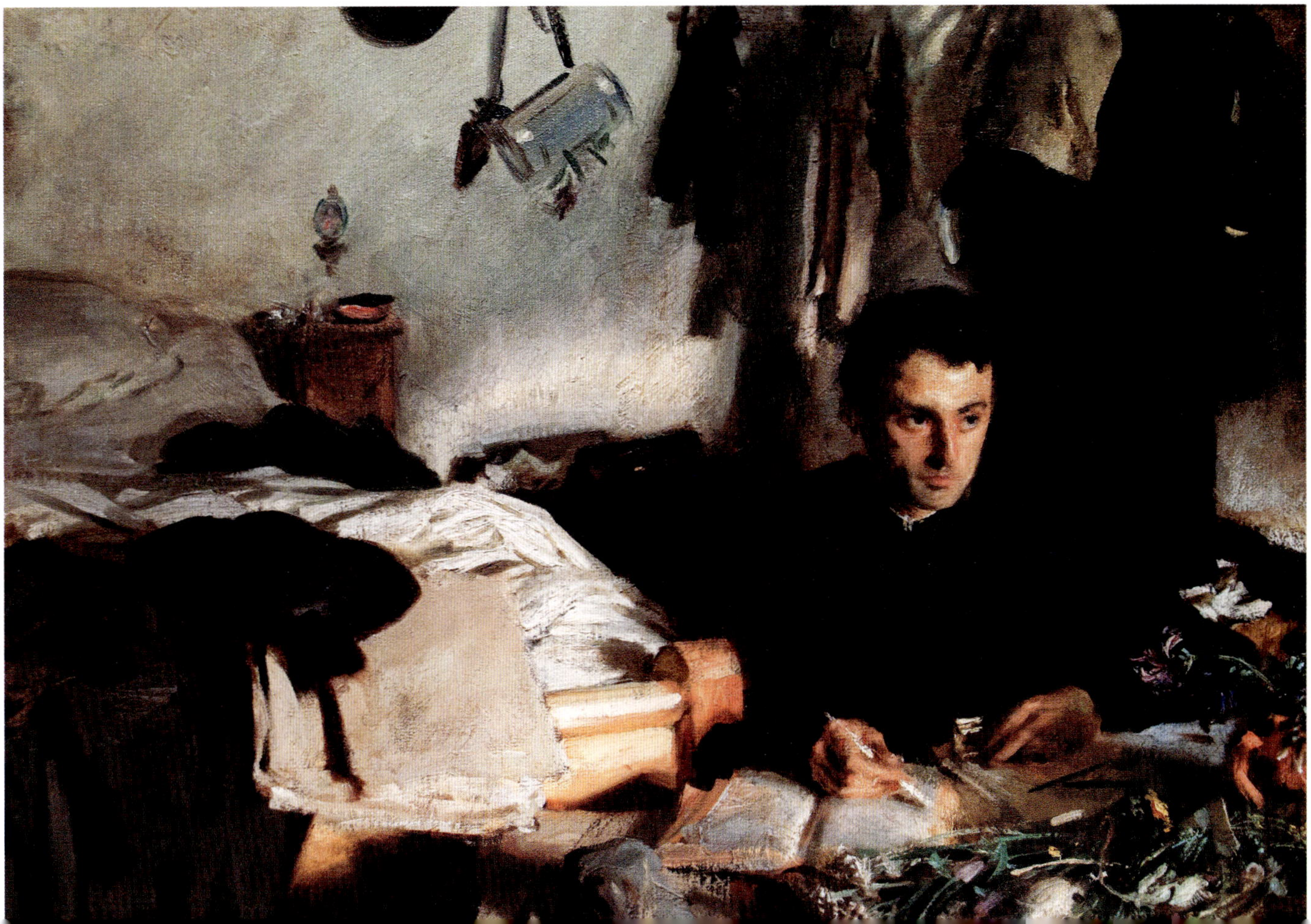

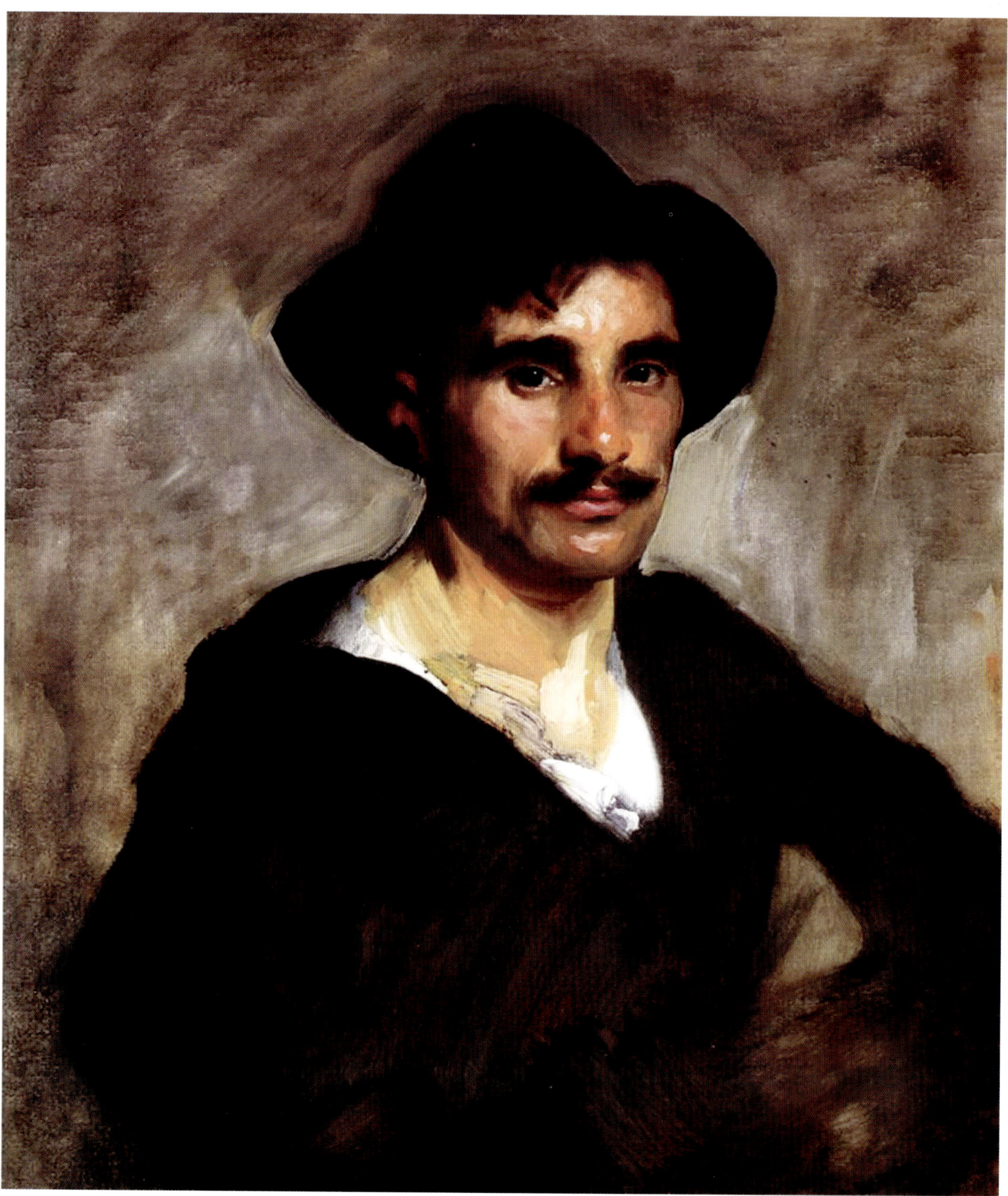

Gondolier, 1905, oil on canvas, 55.9 x 71cm (28 x 22in), Private Collection

Even when Sargent was painting portraits of strangers, he employed the same method, beginning with a few quick lines in charcoal to capture the anatomy of the face. Then he wiped the canvas lightly with a rag and applied some turpentine-thinned marks to capture mid-tones, and finally, he painted the entire work, constantly measuring tonal values. Through his natural, intuitive application of paint, this sketchy-looking portrait grabs the attention, following Romanticist and Realist loose brushwork and dramatic chiaroscuro.

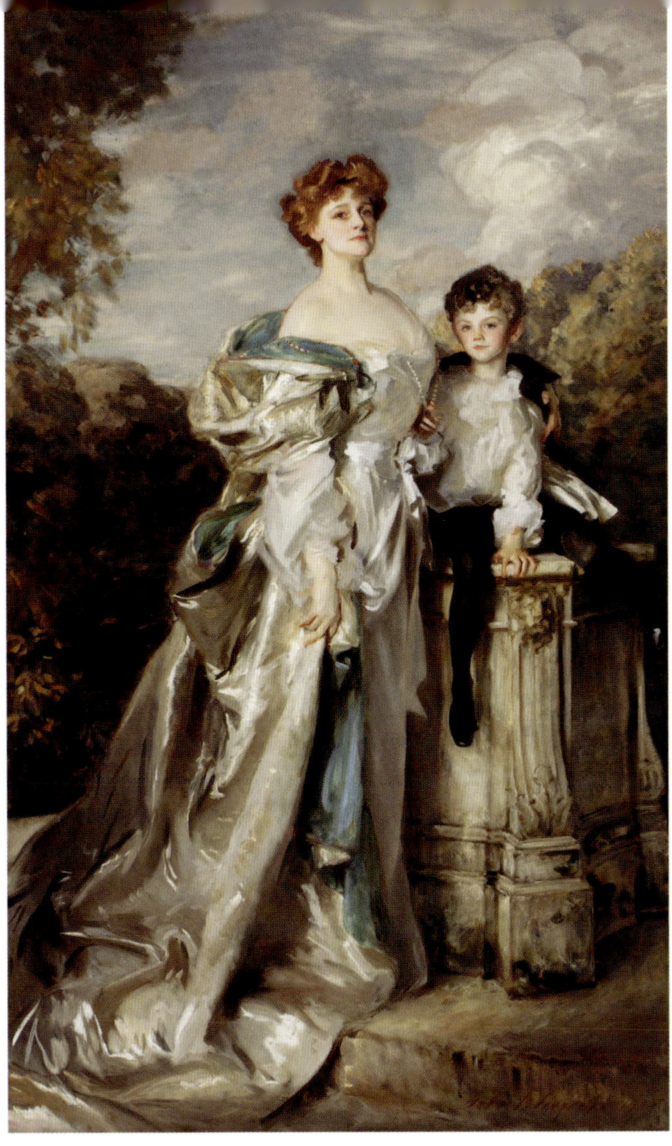

Lady Warwick and her Son, 1905, oil on canvas, 270.5 x 153cm (106½ x 60¼in), Worcester Art Museum, Massachusetts, USA

On her marriage to the 5th Earl of Warwick in 1881, Daisy Greville (1861–1938) became the notorious Countess of Warwick. A socialite, philanthropist and socialist, she had five children, but not all by her husband. Among her many lovers was the Prince of Wales. She was a major donor to the Social Democratic Federation and she was nearly imprisoned for her romantic indiscretions.

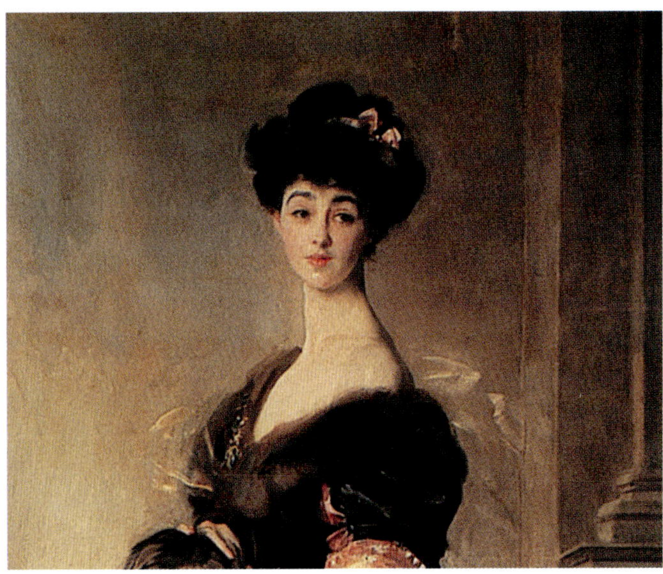

The 9th Duchess of Marlborough, 1905, oil on canvas, entire portrait: 332.7 x 238.8cm (131 x 94in), Blenheim Palace, Oxfordshire, UK

A detail from a vast canvas (see page 65) depicting the American heiress Consuelo Vanderbilt (1877–1964), 9th Duchess of Marlborough, her first husband Charles Spencer-Churchill, 9th Duke of Marlborough and their two sons. Ending in divorce, her unhappy marriage epitomized a loveless union of the era; entered into for money on one side, status on the other.

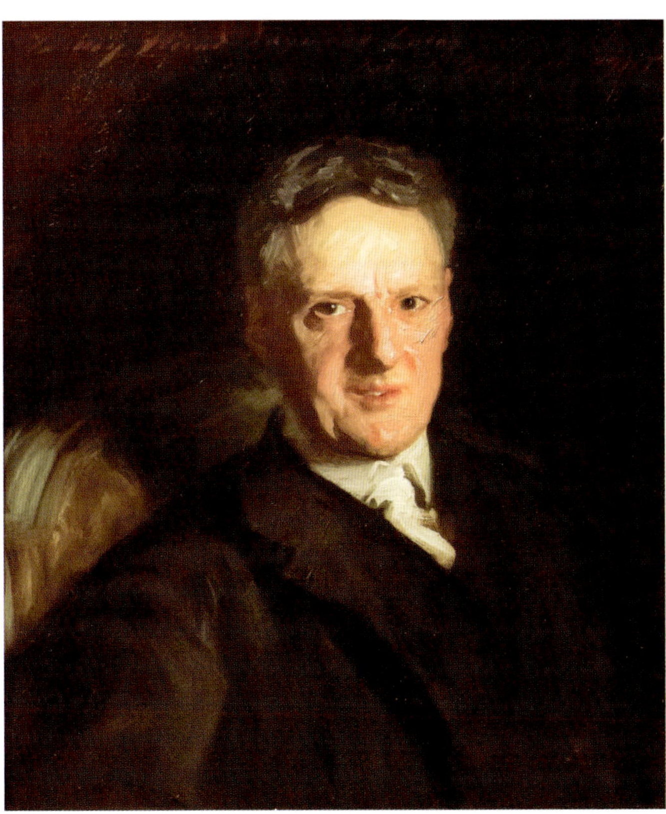

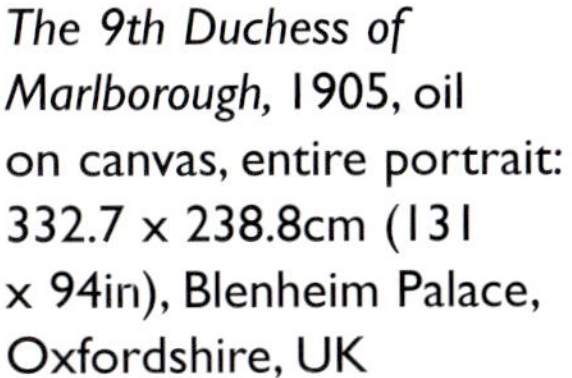

John Seymour Lucas, 1905, oil on canvas, 69.8 x 54.9cm (27 x 21½in), The National Portrait Gallery, London, UK

Although not a particular friend, Sargent inscribed his portrait of the English painter John Seymour Lucas (1849–1923) with the words: 'to my friend.' It is possible that the artists painted each other in a friendly exercise. When the painting was exhibited at the New Gallery in London in 1906, it was highly praised, for instance, an article in *The Spectator* included: 'the construction of the head shows the hand of a master.'

Bedouins, 1905–06, opaque and translucent watercolour on paper, 45.7 x 30.5cm (18 x 12in), Brooklyn Museum, New York, USA

By 1905, Sargent wrote to a friend that he was seeking 'new fuel for the murals.' For a while in Palestine, he travelled and lived with a Bedouin tribe, producing this and several other watercolours that are a direct record of desert life. Here, using vivid blue and allowing the white of the paper to suggest the strong sunlight, Sargent creates a powerful portrait of two Bedouin figures evocatively swathed in their kaffiyeh – traditional headscarves.

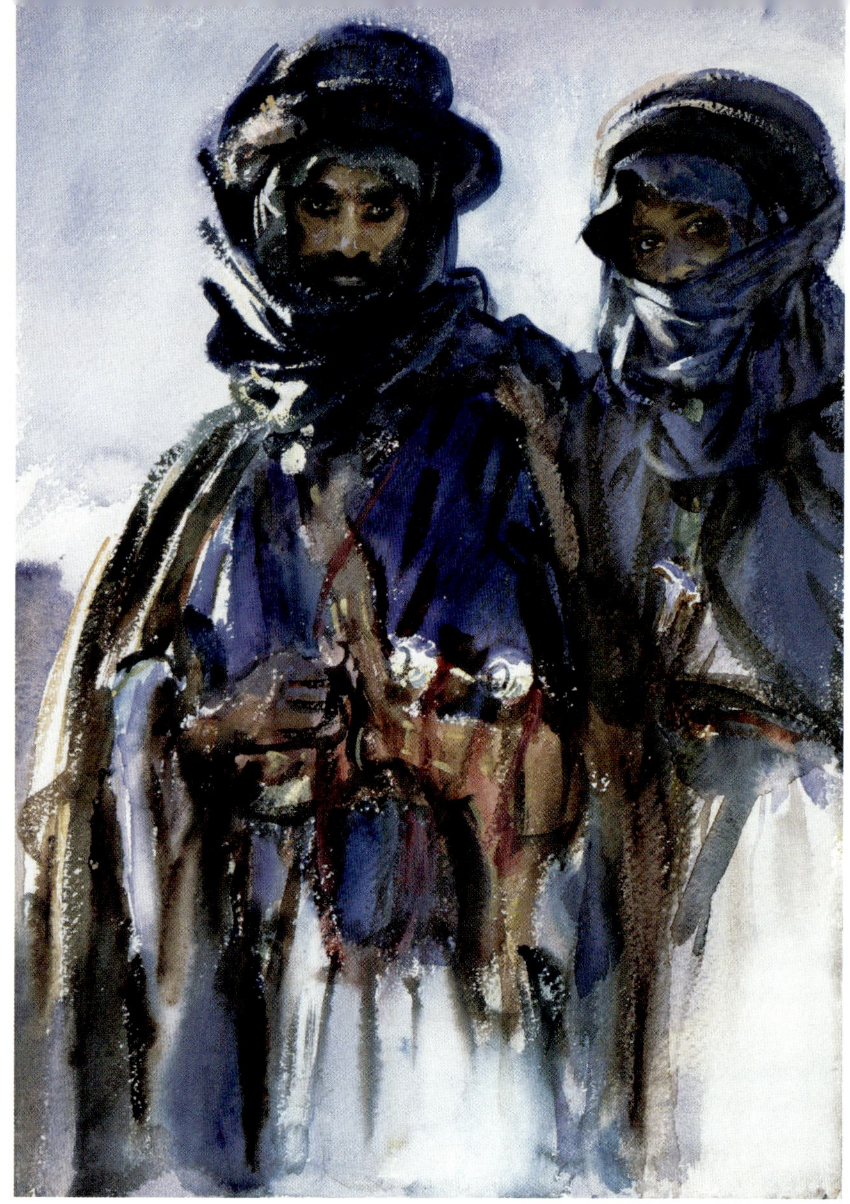

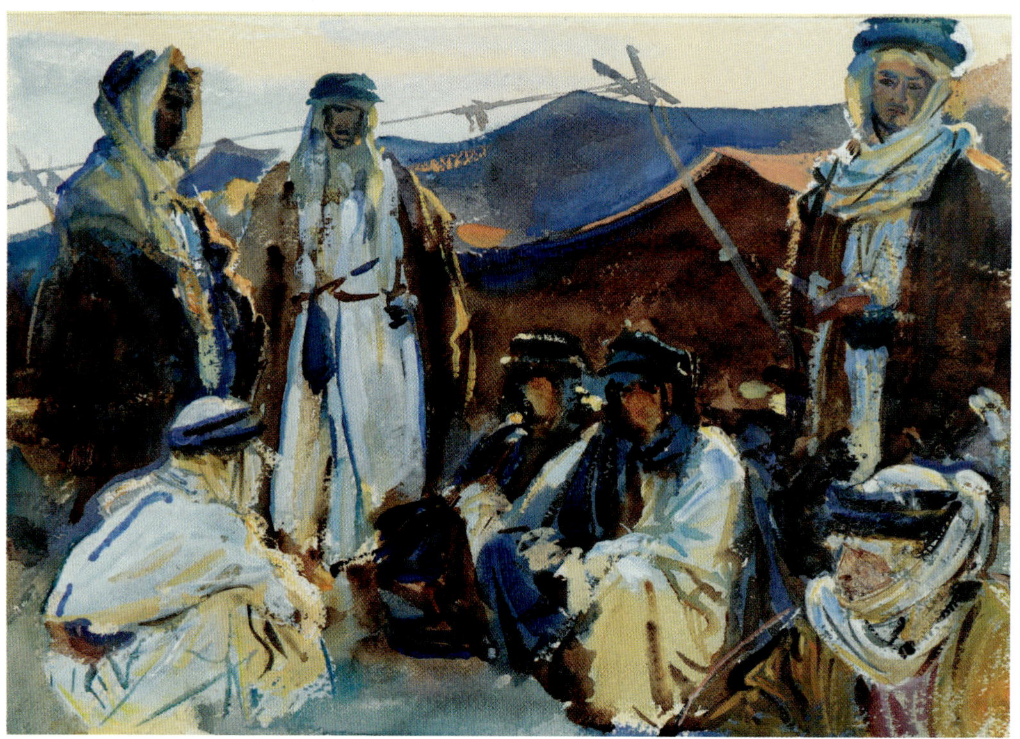

Bedouin Camp, 1905–06, opaque and translucent watercolour on paper, 25.4 x 35.7cm (10 x 14in), Brooklyn Museum, New York, USA

Using ochre and ultramarine almost exclusively, frequently as it came undiluted straight from the tube, Sargent directly observed this group of Bedouins outside their tent in the late afternoon. He used some dry brush and some wet-into-wet paint, with opaque zinc white in places to create highlights. He manages to convey a complex range of underlying feelings, including pride, curiosity and shyness.

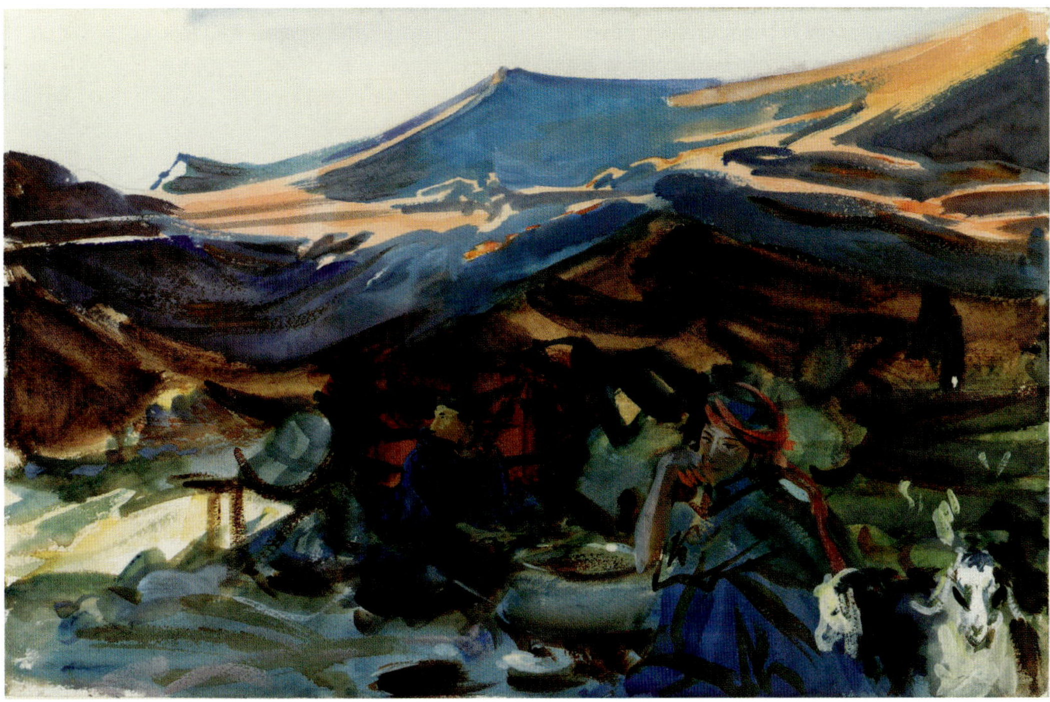

Bedouin Women, 1905–06, opaque and translucent watercolour over graphite on paper, 30.5 x 45.9cm (12 x 18in), Brooklyn Museum, New York, USA

Sargent spent some time living with this Bedouin tribe, observing, painting and drawing them. This is a particularly sketchy watercolour, made from his standing position, looking down into a tent where a group of Bedouin figures and a goat rest in the shade, away from the sweltering sun. In the distance, the glowing landscape stretches away dramatically.

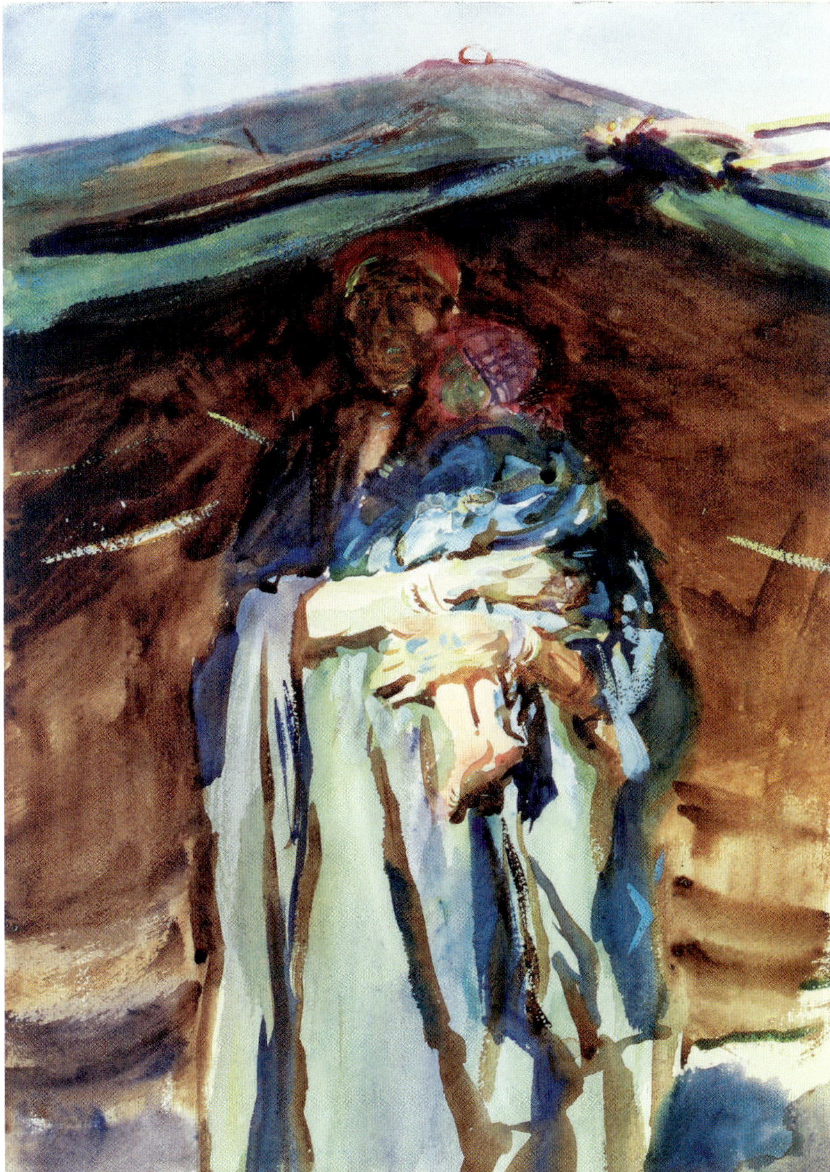

Bedouin Mother, 1905–06, opaque and translucent watercolour over graphite on paper, 45.9 x 30.5cm (18 x 12in), Brooklyn Museum, New York, USA

Using powerful chiaroscuro, Sargent painted this young Bedouin mother holding her baby in the shade of a tent. Both their faces are obscured in shadow, while her hands and the baby's feet are bathed in brilliant sunlight. Although details are kept to a minimum, Sargent still conveyed the people and place. The top of the green tent can be seen, and a suggestion of the landscape in the misty distance.

Black Tent, 1905–06, opaque and translucent watercolour on paper, 30.5 x 46cm (12 x 18in), Brooklyn Museum, New York, USA

With a reduced palette and some dry-brushed areas which allow areas of the paper to shine through as highlights, Sargent has created a glowing, soft image, conveying the sense that dusk is falling, bathing everything in ultramarine and cobalt blue.

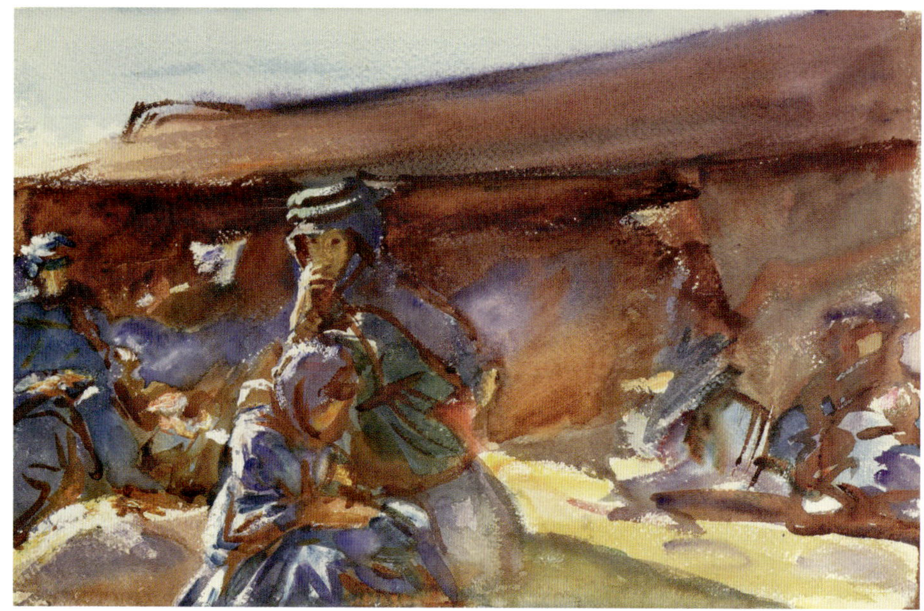

Lake Tiberias, 1906, watercolour on paper, 25.4 x 35.5cm (10 x 14in), Private Collection

By December 1905, Sargent was staying at Tiberias in Israel near the Sea of Galilee. Although he had high expectations of finding material for his murals, he was not inspired by what he saw and wrote to a friend that he had found some new material, but it was not what he wanted. This was one of the watercolour studies he made.

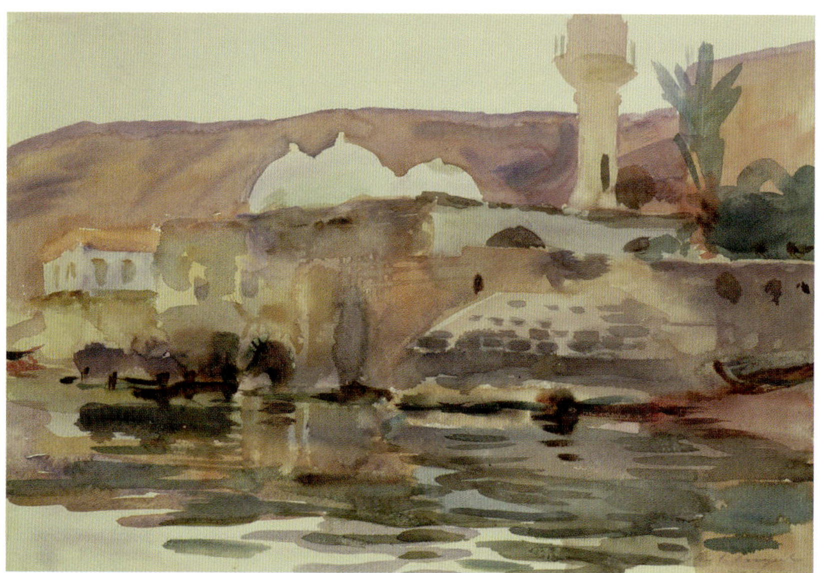

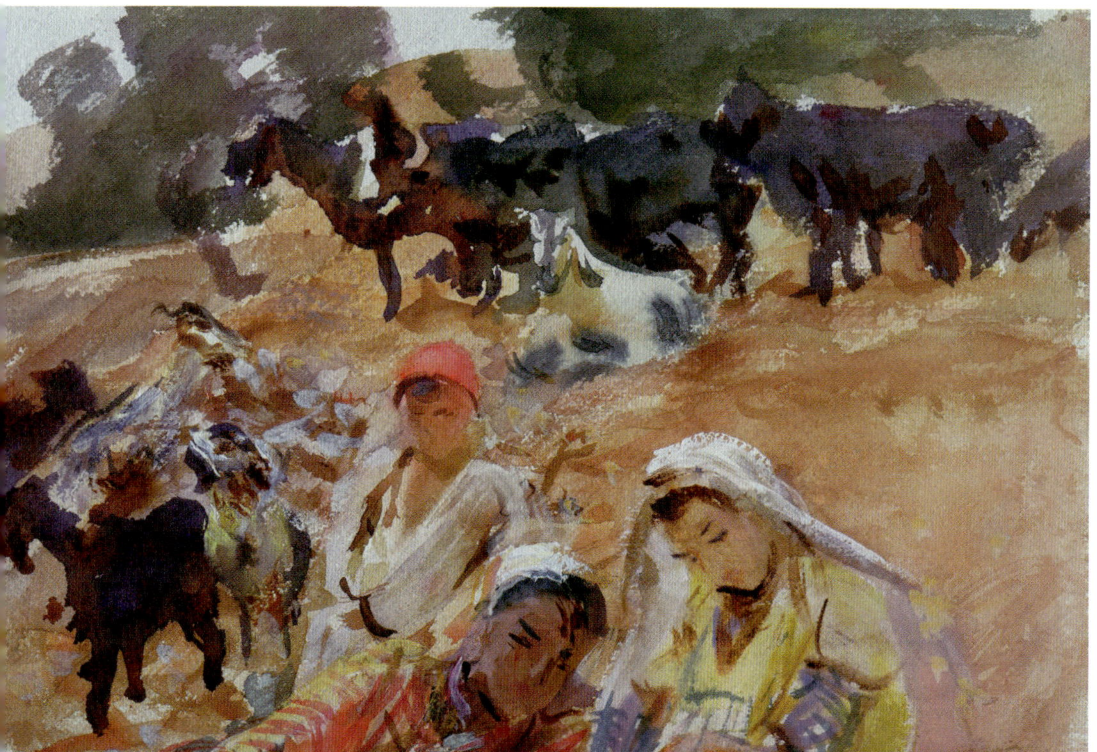

Goatherds, 1905–06, opaque and translucent watercolour over graphite on paper, 25.4 x 35.6cm (10 x 14in), Brooklyn Museum, New York, USA

This loosely rendered image was painted in Syria, and was part of Sargent's research for his painting of the biblical story of the Sermon on the Mount for his Boston Public Library murals. Reflecting the light and colours around him, for this and for several other paintings in Syria, he used a brighter palette than usual.

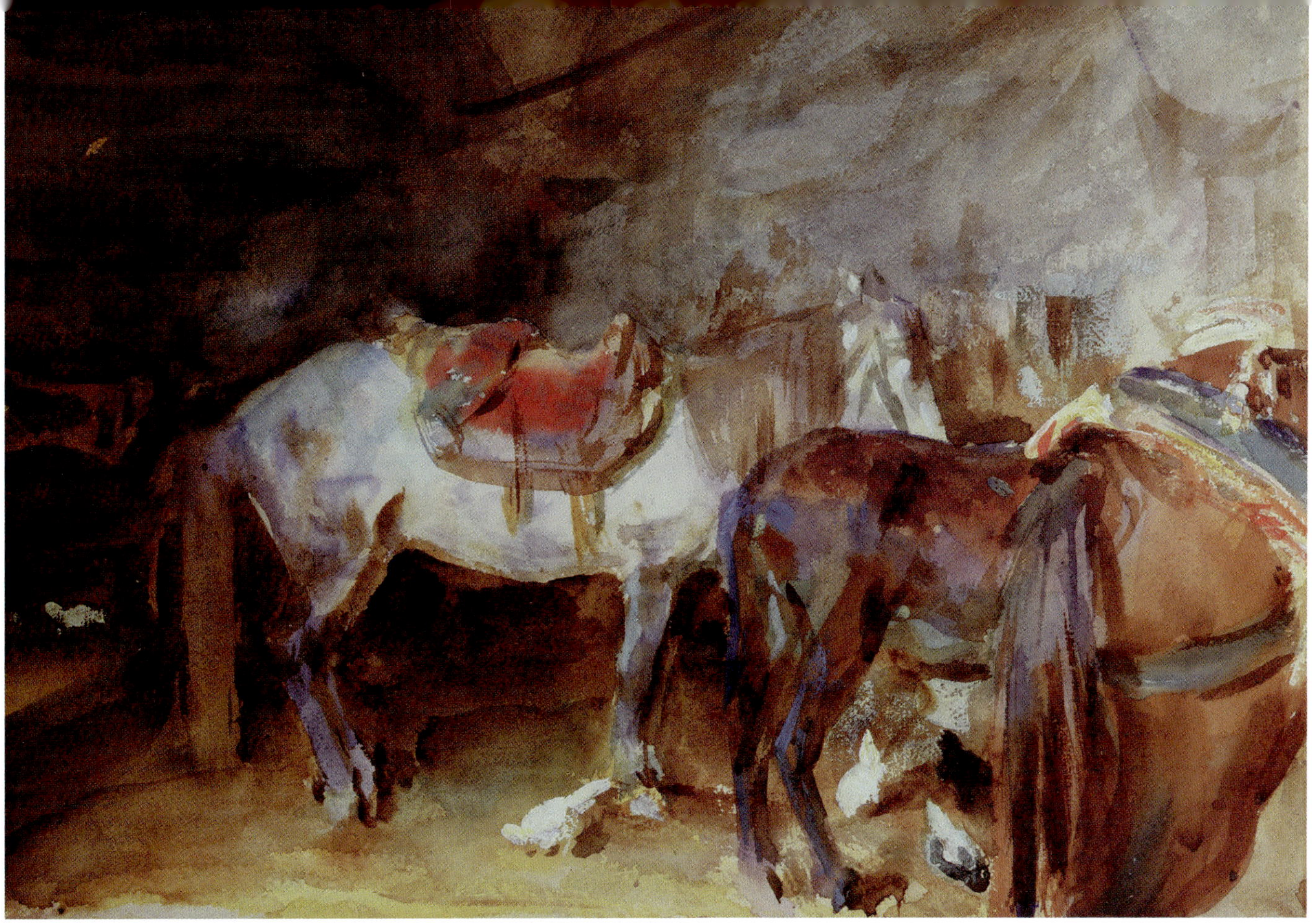

Arab Stable, 1905–06, opaque and translucent **watercolour on paper, 26.5 x 36.5cm (10½ x 14¼in), Brooklyn Museum, New York, USA**

Areas of coloured wash juxtaposed with bold colours create a convincing scene of the interior of a cave used as a stable in the hills of Galilee. In a letter to Isabella Stewart Gardner, Sargent wrote of the cobalt blue on the backs of the horses: 'They ought to have blue ribands plaited into their tails and manes, like Herod's horses in Flaubert's beautiful Herodiade.'

Arab Gypsies in a Tent, 1905–06, translucent and opaque watercolour on paper, 30.5 x 45.7cm (12 x 18in), Brooklyn Museum, New York, USA

Painted from an intimate perspective, all the figures in this composition are situated in the foreground. Unlike some of his other paintings of Bedouins however (see pages 192–193), they do not seem curious or even slightly interested in the artist, some even look away. They appear to be in their low-ceilinged tent, busy with their own lives, ignoring the artist scrutinizing them. Patches of white suggest dappled light piercing the tent.

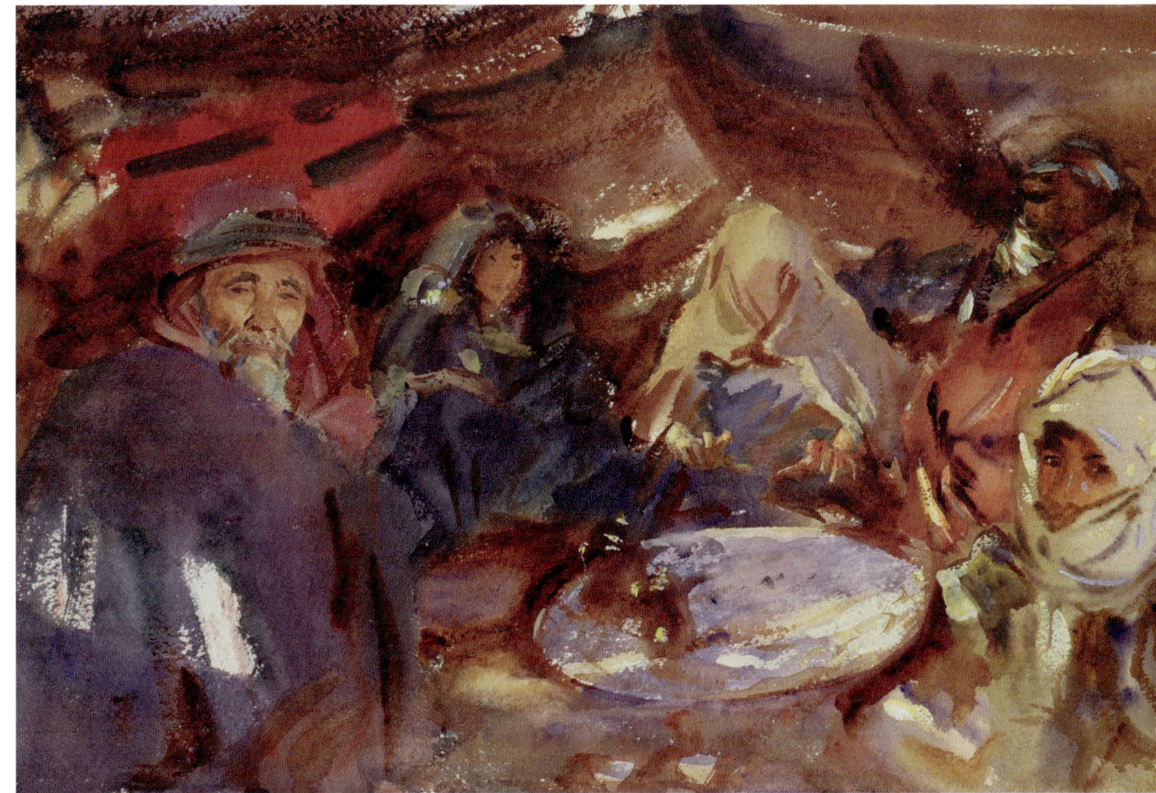

Rigging, c.1905–08, translucent and opaque watercolour over graphite on paper, 28.7 x 45.9cm (11¼ x 18in), Brooklyn Museum, New York, USA

Although this has been painted primarily with translucent watercolour, areas of it resemble the dense opacity of oil paints, as Sargent squeezed some of the paint directly on to his paper from the tube. The boat and the building behind are painted with fluid brushwork, capturing both the complex spatial architecture and the atmosphere of the location.

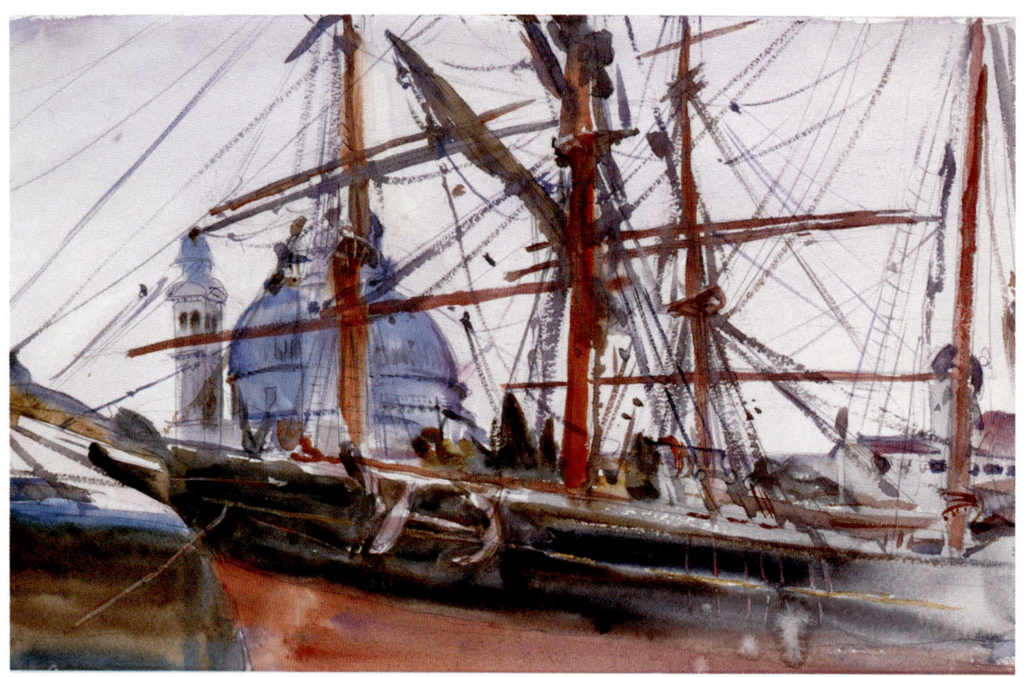

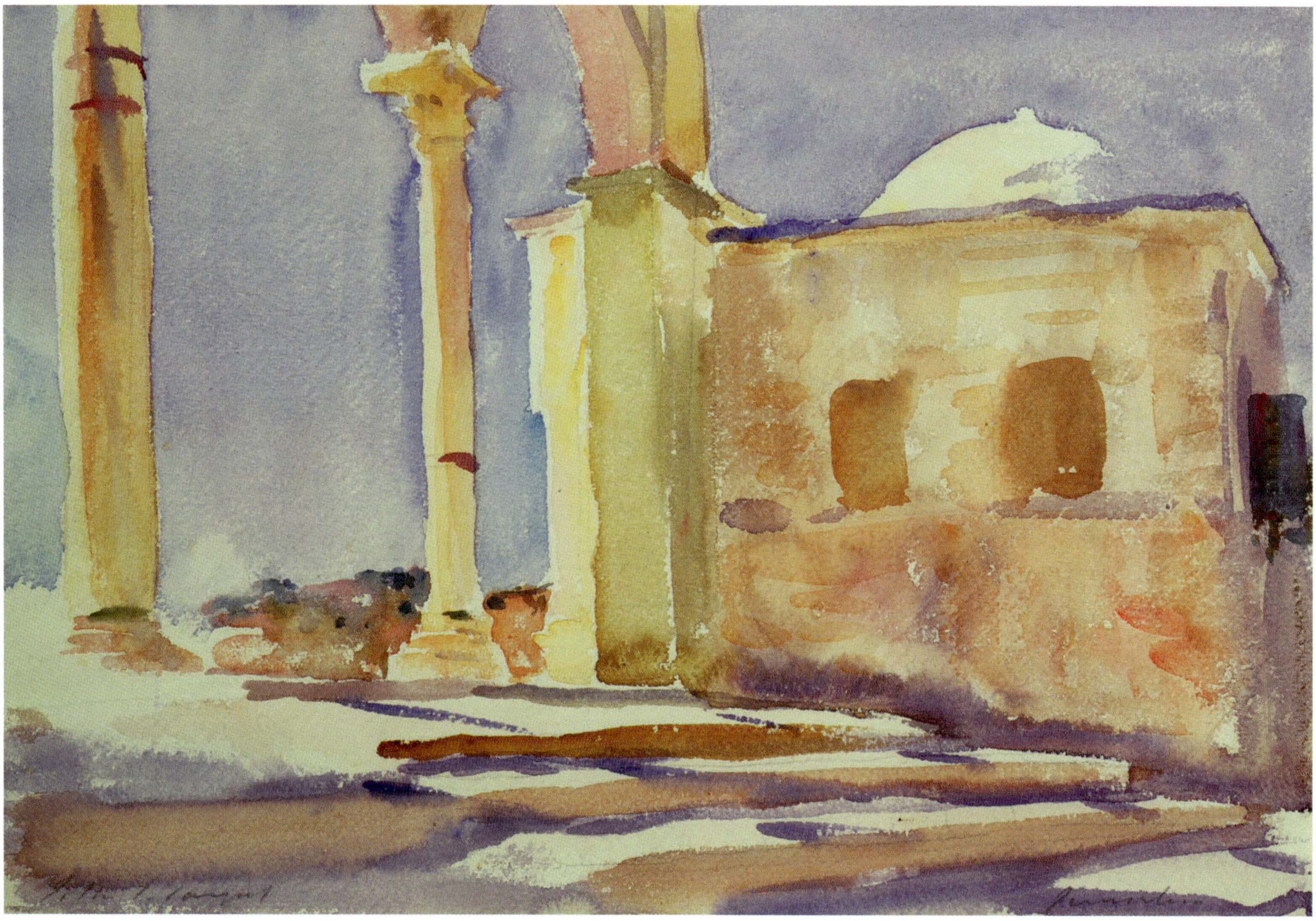

Dome of the Rock, c.1906, watercolour on paper, 25.4 x 35.5cm (10 x 14in), Private Collection

In January of 1906, Sargent travelled to Tiberias and to Jerusalem, continuing to seek material. In Jerusalem, he was fascinated by the ancient architecture around the Dome of the Rock and the way it contrasted with the vivid blue sky. He painted several watercolours and at least one oil painting of the subject.

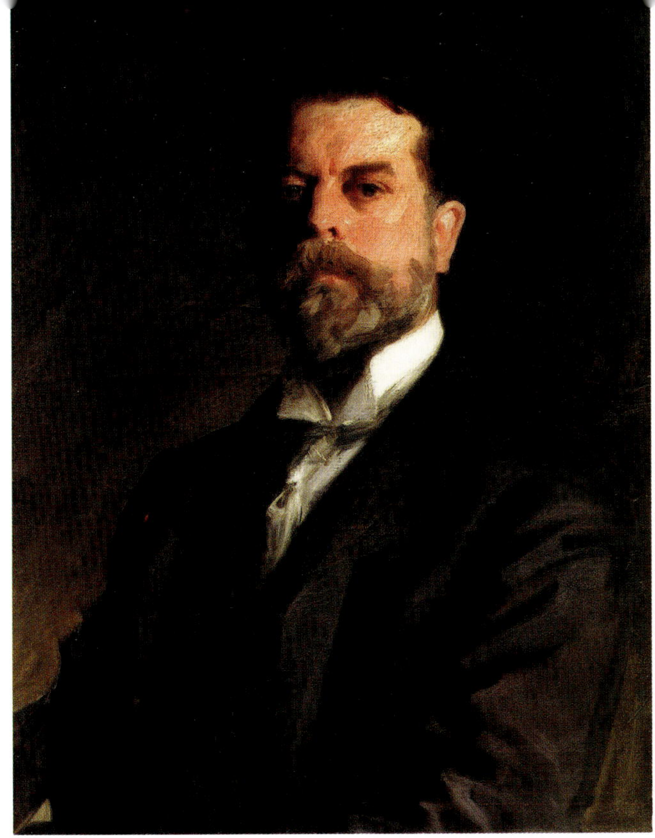

Self-portrait, 1906, oil on canvas, 76.2 x 63.5cm (30 x 25in), Galeria degli Uffizi, Florence, Italy

In the year before he declared he would give up portraiture, Sargent had been asked by the Uffizi Gallery in Florence to paint a self-portrait to add to their exclusive collection for the 'Vasari Corridor.' He wrote to the gallery officials:
'I highly appreciate the honour you confer upon me by the invitation to contribute my portrait to the historical collection in your galleries. I beg to express my thanks to you for this privilege, of which I will most gladly avail myself.'

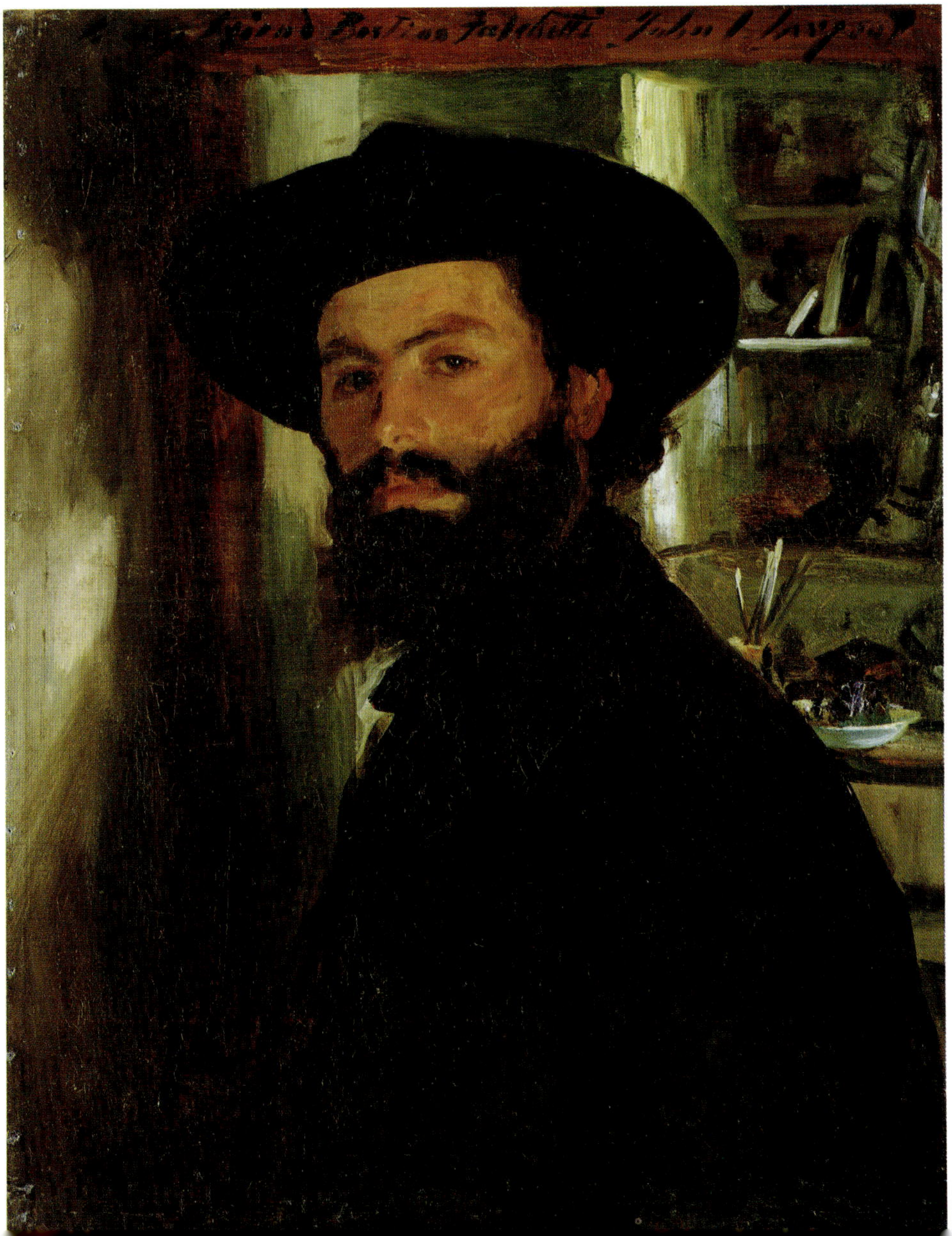

Alberto Falchetti, 1905–06, oil on canvas, 75 x 54.6cm (29½ x 21½in), Private Collection

One of a group of several Italian artists who became close friends with Sargent while he was painting in the Italian Alps, Alberto Falchetti (1878–1956) was also friends with Raffele and Pollonera (see page 187). Sargent painted this while residing in the Hotel Mont Cervin in the Matterhorn. He conveys the dark, handsome features of the extremely talented landscape painter.

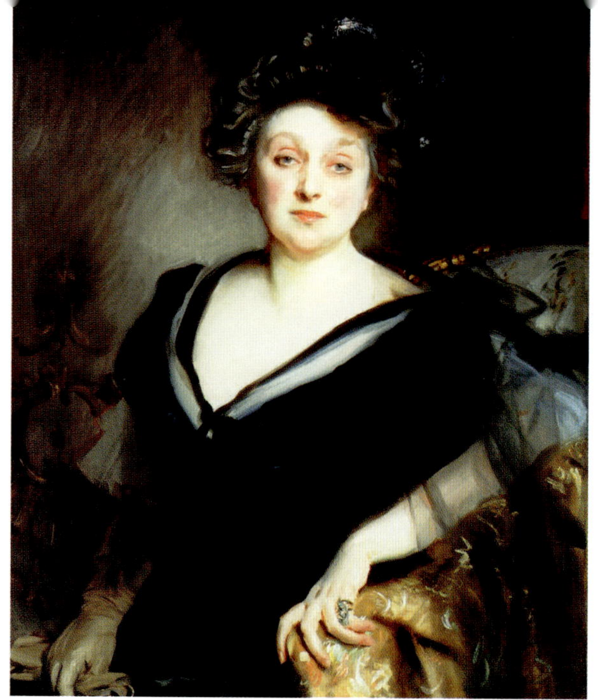

Mrs George Mosenthal, 1906, oil on canvas, 91.4 x 73cm (36 x 28¾in), Private Collection

Described as a 'French woman of taste and a certain powerful presence,' Marguerite Mosenthal did not commission this painting, Sargent probably asked her to sit for him when they met at a dinner party. Completed at his Tite Street studio, Sargent used exotic textiles and expensive furniture to create an atmosphere of opulence, while Marguerite's evening gown and ring reveals her upper class status.

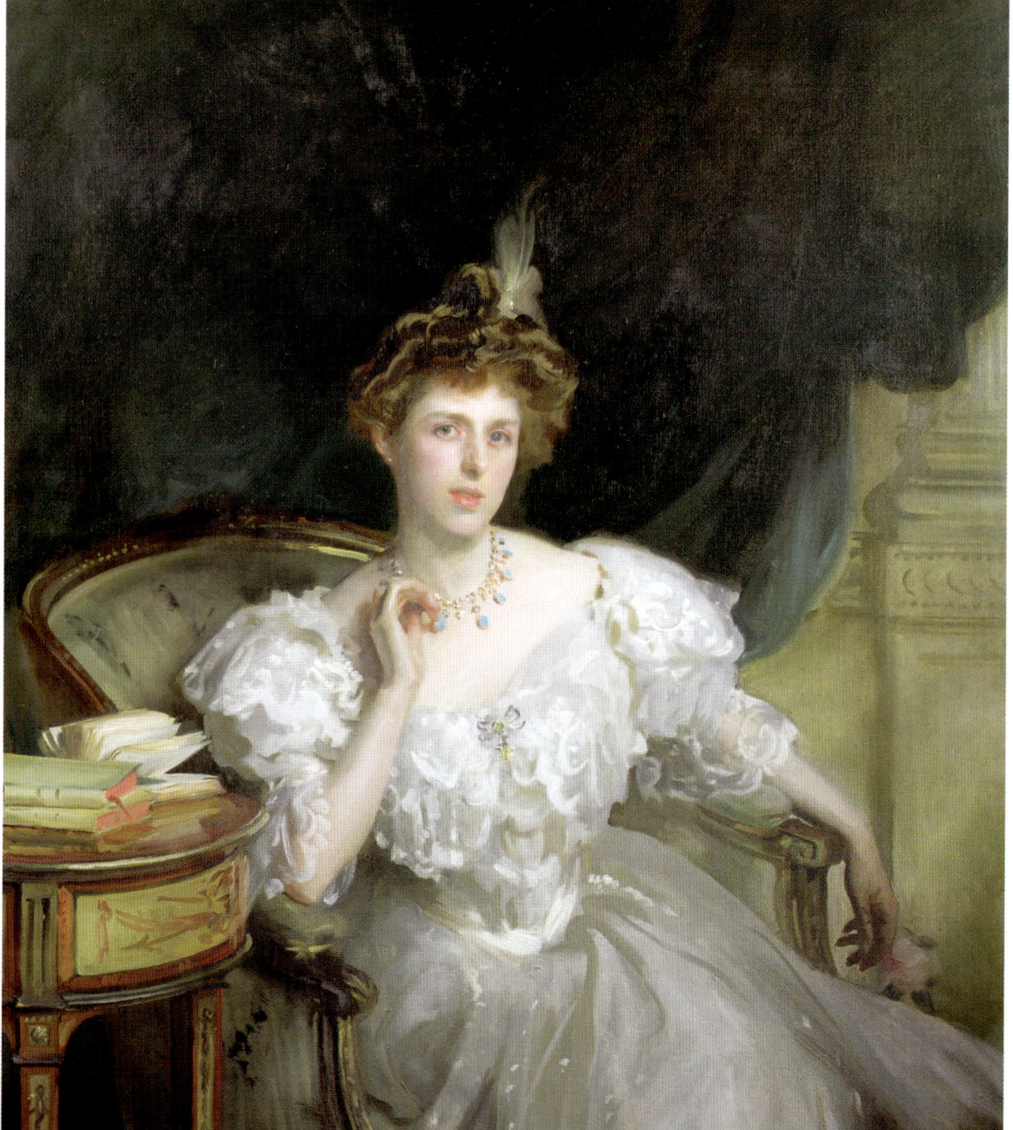

Margherita Goldsmid, later Mrs William George Raphael, 1906, oil on canvas, 142.2 x 104.1cm (56 x 41in), Private Collection

From a prosperous Jewish family, Margherita Goldsmid (1871–1925) is portrayed here in a three-quarter-length seated portrait, wearing a highly fashionable white satin and lace dress with an expensive diamond and turquoise necklace. Her father was a lawyer, businessman and Liberal politician and her future husband was part of a prominent banking family.

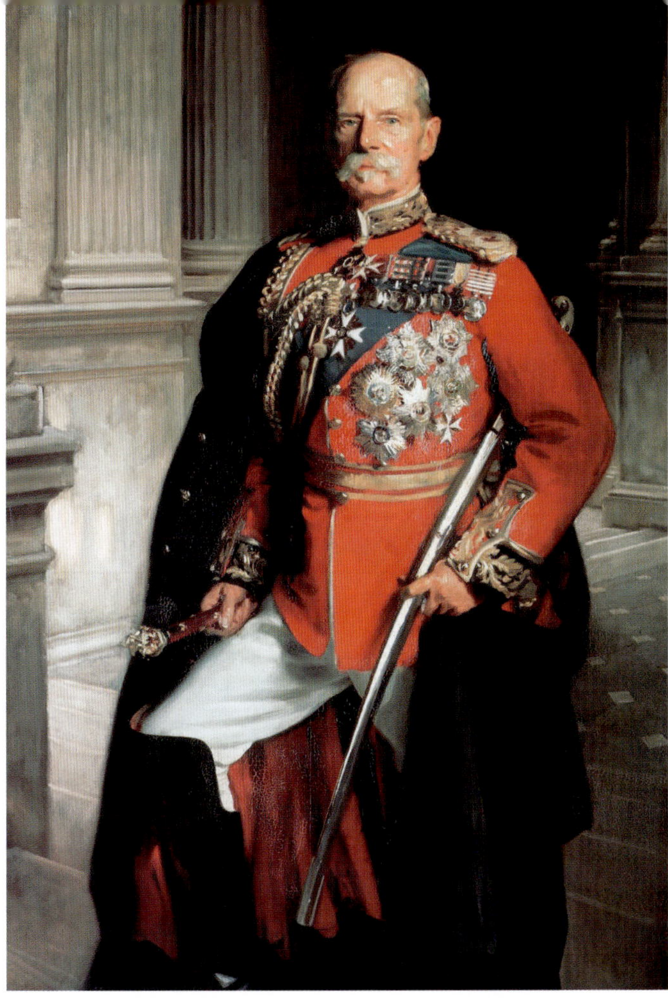

Frederick Sleigh Roberts, 1st Earl Roberts, 1906, oil on canvas, 163.8 x 105cm (64½ x 41¼in), The National Portrait Gallery, London, UK

British Field Marshal Frederick Sleigh Roberts (1832–1914) was one of the most successful commanders of the 19th century. In 1912, when he was nearly 80, he warned that Germany was making real and worrying efforts to prepare for war, advising: 'if these were my last words, I still should say to you: "arm yourselves"'. He was not believed and was heavily criticized in the Press.

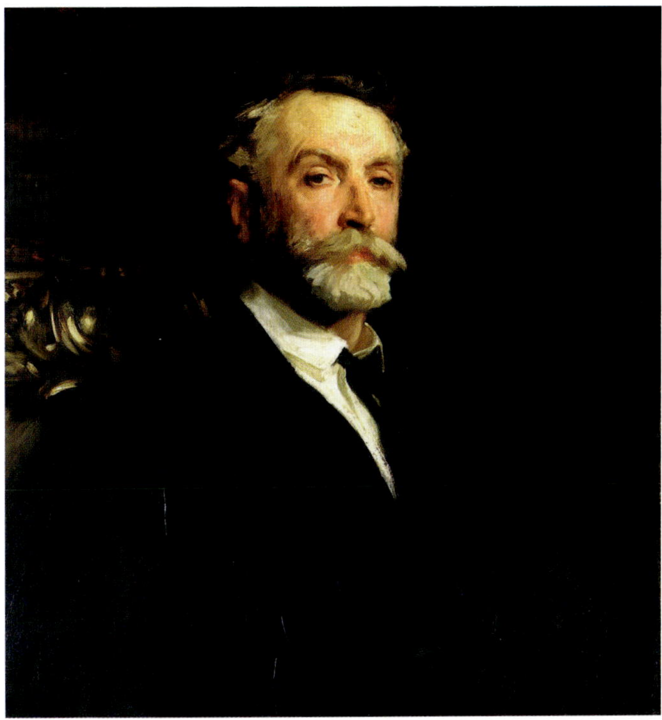

Edgar Vincent, Viscount D'Abernon, 1906, oil on canvas, 97 x 71.8cm (38 x 28¼in), Private Collection

A prominent British politician, Edgar Vincent (1857–1941) was also a diplomat, financier and author. In 1890, he married a celebrated beauty, Helen Venetia Duncombe, and became known for hosting society parties and soirées, and for amassing a great art collection. Sargent painted Helen's portrait at their Venetian villa two years before producing this portrait of her distinguished husband.

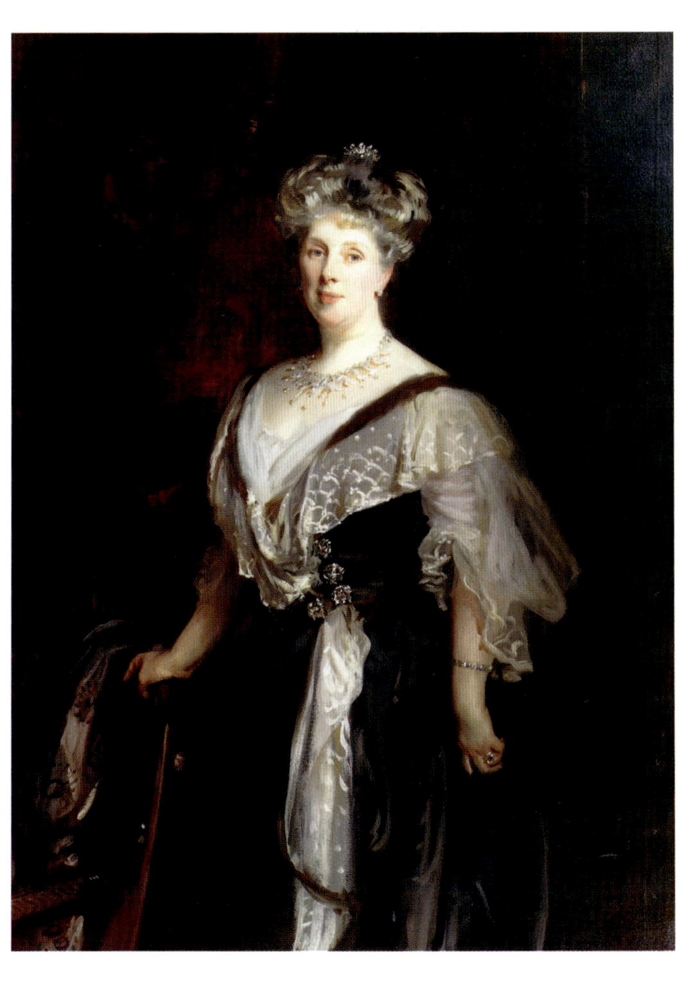

Lady Caroline Williamson, 1906, oil on canvas, 148.6 x 107.3cm (58½ x 42¼in), Private Collection

During 1906, Sargent painted a large number of aristocratic sitters and became quite fed-up with the constant strain he felt in having to make small talk and to pander to their vanities. He longed to paint what pleased him. Although this sitter was not too demanding, many of his subjects were snobs, which he found particularly difficult to deal with.

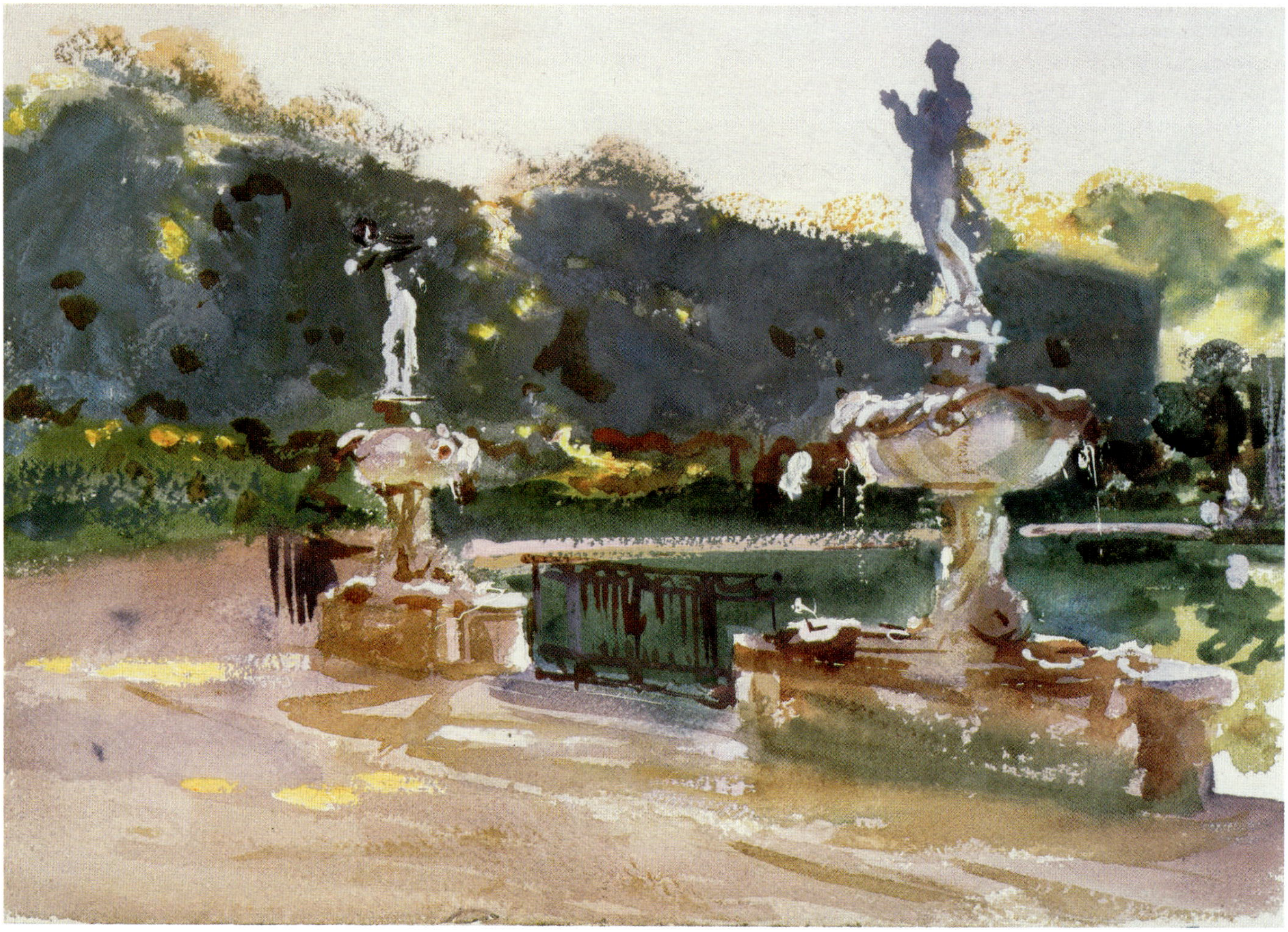

Boboli Gardens, c.1906,
opaque and translucent
watercolour over graphite
on paper, 25.4 x 35.6cm (10
x 14in), Brooklyn Museum,
New York, USA

A beautiful oasis in the
city of Florence, the Boboli
Gardens stretch over a hill
behind the Pitti Palace. First
built in the Renaissance
by the Medici family and
extended by several
subsequent owners, the
gardens appealed to Sargent
for their variety. Beginning
with a detailed underdrawing,
he applied strokes of opaque
zinc white to depict water
sparkling from the fountains.

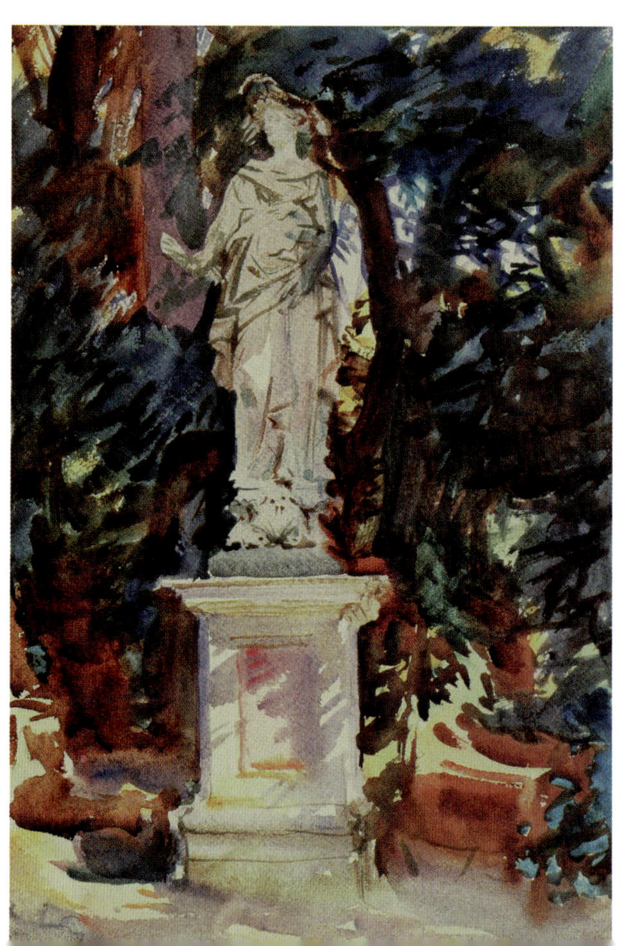

Boboli, c.1906, translucent
and opaque watercolour
over graphite on paper,
46 x 29.1cm (18 x 11½ in),
Brooklyn Museum,
New York, USA

Among many different
aspects, the Boboli Gardens
includes a woodland path
of cypress trees, planted in
1612, called Il Viottolone.
This sculpture is one of
several lining the path and
Sargent captured it, dappled
with light through the leaves.
He painted the shadows,
highlights and reflections in
a range of warm and cool,
tones in subtle and bright
colours, including purple,
gold, green and blue.

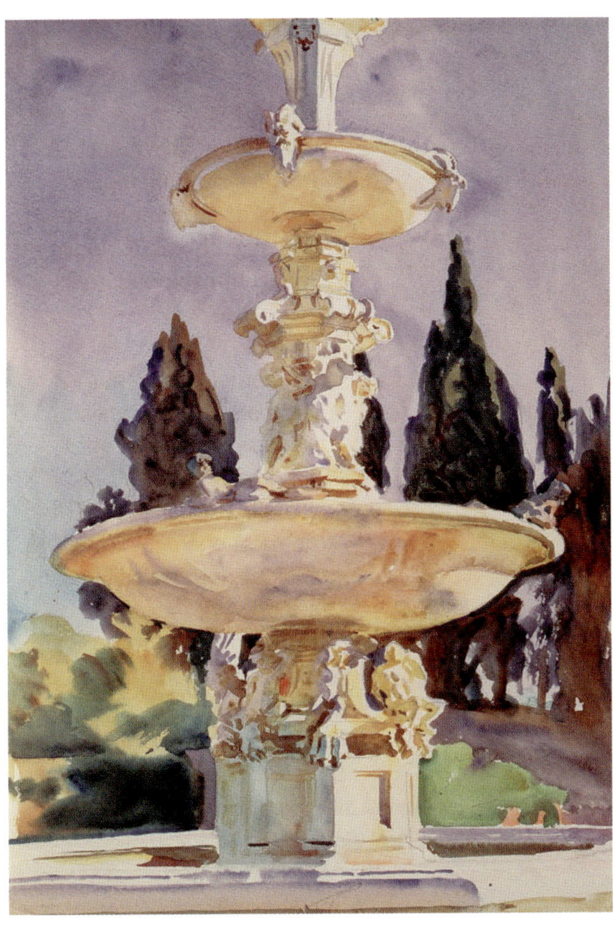

In a Medici Villa, 1906, translucent and opaque watercolour over graphite on paper, 53.8 x 36.5cm (21¼ x 14½in), Brooklyn Museum, New York, USA

A view of the classical Renaissance garden at the Villa Medici di Castello, near Florence, this is painted from a low position – as Sargent often did with his Venetian watercolours. The garden is on a gentle slope, with formal box and herb hedges surrounding more flamboyant grand stone fountains. Making a feature of the Hercules and Antaeus fountain, he cropped the sides of the painting.

Zuleika, c.1906, watercolour and gouache on paper, 25.4 x 35.4cm (10 x 13¾in), Brooklyn Museum, New York, USA

This is either one of Sargent's nieces or the daughter of one of his friends wearing an exotic costume that he bought when travelling in the Middle East earlier that year. The title refers to a woman featured in biblical and Arabic literature who was often depicted as being in love with Joseph, her handsome slave. Sargent's marks, the costume and pose convey a sense of sensuality.

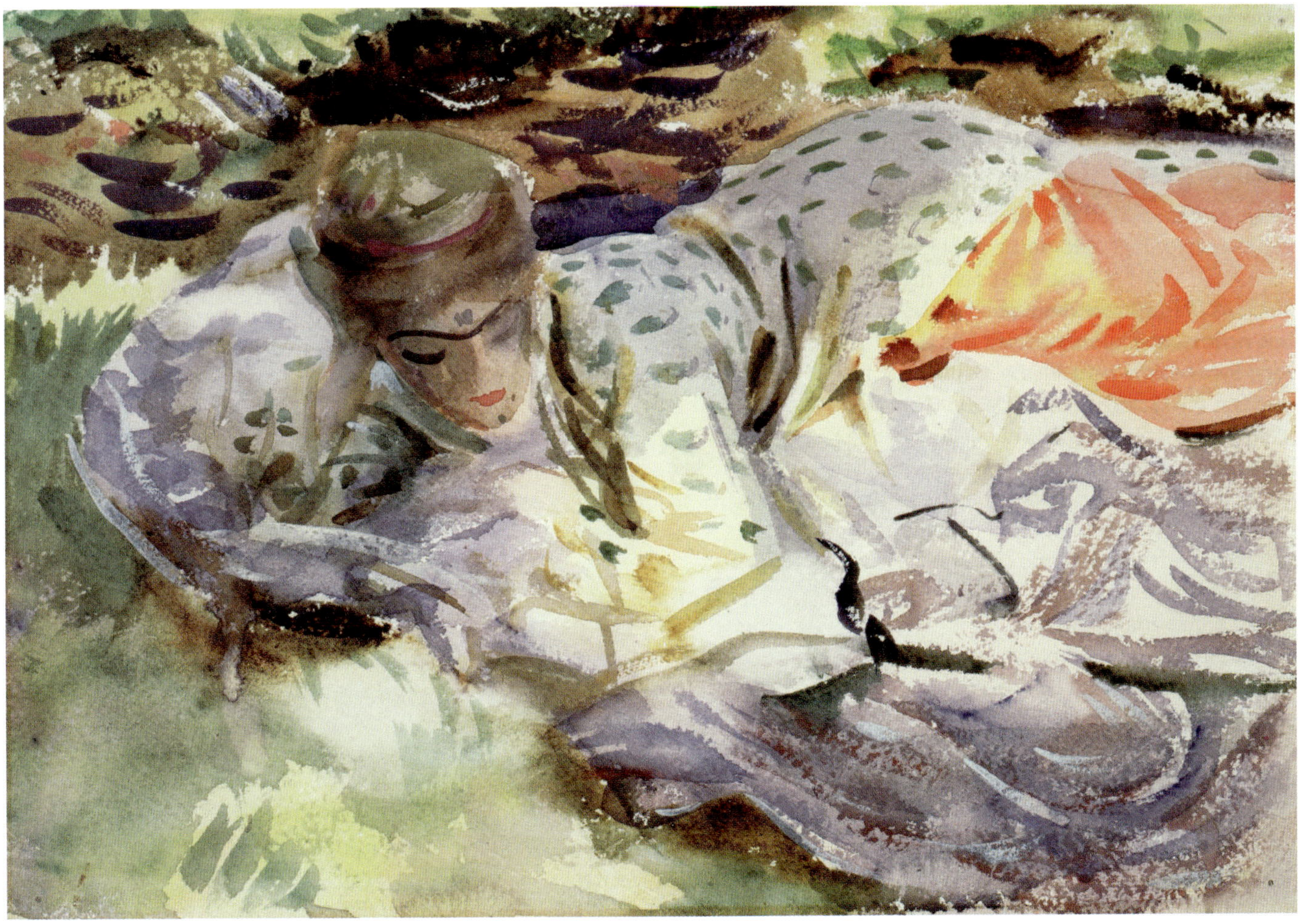

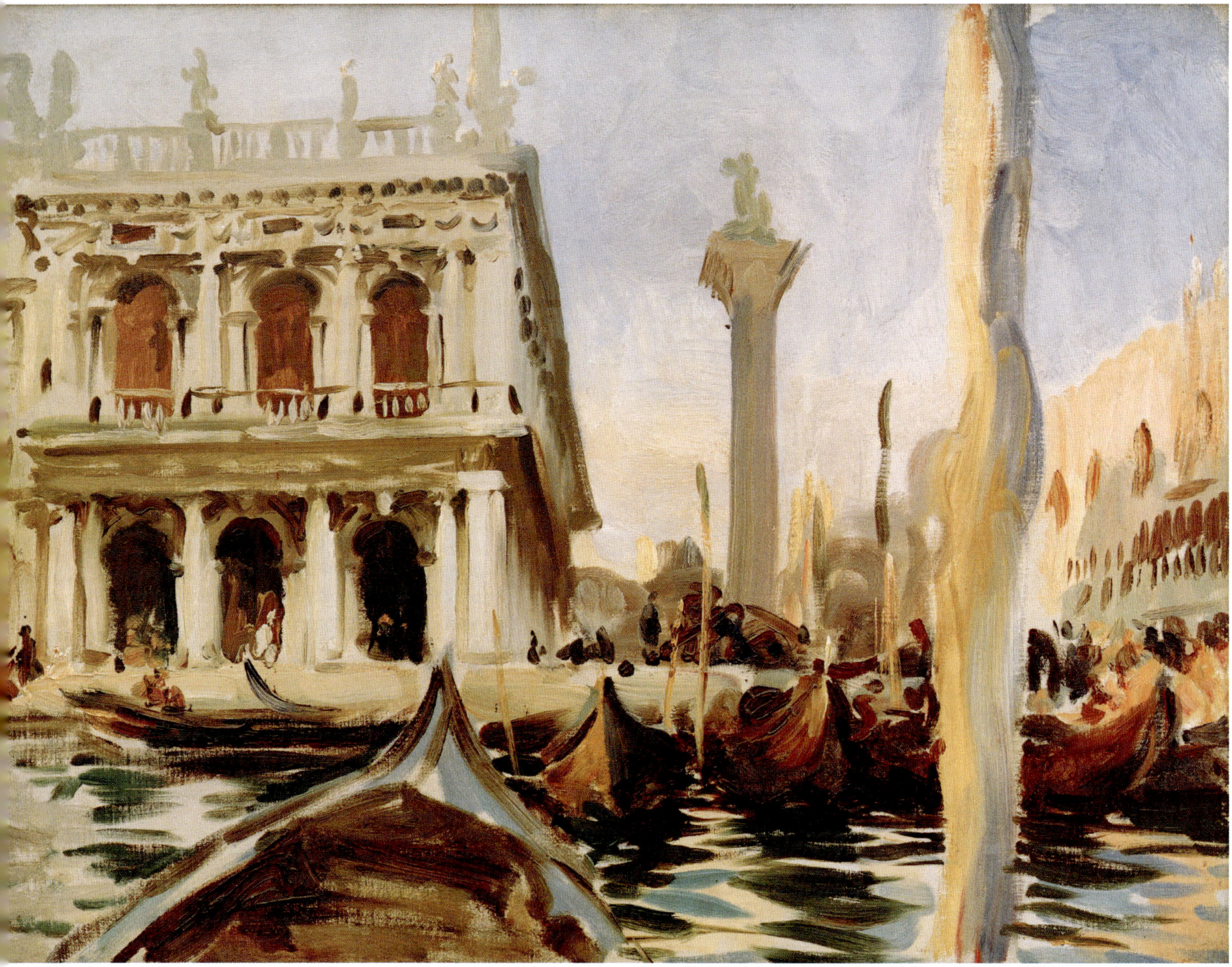

The Libreria, c.1902–12, oil on burlap, 54.6 x 69.8cm (21½ x 27½in), Private Collection

This is the only oil painting that Sargent made of the Biblioteca Nazionale Marciana – or library – that was designed by Jacopo Sansovino in 1536 and stands at the edge of the Piazzetta. Painted from his gondola, Sargent looked ahead at the library and the large column bearing its statue of Saint Theodore. In this bold composition a pole, rising from the lagoon, essentially cuts off the picture at the edge.

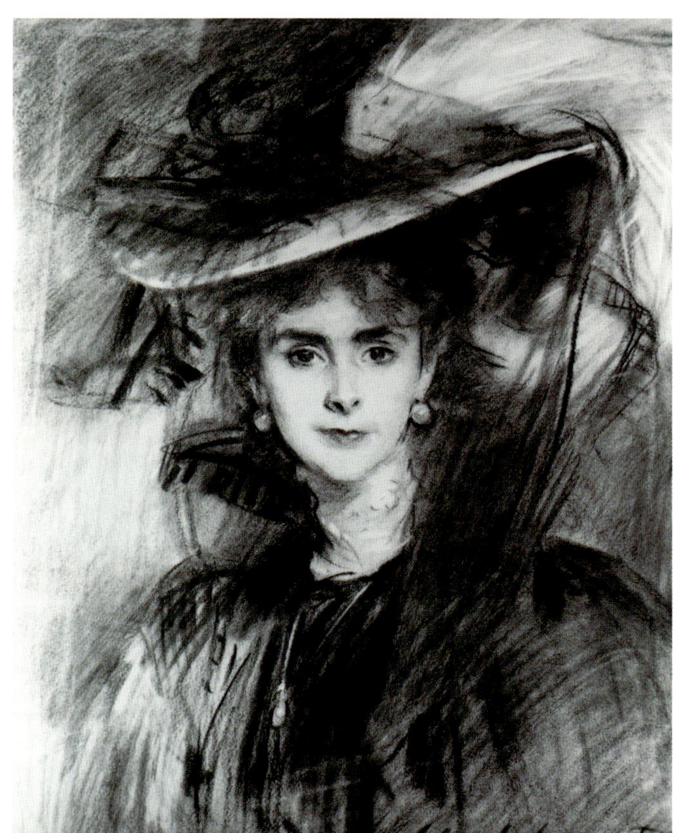

Olga, Baroness de Meyer, c.1907, charcoal on paper, 87.6 x 71cm (34½ x 28in), Birmingham Museum and Art Gallery, Birmingham, UK

Maria Beatrice Olga Alberta Caracciolo (1871–1930) was a British-born artists' model, socialite, patron of the arts and writer, and was also rumoured to be the natural daughter of the Prince of Wales, later Edward VII. Sargent probably drew this in Venice. Olga's beauty also inspired William Bruce Ranken, Whistler, Boldini, Sickert and Helleu, all of whom painted her.

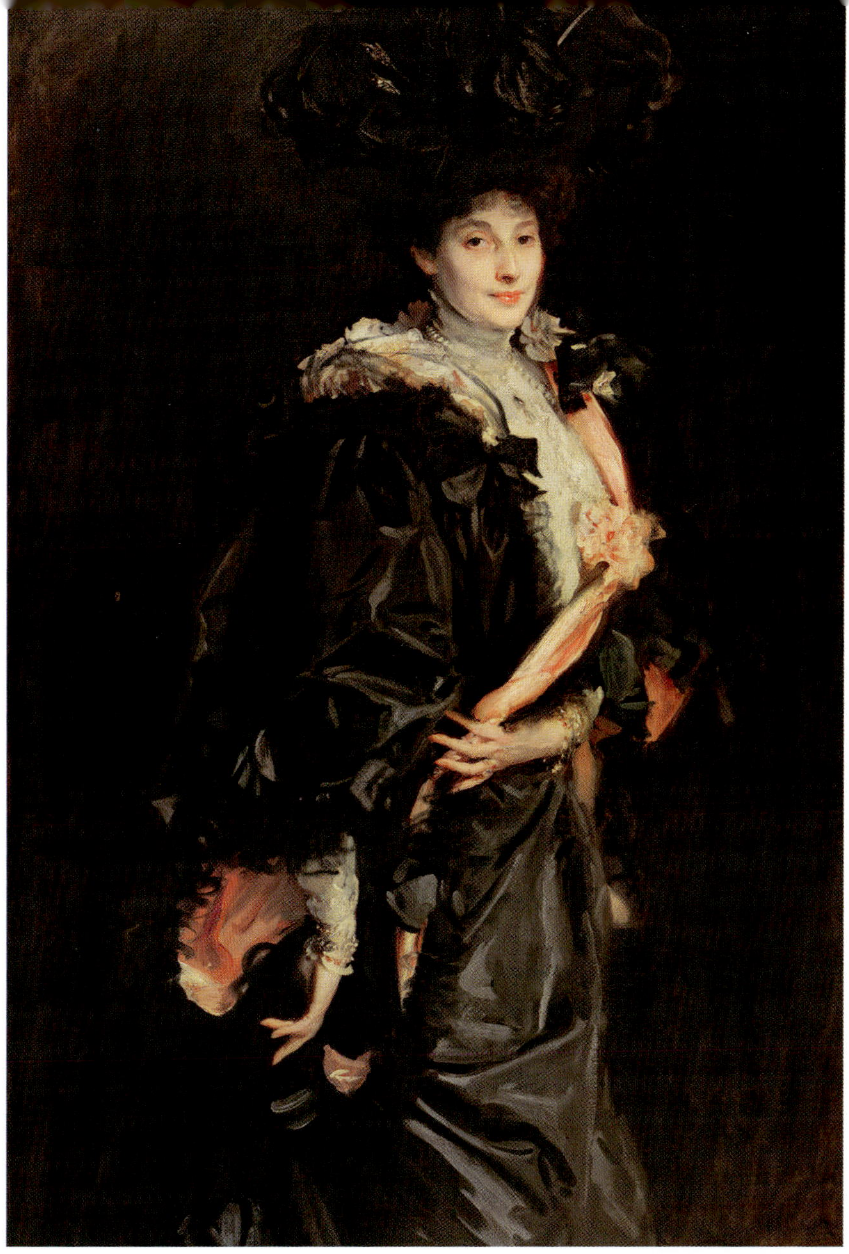

Lady Sassoon, 1907, oil on canvas, 157.5 x 104.1cm (62 x 41in), Private Collection

Lady Sassoon, née Aline Caroline de Rothschild (1867–1909), was a well-known French socialite, artist, friend of the Prince of Wales (whose yacht *Aline* was named after her) and daughter of the prominent Rothschild family. Born in Paris, she had married Edward Sassoon (1856–1912) in 1887 when she was 19, and she and her children, Sybil and Philip (see page 65), were all good friends with Sargent. He painted this portrait of her when she was 50. Although many said it resembled her closely, she did not like it.

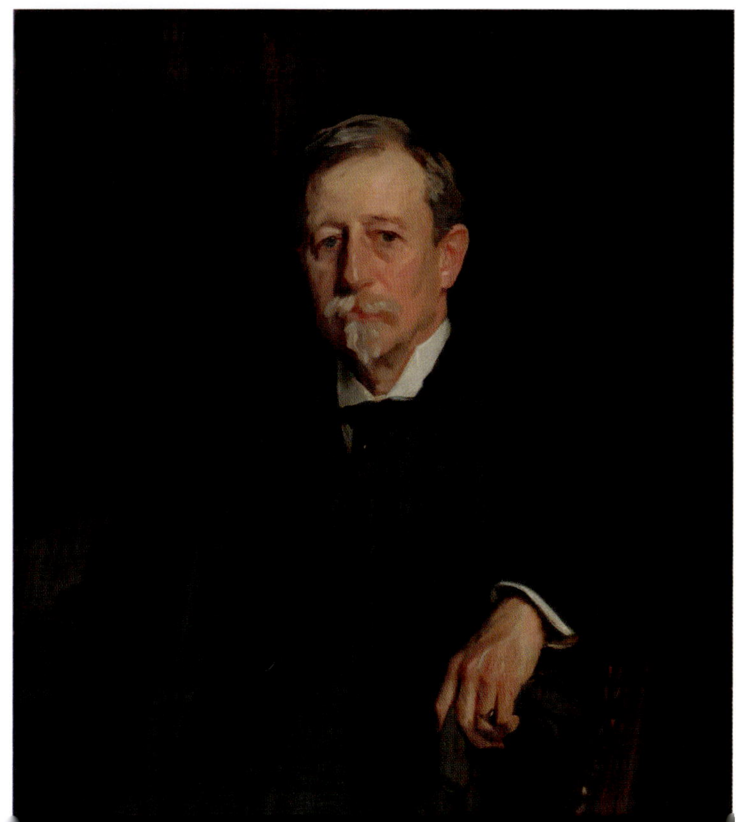

Aaron Augustus Healy, 1907, oil on canvas, 86.5 x 73cm (34 x 28¾in), Brooklyn Museum, New York, USA

For 25 years, Aaron Augustus Healy was the President of The Brooklyn Museum. In 1909, Sargent's watercolour exhibition had only been open for two days when Healy declared that he wanted to buy all the paintings in it for the museum. In his personal collection, he already owned one of Sargent's most recent oil paintings: *Dolce Far Niente* (see page 78).

Study of a Sicilian Peasant, 1907, oil on canvas, 60 x 46cm (23½ x 18in), Fitzwilliam Museum, Cambridge, UK

From the 1880s, Sargent visited Sicily on several occasions. He told his friend the sculptor Augustus Saint-Gaudens that he went there to avoid painting formal portraits adding that: 'the plage [beach] in Naples answers very well, too.' In 1907 he began the summer painting with his friend Wilfrid de Glehn in the Val d'Aosta, and went to Rome and Frascati later that year.

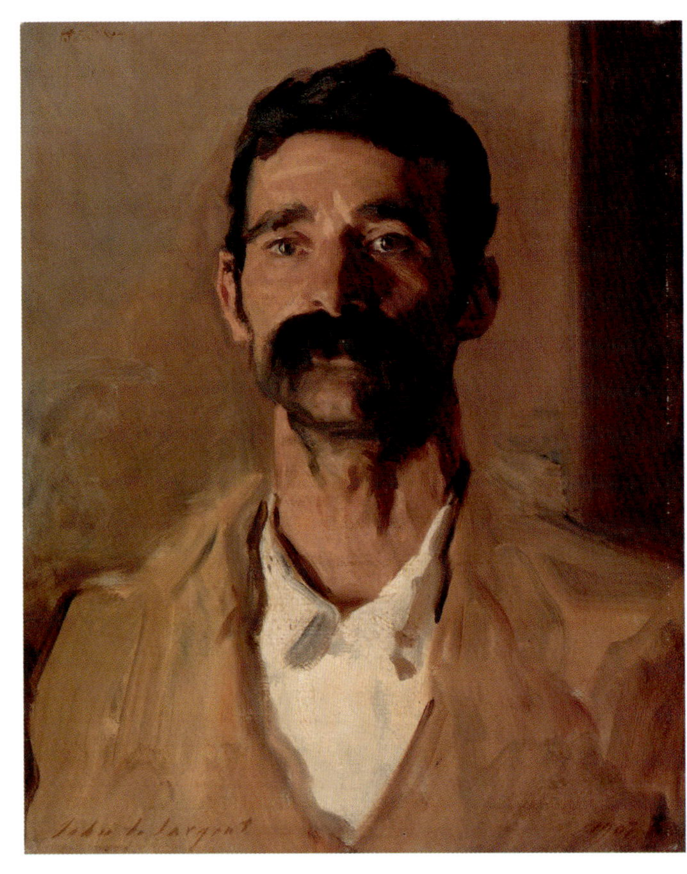

Alpine Pool, 1907, oil on canvas, 69.9 x 96.5cm (27½ x 38in), The Metropolitan Museum, New York, USA

This the brook at Purtud in close-up view. There is no sky or horizon, but it focuses instead on water, rocks and foliage, resulting in an almost abstract arrangement of form and colour. Sargent applied his paint quickly and lightly, building up patches of colour, creating the effect of dappled light and shimmering reflections in the flowing water.

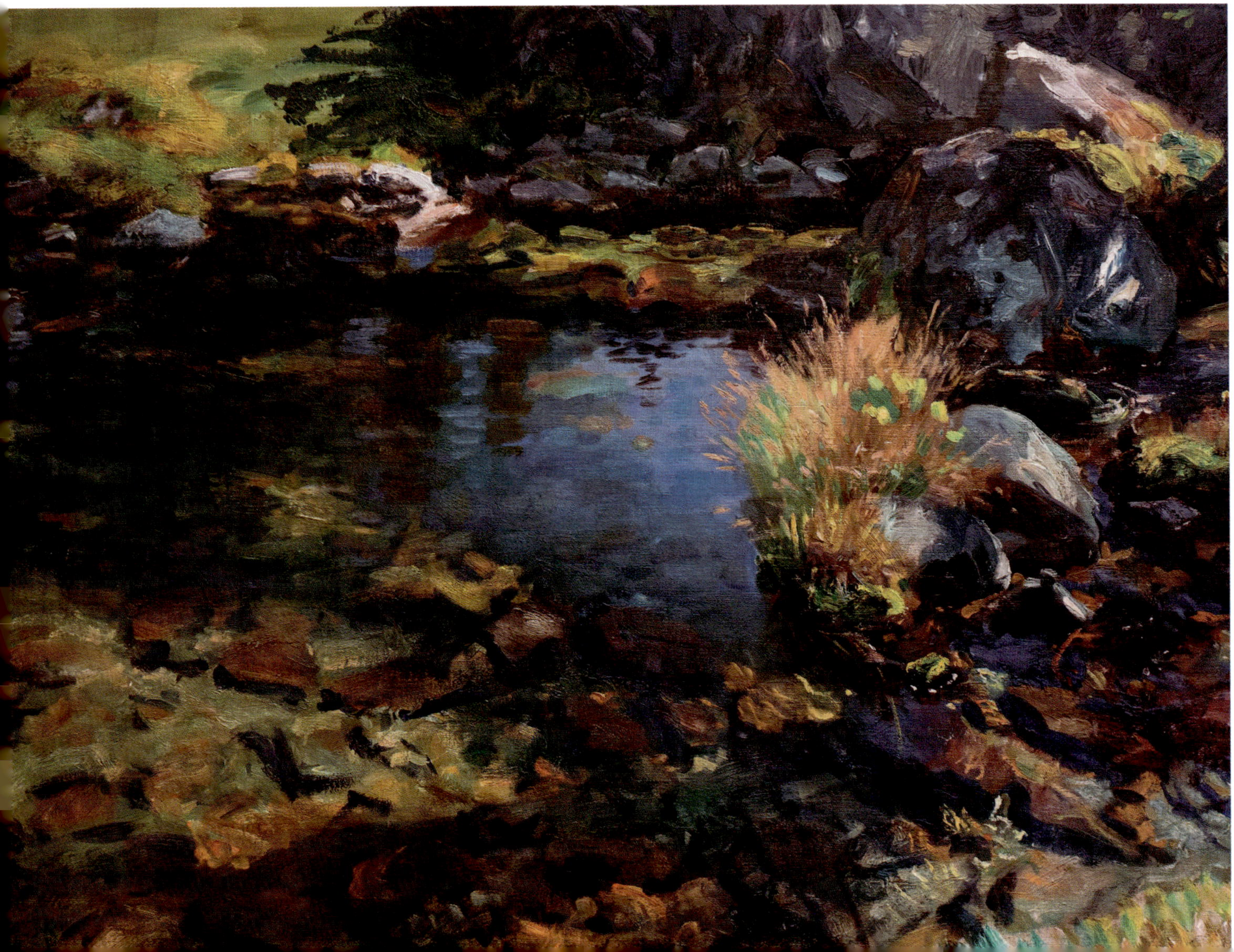

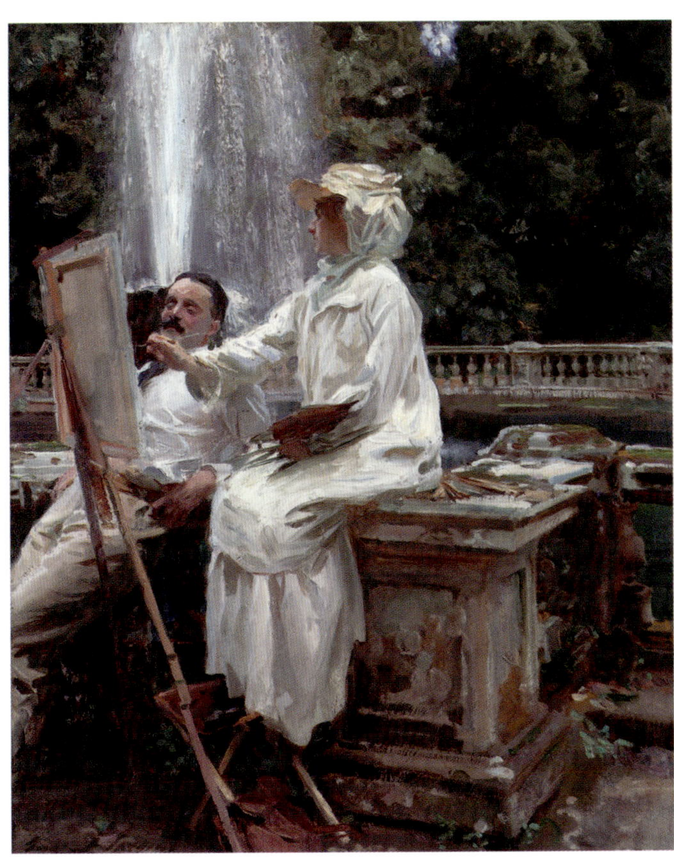

The Fountain, Villa Torlonia, Frascati, 1907, oil on canvas, 71.4 x 56.5cm (28 x 22¼in), The Art Institute of Chicago, Illinois, USA

In a sunlit garden in the Italian town of Frascati, this double portrait is of Sargent's friends and fellow artists Wilfrid and Jane de Glehn. In a letter to her sister, Jane described it as a: 'killingly funny picture...I am all in white with a white painting blouse and a pale blue veil around my hat... Wilfrid is in short sleeves, very idle and good for nothing, and our heads come against the great panache of the fountain.'

A Stream in Val d'Aosta, 1907–08, oil on canvas, 54.9 x 69.9cm (21½ x 27½in), Brooklyn Museum, New York, USA

Also known as *Val d'Aosta, a Stream over Rocks* and *Stream in Val d'Aosta,* this follows Sargent's pursuit of studying and depicting nature at close hand. The stones and rocks seen beneath a trickling stream required great skill with his oil paints. This is an astutely observed image and using a range of marks, colours and tones, Sargent conveys the cool, clear water as it tumbles over the Italian hills.

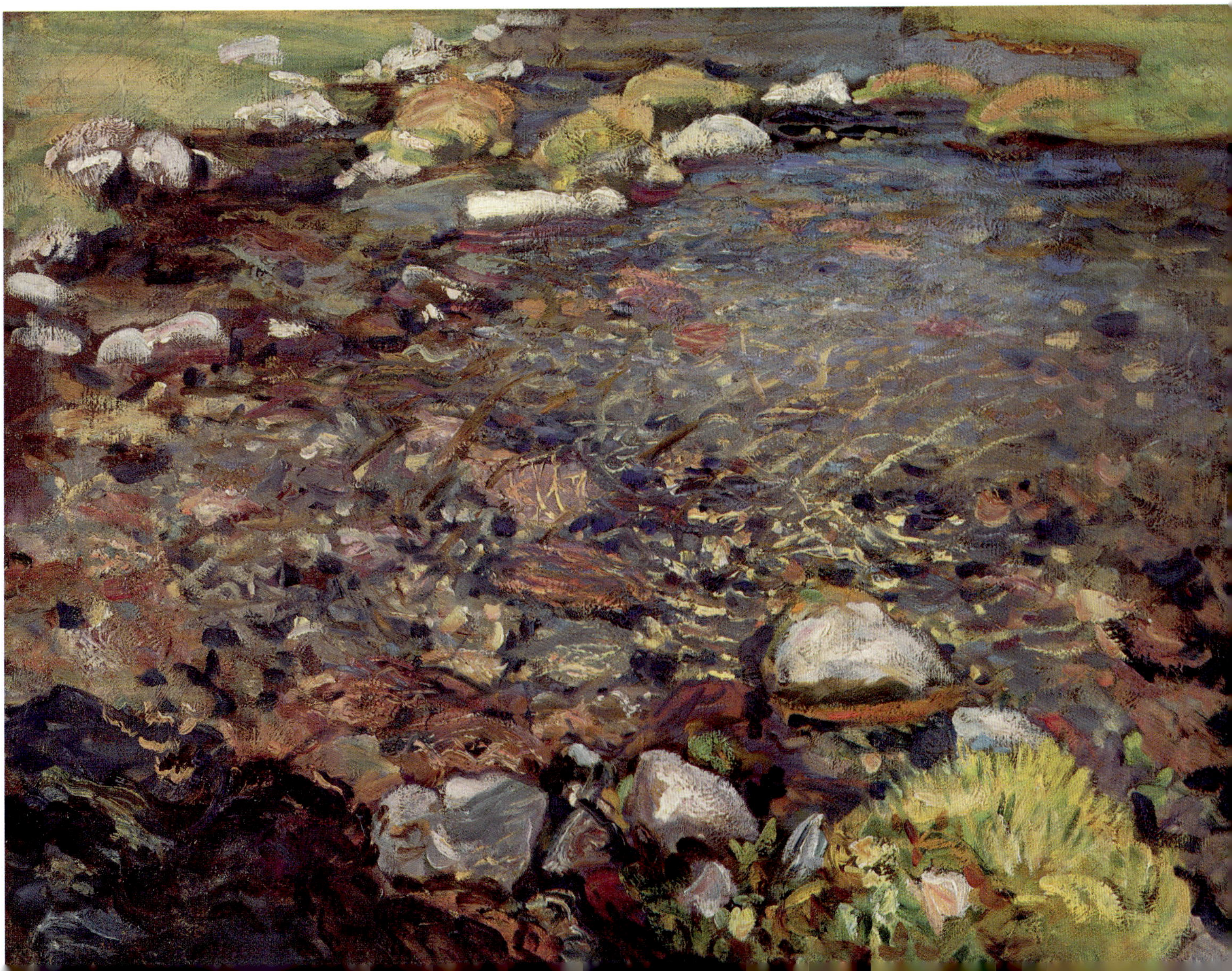

In Switzerland, 1908, translucent and opaque watercolour over graphite on paper, 24.6 x 33.2cm (9¾ x 13in), Brooklyn Museum, New York, USA

It is not clear exactly when Sargent painted this. In a Swiss hotel room or chalet, a figure is dozing fully-dressed, on the bed during the bright daylight hours. The work has been dated c.1905 and 1908, but Sargent stayed near the Simplon Pass in 1904, 1909, 1910 and 1911. In his later visits, he stayed regularly at the Bellevue Hotel, which was situated close by.

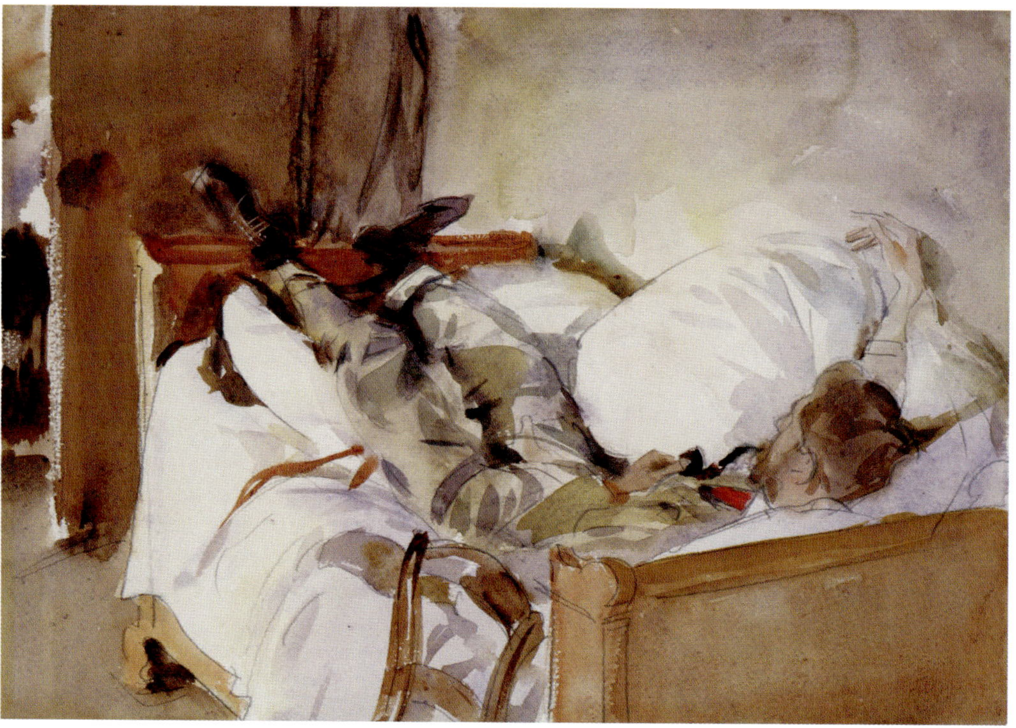

The Hermit (Il Solitario), 1908, oil on canvas, 95.9 x 96.5cm (37¾ x 38in), The Metropolitan Museum, New York, USA

After staying in the Val d'Aosta in the foothills of the Italian Alps, Sargent produced this work from sketches he had made en plein air. At first glance it is quite difficult to differentiate the textured brushwork that conveys the sun on the landscape, the hermit himself and two deer (drawn from one stuffed deer). The work deliberately recalls Renaissance paintings of Saint Jerome.

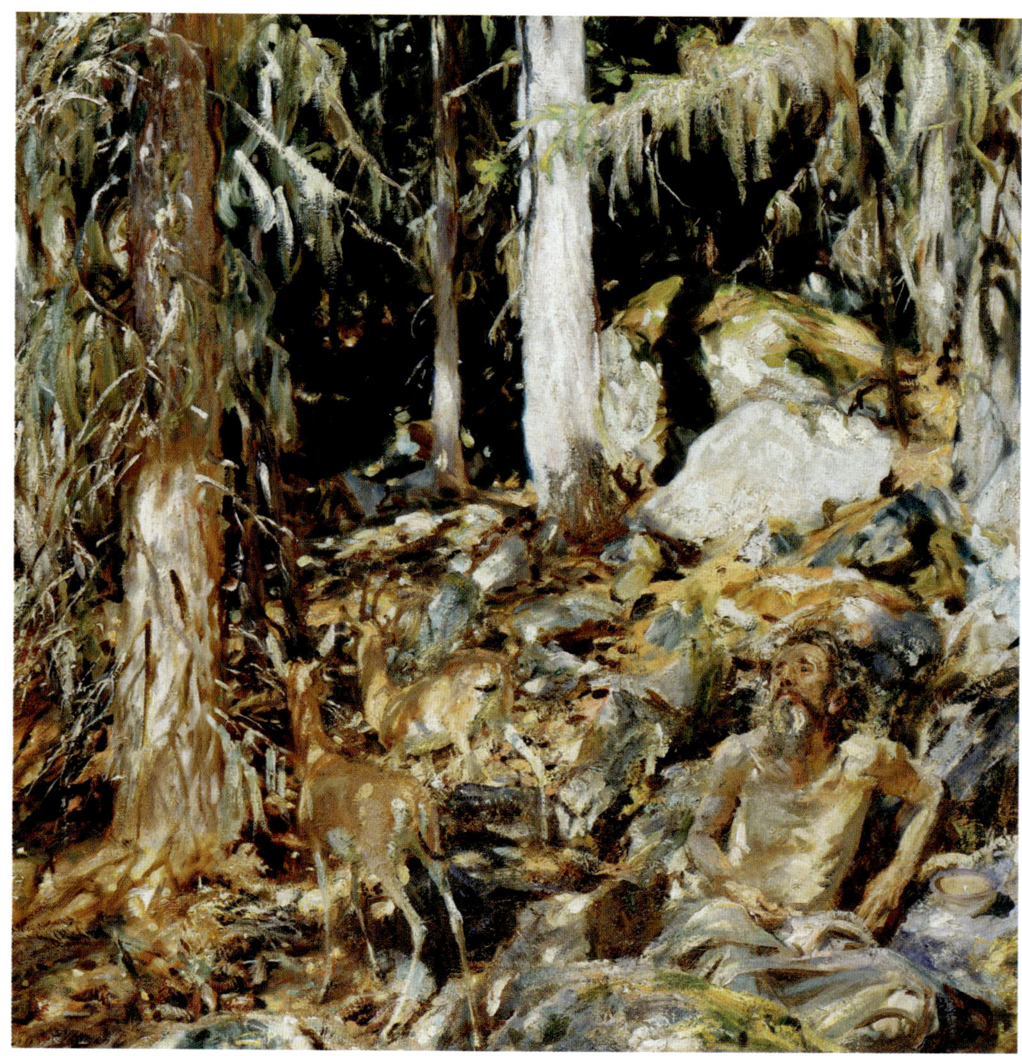

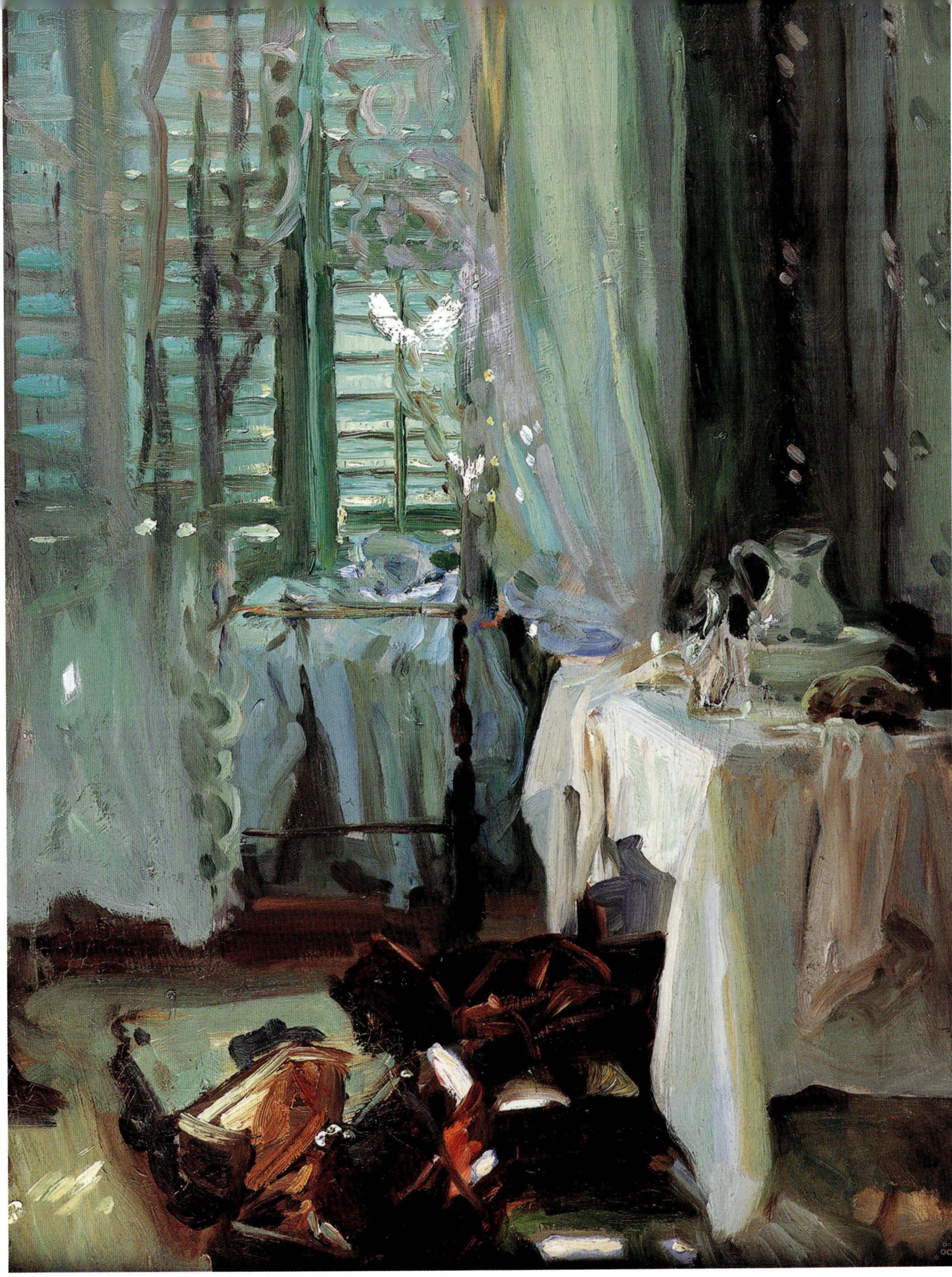

The Hotel Room,
c.1908, oil on canvas,
61 x 44.5cm (24 x
17½in), Private
Collection

Because of his constant travelling, Sargent always told others that he was half-gypsy. As much of his time was spent in hotel rooms living out of suitcases, he said that material objects were relatively unimportant to him. Painted in his hotel room in Genoa, Italy, this is a blend of drawing, watercolour and oil paint, capturing the soft voile at the window, his clothes strewn in his suitcase and washing items on the table.

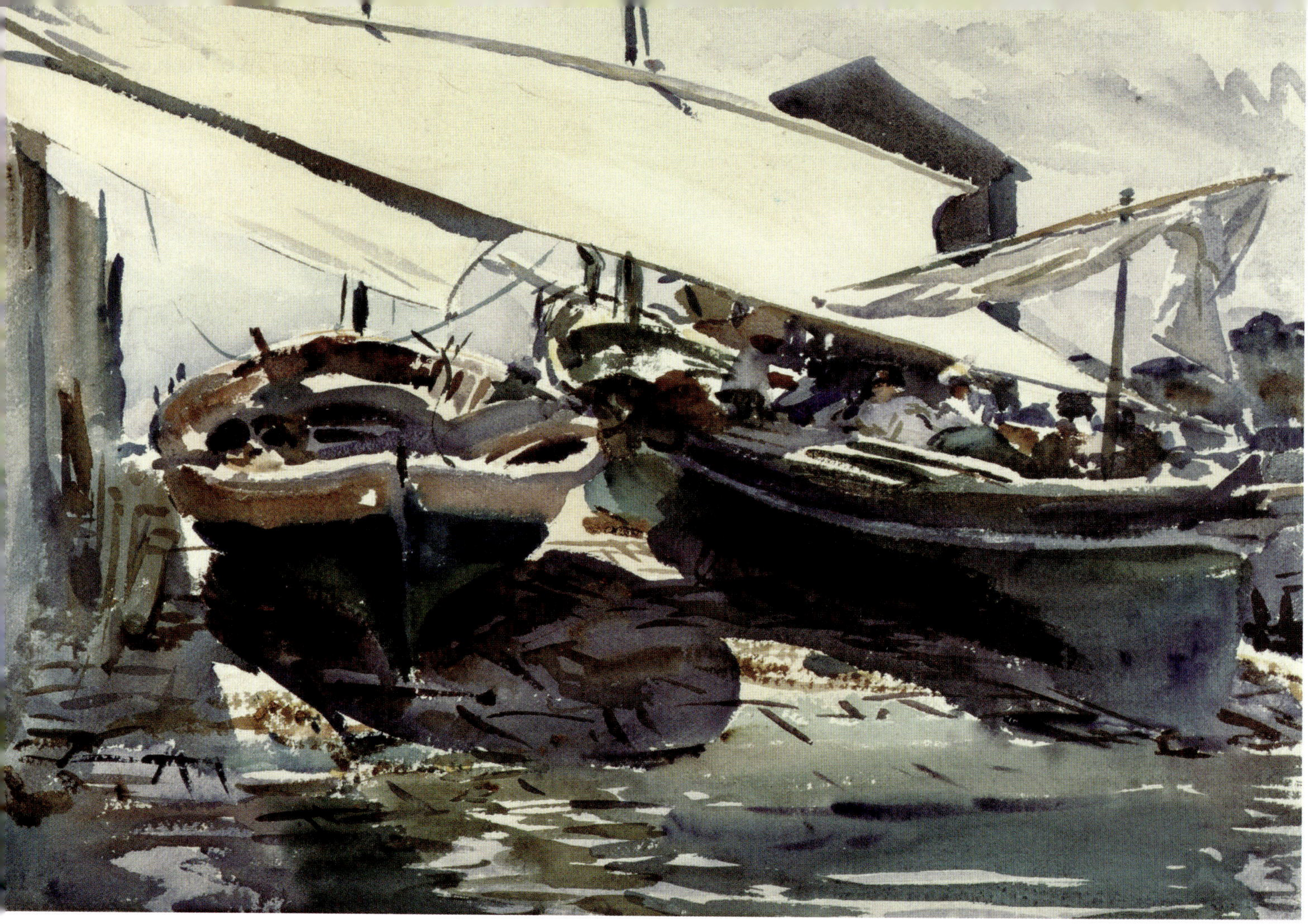

Boats Drawn Up, c.1908, watercolour over graphite on paper, 35.6 x 50.7cm (14 x 20in), Brooklyn Museum, New York, USA

In June 1908, an exhibition of Sargent's watercolours was held at the Carfax Gallery in London. That September, after travelling to Barcelona with Emily, he continued to Majorca where he probably painted this work. In a powerful composition, he confidently leaves bare large areas of white paper to depict sparkling sunlight on the boats and water. Later that year he was made a full member of the Royal Watercolour Society.

Port of Soller, 1908, opaque and translucent watercolour over graphite on paper, 35.6 x 49.2cm (14 x 19½in), Brooklyn Museum, New York, USA

Reminiscent of works by Cézanne that he painted in the small fishing village of L'Estaque, and later echoed by Georges Braque (1882–1963), this almost abstract painting of a view through trees is of a port on Majorca. Sargent created a semi-geometric composition of flat colours in patches of blue, green and sandy coloured shapes with orange lines.

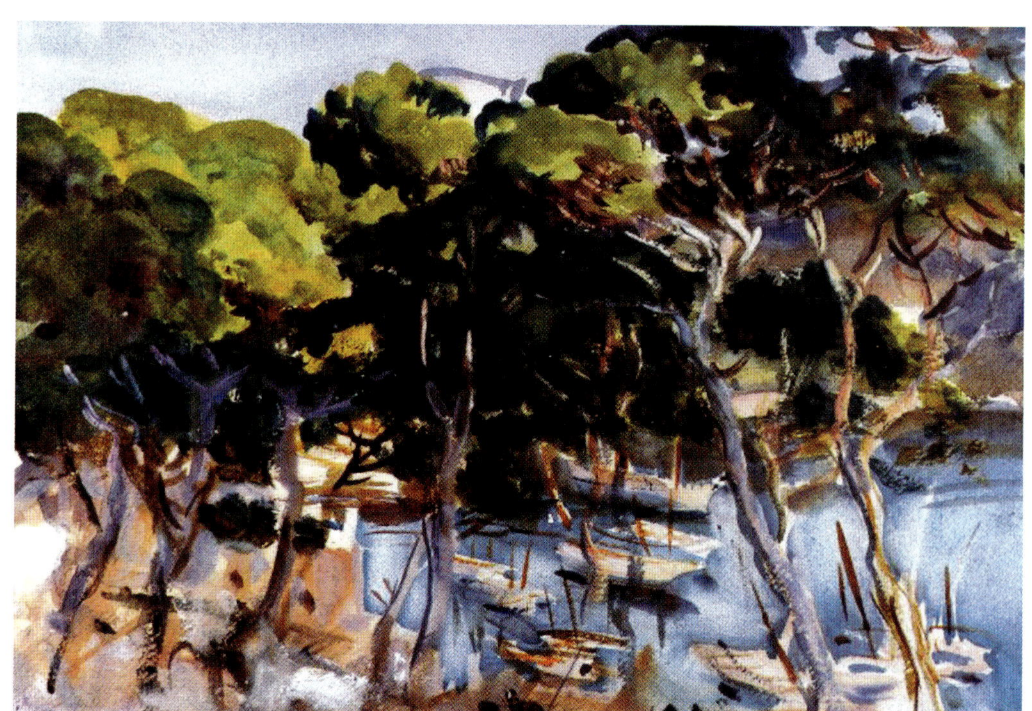

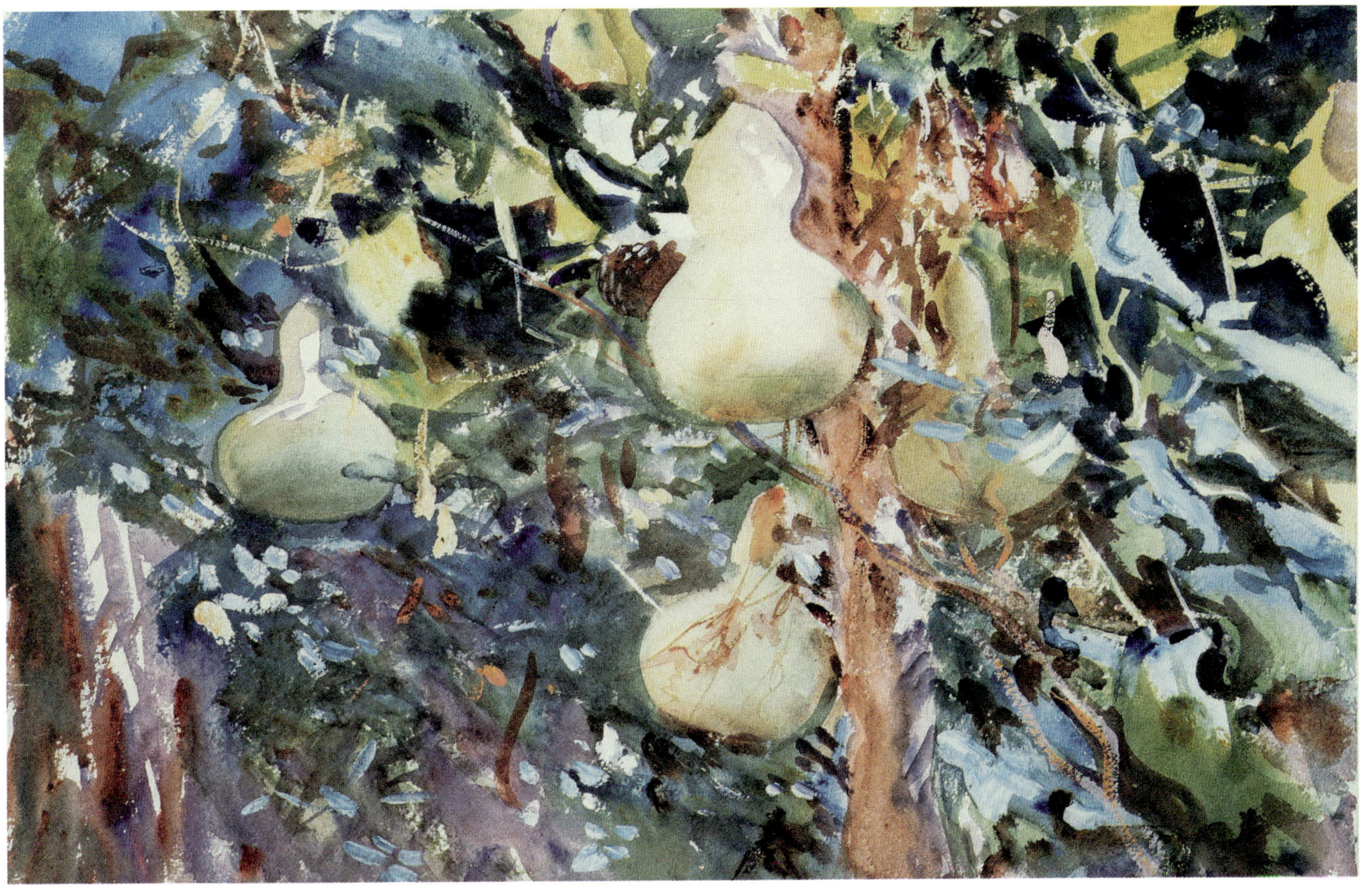

Gourds, c.1908, watercolour over graphite on paper, 35.1 x 50cm (13¾ x 19¾in), Brooklyn Museum, New York, USA

This was painted in Majorca in the late summer of 1908. Here Sargent built up denser brushmarks than seen in many recent watercolours, with less white paper exposed and little of the zinc white opaque colour that he often used to create dramatic highlights. Yet it is just as textural and as contrasting in tone, demonstrating his accomplished skills in conveying the altenating play of light and shadow.

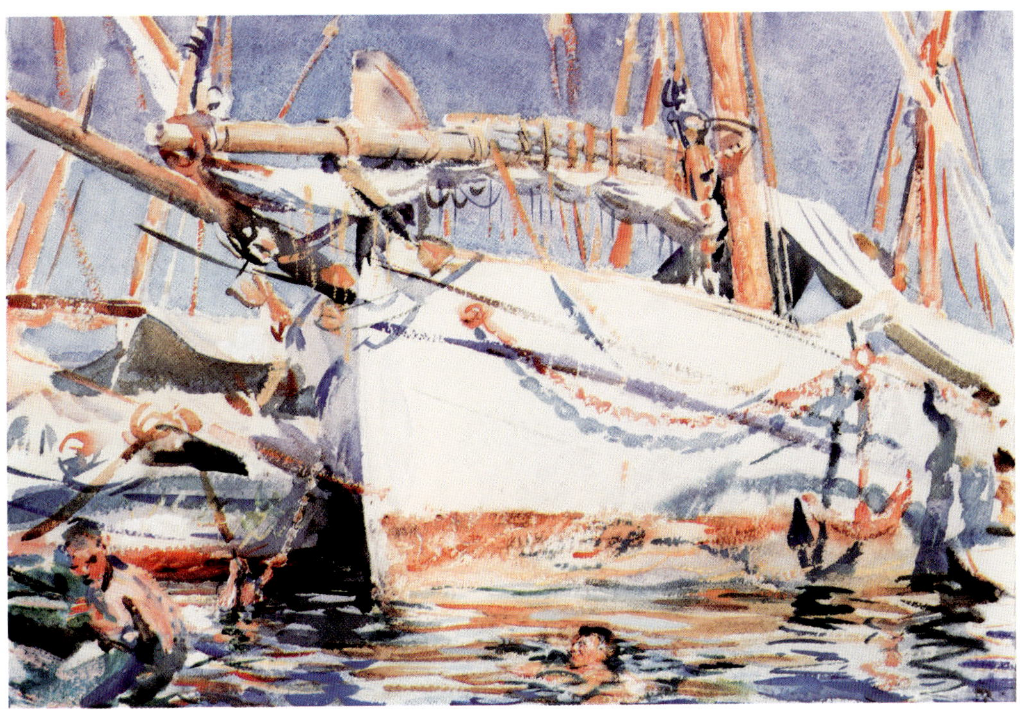

A Falucho, 1908, watercolour and graphite on paper, 35.6 x 50.5cm (14 x 20in), Cincinnati Art Museum, Ohio, USA

Painted while he was in Majorca in October 1908 with Emily and Eliza Wedgwood, the fresh, fluid brushwork appears spontaneous, while the dramatic viewpoint is from a characteristically low position. Viewers are on the same level as the swimmers bobbing in the water against the rising hulls of the boats. Brilliant sunlight is captured using the white of the paper and touches of gouache, or opaque watercolour.

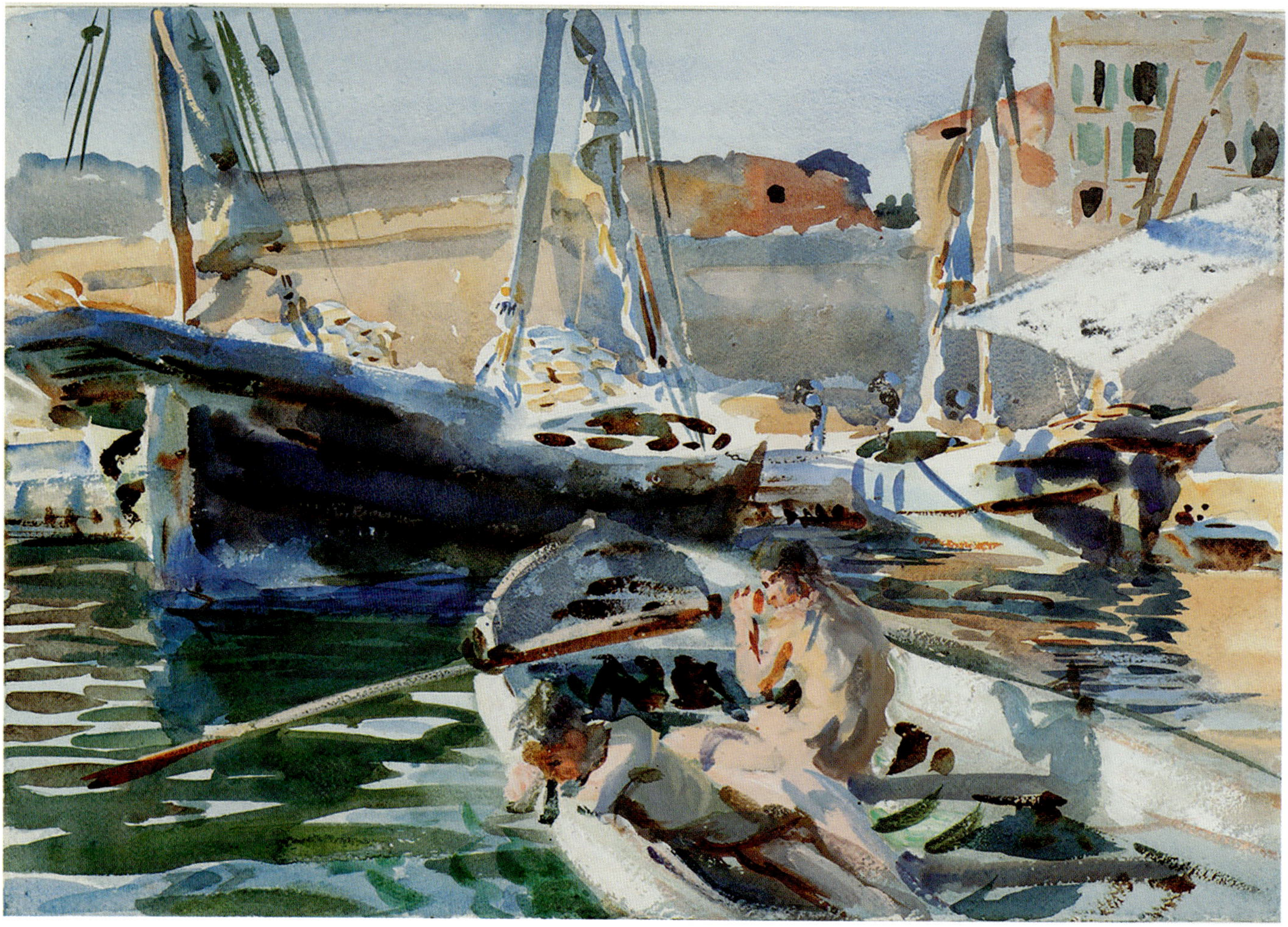

Unloading Plaster, c.1908, opaque and translucent watercolour over graphite on paper, 35.3 x 49.2cm (13¾ x 19¼in), Brooklyn Museum, New York, USA

Although this gives the impression of being another speedy execution, Sargent worked considerably on this watercolour, altering large areas by scraping away previous paint applications and repainting them with thickly applied opaque watercolours, or bodycolour, such as on the boat in the front of the composition and the large triangular white sail on the right-hand side of the composition.

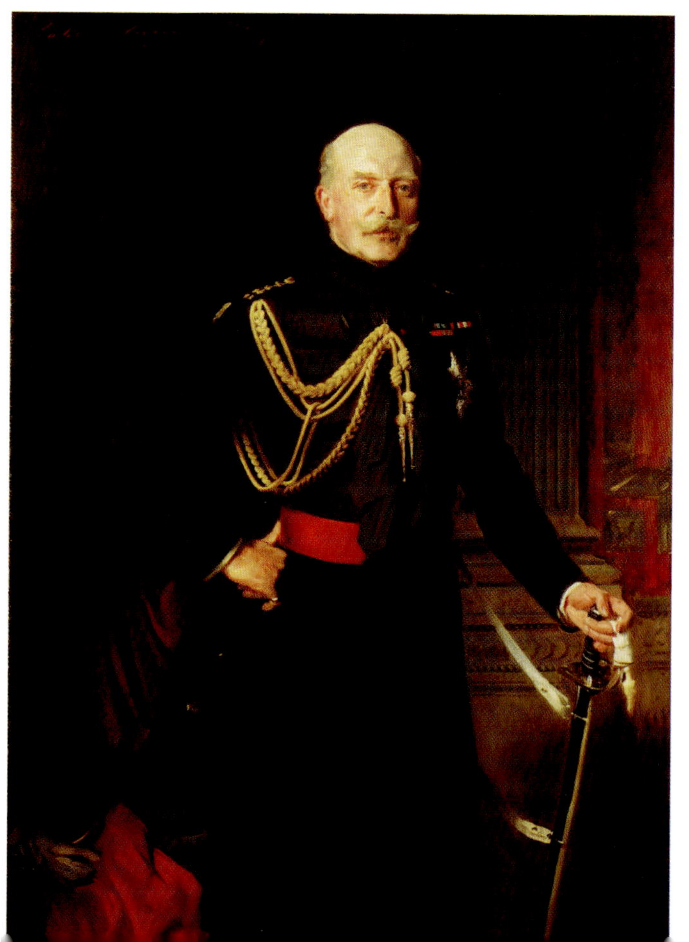

Arthur, Duke of Connaught, 1908, oil on canvas, 163.7 x 109.8cm (64½ x 43¼in), Royal Collection, London, UK

Prince Arthur William Patrick Albert, the Duke of Connaught and Strathearn (1850–1942) was a member of the British Royal family, the third son of Queen Victoria. For five years from 1911, he served as the Governor General of Canada. Sargent painted identically dimensioned portraits of the Duke and Duchess (see opposite), in the traditional style of pendant portraits for royalty and the aristocracy.

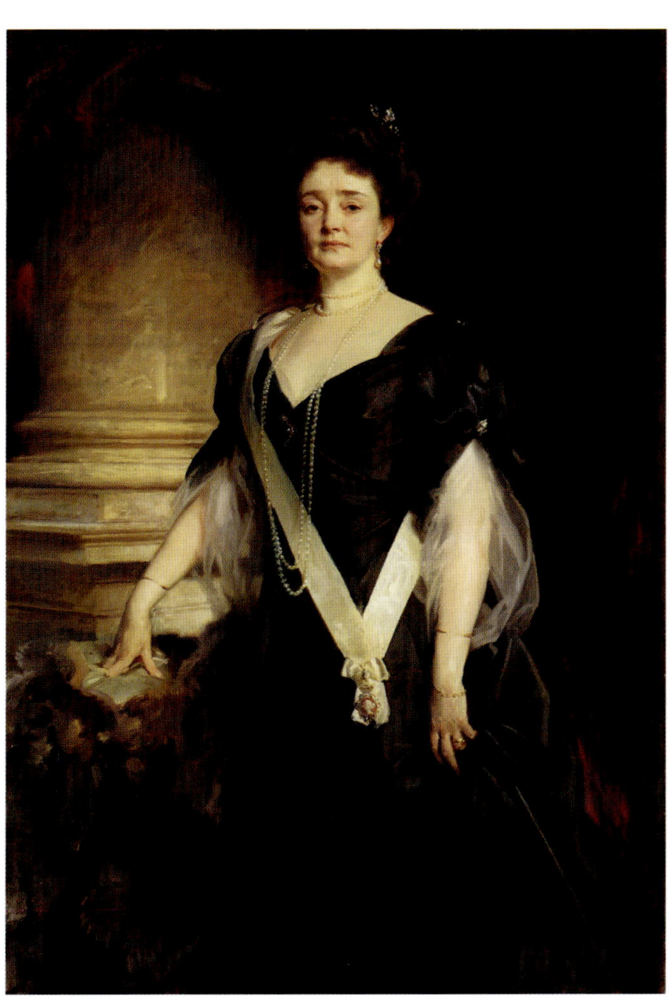

Louise, Duchess of Connaught, 1908, oil on canvas, 163.7 x 109.8cm (64½ x 43¼in), Royal Collection, London, UK

Princess Louise Margaret of Prussia (1860–1917) was a German princess and later a member of the British Royal family when she married Prince Arthur, Duke of Connaught and Strathearn, Queen Victoria's seventh child. She was also the Viceregal Consort of Canada, when her husband served as the Governor General of Canada from 1911 to 1916. This is a pendant portrait to the one Sargent made of the Duke (opposite).

Nancy Astor, 1908, oil on canvas, 150.5 x 99.7cm (59¼ x 39¼in), Cliveden, Buckinghamshire, UK

In 1893, the American millionaire William Waldorf Astor bought Cliveden for $1.2m. In 1906, his eldest son Waldorf married Nancy Witcher Langhorne (1879–1964) and William gave them Cliveden as a wedding gift. The mansion then entered a new glittering era as the couple hosted many society parties there. A great socialite, Nancy also became the first female Member of Parliament; she was elected MP for Plymouth in 1919, a seat she held until 1945.

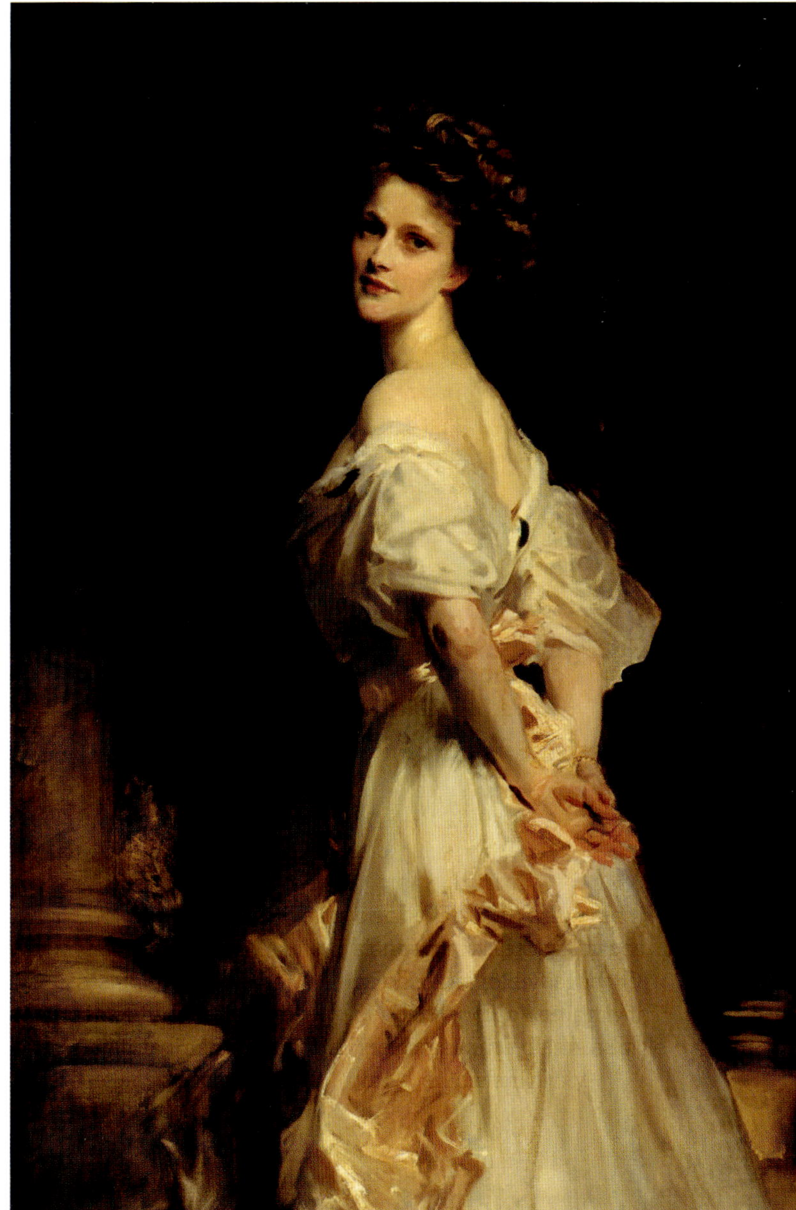

Oxen on the Beach at Baia,
c.1908, watercolour on
paper, 25.4 x 35.6cm
(10 x 14in), Private Collection

For centuries Baia was a
fashionable coastal resort on
the Gulf of Naples, particularly
during the ancient Roman
period; it was where the
super-rich gathered in
preference to Pompeii,
Herculaneum and Capri. By
Renaissance times its ruins
were largely submerged by
volcanic ash. Numerous artists,
including Turner, had preceded
Sargent to paint the sweeping
bay and ruined architecture; he
probably visited in 1907.

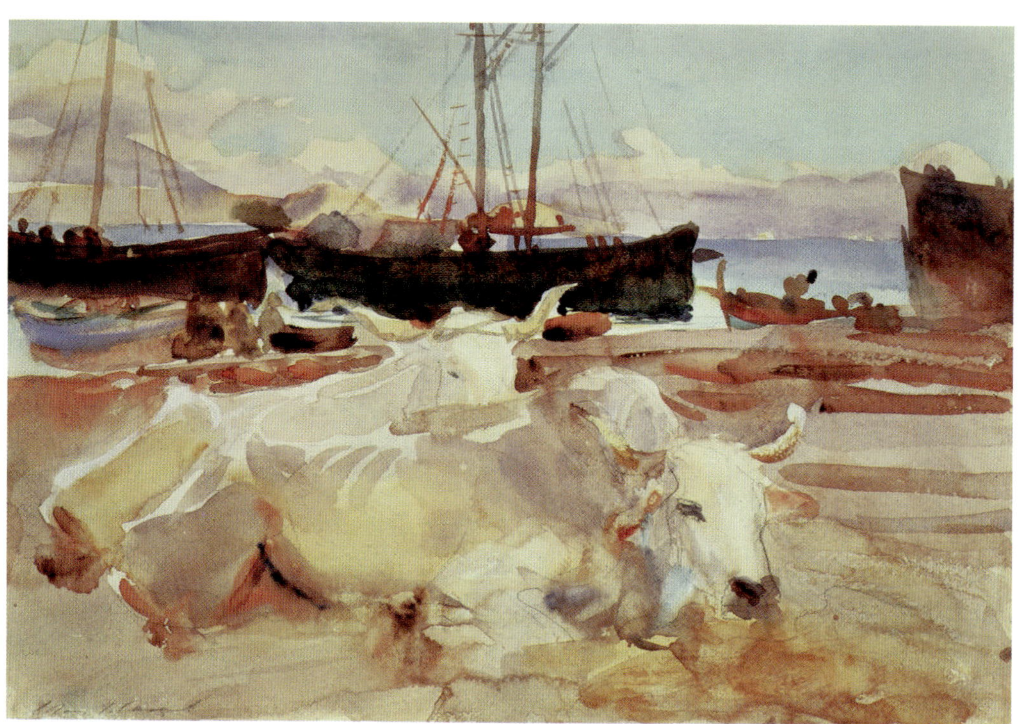

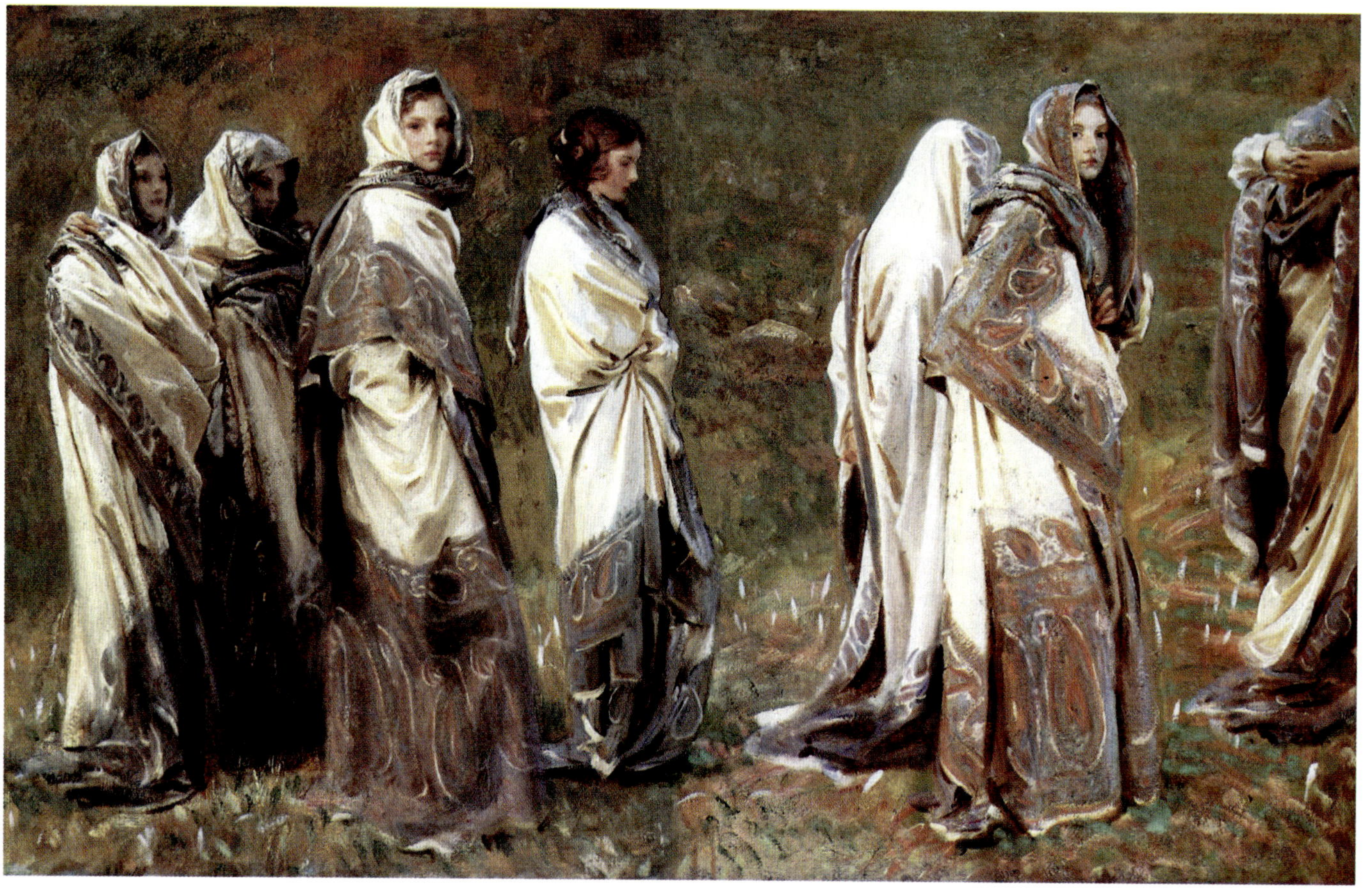

Cashmere, 1908, oil on
canvas, 71.1 x 109.2cm (28
x 43in), Private Collection

Painted in the Italian Alps

at Purtud, all seven figures
were modelled by Sargent's
youngest niece, Reine
Ormond, then aged 11, in
an exotic cashmere shawl.

Sargent's enduring fascination
with exotic-looking figures
draped in luxurious shawls
and robes was apparent
early in his career, in works

such as *Fumée d'Ambre Gris*
of 1880 (see page 113). This
image forms a mysterious-
looking procession, both
poetic and intriguing.

Predella of an Altar, Cathedral, Tarragona, c.1908, graphite and brown pigment on white wove paper, 35.9 x 25.2cm (14¼ x 10in), The Metropolitan Museum, New York, USA

Sargent became a full member of the Royal Society of Painters in Water Colours in 1908, and had become as celebrated for his watercolours as for his portraits. While in Tarragona, in Catalonia, Spain, he painted several works in the cathedral.

Pomegranates, 1908, watercolour and graphite on paper, 53.8 x 36.7cm (21¼ x 14½in), Brooklyn Museum, New York, USA

Here Sargent emphasized the contrasts of red and green pomegranates growing in dense foliage. Abandoning any horizon line, he created a textural, pattern effect that evokes a tapestry. He painted the image quickly, with free, gestural brushstrokes.

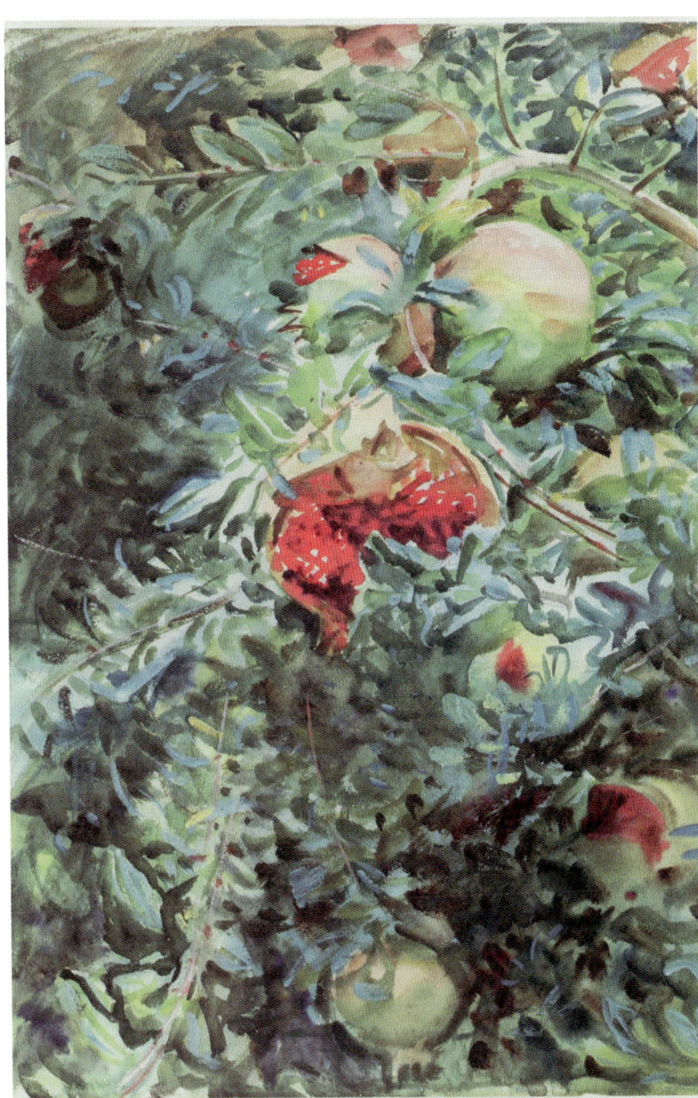

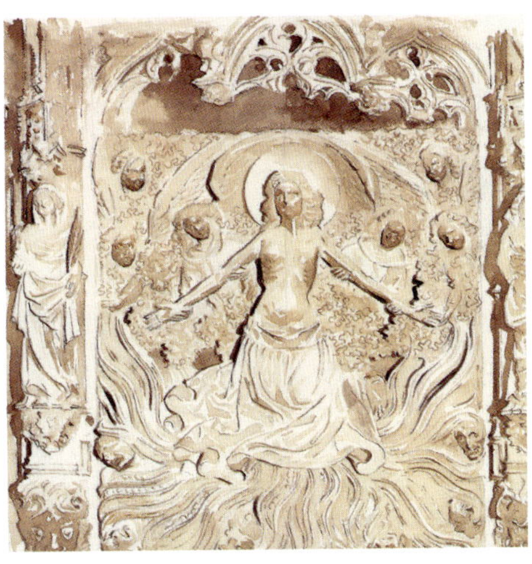

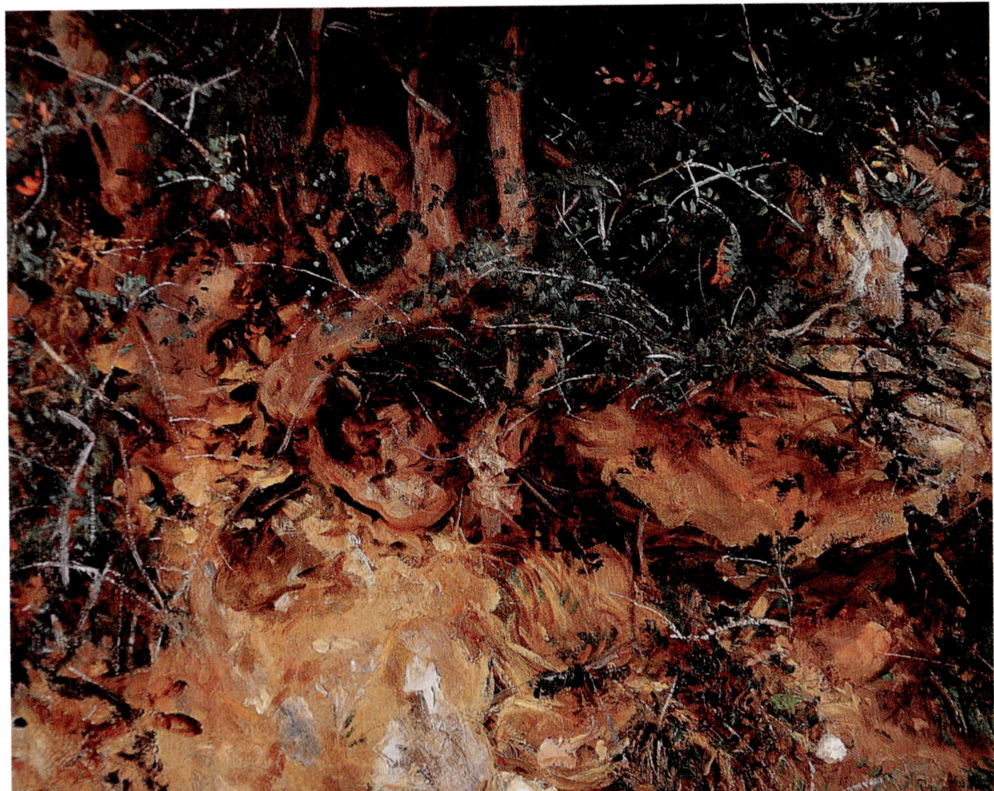

Valdemossa, Majorca: Thistles and Herbage on a Hillside, 1908, oil on canvas, 25.4 x 19.7cm (22 x 28in), National Gallery of Art, Washington DC, USA

In the autumn of 1908, Sargent stayed with Emily and Eliza Wedgwood in a large house called Can – or San – Mossenya. Avoiding the usual tourist type scenes, Sargent looked more closely at his surroundings and while most of his watercolours of the period are fluid, light and spontaneous, several of his oil paintings, like this, are more detailed close-ups, showing his fascination with nature.

Girls Gathering Blossoms, Majorca, c.1908, oil on canvas, 71.1 x 56.5cm (28 x 22¼in), Private Collection

In June 1908, Sargent made his first trip to Majorca and returned again in the autumn, staying in an old house in the village of Valdemossa. This was one of his favourite subjects; local people engaged in traditional work, such as picking fruit, tending livestock and gathering flowers. With a characteristically dramatic composition, he has taken a high viewpoint, so viewers look down on the scene.

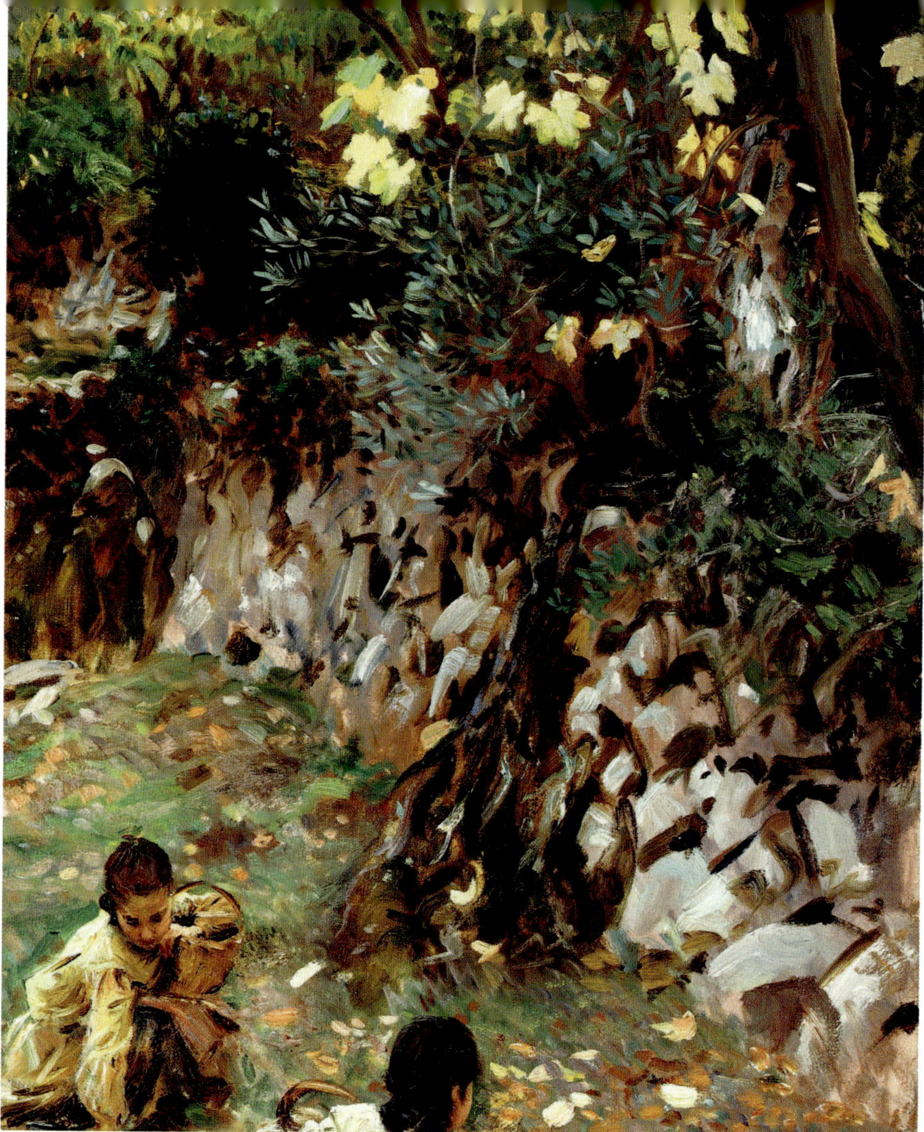

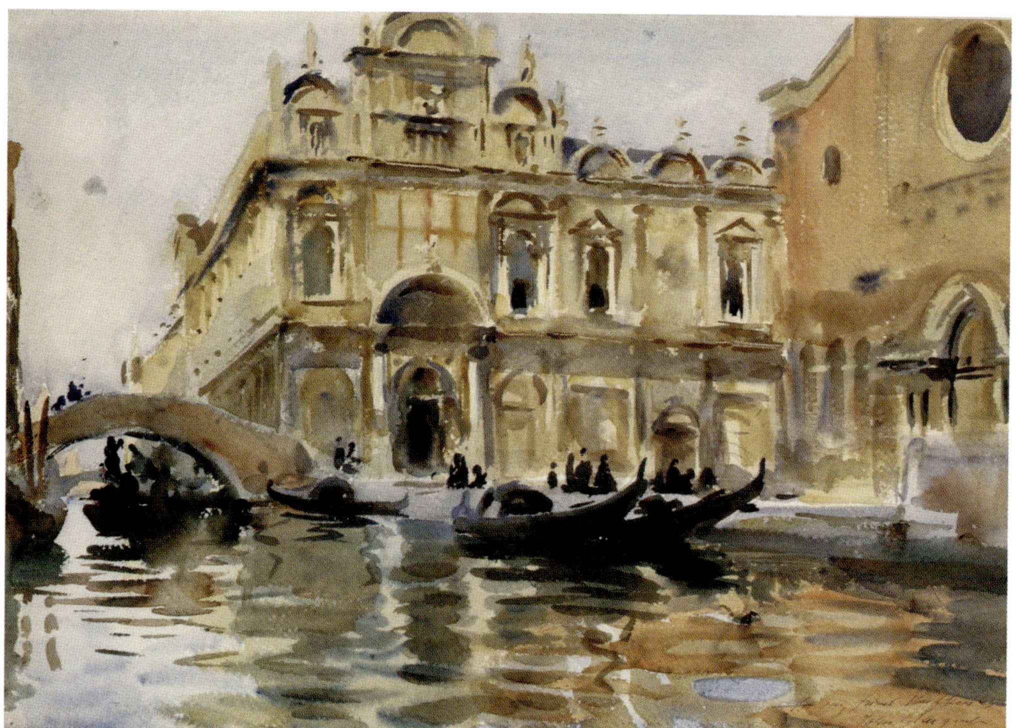

Rio dei Mendicanti, Venice, c.1909, watercolour and graphite on paper, 91.4 x 72.4cm (36 x 28½in), Indianapolis Museum of Art, Indiana, USA

Just as tourists take photos in Venice of the grand palaces they pass as they travel on the water, so Sargent drew and painted the juxtapositions of sky, water and architecture that caught his eye from his gondola. He was particularly sensitive to the various ways in which atmosphere is evoked through shadows and reflections, and to effects of the weather, as produced here by the rain.

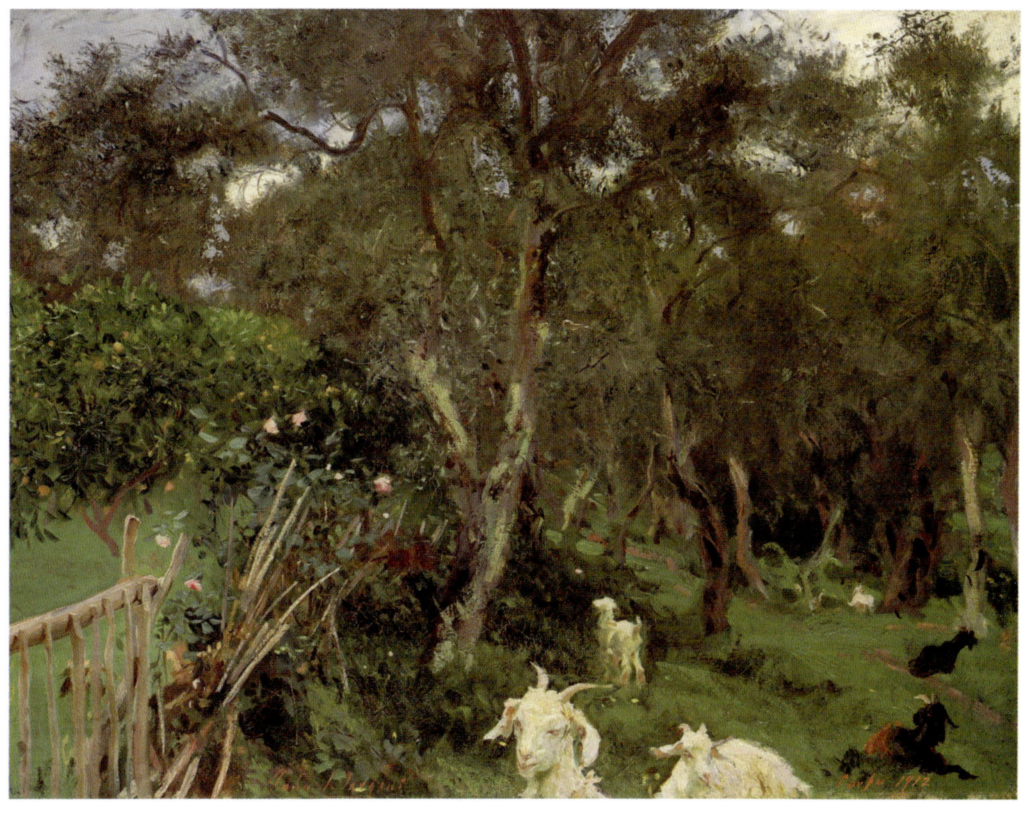

Olives in Corfu, 1909, oil on canvas, 56.6 x 71.7cm (22¼ x 28¼in), Fitzwilliam Museum, Cambridge, UK

Sargent began 1909 in the United States, but in August, he went to the Val d'Aosta and Venice, and at the end of September he continued to Corfu. The Villa Soteriotisa was four miles from Corfu town and Eliza Wedgwood recalled that: 'The villa had hardly a stick of furniture in it, but the walk through the lemons and oranges in the garden straight to the silky blue sea was worth all the discomforts.' Here Sargent turned away from the attractions of the sea, instead capturing an image inland.

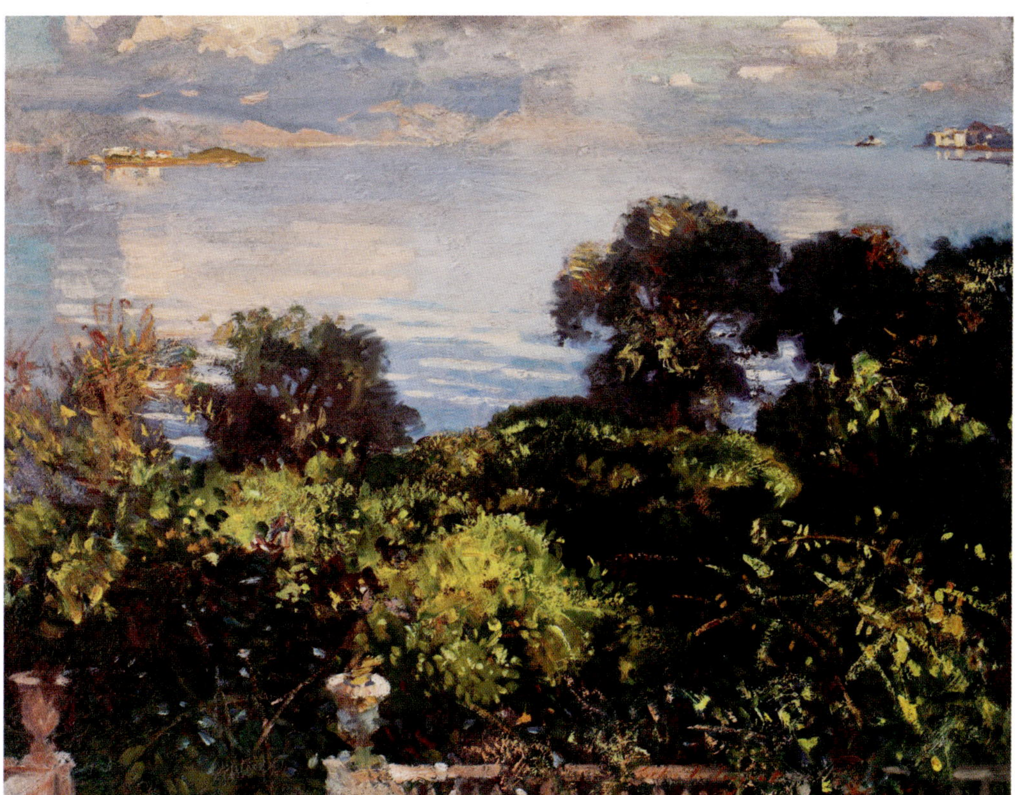

Oranges at Corfu, c.1909, oil on canvas, 55.9 x 71.1cm (22 x 28in), Worcester Art Museum, MA, USA

From the end of September until the middle of November 1909, Sargent stayed in Corfu in the Villa Soteriotisa with Emily, Eliza and the de Glehns. While there, he painted this view looking across a terrace to a grove of orange trees that can be seen beyond a stone balustrade. The calm blue sea and other parts of the island can be seen in the distance.

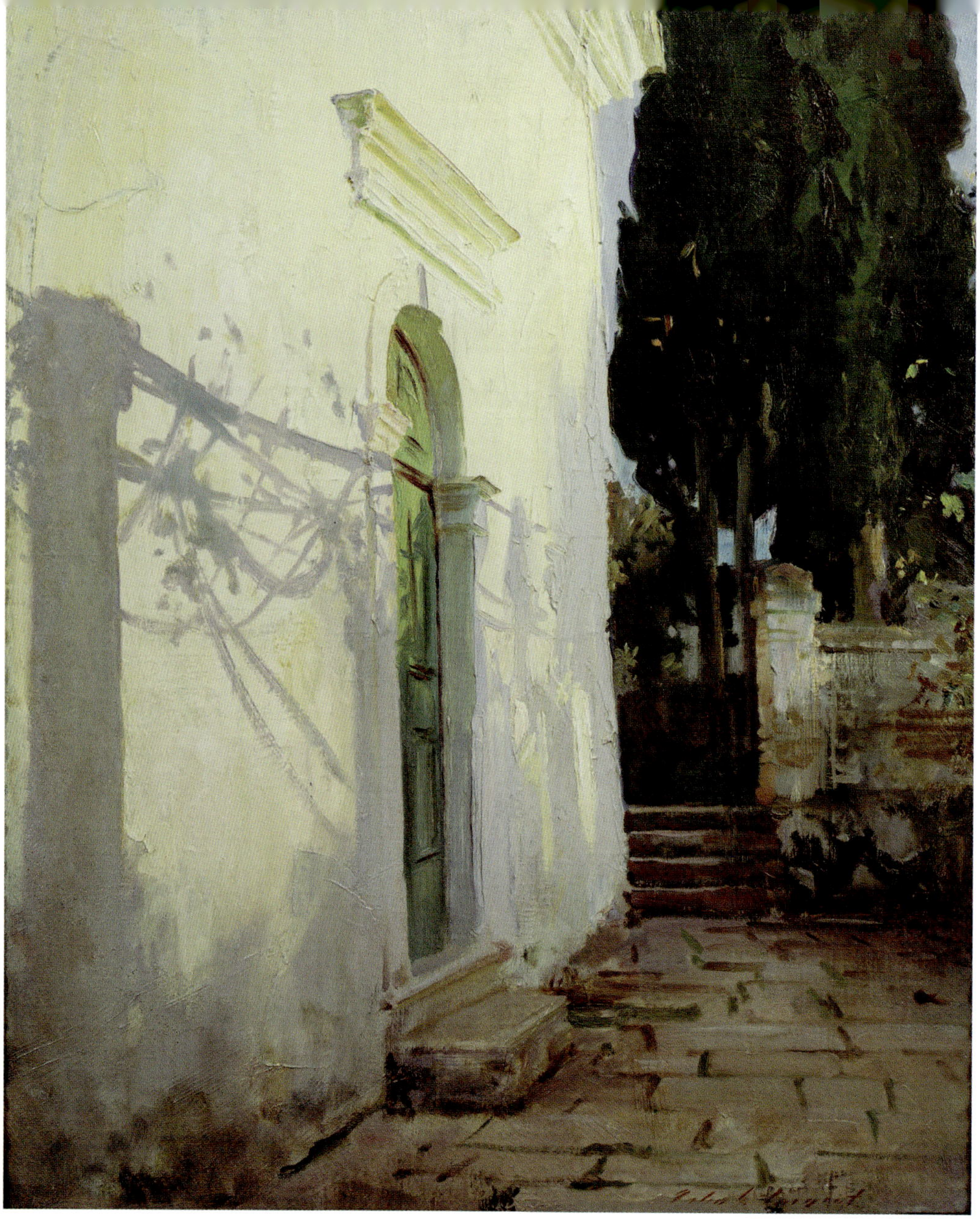

Shadows on a Wall in Corfu,
1909, oil on canvas, 71.8 x
56.2cm (28¼ x 22in), Fine
Art Society, London, UK

Sargent always maintained
that vast skies and extensive
landscapes did not appeal
to him. In contrast, he was
fascinated by details, patterns,
colours and textures. The
patterns created here by
a low sun, architecture
and foliage create a gentle
ambience, as the soft, early
evening light makes the
white wall glow. He painted
the shadows on it in violet,
cobalt blue and yellow ochre,

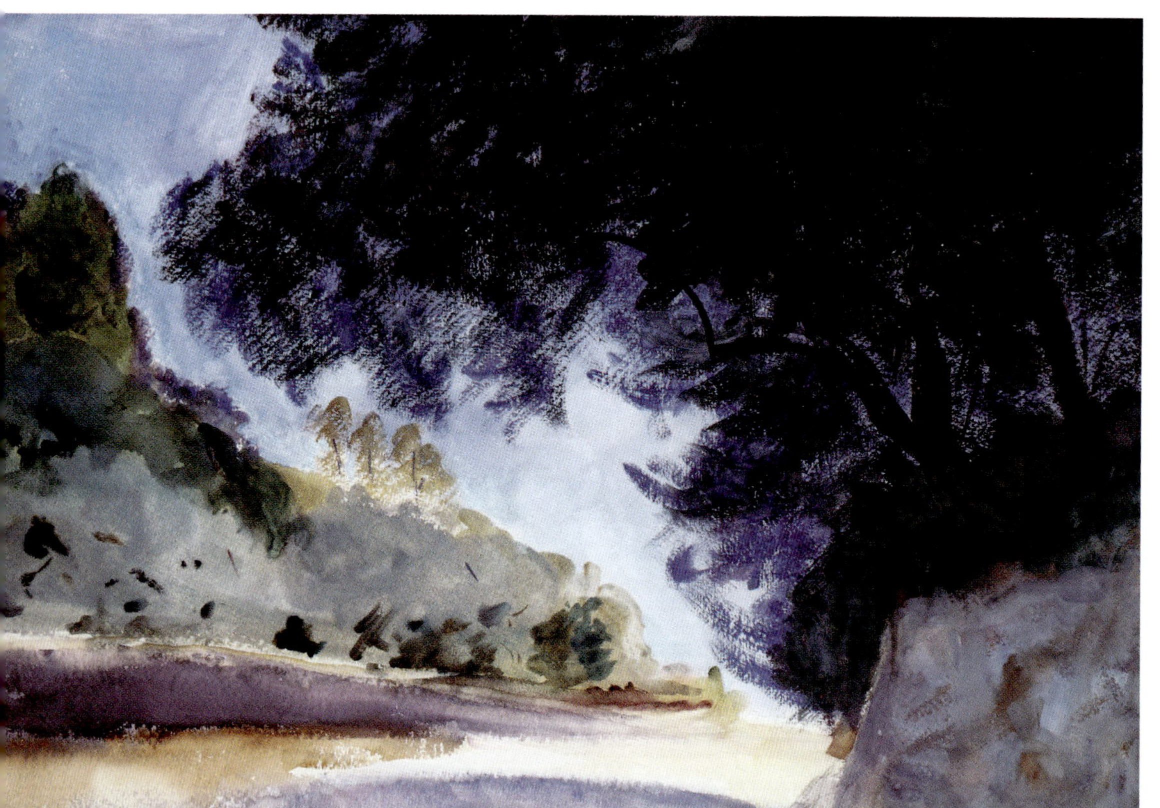

Landscape, Olive Trees, Corfu,
1909, translucent and
opaque watercolour and
graphite on paper, 34.3
x 24.5cm (13½ x 9½in),
Private Collection

Using washes and dry brush
techniques, Sargent built
up patterns of leaves and
plants, creating a simplified,
light-filled impression of the
scene; a sultry day in Corfu,
the heat almost palpable. His
palette reflects his interest
in Impressionist philosophies,
with shadows of violet, yellow
ochre and ultramarine. The
middle and far distance are
deliberately undefined.

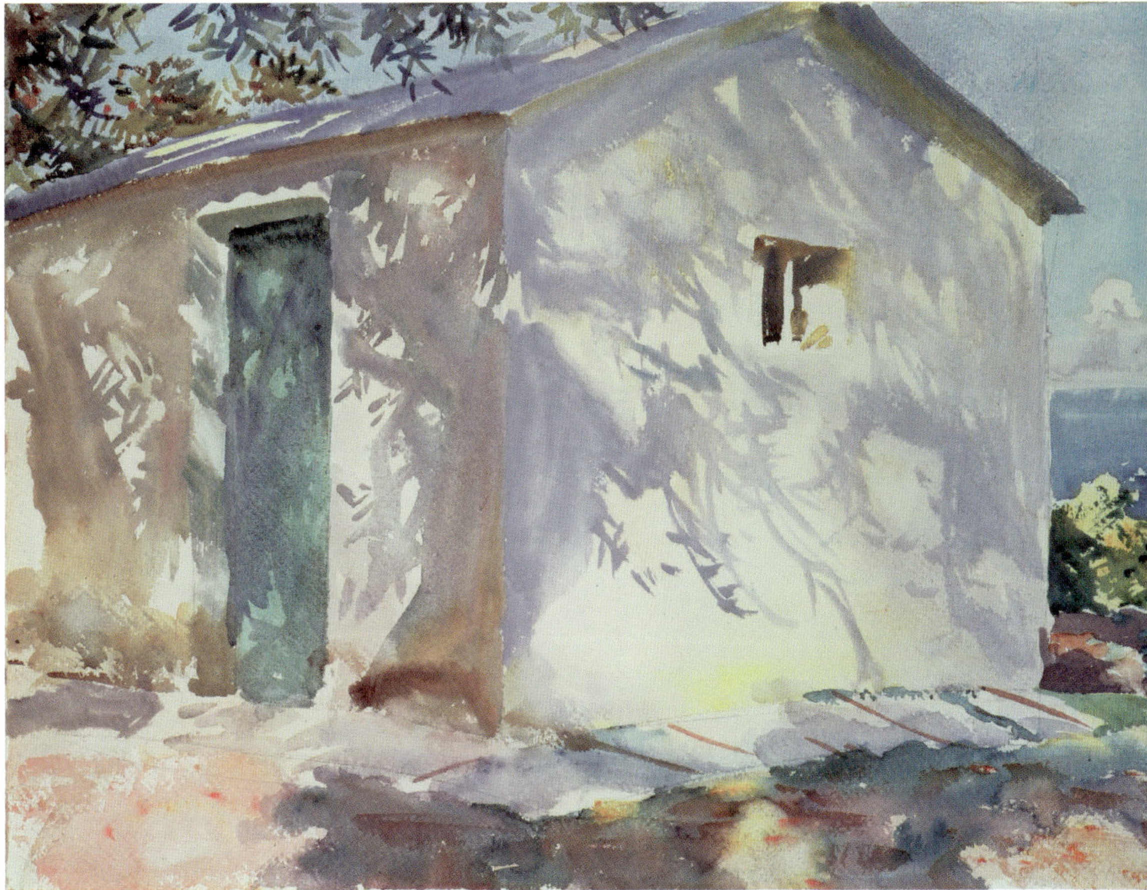

Corfu: Lights and Shadows, 1909, translucent and opaque watercolour and wax resist over graphite on paper, 61 x 76cm (24 x 30in), Museum of Fine Arts, Boston, Massachusetts, USA

Focusing on objects bathed in light, and patterns of shadow and colour, Sargent painted the wall of this hut in the park of the royal villa, Monrepos, where he was staying in Corfu at this time. He wrote: 'enormous views and huge skies do not tempt me.' Intimate views and close features such as these shadows on the sunlit walls were more to his taste, here expressed in violet, green, blue, pink and yellow.

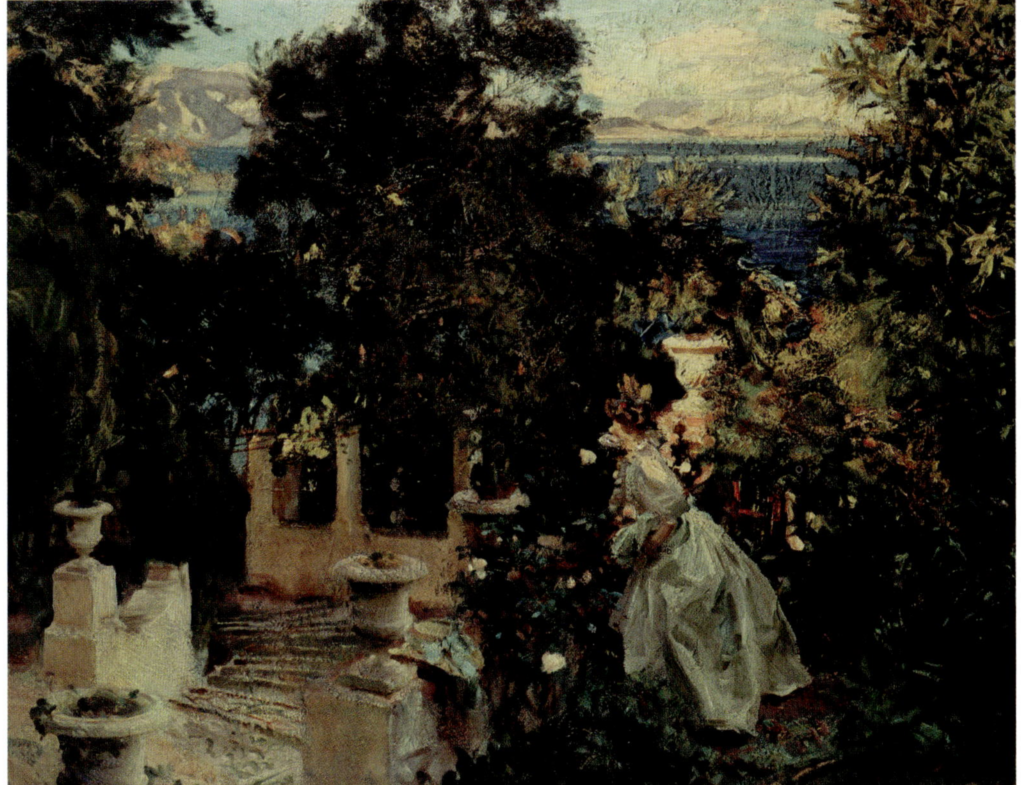

A Garden in Corfu, 1909, oil on canvas, 55.9 x 71.2cm (22 x 28in), Private Collection

Focusing on objects bathed in light and colour rather than the broad panoramic view beyond the trees, this was painted in the grounds of the Villa Soteriotisa where Sargent was staying in the autumn of 1909. Fascinated by shadows from the trees and the steps and other structures, he painted Jane de Glehn, elegant in white, leaning over the stone steps, looking out across the sea.

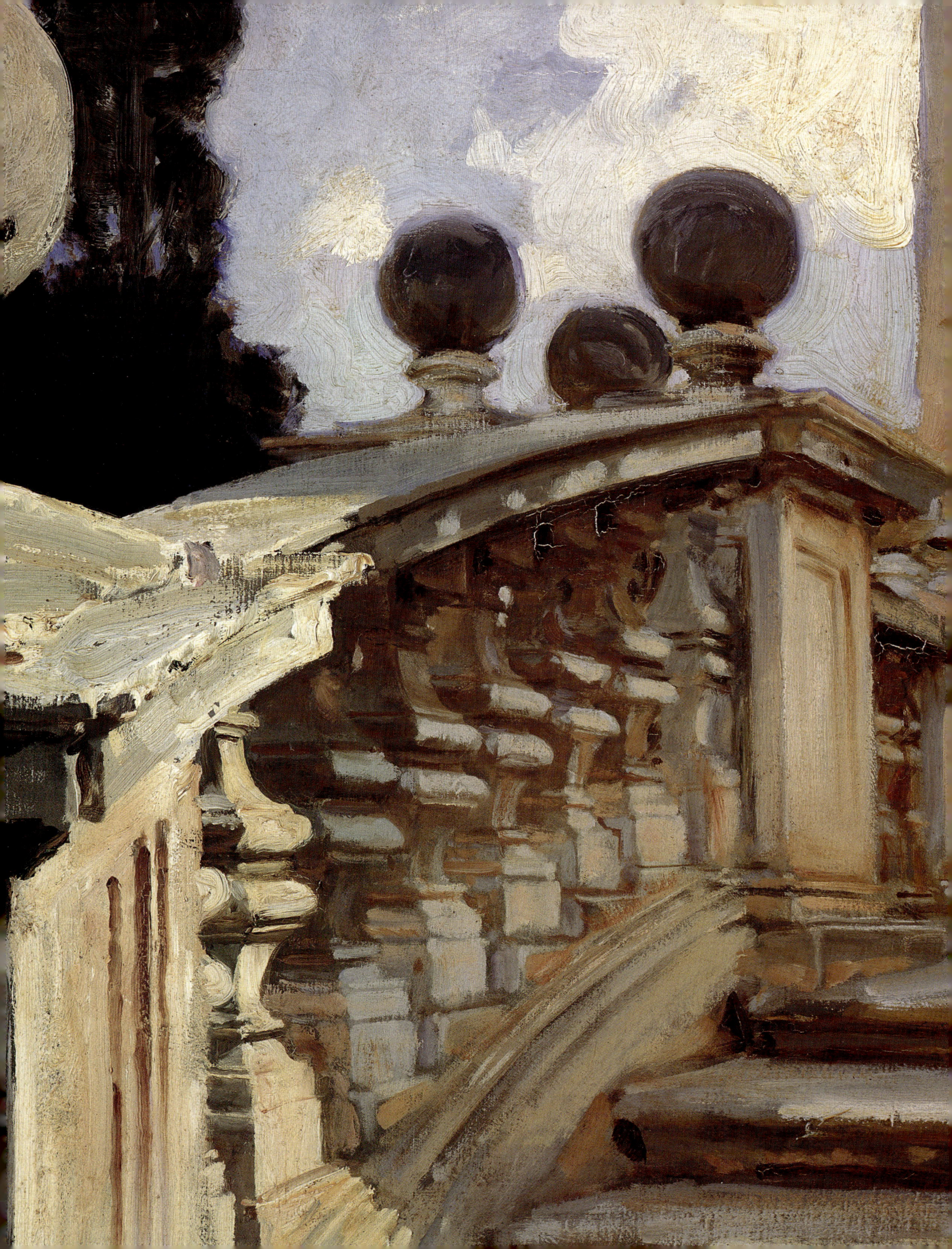

INTERNATIONAL RENOWN

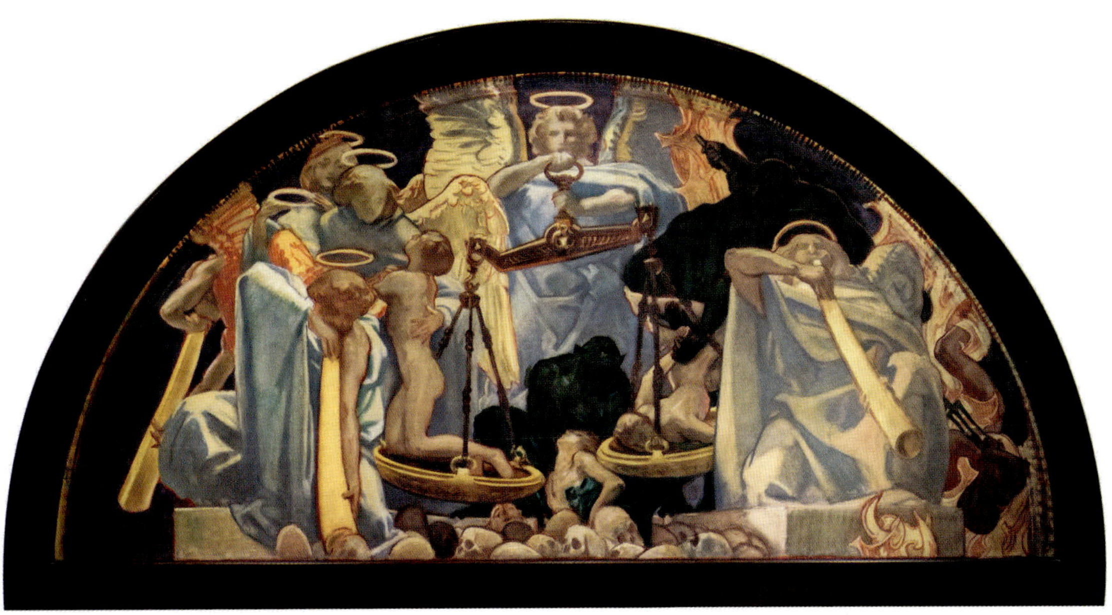

By the early 20th century, Sargent was revered and celebrated, particularly in Britain and America, where the most high-profile figures sought to have their likenesses captured by him, no matter what the cost. It was for this reason that, ironically, by 1907, he decided to no longer paint portraits on commission. 'No more paughtraits,' he wrote jokingly to Ralph Curtis, implying the upper classes who made so many demands on him. His great success had made it financially possible for him to abandon the practice.

Above: Study for Boston Public Library Lunette, Judgement, c.1909–14, oil on canvas, 83.8 x 170.2cm (33 x 67in), Museum of Fine Arts, Boston, Massachusetts, USA. This study was made for an image for the centre of the west wall in the library; the gilded, sinuous image reflects the fashionable Art Nouveau styles of the time and although less overtly embellished, it can be compared to contemporary paintings by Gustav Klimt (1862–1918).

Left: A Balustrade, 1910, oil on canvas, 55 x 71cm (21½ x 28in), The Ashmolean Museum, Oxford, UK. Painted from an unusual viewpoint, this balustrade leads to the front door of the church of Saints Domenico e Sisto in Rome.

The Olive Grove, c.1910, oil on canvas, 55.9 x 73cm (22 x 28¾in), Indianapolis Museum of Art, Indiana, USA

The greyish foliage of these olive trees, probably on Corfu, create a sense of calm over the entire composition. Sargent's lively Impressionistic brushmarks describe the dynamism of villagers gathering olives in the cool shade beneath the trees. The palette recalls his stay in Capri in 1878.

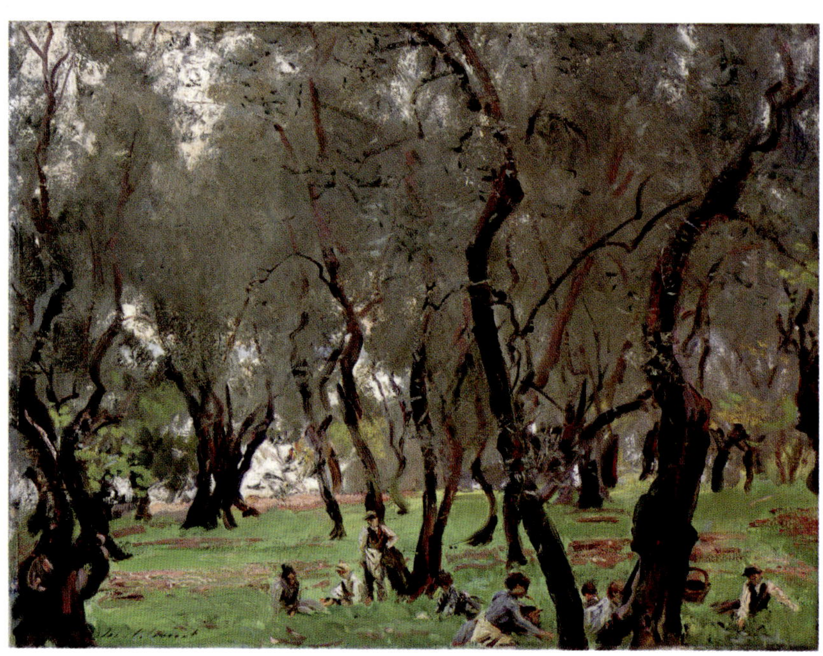

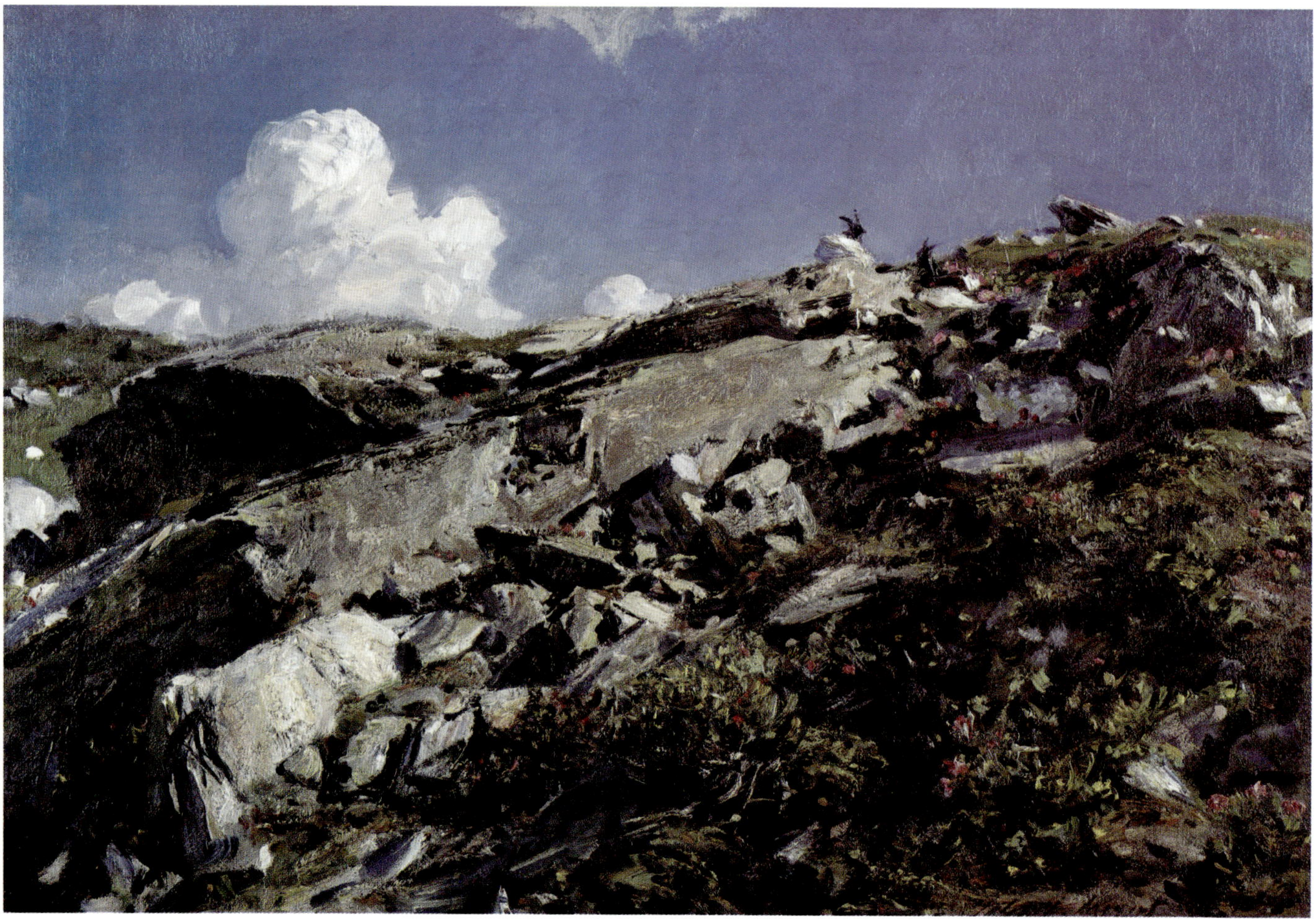

In the Alps, 1910, oil on canvas, 71.1 x 50.8cm (28 x 20in), Private Collection

Here the mountain makes up most of the composition, rising up to a strip of brilliant blue sky smudged with white clouds. Sargent favoured a low viewpoint as it enabled him to focus on close-up elements of the theme, and to create a sense of drama. Unlike many of his sketchy watercolours of the landscape, this work in oil is extremely detailed and complex, emphasizing the contrasts of lights and darks.

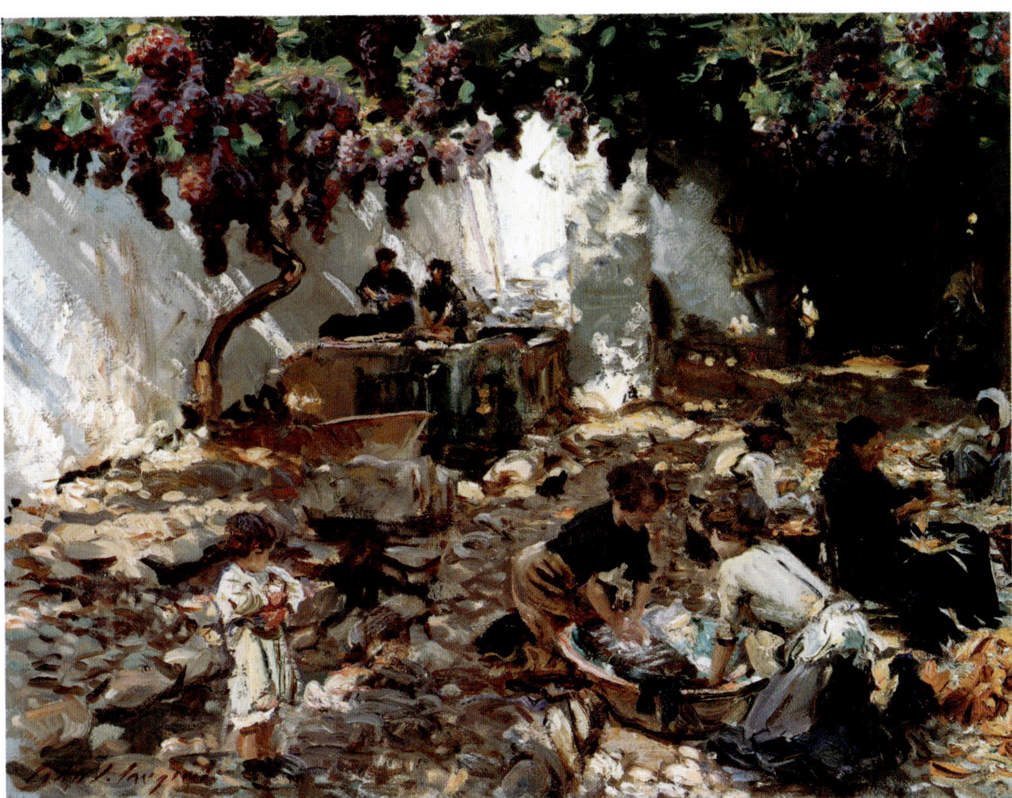

Women at Work, 1910, oil on canvas, 56 x 71cm (22 x 28in), Private Collection

At around this time, Sargent spent a great deal of time in Italy; including in Bologna, Florence, Lucca and Siena, where he painted this view of local women under the trees, working at various things, including washing and knitting. The entire work appears like a pattern created by the dappled light filtering through the trees around them. This focus on strong colour and light effects was probably why Roger Fry mistakenly added Sargent's name to a list of Post-Impressionist supporters.

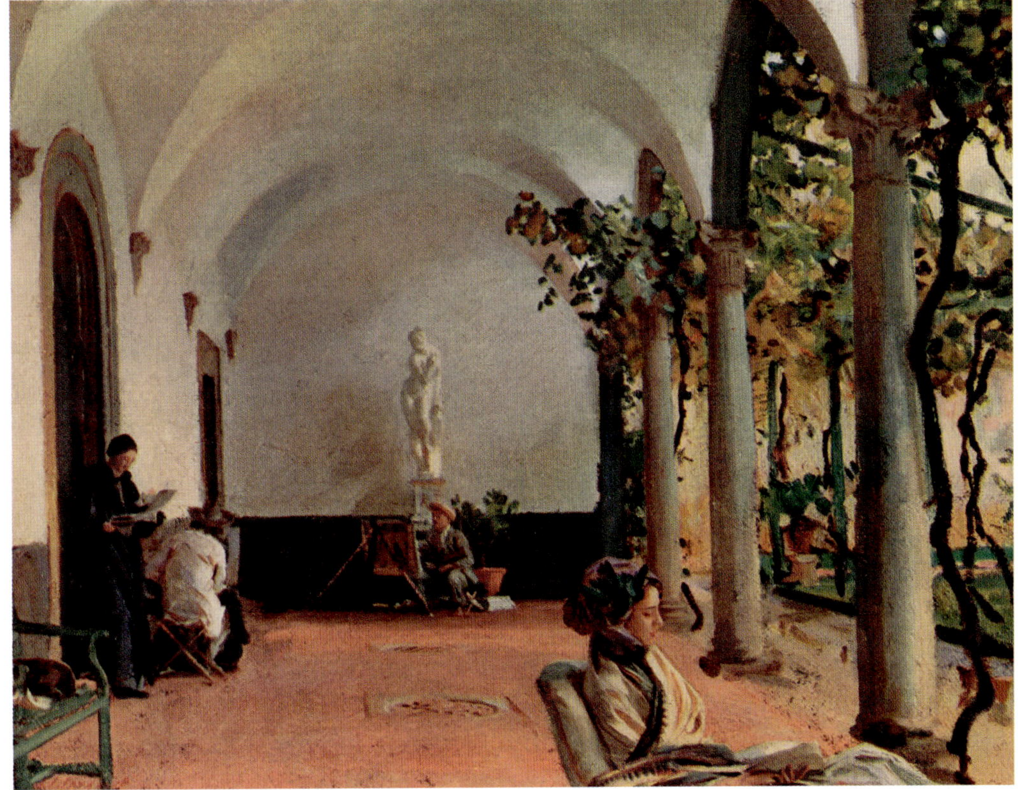

Villa Torre Galli: the Loggia, 1910, oil on canvas, 55.9 x 71.1cm (22 x 28in), Private Collection

After travelling to Italy during the autumn of 1910, Sargent and Emily met up with their friends Wilfrid and Jane de Glehn, William and Clara Blake Richmond, and Emily's friend Eliza Wedgwood. They stayed in a villa near Florence (see overleaf) where the group painted and relaxed. Here William Blake Richmond and Wilfrid de Glehn can be seen painting. Sargent produced a few scenes of this loggia, capturing the tranquility of the moment, with each figure absorbed in his or her own personal activity.

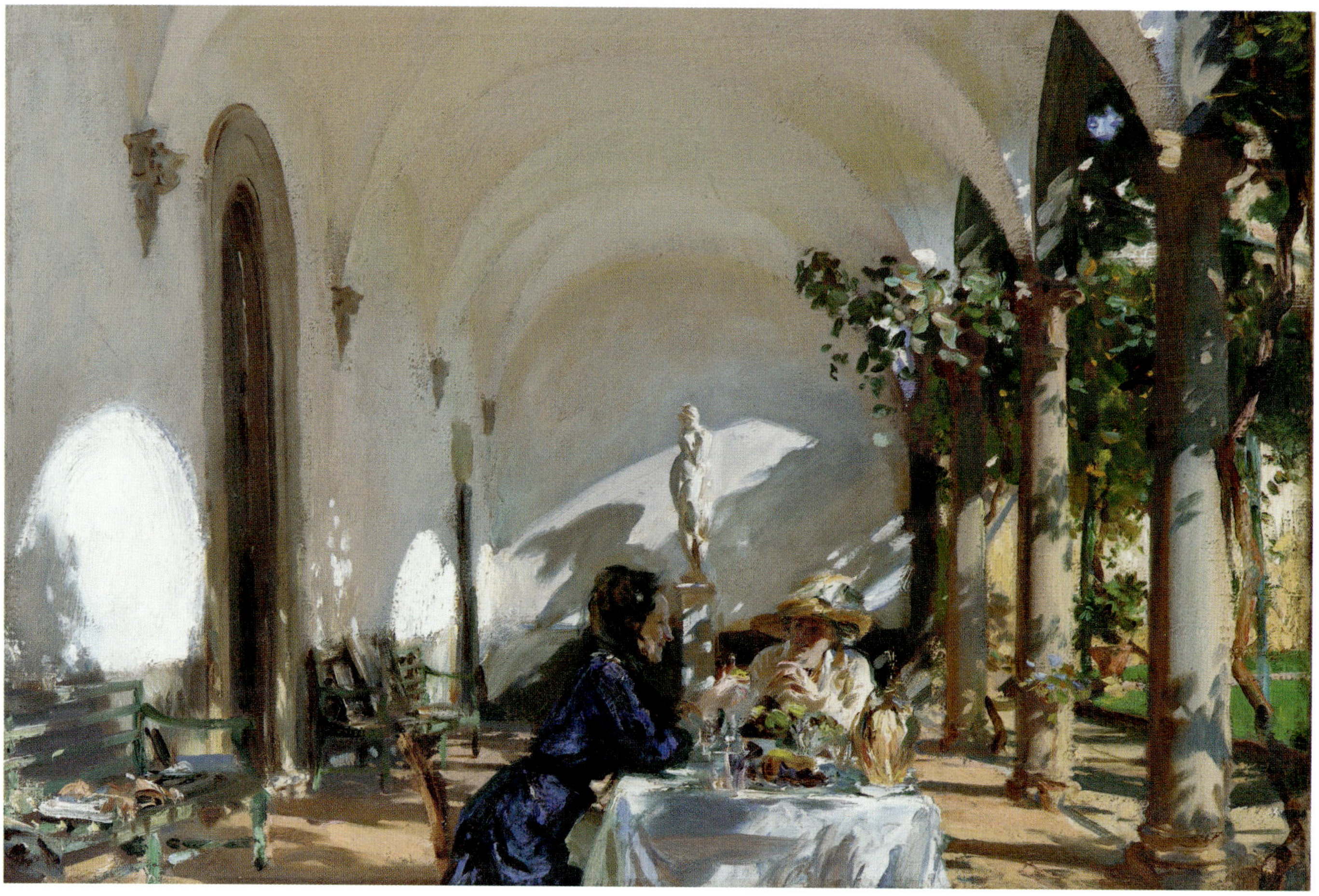

Breakfast in the Loggia,
1910, oil on canvas, 52.1
x 71.1cm (20½ x 28in),
Freer Gallery of Art,
Smithsonian Institution,
Washington DC, USA

In the autumn of 1910, Sargent stayed in the Villa Torre Galli at Scandicci, near Florence, with a group of friends. He captured the dappled, slanting early morning light falling on two of the party as they enjoy a peaceful breakfast. They are Lady Richmond (the wife of Sir William Blake Richmond, who created the mosaics for the chancel of St Paul's cathedral in London) and Jane de Glehn. They are overlooked by a marble statue of Venus, the embodiment of beauty.

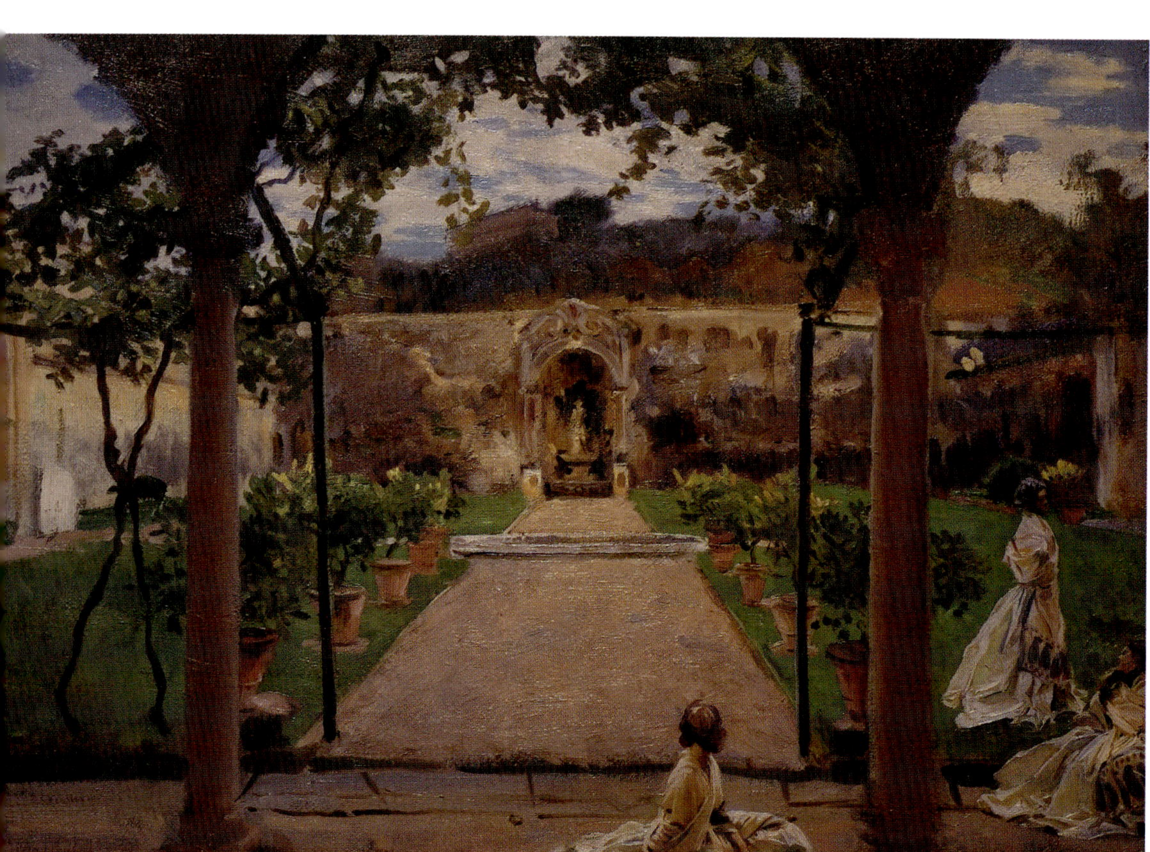

At Torre Galli: Ladies in a Garden, 1910, oil on canvas, 71.1 x 91.4cm (28 x 36in), Royal Academy of Art, London, UK

As in the above work, this was painted at the Villa Torre Galli. The colonnaded loggia that opened on to a picturesque garden particularly appealed to Sargent. Here, three somewhat self-contained women, swathed in Sargent's exotic cashmere shawls, walk from the loggia to the garden. The model for all three women is believed to have been Jane de Glehn.

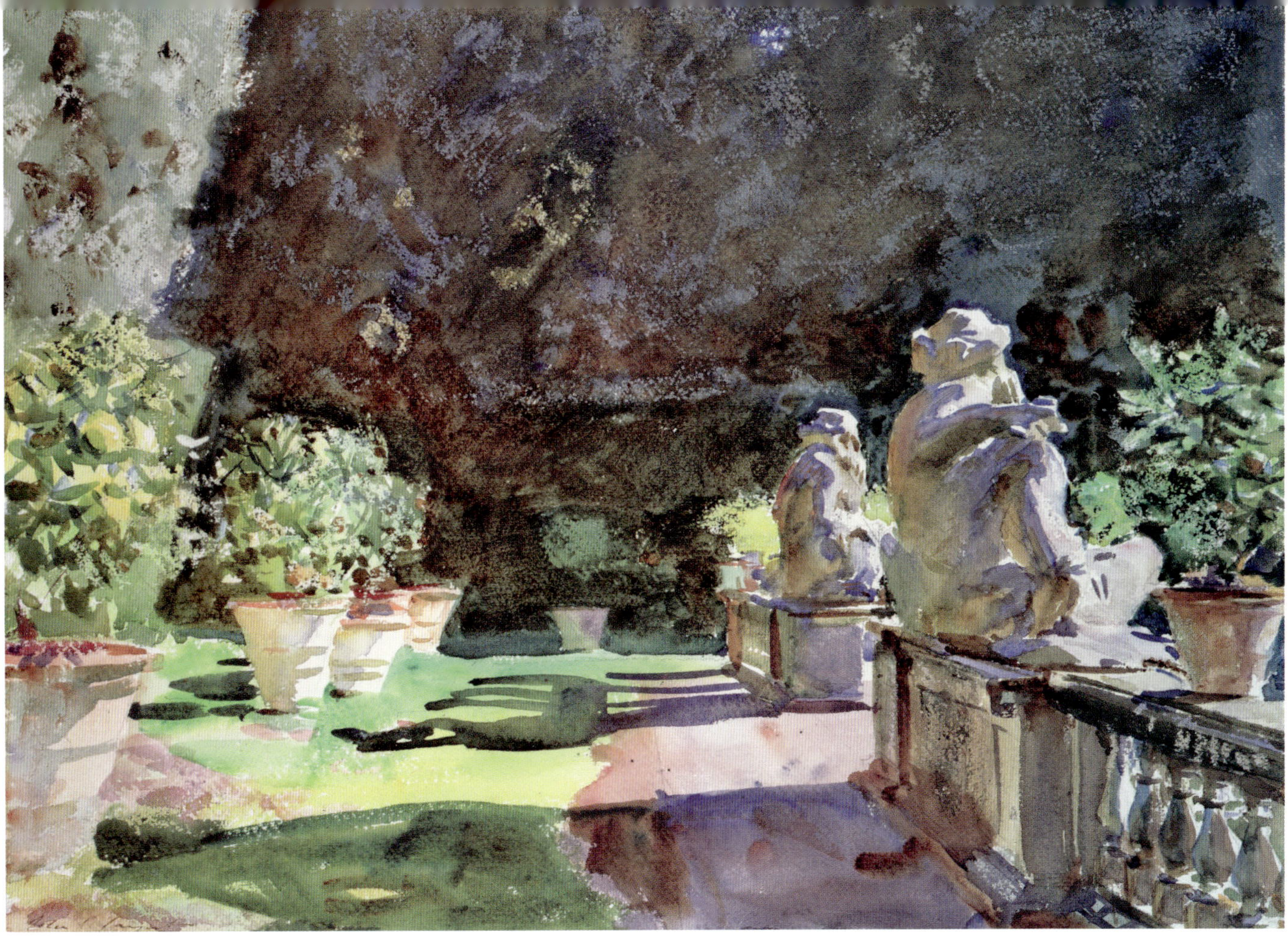

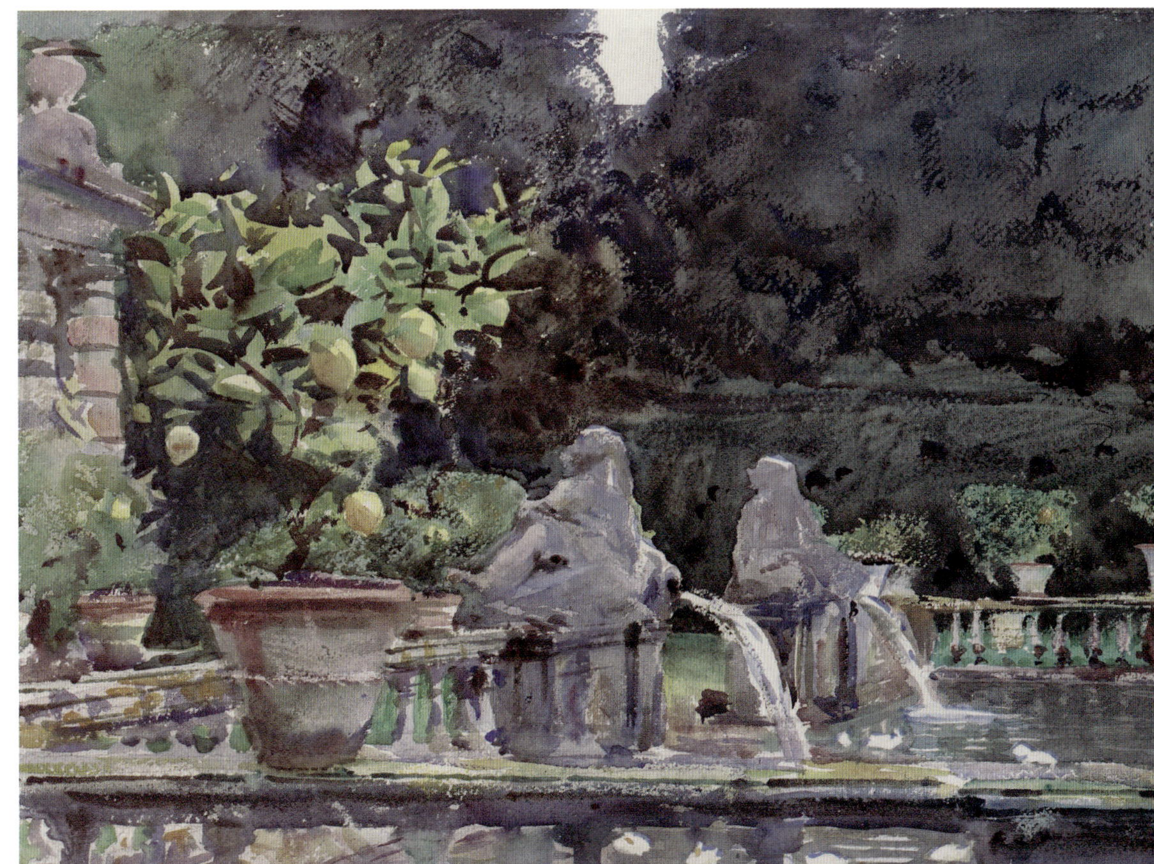

Villa di Marlia: Lucca, 1910,
watercolour over graphite
on paper, 40.4 x 53.1cm
(15¾ x 20¾in), Museum
of Fine Arts, Boston,
Massachusetts, USA

After staying in the Villa
Torre Galli, Sargent and
his friends moved to the
Villa Marlia near Lucca.
Here a sunlit path leads
through the Tuscan garden
to a background of trees
shadowed in blue and brown.
Two statues on a balustrade
are dark on one side and
bathed in sunlight on the
other, with shadows in violet,
green and gold. The plants
are also vibrantly depicted
with loose brushstrokes and
in warm and cool colours
that vividly express the heat.

*Villa di Marlia, Lucca: A
Fountain,* 1910, translucent
and opaque watercolour
and graphite on paper, 40.4
x 53.1cm (15¾ x 20¾in),
Museum of Fine Arts,
Boston, Massachusetts, USA

This is a part of Villa
Marlia's garden where a
stone balustrade is lined
with lemon trees in large
terracotta pots, and two
statues of river gods hold
jars that spout water into
a raised pool. The lush
background vegetation is
rendered with dense wet
washes, with darker colours
scumbled across with a dry
brush technique.

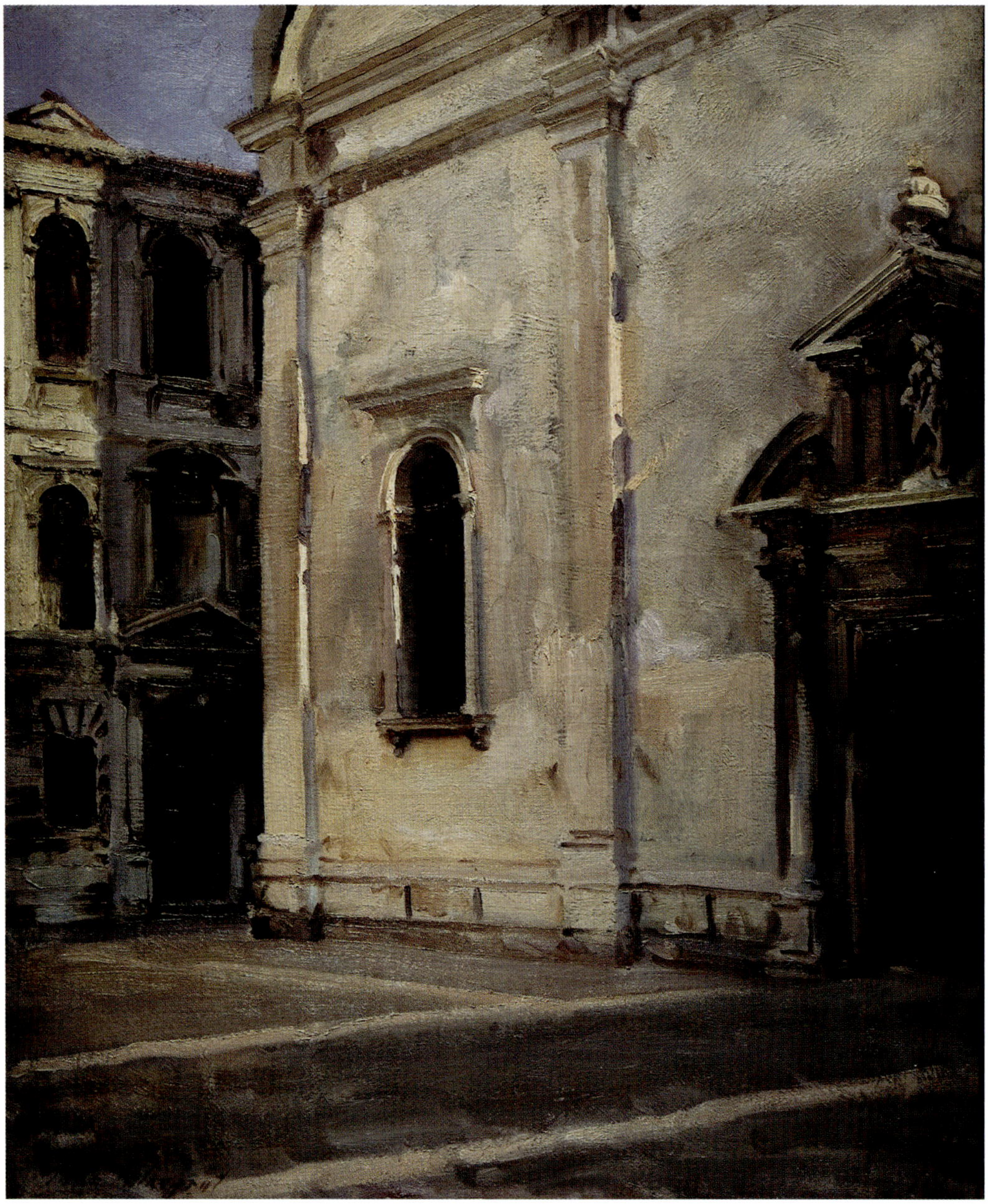

Santa Maria del Carmelo and the Scuola Grande dei Carmini, 1910, oil on canvas, 71.1 x 55.9cm (28 x 22in), Private Collection

Also known as the Santa Maria dei Carmini, or simply the Carmini, this large church in the sestiere of Dorsoduro in Venice was consecrated in 1348. Adjacent to it is the former Scuola Grande di Santa Maria del Carmelo, or the Scuola dei Carmini, a charitable confraternity founded in 1597. Sargent applied oil paint in fairly thin consistencies, with long strokes and black in the doors, windows and shadows.

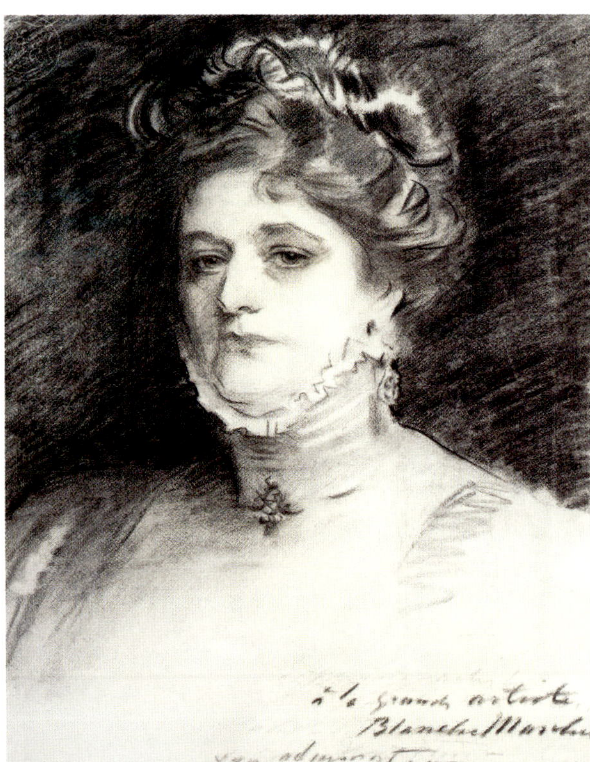

Portrait of Blanche Marchesi, 1910, black chalk on paper, 63 x 48cm (24¾ x 18¾in), Private Collection

Originally trained as a violinist, Parisian-born Blanche Marchesi (1853–1940) became a mezzo-soprano and voice teacher.

Sargent admired her hugely and he signed and inscribed this drawing on the lower right: 'à la grande artiste Blanche Marchesi, son admirateur John S. Sargent.' The drawing depicts her dressed in the height of fashion, with her high-necked blouse.

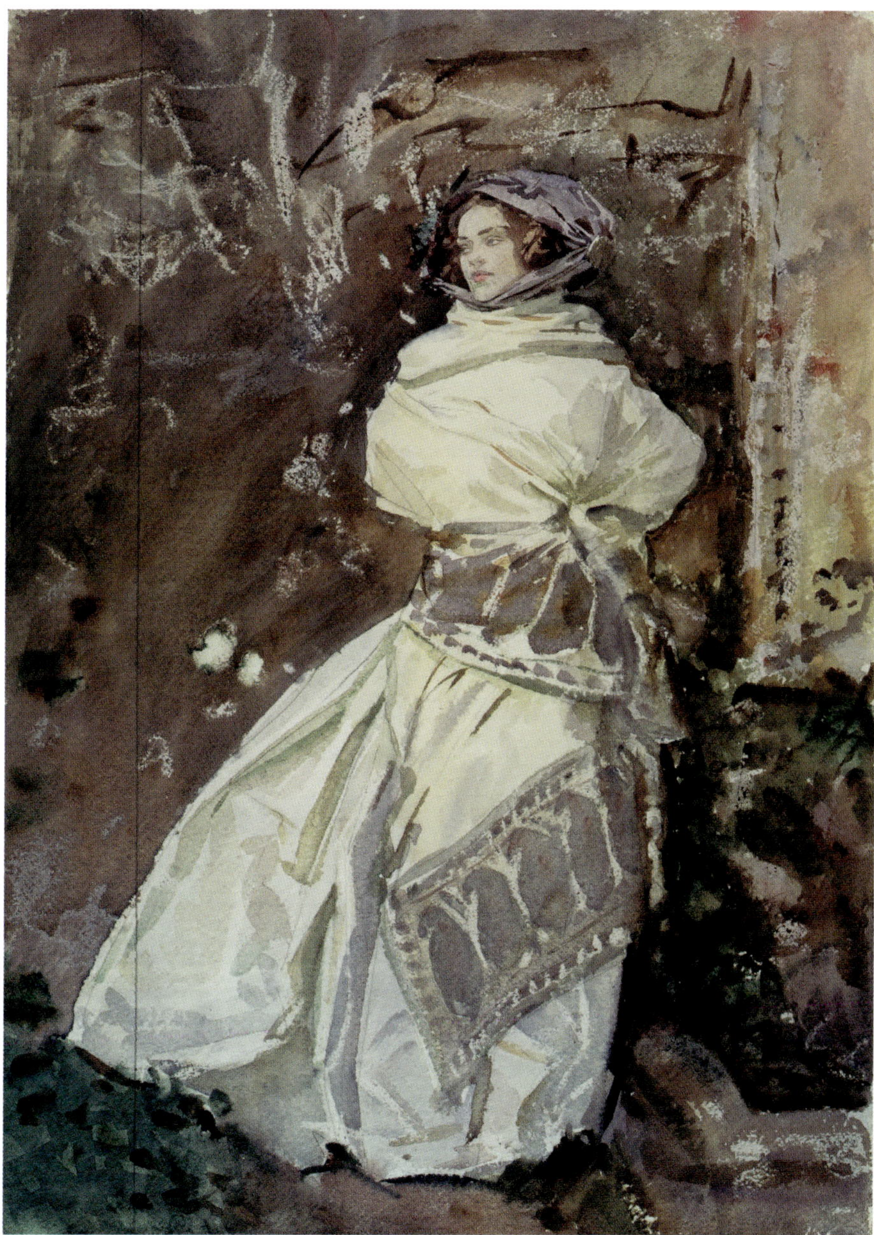

The Cashmere Shawl, 1910–11, watercolour on paper, 50.2 x 29.9cm (19¾ x 11¾in), Museum of Fine Arts, Boston, Massachusetts, USA

Rose-Marie was Sargent's favourite and most elegant model. He depicted her over and again in billowing white dresses, draped in the exotic cashmere shawls that he took on holiday for the purpose. With her figure poised and her face depicted in careful, delicate detail, she leans against a soft brown and terracotta coloured wall, with emerald green foliage having the effect of throwing her figure into high relief.

Mrs Gilbert Russell, 1911, charcoal on paper, 46.5 x 61cm (18¼ x 24in), Clark Art Institute, MA, USA

Maud Julia Augusta Nelke (1892–1982) was the daughter of a stockbroker and the wife of banker Gilbert Russell. She was also a society hostess and a patron of art. In 1934, she and her husband bought Mottisfont Abbey in Hampshire, England, where they entertained artists and writers. She commissioned some of her artist and designer friends to decorate the property, paying careful attention to its history.

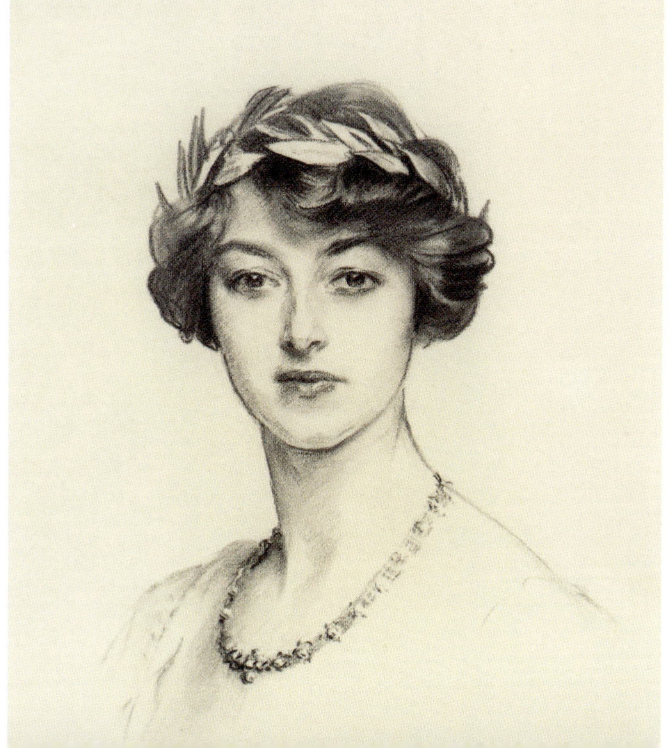

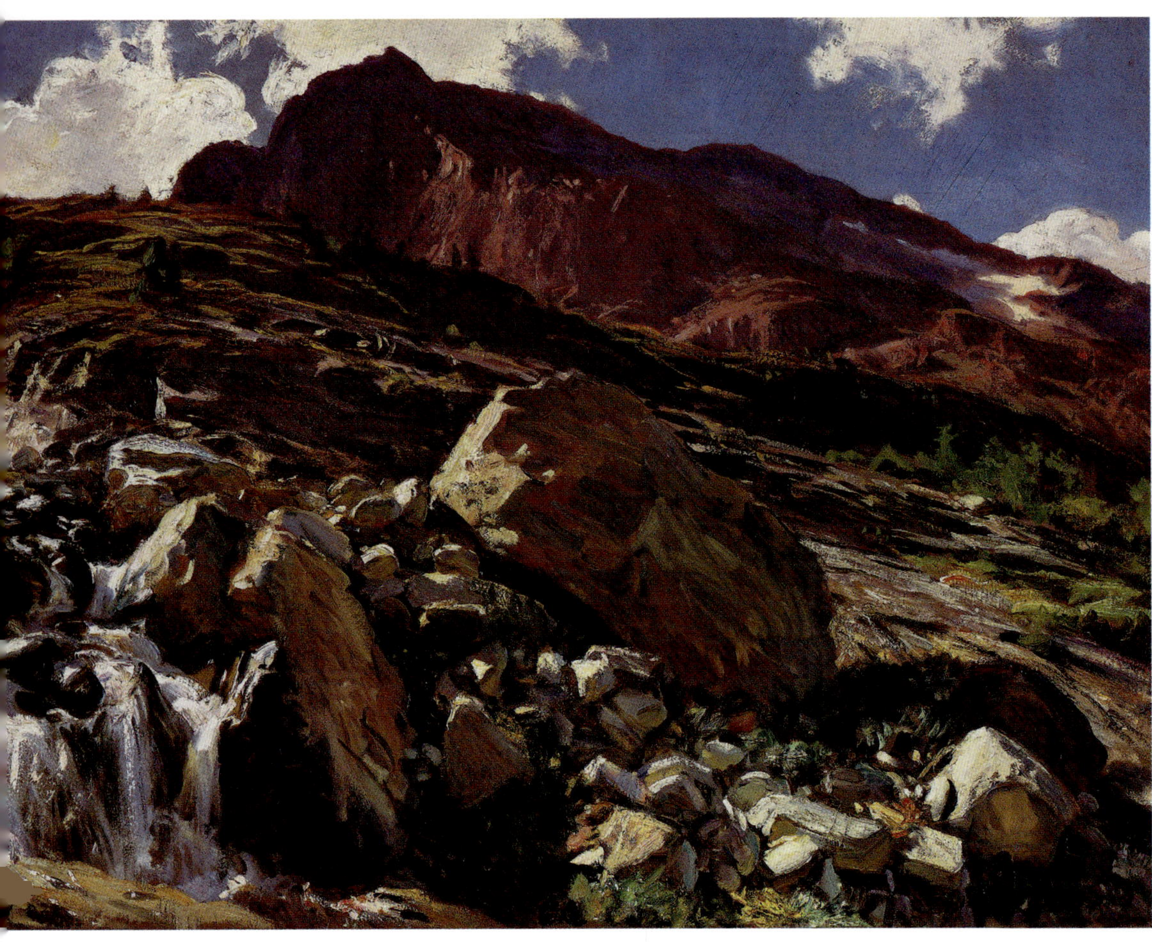

Simplon Pass, 1911, oil on canvas, 71.8 x 92.6cm (28¼ x 36½in), National Gallery of Art, Washington DC, USA

One of several paintings of the Simplon Pass that Sargent made in 1909, 1910 and 1911, while he was staying at the Bellevue Hotel. in Switzerland. This vibrant study of the clear light and rocky terrain of the great Alpine pass is built up with a wide variety of brushstrokes, vividly conveying the rushing stream, colourful vegetation, dazzlingly sunlit foreground and distant peak, set against the brilliant blue sky.

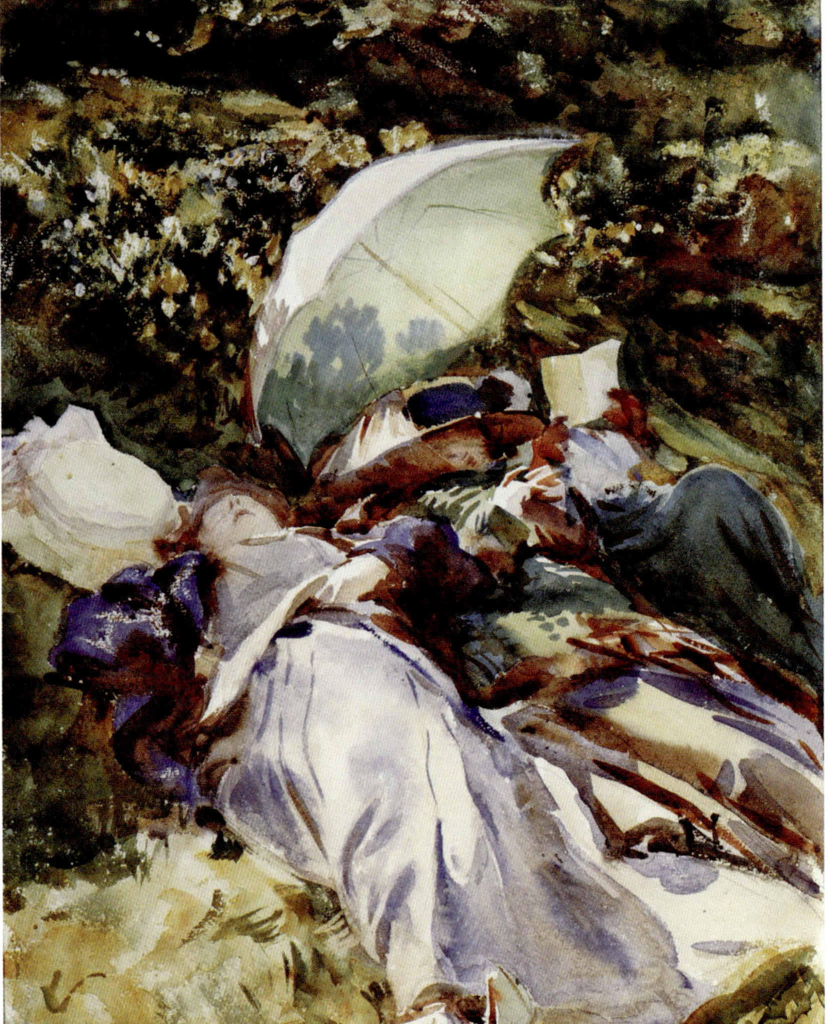

The Green Parasol, 1911, translucent and opaque watercolour over graphite on paper, 50.8 x 35.6cm (20 x 14in), Private Collection

While at the Hotel Bellevue near the Simplon Pass in August 1911, Sargent painted a group of watercolours featuring Dorothy Barnard and her friend, his niece Rose-Marie reclining languorously beneath parasols, including this particularly noticeable one dappled with green and blue shadows. The girls are painted close up, thrust into the foreground and exaggerating the perspective.

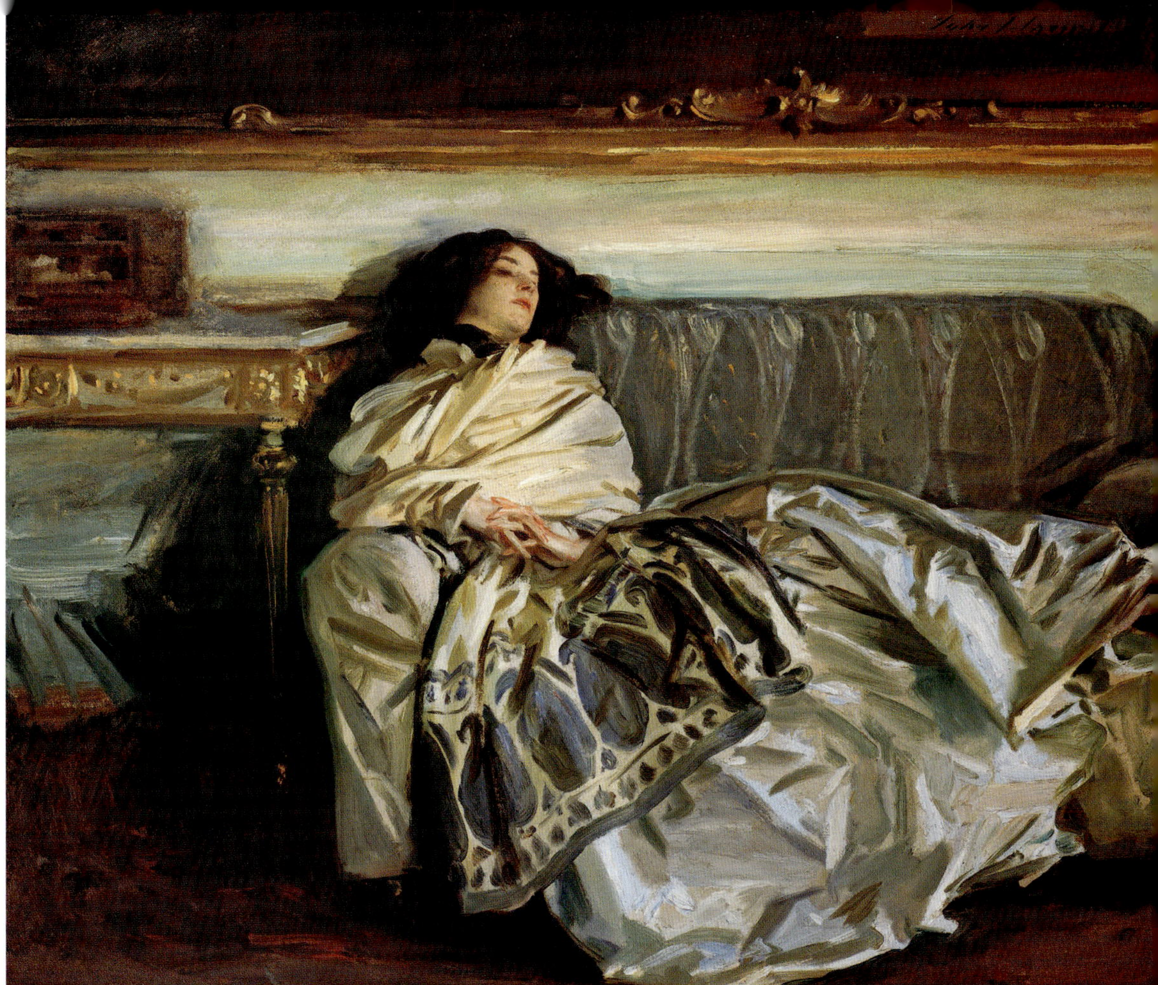

Nonchaloir (Repose), 1911, oil on canvas, 63.8 x 76.2cm (25 x 30in), National Gallery of Art, Washington DC, USA

In Switzerland in 1911 Sargent stayed with Violet's family. This is Rose-Marie on a lazy afternoon in their hotel. Sargent has used swift brushstrokes to depict Rose's fingers, hair, cashmere shawl and satin skirt. He nicknamed her 'Intertwingle' because she was so bendy and flexible, a great model – here he portrayed her in a fluid pose, absorbed in her reverie.

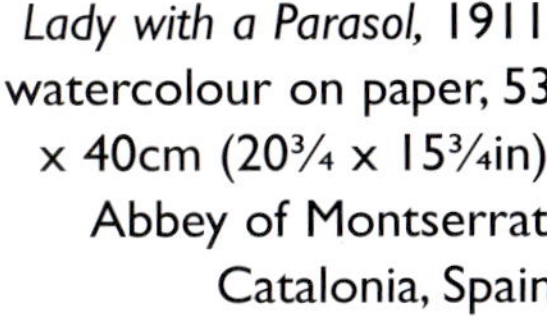

Lady with a Parasol, 1911, watercolour on paper, 53 x 40cm (20¾ x 15¾in), Abbey of Montserrat, Catalonia, Spain

Sargent painted Rose-Marie several times while he was holidaying in the Alps with the Ormond family. This is one of a series of watercolours he painted of her in Simplon that year. Many show her reclining under a parasol, either alone or with her sister Reine. This is foreshortened and painted with a light touch and swiftly applied brushmarks.

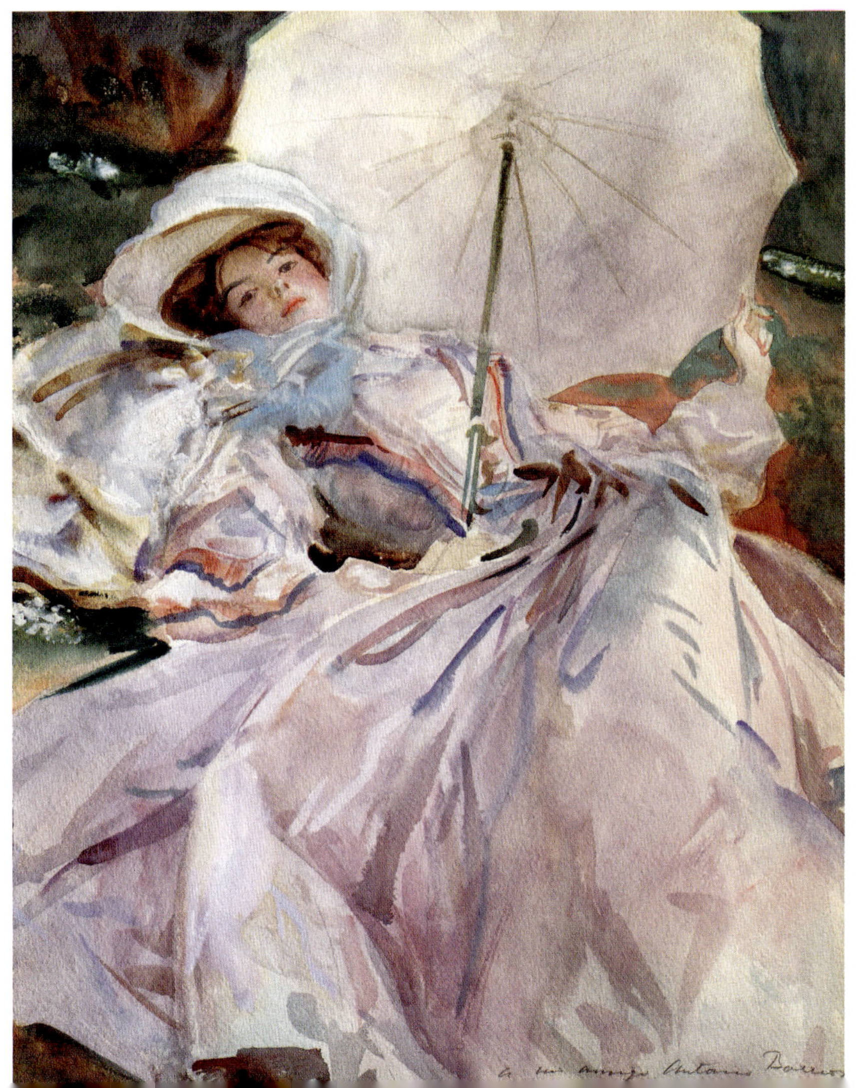

Portrait of Eva Katherine Balfour, 1911, charcoal on paper, 60.3 x 48.3cm (23¾ x 19in), Private Collection

Eva Katherine Balfour (1889–1978) became Lady Buxton after her marriage. Her maternal grandmother, Alice Mason commissioned the portrait – although by then, Sargent rarely accepted them, but he still produced less time-consuming charcoal portraits. Alice was a friend of Henry James who had been painted by Sargent.

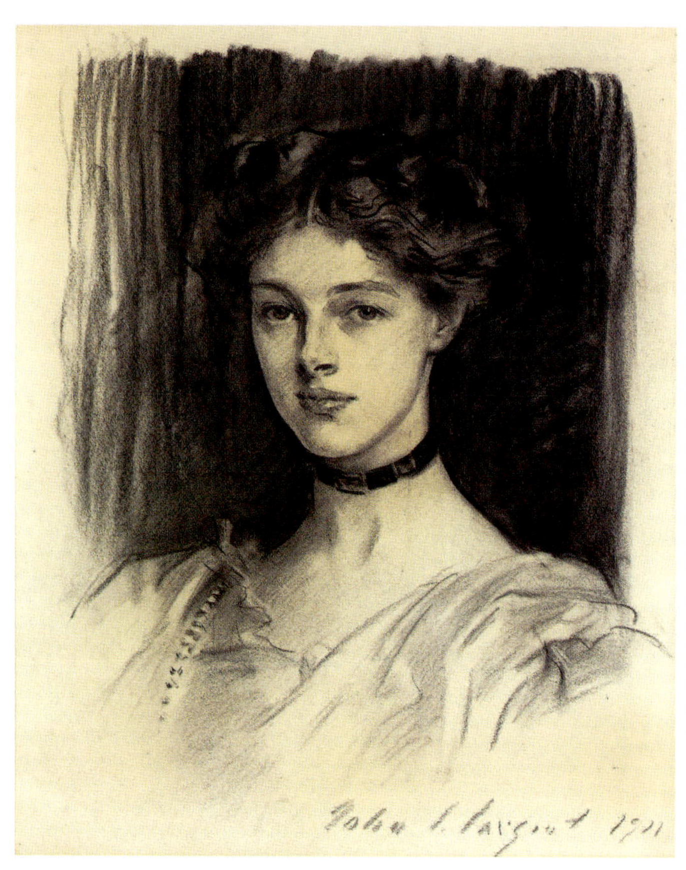

The Rialto, Venice, 1911, oil on canvas, 55.9 x 92.1cm (22 x 36¼in), Philadelphia Museum of Art, Pennsylvania, USA

A cool, shady image of the view beneath the Rialto Bridge, this shows several gondoliers working hard, with gondolas and boats moving along the calm waterway. The painting conveys a sense of the quiet echoing sound of water lapping and boats travelling smoothly under the massive stone bridge as well as the reflective quality of the water. This is a moment away from the bustle of the tourist-filled areas.

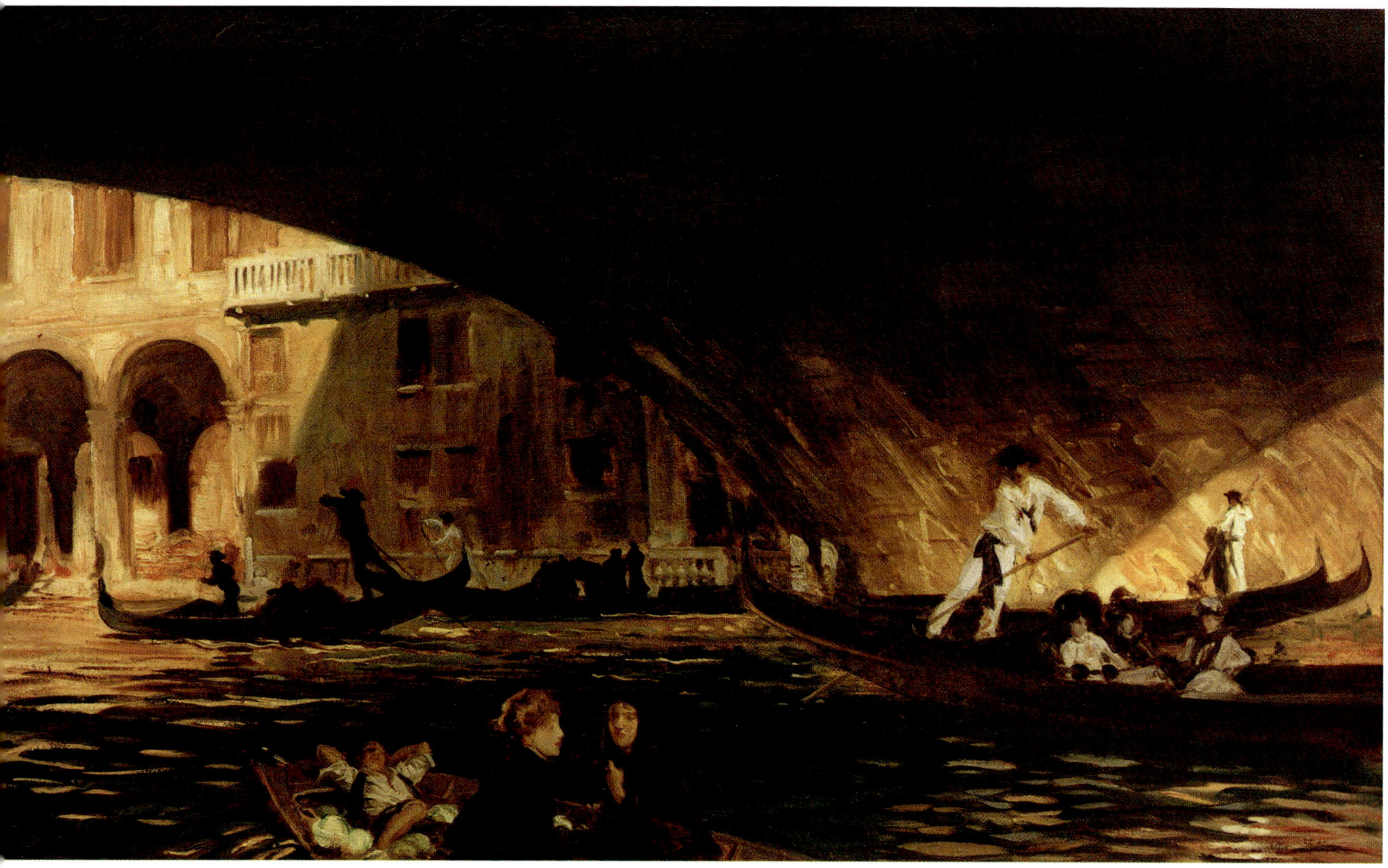

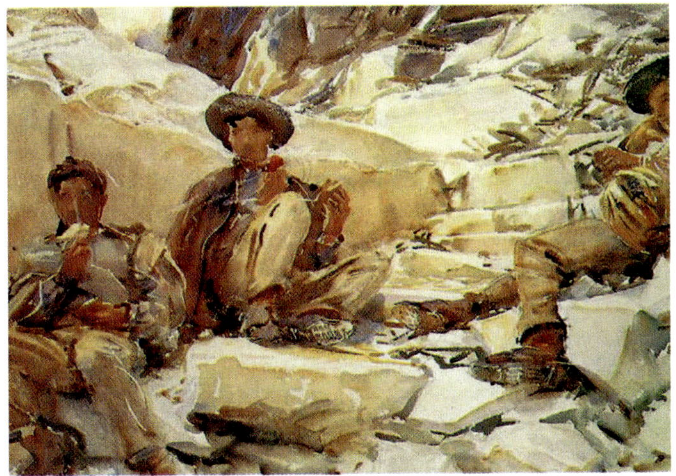

Workmen at Carrara, 1911, translucent and opaque watercolour and wax resist over graphite on paper, 35.6 x 50.8cm (14 x 20in), Museum of Fine Arts, Boston, Massachusetts, USA

Despite their featureless faces, these marble quarry workers still exude expression through their poses. Subtle use of wax resist creates fine white highlight lines. The men were nicknamed 'lizzatori' as they worked with rock, and their job was to use their physical strength to cut huge marble blocks and then haul them down the mountain and tie them up with thick ropes.

View from a Window, Genoa, 1911, watercolour with pencil and oil on paper, 40.3 x 53cm (15¾ x 20¾in), The British Museum, London, UK

Looking out of a window over the port of Genoa, this was painted in the autumn of 1911. Although Sargent painted hundreds of views of Venice, there are only three known paintings by him of Genoa. This was possibly one of the works that he exhibited in the summer of 1912 at the Royal Watercolour Society. More immediate than the view are his sketchbook and paintbox propped up by the open window of his hotel room.

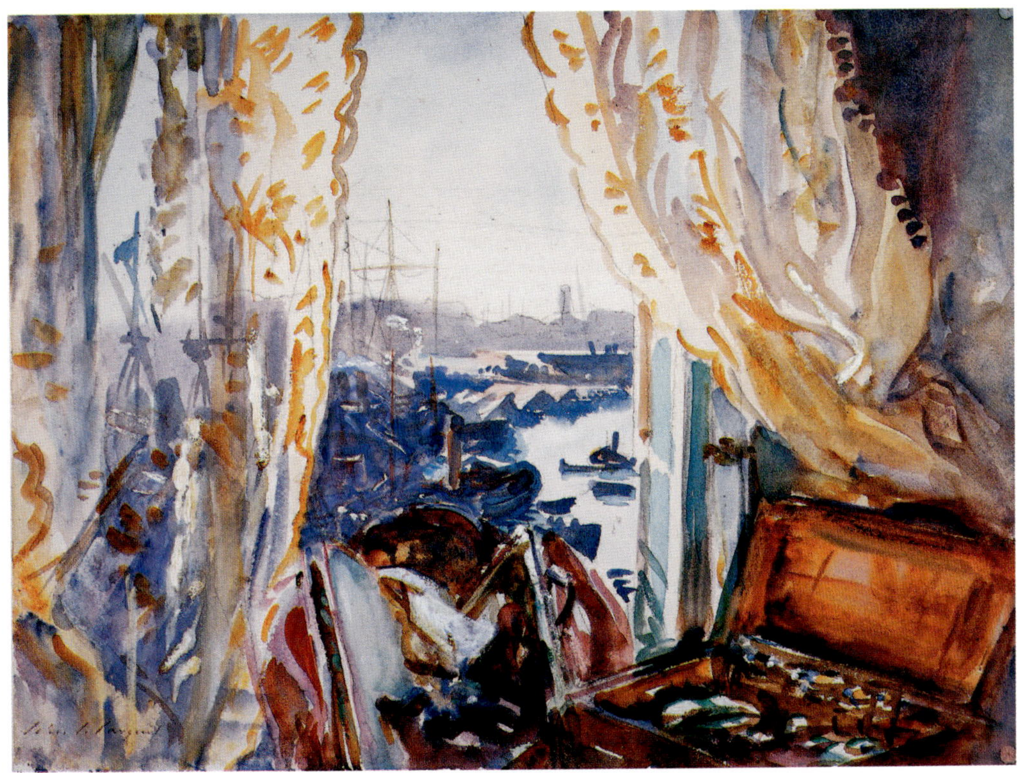

Tamara Karsavina in the Title Role of 'Thamar', c.1911–12, charcoal and white chalk on white paper, 59.7 x 45.2cm (23½ x 17¾in), Fogg Art Museum, Massachusetts, USA

Tamara Platonovna Karsavina (1885–1978) was an acclaimed Russian prima ballerina who first danced with Diaghilev's Ballets Russes. In 1911–12; when she was 27, she was performing in Paris in the lead role of Thamar, which was set in an exotic location. Her costume and the set were designed by the also internationally acclaimed Léon Bakst. Sargent loved exotic costumes and combined this with his skills in portraiture.

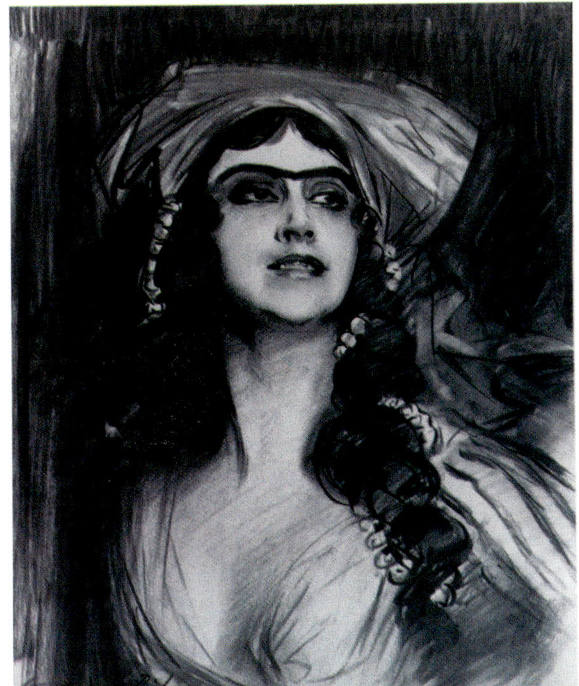

Abriès, c.1912, watercolour and graphite on white paper, 53 x 40cm (20¾ x 15¾in), The Metropolitan Museum, New York, USA

Approximately five years after Sargent had decided to stop painting portrats, he painted this watercolour, among many others, while he was on holiday with family and friends in Abriès, an Alpine region in France. It expresses his interest in structure, contrasts and alignments. In close-up, he focuses on the corner of this wooden chalet and skims over the ground, building up a patterned surface with the colours and shapes in the intersecting wood beams.

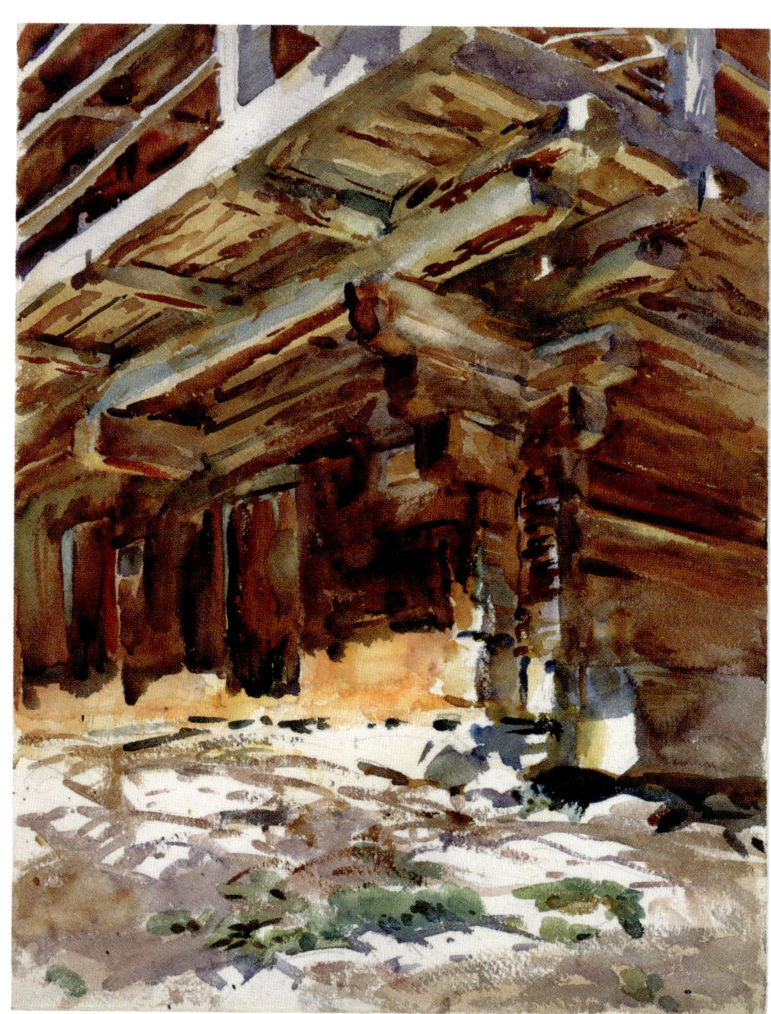

Two Girls Fishing, 1912, oil on canvas, 55.9 x 71.5cm (22 x 28¼in), Cincinnati Art Museum, Ohio, USA

In August 1912, Sargent was staying with the Ormond family at the village of Abriès in the French Alps, near the Italian border. The two girls depicted here are his nieces, Rose-Marie and Reine. The painting is an extremely natural image of the sisters as they fish companionably, not at all self-conscious as their doting uncle paints them. Of course they had grown up with him painting and drawing them frequently.

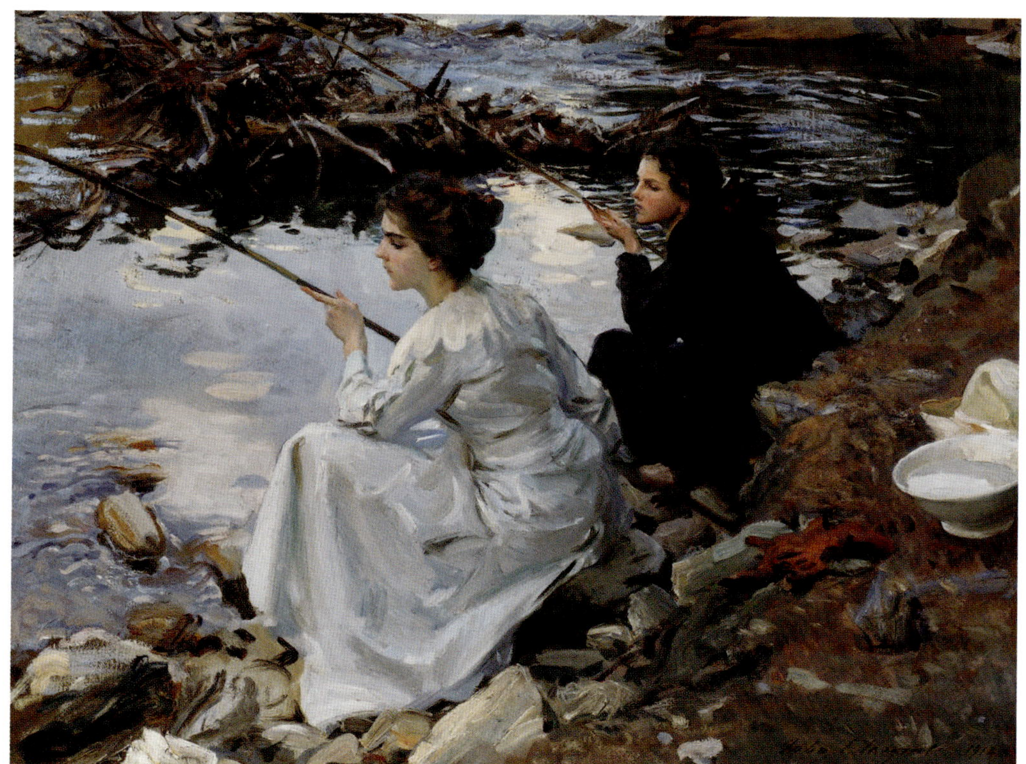

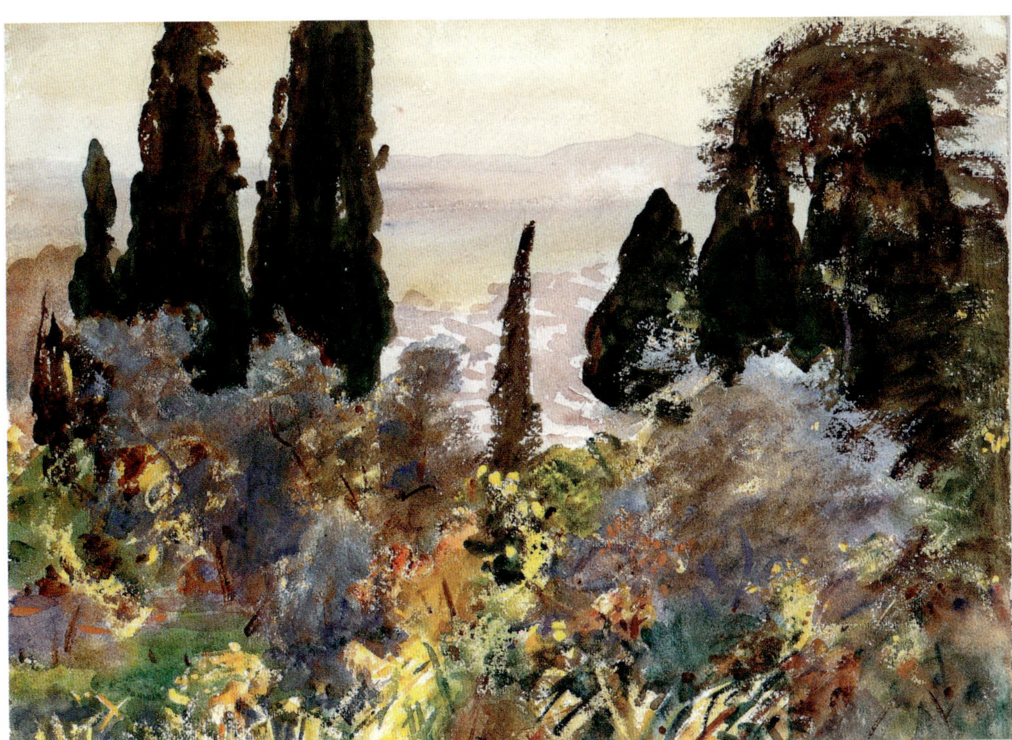

Granada, 1912, watercolour, graphite and wax crayon on white wove paper, 40 x 53cm (15¾ x 20¾in), The Metropolitan Museum, New York, USA

From September to November 1912, Sargent stayed in Seville and Granada with Emily and the de Glehns. In Granada, they stayed at the Hotel Siete Suelos. Sargent had been there several times before, but on this visit he was particularly focused on rendering the effects of intense light and deep shadow, as in this light-filled garden and hazy, distant view.

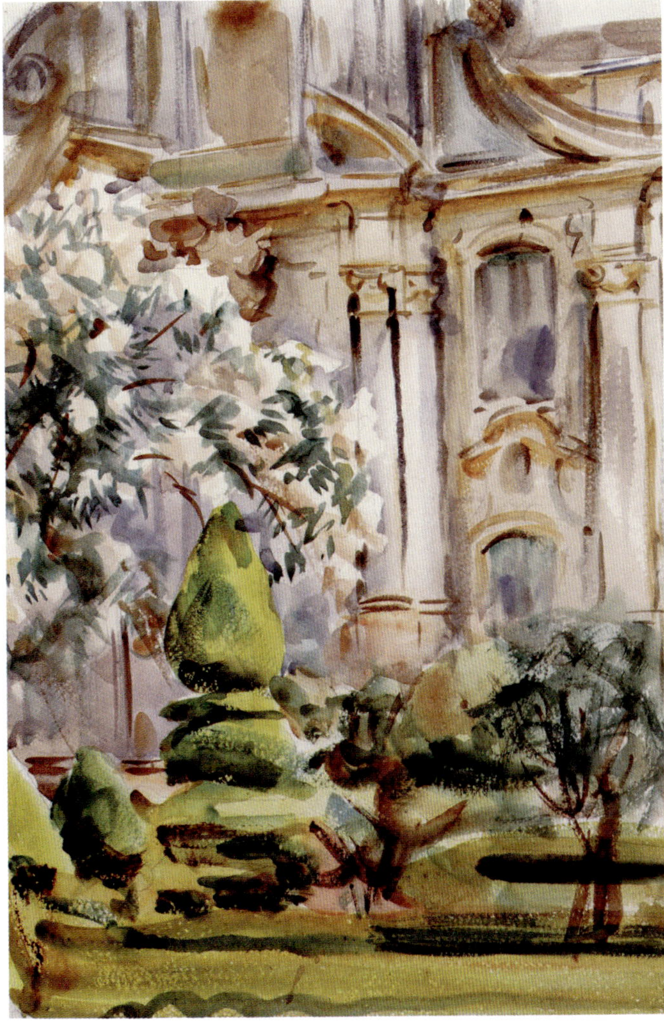

Palace and Gardens, Spain, 1912, watercolour over graphite on paper, 45.5 x 30.5cm (18 x 12in), Private Collection

This is the façade of the Baroque palace at Aranjuez near Madrid in Spain, where Sargent travelled in September to November 1912. The building is glimpsed through its formal garden and although the paint has been applied quickly, Sargent has still managed to convey the sunlight on the stonework, leaves, grass and bushes. Paint has been applied freely and fluidly, in diluted mixtures with an assured hand and eye.

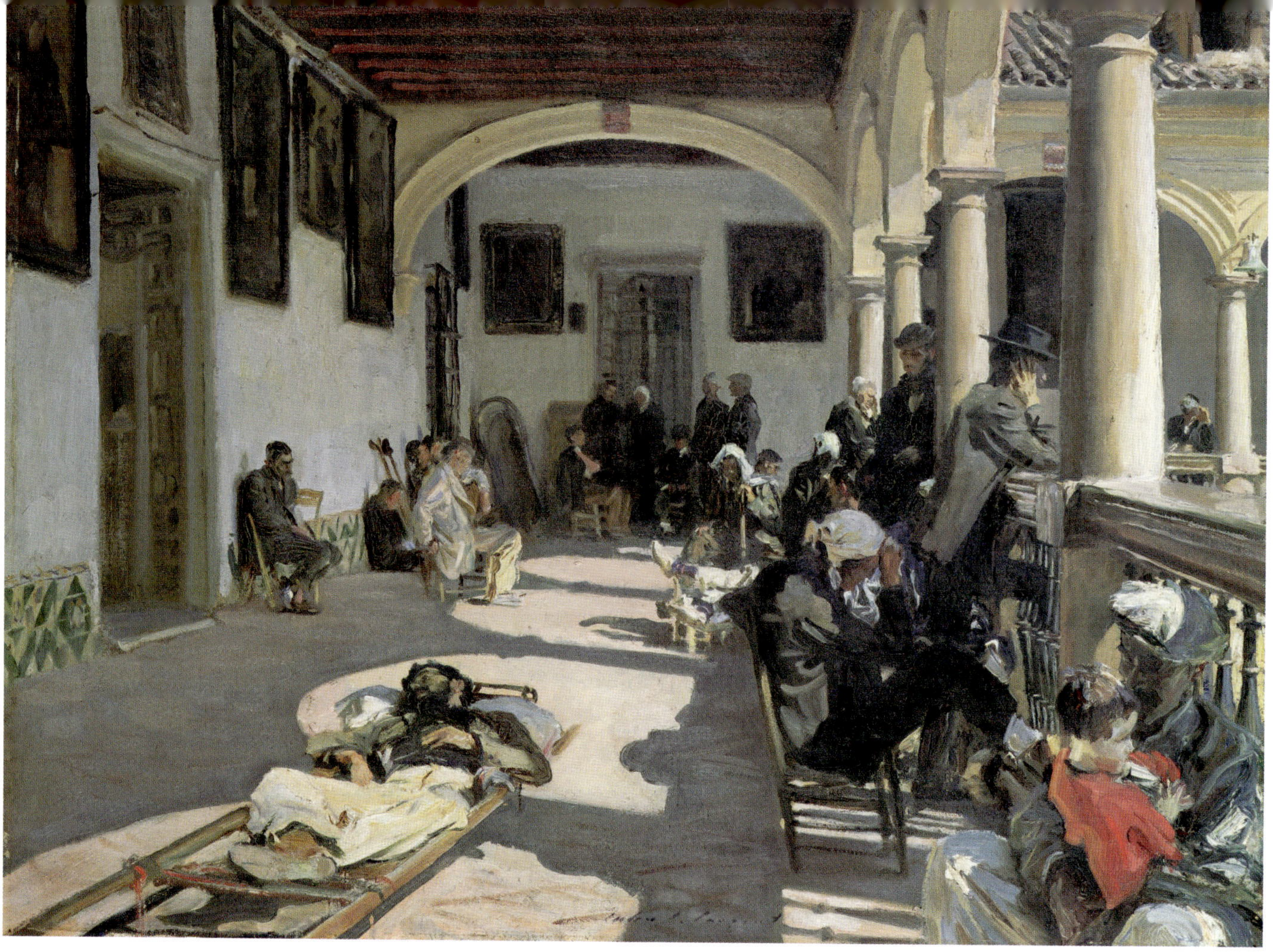

Hospital at Granada, 1912,
oil on canvas, 56 x 71.2cm
(22 x 28in), National Gallery
of Victoria, Melbourne,
Australia

Passionate about archi-
tecture as much as light,
nature and figures, Sargent
depicted the columns,
arches and porticoes of

this Spanish hospital, as well
as some of the patients
and convalescents who
are crowding in the cool
shade of the stone loggia.

All the separate elements
are pulled together through
his depiction of the play of
contrasting light and shadow
on different surfaces.

Henry James, 1912, charcoal
on paper, 61.8 x 41cm (24½
x 16in), Windsor Castle,
London, UK

Two weeks after the death
of his great friend Henry
James in July 1916, Sargent
presented this candid
charcoal portrait to King
George V. The King had
already awarded James the
Order of Merit; an award
that he had established
on his ascension in 1902,
for those who had
rendered exceptional
service to the Crown
or to the advancement
of the Arts, Learning,
Literature or Science.

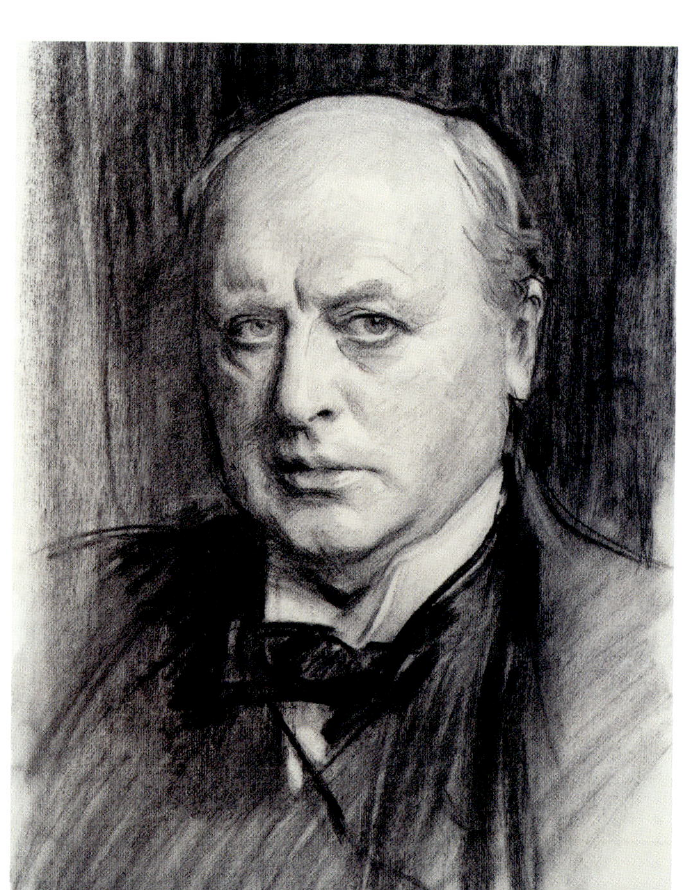

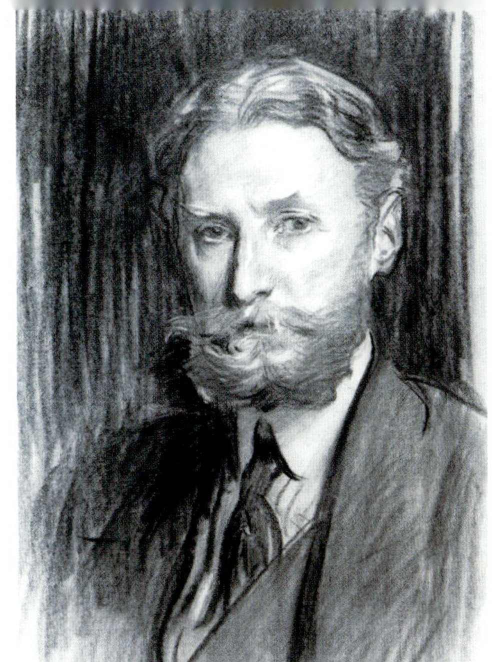

Captain George Sitwell Campbell Swinton, 1912, charcoal on paper, 62 × 38.2cm (24½ × 15in), Guildhall Art Gallery, London, UK

A grandson of Sir George Sitwell (see pages 66–67), George Sitwell Campbell Swinton (1859–1937) was born in Edinburgh and at one point, studied art, but later became a fairly prominent Scottish politician, a member of the London County Council and a captain in the British army. In 1897, Sargent had painted a portrait of his wife Elizabeth.

Escutcheon of Charles V of Spain, 1912, watercolour and graphite on white wove paper, 30.5 × 45.7cm (12 × 18in), The Metropolitan Museum, New York, USA

In 1912, Sargent painted in and around the Alhambra in Granada, Spain. This is a stone relief of the heraldic insignia of Emperor Charles V of Spain. Despite its appearance of spontaneity Sargent planned it carefully with a pencil drawing first, then painting over it with his free, loose and confident application of colour.

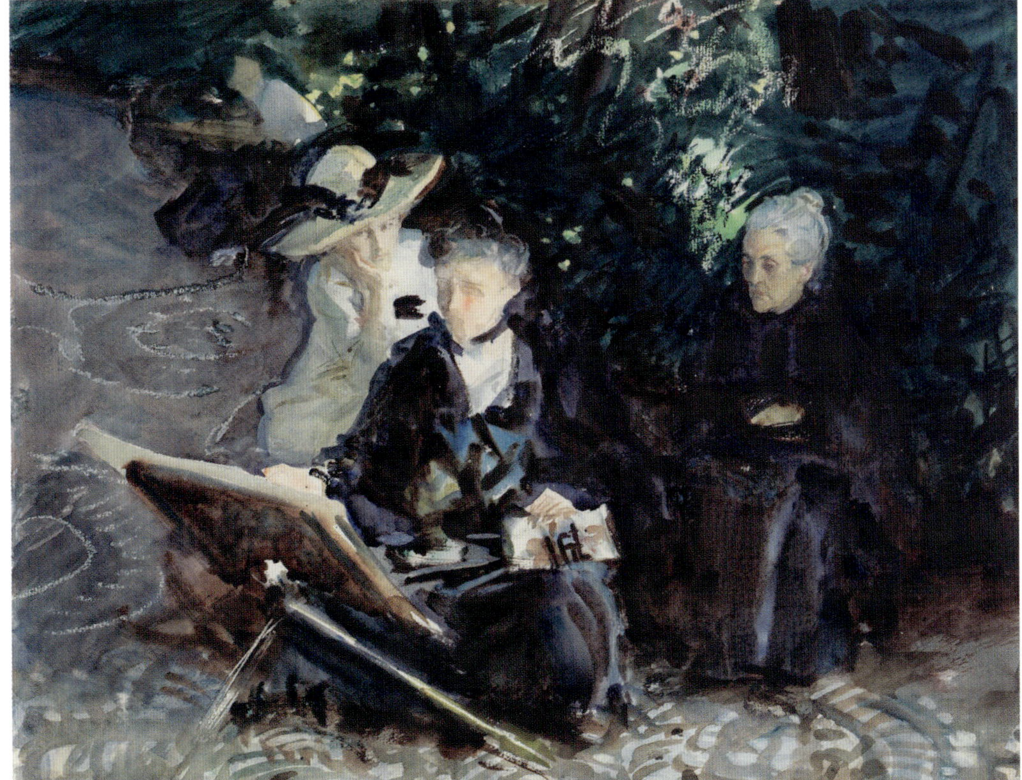

In the Generalife, 1912, watercolour, wax crayon and graphite on white wove paper, 37.5 × 45.4cm (14¾ × 8in), The Metropolitan Museum, New York, USA

The Gardens of the Generalife are the former summer palace of the Moorish sultans at the Alhambra in Granada, Spain. In 1912, Sargent made several plein air paintings at the location. Here, Emily sketches alongside Jane de Glehn and their Spanish friend Dolores Carmona. The image blends his skills of landscapist and portraitist in one watercolour.

Moorish Courtyard, 1912 or 1913, oil on canvas, 91.5 x 71.1cm (28 x 36in), Private Collection

This may have been painted while Sargent was in Spain with the de Glehns in 1912, or soon after, or he may have painted it the following year. Wilfrid and Jane painted a view of the same place from a slightly different angle in 1912, so it is likely that they painted alongside each other. Using a restricted palette, he has captured details of the place, but also the overriding atmosphere.

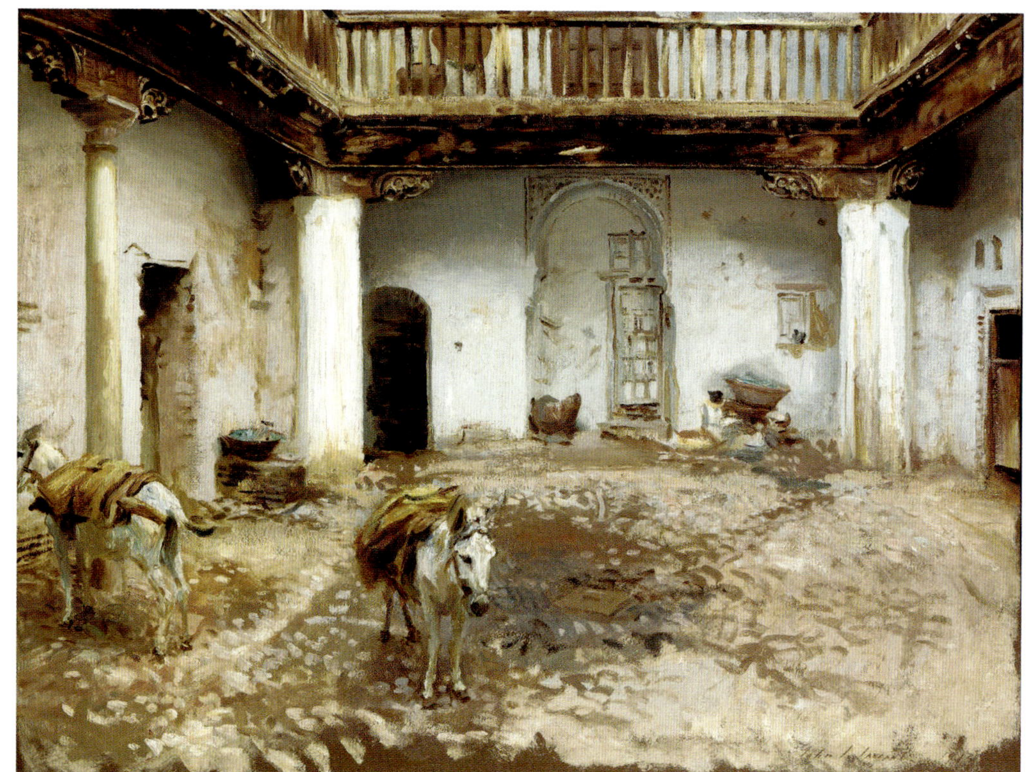

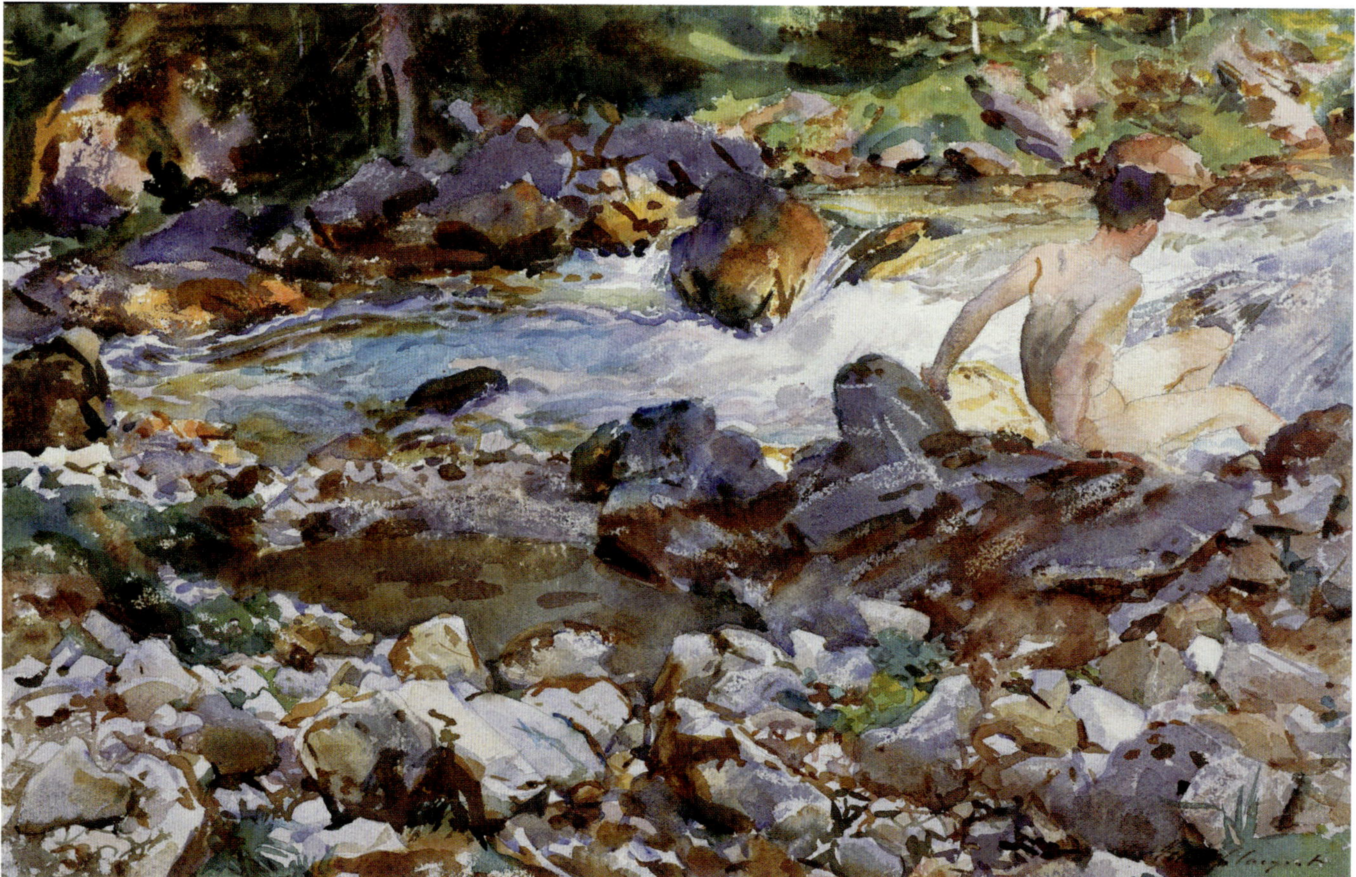

Mountain Stream, c.1912–14, watercolour and graphite on off-white wove paper, 34.8 x 53.3cm (13¾ x 21in), The Metropolitan Museum, New York, USA

Although the location of this painting has not been identified, it is probably somewhere in the Alps. This watercolour exemplifies Sargent's love of capturing moving, flowing water, catching flickering light and contrasting close-up foreground details with almost abstract areas; here the solid elements – the rocks – stand out sharply against the sketchy marks of the swirling water and the soft, pale form of the bather. Unusually, he includes a figure, about to go for a dip.

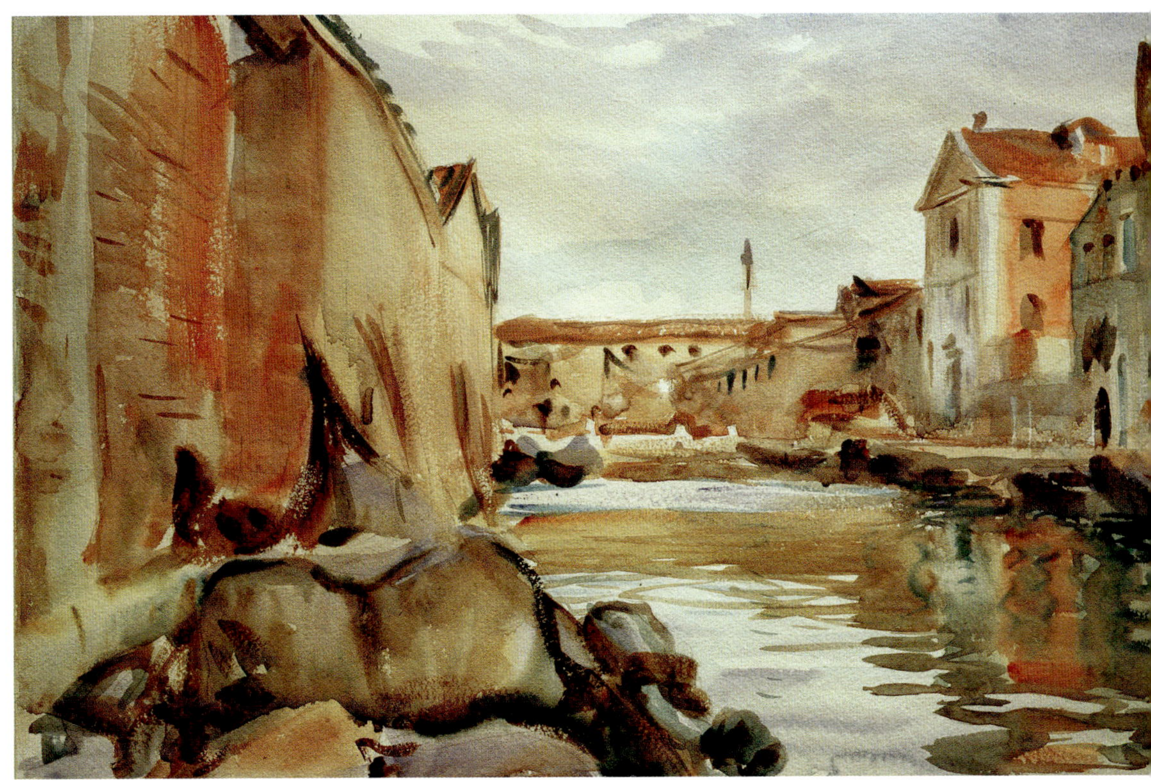

Giudecca, c.1913, watercolour and graphite on paper, 30.5 x 45.7cm (12 x 18in), Fitzwilliam Museum, Cambridge, UK

In 1913 Sargent spent a large part of August in Venice. He arrived early in the month, then spent some time in the Dolomites before returning at the end of August. While there as usual, he shared his good friend Ralph's studio at the top of the Palazzo Barbaro. This was painted from his gondola, at the peaceful Giudecca island across the lagoon from the hustle and bustle of Venice.

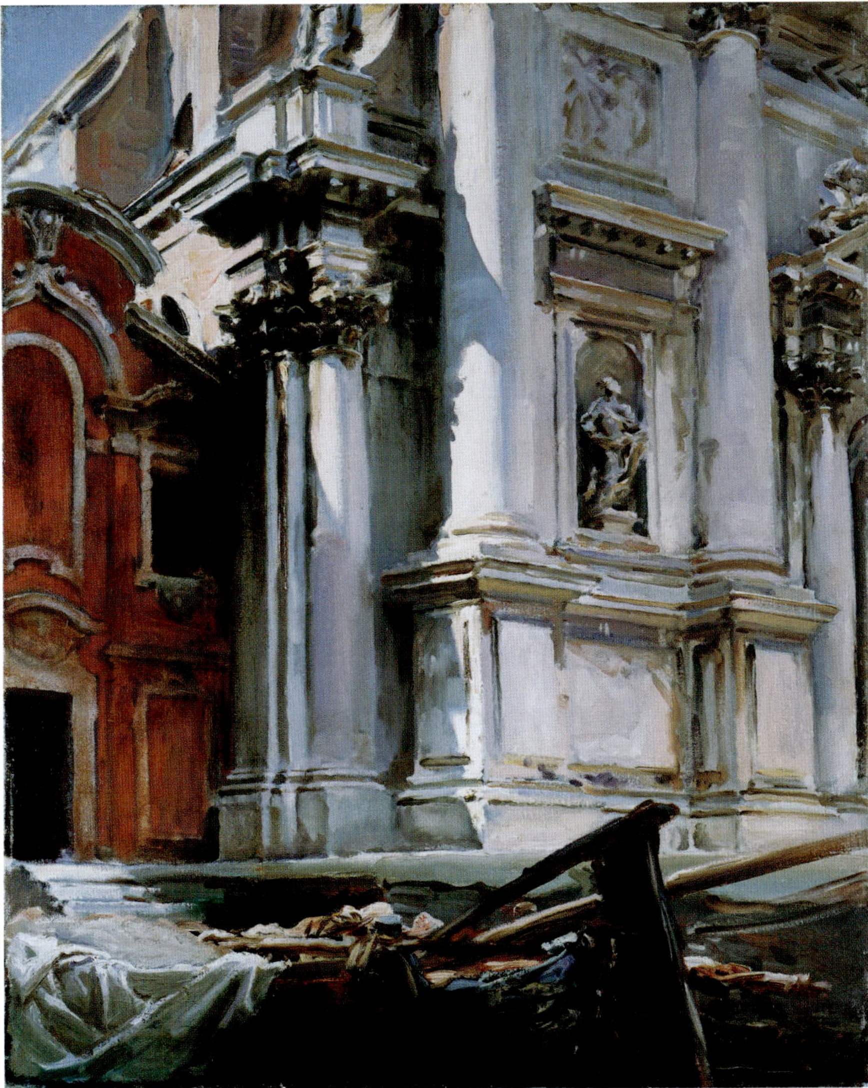

Corner of the Church of San Stae, Venice, c.1913, oil on canvas, 71.1 x 55.9cm (28 x 22in), Private Collection

The Baroque façade of the church of San Stae, designed by the Swiss-Italian architect Domenico Rossi (1657–1737), appealed to Sargent for its dramatic forms and tones. The church was situated on the south side of the Grand Canal, on a route that Sargent often took when strolling through the streets of Venice. Having stayed regularly and extensively in Venice for years, he knew it extremely well. During the 19th century, he tended to paint his Venetian views from the water, but after 1900, he focused more on the architecture, and the effects of light falling on the grand stone façades.

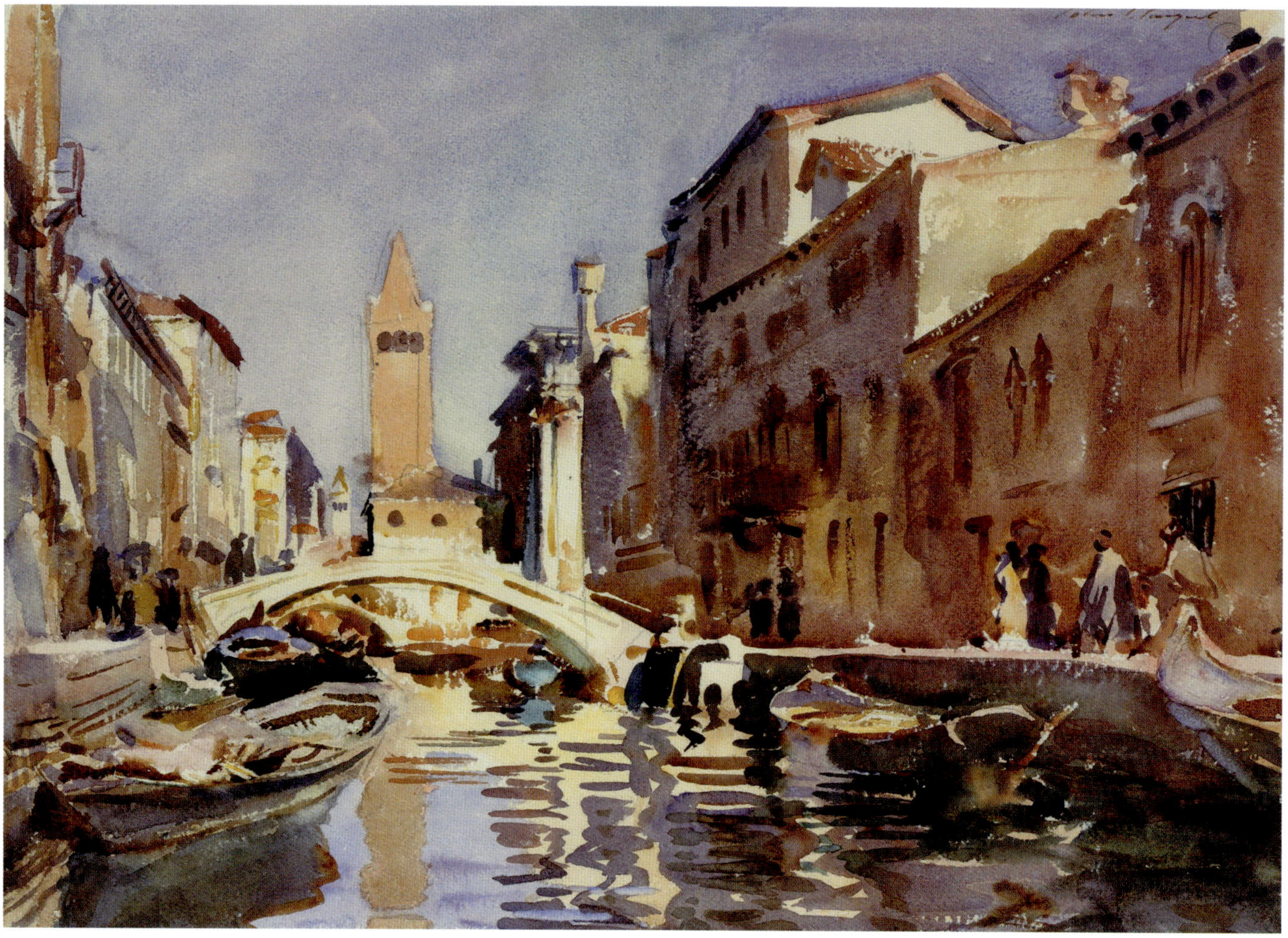

Venetian Canal, 1913, water-colour and graphite on paper, 40 x 53.3cm (15¾ x 21in), The Metropolitan Museum, New York, USA

Sargent captured this dramatic view of the Rio de San Barnaba in clearly defined perspective, looking directly down the canal to the tower of the Church of San Barnaba. The dazzling effect of clear, bright light is created by strong tonal contrasts and by allowing plenty of the white paper to show through. The low viewpoint is close to the water, looking looking into the depths of the Grand Canal.

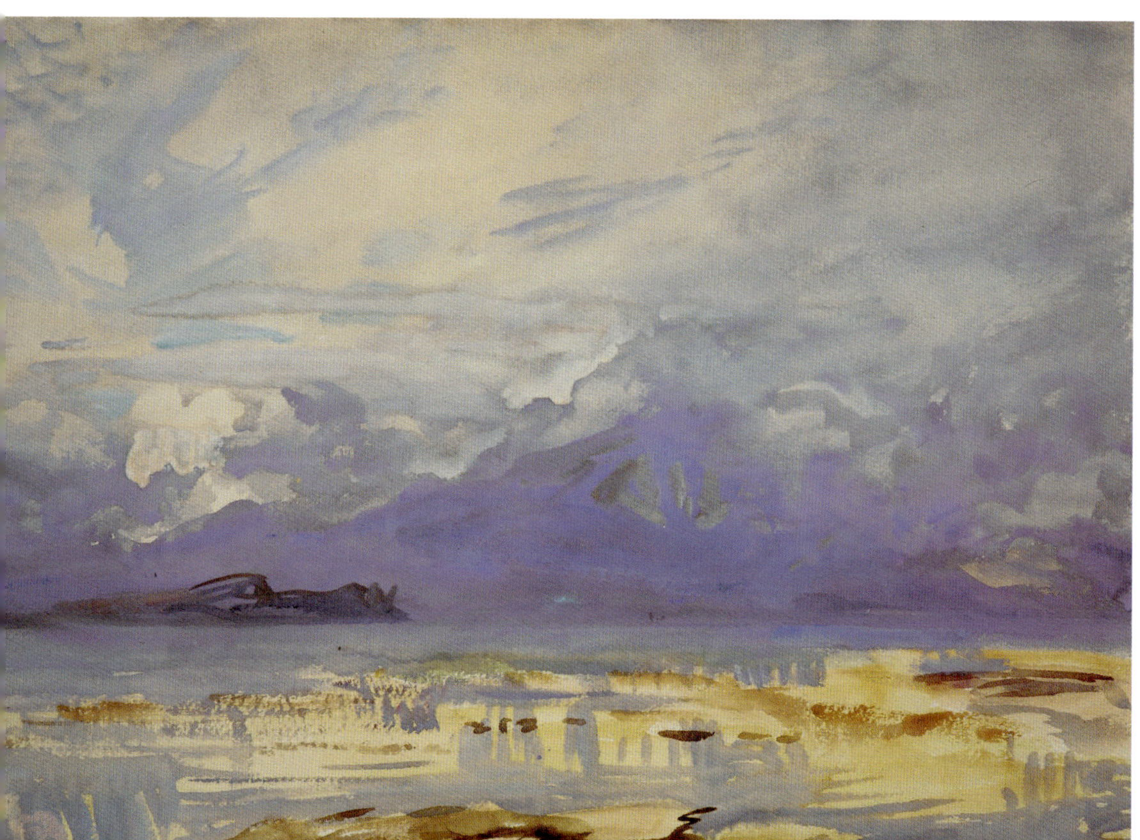

Sirmione, 1913, watercolour and gouache on off-white wove paper, 40 x 53.5cm (15¾ x 21in), The Metropolitan Museum, New York, USA

In September 1913, Sargent stayed in San Vigilio near Lake Garda in Italy, with Emily, Eliza Wedgwood and the de Glehns. He and the de Glehns painted en plein air every day. They sought to capture the breathtaking landscape and the transient quality of light. This is a view of the town of Sirmione, known for its thermal baths and Rocca Scaligera, a medieval castle overlooking the lake.

Lake Garda (at San Vigilio), 1913, translucent and opaque watercolour on paper, 34.9 x 53.4cm (13¾ x 21in), Private Collection

Sargent never lost his fascination for the Impressionist approach to capturing transience. Monet was praised for this, but Sargent was later criticized. This tranquil scene was painted the same year the Armory Show in New York had shown the world all the latest developments in modern art, including work by Braque, Picasso, Duchamp, Kirchner and Kandinsky.

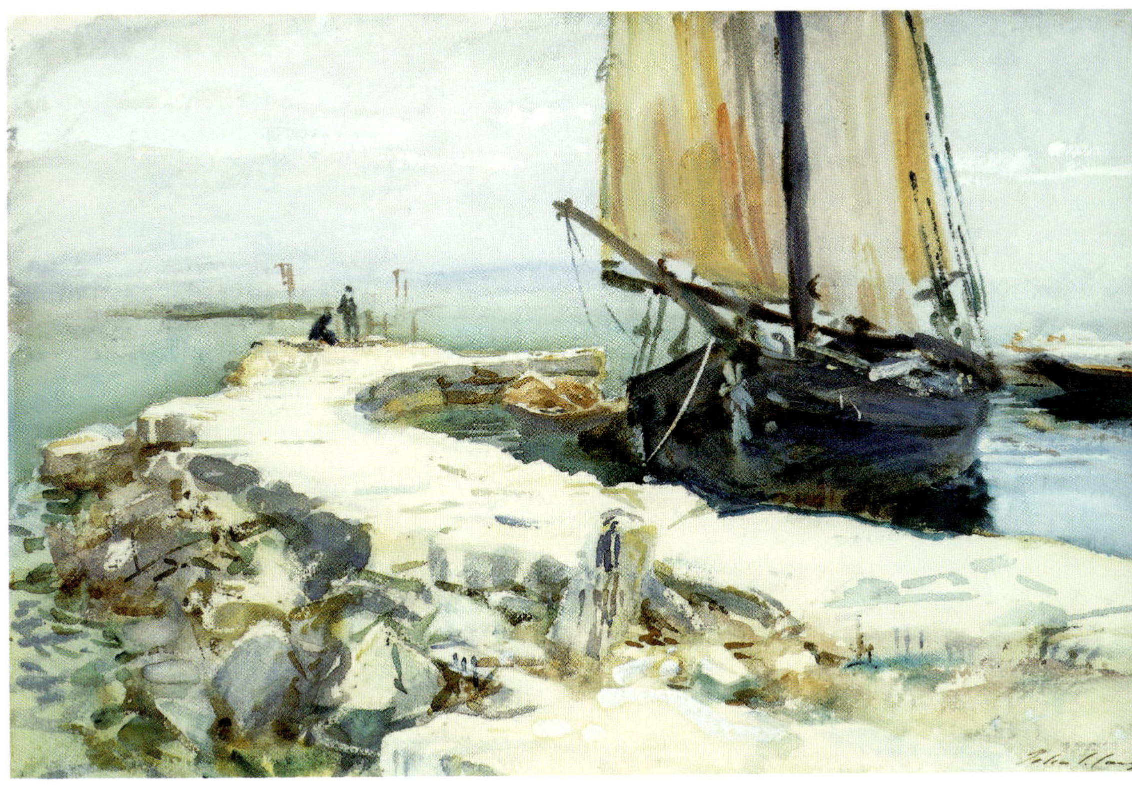

The Sketchers, 1913, oil on canvas, 55.9 x 71.1cm (22 x 28in), Virginia Museum of Fine Arts, Richmond, USA

A fluidly painted work with a woman in a blue smock painting at an easel in an olive grove in San Vigilio, overlooking Lake Garda. She is Mary Foote (1872–1968), a friend of Jane de Glehn's, while the seated man also sketching and viewed from the back is Wilfrid de Glehn. Mary grew up in many locations, not unlike Sargent, and she had a ready wit that he appreciated. He described San Vigilio as 'paradise.'

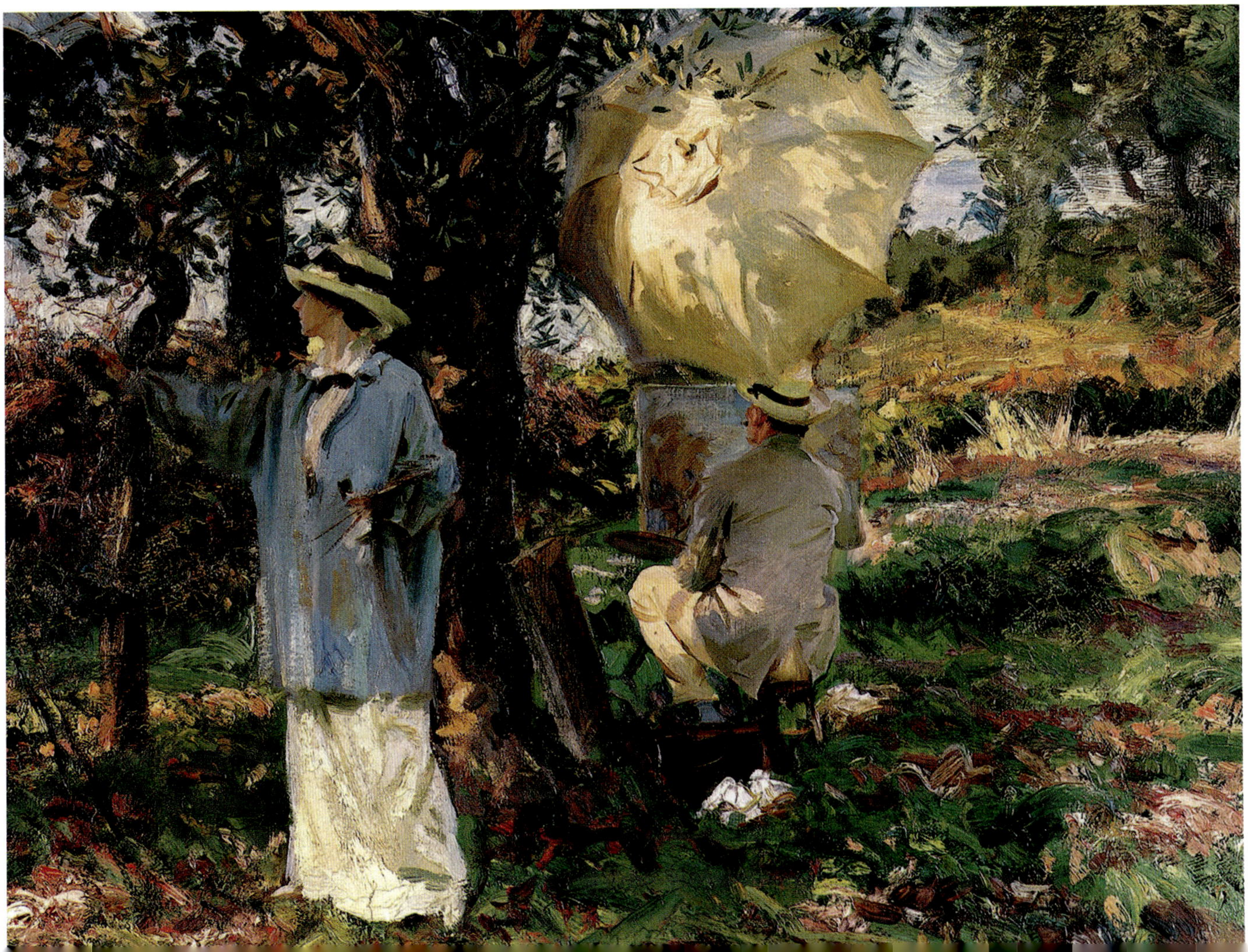

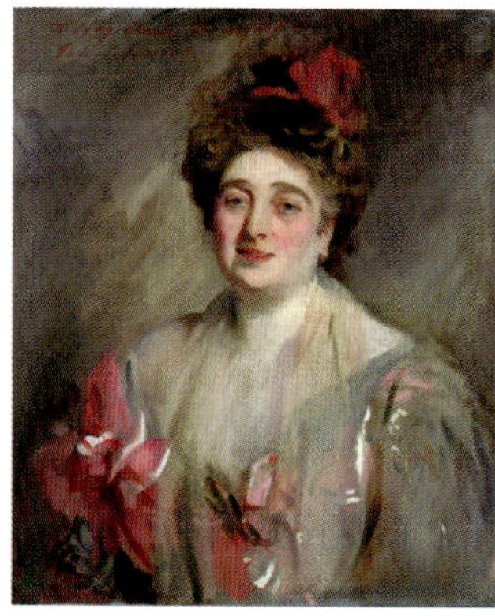

Portrait of Lady Charles Beresford, 1913, oil on canvas, 73.5 x 60cm (29 x 23½in), Dublin City Gallery, Dublin, Republic of Ireland

Sargent still accepted some portrait commissions. Lady Charles Beresford, née Ellen Jeromina Gardner (1852–1922) was unhappily married to Lord Charles Beresford, a prominent admiral, close friend of the Prince of Wales and notorious adulterer. Unusually for Sargent's commissioned portraits, this is painted particularly loosely.

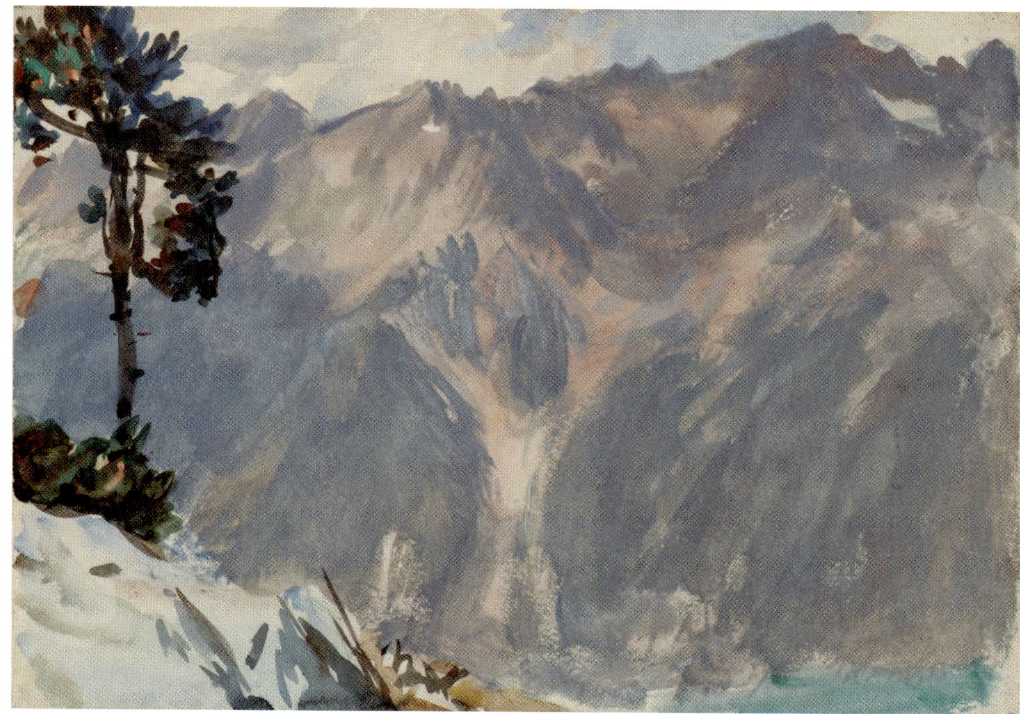

The Tyrol, 1914, watercolour and gouache over graphite on cream wove paper, 25.4 x 35.6cm (10 x 14in), Princeton University Art Museum, Princeton, Massachusetts, USA

While visiting the Tyrol with friends, Sargent worked avidly in watercolour. As a child he had been fluent in the medium and now, as an accomplished and celebrated artist, his technique was especially honed; he called his own plein air paintings 'snapshots.' This alpine view shows both his skill and conveys what he loved about painting away from his studio. An atmospheric image, it is created with fluid washes and dry brush technique.

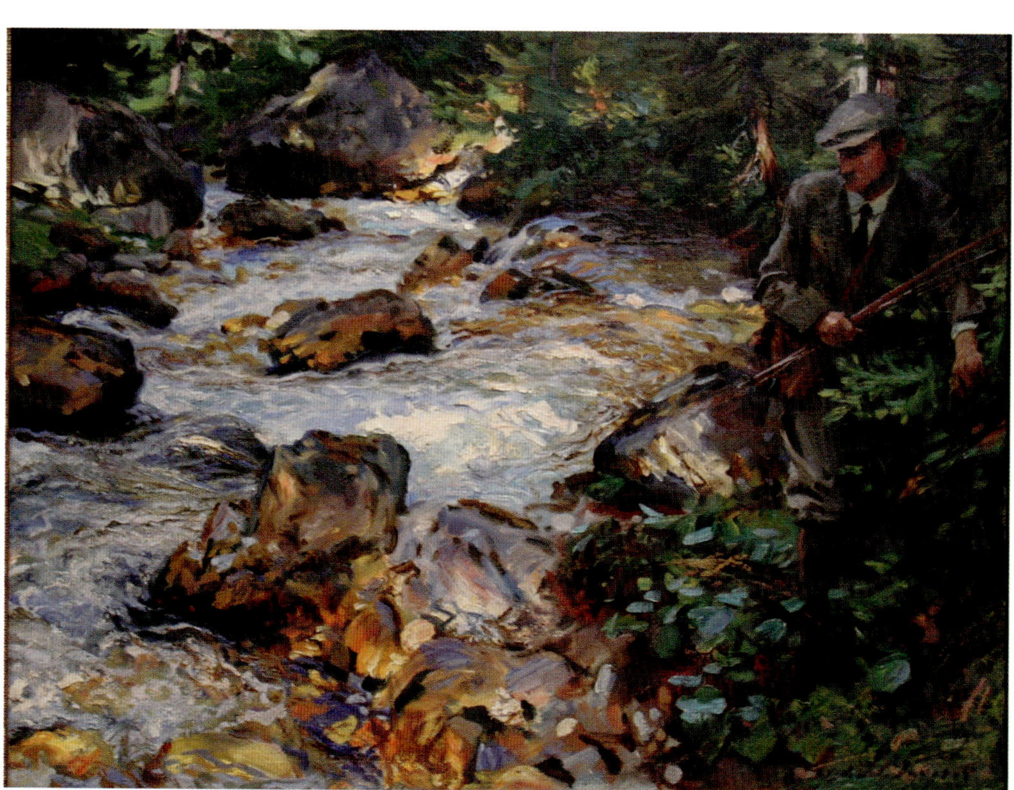

Trout Stream in the Tyrol, 1914, oil on canvas, 55.9 x 71.1cm (22 x 28in), Fine Arts Museum of San Francisco, California, USA

Sargent chose to ignore the political events of 1914, deciding that all would blow over and none of it would have any bearing on him. He was enjoying a holiday in the Austrian Tyrol with his friends Adrian and Marianne Stokes when events did, in fact, affect him and war was declared. This idyllic scene is testament to his blissful ignorance of the horrific events that were unveiling close by and across Europe.

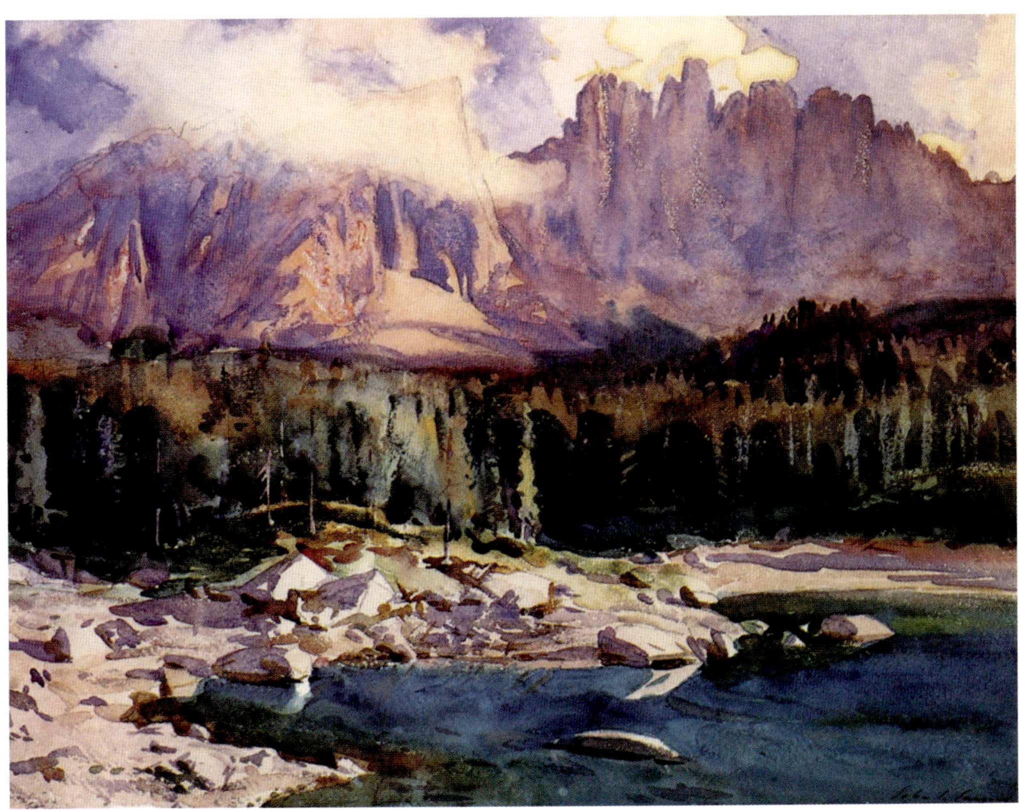

Karer See, 1914, watercolour
and gouache on paper,
40.6 x 52.7cm (16 x 20¾in),
Smithsonian Institution,
Hirshhorn Museum
and Sculpture Garden,
Washington DC, USA

Although World War I had
broken out, Sargent and his
companions continued their
holiday. Without realising the
enormity of it, Sargent chose
to remain in the Tyrol. He
painted this image of Karer
See, a huge lake in the south
Tyrol. Using his reduced,
rapid brushstrokes and
leaving plenty of white paper
showing through, he captured
the colours and atmosphere
of his idyllic surroundings –
before being called back to
the realities of the war.

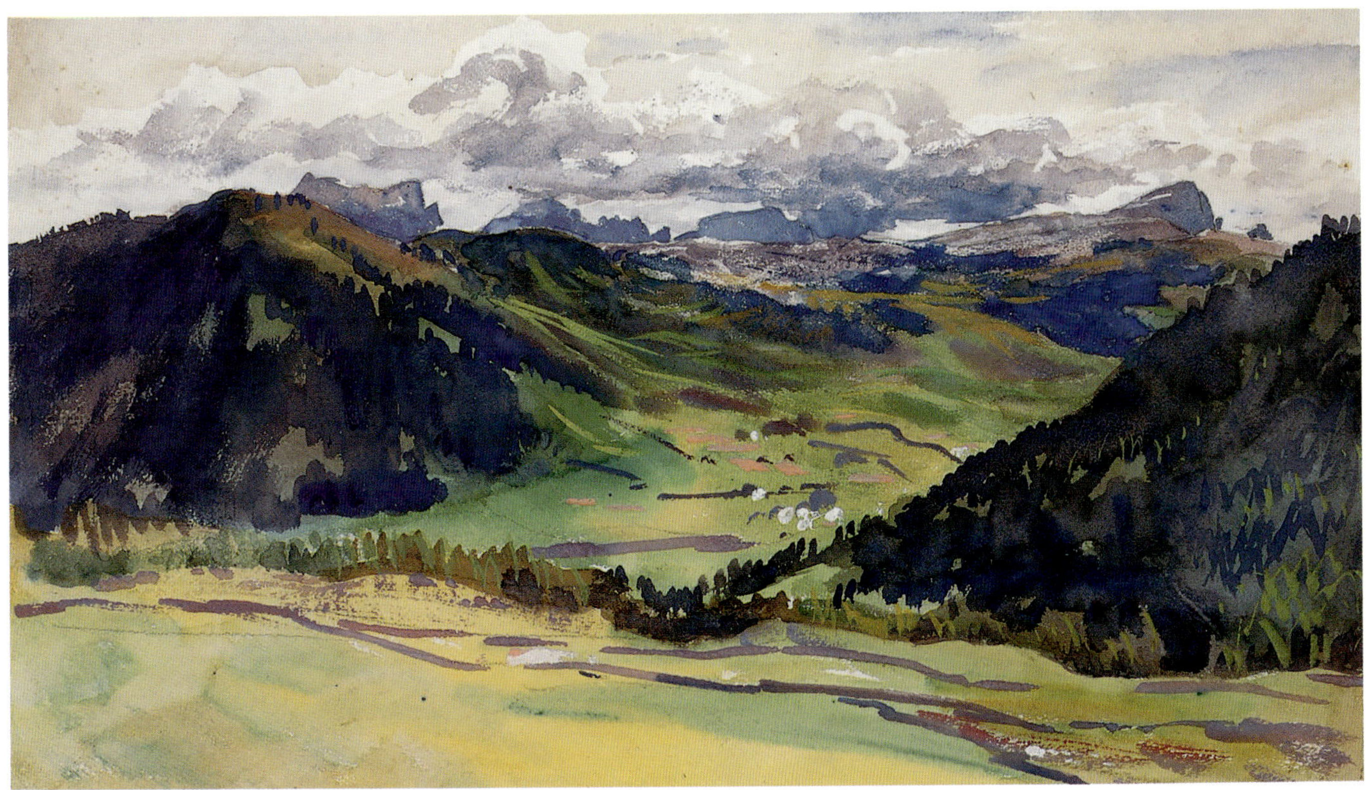

Open Valley, Dolomites, 1914,
**watercolour and gouache
on paper, 34.6 x 53.2cm (13½
x 21in), The Metropolitan
Museum, New York, USA**

Sargent had known and
painted the Alps since
childhood, and while there
with Adrian and Marianne
Stokes in 1914, wanted to visit
Seiser Alp. Adrian wrote of it
in a letter, describing the area
as: 'An immense, grassy plateau
lying among the Dolomites.
He had been there as a boy
and wished to see it again.
He said he did not find much
to paint there, but there was
always something.

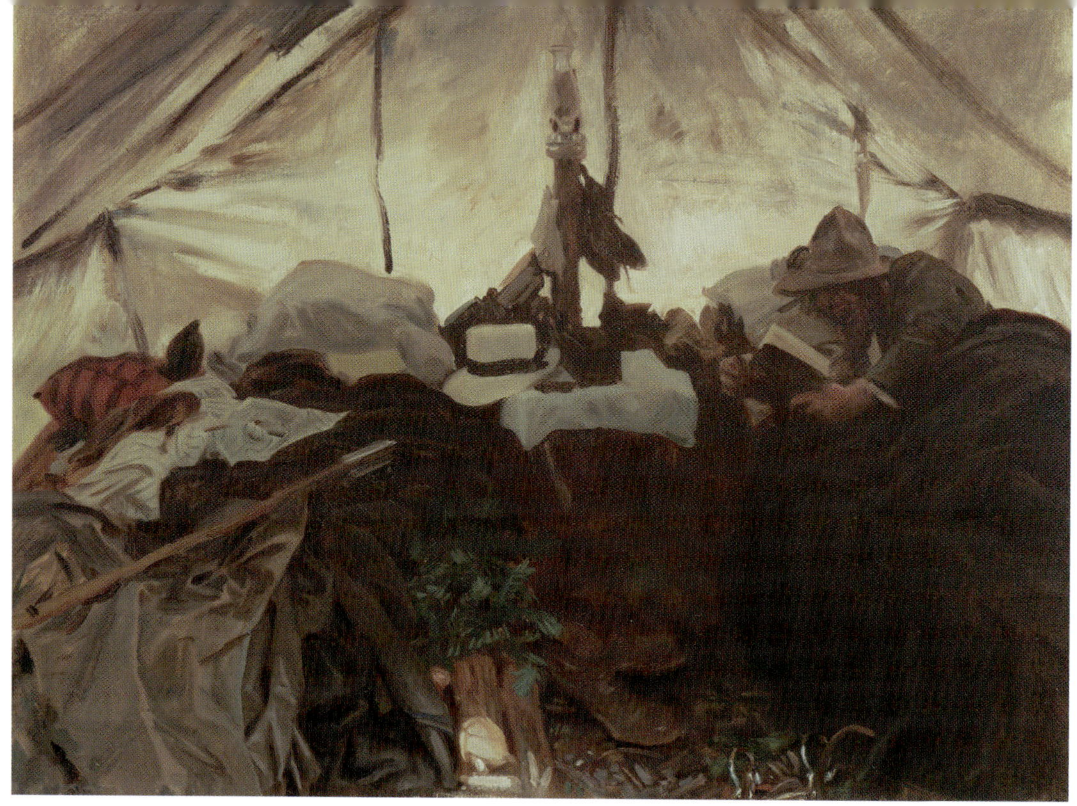

Sargent kept his visit to Canada fairly quiet and took the long train journey from America to western Canada, painting the landscape as it inspired him. He wrote to a friend, however, explaining that it was not as idyllic as he made it look: 'Our hands and feet [were] very cold most of the time, and [it was] hard to keep warm at night.' Despite the chill, he managed to sketch this painting.

Below: *Yoho Falls,* 1916, oil on canvas, 94 x 113cm (37 x 44½in), Isabella Stewart Gardner Museum, Boston, Massachusetts, USA

In the summer of 1916, Sargent had been in Boston to see his murals being put in place and then he travelled to the Rocky Mountains of Montana and British Columbia. That August, he wrote with enthusiasm of his experiences there to his friend Isabella Stewart Gardner: 'I am camping under the waterfall...It is magnificent when the sun shines...I have done a picture of a fantastic waterfall.'

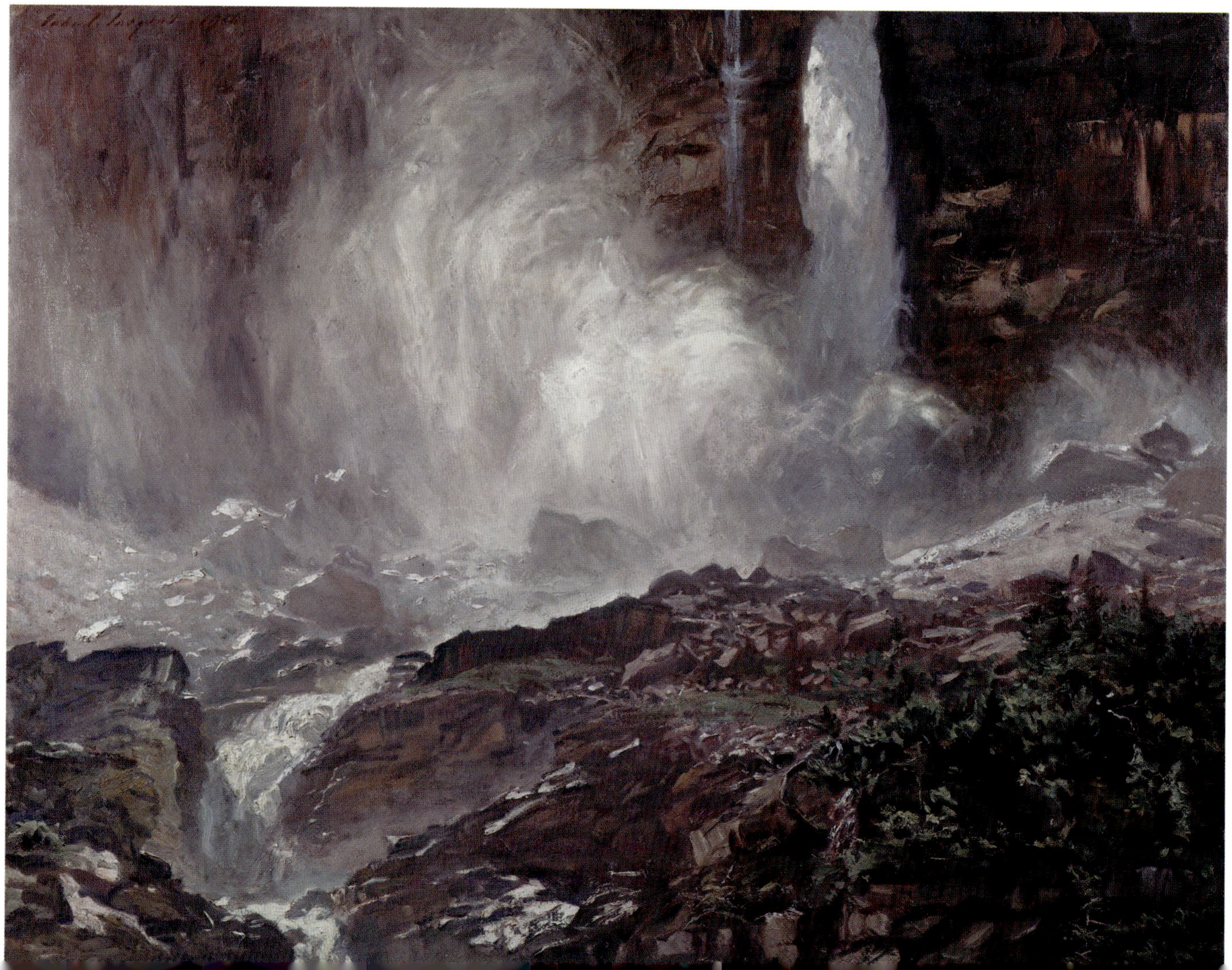

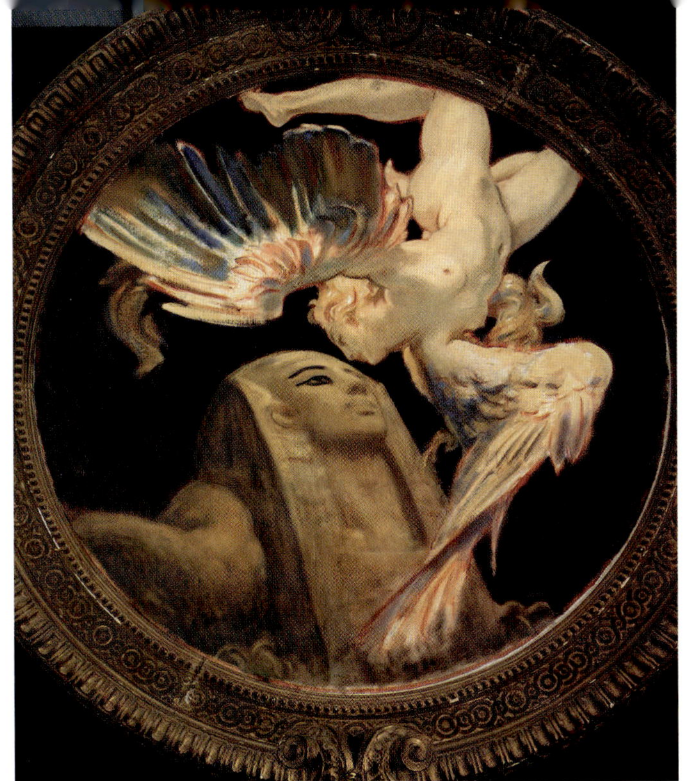

Sphinx and Chimaera, 1916–21, oil on canvas, diameter: 90.2cm (35½in), Huntington Library and Art Gallery, California, USA

This roundel depicts the mythological Sphinx and Chimaera, and was created as a study for Sargent's murals in the Museum of Fine Art in Boston. The style contrasts strongly with his Grand Manner style portraits, and his loosely painted views of figures in the landscape. It was a deliberate departure and intended to appeal to contemporary tastes, exploring the Beaux-Arts style for internal décor.

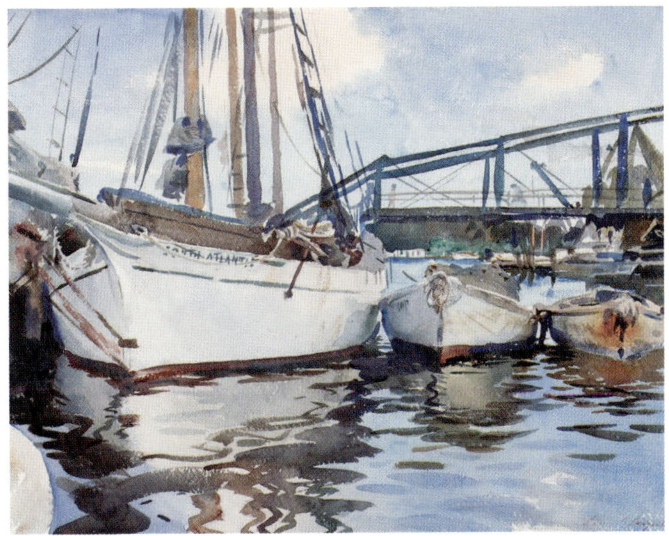

Boats at Anchor, 1917, watercolour over graphite on paper, 40.1 x 53.2cm (15¾ x 21in), Worcester Art Museum, Massachusetts, USA

While in Miami in 1917, Sargent visited a friend at his newly-built Villa Vizcaya, built as a self-sufficient Italian Renaissance country villa. It stood on 180 acres, with a dairy, poultry house, stable, greenhouse, staff residences, gardens, lagoons, cow pastures, citrus groves, nature trails, tennis courts, a village, mangroves and this yacht harbour. Sargent painted several views of the vast estate.

Derelicts, 1917, watercolour over graphite on paper, 34.7 x 53.4cm (13¾ x 21in), Worcester Art Museum, Massachusetts, USA

From 1915 to 1917, Sargent stayed in America, for the longest time he had yet spent there, and far from the battlefields of Europe. During this time critics were beginning to consign him to the masters of the past and several were starting to judge him fairly harshly in the light of modern movements such as Cubism and Futurism. Yet Sargent never wavered from his passion of capturing light and shade on forms.

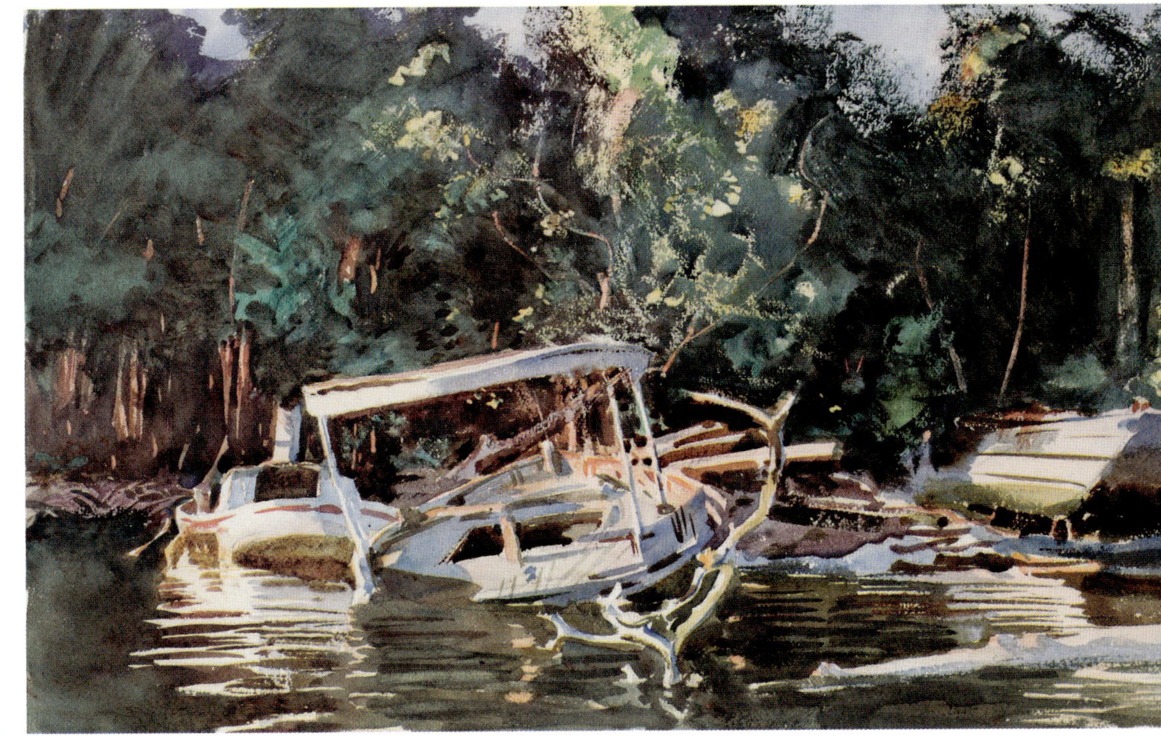

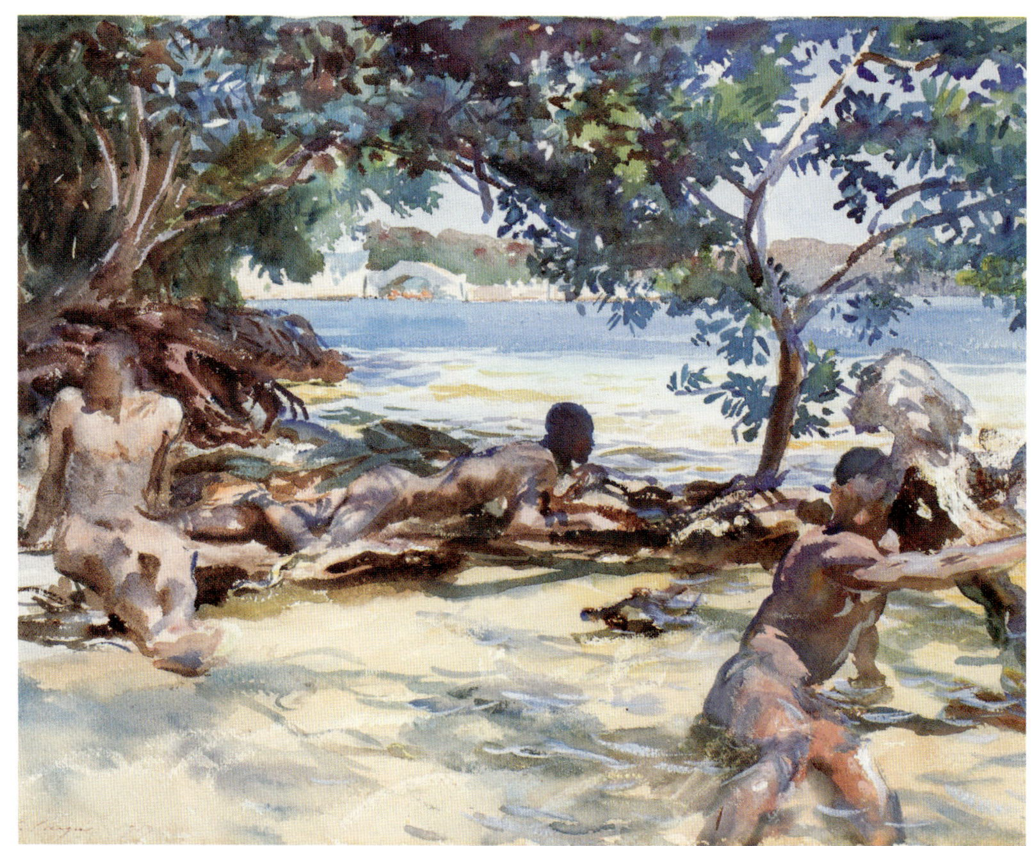

The Bathers, 1917, translucent and opaque watercolour on paper, 40 x 52.7cm (15¾ x 20¾in), Worcester Art Museum, Massachusetts, USA

While in Florida in 1917, Sargent's palette lightened and brightened to convey the heat and brilliant light. Frequently the subject of debate about his sexuality, Sargent's sensuous watercolours of both men and women, clothed or unclothed, have been open to interpretation, such as in this image of naked young men on the beach, or in his paintings of young women languidly reclining.

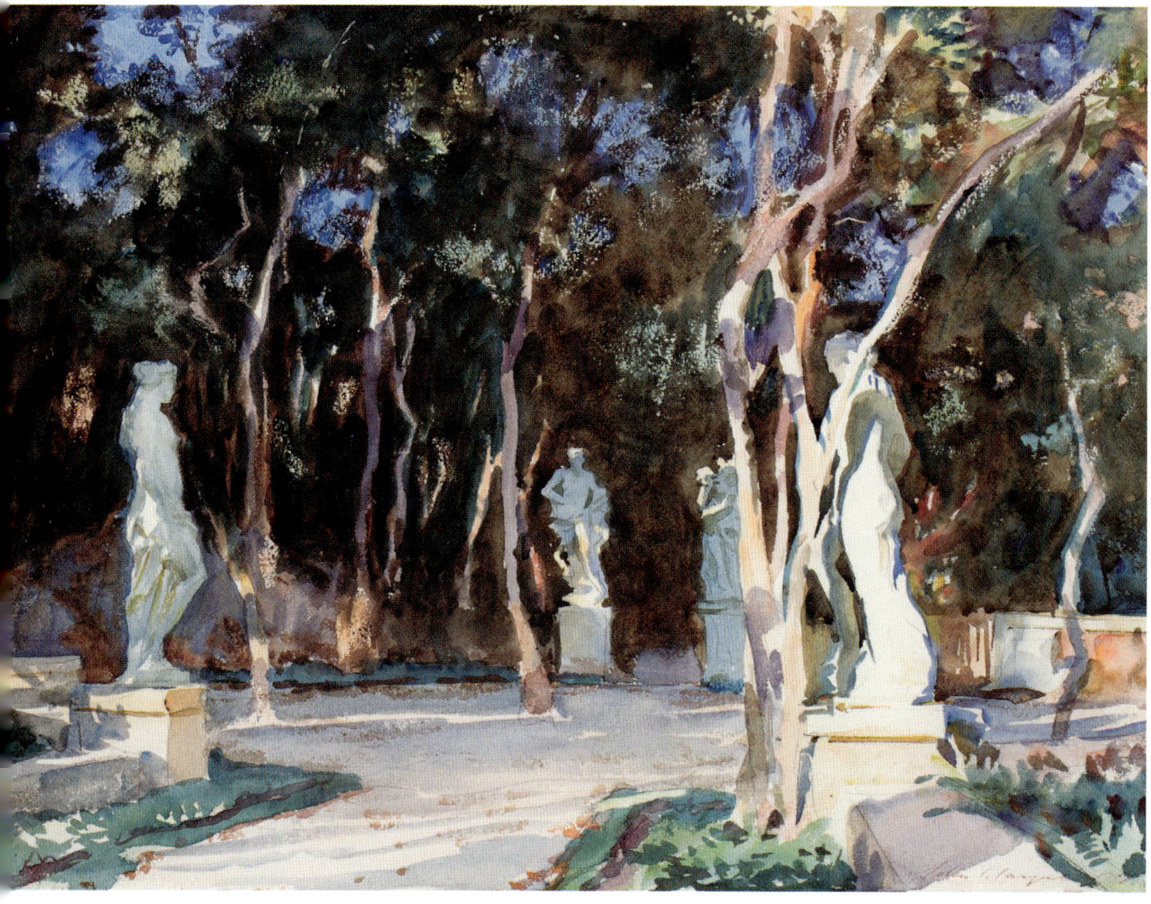

Shady Paths, Vizcaya, 1917, watercolour over graphite on paper, 39.7 x 53.3cm (15½ x 21in), Worcester Art Museum, Massachusetts, USA

These are the gardens of the Villa Vizcaya in Miami. The mansion and extensive grounds had only been completed in 1916, and its deliberate resemblance to an Italian Renaissance villa and garden especially appealed to Sargent. Whilst there, he also painted a portrait of the owner, his friend, industrial executive and art patron James Deering (1859–1925) – whom he had known since his student days.

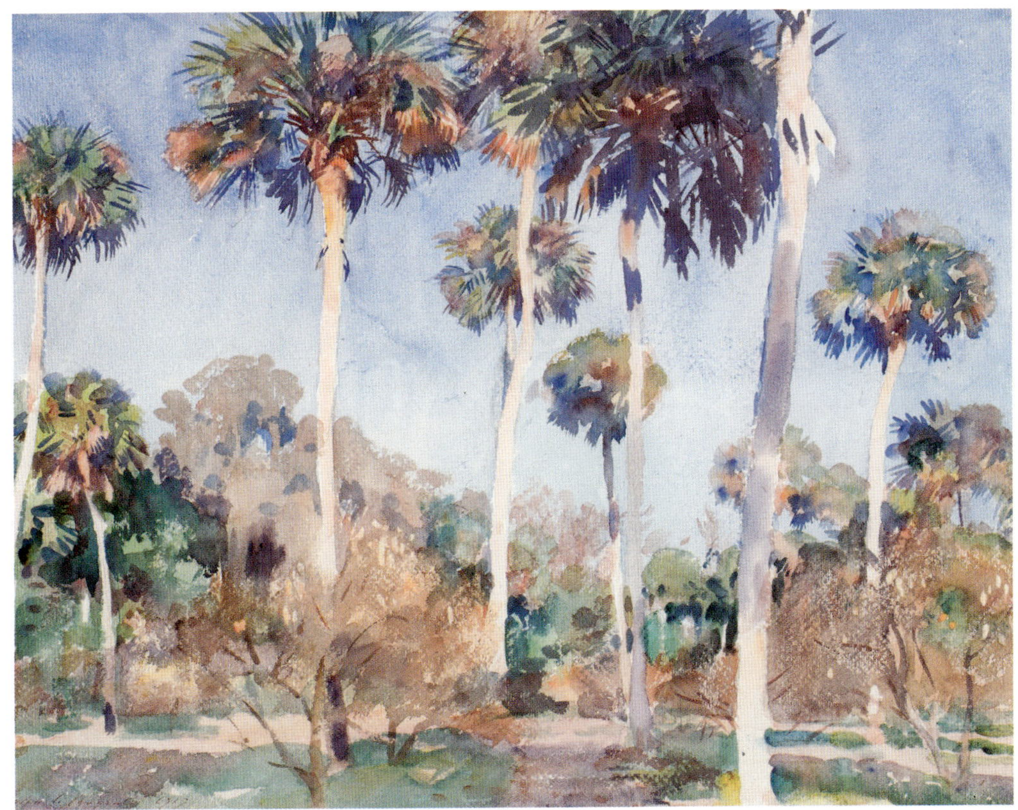

Palms, 1917, watercolour over graphite on paper, 40.1 x 53cm (15¾ x 21in), Worcester Art Museum, Massachusetts, USA

In February 1917, Sargent finally succumbed to the urging of John D. Rockefeller to paint some family portraits. He eventually made two oil paintings of Rockefeller and was paid $15,000 for each, but he refused to paint any more. While waiting for his subject to sit for him, he painted several views of the surroundings, including *Muddy Alligators* (see page 244) and these palm trees.

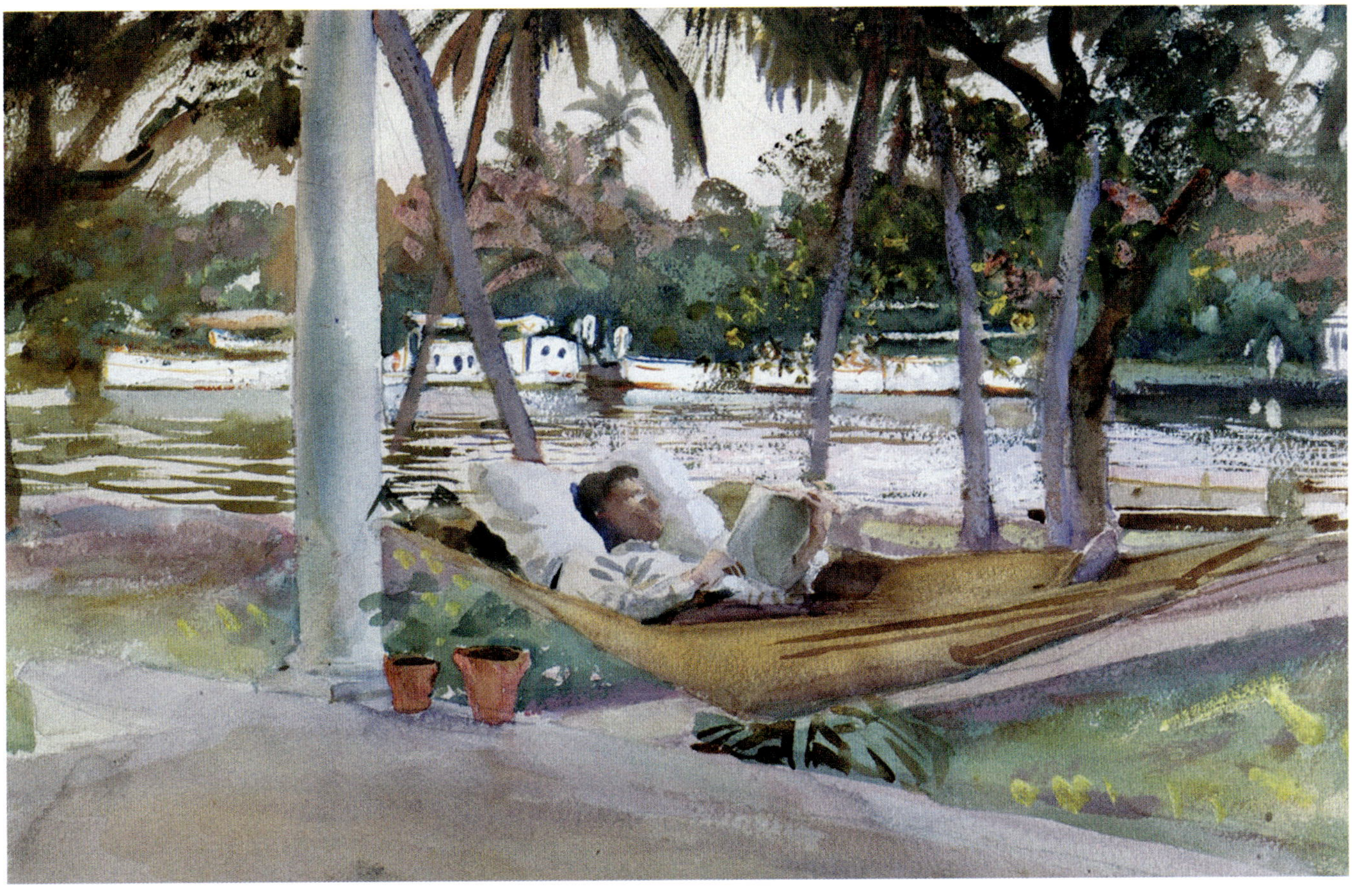

Figure in a Hammock, 1917, watercolour over graphite on paper, 34.6 x 53.3cm (13½ x 21in), The Metropolitan Museum, New York, USA

This is possibly a view of Deering reclining in a hammock in the grounds of the Villa Vizcaya, Florida. Sargent had met Deering when they were both students in Paris, so it was a pleasant interlude to visit his old friend in between working on his Boston Public Library mural project, and painting portraits of John D. Rockefeller. Contrasting with his quick sketch, this is a fully rendered painting.

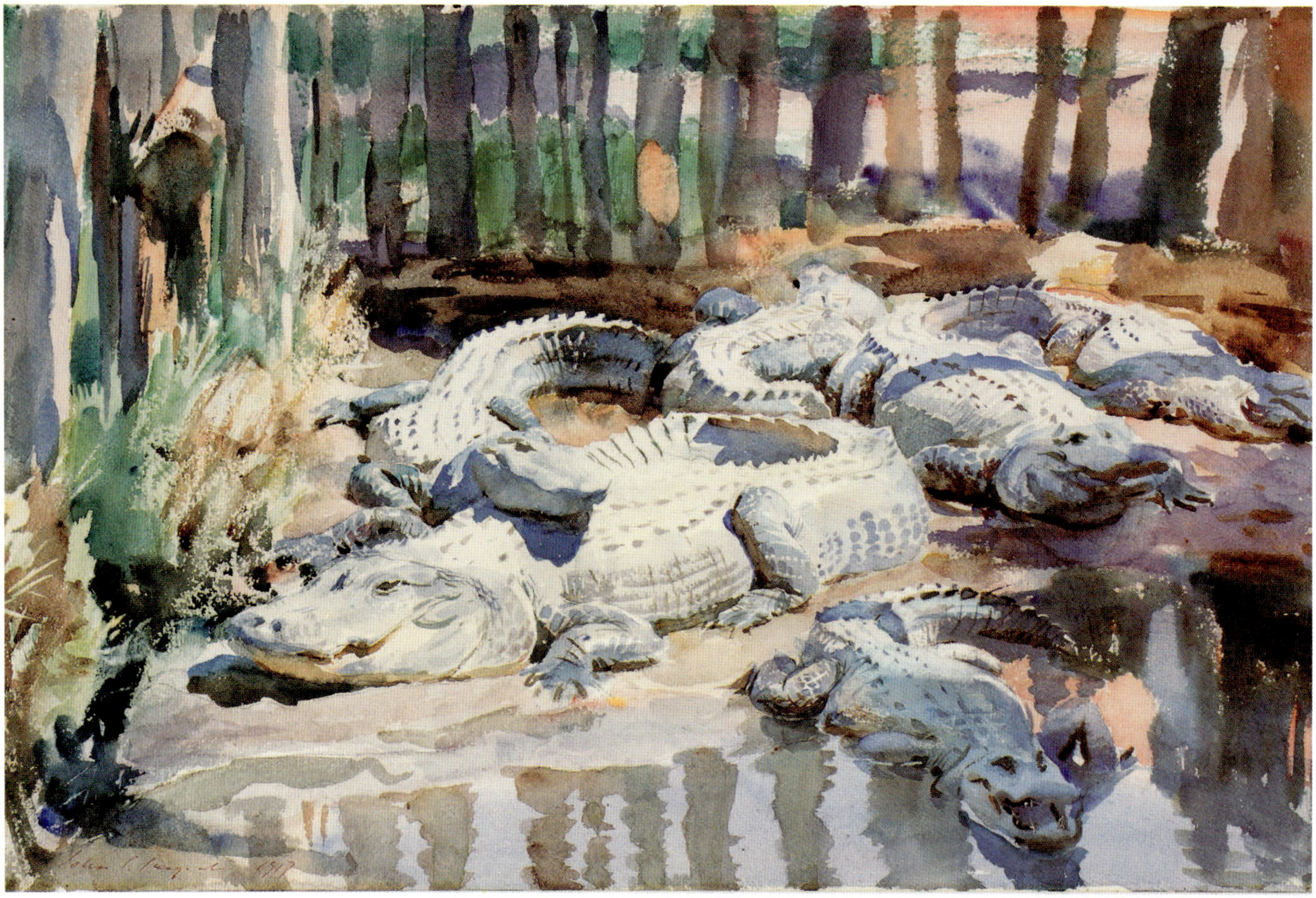

Muddy Alligators, 1917,
watercolour over graphite
on paper, 35.5 x 53cm
(14 x 20¾in), Worcester Art
Museum, Massachusetts,
USA

Painted while he was feeling
particularly frustrated over
a portrait he was painting
of John D. Rockefeller at his
winter home in Ormond
Beach, Florida, these
alligators caked with mud
were a departure in subject
for him, but continued the
theme he always pursued:
the depiction of light and
shadow on objects that are
partly in brilliant sunlight and
partly in cool shade. He used
various techniques, including
scratching into the paper,
employing wax resist and
broad brushstrokes.

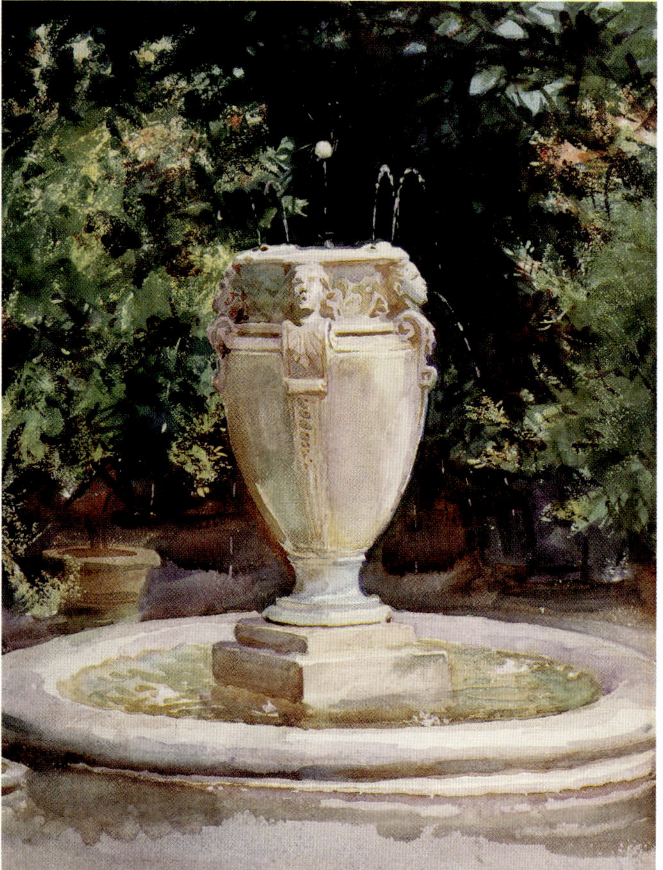

Vase Fountain, Pocantico,
1917, watercolour on paper,
54.6 x 40.6cm (21 x 15¾in),
Private Collection

After spending February
at the Rockefeller mansion
in Ormond Beach, in May,
Sargent went to the family's
summer residence of Kykuit
in Pocantico Hills, New York
and then on to Philadelphia
and Boston. While in New
York, he painted his second
portrait of Rockefeller and
this ornate fountain-vase in
the grounds of the mansion.

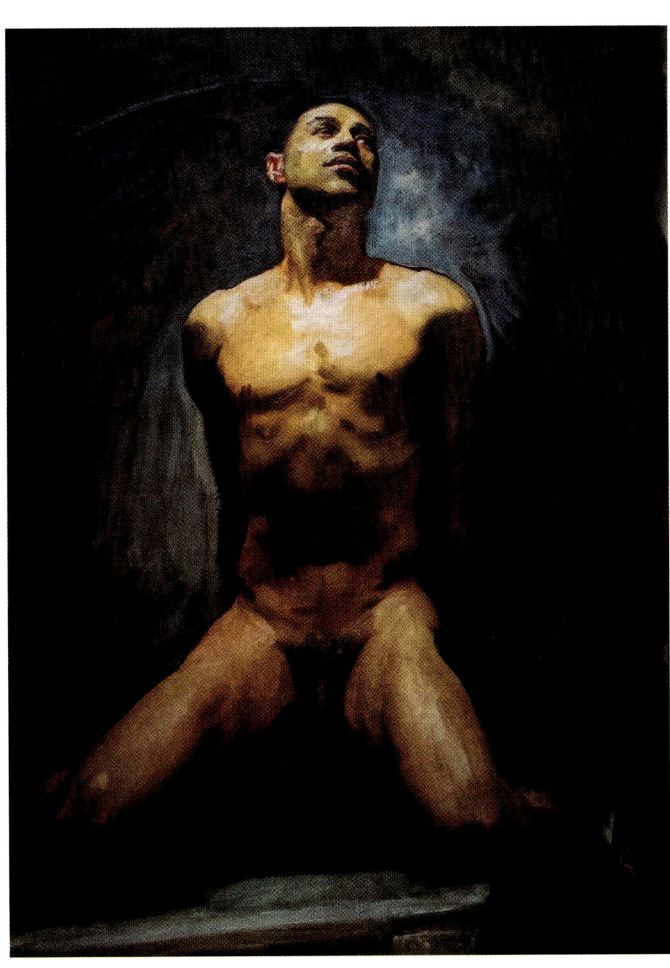

Nude Study of Thomas E. McKeller, c.1917–20, oil on canvas, 125.7 x 84.4cm (49½ x 33¼in), Museum of Fine Arts, Boston, Massachusetts, USA

The muscular young man was Thomas E. McKeller, a bellboy at the Copley Plaza Hotel in Boston where Sargent had met him in 1916. Just as he had become enthralled by Rosina Ferrara in Capri in 1878 and by Rose-Marie, so Sargent also became mesmerized by McKeller and used him as a model in several works, capturing his strong, muscular body and distinctive facial features.

Dugout, 1918, watercolour and graphite on white wove paper, 38.9 x 53cm (15¼ x 20¾in), The Metropolitan Museum, New York, USA

Assembled from sandbags, corrugated iron and canvas, these dugouts were made not far from Arras where Sargent was stationed in 1918. Created with strong light and tonal contrasts, and Sargent's rapidly applied marks, the image captures the sharp contrast of the peaceful French countryside with the essentials of war.

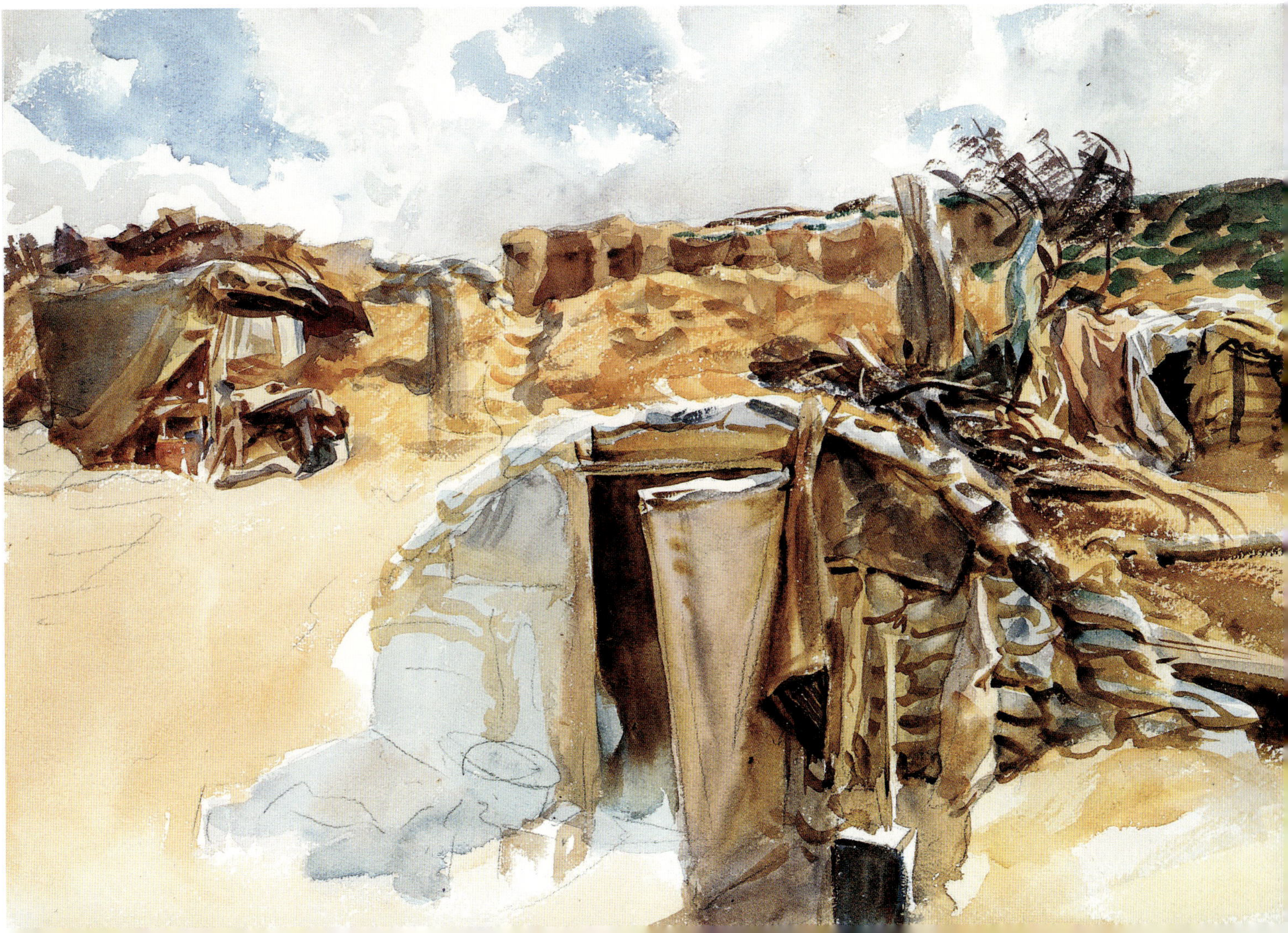

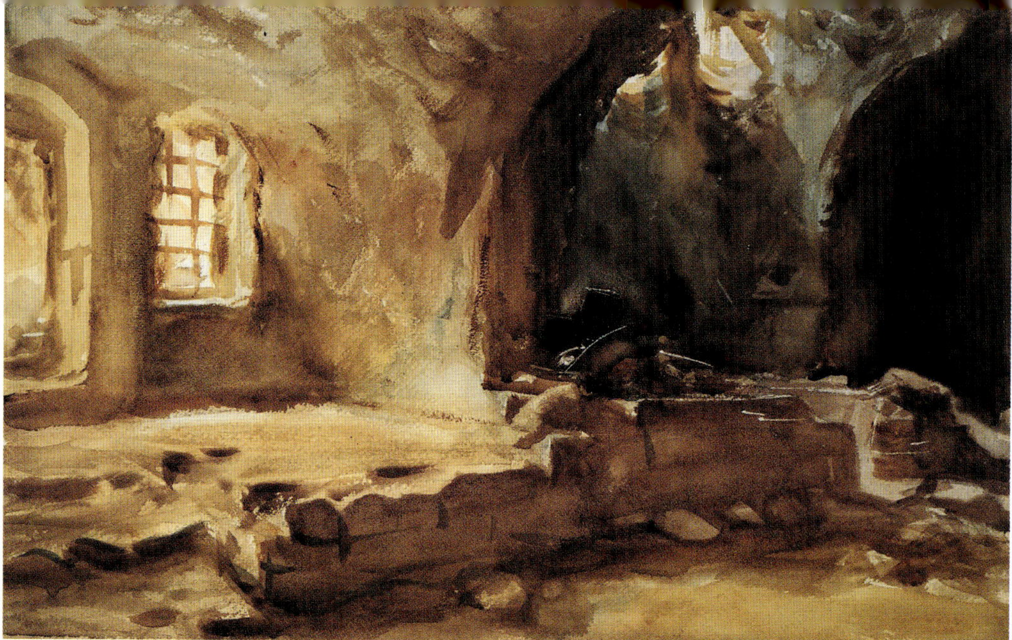

Ruined Cellar, Arras, 1918, watercolour and graphite on wove paper, mounted to cardboard, 36.5 x 54cm (14 x 21¼in), The Metropolitan Museum, New York, USA

Using commercially prepared board, Sargent could work more easily on location, applying dry and wet paint rapidly to capture a quick impression, as in this evocative scene.

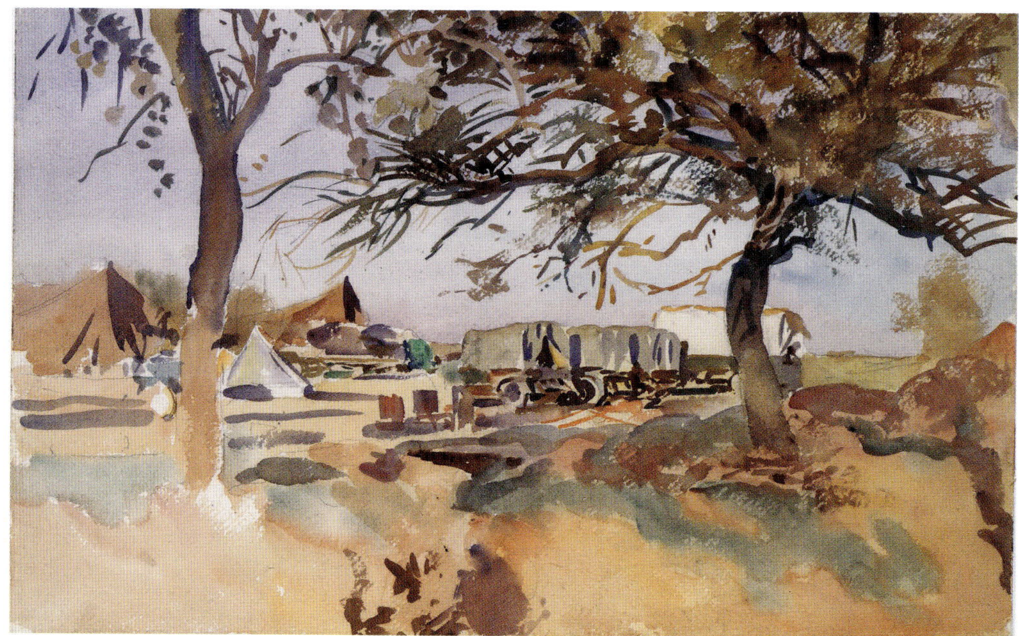

Military Camp, 1918, watercolour and graphite on white wove paper, 34 x 53.1cm (13½ x 20¾in), The Metropolitan Museum, New York, USA

Sargent painted this view of part of a military camp, looking from a distance through trees. The contrast of peace and destruction fascinated him, and he used both wet-into-wet and dry brush techniques, evoking the calm of the countryside as a direct contrast with the machinery of war and horrors of the battlefield.

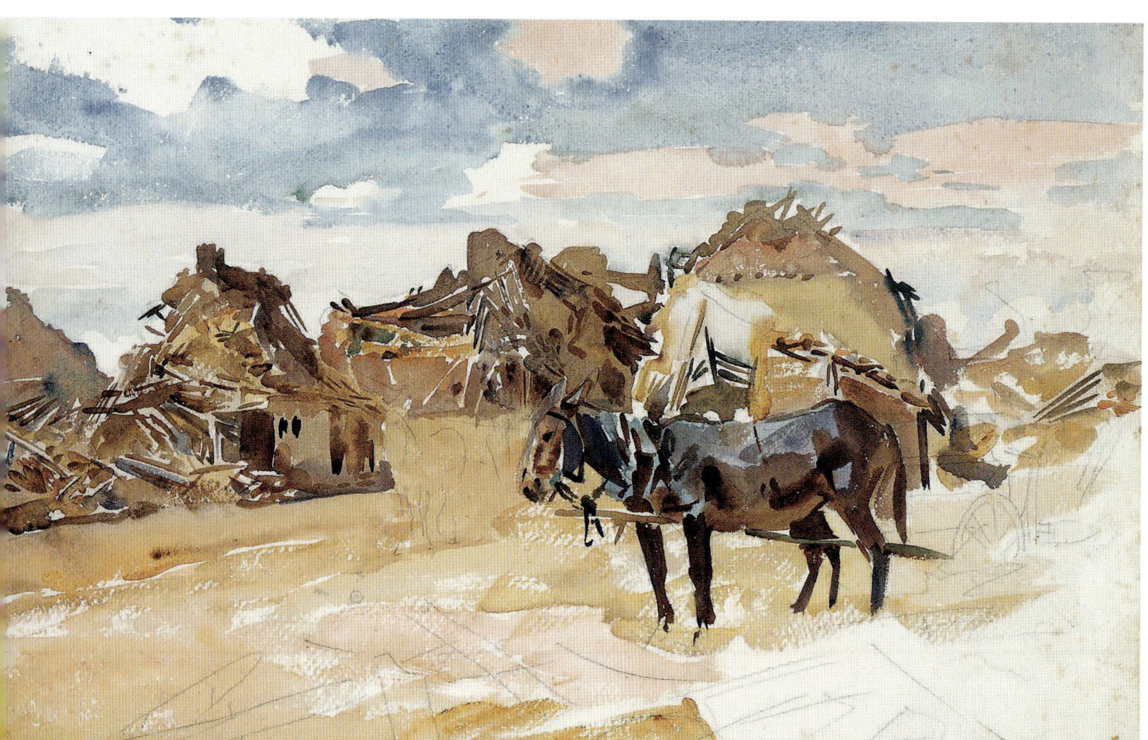

Mules and Ruins, 1918, watercolour and graphite on white wove paper, 36.4 × 53cm (14¼ x 20¾in), The Metropolitan Museum, New York, USA

Sargent donated ten of the watercolours that he had painted at the Front in 1918 to London's Imperial War Museum. He wrote to the museum officials: 'I think my watercolours gain by being seen together in a certain quantity, and I would be glad to add to the four you have selected.'

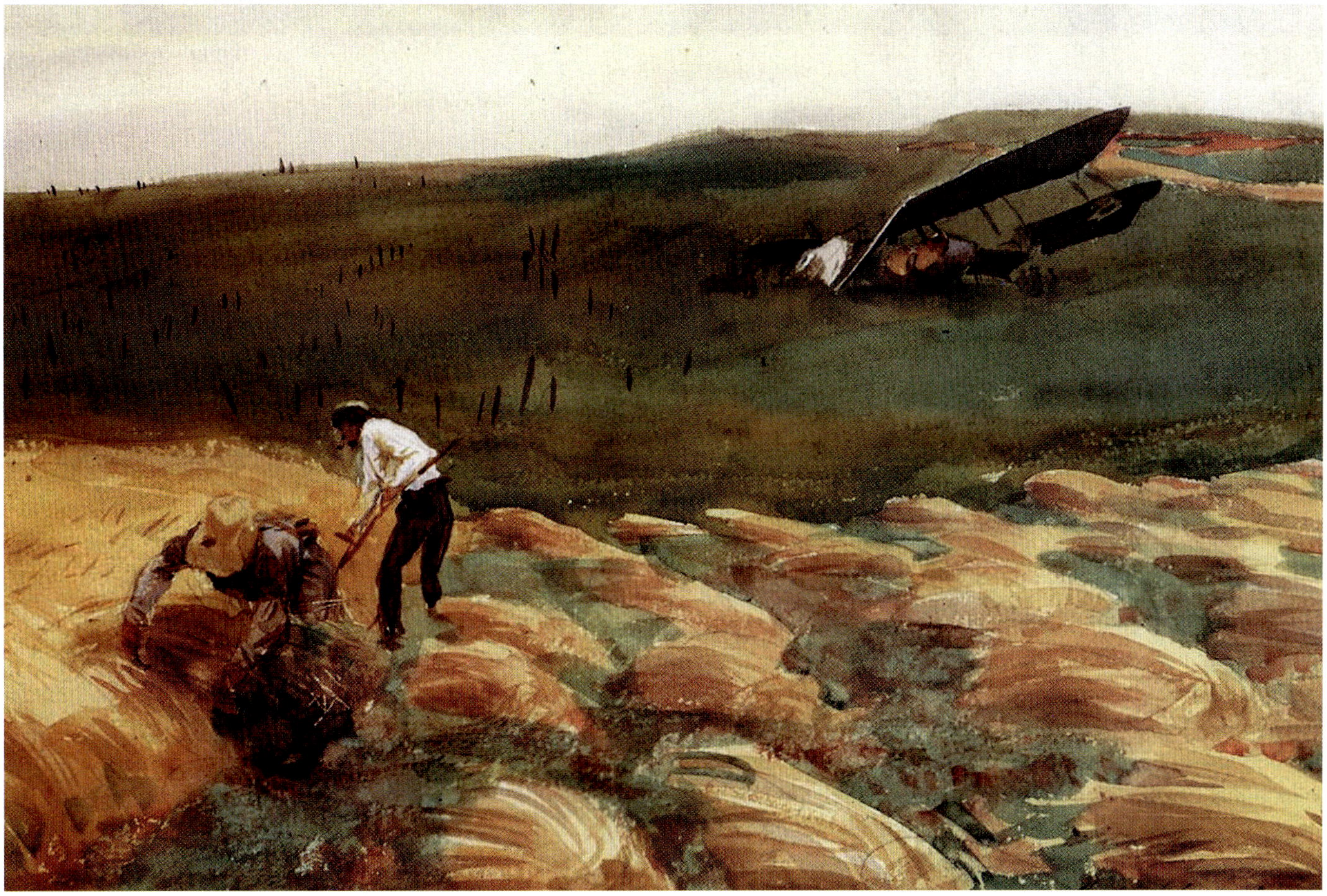

Crashed Aeroplane, 1918, watercolour on paper, 53.3 x 34.2cm (21 x 13½in), The Imperial War Museum, London, UK

With greater looseness and directness than ever, Sargent worked alla prima, with minimal pencil drawing beforehand or gouache highlights. Painted with a fairly wet brush, this is a view of fields in France with a crashed aeroplane in the middle distance. In the foreground, two labourers, a man and a woman, are gathering wheat and tying it into bundles. Both are bent over, concentrating on their work.

Highlanders Resting at the Front, 1918, watercolour over traces of graphite on paper, 34.3 x 53.5cm (13½ x 21in), Fitzwilliam Museum, Cambridge, UK

Although before going to France, Sargent had expected to encounter vast numbers of marching troops, in the event, where he was stationed, he usually only came across small units taking advantage of an occasional respite from the trenches. Here, enjoying a short break, are some Scottish infantrymen, dozing in the sun, their weapons and other equipment strewn close by.

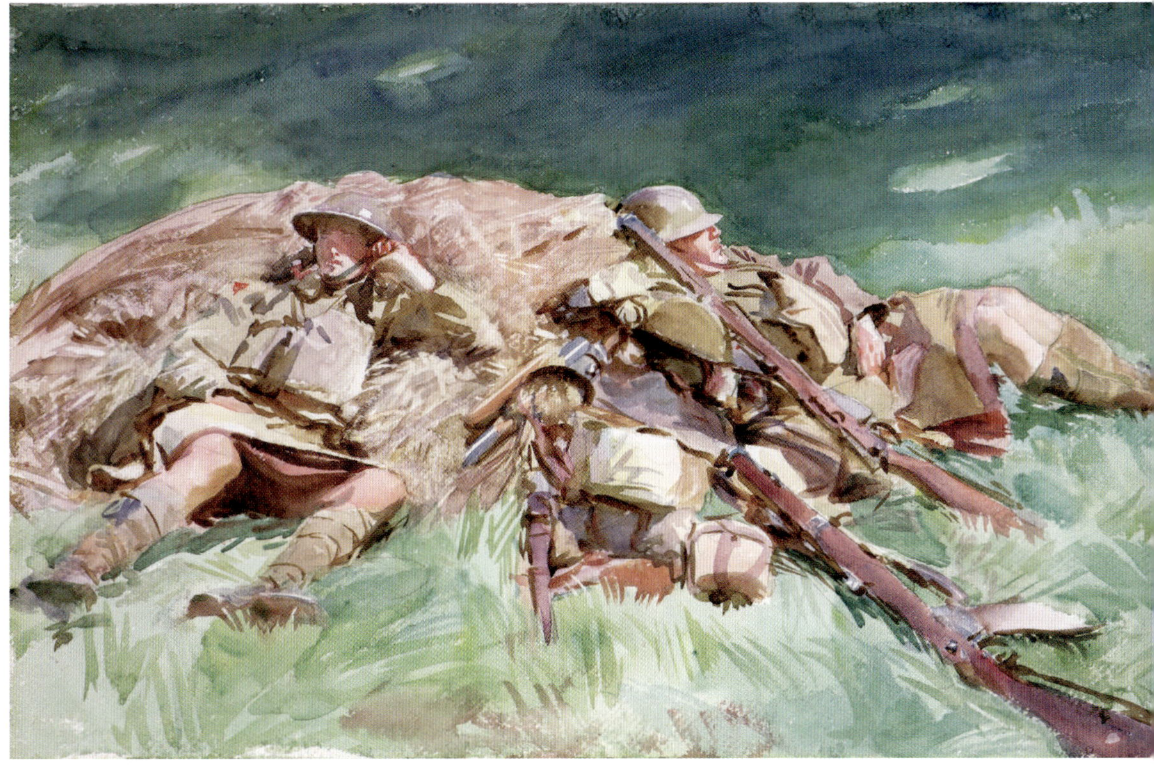

Thou Shalt Not Steal, 1918, watercolour on paper, 50.8 x 33.6cm (20 x 13¼in), The Imperial War Museum, London, UK

A comment on the differences in society during peace and war; this shows soldiers helping themselves to apples from a French orchard. Amid the brutality and killing, these men nonetheless still feel guilty for trespassing and stealing fruit from trees that do not belong to them. Sargent however, was more focused on capturing the contrasts of khaki and flesh with leaves and fruit.

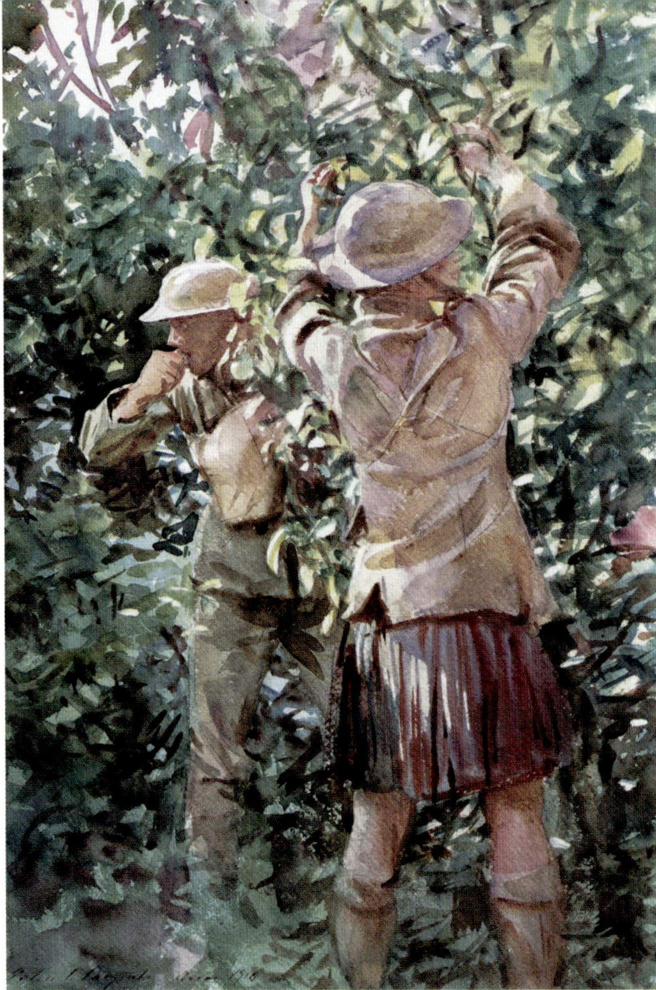

Below: *Tommies Bathing,* 1918, watercolour over graphite on paper, 38.9 x 52.7cm (15¼ x 20¾in), The Metropolitan Museum, New York, USA

In March 1918, Sargent's beloved niece Rose-Marie was killed when a bomb hit a church in Paris where she was attending a concert. He returned to England to be with Violet and Emily, but within weeks, he was commissioned by the British Government as an official war painter. In July, he left England with Henry Tonks for the Western Front where he made watercolours and sketches of soldiers.

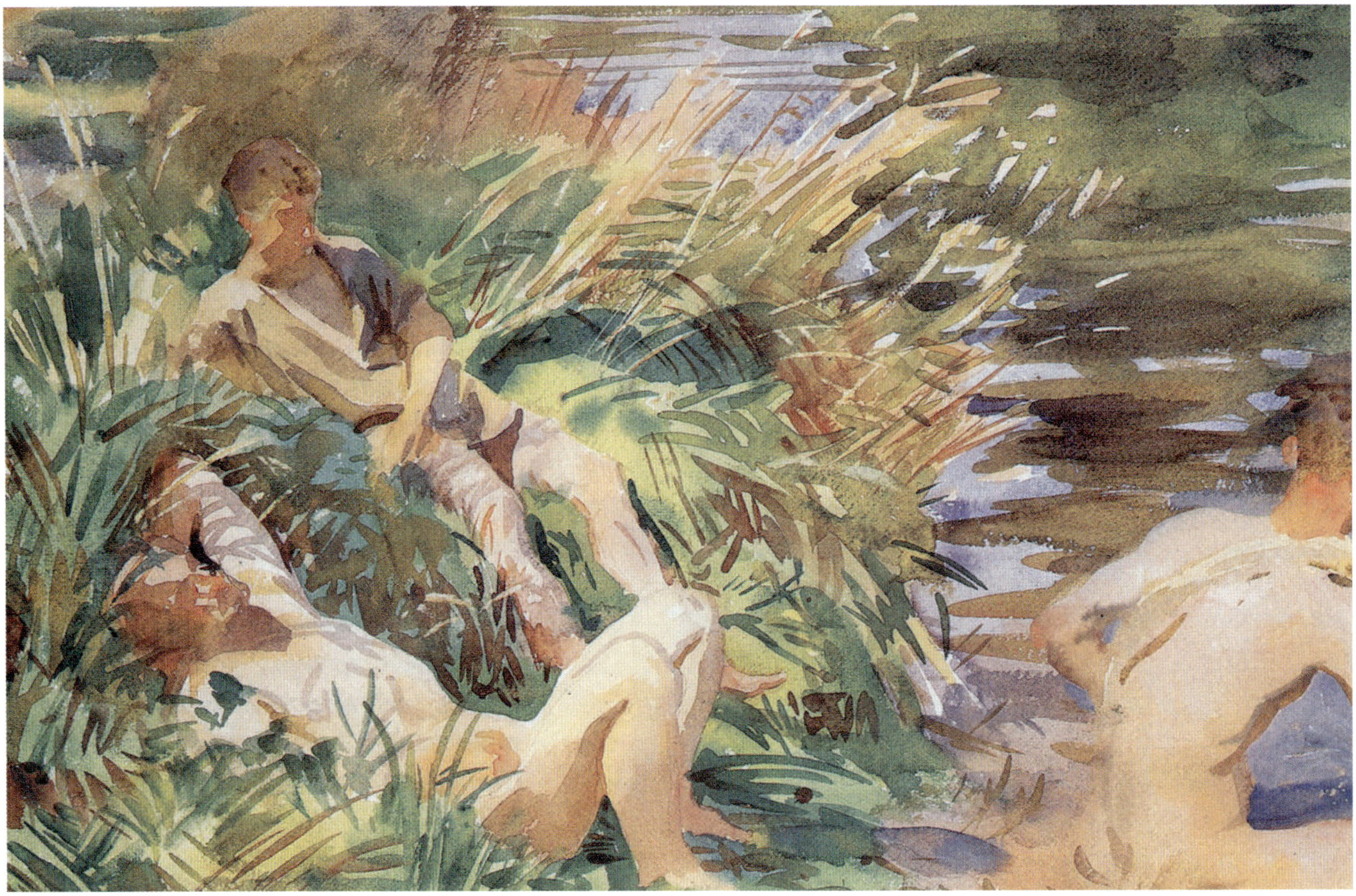

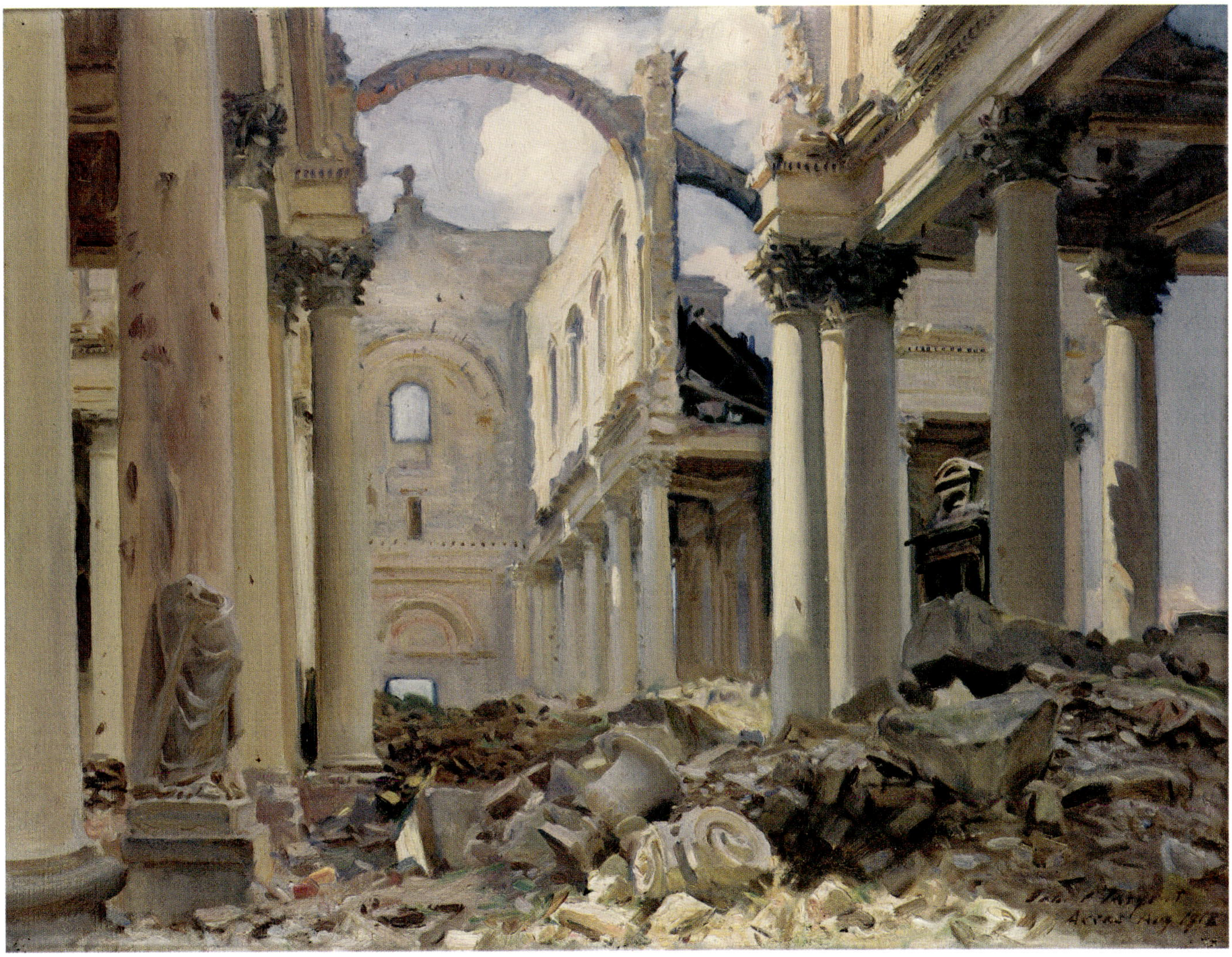

Ruined Cathedral at Arras,
1918, oil on canvas, 55.8 x
71.1cm (22 x 28in), Private
Collection

The shocking reality of
a completely devastated
cathedral after bombing was
going to be Sargent's 'big
picture' for an exhibition on
his return to England, but in
the end, he found something
even more disquieting for
that. This was the Cathedral
of Saint Vaast in Arras after
it suffered a direct hit in
August 1918. His companion
Henry Tonks also painted the
ruined town, but at night.

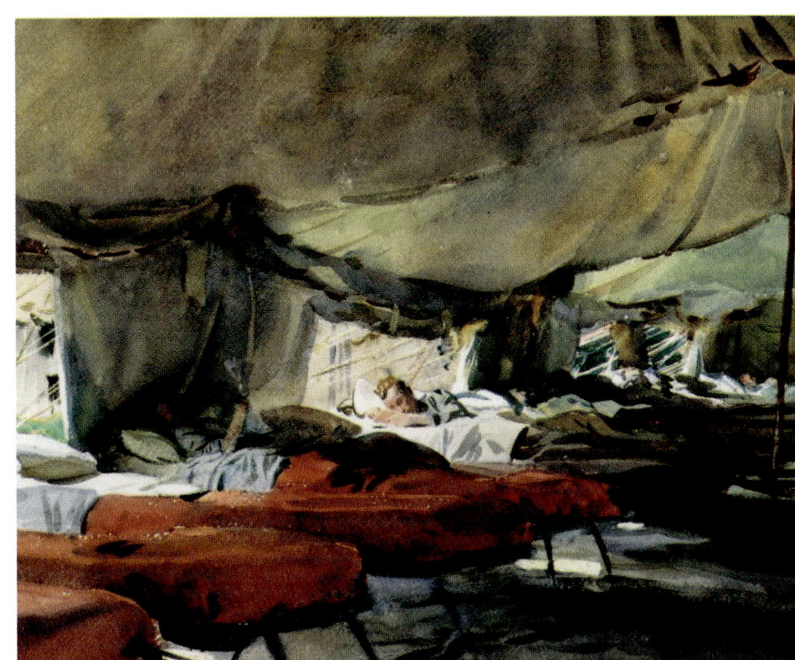

Interior of a Hospital Tent,
1918, watercolour on paper,
38.5 x 51.9cm (15 x 20in),
The Imperial War Museum,
London, UK

Late in September 1918,
while painting soldiers on
the Western Front, Sargent
contracted influenza and
was taken to a temporary
hospital not far away near
Roisel. He spent a week
in the hospital tent, and as
he recovered, painted the
injured soldiers around him.
The camp beds are covered
with red or brown blankets,
and patients read or sleep.

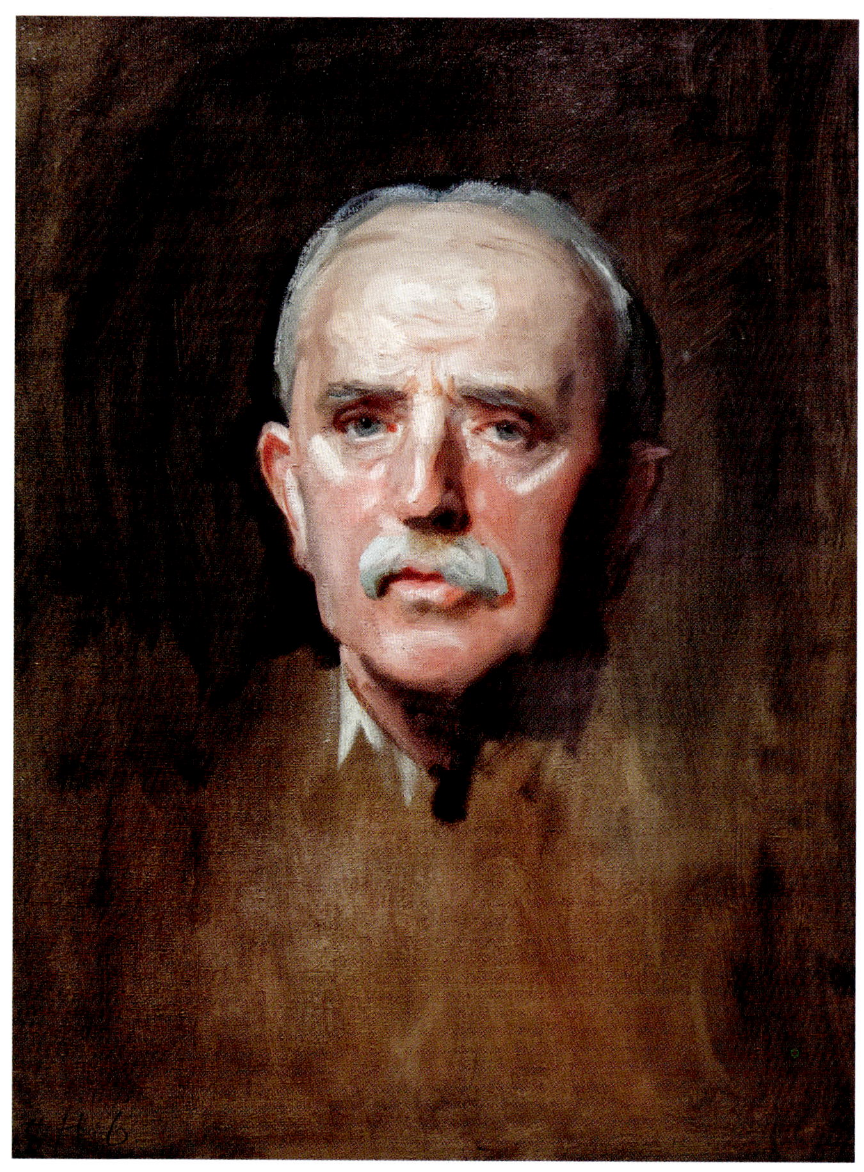

John Denton Pinkstone French, c.1919–22, oil on canvas, 54.6 x 39.4cm (21½ x 15½in), National Portrait Gallery, London, UK

After World War I, and after his painting *Gassed* (see page 95) had been named Picture of the Year by the authorities at the Royal Academy, Sargent was commissioned by a South African financier Sir Abraham Bailey, to paint another large canvas for the National Gallery, of officers who had fought. For this momentous portrait, he painted all 22 men individually (see page 253). John Enton Pinkstone French (1852–1925) was among them.

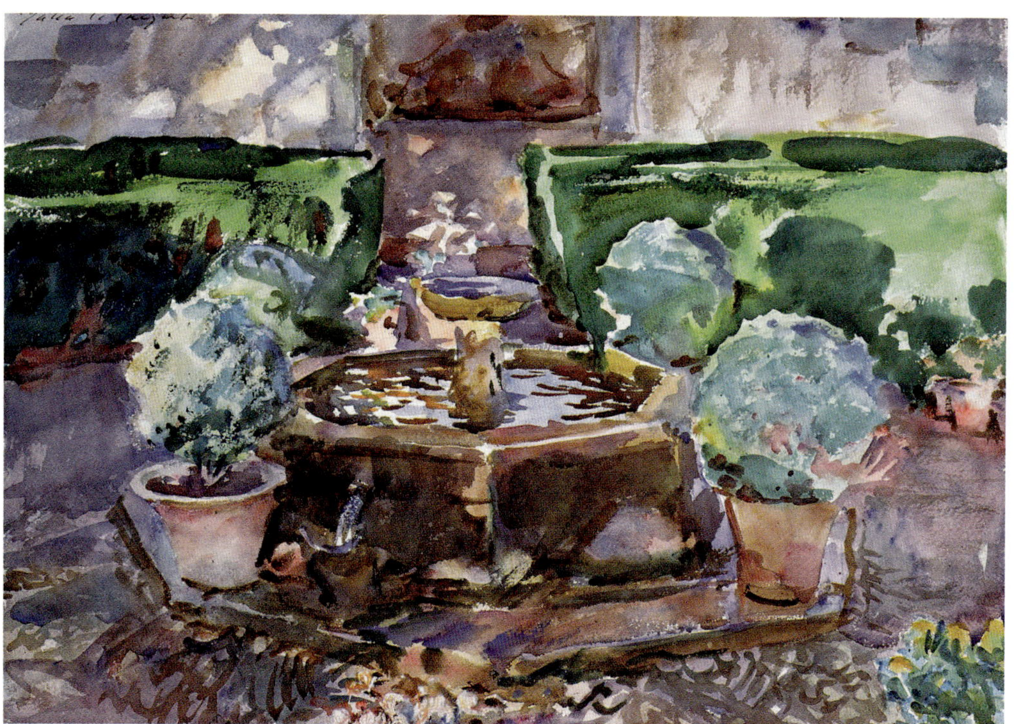

Fountains in the Generalife, Granada, exh.1920, watercolour on paper, 40 x 54.6cm (15¾ x 21½in), The Victoria and Albert Museum, London, UK

The Palacio de Generalife, which translates literally as the 'Architect's Garden,' was the summer palace and estate of the Emirs, or rulers of the Emirate of Granada in Al-Andalus, now near Granada in Spain. It is not clear when exactly Sargent painted this work; it could have been in 1912 on his last trip to Granada, or he could have painted it from memory, but he exhibited it for the first time in 1920.

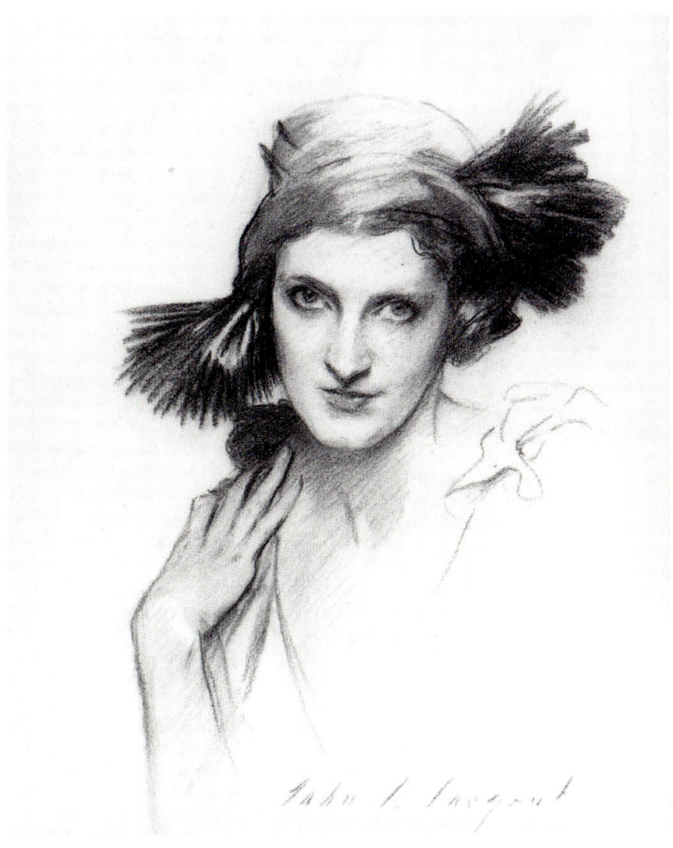

Mrs Reginald (Daisy) Fellowes, c.1920, charcoal on paper, 61 x 45.7cm (24 x 18in), Private Collection

Twice-married socialite, editor, writer and heiress to the Singer sewing machine fortune, the Honourable Daisy Fellowes (née Marguerite Séverine Philippine Decazes de Glücksberg, 1890–1962), was an acclaimed beauty, style icon and notorious adulterer. Sargent's charcoal portrait complements her understated style.

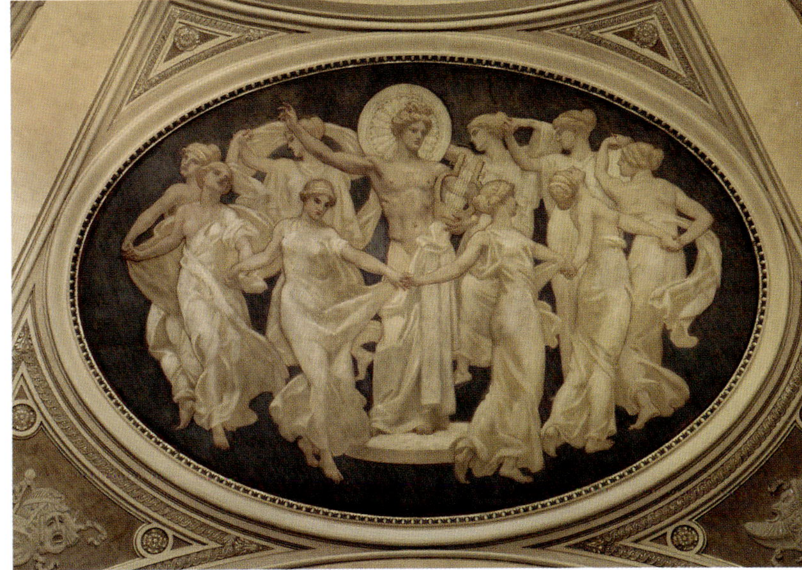

Apollo and the Muses, 1921, oil on canvas, 283.2 x 428.6cm (111½ x 168¾in), Museum of Fine Arts, Boston, Massachusetts, USA

Sargent was commissioned to paint this work for the Rotunda of the Museum of Fine Arts, Boston in 1916, for just over $40,000. It represents the mythological god Apollo, patron of music and fine arts and the god of light. He is circled by dancing women, the nine muses: Calliope, Clio, Euterpe, Terpsichore, Erato, Melpomene, Thalia, Urania and Polyhymnia,

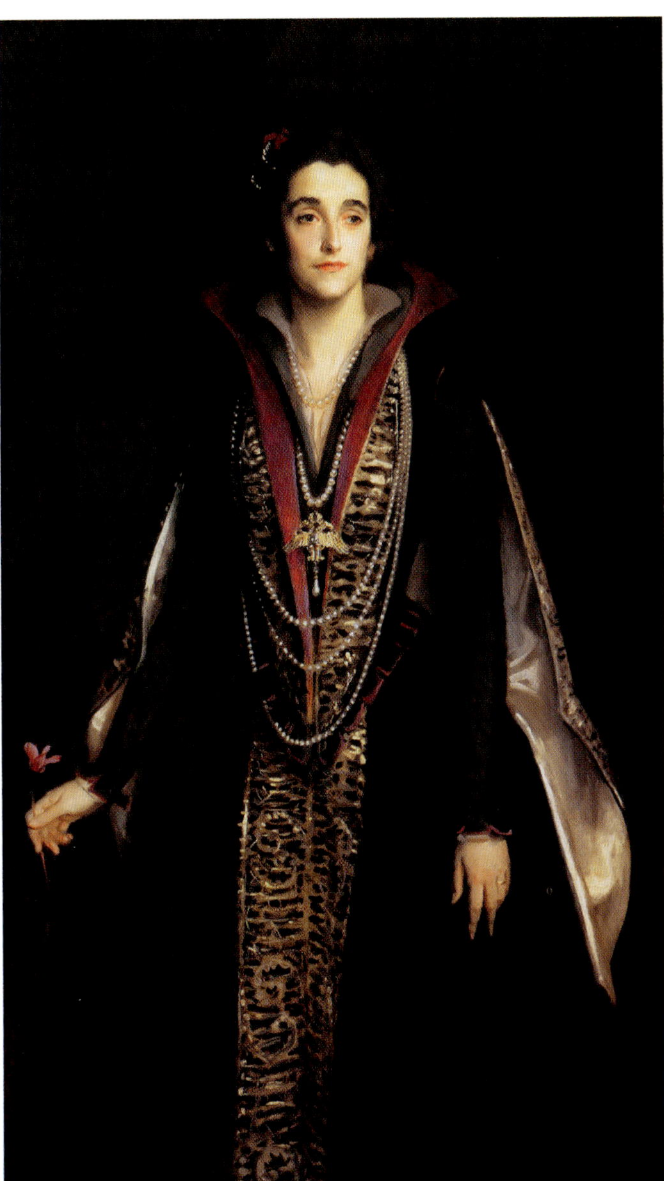

Portrait of the Marchioness of Cholmondeley, 1922, oil on canvas, 161 x 93cm (63¼ x 36½in), Private Collection

Sybil Cholmondeley, the Countess of Rocksavage (later Marchioness) was a member of two of the most prominent families of the time: the Sassoons and the Rothschilds, and she was one of Sargent's closest friends. This is the most dramatic of the portraits Sargent painted of her; she stands tall in a black dress with a layered stand-up collar, long strands of pearls, a gold winged pendant and golden satin-lined cloak. The delicate single flower adds femininity.

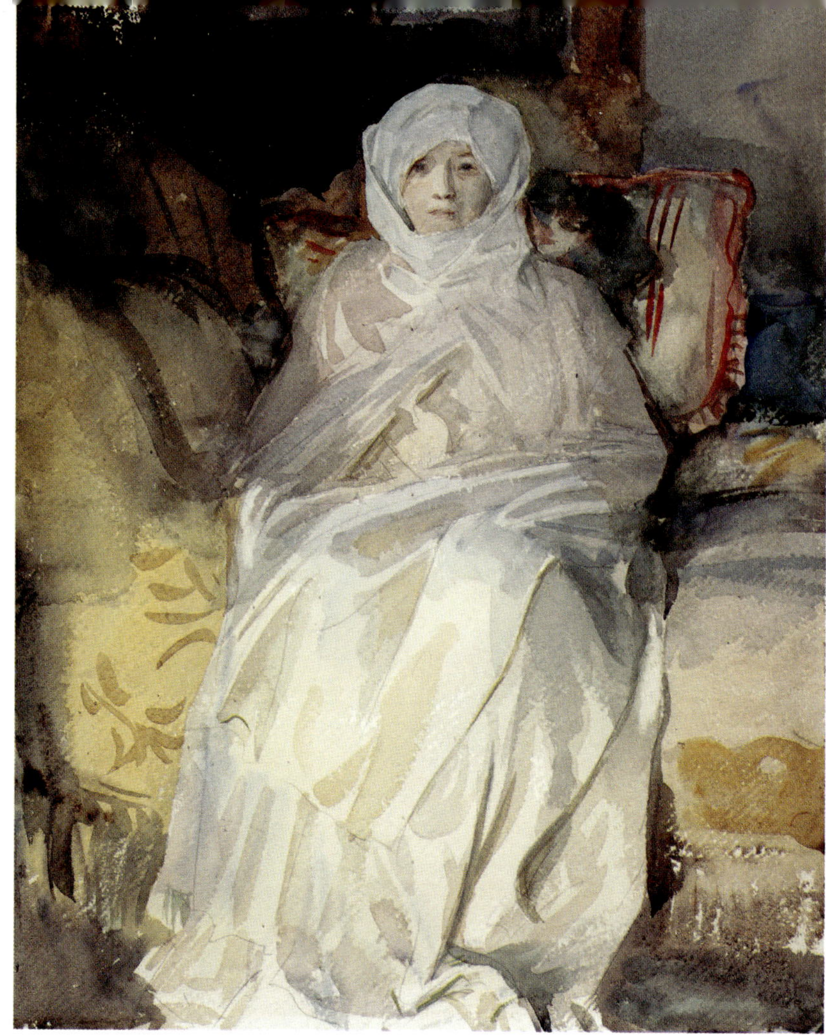

Mrs Gardner in White, 1922, watercolour on paper, 43 x 32cm (17 x 12½in), Isabella Stewart Gardner Museum, Boston, Massachusetts, USA

In September 1922, Sargent visited his dear friend Isabella Stewart Gardner who had recently suffered a stroke. She described this work as: 'a water-colour, not meant, I hope, to look like me.' Her apparent calmness, swathed in soft, white, contrasts with her earlier portraits by Sargent, which show her to be lively and high-spirited. The painting is inscribed: 'To my friend Mrs Gardner / John S. Sargent.' Isabella died two years later.

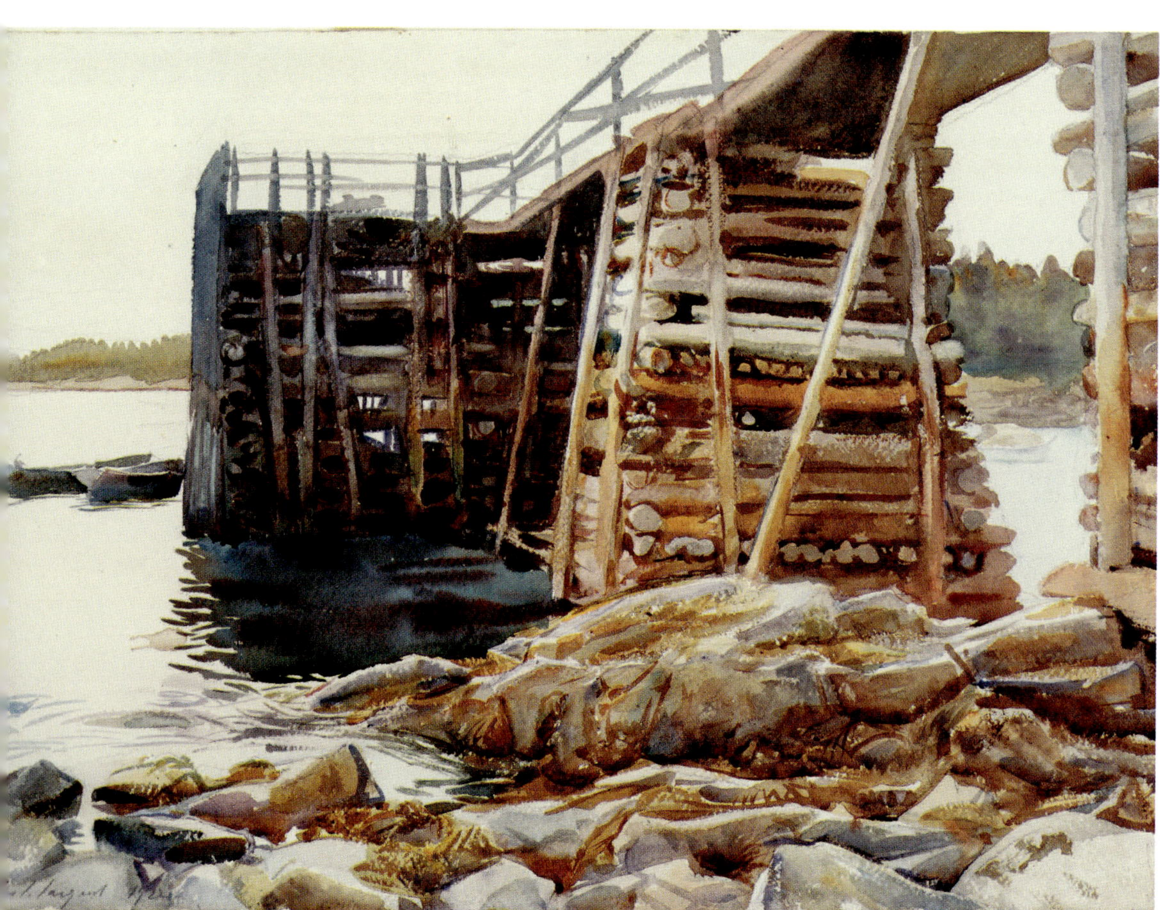

Wharf at Ironbound, 1922, watercolour on paper, 39.4 x 53.4cm (15.5 x 21in), Private Collection

In 1922, Sargent stayed with his friend the artist Dwight Blaney (1865–1944) and his family for a few days at their summer home at Ironbound Island, about three miles east of Bar Harbour in Maine. While staying there, he produced seven watercolours and sketches, including Dwight painting, the family relaxing on the verandah, and this view made near the shore.

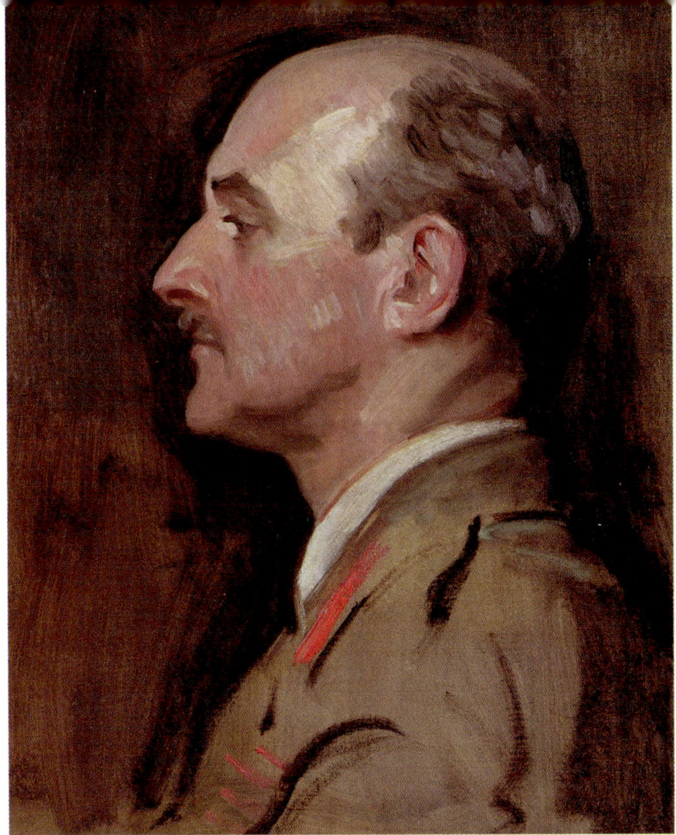

Portrait sketch of Field Marshal Viscount Allenby, 1922, oil on canvas, 56.3 x 41.2cm (22 x 16¼in), New Walk Museum & Art Gallery, Leicester, UK

Field Marshal Viscount Edmund Henry Hynman Allenby (1861–1936) was an English soldier and Imperial Governor who fought in the Second Boer War and World War One. He continued to serve as High Commissioner for Egypt and the Sudan after the war until 1925. This is one of Sargent's studies for his large commission of 22 officers for the National Gallery (see below).

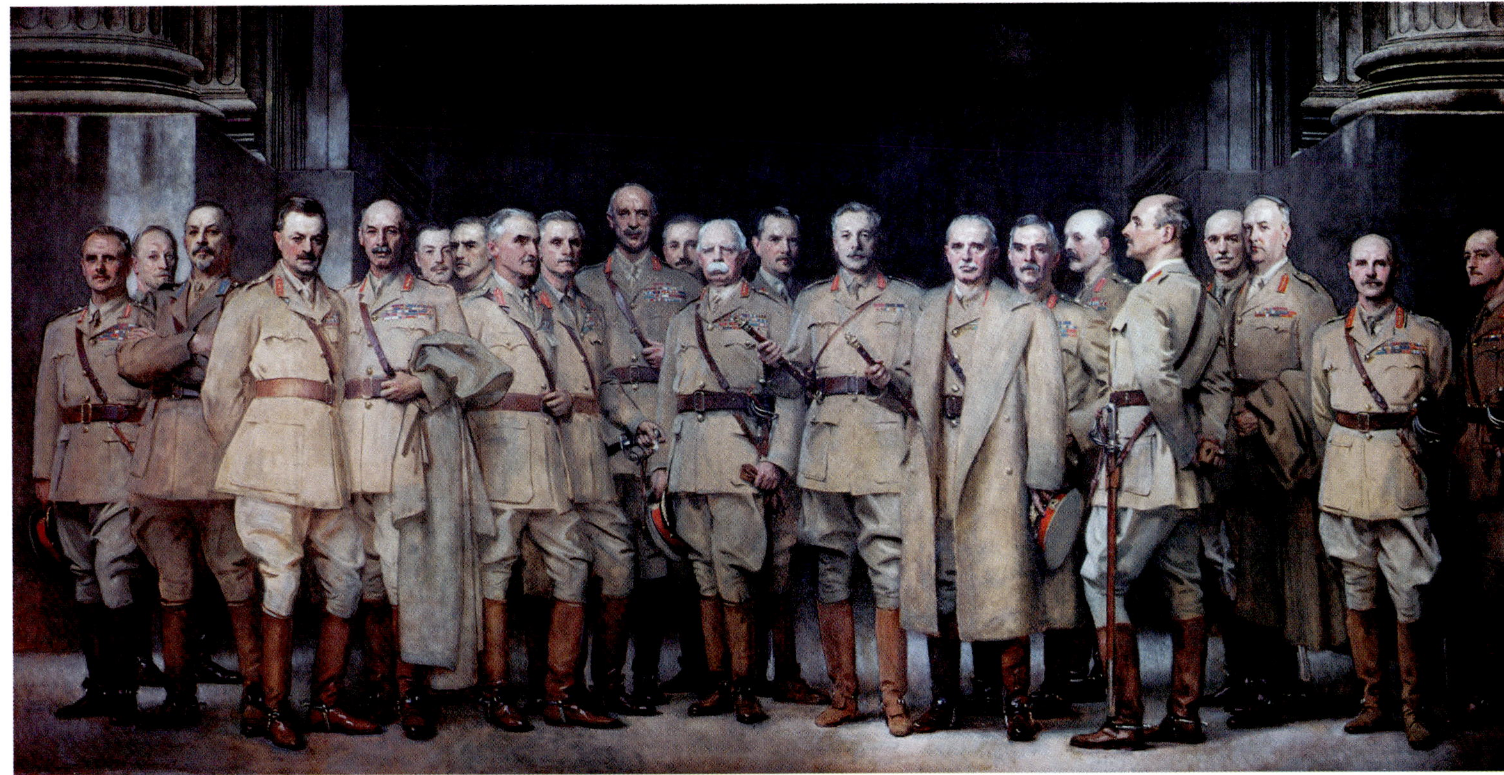

General Officers of the Great War, 1922, oil on canvas, 299.7 x 528.3cm (118 x 208in), National Portrait Gallery, London, UK

In 1919, when Sargent was asked to paint this large group portrait he was busy on his mural decorations in Boston and wrote: '... I am so hampered by circumstances that I would not be justified in accepting a commission of this great and immediate importance.' Eventually, Charteris intervened, telling gallery officials that if Sargent had no time constraints and if payment was 'not less than £5,000' he might consent. They agreed and he did. The monumental portrait received universal acclaim. Three years after its unveiling, and after a major exhibition in New York, Sargent died at his home in Tite Street of a heart attack. He remains an enigmatic figure, often described as shy, retiring and socially awkward, yet clearly charismatic, a devoted and generous friend whose works reveal his love of life, of people and of the world.

INDEX

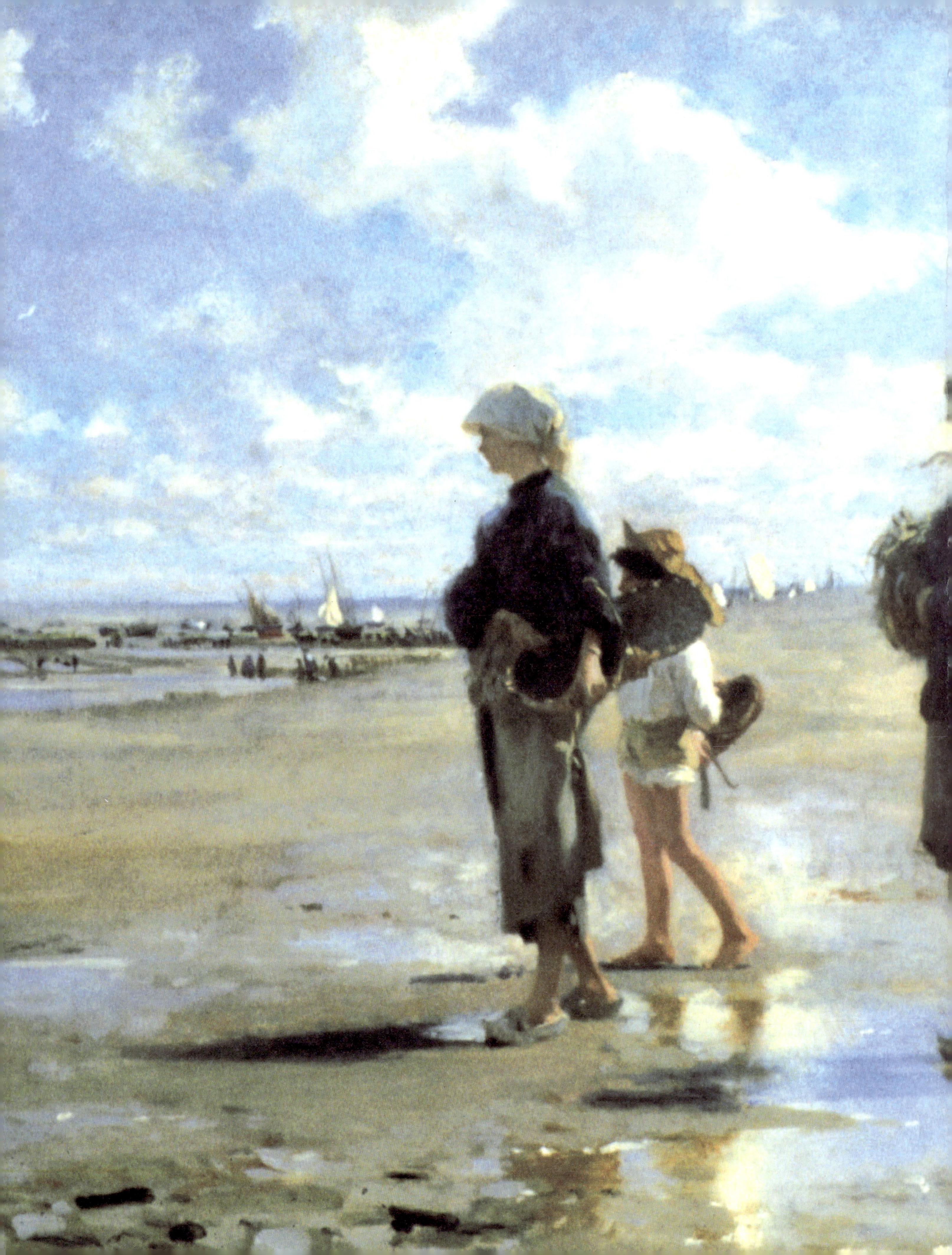